EMERGENCY WAR PLAN

EMERGENCY WAR PLAN

The American Doomsday Machine, 1945–1960

SEAN M. MALONEY

Potomac Books

AN IMPRINT OF THE UNIVERSITY OF NEBRASKA PRESS

Library of Congress Cataloging-in-Publication Data
Names: Maloney, Sean M., 1967– author.
Title: Emergency war plan: the American doomsday machine,
1945–1960 / Sean M. Maloney.
Other titles: American doomsday machine, 1945–1960
Description: Lincoln, NE: Potomac Books, an imprint of the
University of Nebraska Press, 2021. | Includes bibliographical
references and index.
Identifiers: LCCN 2020015658
ISBN 9781640122345 (hardback)
ISBN 9781640124172 (epub)
ISBN 9781640124189 (mobi)
ISBN 9781640124196 (pdf)
Subjects: LCSH: Nuclear weapons—United States—History—
20th century. | Targeting (Nuclear strategy)—History—20th
century. | Soviet Union—Strategic aspects. |
Strategic forces—History—20th century. | Deterrence
(Strategy)—History—20th century. | Nuclear warfare—
Government policy—United States—History—20th century. |
Military planning—United States—History—20th century. |
Cold War.
Classification: LCC U264.3 .M36 2021 |
DDC 355.02/17097309045—dc23
LC record available at https://lccn.loc.gov/2020015658

Set in Arno Pro by Laura Buis.

This is for Larissa.

"If the devil is powerless, send him a woman."
—Ukrainian proverb

CONTENTS

Photographs

Following page 188

Maps

TABLES

ACKNOWLEDGMENTS

Emergency War Plan was originally going to be a chapter in *Deconstructing* Dr. Strangelove: *The Secret History of Nuclear War Films.* The availability of substantial amounts of new material resulted in a rethinking of that idea and the conceptualization of this book and its planned sequel dealing with the Single Integrated Operational Plan (SIOP). Consequently many of the people acknowledged in *Deconstructing* Dr. Strangelove get thanked again here as the research was to some extent overlapping.

That said, there are some additional people to add to this pantheon. I would like to thank Senator Jon Kyle for his assistance. And I thank my colleagues Michael Whitby at the Directorate of History and Heritage and Maj. Dr. Tanya Grodzinski and Dr. Randall Wakelam at Royal Military College for commenting on the logic if not the veracity of the manuscript. Lt. Col. Earl "Mac" McGill and his work were of considerable importance, not just in terms of data but also in terms of motivation to ensure that knowledge of this critical period is not lost to time. Maj. Gordon Ohlke's expertise in the Cold War era was of great assistance especially when I needed a sounding board. Lt. Col. Bernie DeGagne assisted me with understanding certain delivery techniques. Dr. Bill Andrews and I had a pleasant afternoon discussing how to optimally target nuclear weapons. I would especially like to thank Michael Holm for compiling the best open-source order of battle available for the Soviet-era air forces and Harald Rabeder for his expertise in Luftwaffe reconnaissance history. I can always count on my good friend Robert Silliman for a session trying to recover forgotten rationales: his proximity to Pima Air Museum and other facilities served us both well. Another old friend, Glen Barney, handled some West Coast site research on short notice. Brett Davenport's unique insights also served me well.

As before, this project would not have seen the light of day without the efforts of my agent, Fritz Heinzen, and Tom Swanson at University of Nebraska Press/Potomac Books. Thanks again for placing faith in me and my work. The staff at Potomac Books was, once again, superlative.

I developed a high level of respect for the U.S. Air Force agencies I have dealt with. Time and again USAF personnel assisted, facilitated, and understood what I was doing and why. I had every confidence that I would be dealing with professional, mature personnel every time I was in contact with them. I could even joke with them about the sometimes bizarre limits placed on material by the Department of Energy. The staffs of the archives I buried myself in and the museums I had access to and the Freedom of Information Act (FOIA) entities at certain government agencies are to whom I direct the bulk of my thanks. Thanks particularly to the staff of the Air Force Historical Research Agency, especially Cathy Cox, Marcie Green, and Geoff Henson. Other USAF FOIA personnel crucial to this book are Justin W. Barnes, Theresa Corbin, Renee Kaffenbarger, TSgt. Meegan C. Haynes, Janet F. Beasley, Candice Velazquez, Crystal Delk, and SSgt. LaTeasha Mayo.

This book benefited from substantial field research. I can't thank enough the friendly, knowledgeable, and dedicated staff of the Strategic Air Command Museum, especially Brian York, the curator, and Joe Vrana, Mark "Hambone" Hamilton, Dan Kirwan, Allen Jones, and Kat Jones from the restoration staff. The support I received from them was superlative; the museum is truly a monument to SAC and its personnel. Another crucial entity in my journeys was the National Museum of Nuclear Science and History in Albuquerque. I want to thank the curator, David Hoover, for taking the time to walk me though his unique and fascinating collection of nuclear weapons and delivery systems. Similarly, Martha DeMarre at the Nuclear Testing Archive remains one of the most knowledgeable and responsive archivists I've met in my travels.

The Library of Congress Manuscript Division is populated with knowledgeable, calm, cool, and collected professionals, who in their quiet and unruffled way instantly correct errors on my part when I request the wrong group of boxes. The staff of the small but powerful Syracuse University Special Collections archives, particularly Jacklyn Hoyt and Nichole Westerdahl, is equally efficient.

The laughable and incredibly unprofessional correspondence by the National Security Agency, which portrayed me to other agencies as an evil "agent of a foreign government" in order to deny me fifty- to sixty-year-old material is acknowledged. The CIA's much more mature approach to Cold War history and its communications style are equally acknowledged, as is the professionalism of its staff.

There were just too many people to thank at all of the museums I visited. To the knowledgeable docents, the enthusiastic tour guides, and everybody else I encountered who were determined to preserve the history of the Cold War: thanks for your hospitality and assistance. These include the Air Mobility Command Museum in Dover, Delaware; the Grissom Air Museum in Indiana; the Loring Military Heritage Center in Maine; the March Field Air Museum, California; the National Atomic Testing Museum, Las Vegas; the National Museum of the U.S. Air Force in Dayton, Ohio; the Pima Air and Space Museum, Arizona; the Valiant Air Command, Florida; and, last but not least, Wings Over the Rockies Air and Space Museum in Denver.

ABBREVIATIONS

2 ATAF	NATO 2nd Allied Tactical Air Force
4 ATAF	NATO 4th Allied Tactical Air Force
12th GUMO	12th Glavnoye Upravleniye Ministerstvo Oborony (12th General Directorate, Ministry of Defense, Soviet nuclear custodian organization)
AAF	Army Air Forces
AAFCE	NATO Allied Air Forces Central Europe
ACE	NATO Allied Command Europe
AEC	Atomic Energy Commission
AFB	air force base
AFDS	Aviation Field Depot Squadron
AFOAT-1	Air Force Office of Atomic Energy
AFSWC	Air Force Special Weapons Center
AFSWP	Armed Forces Special Weapons Project
ARDC	Air Research and Development Command
ASP	Atomic Strike Plan
BMEWS	Ballistic Missile Early Warning System
BRIXMIS	British Commanders in Chief Mission to the Soviet Forces in Germany
BWP	Basic War Plan
CEP	Circular Error Probable
CG	commanding general
CHICOM	Chinese Communist
CIA	Central Intelligence Agency
CIG	Central Intelligence Group
CINCEUCOM	Commander in Chief European Command
CINCFE	Commander in Chief Far East

CINCLANT	Commander in Chief Atlantic
CINCNELM	Commander in Chief U.S. Naval Forces, Eastern Atlantic and Mediterranean
CINCPAC	Commander in Chief Pacific Command
CINCSAC	Commander in Chief Strategic Air Command
CNO	chief of naval operations
COMINT	communications intelligence
CPIC	Central Photographic Interpretation Center
CREST	CIA Records Search Tool
DCOS	deputy chief of staff
DDRS	Declassified Documents Reference System
DEFCON	Defense Condition
DGZ	Desired Ground Zero, later called Designated Ground Zero
DHH	Directorate of History and Heritage, Department of National Defence, Canada
DOD	Department of Defense
DOE	Department of Energy
DTRA	Defense Threat Reduction Agency
EC	emergency capability
ECM	electronic countermeasures
E-Hour	Execution Hour, the time the EWP, BWP, or SIOP was initiated
ELINT	electronic intelligence
EMP	electromagnetic pulse
EWP	Emergency War Plan
FEAF	Far East Air Force
FEC	Far East Command
FOIA	Freedom of Information Act
GCI	ground-controlled intercept
GEOP	General Emergency Operations Plan
GRU	Glavnoye Razvedyvatel'noye Upravleniye (Main Intelligence Directorate, Soviet armed forces)
ICBM	intercontinental ballistic missile
IR	infrared
IRBM	intermediate-range ballistic missile

ISCAP	Interagency Security Classification Review Panel
JCS	Joint Chiefs of Staff
JIB	Joint Intelligence Board
JSCP	Joint Strategic Capabilities Plan
JSSC	Joint Strategic Survey Committee
JWPC	Joint War Plans Committee
K-25	uranium-enrichment plant at Oak Ridge, Tennessee
kt	kiloton
LABS	Low-Altitude Bombing System
LCMD	Library of Congress, Manuscript Division
LST	landing ship tank
MRBM	medium-range ballistic missile
MRF	Master Readiness File
MT	megaton
NATO	North Atlantic Treaty Organization
NEAC	North East Air Command
NIE	National Intelligence Estimate
NKVD	People's Commissariat for Internal Affairs, the Soviet state repressive apparatus
NNSA	National Nuclear Security Administration
NORAD	North American Air Defense Command
NPIC	National Photographic Interpretation Center
NSC	National Security Council
NSS	National Stockpile Site
OCR	Office of Central Reference (CIA)
OPLAN	Operations Plan
ORR	Office of Research and Reports (CIA)
OSD	Office of the Secretary of Defense
OSI	Office of Special Investigations (USAF); Office of Scientific Intelligence (CIA)
OSINT	open-source intelligence
OSS	operational stockpile site
PAC	Public Archives of Canada
PACAF	Pacific Air Forces
PHOTOINT	photography intelligence
PIB	Photographic Intelligence Board

PIC	Photographic Intelligence Committee
PIR	Photographic Interpretation (or Intelligence) Report
PVO	*protivovozdushnaya oborona strany,* "anti-air defense of the nation," the Soviet air defense system
RCAF	Royal Canadian Air Force
RDS	*reaktivnyi dvigatel spetsialnyi,* "special jet engine," Soviet nuclear weapon
ROK	Republic of Korea
RTS	Reconnaissance Technical Squadron
SAC	Strategic Air Command
SACEUR	NATO Supreme Allied Commander Europe
SACLANT	NATO Supreme Allied Commander Atlantic
SCRC	Special Collections Research Center, Syracuse University
SECDEF	secretary of defense
SENSINT	sensitive intelligence
SHAPE	Supreme Headquarters Allied Powers Europe
SIGINT	signals intelligence
SIOP	Single Integrated Operational Plan
SSA	special storage area
STAVKA	Soviet armed forces high command
TAC	Tactical Air Command
Talent	data derived from U-2 reconnaissance imagery
TELINT	telemetry intelligence
TN	thermonuclear
TX	thermonuclear experimental
U/I	urban industrial
USAAF	U.S. Army Air Forces
USAF	U.S. Air Force
USAFE	U.S. Air Forces Europe
USAFSS	U.S. Air Force Security Service
USCINCEUR	U.S. Commander in Chief Europe
USN	U.S. Navy
USNARA	U.S. National Archives and Records Administration
USNOA	U.S. Navy Operational Archive
WSEG	Weapons Systems Evaluation Group

EMERGENCY WAR PLAN

Introduction

Well, we did not build these bombers to carry crushed rose petals!

—GEN. THOMAS S. POWER

Dwight D. Eisenhower was forced to deal with more nuclear crises than any other American president. Confronted with the bellicose rhetoric and the dangerous maneuverings of Mao Zedong and Nikita Khrushchev, Ike became adept at nuclear diplomacy when pushed over the Taiwan Straits, Suez, Lebanon, Berlin, and the May Day U-2 crisis. But what if either Communist leader decided to "call" at the geostrategic poker table? Was Ike going to bluff? Some didn't think he had the cards to play. As this book demonstrates, however, he had the ability to lay down a pair, a straight, or a royal flush.

If that day came and the United States or its NATO allies were under attack, Eisenhower's response wasn't going to be FDR-like, casually puffing away on his cigarette on a bright Sunday afternoon on 7 December 1941 while the principals assembled. Ike wasn't going to be like Truman, presiding over a tense White House roundtable as teleconference messages poured in from Japan in 1950. Eisenhower would be on the phone. It might happen while he was in the air being transported by a four-engine VC-121E Super Constellation aircraft dubbed *Columbine III*. He might be traveling aboard a train with a pair of special railcars code-named Crate attached. He might be aboard the yacht USS *Sequoia* on the Potomac, or at the renovated Camp David sanctuary. Indeed, if necessary, there was the 2857th Test Squadron, a secret helicopter unit hidden away at an obscure air force base near Harrisburg, Pennsylvania, designated to dig him out of the rubble of a destroyed Washington DC and put him in contact with his forces.

All of Eisenhower's transports were equipped with Collins Single Side Band radios with a patch system. These permitted the president to access, from land, sea, or air, the labyrinthine AT&T telephone network, which in turn was connected to the Joint War Room at the Pentagon and the Strategic Air Command underground command post near Omaha, Nebraska.

And what would Ike have done had he chosen to launch? He would have turned to Cdr. Ned Beach, USN, carrying "the Satchel" containing the president's Emergency Action papers. These included the Joint Chiefs of Staff War Emergency Checklist, identical copies of which were distributed to the secretary of defense, the chairman of the Joint Chiefs of Staff, and the commissioner of the Atomic Energy Commission. Appended to the checklist was the Master Readiness File, or MRF. This contained prewritten JCS emergency messages "designed to trigger certain actions by unified command-ers." When authorized by the president, an automated taped message corresponding to the MRF number was dispatched on the phone and telex systems, initially from the Air Force Command Post and later from the Joint War Room.[1]

Eisenhower had the following messages to choose from:[2]

MRF-1A: Situation Message

MRF-2A, 2B: Transfer of Atomic Weapons

MRF-3A: Declaration of National Emergency

MRF-4A: Presidential Authorization to Use Atomic Weapons

MRF-5A: War Message

MRF-7A, 9A: Base Rights

MRF-10A: Canada-U.S. Emergency Defense Plan

The recipients included the four chiefs and all major joint com-mands. In the case of Strategic Air Command (SAC) and the North

American Air Defense Command (NORAD), their actions were governed by "authenticated telephone calls" using the JCS Telephone Authentication System. This was a conference call including the chiefs, the secretary of defense, and the president, with some form of authentication established prior to members joining the conversation. This exclusive club had the MRF list, and the president essentially selected the options he wanted implemented. For example, MRF-2A was sent from the secretary of defense to the chairman of the Atomic Energy Commission requesting that X number of nuclear components and Y number of nonnuclear components "be made immediately available for pickup on demand." The secretary then sent a message establishing a "P" Hour (pickup hour) with the numbers but also with a single line: "Authorization for the Use of Nuclear Weapons Has Not Been Granted."[3] That permitted the chiefs to implement "Atomic Standby." Only the president could select MRF-4A, a single line authorizing their use, and then a corresponding service-level message, "Atomic Execute," was dispatched.

This message would have activated the Emergency War Plan, or EWP. No matter what the prevailing circumstances were, that would have ended the Soviet Union as a viable, functioning society. And if Ike were dead, some of his commanders had written instructions to make sure the EWP was executed.

This was a decision that Eisenhower never wanted to make. He dedicated his presidency to ensuring that the United States and her allies were not pushed into a position where he had to make it, while at the same time doing his utmost to not lose ground in the Cold War. By the mid-1950s the EWP and its successors were created, designed, and structured to deter. Without a plan, the deterrent system was simply not credible. And if plans were not maintained, technological gaps shored up, forces exercised, and capabilities demonstrated, vulnerabilities might be exploited by opponents, thus undermining the system and rendering it useless. And to a generation of American leaders still suffering the psychological effects of Pearl Harbor, having been bullied over Berlin, surprised in Korea, confronted with thermonuclear weapons, and beleaguered with Munich analogies thrust on them in a volatile domestic political environment, vulnerabilities of any sort were simply unacceptable.

What was the Emergency War Plan? How and why was it created? What were its constituent parts? How was it supposed to work? How and why did this change over time? And what does it mean for us today, looking back at the Cold War?

The Cold War was a unique style of conflict fought on several fronts. It was a war of competing strategies, its opponents seeking to gain advantage over one other in order to accomplish a variety of political objectives. Related to this, the Cold War was a competition to gain technological advantage to make those strategies credible. This involved intelligence collection, particularly on targets and their defensive systems. It involved increasing the reliability of the weapons and their delivery systems as well as the ability to communicate with those systems. The Cold War was also a war of geographical position, particularly the proximity of bases to their targets but also with regard to outer space, the new high ground. Consequently, understanding the Emergency War Plan becomes an important aspect of understanding the Cold War style.

There are several reasons why the Emergency War Plan and its successors are of interest. First, it provides insight into the interplay of technology, strategy, and policy throughout the long Cold War. Related to this, the planning highlighted contrasting U.S. Air Force, U.S. Navy, Joint Chiefs of Staff, and secretary of defense views, beliefs on nuclear weapons development, and on employment. Examining the targeting and the intelligence that fed it shows us what was known about the threat at the time. This allows us to reach some tentative conclusions about war outcomes at given periods of the larger conflict and thus the viability of the deterrent itself.

Insight into nuclear war planning provides insight into the Cold War confrontation itself as a system as well as into how dangerous nuclear crises could have been. Similarly, examining the EWP and its forces as they evolved affords insight into the staggering pace of technological and operational change that quite possibly outstripped strategy and policy. These intense technological changes, seemingly on a day-to-day basis, make any attempt to examine U.S.

nuclear war planning akin to using Heisenberg's uncertainty principle to understand an atom. One almost has to look at the EWP through snapshots in time.

There are, however, challenges to a new understanding of American nuclear deterrence. The first of these is the widespread discrepancy in Cold War literature on what constitutes nuclear strategy. The existing period literature tends to conflate American Cold War nuclear policy, strategy, and doctrine into artificial and in some cases Procrustean bed–like categories in the absence of access to the highly classified processes that produced nuclear strategy. This was the result of several factors. First, there was declaratory policy by the executive branch and how the media and the legislative branch interpreted it within the intellectual limitations of their arenas or environments. Second, there was analysis conducted by a variety of analytical institutions with varying levels of access to the intelligence, industrial, military policymaking, and military strategy-making organizations. Analysis of equally variable quality was produced dependent upon the proximity of the given organization and its economic or influence-based objectives to the actual seats of power in the Pentagon. Finally, there were the military commands and how they disposed of their assigned forces to accomplish the stated objectives and guidance provided to them by the Joint Chiefs of Staff. In many cases these three aspects were not always in alignment. And, importantly, this was not the result of rogue behavior by military leaders, as is frequently asserted by activists and cultural content producers.

Consequently the language and terminology employed to discuss and describe American nuclear strategy can be extremely problematic. Jerome H. Kahan used the term "official U.S. strategic policy," and nobody challenged or corrected this. If there is official U.S. strategic policy, then what is official U.S. tactical policy?[4] John Lewis Gaddis refers to "strategies of containment," neatly conflating or blurring policy and strategy. Richard K. Betts finally explained in 1985, thirty years after the debate started, the difference between preventive war and preemption.[5] Exasperated, Scott Sagan eloquently asserted that Mutual Assured Destruction is a "layman's myth."[6] As another example, "flexible response" means different things to different people at different times. For Gaddis, it is a generalized period of a particular containment strategy during the Kennedy and Johnson administrations.[7] For NATO aficionados, it is the informal name of the MC 14/3 strategy document promulgated in 1967. For some historians, it is a blanket name given to a series of concepts, force employment plans, or aspirational goals examined by NATO from 1957 to 1967, predating MC 14/3. For the Soviets, it didn't exist.

Language can distort. How many books assert that strategy or policy during the Eisenhower years was simply a blunt instrument called Massive Retaliation, implying that it was simplistic, unworkable, and dangerous?[8] Just because John Foster Dulles used the term in a speech did not necessarily mean that American nuclear delivery forces were fully operationalized to carry out something so general in description, even though that is what the end result may have looked like. How about "counterforce"? This is an analyst's word implying that a specific, distinguishable target type exists (nuclear delivery systems), and thus a distinguishable strategy to destroy them exists independently from strategies to destroy other types of targets. But what if bombers are based on an airfield in the outskirts of a city, an "urban-industrial" target type? A 19-megaton free-fall bomb from a B-47 will not distinguish between the two, so can a narrowly defined "counterforce" strategy actually exist? Yet such jargon eventually became canon and remains in widespread use.

A related problem is the application of language and concepts from one period to suggest that ideas were active in an earlier period, when in fact the context was completely different. For example, Richard Rhodes characterizes abstract brainstorming by the Army Air Forces in 1945 ("striking the first blow") as planning for a "first strike" against the Soviet Union.[9] The term "first strike" is pejorative language from the 1970s related to issues of stability and, for the disarmament crowd, legality. These constructs did not necessarily apply in the 1945 planning environment in the same way. Conceptualizing the use of strategic air forces against the Soviet industrial capacity in the early stages of a World War II–style war is a different prospect from planning to use ballistic missiles to eliminate leadership targets or other intercontinental ballistic missiles (ICBMs) in the hair-trigger 1970s.

"Doctrine" is yet another heavily abused word. The Monroe Doctrine. The Schlesinger Doctrine. The Carter Doctrine. In reality these are declaratory policies, guidelines for the conduct of foreign policy at particular times and places. Military forces employ doctrine, that is, a philosophical basis for action; they don't necessarily employ "the Reagan Doctrine." There was a SAC Tactical Doctrine: this was the handling of an aircraft and its defensive systems as it penetrated Soviet air defenses and delivered its weapons. If there was something like SAC "strategic" doctrine it likely consisted of the processes by which the JCS and the Joint Strategic Target Planning Staff assessed targets and assigned weapons to destroy them. But doctrine is not strategy.

Robert Jervis successfully identified the labeling issue and its import: "While public pronouncements have changed dramatically in the past twenty years, from 'no cities' to 'damage limitation' to 'assured destruction' to multiple options and the countervailing strategy, targeting and the Single Integrated Operational Plan (SIOP) have been much more stable."[10]

There is a difference between what is said and what is to be done. This work provides more information than previously available on both subjects. Indeed many, if not most publicly expressed assumptions on nuclear war planning in the 1950s were, as we will see, incorrect.

The second historical question involves the Cold War–era arguments over whether deterrence works and the role that nuclear weapons played in making it work. The efficacy of deterrence was debated in official venues and street-level antinuclear movements during that time and eventually spilled over into academia as the Cold War ended. If one opposed nuclear weapons, deterrence was dangerous because of the potential consequences of failure, and its efficacy could not be proven empirically because, using the logic of the day, "you cannot prove a negative."[11] If one was pro–nuclear weapons, deterrence was the sine qua non of American policy and strategy and was successful. Deterrence was designed to deter; there was no nuclear war; therefore deterrence worked. This was an article of faith in the Church of the U.S. Air Force.

The provocative but simplistic view that nuclear weapons and deterrence were irrelevant during the Cold War will be discarded here.[12] Nuclear weapons in general and aspects of American nuclear war planning in particular did seriously concern the Soviet Union's leaders. They feared and continuously reacted to evolutions in American capabilities in this field. And rightly so, given the capabilities that were deliberately put on display for them in response to the choices they made.

The accompanying Cold War–era debate over how misunderstood the Soviets were or to what degree Soviet motives were benevolent can also be tossed into the dustbin of history. The Soviet Union was a malevolent force surpassing that of Nazi Germany in quantity if not in quality, and it needed to be deterred to protect the sacrifices made by the Western powers during World War II and the emergent world order that war gave birth to. Scholarship, let alone revealed human experience, uncontrovertibly bears this out. "Moral equivalency" was a Soviet propaganda tool that elements of the Western intelligentsia bought into; in real terms it did not exist and never existed during the Cold War period. The Soviet Union really was an evil empire, and Stalin was in effect "Hitler with nuclear weapons."[13]

The Soviet Union's leaders sought not only to dominate the European landmass but also to extend their reach globally; that project remained a constant throughout the course of the Soviet Union's seventy-year existence. The post-McCarthy dismissal of the "International Communist Conspiracy" (spoofed in the film *Dr. Strangelove*) must be seriously reexamined given new scholarship on the period, particularly with regard to "atomic espionage" and political subversion directed against the ABCA partner countries (United States, United Kingdom, Canada, Australia, and New Zealand) and NATO. Fluoridation wasn't the problem; spies, agents of influence, and "active measures" were.[14]

Soviet leaders chose to construct a monstrous and unnecessary nuclear capability to accompany their excessive and unnecessary conventional capability that overmatched the conventional forces of the NATO countries and repressed millions of people in Eastern Europe. The Soviet leaders chose to employ or otherwise facilitated subversive measures and coercion as well as outright military intervention in global affairs behind their nuclear-conventional shield, and they increased these activities as the Cold War progressed. The 1979 Soviet intervention in Afghanistan, which led to the deaths of more than 1.5 million people, would not have been undertaken in the 1950s, for example. The suggestion that this activity was all "defensive" or merely an extension of historical Russian imperial policy, common arguments during the Cold War, no longer carries weight with the walls down, the prisoners freed, and the archives, to a certain extent, opened.[15]

The Soviet leaders saw the American nuclear deterrent as a brake on their ambitions and then sought to offset it to make the world safe for subversion and conventional warfare, actions they deliberately chose to undertake by countering the U.S. ability to inflict damage on the Soviet Union at levels unacceptable to the Soviet leadership. The Soviet policy to offset American nuclear capabilities likely increased the danger of nuclear weapons use in the second half of the Cold War, particularly with MIRV'd ICBMs (improved missiles with multiple independently targetable reentry vehicles) at the forefront of the arsenals. Importantly, this state of affairs gave rise to lethal Soviet Third World adventurism, the effects of which are still felt today in places like Africa and the Middle East.[16] The Soviet leaders were confronted with the American nuclear deterrent particularly in the Berlin and Cuban crises in the 1960s. Once confronted they could have chosen a more defensive path, like that ultimately taken by China in the 1960s and 1970s.[17] They did not. If the American nuclear deterrent was irrelevant, then why did the Soviet leadership back down during the various international crises of the 1950s and 1960s, actively overtake American capabilities in the 1970s, and ultimately increase their aggressive international behavior?

This book has its own assumptions that the reader needs to be aware of. First, it was not undertaken to specifically contribute to ongoing polemics over the nuclear weapons issue, though I am aware that its depiction of the EWP and the book's conclusions will be employed by one camp or another for their purposes. My objective is to understand the underpinnings of the EWP and how it would have worked, had it been implemented, and some of its possible effects. Second, the book assumes it is possible to view the EWP dispassionately while at the same time recognizing the magnitude of the immense devastation it would have wrought had it been unleashed. Third, the book operates from the assumption that those involved in the formulation of the EWP and its associated systems were not inherently evil or deranged but people with complex motivations, many of which were focused on generating the best deterrent system they could conceive under extreme temporal, technological, and political pressures.

We move forward with the object of our inquiry to answer the question: How was nuclear war going to be fought so that it could deter?

A Note on Conventions

Given that this book is about nuclear wars that were not fought, it by necessity uses tentative language and extrapolation when required. Nuclear war planning was in constant evolution, sometimes on a day-to-day basis. It is not always possible to be definitive about what unit was prepared to do what and when. Rotations of forward-based units was the norm, and overlap was the word of the day. There remain significant gaps in the primary literature, and in my view it is better to be clear when one does not have the exact data to fill the gap. That said, the leaps taken in the work are not gargantuan, nor are they wanton. I remain open to other interpretations, and I welcome the release of more and better information.

1

Kami no itte

Nuclear Targeting and Japan, 1945

There is much delusion and wishful thinking among those after-the-event
strategists who now deplore the use of the atomic bomb on the grounds
that its use was inhuman or that it was unnecessary because Japan was
already beaten, and it was not one atomic bomb or two, which brought
surrender; it was the experience of what an atomic bomb will actually do
to a community, *plus the dread of many more*, that was effective.

—KARL T. COMPTON, president of MIT, 1946

Nuclear weapons targeting during the Second World War was
more of an expedient wartime activity than a solid foundation on which Cold War–era targeting was constructed.
There was no attempt or even need to employ what we would call
"deterrence" as the Japanese nuclear weapons program, including
its isotope-separation facilities in Tokyo, was destroyed during the
course of the conventional bombing campaign, and it is likely that
the Japanese efforts in this field remained unknown to the Allied
intelligence apparatus.[1] Some have argued that the use of the two
weapons against Hiroshima and Nagasaki was an extension of the
strategic bombing campaign and should not be seen as something
special or distinguishable from conventional bombing, especially
after the March 1945 Tokyo raid. In this view the atomic bomb was
a "tactical weapon," not a "geopolitical strategic gambit."[2]

Yet the atomic bomb and its employment were an extension of
conventional strategic bombing and special because of the novel det-

onation mechanisms, the anticipated effects, and the secrecy surrounding the atomic weapons themselves.

The specific purpose behind the planned use of atomic weapons in 1945 was to attack the will of the Japanese people, to undermine their willingness to continue the war. Unlike conventional strategic bombing, this was to be achieved through psychological shock brought on by the intense and immense destruction of area targets with single weapons. The spin-off benefits of the attacks were to include the destruction of command-and-control facilities, troop and materiel concentrations, and production capacity. Equally important, and a priority item, was that the effects of the attacks be measurable.[3] But the primary objective was clear: to generate psychological shock targeting the Japanese national will to fight under the specific circumstances of the Pacific War.

Centerboard was the code name for the initial target selection designed to carry out these instructions. After substantial debate, only a city met all of the targeting criteria, and therefore cities were placed on a list, just as they had been for the combined bombing offensive in Europe and in the Pacific. There was no distinction between a civilian and a military target, and there had not really been one for years: an industrial target was an industrial target.[4] Indeed, given the mobilization of the Japanese population as part of the home island defense plan Ketsu-Go, the distinction between soldier and civilian blurred, particularly in the minds of the American planners but definitely in the written expositions of the Japanese leadership.[5] The Targeting Committee met in several iterations from May to July 1945, and there were spin-off processes involving men like Brig. Gen. Lauris Norstad, future NATO Supreme Allied Commander Europe, and Brig. Gen. Nathan Twining, future chief of staff USAF and chairman of the Joint Chiefs of Staff. Indeed, the ambiguous nature of the civil-military relationship regarding Cold War nuclear targeting had its origins during this period.[6]

Starting with a list of seventeen cities, the number of targets was progressively narrowed to five over the course of several meetings. Secretary of War Henry Stimson objected to the inclusion of Kyoto for either sentimental or moral reasons, and it was removed from the list, an act that would repeat itself in a similar fashion when John F. Kennedy demanded that Warsaw be removed from the SIOP in the early 1960s. The Emperor's Palace was also considered as a target but not added, clearly an early move reflecting the importance of not decapitating the enemy's leadership so as to positively affect war termination. The final list: Hiroshima, Kokura, Niigato, and Nagasaki.[7] At a roll of the weather dice, Nagasaki was destroyed by the second weapon, contributing to Japan's decision to capitulate. And that is usually where the narrative ends, with some jettisoning the projected targeting trajectory: "All the rest is speculation."[8]

But it doesn't end there. And it is not speculation. The bomb pipeline was kept open and the planning continued into September 1945. What if the Japanese militarists staged a coup and the war was back on? And what about Operation Downfall, the invasion of the Japanese home islands? That too had to be kept on tap. And it had a nuclear component that had to remain active, just in case.

It is perhaps better to step back from the Japanese decision to concede defeat in August and look at the American effort in 1945 as a whole, not as something that suddenly ends. The infrastructure for atomic bomb operations against Japan did not consist merely of the USS *Indianapolis*, a bomb-loading pit on Tinian, and a couple of B-29 planes. Hardstands and hydraulic loading pits were also under construction on Okinawa so that six more Centerboard targets could be put in reach of the 509th Composite Groups' B-29s: Sapporo, Hakonate, Oyabu, Yokosuka, Osaka, and Nagoya. Los Alamos continued to fabricate and assemble spheres for Fat Man weapons; it didn't down tools suddenly on 9 August. The 509th had fifteen modified Silverplate B-29s and fifteen trained crews and was prepared to deliver atomic bombs as soon as they arrived.[9] Forty initiators, four of which were required for each combat weapon, were also deployed to Tinian from Los Alamos, implying that ten weapons were also scheduled to be deployed.[10]

Gen. George C. Marshall, however, extensively studied the effects of the 16 July Trinity test. What is generally overlooked is that the metrics derived from that test were far more extensive than is commonly understood. Air blast, ground shock, and firestorm effects were anticipated and measured. However, so was radioactive fallout; that was not, contrary to popular belief, a 1950s discovery. The need for eye protection, the role of weather, the employment of cloud sampling and tracking aircraft, radioactivity surveys using special armored vehicles—all of these were accounted for just as they would be in more extensive forms in the 1948 tests in the Pacific and 1951 tests in Nevada.[11] In other words, there were enough data to start examining battlefield use of nuclear weapons much earlier than is generally understood. And Marshall was already moving in that direction.

Indeed, if the war had not ended when it did, the eventual inter-command debate over "strategic" versus "tactical" use of nuclear weapons would have started in 1945 instead of five years later.[12] Marshall calculated that eight or nine weapons would be available by November 1945. Instead of attacking the Centerboard targets, he wanted them used for Operation Olympic, the invasion of Kyushu. This massive operation was intended to establish an air base network to support 1946's Operation Coronet, the planned assault on Honshu east of Tokyo. It was envisioned that three atomic bombs would be made available to the three assault corps. The first weapon would be employed in the preliminary assault, the second employed in depth against supporting forces; the third would be used to seal mountain passes or destroy other terrain features to block mass reinforcements from entering the landing areas. Special monitoring units would lead U.S. landing units, and effects data were provided by Manhattan Engineering District supremo Gen. Leslie Groves to Marshall on optimal employment of the weapons.[13] The use of airbursts instead of groundbursts to reduce fallout, a phenomenon noted during the Trinity test in 1945, was the most likely methodology. Its efficacy was later confirmed by early assessments of the bombings of Hiroshima and Nagasaki, where there was minimal fallout in the case of Nagasaki and none in Hiroshima.[14]

Despite dogged attempts by activists to downplay the lifesaving effects of the Hiroshima and Nagasaki bombings, it is increasingly clear that the number of Allied dead in an assault on Japan would have been around 700,000, while Japanese estimates suggest that 10 million to 15 million Japanese would have died.[15] (Notably, the destruction of Hiroshima inadvertently destroyed the Ketsu-Go command-and-control apparatus for national resistance on Kyushu, an early example of "bonus damage.")[16] The paradoxical nature of highly destructive nuclear weapons having positive benefits was therefore also established in 1945, particularly in the minds and hearts of those who were going to be in the first wave of Operation Olympic. And that did play a role in Cold War targeting. Could these weapons be used to deter an opponent from using them, as was true for the non-use of chemical weapons during the Second World War? Could nuclear weapons even deter war itself?

One of the most important, if not the most important aspect of the 1945 atomic bomb attacks in relationship to Cold War nuclear targeting involves weapons effects. This obviously relates to the measurable specific damage that could be rendered by a nuclear weapon to structures, services, and people. Indeed the Nagasaki Fat Man bomb and its effects became the "nominal bomb," the baseline standard for nuclear weapons not only for the United States but also for the Soviet Union, which directly copied it, and then China, which was assisted in replicating the design by the Soviet spy Klaus Fuchs.[17]

But there was also the terrifying nature of the weapon itself: its relatively small size contained a lethal combination of blast and fire, plus an invisible element, radiation, that could kill immediately and over the long term. This perhaps had an inherent deterrent effect all on its own. Much is made of the early expositions by RAND analyst Bernard Brodie on nuclear deterrence.[18] One could equally argue, however, that journalist John Hersey's depiction of what occurred in Hiroshima was more important: unlike Brodie, Hersey had seen for himself what "the Bomb" did and conveyed it to a wide audience. No doubt the Soviets took careful note.

So too did Gens. Curtis LeMay and Thomas S. Power, future commanders in chief of the Strategic Air Command. They did not need Brodie's or anybody else's writings to understand what they were dealing with and what a threat it posed. LeMay was conflicted, arguing in his memoir that in essence Hiroshima and Nagasaki constituted a coup de grâce after the conventional bombing campaign. That said, he noted, "These bombs brought into the world not only their own speed and extent of desolation. They brought a strange pervading fear which does not seem to have affected mankind previously, from any other source. This unmitigated terror has no justice, no basis in fact. Nothing new about death, nothing new about deaths caused militarily. We scorched and boiled and baked to death more people in Tokyo on that night of March 9–10 than went up in vapor at Hiroshima and Nagasaki combined."[19]

But this was something different. And he knew it. So did Tommy Power:

> I did not participate in the actual [Hiroshima and Nagasaki] raids, but shortly after the war I visited what was left of the two cities. This sight, too, was an unforgettable experience, not merely because of the terrible devastation I found but, even more so, because of the incomprehensible fact that such an enormous and widespread destruction had, in each instance, been caused by one bomb, dropped from a single airplane. . . . Less than a year later, I was appointed Assistant Deputy Task Force Commander for the Operation Crossroads atom bomb tests at Bikini Atoll and observed the first series of atomic explosions. As these explosions increased in power and destructiveness, they kept making an even greater impression on me. Then I saw the first explosion of a hydrogen bomb and everything that I had seen before paled into insignificance.[20]

The path to the Emergency War Plan and then to the SIOP lay here: what was done to Japan could not be allowed to happen to the United States. But what was the best way to ensure that state of affairs in an ever changing world? That was the fundamental question occupying the minds of postwar air force leaders.

Although the detonations at Hiroshima and Nagasaki were not deliberately intended to do so, they generated a pause in the Soviet camp. In 1944 Stalin ordered the STAVKA, the Soviet armed forces high command, to prepare plans to invade Western Europe, defeat National Socialist Germany forces, and install Communist governments before the Western allies could react. According to Lavrentiy Beria's son Sergo, who handled the surveillance equipment directed at Churchill and Roosevelt during the Tehran and Yalta summits and later at Potsdam, "It was calculated that the whole operation would take no longer than a month. . . . [However,] all these plans were aborted when Stalin learnt from my father [through his espionage apparatus] that the Americans had the atom bomb and were putting it into mass production." Stalin's decision "to cancel these plans was taken late, between the end of the Potsdam Conference and the USSR's entry into the war with Japan."[21] This was the first instance of nuclear deterrence, albeit an inadvertent one.

2

Per Ardua ad Atomica

Ur-Nuclear Targeting, 1946–49

Nobody respects a country with a poor army, but everybody respects a
country with a good army. I raise my toast to the Finnish Army.

—JOSEPH STALIN, 1948

The Emergency War Plan's foundations lie in the immediate postwar years. The term "atomic monopoly" has been employed to describe this intense technological development during a time of significant geostrategic uncertainty. The acceleration of the American atomic enterprise during the Berlin Crisis in 1948 generated greater emphasis on examining how the weapons were to be used if the crisis expanded, but it was the full-on threat of global war in 1950–51 that really thrust planning into its second postwar period.

The idea that the Soviet Union would be the next enemy and that contingency planning and the development of strategic concepts should be undertaken was validated with the discovery of the vast Soviet espionage apparatus operating in North America in 1946; it was also validated by questionable Soviet behavior in "liberated" Eastern Europe, the USSR's support for the Communist insurgency in Greece, and its direct military pressure on Turkey. However, the Soviets' continued occupation of northern Iran was equally problematic. Stalin's unwillingness to fully demobilize the Soviet Union's massive land forces and the retention of around a million men stationed in Eastern Europe lay at the heart of the problem. The potential of this force could not be ignored by prudent people, no matter how damaged the Soviet economy might be. In any event that "poor economy" was able to produce an atomic bomb and build strategic bombers to carry them within four years. Stalin's behavior in Czechoslovakia and Berlin in 1948 confirmed for the public what the planners had already figured out: the Soviet Union was a powerful threat to Western interests and values. The question was how to stand up to it without triggering a war. And if war was to be fought, what was the most expeditious way to bring about a desirable conclusion?

Second Steps, 1946

The deep basis for the EWP was a study conducted in Washington during the steamy summer of 1945 as part of the U.S. Army Air Forces (USAAF) assessment of its postwar requirements. Gen. Lauris Norstad, a planner with extensive experience in the Mediterranean theater and then with the Twentieth Air Force staff in Washington, was now one of the three members of the Spaatz Committee, which included Gens. Carl "Tooey" Spaatz and Hoyt Vandenberg, the eventual first two chiefs of staff of the U.S. Air Force.[1] Already back in 1944, after a series of bad experiences negotiating with the Soviets over shuttle bombing arrangements, Norstad and others had become concerned about the potential Soviet threat. As the Allies fought their way up the Italian Boot, Norstad believed that Anglo-American forces should thrust into Austria and Hungary and gain a foothold in western Poland to ensure the Red Army did not take control of Eastern Europe in its entirety.[2]

Vandenberg was as concerned as Norstad about the Soviets. During the war he had spent three months in Moscow being stalled, insulted, and deceived by a variety of high Soviet officials over the implementation of Operation Frantic, for which USAAF forces would use three bases in Ukraine for attacks against targets in Germany. After the first Frantic mission, German aircraft caught fifty American bombers on the ground at their base at Poltava and destroyed them. Soviet personnel had refused to allow the fighters to take off, and the Soviet air defense system was ineffective in protecting the bases. Even when the U.S. bomber force got off the ground, the Soviets would not permit it to bomb agreed-to targets. Vandenberg was further appalled when Stalin blocked the Frantic bases from supporting the Poles during the 1944 Uprising, thus allowing Nazi forces to destroy the non-Communist Polish Home Army.[3]

Further evidence of Vandenberg's distrust of the USSR is his use of the Ninth Air Force intelligence apparatus and its liaison with the U.S. Office of Strategic Services and the British Special Operations Executive and their secret service, MI6, as well as Greek and Turkish agencies to collect information on Communist operations in Italy and throughout the Balkans in the immediate postwar period. Clearly Vandenberg was seriously concerned about Communist expansion from an early date. He also found problematic the shooting down of American transport aircraft by Communist Yugoslavia.[4] These proto–Cold War concerns were not simply manifestations of anti-Communist hysteria. Norstad and Vandenberg harbored legitimate and deep suspicions of Soviet motives and methodology based on their personal experience, not theory or abstract prejudice.

While the Spaatz Committee sat, the JCS's Joint Strategic Survey Committee also identified the USSR as a potential enemy. The convergence of the JSSC studies and the Spaatz Committee led Norstad's staff to produce a very general estimate of what the air force might need if ordered into action against the Soviet Union in the near future.[5] At this point Norstad was primarily interested in data that could be fed into the force structure calculations that he, Spaatz, and Vandenberg were engaged in. A draft of the study was then passed to Gen. Leslie Groves at the Manhattan Engineering District for professional comment.

The 15 September 1945 memo for Groves, "Subject: Atomic Bomb Production," assumed that the air force mission would be to implement "the immediate destruction of the enemy centers of industry, transportation, and population": "For the purposes of this study the destruction of the Russian capacity to wage war has therefore been used as a basis upon which to predicate the Unites States atomic bomb requirements." An attached map provided the locations of sixty-six Soviet cities. The "incapacitation" targets included between fifteen and sixty-six of these cities. There were bombs assigned to "neutralization": targets of opportunity should the enemy gain bases in the Western Hemisphere. Finally there were bombs assigned for "strategic isolation of the battlefield," that is, destruction of terrain features like the Kiel and Suez canals. The "minimum" list included 123 bombs: 39 for the fifteen priority city targets, 10 for neutralization, and 10 for strategic isolation. The "optimum" list had 204 weapons against the sixty-six cities on the list, and 10 each for the other two tasks. Building in a number for effectiveness, the staff concluded that for 59 targets on the minimum list, there should be 123 bombs, while the 224 targets on the optimum list required 466 bombs. The bomb types and yields were not specified.[6]

Groves was concerned that Norstad's people assumed a far too conservative damage estimate for the Fat Man implosion weapon: 7,000 feet. In Groves's view, "an area at least twice that should be used." He also emphasized to Norstad that "it is not essential to get total destruction of a city in order to destroy its effectiveness": "My general conclusion would be that the number of bombs indicated as required, is excessive."[7]

This was a planning document in the context of force structure deliberations. It was not a targeting document, nor was it a policy document. It was not operationalized; that is, forces were not assigned to carry out these tasks, and no orders existed linking this study to what would become SAC.[8] The document's assumptions that future priority targets included aircraft, tank, artillery, and truck production, plus crude oil and it refining industry, as well as steel, aluminum, copper, zinc, and ball bearing production, were lifted from World War II European Theater targeting philosophies. The idea was that destruction of the means to make war was part and parcel of larger strategic ends, not an end unto itself. This was World War II replayed with kiloton-yield nuclear weapons. The staff wanted to know: What do we need, and how many?

The data in the 1945 Norstad staff study was folded into other force structure planning discussions and forgotten by early 1946. However, the strategic context for an atomic aerial campaign finally emerged. Continuing aggressive Soviet behavior, especially the uncovering of extensive Soviet subversion and espionage apparatus targeting, among many things, the tripartite atomic bomb program, led to increased concern among the Joint Chiefs of Staff. To further define the issues vis-à-vis postwar force structure, Norstad was brought in once again to conduct a study.

Norstad briefed President Truman in October 1946. He guardedly told Truman that whether one interpreted the Soviets' activities as regular international power politics or a ploy for world domination, their military potential was greater because of the postwar drawdown by Western forces. There was a "conflict of purpose" that would not go away: "Such an eventuality is, therefore, the basis of our planning. At this time it appears not only the *most* probable, but is in fact the *only* probable source of trouble in the foreseeable future." Norstad addressed the Soviets' atomic capability: "It is generally accepted that it is possible for them to develop this weapon, perhaps by 1949 but it is believed most probable that it cannot be produced in significant numbers before 1951. These dates are very cautious estimates. There is serious doubt whether the atomic bomb in the hands of the Russians could be a significant factor before 1956." In this Norstad was nearly bang on. The Soviets had German guided missiles and would have a three-thousand-mile, 1-ton warhead capability, and offensive naval submarine forces based on Type XXI technology would be available in "15 or 20 years."[9]

In his view the Soviets would not initiate war in the next five years but would obtain "objectives—some of them directly or indirectly military—through diplomatic and subversive means." That said, he cautioned, "A miscalculation on the part of the Russians as to the real nature and extent of our interests, or the action of an overzealous satellite might tip the scales and bring on war at any time. Another great danger lies in the fact that a totalitarian government which directs a major part of its national effort towards the attainment of great military power may have to exercise that power in order to retain its own authority."[10]

After discussing how time and space would compress with the development of new weapons, Norstad emphasized that the United States had to "prepare for a total war." The attack would be a surprise launched by the enemy. "Victory for us might only be possible only as a result of absorbing or repelling strong initial attacks, and finally by proceeding methodically to destroy the enemy['s] war-making potential." Future plans would incorporate the atomic bomb: "We are preparing to use the atomic bomb if necessary."[11]

Truman clearly had no quarrel with the case made by Norstad. Out of this thinking, or concurrent with it, flowed the Pincher studies of JCS plans, which in turn became the basis for immediate postwar contingency and mobilization planning. Pincher saw a collapse of Western Europe under a Soviet onslaught and the establishment of Allied base areas in the United Kingdom, Egypt, and India, from which an aerial assault would be made "against the war-making capacity of the USSR." There were eight "vital areas" connected by "an extensive communication system" where war industries were concentrated: Moscow, the Caucasus, Ploieşti in Romania, the Urals, Stalingrad, Kharkov in Ukraine, Lake Baikal, and Leningrad. These would be attacked by "a rapid and effective series of initial operations, exploiting special weapons."[12]

As more refined information came in during 1946, these vital areas changed and were prioritized: Moscow and industrial suburbs; Baku with its oil production and refining; Ural industrial centers; the Volga railway bridges; mining and processing in the Kuzbass and Donbass regions; and the Ploieşti oil producing area. One of the Pincher studies had a map depicting thirty cities with associated B-29 radii.

Pincher was a strategic outline plan that had the first nuclear targeting concepts embedded in it. But once again this was World War II replayed with a limited number of atomic bombs. This was not a "deterrent" plan, and it was not a "first strike" plan. It was a strategic concept. And the forces did not exist yet to carry it out.

There were reasons for that state of affairs. First, there were only components and assemblies for nine Fat Man–like implosion bombs, the ones destined to be used to support Operation Downfall.[13] Second, the collection of weapons effects data against industrial systems and against human beings was underway in Hiroshima and Nagasaki, but there was no information on effects against military systems like aircraft and ships. And in the postwar scramble for budgetary resources, the atomic bomb became a central factor in interservice rivalry over how the bombs would be used: against cities, military forces, or both? The July 1946 Crossroads tests at Bikini Atoll were in some ways a showdown between the U.S. Navy and the Army Air Forces, and until they played out, other matters had to be held in abeyance.[14]

It was also at this point that several personalities converged with important long-term effects. Norstad's advocacy back in 1945 "that an officer of the caliber of Maj. Gen. Curtis E. LeMay be made Deputy Chief of Staff for Research and Development" bore fruit.[15] LeMay, like Norstad and Vandenberg, had also had negative experiences with Soviet behavior during the war. This included the shoot-down and incarceration of one B-29 crew over Korea, and the seizure and exploitation of several other B-29s that diverted to Soviet bases with damage and wounded.[16] The unwillingness of the Soviets to provide vital weather data for the region was another sore point. LeMay liaised with Mao Zedong so that a weather detachment could be established in Communist Chinese territory.[17] LeMay, now stationed at Wright Patterson field in his native Ohio, was positioned to oversee the USAAF's role in Crossroads—and, not incidentally, he was involved in Operation Paperclip, the exploitation of Nazi Germany's aeronautical and other secrets, and the funding of what became Project Air Force, eventually the Research and Development (RAND) Corporation.[18] He was put in charge of the LeMay Subcommittee to organize the tests. Not coincidentally, the air deputy for Crossroads was Maj. Gen. Thomas S. Power, LeMay's right-hand man, who had also worked under Norstad in the Mediterranean and later led the operation that incinerated Tokyo in March 1945.[19]

The detonation of two 23-kiloton nuclear weapons, the airburst shot Able, and the underwater burst shot Baker at Bikini in July 1946 had numerous spin-off effects that had an impact on war planning and targeting. The first was to stoke interservice suspicion of the navy within the future SAC leadership. The U.S. Navy publicly downplayed the damage to the test array of ships, to LeMay's chagrin. He believed the navy had rigged the tests by not fully loading target ships with ammo and fuel. This was not a new problem for LeMay, as he had seen the navy rigging exercises in the 1930s to embarrass the air corps and he had experienced the lack of support by bloated rear-area navy logistics types on Guam in the 1940s. Indeed the navy leaked casualty figures during the Pacific War for political purposes and to influence strategy. None of this boded well for interservice cooperation when it came to LeMay.[20]

The second spin-off effect was the downplaying of certain weapons effects by Crossroads participants. Yes, the airburst did not damage as many vessels as the underwater burst. Yes, some ships could be started up and could sail. But nobody really wanted to discuss the long-term effects. Years later Ralph E. Lapp, a Manhattan Project scientist, pointed out that the navy had suppressed the fact that radiation measurements on the order of 10,000 roentgens an hour were detected (in the 1950s 600 to 800 r was considered lethal) and that radioactive saltwater left radioactive salt behind on surfaces when it dried.[21] The uss *Independence*, a test aircraft carrier at Crossroads, was scuttled off California five years later. It was still radioactive and had been used as a training aid for decontamination crews.[22] The compartmentalization of the classified data and the hampering of internal debate over effects for other reasons would replay itself in the 1950s and again in the 1960s.

The third spin-off effect involved the limitations of the delivery systems. The Able drop of the 23-kiloton weapon by the *Dave's Dream* B-29 missed its aim point by 1,500 to 2,000 feet, to the chagrin of the usaaf and the delight of its detractors and competitors. An extensive investigation undertaken by General Power—and under Power it would have been thorough—concluded that there was likely a defect in one of the bomb's stabilization fins. Nuclear weapons were incredibly powerful, but they were subject to the same drawbacks as any other system.[23] LeMay and Power paid attention to that lesson; it became part of sac's ethos, possibly even an obsession, to increase the probability of operational success by emphasizing planning, training, navigation, maintenance, morale, and the overall pursuit of command and formation excellence.

Finally, Crossroads highlighted and confirmed the apocalyptic aspects of the weapon among the cognoscenti. The report of the President's Evaluation Board on Crossroads noted, "Atomic bombs can not only nullify any nation's military effort, but can demolish its social and economic structures and prevent their re-establishment for long periods of time. With such weapons, especially if employed in conjunction with other weapons of mass destruction, for example, pathogenic bacteria, it is quite possible to depopulate vast areas of the Earth's surface, leaving only vestigial remnants of man's material works."[24]

The forces available to implement this level of destruction, however, were minimal. Forty-six B-29s had been modified to deliver nuclear weapon in 1945, the so-called Silverplate version. Twenty-two of these were modified further with improved radar-computer systems in December 1945; the rest of the aircraft was put into storage. After Crossroads there were sixteen operational Silverplates with the 509th Bombardment Group at Roswell Army Airfield in New Mexico, five more with the Armed Forces Special Weapons Project at Kirtland Army Airfield, and three more for training and indoctrination at Oklahoma and Fort Worth. Eighteen remained in storage. Nineteen new B-29s were also modified later in the year.[25]

The 58th Bombardment Wing was approved as the "Atomic Air Force," as it was informally called, in June 1946 by General Vandenberg at Norstad's urging. This formation grouped the existing Army Air Forces (AAF) nuclear delivery and support units, including the 509th, 7th, and 43rd Bombardment Wings. The 58th in turn reported to the Continental Air Force, but this formation was redesignated the Strategic Air Command on 13 March 1946.[26] That said, its weapons did not belong to the AAF: they were in the custody of the Atomic Energy Commission (AEC). The early weapons components were stored near Sandia Base, where the Mk-3 weapons were assembled. Three AEC National Stockpile Sites were commissioned in 1946, code-named Able (Manzano Base) in Albuquerque, Baker (Killeen Base) in Texas, and Charlie (Clarksville Base) in Tennessee, each with associated airfields where SAC aircraft would pick them up when released by the president and the AEC commissioner. They were not ready until 1948–49, however, so the components for thirteen Mk-3 weapons remained at Albuquerque, while sixteen more assemblies awaited their cores.[27]

The gap between JCS planning and SAC capability in the late 1940s is examined in substantial detail in a variety of works.[28] To some extent the blame for the gap rests on events surrounding the relief of SAC commander Gen. George Kenney in October 1948. In essence, Norstad heard rumblings that all was not well with SAC in early 1948, and as the Berlin Crisis heated up, he sent Paul Tibbitts and Charles Lindbergh to investigate. Their damning report, with Norstad's recommendation, was accepted by USAF chief of staff Vandenberg, and Kenney was relieved of command. Vandenberg asked Norstad who should take over SAC: Curtis LeMay was the answer.[29]

The Lindbergh report criticisms were legitimate. Kenney had three command hats and excessively devolved authority to others in SAC. The crews were not proficient with flying and chose not to fly at altitudes requiring oxygen. The number of operational aircraft was abysmal. A May 1947 "maximum effort" training mission with one hundred B-29s against New York was a public relations exercise as opposed to a true test of capability. When LeMay took over and launched a similar exercise against Wright Patterson field, none of the aircraft completed the mission.[30]

Similarly, the prevailing view is that SAC had extremely limited target intelligence before the vaunted U-2 came on the scene in 1956. As a result targeting was extremely tentative and vague: one Kenney-era pilot told an interviewer, "We had a list of targets, but apparently someone was going to assign us which targets we were to attack before we took off." Not surprisingly for 1947, this was World War II methodology.[31]

However, the situation was actually somewhat different. The JCS's Joint War Plans Committee, as part of the run-up for a new plan for 1947, established a target list in the confines of a mobilization plan, JWPC 486/7. Out of this fell the Army Air Forces war plan, Earshot, and its atomic annex, and then SAC's first war plan, SAC OPLAN 14-47. There were further refinements, and later in 1947 the Joint Outline Emergency War Plan Broiler essentially pulled all of these elements together.[32]

Table 1. JWPC 486/7 and Broiler targets

Targets identified and confirmed by 1947

Moscow	Aviation Plant 45, Khimki Airfield, Fili Airframe Plant, Tushino Airfield, Airframe Plant 30
Leningrad	Flugov Plant No. 117 and Red October Plant No. 466 tank factories
Kharkov	Airframe Plant No. 135, Kharkov Tank Factory
Stalingrad	Red Barricades Ordnance Plant 221
Baku	Budenny, Andreyev, Stalin, Vano Sturua oil refineries
Gorki (Niznhy Novograd)	Gorki Airframe Plant Ordzhonikidze 21
Denepropetrovsk	Petrowskiy, Komintern, Karl Mark, and Lenin factory complexes
Prosny (Grozny)	Oil production facilities
Zaporoshye	Denprovskiy Magnesium Factory
Omsk	Tank plant and aircraft plant
Chelyabinsk	Kirov Tank and Tractor Plant
Molotov (Perm)	Tank Plant 148
Ufa	Ufa Novo Utimskiy, Staro Ufimskiy, Ufa Novo Chernikovsk refineries
Stalinsk (Novokuznetsk)	Aluminum Combine Stalin
Nizhny Tagil	Kaganovic Tank and Railroad Car Plant
Stalino (Donetsk)	Tank factory
Sverdlovsk (Yekaterinburg)	Aircraft factory
Novosibirsk	Novosibirsk Airframe Plant Chklov 153
Kazan	Kazan Airframe Plant Gorbunov 22
Kuybyshev	Aircraft Engine Plant 24, Zavod 2
Saratov	Saratov Airframe Plant 292
Magnitogorsk	Stalin Steel Combine, rail junction for Siberia
Chkalov (Orenberg)	Airplane Factory Zavod 47, Kirov Tank Factory

JWPC 486/7 refined the Pincher targeting enough so that some level of operational planning could be carried out. It assumed that one hundred to two hundred atomic bombs would be available and that destruction of its "target system [would] inflict both economic and psychological damage," and it recognized that such an attack would "disrupt substantially the functioning of Soviet society." The specifics of the targeting are important here as they demonstrate that the JCS planners were not merely putting dots on a map as they had done in 1945 and 1946 (see table 1). The breakdown of the JWPC 486/7 attack envisioned thirty-four bombs on targets in twenty-four cities, with the focus on "war-making industries." But it was more specific than that: JWPC 486/7 had percentage estimates of how many and what type of plant would be destroyed.[33] Even the number of bombs was specified, implying detailed knowledge: Moscow, seven; Leningrad, three; Kharkov and Stalingrad were to get two each, and one each for nineteen others. This begs the question: With no U-2s or SR-71s, and no Corona, Gambit, or Hexagon satellites, how did the JCS planners pick these targets? What changed between 1945 and 1947?

There were several sources of targeting information. One consisted of captured Luftwaffe aerial reconnaissance photos of facilities in the Soviet Union and their associated target packages. The Luftwaffe had flown missions east of the Urals and even into Kazakhstan, operating JU 188 aircraft equipped with cameras that had better resolution than their American wartime counterparts.[34] Another source was the product of Project Wringer. This human intelligence program was initiated by the AAF in Austria in 1946 to screen and interview returning German prisoners of war and refugees and later became a joint USAF-CIA affair. Wringer generated 7 million interviews and 1 million reports between 1946 and 1959; one Soviet industrial target was assigned after eighty-six separate interviews were conducted. Wringer also had penetration agents, including one in the Soviet atomic establishment.[35] A third source was the Shell Oil refineries built for the USSR during the war in Ufa; this and other industrial information was collected through open-source means.[36] The United States had also shipped complete aluminum plants to the Soviet Union during the war and had that information on hand.[37] And Operation Treasure Island exploited Eastern Bloc open-source information, including the Anders Collection, by the Library of Congress Air Studies Division (later the Air Information Division).[38]

There was also Houghteam. This U.S. Army intelligence unit "captured vast quantities of cartographic and photogrammetric equipment, map series of all scales, and geodetic and cartographic data" and "secured a nucleus of German geodesists." The emergent earth sciences were increasingly crucial for photo reconnaissance and bomber and ballistic missile operations in solving navigation problems.[39] In the early years these materials was cross-indexed and fused at the Pentagon for the JCS and not at SAC. Finally, there was Gen. Hoyt Vandenberg himself, who spent considerable time when he was in Moscow during the war visiting Soviet aircraft production and testing facilities scattered around the gargantuan city.[40]

The 1947 target list and later efforts benefited from all of these sources. For example, Airframe Plant No. 292 in Saratov was initially identified from German wartime photos and then by human intelligence sources in 1947. This facility produced Yak fighters during the war, then moved into swept-wing jet fighter production by 1948–49 (the MIG-15), then the Yak-25 Flashlight interceptor, and eventually SA-2 Guideline surface-to-air missile production by the early 1960s. Its development was continuously tracked by the American intelligence apparatus from German sources, to yearly compilations of human intelligence reportage, to U-2 imagery in 1956, and then the satellites in the 1960s. Saratov remained a SAC primary industry target from 1947 until the end of the Cold War.[41] When historical analysis is conducted on each of the cities on the JWPC 486/7 target list, similar data emerge.[42] In 1947 the JWPC targeteers inadvertently identified the plants that eventually would build the entire Soviet strategic bomber force: the TU-22 Blinder and TU-22M Backfire (Kazan Plant 22); the TU-95 Bear (Kuybyshev Airframe Plants 1 and 18); the Mya-4 (Fili Airframe Plant 23, Moscow); and the TU-16 Badger nuclear bomber (Novosibirsk).[43] Indeed they had identified the TU-4 Bull strategic bomber plant at Kazan by 1949.[44]

Summed up, the 1947 target list focused almost exclusively on aircraft industry, tank production, and oil. There was one exception, however, and that was Moscow. There were seven weapons assigned to Moscow in JWPC 486/7 but only six aviation industry targets: Ramenskoye Airfield, Aviation Plant 45, Khimki Airfield, Fili Aircraft Plant 23, Tushino Airfield, and Airframe Plant 30 (Central Moscow Airfield).[45] That left one bomb unaccounted for. It is safe to assume it was destined for the Kremlin, but we will examine the implications of this in more detail in chapter 3.

Plan Broiler's targeting was essentially an elaboration of J W P C 486/7, and likely so was Broiler's successor, Frolic.[46] By this point, however, the U.S. Navy had provided its criticism of the A A F-dominated nuclear targeting methodology employed. The navy's N S P S-3 study conducted in 1947 argued that nuclear weapons were required to slow down and stop the Red Army as it blitzkrieged its way into Western Europe. Possible targets could include rail junctions, bridges, and oil complexes. Perhaps the navy could drop nuclear weapons from carrier-based aircraft against air defense targets to assist S A C in getting to their targets in the interior of the Soviet Union.[47] At this point, however, there was no navy capability in this area, though experiments on using P2V-2C Neptunes on one-way missions ("a serious deficiency") from aircraft carriers were about to commence in mid-1948.[48]

S A C's capabilities also evolved in 1947–48 under the loose leadership of George Kenney. There are three issues to keep in mind. First, the 1948 Berlin Blockade and associated crisis was a catalyst for change, but the blockade was not underway until June, and it was after that when the critical spotlight was directed at S A C. Second, as LeMay noted later, as S A C commander in 1947–48, Kenney was "trying to hold something together that was being torn down."[49] Finally, Kenny was operating under the assumption that "in the opinion of the country's best strategists" requirements to address such a threat would not exist "in the next three to five years."[50]

There were new aircraft entering service: the B-50, an evolution of the B-29, and the B-36, a bomber designed to meet World War II intercontinental conventional bombing requirements. Thirty-six B-50s, scheduled for delivery in September 1947, underwent modifications similar to the Silverplate B-29s: these were code-named Saddletree, a replacement code-name for Silverplate. This took longer than expected, in part because Kenney examined the war plan and determined that aircraft had to be modified to operate from Arctic as well as desert and tropical bases. Then in January 1948 the J C S issued a requirement whereby S A C was to have 225 atom bomb–carrying aircraft available. Furthermore, B-36 and non-Silverplate B-29 aircraft were also to receive Saddletree modifications.[51]

PER ARDUA AD ATOMICA

And that was not all. The possibility that SAC might have to operate solely from North America was raised during Kenney's tenure when planning for the defense of the continent was quietly examined in the wake of Pincher back in 1946. Project Nanook, a series of joint Canada-U.S. Arctic projects, included a SAC program to photograph Alaska and northern Canada in their entirety. Paralleling this were projects to map Arctic weather and conduct navigation exercises over the North Pole. During these operations the first electronic reconnaissance missions against the Soviet Union took place off the Chukutski Peninsula. By 1947 a covert long-range navigation system for SAC was also established in the Arctic with Canadian help.[52]

Connected to these efforts were two others. First, the concept of operating "Very Heavy Bomber" squadrons from forward locations in the Canadian Arctic was implemented, also starting in 1947, with seven operating locations identified and surveyed.[53] Second was SAC's interest in aerial refueling, also dating from 1947. A SAC team that included Thomas Power concluded that B-29s could be modified as tankers (Project Superman, KB-29s) and receivers (Project Ruralist, B-29MR and B-50AS). From 1947 to 1948 forty KB-29s were generated, plus seventy-nine B-29MRs and thirty-six B-50AS as receivers. Another project, Chickenpox, generated eight C-97 aircraft equipped as mobile bomb assembly carriers; these also had to be modified to accompany the other aircraft. In other words, in 1947–48 SAC was tied up with modifying several hundred aircraft to drop or transport nuclear weapons, operate in the Arctic and from the desert, *and* add an aerial refueling capability to the same aircraft.[54]

At the same time, SAC implemented its first overseas rotations for its Very Heavy Bomber groups. By May 1948 a squadron of B-29s was rotating to Yokoto, Japan; this was followed by the entire 93rd Bombardment Group and its thirty B-29s on a ninety-day rotation. The 43rd Bombardment Group and then the atomic-capable 509th rotated to Eielson AFB in Alaska, also on ninety-day rotations.[55] Kenney may have neglected readiness, but this force structure and its supporting efforts set the stage for what LeMay and Power would accomplish in the 1950s and 1960s with intercontinental SAC operations.

As for targeting, the 1945 estimate that ten atomic bombs would be withheld to counter any Soviet lodgments in the Western Hemisphere was apparently not elaborated on, at least not on paper. That said, the long-range navigation system provided SAC with the navigational capability in poor weather to deploy atomic bombs against possible Soviet lodgments in Alaska, sites from which TU-4 Bull bombers could presumably operate against the Lower Forty-Eight. SAC's aircraft were "Arcticized" and could use the network of Canadian bases. A communications and weather network was in place. Reconnaissance was conducted against Soviet bases in eastern Siberia, all between 1946 and 1948.[56] Later an operational storage site for nuclear weapons was constructed adjacent to Fairchild AFB in Washington State. We must conclude that SAC was keeping its options open in this area.

Stalin's imposition of the Berlin Blockade in the summer of 1948 prompted a reexamination of war plans. Bushwhacker, the successor to Broiler and Frolic, was revised into Halfmoon and renamed two more times, to Fleetwood and then Doublestar, as the crisis unfolded. The USAF derivative plan was called Harrow. The objective was "to destroy the will of the USSR to resist by a main offensive effort in Western Eurasia and a strategic defense in the Far East. Initially, to launch a powerful air offensive designed to exploit the destructive and psychological power of atomic weapons against the vital elements of the Soviet war-making capacity."[57] It was understood that Harrow was a "limited sustained strategic air offensive" to "reduce offensive capabilities." The plan assumed that advanced air bases would be retained and that there would be a buildup period.[58] Overall the plans focused the strategic air campaign on nine target types: atomic stockpiles and production; key government control centers; urban-industrial areas; oil; submarine bases; coke, iron, and steel; and electrical power. The plans assumed there were fifty weapons available and that targets in twenty cities would be struck to destroy the target types, with the list approximating JWPC 486/7.[59] At this point the collections of targets were grouped and referred to as "target systems," of which there were twelve.[60]

SAC, meanwhile, was responding to the Berlin Crisis. The first

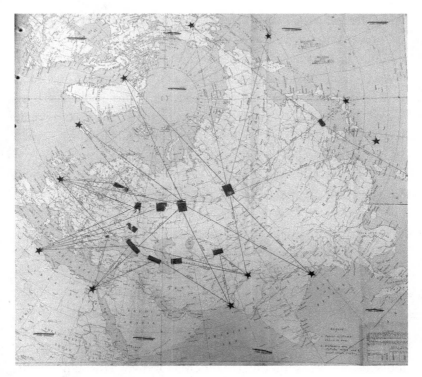

Map 1. Gen. Hoyt Vandenberg's "Blitz Book" depicting SAC Target Systems in the Soviet Union, 1948. Courtesy of Library of Congress.

target folders were developed in June 1948, and the AEC now had fifty Mk-3 bombs available. Some of these weapons even possessed yields greater than the original 23 kilotons due to technological developments.[61]

LeMay was at this point commanding general of the U.S. Air Forces in Europe, which was in an embryonic state at best, with little firepower. He requested B-29s, while apparently at the same time British foreign secretary Ernest Bevin suggested a B-29 deployment to signal Stalin; Gen. Lucius Clay in Berlin made the request for a SAC B-29 deployment, which was approved by President Truman.[62] Kenney deployed three bombardment groups, the 301st, 28th, and 307th, staged through Goose Bay, Labrador; the 301st was sent to Fürstenfeldbruck in Bavaria and the other two groups to three bases in the United Kingdom. Another bomb group moved to Goose Bay while the rest of SAC achieved a twenty-four-hour alert status. U.S. Air Forces Europe plans envisioned B-29 use against Soviet airfields in East Germany and, if necessary, against airfields they overran in West Germany, what would be later called "retardation" missions. LeMay is coy in his memoirs about what munitions would have been used: "We would have cleaned them up pretty well, in no time at all. We were prepared to do this but of course nobody hit the switch in Washington." He noted that nuclear weapons were not transported overseas at this time, though it is clear that some of aircraft could have been Saddletree-capable and the weapons could be moved by the Chickenpox C-97s if released by the AEC custodians.[63]

Right after these deployments, Kenney had SAC mount an unusual operation. Three B-29s departed Davis-Monthan AFB in Arizona for a round-the-world flight. One aircraft crashed in the Middle East, but the other two completed the task in fifteen days, leapfrogging from base to base. This effort, as well as the deployments in Western Europe, was widely seen as "signaling" the Soviet Union.[64] This is probably when the concept of a more explicit deterrent function for SAC emerged, something that LeMay and Power would dramatically elaborate on in the 1950s and 1960s.[65]

Kenney's replacement by LeMay in October 1948 led to an immediate tightening up in the command, especially after the first major exercise failure that same month. LeMay was able to have Power recalled from the United Kingdom, while Gens. Richard Montgomery, Charles Sweeney, and August Kissener were brought in as "new brooms."[66] The war plan itself was under evolution. SAC had been leaning forward and assumed for its purposes that, based on the requirement to man 225 atomic-capable aircraft, the number of targets would increase to two hundred.[67] However Harrow, the USAF portion of Halfmoon/Frolic, focused on attacking targets in twenty cities with fifty weapons. While SAC was working on the Venturous operations plan to carry this out, Plan Trojan emerged from the bowels of the JCS. Trojan's atomic annex upped the numbers to seventy cities with between 133 and 147 Mk-3 bombs.[68] The targets likely were similar in type to those established in JWPC 486/7. That said, a subordinate commander wrote Power, "There is a serious weakness at all levels when thinking is done about *what kind* of targets we are preparing to bomb." The information was not being pushed down, so some units actually believed they were training to bomb islands.[69]

SAC's buildup continued. During a speech on 15 February 1949 the SAC commander asserted, "It is the threat of our might that is keeping the peace. Any aggressor anxious to achieve world domination must first do us in before he can go on."[70] Two weeks later LeMay ordered the round-the-world deployment of a 43rd Bomb Group B-50A, the *Lucky Lady II*, supported by KB-29 tankers stationed in the Azores, Saudi Arabia, and the Philippines. The successful February mission, coming at the height of the Berlin Blockade, was an international sensation. LeMay was asked by the press "if this mean[t the United States could] use refueling to deliver an A-Bomb anywhere in Russia." LeMay looked thoughtful for a minute, blew some smoke from his cigar, and replied, "Let's say any place that would require an atom bomb."[71] SAC was now increasingly linked, at least in the public mind, with deterring the Soviet Union.

What role did SAC's B-29 deployments and other preparations play in Stalin's decision to close out the blockade in 1949? The Western powers demonstrated resolve, and clearly the Berlin Airlift was central and key, but it was backed up with the possibility of nuclear weapons use, as primitive and as remote as it was.[72] Stalin had insight into American planning via elements of the Cambridge Five espionage apparatus in Washington.[73] One Russian historian, Col. Gen. Dmitri Volkogonov, noted that at this time "plans were being made in the Pentagon for the nuclear bombardment of the USSR. In these circumstances, Stalin pursued a cautious policy, developing his military might, while avoiding any provocation of his former ally."[74] Additionally, Milovan Djilas, a senior Yugoslav official, noted that in the late 1940s, given the lack of a significant navy and only a nascent atomic capability, "Stalin was just as anxious to avoid conflict with the West, particularly the United States."[75] Sergo Beria believes Stalin was convinced to back off by five advisors, led by Lavrentiy Beria, who argued, "We had four hundred divisions in the heart of Europe, with nothing in front of them. We stopped because we did not have the bomb. We still haven't got it. Do you want the Soviet Union to be devastated by atomic bombs? . . . Eventually Stalin did realize he had been defeated and lifted the blockade."[76]

On 29 August 1949 at 7:00 local time at Semipalatinsk in the Kazakhstan Soviet Socialist Republic, a direct copy of Fat Man, designated "Special Jet Engine-1" (Reaktivnyi Dvigatel Spetsialnyi, or RDS-1), detonated in the desert, yielding 22 kilotons. And the world changed again as Stalin prepared to face off with the West once more.[77]

3

Imminence of War I

Targeting the Soviet Union, 1950–53

"Comrade, will there be war?"

"No, comrade, but there'll be such a struggle for peace that
not a stone will be left standing."

—Soviet joke, quoted in Robert Conquest, *Stalin: Breaker of Nations*

T he pace of international events picked up after the first Soviet nuclear weapons test, and so did American nuclear targeting and war planning. NATO's creation produced a flurry of reorganizations and a reexamination of the assumptions on which Pincher, Broiler, Halfmoon, and their spin-off support plans were based. Similarly, the idea that war with the Soviet Union was essentially World War II with atom bombs was called into question by the Soviet's acquisition of a nuclear capability. Connected to this were the tremendous technological advances in jet aircraft and nuclear weapons that were not just on the horizon but approaching at Mach speed.

The United States and her allies were confronted with several interlocking problems. The first and primary one was deterring a Soviet attack on Western Europe and forestalling Soviet nonmilitary activities designed to subvert the democracies. The second problem was the premeditated multinational Communist assault on the Republic of Korea, which was in part designed, as Mao explained to Stalin, "to spend several years consuming several hundred thousand American lives."[1] That effort, sanctioned by Stalin, had North Korea in the lead backed up with direct Communist Chinese ground force intervention and supported by an advanced, plausibly deniable air force flown by Soviet pilots.[2]

To what extent were Communist efforts in the West and those in the Far East connected? If they were not, did the possibility of opportunistic adventurism on the part of Stalin exist when it came to Berlin, or even Western Europe? Prudent steps were taken: NATO established the Supreme Allied Commander Europe in 1951 and Supreme Allied Commander Atlantic in 1952, and member countries assigned standing forces to these commands. This included the 1951 deployment of American and Canadian troops and air forces to western Germany, where they would remain until the end of the Cold War.

SAC planning and deployments became integral to these defensive activities. The dominant nuclear warfare concept from 1950 to 1953 solidified as SAC Emergency War Plan 1-49. The internal debates over how to implement EWP 1-49 and against what targets in part laid the groundwork for issues that would generate friction with the Emergency War Plan in the 1950s and lead to the creation of the SIOP in the 1960s.

SAC Emergency War Plans 1-49 and 1-51, 1949–53

The altered geostrategic situation in 1949 produced fluctuating planning within the JCS. The planning system attempted to maintain an emergency war plan for near-immediate execution, plus contingency plans for several years out. However, with the Berlin Blockade, the formation of NATO, and the detonation of the first Soviet atomic bomb, the original plans that featured Western forces evacuating Western Europe or holding at the Pyrenees had to be shelved. SAC Emergency War Plan 1-49 was originally based on the atomic annex for Plan Trojan, but when Trojan gave way in late December 1949 to a new plan, Offtackle, a new annex was not prepared. SAC EWP 1-50 was supposed to accompany Offtackle, but this did not occur in part because of the outbreak of the Korean War in 1950.[3]

The number of targets and cities to be hit by these plans varied. Trojan was a modification of Halfmoon and was approved on 28 January 1949. Trojan had the atomic offensive focused on war industries and oil, with seventy cities hit with between 133 and 147 bombs.[4]

Offtackle, approved almost a year later, had several expanded target sets: Soviet war-making capacity, oil, transport, military and political command and control, and targets to impeded the Red Army's advance across Western Europe. Offtackle was assigned 104 cities, 220 bombs, with a further 72 bombs for restrike.[5]

Then there was Plan Dropshot, a JCS project planning for what war might look like in 1957. As a reflection of 1949 JCS thinking, Dropshot was prescient in several ways. It anticipated that before 1957 SAC would have to deal with expanded Soviet nuclear capabilities. Seventy-five to one hundred bombs would be needed to destroy the Soviet offensive air threat; one hundred would be required to hit nuclear production, lines of communication, supply dumps, submarine bases, and troop concentrations, and an undesignated number of bombs for use against the "military-industrial economy": oil, steel, and power. Dropshot planners noted that "the use of atomic bombs against satellite and overrun areas . . . should be confined as far as possible to those targets the destruction of which would not involve large masses of population." Some twenty-two Soviet administrative and control centers would be destroyed as "a byproduct" of the other targets getting hit. In the planners' view, it was possible that a psychological shock effect might produce capitulation, the Holy Grail of airpower theory.[6]

What was a SAC planner to do? LeMay and his staff had to contend with the here and now (1949), the immediate future (1950–51), and the "distant" future, five to seven years hence. With the talented and motivated SAC staff, LeMay was able to handle all three concurrently: responding to the shifting sands of policy-based target selection and melding future strategic requirements with projected science fiction–like technology into the next-generation SAC force, while at the same time preparing to fight a war with what was on hand, today, now. The nuclear weapons stockpile in 1949 consisted of 170 weapons, the bulk of which were Mk-3 Fat Man weapons (23 kt). Operation Sandstone, the nuclear test series held in 1948, produced new means of using plutonium and uranium so that these scarce materials could be stretched to make more weapons. Innovative assemblies increased yields for the new Mk-4 bomb to between 37 and 47 kilotons. SAC had "less that 100 targets" in its target system by the end of 1948, and ninety "target complexes" with 220 assigned targets within those by late 1949. By 1949 there were eleven medium bomb wings of B-29 and B-50 aircraft. There were two tanker squadrons with KB-29M tankers; 180 aircraft of the medium bomb force, about half, were capable of nuclear weapons delivery.[7] That said, expansion was underway: Saddletree B-29s were coming out of storage, training was ramped up, and the huge B-36s were undergoing testing for a planned 1951 operational capability.

For all intents and purposes, however, SAC Emergency War Plan 1-49 ceased to be associated with specific JCS plans but remained the basis for SAC planning, with ongoing modifications. For example, SAC submitted EWP 1-51 in December 1951 to the JCS. This document, which an astounded Chief of Staff USAF Nathan Twining said provided "practically no detailed information" to the JCS, remained on the books until 1955.[8] Consequently SAC war planning started to resemble the 1960s SIOP in that EWP 1-49 became a process, not just a singular plan. Aircraft and weapons were continually added or subtracted, as were targets as more information became available: EWP 1-51, approved in December 1951, was basically EWP 1-49 with these changes, but the plan remained essentially the same. Thus the only way to examine the SAC Emergency War Plan is to freeze it at particular points of its existence.

But what exactly was the SAC Emergency War Plan supposed to accomplish? The Offtackle target systems consisted of oil, electrical power plants, aircraft industry, automotive industry, and submarine yards and were geared to the "World War II with atom bombs" concept. Criticism of Offtackle suggested three targeting options for future planning. First, hit one or two key industries that were "indispensable for war production," possibly petroleum and electrical power plants. A second option was to hit "general industrial complexes in urban areas." A third was to destroy the cities themselves as area targets.[9] The JCS selected electrical power, petroleum, and "war-based industry" as the new target systems in 1950–51.[10] Again, this was a modification of World War II with atom bombs, intended for a protracted war. Indeed the targeting of Soviet electrical power plants seems to have been influenced by extremely detailed but unimplemented German World War II plans designed to stop Soviet steel production through the destruction of specific electrical power plants on the Volga and in the Urals.[11]

LeMay, however, noted that, while the present targeting policy correctly embraced elements of Russia's "sustaining resources" in "large industrial centers," the Soviets now had the atomic bomb. And that had to be prioritized in new planning as North American targets, specifically SAC's staging and strike bases in Canada and Alaska, let alone the UK base complexes, were at risk.

Assertions that the Soviets could not attack North America with its TU-4 capability in the 1950s are incorrect. SAC's Alaskan and Canadian bases were well within TU-4 range from deployment bases in Siberia and on the Kola Peninsula. These assertions are usually couched in the context of the highly politicized American "Bomber Gap" debate in the 1950s and are based on an incomplete understanding of the Soviet TU-4 force and its capabilities. There were over 600 TU-4s available by 1950 and 1,296 by 1953. Some crews had over-the-pole navigation training, and there was a nascent aerial refueling capability tested in 1954. The TU-4s had atomic, chemical, biological, and conventional bombs; some had an air-to-surface missile capability. If even a proportion of these systems were directed against targets that had no significant air defense system (there was no NORAD yet), this was a significant problem.[12] The TU-4 deployment to the Soviet Far East, initially 160 aircraft, was eventually detected by the United States in January 1952.[13] By 1954 TU-4s were identified at six Soviet Arctic air bases, while Far Eastern–based TU-4s were monitored as they conducted exercises that resembled a mock attack on Tokyo and other targets in Japan.[14]

These were the first steps away from "World War II with atom bombs." A "counter-weapons phase" of the plan would be needed in the future.[15] Vandenberg wrote LeMay in April 1950 suggesting that the acquisition of nuclear weapons by the Soviets meant the U.S. Air Force had to "reach and maintain an acceptable state of combat readiness" that wasn't there yet. In his view the institution and its "emergency capability" was there for two purposes: to carry out its assigned "tasks in the event of war" and to "serve as a continuing deterrent to war."[16] This was in line with LeMay's thinking as well as his demonstrative activity in 1949. SAC was a deterrent force and a war-fighting force: both tasks coexisted in the space and time. Furthermore SAC's capability had to be demonstrated for the Soviets and all to see. Conceptually, U.S. nuclear targeting was in a new phase of development by 1950.

LeMay and Power ran a SAC readiness exercise not long afterward, simulating part of EWP 1-49 in its present state. There were twenty-nine targets in the exercises, twenty-five for the medium force and four for the heavy force. The scenario had SAC deploy to its forward bases and on E+6 launch operations. Sixty-one "bomb carriers" lifted off; fifty-eight hit their targets in all seventeen areas. Eglin AFB, simulating Moscow, was hit with ten out of eleven assigned weapons. Eighteen KB-29 tanker hookups were conducted successfully. The exercise was considered a successful base to improve on. The only unit that was short was the unit "attacking" Denver, which simulated the Ploieşti oil production facilities in Romania.[17]

At the same time, the deteriorating world situation in 1950 had the JCS revisit targeting. After some debate a decision was made to categorize targets as either Disruption (later called "Destruction"), Blunting, or Retardation (Delta, Bravo, and Romeo, respectively). Delta targeted the war-making industry, Bravo targets involved the destruction of Soviet nuclear capabilities, and Romeo targets were selected to retard the Soviet Army's assault on NATO, should it occur.[18] Several questions emerged from this shift in terminology: To what extent did "disruption" targets have an impact on retardation of the Soviet advance, and when? Who, exactly, would carry out which mission and under what command structure? LeMay's initial view was that Delta targets should be prioritized over Romeo targets.[19] That led to a separate debate between SAC and Supreme Allied Commander Europe, as we will see later, that had long-term effects on nuclear war-planning well into the 1970s.

There were similar issues with the Bravo task. Blunting was initially problematic from an intelligence point of view in 1950, less so by 1952. As a result, EWP 1-49 in its 1950 iteration targeted "vital elements of Soviet industry" to "weaken enemy war potential," leaving Bravo and Romeo targets aside for the time being.

The JCS shift from Offtackle to its replacement plan, Shakedown, was also in play during this time, and the machinery that linked the JCS planning to SAC planning became contentious. USAF HQ established a Target Panel consisting of the senior leaders of the operations, intelligence, and plans staffs, plus LeMay. Sometimes Vice Chief of Staff Twining observed.[20] It appears its purpose was to coordinate an air force response to any JCS requirements related to the JCS war plans' Target Destruction Annexes. Those who criticize LeMay for being out of control do not appreciate how restrictive the process actually was in the early 1950s and why he reacted negatively to that state of affairs. The JCS formulated the war plan, generated the objectives it wanted to achieve with the strategic air offensive, selected the target systems, selected the Registered Ground Zeroes, and then placed them in the Target Destruction Annex. There was little SAC input short of making sure the aircraft and the bombs delivered onto the aim points generated by the JCS.[21] The Atomic Energy Commission and the Military Liaison Committee tried to horn in on SAC's prerogatives, forcing LeMay and Power to push back. As Power said, "Curt feels that we should avoid, if possible, getting into a position where we are defending our contemplated strategy and tactics before anyone outside the Air Force. . . . Our position . . . is that there are many tactics that might be employed. Our mission is to be trained and equipped to employ any one of them and that the final choice would be made by the field commander just prior to the first mission and based on his estimate of enemy defenses and capabilities of our forces."[22]

There was a Strategic Vulnerability Branch in USAF HQ's Director of Intelligence, involved in helping SAC generate target folders, but how it interacted with the JCS in the targeting process is obscure.[23]

The Target Panel was likely formed by USAF HQ and SAC to counter excessive "reach-down" that was occurring between the JCS and SAC, and in this it succeeded. LeMay complained that there were directives "requiring him to obtain prior approval from [HQ USAF] before modifying any ground zeros, for operational purposes, contained in an approved target study" and that "this directive tied his hands completely in not allowing him any operational leeway at all in selecting aiming points." Prior to this directive "he had the authority to modify, to a certain extent, any ground zeros when he felt that a slight change would obtain better operational results." He was told this directive apparently related to a Weapons Systems Evaluation Group audit. LeMay wasn't buying it; this was micromanagement by unqualified people in the JCS, possibly from elsewhere. He'd seen this happen before in the war: "We get the target lists, but how I handle missions is my business."[24] Shakedown's air campaign, he believed, was "operationally infeasible."[25] At some point the JCS agreed. Shakedown was approved, but its Target Destruction Annex eventually was not. Therefore Offtackle's annex continued to be the basis for SAC planning. Thus Emergency War Plan 1-49 remained the basis for SAC war planning.

And, importantly, the USAF was now in a position to recommend and shape target systems before the main new JCS plan was even written. From there LeMay was able to imperceptibly and progressively separate "strategic" matters from "operational" matters and then gradually shift control of both selecting the target systems and generating Registered Ground Zeros (later Desired Ground Zero, or DGZ) from the JCS to the USAF and then to SAC.[26]

LeMay and SAC had leeway, and that leeway was given top cover by Gen. Thomas White, the deputy chief of staff of operations at USAF headquarters. Exploiting inexact and possibly contradictory language in two JCS targeting directives, White told LeMay that targeting was flexible and that SAC could substitute new target systems, "including the atomic energy industry[,] in lieu of some of the targets on the original list," as long as the damage to the "industrial system" was "materially increased by the substitution." White cautioned LeMay that he was limited to the total number of bombs "released for industrial target systems." One could interpret this document as suggesting that SAC substitute the Soviet atomic production facilities for the despised electrical plant category.[27] The JCS hammerlock on nuclear targeting was seriously challenged by SAC in late 1951.

This masterful bureaucratic maneuver paid off in the early 1950s to the point where SAC eventually developed the target systems by shaping the JCS through the Target Panel, then handled the selection of the DGZs, and briefed the crews who then maintained target folders and trained on those specific targets.[28] This was a significant change from the 1940s and set the stage for the Joint Strategic Target Planning Staff and the SIOP in the 1960s.

And that was not all. Criticism of the Shakedown air offensive by Vandenberg, Bernard Brodie, and LeMay in 1951 prompted a shift in JCS targeting priorities for the Delta category to include petroleum; military, government, and economic centers; and "industrial capital." Electrical power stations, for example, were too difficult to find with current intelligence techniques.[29] In its 1952 iteration the SAC Emergency War Plan was prioritized to destroy vital elements of the Soviet war-making capacity, blunting Soviet atomic weapons and retarding Soviet advances. The Delta tasks solidified to include petroleum, electrical power, steel, aluminum, and government control centers. Bravo targets were added by the end of 1952.[30]

SAC's ability to implement the Emergency War Plan in 1951 was initially based on five B-29, five B-50, and three B-36 bomb wings of forty-five aircraft each. This increased to fourteen B-29, five B-50, and five B-36 wings by 1953. Eighteen tanker squadrons to support them existed, with conversion from KB-29MR to KB-29P and then KC-97 aircraft by 1953.[31] SAC reported in January 1951 that it had the ability to deliver 135 bombs with this force in the event of war. This increased to 140 to 146 bombs in August 1951 and 200 bombs by July–December 1952. The capability related directly to the number of trained crews capable of meeting the high standards imposed by SAC before they were qualified for nuclear delivery, not the number of aircraft.[32]

The Atomic Energy Commission had 299 weapons in its custody in 1950, 438 in 1951, 841 in 1952, and 1,169 by mid-1952.[33] Nuclear weapons could be released to SAC only when both the president and the AEC chairman authorized their removal from the AEC-controlled storage sites. The plutonium or hybrid cores of these implosion bombs were stored separately from the casings, or "shapes." These casings contained the detonation system and the assembly that held the high explosive, tamper, and reflector around the core (the assembly was sometimes called the "pit").[34] In 1950 Truman authorized the forward deployment of eighteen "shapes," nine to Guam and nine to the United Kingdom, but the cores were held in storage in the United States and later on U.S. Navy aircraft carriers.[35]

The nuclear weapons available between 1950 and 1953 are depicted in table 2, but for the most part the main weapons used by SAC were the Mk-4, Mk-5, and Mk-6. It is important to understand that the yields of these weapons were variable and depended on which combinations of cores and assemblies were used. There were at least three assemblies—Type A, Type B, and Type C—and four different cores, Able through Dog. (Tare was a thermonuclear weapons package.) An Mk-5 bomb combination for SAC yielded 81 to 83 kilotons, while a different configuration used by the U.S. Navy might yield 92 kilotons.[36] The Mk-18 bomb was actually an Mk-6 bomb casing with different assembly and a Dog oralloy core that produced a 500-kiloton yield.[37] For the most part, however, the yield range for weapons that would have been employed in EWP 1-49 were been between 37 and 83 kilotons.[38]

Why was this important? The scarcity of nuclear material limited the size of the stockpile, thus producing competition for weapons allocations between the commands. Though this would change once the large gaseous diffusion plants at Portsmouth, Ohio, and Paducah, Kentucky, went online in the 1954–56 period, it remained a source of bureaucratic competition in many venues. These technical measures helped spread the atomic wealth, as it were.

It also affected targeting on several levels. LeMay pointed out to his superiors in 1952, "The number of targets which must be destroyed to insure the destruction of the Soviet war-making capacity . . . has been badly warped by the limited number of bombs assumed to be available. . . . The low number used in planning has seriously restricted the selection of targets. Many targets and target systems that are profitable targets for atomic weapons were not even considered." But most important, and this from a man experienced with strategic bombing in both the European and Pacific theaters:

Table 2. U.S. nuclear gravity bombs, 1948–53, estimated yields and availability

Core	Yield range	Availability
Able	12, 14, 18 kt	1949+
Baker	37, 47 kt	1949+
Charlie	81–83, 92 kt	1952+
Dog	500 kt	1953+
Tare	(MT)	1953+

Weapon	Core selection	Yield range	Availability
Mk-3		23 kt (others possible)	1947–50
Mk-4		18, 37 kt	1949–53
Mk-5	A, B, C	12, 14, 18, 37, 47, 81–83, 92 kt	1952+
Mk-6	A, B, C	12, 14, 18, 37, 47, 81–83 kt	1951+
Mk-7	A, B, C	12, 14, 18, 37, 41 47, 81–83 kt	1952+
Mk-8, -9	Gun-type	15–20 kt	1952
Mk-12	B	10–20, 37, 47 kt	1954
Mk-18	D	500 kt	1953+
Emergency Capability	T	(MT secondary)	1953+

Sources: Compiled from AEC; U.S. Department of Energy; LeMay Papers, Library of Congress Manuscript Division; Hansen, *US Nuclear Weapons*.

We have assumed that the damage inflicted would produce greater results than we have any right to expect. In my opinion, we have sadly under-rated the job to be done. . . . The rigid limitation of bombs available over the last few years has misled us into thinking that the job could be successfully accomplished with only a relatively few hundred bombs. The bombing encyclopedia compiled by the Air Staff contains over 6000 possible targets in the USSR and satellites. Undoubtedly, many more have been developed in the USSR of which nothing is known. We must apply sufficient mass against the Soviet economy to insure that it is completely, not partially, destroyed. Historically we have always underestimated the tonnage required to destroy targets.[39]

One could argue that the "origins of overkill" lay in LeMay's understanding of the limitations of World War II–era strategic bombing, particularly after the harrowing experiences of the Schweinfurt and Regensburg raids in 1943.[40] Power's experiences with the Fifteenth Air Force during the Pointblank campaign and its frustrating Ploiești component likely influenced him along similar lines.[41] Nuclear weapons were powerful, but they were not a panacea for the bombing problem. There would be limitations on atomic bombing operations just as there were limitations on conventional bombing in World War II, and it was better to have more rather than less to cover these limitations.

Then there were the effects of accuracy and the damage radii, which related directly to yield and height of burst. The lower the yield and less accurate the weapon, the more weapons were needed to be directed at a target to ensure its destruction.[42] If the yield was large enough, these problems magically decreased. And SAC crews had to be trained and they needed a standard. What was that standard? What was the Circular Error Probable they needed to train toward? What CEP was feasible with the aircraft they were equipped with? How did that relate to weapons effects?

What if there were multiple targets inside a target complex? Room for "bonus damage" was made in the early plans, but it became more critical with a larger number of targets. Altering the aim point of a bomb to optimally destroy multiple targets was the preferred methodology. Using a larger weapon to destroy all of the targets in a target complex instead of using several smaller weapons was a logical extension of this thinking. But what was the relationship of nuclear material produced to weapons produced to yield packages generated to number of targets destroyed? What was the most efficient solution given limited national resources?[43] LeMay stated that targeting "criteria may change dependent upon the availability of fissionable materials": "A target which today, because of scarcity of bombs would not justify the expenditure of an atomic bomb, might become a logical target when fissionable material becomes as plentiful as gunpowder."[44]

Then there were the targets. Numerous entities outside of SAC used "target" to mean anything attacked with a nuclear bomb. Terminology therefore had to evolve, as "target" was too general for the practitioners. For example, in 1951 Leningrad was Target Reference 002, yet it contained up to twelve installations that had to be destroyed. A target could be a singular facility to be destroyed by a single bomb; it could also be a "target complex," a term first used around 1950–51 to describe a collection of targets within a specific geographical space that could be destroyed either by an optimally targeted bomb or several bombs. A "reconnaissance target" was a target or target complex photographed by a reconnaissance sortie after the attack. At some point in the 1960s during the SIOP-era collections of targets and target complexes became known as "target islands."[45]

It is not clear when the JCS destruction criteria like that employed by the SIOP in the 1960s (rubble, gravel, dust) first appeared. The immediate effects of the Fat Man over Nagasaki were within the knowledge base of 1950s targeteers, as was the data from Crossroads and Sandstone. Those data were readily applied to the industrial targets in EWP 1-49. Important questions, however, revolve around the role of radiation effects in targeting. First, American nuclear use and test experiences, with the exception of Shot Baker during Crossroads, were with airbursts and their associated blast and fire effects. The industrial targets in EWP 1-49 were likely going to be destroyed with airbursts in the kiloton-yield range using optimal height of burst techniques for maximum blast damage, with thermal effects generating secondary damage beyond that.

Fallout, as we know it in the mid-1950s sense, did not exist for the planners. They knew about "residual radiation": that was detected and measured after Trinity, Nagasaki, Crossroads, and Sandstone (where it was called "rainout") and during the early test series in Nevada. The amount of residual radiation, however, would not have been militarily important to them, with the exception that it had a potential secondary denial effect. For example, depending on the weather, the destruction of the Ploieşti oil refineries by a pair of 35-kiloton weapons would have generated enough residual radiation to interfere with the rail transportation system in, through, and around the remains of the city. That said, it appears the targeteers were focused on the primary effects of blast because of the unpredictability of other effects due to fluctuating conditions over and on the target.[46]

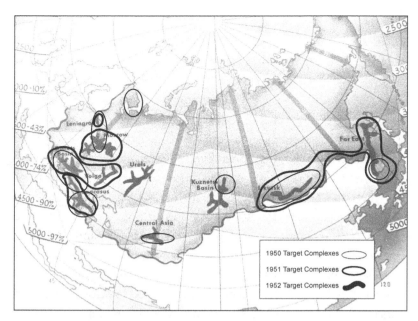

Map 2. Delta Target Complexes evolution, 1950–52, superimposed on a 1953 map from the LeMay Papers analyzing future medium bomber programs. Courtesy of Library of Congress.

EWP 1-49 and EWP 1-51: Destroying the Delta Targets

The evolution of the plan's Delta target complexes from 1950 to 1952 can be seen in map 2.[47] The evolution of SAC base areas in the United Kingdom, North Africa, and North America, plus the expansion of the bomber force from 1950 to 1953, clearly had a direct relationship to the geographical areas that could be hit by those forces and thus the increasing number and granularity of the target complexes.

The Delta target list was the basis for later nuclear targeting. By the time of the SIOP in the 1960s, the term "urban/industrial" target came into use, but the bulk of the SIOP was directed toward destruction of Soviet nuclear capabilities. The U/I category, however, remained prioritized for early destruction if the SIOP was launched in retaliatory mode. Similarly, British nuclear targeting, in its national retaliatory mode, focused on Soviet urban centers. Both the SIOP and the British target lists have as their basis the EWP 1-49 Delta targets. All three lists had between 90 and 123 targets (see appendix A).

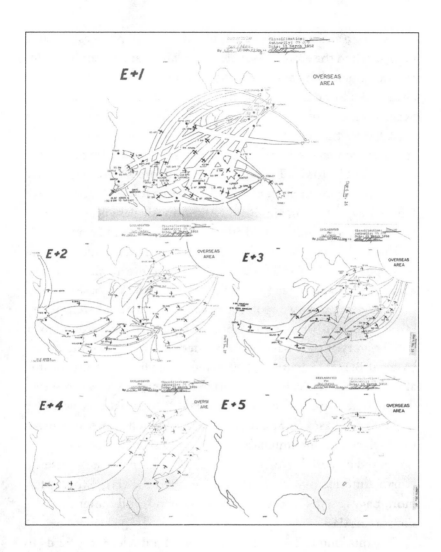

Map 3. SAC Emergency War Plan, 1950–52: deployment from the "Zone of the
Interior" (United States) through Canada to bases in the United Kingdom over
a five-day buildup period, E+1 to E+5. Note the centrality of Goose Bay and
Harmon air bases to the plan. Note also the locations of the AEC-controlled
nuclear stockpile sites at Campbell, Gray, and Kirtland on the E+1 map.
Courtesy of Library of Congress, LeMay Papers.

EWP 1-49 and EWP 1-51 were built on three subplans established in 1950, when the Korean War started, plans that had ramifications for SAC operations and the SIOP well into the 1960s.[48] SAC was already deployed in the United Kingdom at four bases: Marham, Scampton, Lakenheath, and Sculthorpe, the original bases used in 1948. Under the so-called Ambassador's Agreement, SAC airfields stabilized to include Fairford, Greenham Common, Brize Norton, and Upper Heyford.[49] These forward-based forces were augmented, if EWP 1-49 were implemented, by U.S.-based forces staged through Goose Bay, Labrador, and Ernest Harmon Air Base in Newfoundland. Other SAC units would attack from Alaska and Japan.

The Soviet acquisition of a strategic air and then a nuclear capability put the UK-based forces at risk. Therefore an alternate SAC plan saw forces deployed to French Morocco if the UK bases became untenable for military or political reasons. Negotiations were undertaken to acquire basing rights from the French starting around 1950, and five very austere bases were opened in 1951–52. Bombers were based at Ben Guerir and Sidi Slimane, while fighters were located at El Djema and Mechra Bel Ksiri. Nouasseur was a "war reserves depot" that also acted as a bomber base.[50] Negotiations were also initiated for bases in Spain, in case the French Moroccan bases themselves became untenable.[51] The third plan, the backup plan, was based on aerial refueling and a combination of bases closer to North America that evolved to include Goose Bay; Ernest Harmon; Lages on the Azores; Thule, Greenland; and Elmendorf and Eielson in Alaska.[52]

Our thinking today on the duration of a nuclear war tends to be conditioned by the perceived speed of the system: hours in the 1960s, or even minutes in the 1970s and beyond. During the early 1950s, however, the initial SAC deployment to the forward areas would take three to five days after Execution Day (E-Day) was initiated, with the first operations against enemy targets commencing on E+3, possibly E+6. Between 1950 and 1953 the most stable estimate is that there would be three strikes: E+3, E+6, and a third.[53] The tempo of the operation involved prestrike reconnaissance on some targets during the E-Day to E+3 period, followed by the first wave of

Map 4. SAC Emergency War Plan, 1950–52: operations against the Soviet Union on E+6 from the United Kingdom bases. The EWP envisioned overflying neutral Sweden and "nonaligned" Yugoslavia, with the tacit permission of the military authorities of those countries. Courtesy of U.S. National Archives and Records Administration.

strikes, then a series of night reconnaissance operations, followed by the second strike, and so on. One exercise suggests that by 1952 the plan had sped up to three consecutive strike days with ten targets on E+3, one hundred targets on E+4, and ten on E+5.[54] As more weapons were made available and deployed forward by SAC's Strategic Support Squadrons and additional MATS C-54 transports, recovering bombers could reload and go back in against targets defined by the reconnaissance forces. In general terms, the campaign was expected to last up to thirty days if necessary.

For our purposes and given the evolution of the plan from 1950 to 1953, EWP 1-49 and EWP 1-51 progressively assigned 134 to 200 bombs against 90 to 123 targets. The general breakdown divided bombs between the ten target complexes and the approximately twenty-seven individual targets that lay outside of those complexes. Within the target complexes were single target cities and bonus target cities. In 1950–51 one weapon was applied to the first, and a pair to the second using optimal height of burst aim points. As more weapons became available after 1951, more weapons could be employed against individual targets within the bonus target cities. This was not pure "overkill": in some cases it was done to overcome unique geographic features that might attenuate weapons effects in order to ensure target destruction. For example, Stalingrad is a linear city along the Volga River, not a concentric circular city like Moscow. The primary targets, including the Red October Steel Plant, the Red Barricades Ordnance Plant, the Lazur Chemical Works, the Aluminumstroy Rolling Mill, and the Dzerzhinskiy Tractor Factory, would have required three 40- to 80-kiloton weapons detonated in a line to ensure their destruction.[55]

From 1950 to 1951 the bulk of SAC's attack was against Leningrad, Moscow, the Volga Basin, the Donets Basin, the Urals, and the Caucasus. (The Far East is a special case and is dealt with in the next chapter.) As SAC's reach grew in 1951–52, an increased weight of attack could be directed at the Urals, and the Central Asian and Kuznetsk Basin target complexes were then covered.

In its 1950 iteration, however, the plan envisioned three attacks on the first day, consisting of 112 medium bombers launched from Lakenheath, Sculthorpe, and Marham in the United Kingdom, passing over Norway and Sweden, protected by F-84E fighters from Bentwaters, then across the Baltic before going "feet dry" over the Soviet Union. The southern wing, launched from Fairford, Upper Heyford, and Brize Norton, took eighty-nine medium bombers over France, Italy, Yugoslavia, Greece, Bulgaria, and the Black Sea. The B-36 force launched from North America would then strike its targets.[56]

Not surprisingly, Targets 001 and 002 were Moscow and Leningrad, the centers of Soviet administrative power and heavy concentrations of industry, research, and development. As Stalin told Averell Harriman and Lord Beaverbrook in 1941—and as LeMay and Power surely understood—the destruction of Moscow would have a catastrophic effect because it "would destroy the nerve center of the nation."[57] The 1950 plan grouped both together as a target complex, but by 1951 they were split into Leningrad (four and then twelve targets) and then Moscow-Gorki, which included ten targets in Mos-

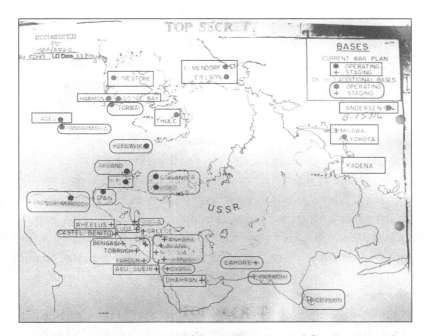

Map 5. The SAC Emergency War Plan, 1950–52, envisioned three scenarios. The first focused on the use of bases in the United Kingdom. If for whatever reason these were unavailable, a second plan activated SAC's forces in airfields in French Morocco and possibly Spain. The third and worst-case scenario was to have SAC mount a high-risk attack on the Soviet Union from North America using the relatively new aerial-refueling techniques involving squadrons of KB-29s. LeMay wanted to expand SAC's alternatives, but political considerations militated against forward basing in Norway and the eastern Mediterranean. Surveying staging and recovery bases, however, was permitted. Courtesy of Library of Congress, LeMay Papers.

cow and six outlying cities. The strike against Leningrad was to be handled by B-29s from the 509th Bomb Wing, while Moscow and the surrounding target cities east to Gorki and south to Tula were to be struck with B-50s from the 43rd Bomb Wing.[58] In 1951–52 the 11th Bomb Wing with its B-36s took over the Moscow and Leningrad targets. They would launch, hit their targets, and recover to the United Kingdom.[59] A backup plan in case the UK bases were untenable involved a B-29 wing launched from Goose Bay, refueled by a KB-29 wing launched from Ernest Harmon, striking the Moscow-Leningrad complexes.[60]

The southern strike force, after going "feet wet" over the Black Sea, would split into three. The 97th Bomb Wing would send some of its B-50s to hit Ploieşti, and the rest, working alongside the 93rd Bomb Wing, would pass on to the Donets Basin, with its twelve "bonus" industrial city targets. Meanwhile the 2nd Bomb Wing and 509th Bomb Wing would proceed to divide over the Black Sea, the 2nd going after the northern Caucasus and southern Volga, and the 509th taking on the oil refineries and facilities in Batumi, Baku, Grozny, and Tbilisi.[61] The northern Volga targets required special handling. The 301st Bomb Wing, equipped with fourteen B-29s and fourteen KB-29s, staged to Lages in the Azores and then to Tripoli, Libya, where space for sixty-four B-29 aircraft and refueling facilities awaited. From there they were to mount a deep penetration raid against the aircraft industry located at Saratov, Syzran, Kuybyshev, and possibly Kazan.[62]

The northern strike would, hopefully, recover to the United Kingdom. The southern strike was scheduled to recover to Wheelus in Libya; Lucca, Italy; and Nicosia, Cyprus. The Herculean task of gaining recovery and staging basis for EWP 1-49 and EWP 1-51 led LeMay and SAC into hitherto uncharted territory and even occasionally into conflict with the State Department. On the northern strike routes, Norway would not permit staging at Oslo or Stavanger but had no issue with overflight as long it was informed ahead of time. State even complained that LeMay was making his own foreign policy.[63] The Swedish air force leadership in the person of air force chief of staff Gen. Gustaf Adolf Westring developed an "understanding" conveyed to SAC that it would be permitted to overfly Sweden in the event of war.[64] A similar arrangement apparently existed with Yugoslavia: Twining met with the Yugoslav air force leadership in 1951, ostensibly on Mutual Defense Assistance Plan issues but likely for other matters.[65] In the Mediterranean, SAC desperately wanted the base at Abu Sueir in Egypt; looked at Lydda, Israel; and considered bases as far away as Lahore and Karachi, even Ceylon.[66]

The most important recovery and staging base, however, became Dhahran, Saudi Arabia, and this related to SAC's expanded target coverage in the Urals, Central Asia, and Kuznetsk Basin target com-

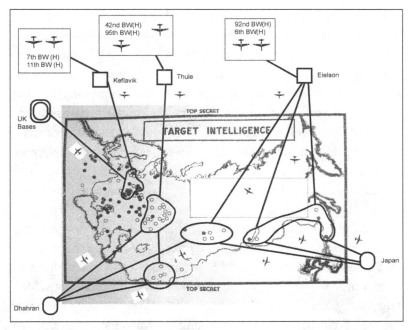

Map 6. Superimposed on a contemporary SAC briefing map, this map depicts how B-36 heavy bombers launched from the United States and refueled at bases in Iceland, Greenland, and Alaska could destroy Soviet industrial targets unreachable by B-29 and B-50 medium bombers and then recover to bases in the United Kingdom, the Middle East, and Japan. Courtesy of U.S. National Archives and Records Administration.

plexes (see map 6). The B-36 forces grew from two wings in 1950 to three in 1951–52 and then six in 1953. To ensure that they could strike targets in the Soviet Union, three staging bases were established: Keflavik, Iceland; Thule, Greenland; and Eielson, Alaska. In an ideal situation, two wings staged through each base before proceeding to their targets: the 7th and 11th through Keflavik; the 42nd and 95th through Thule; and the 92nd and 6th through Eielson. The weather situation in Alaska, however, prevented full use of Eielson during specific months, thus forcing the western-based wings at Walker and Fairchild AFBs to employ alternative arrangements.[67]

There were several designated bases for heavy bomber recovery: four to six bases in the United Kingdom for up to sixty-five B-36s; Kadena, Okinawa, for fifteen B-36s; and thirty B-36s at Dhahran,

Saudi Arabia.[68] These and numerous other bases around the world in far-flung places were recipients of prepositioned resources collectively code-named Seaweed. It included refueling facilities, ramp parking, communications, maintenance equipment, and more in warehouses staffed by a skeleton crew or even contractors. In Dhahran, SAC was told that "the ARAMCO Oil Company will assist, and can handle, emergency refueling."[69] Deploying SAC units carried fly-away kits that, when augmented with Seaweed materiel, made the deployed unit self-sufficient for between 30 and 180 days.[70] Portable atomic bomb assembly buildings also accompanied deployed units to facilitate restrike operations.

In an ideal scenario, the B-36s of the 7th and 11th Bomb Wings hit their targets in the Leningrad-Moscow-Gorki target complexes and recovered to the United Kingdom. The 42nd and 95th Bomb Wings proceeded from Thule to strike the Urals and Central Asia target complexes. The 92nd and 6th Bomb Wings departed or staged through Eielson, with the 6th striking the Kuznetsk Basin and proceeding to Dhahran or Kadena, and the 92nd taking out the Irkutsk and Far East targets before recovering to Kadena and Fairchild. If Eielson was closed, one option was to stage out of Kadena, strike the Kuznetsk Basin, and then proceed to Dhahran.[71]

Finally, there were Murmansk and Archangel. Both appear as a single target complex in 1950 but were gone from EWP 1-51 by 1952. This likely reflected the increased U.S. Navy nuclear weapons capabilities at sea, the limited number of weapons available, and the JCS target priorities.

What would have been the overall effect of the SAC Emergency War Plan attack? The destruction of all of the Soviet Union's urban areas as collateral damage to the destruction of the industrial base would have seriously degraded the Soviet Union's ability to continue a war it started. It would likely also have strained the ability of the Communist apparatus to control parts of the nonurbanized country, particularly the Ukraine and Polish and Czech borderlands, where there was already organized armed resistance to Moscow. The destructive effects using airburst kiloton-yield weapons would have been similar to the effects of four hundred Nagasakis spread out over the largest country in the world, as opposed to the later 1950s scenario wherein radioactive fallout from hundreds of megaton-yield weapons would have been a serious hazard to the entire planet. In an attack between 1950 and 1953, however, the rural population would have survived but would have been forced back into a nineteenth-century lifestyle. The destruction of "administrative control centers" would have undermined the centralized nature of Soviet society, and another civil war, this one fought with existing dispersed stockpiles of World War II equipment, would probably have broken out.

Targeting the A-Bomb Nests

It is self-evident that Soviet nuclear capability was a priority issue when it came to targeting. The locations and capabilities of Soviet nuclear weapons production complexes was of interest to the American intelligence apparatus years before the Soviet JOE-1 test, the first Soviet nuclear test, code-named "Fight Lightning." On the whole, the fact that the Soviet process was a direct copy of the Allied effort made the search easier. The required components included a design bureau; uranium mining, milling, and processing; heavy water reactors; the ability to enrich uranium; the ability to separate plutonium; component machining; and weapons-assembly facilities. Soviet disinformation and *maskirovka* (a Soviet doctrinal term encompassing coordinated disinformation, deception, and camouflage) efforts to counter the search were significant: facilities had names of places far removed from where they were; some locations even had no names. Indeed the Soviets had three different names for each facility, and then the CIA and the USAF had their own designations.

The initial sources of information inevitably came from German scientists engaged in atomic weapons activities, particularly the gaseous diffusion program, and came through the Wringer process. Two defectors, code-named Gong and Icarus, also provided substantial data. This information flowed until around 1952, and then the CIA appears to have infiltrated agent Caccola 6 sometime after April that year into the Chelyabinsk area to collect intelligence on facilities there.[72] Rigorous sifting of open-source intelligence produced a mixed bag, with plenty of disinformation strewn about. Part of the take was a German source as early as 1946 explaining that beryllium was made in the Elektrosal plant east of Moscow; an open source claimed there was "a Soviet Oak Ridge near Krasnoyarsk," referring to the Oak Ridge National Laboratory in Tennessee; a 1951 open source identified uranium mining at Tannu Tuva and claimed there was a facility at Sukhumi "as large as Oak Ridge." Crucially, multiple sources identified the "Kyshtym restricted area" and "Chelyabinsk" as part of the enterprise starting in 1948.[73]

It is likely these were only some of the sources that were available to those trying to target Soviet atomic facilities early on. From this information, however, targeteers would have been able to focus their efforts and may have come up with the Elektrosal metallurgical facility; the Krasnoyarsk-45 Uranium Enrichment Plant and the Sverdlovsk-44 Uranium Enrichment Plant with their huge, elongated E-shaped cascade halls similar to the K-25 plant at Oak Ridge; heavy water production at Sukhumi; and the huge complex at Kyshtym, which included multiple Hanford-like facilities: reactors, plutonium separation, and weapons component fabrication.[74] Five facilities, identified by multiple sources. Critically, the KB-11 design bureau and RDS-1 fabrication and storage facility at Sarov, known as Arzamas-16, remained undiscovered at this point.

The number five is significant. On 1 September 1950 USAF general Orvil Anderson, commandant of the Air War College (and incidentally one of the bases for the Jack D. Ripper character in *Dr. Strangelove*), was quoted in the national media as saying, "Give me the order to do it and I can break up Russia's five A-bomb nests in a week! And when I went up to Christ, I think I could explain to Him why I wanted to do it. . . . I think I could have explained to Him I saved civilization." Anderson was immediately disciplined by Vandenberg and later retired.[75]

If EWP 1-49 and EWP 1-51 had been implemented, they would have hit prime industrial targets, including Sverdlovsk and Novosibirsk. Both cities included nuclear weapons component fabrication and assembly: at Sverdlovsk-45 and the Novosibirsk Uranium Processing Facility. Inadvertent bonus damage, as it were. Sverdlovsk-44, the uranium enrichment plant known by the CIA as Verkh-Neyvinsk and the Soviets as Novouralsk, was too far out of the damage radii at Sverdlovsk to qualify for the bonus; it was identified sometime after 1953 and became a priority U-2 target in 1957, on par with Kyshtym.[76]

It is likely that identified Soviet atomic bomb production facilities would have been hit on the second or third day of EWP 1-49 and EWP 1-51. Though the general location of these facilities was known, it would have taken a deliberate reconnaissance effort, perhaps by RB-36s of the 72nd Strategic Reconnaissance Wing from Ramey AFB, Puerto Rico, and staged forward to North Africa, to pin down their exact dispositions before their obliteration by three Mk-4 or Mk-5 weapons dropped against each target the following day by B-36s. The large surface area of the facilities, particularly Kyshtym, would have warranted this level of attack.

The Bravo Targets: Blunting the Long-Range Air Force

As we have seen, efforts to counter the Soviet nuclear production capability appear to have been grouped under the Delta target category but as separate target systems.[77] Bravo, the crippling of delivery systems and their bases, on the other hand, seems to have overlapped with Romeo missions. In an address to the Air War College, LeMay explained that the Bravo mission "require[d] the highest possible order of intelligence": "It requires an initiative not likely to be provided a military commander in a democracy. Within these limits, and they are severe, we are prepared to perform this task."[78] In late 1951 SAC was allocated fourteen Bravo targets by HQ USAF which then had to be incorporated into SAC's EWP 1-51. In SAC's view there were probably more than fourteen such targets, but data were lacking. There was no agreed reporting system to track the movements of the Soviet "atomic air force."[79]

The reverse-engineering of seized American B-29s in 1945 by the Soviets was a massive project and tracked alongside their atomic bomb program until the two merged with the 18 October 1951 live drop of a 42-kiloton-yield RDS-3 bomb from a TU-4A Bull bomber.[80] Unlike the 1949 First Lightning test, however, the existence of the

TU-4 was not a complete surprise. Wringer intelligence was sparse, but it was there. There were numerous reports from several rebuilt or refurbished airfields—Tartu in Estonia, Konotop in Ukraine, and Bobruisk in Belarus—of significant twin-engine bomber activity. Then there were reports of twin-engine and four-engine American bombers operating from Bobruisk in 1948. A four-engine bomber was seen to crash near Tartu and special measures taken in its recovery.[81] What observers were seeing, without the analysts realizing it, was the Soviet training program wherein pilots were exposed to American aircraft by flying the B-25J. They then converted to four-engine B-17 and B-24 aircraft.[82] Then, when TU-4s became available, conversion training was conducted at the Kazan factory, where a Wringer source reported the presence of seventy TU-4s in 1952.[83] For the most part there was some Wringer reportage on at least eight of the fourteen TU-4 bases, but only four of these—Kazan, Bobruisk, Tartu, and Belaya Tserkov—had intelligence-confirmed TU-4 activity by early 1952.[84]

However, SAC was correct in estimating that there were twenty wings of TU-4s; there were in fact twenty Soviet TU-4 regiments, which approximated American wings.[85] USAF intelligence does not appear to have been able to distinguish between a conventional TU-4 and a TU-4A Atomnyy; two regiments, or ninety aircraft, were converted to TU-4A by 1954, but outwardly they would have looked like the conventional version.[86]

SAC expressed concern that, in the event of war, TU-4s might raid its UK bases as well as Goose Bay and Harmon while the SAC Atlantic deployment flow was in progress.[87] This led to increasing air defenses in the United Kingdom, Labrador, and Newfoundland, but it also led to a search for possible TU-4 bases using the expanding communications intelligence apparatus.[88] There was also a concern that TU-4s might be staged out of bases in East Germany and Poland, not only against NATO countries but also against the northeastern United States; twenty-four runways long enough for TU-4 operations were identified in those countries as early as 1950 and reconfirmed in 1952. Three of these were the airports in West Berlin.[89] A Soviet exercise monitored in October 1953 detected the deployment of twenty-three TU-4s from Poltava and Zhitomir in Soviet-occupied Ukraine to staging bases in Poland.[90]

The possibility that the Soviets might stage TU-4s from bases in Finland appears to have been considered after 1949. Though Finland was neutral, its precarious relationship with the Soviet Union meant that SAC could not preclude having to target airfields with the requisite runway length. There were three of these, in Jyväskylä Pori, and Räyskälä. Information on a key route through Finland into Norway was also collected in case there was a ground assault.[91]

Discussions between Prime Minister Winston Churchill and Gen. John P. McConnell of SAC's 7th Air Division representing LeMay revealed Churchill's thoughts on the Bravo target matter: "The only effective defense against would be counteraction against Soviet strike force launched on E-Day. . . . He expressed the hope that adequate forces for E-day strike against Soviet strategic bases will be constantly available."[92] It was in this context that Truman and Churchill authorized Operation Ju-Jitsu in 1952, an operation more spectacular and dangerous than any of the U-2 flights that followed later in the 1950s.

Mounted the night of 17 April 1952, this daring and risky operation had as its primary purpose the radar scope photography of TU-4 bases so they could be confirmed as Bravo targets. Of secondary importance was collection on the air defense system in conjunction with signals intelligence aircraft and ground stations. If possible, industrial complexes were also to be identified. Three RB-45Cs wearing RAF markings and flown by British pilots trained by SAC penetrated the Soviet Union at night from three different directions after aerial refueling with SAC KB-29 tankers over Denmark. The routes took them over the Baltic states, Belarus, and Ukraine, moving from one target to the next. One of the aircraft photographed targets around Moscow during the ten-hour operation. There was no effective opposition from the Soviet air defense system, which futilely fired anti-aircraft artillery and launched MIGs that were not equipped with air-intercept radar.[93]

The take from Ju-Jitsu likely included eleven of the fourteen TU-4 bases that lay along those three routes; three other targets were out of range, one of those in the Far East.[94] In any event the JCS's fourteen Bravo targets remained assigned to SAC and the seven RB-45s assigned to USAF units in the United Kingdom were considered "critical" for the Blunting mission well into 1953.[95] Intelligence efforts were also mounted against the Kola Peninsula: of the fifty-four fields surveyed by intelligence sources, four appeared to operate MiG-15s and TU-4 bombers were reported at one base.[96]

After U-2 operations started, the conversion from the TU-4 to TU-16 jet bombers took place only at eight of the fifteen air bases. The jets were caught on camera at Baranovichi, Poltava, Priluki, Belaya Tserkov, Tartu, Kuybyshev, Kazan, and Soltsy, all former TU-4 bases.[97] Four of these bases continued with jet bomber operations in the late 1970s and presumably remained targeted by the SIOP.[98] The rest were put to other tasks or abandoned.

There were two notable American nuclear weapons tests related to Bravo targeting during the Tumbler-Snapper nuclear test series held at the Nevada Test Site from April to June 1952. The first involved a B-50 drop of a 31-kiloton weapon against a target array consisting of parked aircraft. Another test involved a B-45 delivering a 19-kiloton weapon against a similar target set. Both tests were airbursts and included weapons effects tests on other B-50s in flight. Twenty-five SAC B-50s from the 9th Bomb Wing at Travis AFB and the 93rd Bomb Wing at Castle AFB conducted "orientation and indoctrination" training during the shots.[99] Blunting attacks during this period would have resembled these mission profiles.

Target 001: Moscow

SAC Chief Operational Analyst Carroll Zimmerman said, "I remember when our target system was the 21 or 22 target cities in Russia. The reason was because we had 25 atomic weapons in our stockpile and we thought we should honor Moscow with several."[100] Early nuclear targeting going back to Pincher and Broiler assigned five targets in the Moscow area, all of them aviation industry and airfields that existed during World War II, all presumably under some form or level of surveillance by Western attachés stationed in Moscow. As more information came in through Wringer and other sources into the 1950s, a more complete picture emerged. Ramenskoye Airfield was added when reports of V-weapons testing at the facility emerged. Moscow-Khimki Airfield, already on the list, also featured V-weapons test reports. Moscow Fili Airframe Plant was making components for TU-4 Bull strategic bombers, while Tushino was suspected of missile production. There were hints that Airframe Plant No. 30, at Moscow Central Airfield, was making twin-engine jet bombers.[101] That brought the number of industrial targets up to six.

When the JCS added electrical power plants as a Delta targeting priority, three plants in Moscow were identified: Moskva TETs "Stalin," Moskva GES "Smidovich," and Moskva High Pressure TETs.[102] That brought the number of weapons to be directed at Moscow to nine.

Yet in a 1950 SAC exercise ten to eleven weapons were destined for Moscow, reflecting SAC EWP 1-49. There is only one conclusion: that the additional weapon or weapons were destined to destroy the center of Communist power and were aimed at Joseph Stalin in the Kremlin. If so, that was a significant shift from earlier plans, which did not directly target the Soviet leadership. The shift does, however, resonate with the Dropshot planners and their emphasis on "control center" targets as they looked forward into the 1950s. Using future terminology, there was a tacit "decapitation" aspect to SAC EWP 1-49. As Zimmerman recalled, "Because Moscow is the political center of the USSR and is of special cultural significance, the guidance to SAC war planners from the Secretary of Defense and the President, through the Joint Chiefs of Staff, was 'Extreme damage to designated targets. Level Moscow if you can.'"[103]

LeMay was not happy with the results of the 1950 exercise and wanted the Moscow attack recalculated to achieve this new criteria. SAC Operations Research personnel led by Zimmerman produced a matrix of DGZs over the city that would destroy the Soviet government as well as the existing industrial target set. By varying weapons types and yields and adjusting the aim points and thus increasing the probability of hitting the DGZ, the criteria could be met. After a briefing by Zimmerman that included Maj. Gen. J. B. Montgomery, SAC director of operations, LeMay said, "Monty, that's our planned Moscow mission as of now!"[104]

Using the Kremlin as an aim point, a 37- to 47-kiloton airburst of an Mk-4 bomb delivered by a B-50D would have utterly destroyed the Communist Party of the Soviet Union building, the Party Central Committee building, NKVD headquarters, the Chief Artillery Directorate, the headquarters of the Soviet Navy, the headquarters of Ground Troops of the Soviet Army, the headquarters of Glavnoye Razvedyvatel'noye Upravleniye (GRU; Main Intelligence Directorate, Soviet armed forces), and the headquarters of the Soviet Air Force.[105] Even a Crossroads-like miss with a 23-kiloton Mk-3 would have put all of these facilities in mortal jeopardy. All of the regime's critical paper-based records would have been destroyed, with bonus effects like disabling the repressive apparatus of the NKVD. The tightly centralized Soviet society would have been utterly paralyzed when the Five Year Plan was turned to ash.

Most intriguing, however, was a 1950 intelligence report entitled "Depth of the Moscow Subway System," which was "obtained in part by the Department of the Navy" and disseminated by CIA to the U.S. Air Force. This document included a cross-section sketch of the subway system, showing it to be 25 to 30 meters under the Kremlin.[106] Somebody was clearly interested in how the Soviet leadership were going to protect themselves if Moscow was bombed.

So was Stalin. Soviet analysis of the RDS-1 test in 1949 indicated that any protected facility had to be at least 65 meters underground to survive a direct hit. Immediately after the test, Stalin authorized the construction of Objekt 02, later known as Bunker 42, located near Taganskaya, southeast of the Kremlin. When it was finally completed in 1954, Bunker 42 lay just outside the damage radius for a 47-kiloton bomb directed at the Kremlin and was 65 meters underground.[107]

The prospect of killing Stalin outright or making him crawl through the radioactive ruins of Moscow in the event of war would have been too good to pass up for the planners. If the Kremlin was an aim point before 1951, however, it was a JCS planner who put it there, and the expenditure of the weapons had the concurrence of President Truman.[108]

Stalin had very good reasons to be concerned about being taken out directly and quickly at the start of a war, particularly after Operation Ju-Jitsu. The B-45 was capable of carrying an Mk-5 lightweight nuclear weapon, and, with aerial refueling, it could deliver its 81- to 83-kiloton payload onto Moscow targets from the United Kingdom in under three hours. A night raid mounted on Moscow with these aircraft could not have been intercepted by the existing Soviet air defense system. In the febrile geopolitical environment of 1952, it is inconceivable that Stalin was not informed about the Ju-Jitsu operation (the infamous Beria led a commission investigating the failure of the air defenses), and he was quite capable of determining what the implications were. And Objekt 02 was not ready yet.

The fact that Beria was put in charge of both the Soviet thermonuclear weapons program and the crash program to develop an anti-aircraft missile defense system for Moscow at this time was not coincidental to Ju-Jitsu.[109] The increased weight of attacks planned against Moscow in the EWP, the Basic War Plan, SIOP, the development of the British "Moscow Criteria," and the Moscow anti–ballistic missile quandary can be tracked back to the 1950s. Indeed the sites for the new missiles, called the SA-1 Guild by NATO, were placed near many of the same sites where the anti-aircraft artillery was situated in the 1940s. And the U.S. Air Force already had those positions identified by 1952.[110]

As for deterring Stalin, Churchill explained to Milovan Djilas from Yugoslavia, "If it weren't for atomic weapons, the Russians might have made their move already. . . . [Stalin is] old—he's got no stomach for running around Siberia dodging atom bombs!" Churchill also noted at the time, "If atom bombs were dropped on [Soviet] communication centers—which wouldn't cause heavy civilian casualties— the periphery would loosen up and start to fall away. Stalin knows that well."[111]

Air Defense of the Nation: The Opposition Gets a Vote

Just as EWP 1-49 evolved, so too did the Soviet air defense forces. There were two distinct periods: 1949–51 and 1952–53. SAC's knowledge of the Soviet system progressed throughout the late 1940s to the point where, by 1950, SAC, the U.S. Navy, and RAF "ferret" electronic intelligence collection aircraft had mapped almost all of the radar systems on the periphery of the Soviet bloc. During the course of these operations Soviet interceptors shot down one U.S. aircraft over international waters and attacked at least two more. Ground-controlled intercept (GCI) communications traffic between the radar sites and the fighters, as well as the radar frequencies themselves, was also monitored and analyzed. At this point Soviet radars were derived from British, American, and Japanese systems and thus vulnerable to jamming. Soviet awareness of countermeasures was minimal, having had no experience comparable to the Germans, the RAF, and the USAAF during the war.

A SAC attack in 1950–51 would have encountered an eclectic collection of opponents, including radar-directed 85mm and 100mm anti-aircraft artillery at important facilities. B-36s going after Irkutsk, for example, would have encountered piston-engine Lavochkin-7s, essentially a Soviet P-47 equivalent. B-29s striking the Caucasus target complex would have been attacked by swarms of P-39 Supercobras built at the Bell plant in Niagara Falls. A regiment of Spitfire IXs, considered by the Soviets to be their best high-altitude interceptor, protected targets in the Urals. More important areas were defended by the first-generation MIG-9 and Yak-15 jets using reverse-engineered German Jumo engines; the B-50s coming in to hit Leningrad and Moscow from the Baltic would have encountered these.[112]

The prospect of piston-engine fighters countering SAC's bombers should not be sneered at. At this point most, if not all of the Soviet aircraft assigned to PVO (*protivovozdushnaya oborona strany*, "anti-air defense of the nation") could reach the combat ceilings of the B-29, B-50, and B-36.[113] Unlike American bombers and fighters equipped with .50 caliber machine guns, Soviet aircraft like the Yak-15 or the P-39 carried 23mm and 37mm cannons, which caused more damage and, when it came to jets, kept them out of range of the bomber's defensive systems.

In the plus column for SAC was the spotty nature of Soviet peripheral radar in the Arctic and elsewhere, jammable GCI communications, and known and jammable frequencies of the early warning radar system. Soviet counterjamming systems were nonexistent at this point. Most important, none of the Soviet fighters had air-intercept radar, putting them technologically behind Nazi Germany's air defense system circa 1944.

What changed? In a word: Korea. Covert and overt Soviet support for Communist China and North Korea led to the deployment of MiG-15 jet fighters flown in some cases by Soviet pilots in Chinese and North Korean uniforms, directed by a new radar, Token, that was not jammable by deployed ECM (electronic countermeasures) equipment. In October 1951 over Namsi, Korea, SAC lost three B-29s to the MiGs and four more were severely damaged and crashed at their bases. Close escort by the straight-wing F-84Es was next to useless as the MiG-15s with 23mm and 37mm cannon ran rings around the slower, .50-cal-equipped planes. "Black Thursday" led to a three-month suspension of B-29 operations over Korea.[114] General Vandenberg was shocked; "after briefings in the theatre he left fearful of SAC's abilities to penetrate Soviet airspace as part of the atomic strike plan within the Emergency War Order."[115]

SAC shifted to night operations in Korea, assuming the lack of airborne intercept radar would protect them. The Communist forces adapted and used radar-directed searchlights and flare ships to locate the B-29s and then Token to vector in MiG-15s, which then used their landing lights to find their targets. Several more B-29s were shot down in early 1952.[116] Eventually seventy-four B-29s, nearly one-tenth of the existing B-29 force, was lost over Korea.[117]

Far East Air Force Bomber Command started to use SAC tactics over Korea, but when LeMay found out about it, he was extremely concerned. SAC's "ability to deliver atomic fire on the Russian industrial heart provides the sole deterrent to overt Russian aggression at this time. . . . The sanction which the threat of the air atomic blow to the Russian heart land provides is dependent to a large extent upon the techniques and operational plan of [SAC]. The sanction is, in the last analysis, much more dependent upon the delivery techniques than upon the mere existence of atomic weapons."[118]

LeMay told the Far East leadership, "We had much better results with a tactic during World War II the first time we used it than we did after the enemy had time to work out his defenses and practice his crewmen. It is this same element of surprise and general lack of coordination that I am anxious to preserve for the . . . atomic air offensive."[119]

Brig. Gen. Joe Kelly, responding to LeMay, suggested that if he couldn't jam enemy transmissions, he would use B-26 light bombers and white phosphorus bombs to destroy the radar and searchlight sites before the bombers arrived over target.[120] SAC's acquisition of F-84GS, with their ability to drop Mk-7 nuclear bombs against Soviet air defense systems in the Baltic states to clear the route to Moscow, certainly was an evolution of this thinking, which paralleled U.S. Navy thinking related to supporting SAC's approach over the Balkans in EWP 1-49 and EWP 1-51. SAC training for the Low-Altitude Bombing System delivery profile started at Sandia Base and was on the curriculum at Bergstrom AFB by late 1952.[121] This was, in essence, the progenitor of bomber-launched nuclear surface-to-air missile suppression weapons like the experimental Crossbow in the 1950s, Hound Dog in the 1960s, short-range attack missiles in the 1970s, and air-launched cruise missiles in the 1980s.

In any event, by 1952 all of the Soviet piston aircraft in the PVO had been replaced with MIG-15s. In more sensitive areas, like around Moscow, the improved MIG-15bis was deployed to replace the MIG-9s and Yak-15s.[122] MIG-15s and Yak-15s appeared at bases in southern Romania and in Bulgaria around 1953, and Hungary eventually boasted ten MIG-15 bases.[123] American and British ferrets, however, continued to map the radar and GCI network with their American and British signals intelligence partners, while the CIA and USAF using Wringer developed human intelligence on the Soviet's interior radar networks. This analysis was fused in 1952. The anodyne message was, when it came to GCI radar, the Soviets did not "have adequate height-finding characteristics or scope presentation for effective control of modern interceptors," but with Token they would. Without air intercept radar, "they [were] limited to good weather operations." Jammers and chaff were compromised, as they had been on the B-29s seized during the war, and new ones were needed. Overall, however, "it [was] estimated that Soviet day interception capabilities would be good in the areas of heavily defended targets."[124] And there were hints that the Soviets were working on something new, something based on a German system called "Wasserfall."

Furthermore, information reached SAC that PVO training included the development of specialized tactics to take on the B-36s. Despite the fact that the B-36 was equipped with 20mm defensive cannon, Soviet tactics involved swarming each B-36 with four MiG-15s, making 37mm cannon runs on the gargantuan plane with passes from above.[125]

SAC evolved too as night operations took primacy: one involved cell tactics whereby five aircraft, one the "A-carrier" and four support aircraft, confused the defense with a flying shell game; deceptive feints using non-"A-carriers" and electronic spoofing was another; evasive routing around known heavy air defense areas was still another.[126] These were more reminiscent of World War II RAF operations than USAAF operations and required a shift in mindset, especially when it came to the collection of electronic and communications intelligence. These operations were pursued much more aggressively by early 1952, with USAF ferret operations conducted from the Baltic to Berlin and the Adriatic, and even British operations run out of Iraq and Iran.[127] The new "Wizard War" was on.

Introducing Thermonuclear Weapons

The concept of a thermonuclear weapon emerged during World War II but was deferred in lieu of atomic weapons, which were less theoretical and more likely to be deployed during the conflict. After the war the American thermonuclear project, the "super," was not prioritized and was poorly funded. It did, however, chug along with Edward Teller as one of several proponents of further development.[128] Meanwhile Klaus Fuchs and other spies had already provided the Soviets with the conceptual basis for thermonuclear weapons back in 1943, and then Fuchs handed over the "Classical Super" and a variant called the Alarm Clock in 1948. This information was immediately translated and given to Stalin, Beria, and Vyacheslav Molotov in April 1948. Two months later Stalin made the decision to embark on a thermonuclear weapons program.[129] This was well over a year before Truman and his advisors agonized over the decision to develop the "super" in late 1949.

Concurrent with this, USAF officers from the Special Weapons Command working on retrofitting bombers for nuclear weapons carriage at Kirtland AFB learned of the Super deliberations in 1949. They passed on very basic theoretical data (weight, size, and the fact that the aircraft would have to be two miles away from the target when the bomb detonated) to their counterparts in future aircraft requirements so they could ensure that bombers could be designed to carry and deliver future weapons without retrofitting. When Air Material Command found out about this, a more formal process emerged. There was never any specific mention of the word "thermonuclear," but it was understood that the bomb would be massive, both physically and in terms of yield: possibly 10 to 40 megatons.[130]

Strategically the JCS in 1949 "viewed the hydrogen bomb . . . as a psychological weapon . . . in terms of technological competition with the Soviet Union. Thoughts of actual military use of thermonuclear bombs held secondary importance although the [Military Liaison Committee] recommended . . . that hydrogen weapons might serve offensively as substitutes for numerous fission weapons."[131]

Truman's 1950 decision led to deliberations within the air force to examine the problem even further. The blast and heat problem would be massive. These and other issues, like determining whether the World War II–era B-36 and the B-47 bomber designs could even carry out such a mission, went into gear in the air force system. But there was no stated military requirement for such a weapon. There was no request from SAC to pursue development. It was a future capabilities matter: the theory had not been proven.[132] As one observer noted, "General LeMay thought all he needed to conquer the world and stop war was a 10,000 pound Mark 6 atomic bomb."[133] And thus SAC remained focused on its day-to-day problems of the Korean War, developing target coverage of the Soviet Union with its atomic strike force and pursuing the atomic- but not thermonuclear-capable B-36 and B-47 programs. That said, LeMay expressed concern to Vandenberg in June 1950, saying, "Every day that passes makes more possible the total destruction of Washington by several atomic bombs or by a single hydrogen bomb, leaving our nation temporarily without top level direction."[134]

The George shot during the 1951 Greenhouse test series, at 225 kilotons the largest shot yet, demonstrated emergent tactical problems that SAC would have to confront. LeMay was briefed that the B-36 and the new B-52 aircraft that would replace it could be seriously affected by the extreme heat of a thermonuclear bomb drop.[135] The Tumbler-Snapper test series in Nevada during 1952 was focused on tactical weapons effects with a yield range of 1 to 31 kilotons and could not provide the information necessary to address the heat issue.[136]

Again, it appears that the thermonuclear weapons process was driven by the scientists and the engineers and not the operators: on 22 May 1952 "Sandia and Los Alamos propose[d] guidelines for design of thermonuclear weapon to be called the TX-14," and the Emergency Capability Committee was jointly established between the two to carry out the weapon's development. Three weeks later the JCS established a military requirement for thermonuclear weapons "with yields of 1 megaton and over."[137] The specifics are obscure and are not discussed in the official JCS histories beyond the belief that "any prior production of a deliverable thermonuclear weapon by the Soviet Union would reduce the existing American lead in weaponry and that such a shift in balance might well cause a change in Soviet policy."[138]

Five months later, on 1 November 1952, the mile-wide island of Elugelab at Eniwetok Atoll in the Pacific Proving Grounds disappeared during the successful surface detonation of Mike shot, Operation Ivy. This 10.4-megaton-yield device flung the world into the thermonuclear age. The usually overlooked King shot fifteen days later yielded 500 kilotons but was Mk-6-bomb-modified with a special oralloy core. King was a stockpile weapon dropped from a SAC B-36H bomber, thus demonstrating the ability to deliver a high-yield weapon in 1952.[139]

The first effects of significance for SAC planners were the hugely scaled-up ones generated by the thermonuclear process. Mike's yield was so large that it took several months to calculate after the test and was initially estimated to be between 6 and 20 megatons. The planned crater analysis had to be shelved: "Due to the configuration of the target area, only one of the three requirements—the exact location of ground zero after blast—could be accurately determined," as the water-filled crater appears to have been an unintended effect.[140]

To collect information on weapons effects shock on SAC delivery aircraft the test stationed a B-36D and a B-47B bomber in proximity to the detonation: the B-36 was at 38,500 feet and thirteen miles, while the B-47 was at 35,000 feet and forty-two miles. Even though Mike's "yield was considerably higher than the predicted most probable yield" that the instrumentation was geared for, some data were collected. The B-36 data came through but the B-47 data did not as it was too far away due to radar failure. There were no significant detrimental thermal, mechanical, or radiation effects on either aircraft.[141]

A number of Mike effects were of interest besides the intense heat and blast. A C-54G photoreconnaissance plane piloted by a SAC crew started to make runs over the Mike crater one hour after detonation. It "encountered heavy fallout at 2,500 feet," and "debris had pitted the windshield, all four propellers were chipped, and decals were scrubbed off the nose and leading edges of the wings. All LML film was ruined by radiation exposure." The crew flew through rain squalls to decontaminate the aircraft on their way back to base in Kwajalein in the Marshall Islands.[142]

Most important, however, was the impact of radioactive fallout. Fallout, the distribution of cell-destroying gamma-irradiated particles following a detonation, had been documented on previous kiloton-yield tests to a certain extent, but the size of the Mike shot took the dangers of fallout to a whole new level. "Primary" and "secondary" (or "early" and "late") fallout were observed. Mike's primary fallout was determined to be "militarily significant"; that is, it could disrupt or destroy enemy forces. Secondary fallout was not at this point deemed to be capable of doing so. Using the measurement systems of the day, Mike's primary fallout intensity was from 800 roentgens per hour to 0 roentgens per hour at the two-hour mark from three miles to fifteen miles downwind. It was estimated to be 1,000 roentgens per hour between ground zero and two miles, as most of the measurement equipment for that task was destroyed. Again using 1950s measurement systems, 800 to 1,000 roentgens was a lethal dose.[143]

Summed up, Ivy Mike demonstrated that a huge thermonuclear detonation was possible, but it was by no means a definitive weapons effects test and left numerous and important questions unanswered, primarily: Could a bomber deliver a weapon of this magnitude and escape destruction? That question occupied LeMay and SAC throughout 1953 while Special Weapons Command experimented with a "breakaway" maneuver and parachute-retarded delivery systems that would allow the bomber to get away and white paint to deflect heat. The problem then became a possible reduction in accuracy, which meant that a bigger bomb might be necessary to ensure target destruction.[144]

That said, weaponization of the Mike process proceeded. This was known as the Emergency Capability Program, which established an "Emergency Capability period" to last until 1955, with the intention of having fifteen thermonuclear weapons available by July 1954.[145] Five parallel thermonuclear weapon programs emerged in 1953 after Ivy. In essence each pursued a different method of using a primary device to detonate a thermonuclear-fuel secondary. There were five kiloton-yield primary designs, three solid-fuel secondaries, and two liquid-fuel secondaries.[146]

All of these devices were scheduled to be tested in the 1954 Castle test series, but the political and bureaucratic demand for an emergency capability resulted in the stockpiling of custom-built untested weapons based on these theories. For example, the only EC weapon "available in quantity" in 1953 was the liquid-fuel EC-16. The EC-16 weapon casing was extensively drop-tested, and thereafter a number of 60-kiloton Cobra primaries (based on the Mk-7 warhead) were assigned to them. The United States' first stockpiled thermonuclear weapon was designated the TX-16 and stored at Manzano Base. In an emergency SAC B-36s would land at Kirtland and the USAF Special Weapons Command crews would load them.[147] Thirty-six B-36s were initially modified to carry these weapons.[148]

It was at this point the air force shifted gears. The Air War College's curriculum was modified in 1953 to handle "TN" weapons in its exercises. British and Canadian officers were on course so a bogus name/yield list was employed for training purposes. It was, in fact, remarkably accurate for the kiloton-yield weapons, including the notional "Mk-54-E" fission weapon with a 500-kiloton yield (the Ivy King weapon); a 200-kiloton weapon clearly based on the boosted tritium George shot from the Greenhouse series; and postulated the employment of fusion weapons of 1-, 2-, 3-, 5-, and 10-megaton yields.[149]

In mid-1953 SAC planners working for Deputy SAC Commander Power on the evolutionary Emergency War Plan incorporated fifteen TNs in the first wave of attacks on E-Day. When word came in that forty B-36s were to be modified to deliver the new weapons, forty-one of the Emergency War Plan's targets were retargeted in anticipation of the acceptance of thermonuclear weapons into the stockpile.[150]

Ivy data, as well as scaled-up data from tests in Nevada, suggested some basic targeting parameters. A groundburst required half the yield of an airburst to destroy a target. The thermal intensity of a groundburst was 20 percent less than an airburst. Of course, "radio-active contamination from a surface burst, especially when a surface wind is blowing, far exceeds fall out from an airburst." Notably, "the crater for a surface burst, within the area of the crater, has a serious effect on underground installations." For SAC targeteers, the data strongly suggested that "for nearly all 'hard' targets, the surface burst is likely as effective and perhaps more effective than a low air burst." For "soft" targets, "the height of burst chart clearly indicates that a high burst is desirable."[151]

Exercise Prophecy also employed notional thermonuclear weapons. For comparative purposes, the requirement to employ a pair of 35-kiloton weapons to ensure the destruction of the Ploieşti refinery complexes in previous exercises changed. A single EC weapon with an estimated 6.9-megaton yield would presumably have been employed instead.[152]

The advent of thermonuclear weapons was accompanied by unstated moral quandaries. Did EWP 1-49 and EWP 1-51 deliberately target the population of the cities that would have been attacked? Probably not. If targeteers were using optimal aim points related to specific target complexes, then they were not specifically going after the Soviet population, though civilian deaths were an unavoidable byproduct. And there were indications from the intelligence community that the Soviets would evacuate their cities.[153] The formally stated intent of the EWP 1-49 and EWP 1-51 bombing campaign was to destroy industry. The intent does not appear to have been to destroy the population that ran the industry in a deliberate and systematic way, though it was understood there would inevitably be significant population casualties if the Soviets did not evacuate their cities. There is no evidence that the cities and their populations were specifically targeted; the aim points remained those associated with Soviet war-making capacity and nuclear production and delivery capacity in the context of a global war. The specific effects on the populations of those targeted areas do not appear to have been addressed in the JCS's planning or its targeting policy.

That said, the distinction became virtually irrelevant with the availability of thermonuclear weapons, especially after the first Soviet thermonuclear weapons test on 12 August 1953. Even though that tower shot device yielded 400 kilotons and was a single-stage "layer cake" thermonuclear weapon that was a dead end in terms of design, it still heralded, according to analysis, the Soviet advance toward a 1-megaton two-stage weapon. And the damage that 400 kilotons delivered on target by a TU-4 or a TU-16 or the IL-28 could generate was not something to be downplayed simply because the Soviet Union could not produce megaton yields.[154]

Indeed the idea of World War II–with-atomic-bombs was discarded altogether in 1954, and the increased emphasis on SAC as a deterrent force started then. Putting the industrial and military capacities and, by implication, the populations of those areas at risk with a credible force employing nuclear weapons became overtly and explicitly designed to forestall war altogether. As LeMay explained to Twining in May 1953, "In my opinion SAC's deterrent influence on USSR aggressive intentions can only be maintained by an effective force in being, properly manned, equipped, and trained, at the proper time period, and whose combat capability is universally recognized and unquestioned. . . . It therefore appears that the requirement to maintain the most potent retaliatory force this country can reasonably provide is of increasing rather than decreasing urgency."[155]

4

Imminence of War II

Targeting Europe and the Far East, 1950–53

Q. Is a third world war presently as near as two or three years away?

A. No, it is not.

—JOSEPH STALIN to American media, 31 March 1952

A s much as LeMay and SAC wanted to focus USAF efforts on the Soviet Union, the realities of supporting operations in Europe and the Far East progressively impinged on SAC's prerogatives. This theme, this struggle moved back and forth like a pendulum within the American nuclear planning and force structure mechanism from 1950 until well into the 1960s. Similarly, the place of NATO and nuclear-armed allies in the pantheon of American nuclear planning achieved a baroque prominence by the 1960s. The origins of these challenges lay in the early 1950s, while the Far East remained a separate problem, a separate theater of nuclear war guided by the exigencies of geography and a different array of targets. Like the European issues, the Far East dynamic had its own trajectory, though its basis also lay in the violent events on the Korean peninsula in the early 1950s. The introduction of thermonuclear weapons, though it occurred in isolation and did not directly affect planning during this period, was a tocsin announcing that the status quo would not remain in place very long.

R for Romeo: The Retardation Task, 1951–53

There were several overlapping issues in the case of nuclear targeting in Europe. First, there was the Retardation or Romeo task that attained strategic equivalence with the Destruction (Delta) and Blunting (Bravo) tasks. Second were the command-and-control arrangements for U.S. air forces operating in Europe and the retention of SAC autonomy relative to them. Third was the legal need to retain American control over nuclear aspects of NATO planning. Then there was the role of the U.S. Navy in its involvement with Retardation missions: How did nuclear-armed aircraft carrier task groups intersect with U.S. Air Force European planning, SAC planning, and NATO planning? And how did a nuclear-armed ally, in this case the United Kingdom, relate to all of these factors?

The JCS created the Retardation task in 1950 during its rationalization of target systems, probably to include U.S. Navy thinking on atomic weapons employment.[1] That said, Gen. Omar Bradley, chairman of the JCS, was to some extent influenced by Vannevar Bush, who had just published *Modern Arms and Free Men*. Bush suggested to Bradley that there should be a force to deliver nuclear weapons "successfully on optimum targets." He added, "But we should not assume that these are the targets of five years ago." Bush believed, "It may be . . . that the use of A-bombs to slow the march of Russian armies would be wiser than to attempt to place them on key Russian industrial sites, or on secondary targets of that nature."[2] This correspondence was passed to Vandenberg for information, who in turn handed it to Maj. Gen. Truman Landon, the deputy chief of staff for operations for analysis.

Landon saw the dangers of Bush's argument: such a shift would be a repeat of the 1944 shift of strategic air operations to the operational support of the Normandy bridgehead. Landon did not rule out attacks against "armies in the field, supply concentrations, aircraft on the ground, etc.," but in his view in the future "an offensive against the industrial potential of that country [the USSR] will do most toward successfully and quickly ending a war." Critically, he also noted, "A retaliatory strategic bombing force is of primary importance to our national security": "We realize that the A-bomb alone may not win the war, but we feel that our retaliatory strategic air offensive can greatly reduce the Soviet will and capability to fight. Only by such an offensive can we create those conditions which will permit our combined forces to end the war in the shortest time with the least expenditure of men and resources."[3]

That said, Landon left an out, probably in part due to U.S. Navy developments: "The Air Force does not now believe, and has never believed, that it can single-handedly win a war. Neither do we believe that strategic bombing is our only responsibility."[4]

Retardation, however, remained a fuzzy concept. If the Red Army attacked Western Europe, retardation could mean the use of nuclear weapons against its forces as they advanced. Others thought that retardation should be focused on the logistics systems supporting the advance. But how did this relate to the main strategic bombing effort against the Soviet Union? Was destruction of the Baku refineries "retardation"? How did one delineate between Baku and, say, an oil terminal and storage area in Poland or Czechoslovakia? Brig. Gen. Howard Bunker from USAF headquarters told LeMay in 1951, "I don't believe you can A-bomb troops without killing peasants and I would rather answer for a million Russians than for a hundred NATO farmers."[5] In time these issues were poured into the interservice, intercommand competition pot to bubble and boil.

The problem was that the theater commander, in this case Gen. Dwight D. Eisenhower's staff, started to nominate Romeo targets to the JCS, increasingly so when President Truman issued a directive to Eisenhower in December 1950 assigning him "operational command of U.S. Air Forces Europe to the extent necessary for the accomplishment of his mission."[6] But was it a SAC mission or not? This posed problems for SAC when pressure mounted to provide the American European command with its own atomic strike force.

But there were further complications that emerged throughout 1951–52. The first of these was the NATO Supreme Allied Commander Europe (SACEUR) command structure. Eisenhower divided the NATO Area into three geographical commands: Allied Forces North, Central, and Southern Europe. Each of these was a joint command; that is, NATO headquarters commanded all three services from all of the countries assigned to those geographical areas. On the air side, Allied Air Forces Central Europe (AAFCE) was commanded by Lauris Norstad, who was also commander of U.S. Air Forces

Europe (USAFE). The AF North and AF South air commands were essentially AAFCE coordinating outstations.[7] These commands were restricted in nuclear weapons employment planning because of the Atomic Energy Act, which forbade transfer of nuclear information to non-Americans. Furthermore, SAC was an American 'specified command' that had no relationship whatsoever to NATO, despite the fact that NATO SACEUR was an American general, Eisenhower. Truman's pronouncement in December 1950 that all U.S. air forces in Europe were assigned to him posed serious issues.

SAC responded to JCS direction and was focused on targets inside the Soviet Union. However, there were SAC bases with SAC aircraft in the United Kingdom and North Africa that were to execute the Emergency War Plan, though some targets were generated by SACEUR for SAC's prosecution. At the same time, the existing U.S. Air Force command, USAFE, had bases and units throughout Europe as well as the United Kingdom and North Africa. Did the Truman directive to Eisenhower mean that all of the SAC facilities and aircraft in Europe were under USAFE and thus under Eisenhower's control?

The solutions hammered out by the commanders in 1951 and 1952 had specific long-term effects on nuclear targeting in the 1950s and 1960s. First, Vandenberg put his own house in order before taking on SACEUR and the U.S. Navy: "It has always been my intention to keep the command channel for strategic air operations from the JCS through me to LeMay and thence to SAC units absolutely clean. . . . On the other hand, I do not intend to put SAC in the military-diplomacy or real estate business in overseas theatres nor to permit SAC to encroach on the generally accepted responsibilities of overseas air commanders."[8]

A complicated arrangement was made whereby SAC's 5th Air Division in Morocco reported to SAC "on all matters of an operational nature" and to USAFE on all other matters, such as base development and relations with the French. In the United Kingdom, the Third Air Force was the USAFE subordinate command, but SAC's 7th Air Division, also in the United Kingdom, was for all intents and purposes SAC's forward headquarters with little or no housekeeping responsibilities.[9] USAFE, on the other hand, was the "single

U.S. Air Force agency" and "concentration of U.S. Air Force authority" in Europe and was the main entity for interaction with NATO.[10]

LeMay had issues with targeting priorities and the mushy relationship that existed between SAC and SACEUR. He expressed his concern to director of plans Maj. Gen. Thomas White: "A division of forces between the industrial complex and the so-called 'retardation mission,' if literally applied, could result in a ridiculous situation in which our force has an aiming point on one side of a city because of its industrial significance and a theatre force might have an aiming point on the other side having direct effect on a particular unified or allied area commander because of its transport, storage, communications, or other facilities."[11]

American thinking on retardation targets in Western Europe increasingly involved targets of opportunity, to LeMay's dismay:

> To set aside from the total task either bombs or bombers for this purpose before we have determined the nature and number of these fleeting targets is potentially uneconomical and unsound. Due to limitations in numbers of bombs and equipment, there is no question in my mind but that [SAC] must be charged with this limited portion as well as the balance of the retardation missions. The required command structure, communications, and procedures should be established prior to hostilities to permit the strategic force to schedule missions in support of theatre commanders. Otherwise, I foresee inevitable competition for resources and misuse of air power.[12]

Destruction of the Delta target category, it seemed, was now taking a backseat to the Romeo targets. And then the U.S. Navy encroached on the Romeo task, thus potentially diluting SAC's role further. SAC was now in danger of playing second fiddle to SACEUR and the U.S. Navy.

And what role did the U.S. Navy and its aircraft carriers have in retardation now that they were atomic-capable? After having survived the very public "revolt of the admirals" over the relative roles and missions of aircraft carriers and B-36s in 1949–50, the navy buildup accelerated;[13] by 1951 three aircraft carriers, the *Midway, Coral Sea,* and the *Franklin Delano Roosevelt,* were modified to handle nuclear weapons and were assigned to the Atlantic and Mediterranean. In 1952 two more were added, the *Kearsarge* and the *Oriskany*, and they subsequently sailed for the Pacific Fleet. Twelve AJ-1 Savage twin-engine bombers capable of carrying Mk-4 and Mk-5 nuclear weapons formed the nucleus of two squadrons, VC-5 and VC-6. In 1952 the single-propeller AD4-B Skyraider and the jet F2H-3B Banshee fighters were cleared by Sandia for nuclear delivery of Mk-7 bombs. The fighters and the bombers were combined into composite squadrons, with thirty-three fighters and four Savages assigned each to the Atlantic/Mediterranean commands and the Pacific. The AJ-1s in the Mediterranean were based at Port Layutey in Morocco and flown to the carrier assigned to the Mediterranean to pick up and deliver nuclear weapons if required.[14]

The U.S. Navy's primary interest when it came to targeting in the Broiler-Offtackle period involved three general types of missions that the carrier task forces would be conducting in the Atlantic and the Mediterranean. The first involved providing air support and air cover for Allied ground forces and the destruction of enemy air and ground buildups threatening them, as well as transportation targets. The second was the destruction of naval targets that could interfere with Allied sea and air lines of communications. That could include the destruction of Soviet submarine bases in the initial stages of a war so that their nearly unstoppable submarines based on German Type XXI technology would not get loose, as Hitler's U-Boats had in the 1940s. Third was support to the strategic air offensive, whose "objectives [were] the precision bombing of smaller elements of the selected target systems-elements which are not suitable for high-level bombing but which must be destroyed to make the whole effort effective."[15]

For the most part, the U.S. Navy's efforts in the Mediterranean were designed to retard a Communist advance on Italy, Turkey, Greece, and Iran by going after targets in Yugoslavia, Albania, Hungary, Bulgaria, and the Soviet Union.[16] (This would have posed a problem in that Yugoslavia and Greece had developed plans to occupy Albania, and the gist of those plans was briefed to Truman.)[17] The question of when the U.S. Navy started targeting the naval base complexes and submarine bases in the Murmansk area is interesting. Vice Adm. John T. Hayward explains why the mission was not contemplated in the Broiler days, with P2V-3C Neptune capability: "An attack on the Kola area would not have contributed to our solution particularly because we had so few weapons."[18] Most of the AJ-1 targets in Europe involved "flying at low level through Bulgaria and Romania," writes Jerry Miller, "avoiding briefed radar and antiaircraft areas. . . . Targets on the periphery of the Soviet Union had to be taken out in order to provide for a reasonable penetration of the air space surrounding the strategic objectives."[19] By 1953 U.S. Navy representatives to the Military Liaison Committee told the AEC General Advisory Council, "The Navy aims to have general and local sea supremacy [in the face of submarines, surface forces, and air forces,] which are a very serious threat. Ships at sea must have air cover and it will be necessary to strike heavily at air bases near the sea routes."[20]

In March 1950 the JCS issued SAC nineteen targets in western Germany for the retardation mission. Offtackle also had nine targets in eastern Germany, Poland, and Romania. At this point SAC had the 2nd Bombardment Group with three squadrons of B-29s and B-50s based in the United Kingdom deployed to Marham, Sculthorpe, and Lakenheath. Squadrons rotated to a forward base at Fürstenfeldbruck, west of Munich. SAC also had the 27th Fighter Escort Wing of three squadrons equipped with F-84E aircraft based at RAF Manston with forward deployments to western Germany as well. There were no data on the targets, so three RB-29s were brought in to conduct radar scope photography missions.[21]

The initial retardation target set must remain speculative. The limited number of bombs and the need to disrupt a rapid advance suggest that major Autobahn junctions west of the Inner German Border and particularly bridges along the Weser and Main Rivers were targeted: that would account for most of the allocated nineteen weapons. The Kiel Canal was logically another target.[22] The targets on the other side of the Iron Curtain were probably bridges and rail junctions: Offtackle had what appears to be four aim points in eastern Germany: the marshalling yards and bridges at Frankfurt an der Oder, the marshalling yards at Prague, and a pair of railway hubs in

Transcarpathia. Another likely target was Brest-Litovsk. This was a major rail hub, marshalling yard, and bridge complex over the Bug River and thus was a substantial logistics bottleneck between the Soviet Union and Poland. Almost all of the Group of Soviet Forces Germany's fuel passed through here. Bialystok, Poland, was a similar target.[23]

For the most part, however, this was a lash-up arrangement. The U.S. Navy was attempting to gain recognition of its retardation capability within the JCS but would not commit to anything specific in the defense of NATO.[24] Vandenberg, LeMay, and Norstad capitalized on this hesitancy and moved to place the SAC-SACEUR relationship on a solid foundation. Brig. Gen. Walter Sweeney was brought in to assess the situation in August 1951; his recommendation was to create a Supreme Allied Commander Strategic Air Forces, a NATO command on par with SACEUR and Supreme Allied Commander Atlantic (SACLANT), led by a double-hatted LeMay with an American and British staff. Sweeney was seriously concerned that the existing NATO commands plans "[did] not reflect the requirements of the strategic air offensive" and that "there was a strong possibility that SAC units operating through European areas might be allocated to SACEUR with a consequent loss of strategic mobility": "SACEUR is in a position to force the diversion of the strategic air effort. SACEUR's Presidential directive gives him broad sweeping powers insofar as the utilization of United States forces are concerned." Sweeney ascertained, however, that the creation of a third supreme allied commander posed problems for the NATO alliance. NATO was already embroiled in the debate over whether SACLANT should be British or American. The British were going to lose the debate because they lacked the earmarked forces for the command. Having a supreme allied commander of strategic air forces jammed down their throats too was politically unpalatable.[25]

With Vandenberg's approval, LeMay, White, and Norstad concocted a solution. This took the form of a quasi-formal letter of understanding sent directly to Eisenhower whereby the SAC operational plan to support SACEUR would be drafted in Omaha. Then a SAC representative would take it to Commander in Chief AAFCE (Norstad), whose staff would coordinate the plan with SACEUR and then finalize the SAC operational support plan. It would go back to LeMay for approval, and then to the Joint Chiefs of Staff for final approval, as the JCS allocated the weapons.[26] In its final form, the draft letter of understanding firmly situated the agreement in JCS 2056/7, which previously directed SAC to coordinate with SACEUR for atomic retardation operation and importantly noted that establishment of a SAC command element in Europe near SACEUR was the preferred mechanism. Also of note, the restrictions on the flow of atomic information because of the Atomic Energy Act were incorporated into the concept: NATO SACEUR was American (Eisenhower); NATO Commander in Chief AAFCE was an American officer (Norstad); and obviously LeMay was American. The USAF atomic delivery units were SAC forces as well as the planned atomic strike forces that would be assigned to USAFE.[27]

The next snag involved changes that the JCS were making to command arrangements in Europe. The proposal that a single U.S. commander be responsible for all U.S. forces in Europe was tabled in the fall of 1951. Norstad, LeMay, and Vandenberg believed this cut across what they were trying to accomplish and would possibly interfere with working with RAF Bomber Command, so Vandenberg accelerated efforts to establish the SAC-SACEUR relationship before the JCS could implement its idea.[28]

A meeting of minds took place on 7 December 1951 with Eisenhower, Norstad, LeMay, Gen. Alfred Gruenther from Supreme Headquarters Allied Powers Europe (SHAPE), and Air Chief Marshal Hugh Saunders (RAF and Norstad's deputy). Norstad convinced LeMay that the situation had changed and that the letter of agreement to Eisenhower should not be delivered. The day before, Norstad had convinced Eisenhower that the position of Commander in Chief AAFCE should be SACEUR's agent for handling coordination with Commanding General SAC on atomic support matters throughout Europe and not just in the Central Region, which in theory permitted the AAFCE headquarters to coordinate U.S. Navy forces supporting SACEUR. The finalized "SAC-SACEUR Agreement" established SAC Zebra, a separate U.S. entity from AAFCE but physically close to it. The SAC representative would work only for Norstad and his American representatives on a NOFORN (not releasable to foreign nationals) basis. Eisenhower really wanted the law altered so that British and Canadian NATO officers could handle atomic material, but that would not happen until he was president. Sweeney was brought in to activate SAC Zebra, and Eisenhower gave his blessing to the agreement.[29]

A new problem emerged in 1952, however, and it took the form of JCS thinking regarding American European command arrangements. A directive innocuously labeled SM 597-52 threatened to completely reverse the SAC-SACEUR Agreement. In basic terms, the idea of a singular European command reporting to the JCS and controlling all American forces in Europe was mooted, probably by the army. There was a European command, but it was a U.S. Army headquarters and was geographically distinct from USAFE and its operating areas. The U.S. Navy had two different commands that could support European operations: Commander in Chief Atlantic (CINCLANT) and Commander in Chief U.S. Naval Forces, Eastern Atlantic and Mediterranean (CINCNELM). Would their forces be reassigned to a future Commander in Chief Europe? As the U.S. Air Force leadership looked on in horror, they realized that SM 597-52's proponents asserted that the future CINCEUCOM would handle *all* atomic planning in Europe and coordinate with CINCUSAFE and CINCNELM. This concept "abrogate[d] the Air Force/SACEUR agreement on this matter" and offset all of the progress made in 1951.[30]

The authors of SM 597-52 had their hearts in the right place, or so it seemed. Vandenberg explained to Norstad that the directive "was approved primarily for the purpose of establishing operational procedures for the future control and coordination of forces possessing an atomic capability, to insure that all atomic efforts would be coordinated and maximized in carrying out a strategic offensive, retardation responsibilities in support of SACEUR, and any other operations." Similarly, now that the U.S. Navy and USAFE were going to be atomic-capable, "it was felt important to establish coordinating procedures to ensure that atomic forces [would] not interfere with each other and to make certain that the proper weight of delivery

[was] distributed throughout the approved target system."[31] Vandenberg assured Norstad that the SAC-SACEUR Agreement still stood, that SAC Zebra was going forward, and that they were supported in all of this by Gruenther, Eisenhower's chief of staff at SHAPE.

By May 1952 the implications of SM 597-52 were clearer and the situation was, as Vandenberg, Norstad, and LeMay feared, convoluted. There were three commanders dealing with European matters that reported to the JCS: CINCUSAFE, CINCNELM, and CINCEUCOM. Each generated and submitted to the JCS "atomic annexes to the Joint Emergency War Plan covering the areas for which they [were] given responsibility." And what did that mean? AAFCE covered northern Europe and the United Kingdom; CINCEUCOM's area of responsibility was Western Europe, including Germany and Austria; and CINCNELM's area of operations was southern Europe and the western Mediterranean. These atomic annexes were sent to the JCS for coordination. However, SACEUR assigned NATO AAFCE to work with SAC Zebra to coordinate atomic operations across the whole NATO area in Western Europe, to wit, all three areas.[32] The U.S. Navy leadership was equally concerned.[33]

The first step out of the maze was to make CINCEUCOM and NATO SACEUR the same person; Eisenhower's replacement in 1952, Matthew Ridgway, and later Al Gruenther in 1953 wore both hats. The minute Ridgway took over he sent a message to General Twining, who was picking up the slack due to Vandenberg's illness: "I reaffirm without reservation the agreement you made with General Eisenhower."[34] In other words, the SAC-SACEUR Agreement would remain in effect regardless of the turmoil in command arrangements. Those winds died down in August 1952, when European Command was confirmed by the JCS as commanding the forces assigned to CINCUSAFE, CINCNELM, and CINCEUCOM.

Over in SACEUR's NATO realm, Norstad, as the commander of NATO AAFCE, wanted USAFE to be completely separated from him and assigned its own general. That streamlined AAFCE's relationship with SAC Zebra by jettisoning American administrative and logistical responsibilities from the AAFCE staff and it reinforced the requirement to have a single go-to USAF entity for Europe that was separate from NATO.[35] This move had significant implications for nuclear targeting later on in the decade.

The mechanics of targeting coordination and the delineation of responsibility between SAC and the European-based commands required some work. Norstad asserted:

> We have consistently taken the position here that strength in Western Europe and the Strategic Air Offensive must be looked upon as being complementary and not alternative. . . . Strength in Western Europe fixes a horizon against which the Strategic Air Offensive can operate and without which we would continue to have, as we have had during the last seven years, considerable difficulty in answering questions relative to the time and space factors involved. It is my opinion that fixing the when and the where of the effect of the strategic air offensive greatly enhances the significance of that concept.[36]

Norstad and his staff were now working on a target program for the entire SACEUR area but ran into the Atomic Energy Act once again: no non-American could be privy to any details. Then there was LeMay, who believed that Norstad's staff requests through SAC Zebra were excessive. They wanted, basically, the entire SAC Emergency War Plan:

> I prepared a list of all targets under consideration which lie west of 23 E, essentially a line through Riga and Athens. The new message now asks for all tgts to 50 E. . . . I have asked Sam Anderson to carry this note to you and to explain that I keep our target lists from everyone who does not have a real need to know them. For instance, only those medium and heavy bomb wings actually assigned to Russian targets have access to the target lists. SAC fighter wings, and bomber wings not yet assigned targets, do not have the target section of our Basic Intelligence Planning Guide. It is for reasons of tightening up on the relatively widespread distribution of SAC war plans that existed one year ago that I have closed down all unnecessary access. . . . [The target list prepared in answer to your June message] covers all my targets within range of your B-45's from the UK bases. . . . When you feel your staff has a real need to possess lists of other SAC targets, I shall be glad to discuss them.[37]

Again, this geographical delineation between what was SAC, what was SACEUR, and who hit what had long-term implications into the 1960s.

The immediate solution was the creation of a Joint Coordination Center, which coincided with the deployment in 1952 of the 49th Air Division, an atomic-capable strike force that would be part of USAFE and assigned to SACEUR. It was eventually equipped with two B-45 and three F-84F/G squadrons, all trained and equipped for nuclear strike operations.[38] The 49th Air Division operated from bases in the United Kingdom that were intermingled with the SAC bases. The Joint Coordination Center was then set up to deconflict SAC and the theater nuclear forces in and outside Europe: the SAC control element was based on SAC Zebra (later SAC Zulu, when the NATO Phonetic alphabet was introduced).

The first test of the Joint Coordination Center organization was Exercise Judo, held in July 1952. The scenario had an enemy troop concentration on the east bank of the Rhine opposite Worms. Eleven B-50s from the 509th Bomb Wing, two of them carrying simulated nuclear weapons, were escorted by seventy-five F-84Es to "attack" the concentration of "enemy" forces. The time from SACEUR's identification of the target to the drop time at Worms was four hours. Judo also featured single-aircraft missions assisted by radar and SHORAN electronic navigation systems, conducted at night against a pair of "enemy" airfields.[39]

Despite the strides made by the Joint Coordination Center, practical problems remained when it came to real-world planning. In November 1952 SAC received the first atomic annexes from CINCLANT and CINCNELM in preparation for a coordination conference as stipulated by SM 597-52. There was no concept of operations, no timings, no weights of effort included. Not only did CINCLANT and CINCNELM attack some of the same targets, but both commands' annexes nominated targets already assigned to SAC by the JCS.[40]

Exercise Prophecy, held in spring 1953, was designed to iron out those problems. SACEUR made a request to the JCS that nuclear weapons be employed in retardation strikes. Two hours were simulated for presidential approval. Release was transmitted to the AEC,

SAC, and Air Material Command. The AEC Bossier Base storage site (Site Dog), next to Barksdale AFB in Louisiana, delivered its simulated nuclear weapon components to the C-124s of the 3rd Strategic Support Squadron. Twenty-four hours later these were delivered to forces in the United Kingdom, where the components were married up with their casings. SACEUR selected the targets, and the JCS field representative allocated the weapons. The SAC deputies colocated with them (SAC Zebra) determined the feasibility of the plan; target materials were distributed to the appropriate units; and the attacks went in.[41]

Prophecy, despite protestations on paper to the contrary, was based on actual targeting in Europe and reflected real coordination problems. There were 201 targets of which fourteen missions required deconfliction by the Joint Coordination Center. The duplication in targets tended to be between SACEUR and SACLANT, and SACEUR and CINCNELM: these involved aircraft from each command attacking the same three airfields and two oil-storage areas in various combinations. SACEUR and SACLANT were also both hitting an "amphibious concentration" and a "naval operations base" with the same weapon type at the same time.[42]

SAC's conflicts were mostly with CINCNELM's carrier strikes. Aircraft had to be deconflicted so they didn't collide over Split, Yugoslavia, and Szged, Romania. CINCNELM was attacking a petroleum-storage area supporting "a drive on the Dardanelles" with an F2H-2B Banshee and Mk-7 weapon, while SAC was destroying the entire refinery *and* consuming the navy-targeted storage area with a thermonuclear weapon. (The exercise target's name was a scrambled Ploieşti.) CINCNELM was also hitting enemy forces in Bulgaria to protect Turkey, where SAC had five penetration and withdrawal routes to and from targets in the northeast Black Sea region; SAC aircraft had to be rerouted southeast of Istanbul. In another situation SACEUR hit a target with the intention of destroying locomotives and rolling stock, while SAC planned to obliterate the whole marshalling yard.[43]

The Joint Coordination Center machinery was tested again later in 1953. Exercise World Series, conducted in August, had seventeen

B-50 sorties drawn from the 2nd Bomb Wing at RAF Upper Heyford and the 309th Bomb Wing at RAF Fairford directed against nine airfields, three marshalling yards, and one troop concentration, all targets nominated by SACEUR. The first ten of these strikes took place twenty-eight hours after the targets were nominated.[44]

The Beagle Problem Emerges

Initially the nuclear threat perception was based on Soviet TU-4 aircraft operating from Ukraine and staging from bases in Poland against targets in Western Europe.[45] In mid- and late 1952 Gens. John McConnell of the 7th Air Division in the United Kingdom and Otto Weyland in the Far East noted with alarm the buildup of large numbers of the Soviet two-jet light bomber, the IL-28 Beagle. Using copied Rolls Royce Nene engines, the aircraft were first seen by the intelligence community during the 1950 May Day fly-past in Moscow and then were subjected to intense and successful collection efforts when the first ones were forward-deployed to occupied Austria and then East Germany in 1951.[46] As McConnell told LeMay, there were an estimated seventy-six IL-28s in range of the SAC UK base complex, not to mention 725 TU-4s, and in his estimation, there were not enough air defense forces available. Opie Weyland noted there were eighty IL-28s in range based in China.[47] The IL-28s were a qualitative shift: they were jets that traveled at nearly 800 kilometers per hour, compared to the propeller-driven TU-4s that traveled at 550. This was a serious reduction in reaction time for both the European and Far East commanders, as well as SAC's forward-deployed forces.

There was a concerted effort by the intelligence community to collect on the IL-28 force; this involved the Potsdam-based Military Liaison Missions and significant espionage penetrations of the bases themselves via construction crews, food caterers, technicians, and drunken Soviet personnel. By the end of 1952 IL-28 regiments were located at Werneuchen, Jüterbog, and Brand in East Germany, and Wiener-Neustadt in Austria, each operating twenty-eight aircraft.[48] By mid-1953 Finsterwalde, Welzow, and Briesen were also marked as IL-28 bases, with over one hundred aircraft stationed there. Some were equipped with auxiliary fuel tanks, which gave the IL-28 enough range to hit the United Kingdom with their 2,000-pound bombs and forward-firing strafing cannon. The numbers of deployed IL-28s continued to grow: IL-28 regiments were spotted at Bad Voeslau, Gross Dölln, and Oranienburg in 1954.[49] Indeed, with over six thousand IL-28s produced and distributed among Warsaw Pact countries by the late 1950s, there was a rather large "bomber gap" extant by 1954–55. Conventional weapons delivered by IL-28s could render SAC bases inoperative and destroy their aircraft. The Soviets did not necessarily need nuclear weapons to carry out this task.[50]

These deployments helped accelerate an RAF air defense buildup using more than four hundred F-86 Sabres built in Canada and funded by the Mutual Defense Assistance Program, but that would take time to implement. In June 1953 Vandenberg, in one of his last public acts, explained to a congressional committee the dangers of the IL-28 deployments. Not coincidentally, LeMay dispatched the 306th Bomb Wing with its forty B-47s to RAF Fairford that same month, even though there were still no dedicated nuclear weapons deployed forward for them. In an emergency the capsules still had to be flown in from the United States, and then only after presidential and AEC approval.[51]

The 306th had only just reached the United Kingdom when an uprising in East Germany broke out, followed by a smaller one in Poland. The Soviets promptly but temporarily evacuated all of their IL-28 aircraft, as well as ground crews and fuel, to bases in the Soviet Union, where there were fewer eyes to watch them. The ground evacuation of Soviet air force units also illuminated logistics bottlenecks, albeit in a reverse way, at Frankfurt an der Oder and Brest-Litovsk, two key retardation targets.[52]

As if in response to the events of July, on 23 August 1953 an IL-28 dropped an RDS-4 nuclear weapon at the Soviet nuclear test site at Semipalatinsk. It yielded either 28 or 42 kilotons, indicating the Soviets had developed methods similar to those used in the Sandstone devices to improve the American stockpile back in 1948. The IL-28s were converted to the IL-28N, or nuclear, version later in 1953.[53]

When the IL-28 units returned to their East German bases in 1953, they probably were not nuclear-capable. However, they had a role to play for those units based in the Soviet Union that were. Some of the IL-28 regiments at Chernyakhovsk, Cherlyany, Stanislav, Staro-Konstantinov, Karankut, and Stryy airfields in the Soviet Union were nuclear-capable, and there was almost no information on them available to NATO until 1954. According to one account, their concept of operations had groups consisting of one IL-28 squadron and one bomb-carrying plane to launch, descend over Poland to low level in order to avoid the radar in West Berlin, strike against targets in West Germany, and recover to airfields in Poland to refuel. The forward-based conventional IL-28s probably had a role in distracting NATO air defenses from the strikes. At some point, and it is not clear when, nuclear-capable IL-28s were forward-deployed to Warsaw Pact bases so they could get at the UK and other SAC base complexes in Western Europe.[54] As we will see, the Beagle problem had ramifications regarding preemption as the 1950s progressed.

The Far East, 1950–53

U.S. Air Force and U.S. Navy nuclear operations in the Far East in the 1950–53 period had complexities not seen in Western European operations. Both commands were involved in multiple, overlapping operations. First, there was the ongoing peripheral reconnaissance collection effort monitoring Soviet bases and air defenses from the Chutkoi Peninsula to Hokkaido and then Vladivostok. Complementary to this was the U.S. Navy's collection effort from the Sea of Japan opposite Vladivostok down to Formosa. These operations could be lethal for aircrews, with several violent encounters and shoot-downs occurring in these years. The second was the Korean War itself, with SAC bombers assigned to Far East Air Force Bomber Command striking industry and interdiction targets on the Korean peninsula. In addition to mounting conventional aerial bombing, specified SAC forces remained in readiness with nuclear weapons in case their use in the Korean War was ordered by Truman (and later Eisenhower). The fourth was the deterrent effort against the Soviet Union. The possibility was raised that Stalin might seize Hokkaido, and there was a possibility of overt Soviet intervention in Korea. U.S. Navy and U.S. Air Force units were on call to deliver nuclear weapons if these scenarios expanded into regional or even global war, up to implementation of the Far East portions of EWP 1-49 and EWP 1-51. Like the NATO problem, SAC had to coordinate "strategic" nuclear force with "regional" nuclear forces, but unlike the NATO problem, SAC was getting shot at from various angles for real and had three different enemies. In later years the Far East was treated almost as a separate theater under the SIOP, as these complexities contributed to that state of affairs.

On 2 August 1950, six weeks after Communist forces invaded South Korea, SAC was directed by the JCS to deploy ten nuclear-capable B-29s from the 9th Bomb Wing "with [blank] number of special weapons, less nuclear components," on temporary rotational duty every two weeks to Okinawa.[55] Throughout the course of the war, SAC deployed three B-29 bomb groups equipped for conventional bombing: the 19th, 28th, and 307th Bomb Groups, making a total of ninety-nine B-29s. These aircraft formed the core of Far East Air Force's Bomber Command; they were under FEAF control and used against industry targets until those ran out, and then the B-29s were employed for interdiction operations.[56]

The 9th Bomb Group remained aloof from these operations. It is unclear what the nuclear targets initially were: Vandenberg expressed concern in the initial weeks of the war that Soviet airpower, if applied to supporting the North Korean attack, could prove decisive. Truman apparently instructed the USAF to prepare plans "to wipe out all Soviet air bases in the Far East."[57] LeMay wrote in his memoirs that later on "the B-29s were trained to go up there to Manchuria and destroy the enemy's potential to wage war. They were trained to bomb Peking and Hankow if necessary."[58] In late November 1950 there was concern in USAF circles that the war might expand and that Chinese airfields might be used to attack American airfields in an attack of a "Pearl Harbor type" in the region, including bases in Japan. There were requests for further augmentation of the nuclear capability.[59] When the Chinese massively intervened in December 1950, Commander in Chief Far East (CINCFE) Gen. Douglas MacArthur determined that eight weapons were needed to destroy "targets of opportunity": four weapons to be used against invading ground forces and four more against "critical concentrations of airpower."[60]

LeMay, however, advised Vandenberg, "[SAC's] analysis of available targets together with obvious considerations of possible adverse psychological reaction have led us to conclude that the employment of Atomic weapons in the far east would probably not be advisable at this time unless action is undertaken as part of an overall atomic offensive."[61] LeMay asserted that only SAC had the expertise to undertake such an operation and that it should not be farmed out to FEAF. Importantly, this stance established within SAC the principle that LeMay and Power followed during the course of their careers: with nuclear weapons, you either go all in against a specific and defined enemy, or not at all, and they needed to be under SAC control. In retrospect years later LeMay remarked that "he never saw a situation in Korea . . . where nuclear weapons were needed or desirable and never recommended them."[62]

When further Chinese buildups were detected in early 1951, President Truman and AEC chairman Gordon Dean authorized the deployment of nine nuclear cores to Andersen AFB in Guam.[63] On 5 June 1951 SAC RB-45CS initiated night radar photomapping operations against targets in Manchuria; these consisted of nine airfields which held 52 percent of the Chinese Communist air force and 70 percent of the Soviet air force stationed in China.[64] Soon afterward three KB-29 tankers were added to the force for "operational flexibility" purposes; these permitted the B-29s to reach Harbin, deep in northern Manchuria. LeMay wanted to build up to thirty B-29MRs and twenty tankers: the 19th Bomb Group (later 19th Bombardment Wing) did so by late 1950.[65] At this point it was SAC's intention that this force was to be used to destroy industrial targets in the Soviet Union and Manchuria, but there was now discussion in Far East Air Force HQ about using it to target airfields in the Kuriles and Sakhalin Island.[66]

The relationship between SAC and FEAF was blurred. LeMay commanded SAC forces, but FEAF was under General Weyland's command. Weyland's staff generated its own target list in February 1951; it included five airfields in the Vladivostok area, five in the Sakhalin Islands, the nine Manchurian targets, and ten targets elsewhere in China.[67] The conventional B-29s worked for FEAF but belonged to SAC, and the nuclear B-29s remained under direct SAC control. The innovative, pipe-smoking Weyland was an expert at close air support, having cut his teeth on supporting Patton's army in Europe during World War II, but he had no experience with strategic bombing. So how exactly would these forces relate to EWP 1-49 and EWP 1-51 if the Korean War expanded into a global confrontation? Was the nuclear weapon a strategic, operational-level, or tactical weapon under the unusual circumstances prevailing in the Far East? And who was responsible for the campaign? Was there even a campaign, or were they actually several unmeshed gears?

The coordination mechanism was dubbed SAC X-Ray, a SAC "control element" colocated with the FEAF headquarters. LeMay deployed Power to the Far East as the SAC representative, and the Far East war plan was modified so it provided "for SAC to support [CINCFE] by carrying out, under the JCS, approved atomic retardation attacks in the far East." This permitted SAC the use the 9th Bomb Wing B-29 units on Okinawa, employing nuclear weapons to support UN forces in Korea and attack Soviet targets if required.[68] SAC was also prepared to use these forces against targets of opportunity in conjunction with Weyland's headquarters.[69]

FEAF's reconnaissance activities, which included imagery of Dairen and Port Arthur in China, and Vladivostok, were made available to the 9th Bomb Wing units. And then another question arose: Where did FEAF targeting and SAC targeting for the entire Far East overlap? Some thought was given to having FEAF handle target data for all targets east of 100 degrees.[70]

Concerns about an expanded war continued throughout 1952. What should the role of nuclear weapons be? An analysis conducted for Vandenberg examined bombing Manchuria with nuclear or conventional forces. The advantages for nuclear use against those targets was mostly psychological, as they were limited to "an unknown quantity," but "the logistics drain imposed upon Communist China by the utilization of atomic weapons [was] believed to be substantial." That said, there were distinct disadvantages. First, there were the "unfavorable world-wide political and psychological repercussions which would result from the voluntary U.S./UN utilization of atomic weapons in China." Second, there was a "grave possibility of expanding the conflict to a global scale and thus incurring retaliation in kind." If that happened, "the U.S./UN must be prepared . . . to carry atomic weapons to the heartland of Russia." "Profitable atomic targets available in Manchuria are extremely limited. Sustained atomic operations, if confined to Manchurian targets, would result in the uneconomical expenditure of fissionable material. . . . If these operations proved not to be decisive, serious psychological and political reactions concerning the efficiency of atomic weapons and adverse to UN interest might result."[71]

The deployment of eighty IL-28 bombers to China was also noted in the study, which increased Vandenberg's concerns: these aircraft posed a threat to USAF bases even if equipped with conventional weapons.[72]

To further complicate matters, technological changes generated by the successful testing of the Mk-7 weapon during Shot Easy of the Buster-Jangle test series in 1951 demonstrated that a nuclear weapon's diameter could be reduced to the point where a jet fighter could deliver the same kilotonnage as a B-29. The F-84G was now capable of carrying the Mk-7. The ability of the F-84G to operate in a nuclear environment was also demonstrated during Shot George of the Tumbler-Snapper and during Shot King in the Ivy test series in 1952.[73]

Weyland pushed for a nuclear capability "to offset the enemy's four-to-one numerical superiority and [to] give FEAF a capability to attack the enemy's offensive bases before [it was] too late during the first and critical hours of any coming war."[74] That is, Weyland wanted to hit Soviet and Chinese as well as Korean targets. The unit to carry out these missions was supposed to be a SAC fighter-bomber wing, but LeMay resisted, as there were not enough F-84Gs and the ones SAC had were committed to the Western European portion of EWP 1-49. USAF headquarters wanted the new Far East fighter-bomber capability to be based with the 9th Bomb Wing B-29s and remain under SAC control, but Weyland pushed back again. Twining agreed with Weyland and committed twenty-five non-SAC F-84Gs to the Far East, but as in the past he was wary about Weyland's having access to stockpile data, presumably to prevent him from asking for the allocation of more weapons.[75]

The deployment and training of this force took place from late 1952 to 1953, starting with the 9th Fighter-Bomber Squadron and fifteen nuclear-capable F-84Gs. This was expanded by late 1953 into the three-squadron 49th Fighter-Bomber Wing and a tanker detachment. Based at Komaki, Japan, the 9th Fighter-Bomber Squadron had three deployment airfields to handle four F-84Gs each in the event of an emergency: Misawa and Itasuki in Japan, and Taegu in South Korea. The "shapes" were deployed on the aircraft in sealed hangers at the forward sites and the cores were held by the 3rd Aviation Field Depot Squadron at Kadena to be moved forward by transport aircraft when required. Six aircraft at Komaki would go after airfields around Vladivostok; the Misawa-based group would hit targets in the Kuriles and Sakhalin; Taegu would launch into China and North Korea; and Itasuki could go in with the Taegu force to either target sets. The small KB-29 tanker detachment could also assist with strikes into the Chinese interior as required.[76]

The command-and-control arrangements came under scrutiny in mid-1953 after the armistice and following the resolution of the SAC-SACEUR situation. The JCS looked toward establishing forces to handle retardation-type tasks in the Far East, and SAC X-ray, an organization similar to SAC Zebra in Europe, was formed to handle coordination. If the war in Korea resumed, all SAC forces in the Far East would revert to SAC command, and then SAC X-ray would take over from FEAF Bomber Command to handle target coordination with SAC forces based in the United States.[77]

At the same time, as we have seen, SAC expanded its B-36 force with two new wings based at Fairchild AFB, Washington, and Walker AFB in Roswell, New Mexico. These forces were responsible for EWP 1-49's SAC-directed USSR industrial target coverage.[78] The 92nd Bombardment Wing strike was divided into two elements: fifteen B-36s staged out of Eielson AFB in Alaska and five B-36s launched from Fairchild AFB.

The five B-36s from Fairchild were "featherweighted," that is, their weight reduced (one thousand rounds vs. nine thousand rounds

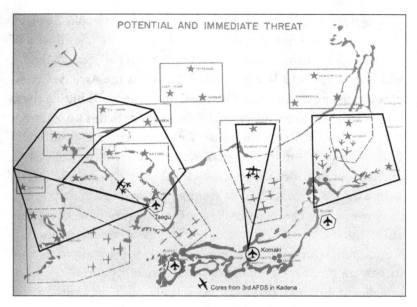

Taegu

Komaki

Cores from 3rd AFDS in Kadena

Map 7. 9th Fighter-Bomber Squadron and then 49th Fighter-Bomber Wing nuclear strike planning, 1952–53, superimposed on a 1952 Far East Air Force briefing map. These units were equipped with F-84G aircraft loaded with Mk-7 "shapes" stationed in Japan. The nuclear cores were flown in from Okinawa in an emergency. Some missions required inflight refueling from the KB-29 tanker aircraft detachment assigned to the wing. Courtesy of Library of Congress, LeMay Papers.

of 20mm ammunition, turrets removed), and likely equipped with the light case, light sphere version of the Mk-6 bombs. They would fly over the North Pole and split into three: one pair would go after Airframe Plant No. 99 at Ulan-Ude in eastern Siberia; the second would handle Airframe Plant No. 39 and a collection of other industry at Irkutsk, also in Siberia. The fifth plane would hit the TU-4 airfield at Blagoveshchensk, on the Chinese border. All would recover to Kadena Air Base in Okinawa.[79]

The Eielson element would break into three five-plane cells equipped with Mk-4 weapons. Penetrating Soviet airspace over the Pole to avoid the Kamchatka Peninsula radar network, these cells would strike from north to south, starting with Komsomolsk's pair of airframe plants, the submarine shipyard, a refinery, and a chemical plant.[80] The second grouping was for Khabarovsk with seven targets: two shipyards, a refinery, an armament plant, an explosive plant, the Khabarovsk Airfield, and Airframe Plant No. 83.[81] Southwest of Khabarovsk were three major air bases at Khorol East, Spassk-Dalniy, and Voroshilov (aka Vozdvishenka). Next was the Arsenyev complex consisting of Airframe Plant No. 116.[82] The B-36s hitting these targets would recover at Fairchild.[83] Subsequent to this RB-36s from the 99th Strategic Reconnaissance Wing staging from Eielson would follow the 92nd Bomb Wing strikes, conduct poststrike collection, and recover to Kadena. The 92nd was scheduled to restrike targets with six B-36s from Kadena as required (as depicted in map 6).[84]

However, the U.S. Navy in the Far East was now nuclear-capable and wanted coequal responsibility for nuclear strike operations.[85] Concurrent with these developments the U.S. Navy also deployed its F2H-2B Banshee light nuclear attack capability and Mk-7 weapons aboard the USS *Oriskany* in the Sea of Japan.[86] The United States now had three different nuclear strike forces directed at target sets that geographically overlapped. In a meeting with Opie Weyland, Adm. Joseph J. "Jocko" Clark, the U.S. Navy Task Force 77 commander, "made quite a point of his atomic capability. Stated that he had no guidance with reference to targets and that in the absence of such guidance he had selected his own targets. Stated that he was ready to launch strikes on a hour's notice. With the exception of the Mk VIII this is an obvious exaggeration. Mk VII weapons cannot be readied in such a time regardless of the availability of nuclear components."[87]

To make matters even more interesting, the USS *Oriskany* had been attacked by Soviet aircraft off Vladivostok in November 1952. The *Oriskany*'s combat air patrol F9F Panthers downed five Soviet MiG-15s.[88] The implications of having a nuclear-armed aircraft carrier with its own independent targeting in a high state of readiness led by an aggressive commander that could be cut off from his chain of command while under attack are historically intriguing. Targets in the Vladivostok area included the submarine base at Ulisa Bay, the Vladivostok Naval Base and Shipyard 202, the Bystry Shipyard, and at least three to four airfields.[89] It is unclear how the U.S. Navy intended to handle the collection of naval bases, repair yards, and air bases at Petropavlovsk. Perhaps this was left to the USS *Kearsarge*, or the *Oriskany* would reposition and strike there next.

Exercise Collie was mounted to test the SAC and U.S. Navy procedures and to untangle the Far East nuclear coordination issues. FEAF was grudgingly permitted to exercise their F-84 force. A multitude of problems emerged. FEAF ran profile missions with the 9th Squadron: twenty-two target profiles were accepted and scheduled, but five missions aborted. This was too high "for a specialized unit of this type." As for the navy, Weyland was told by U.S. Navy representatives that in the event of a general emergency Far East Command could "not count on the carriers." Furthermore, "in connection with atomic planning," he was told, "The Navy has never accepted responsibility for any specific atomic targets or areas—the reason being that they claim that they would not know where their carriers would be at any given time and can not commit themselves in advance."[90]

Then the army made a series of proposals for close support of its forces in Korea. They were told by air force and navy representatives, "Under the plan under discussion, the counter [air force] task was of first priority; therefore that in considering assumptions of availability of atomic weapons to [Far East Command], that from the entire availability should be subtracted the requirements for the counter air force mission (including those delivered by SAC and the Navy), requirements for interdiction, and then consider from the remaining availabilities the requirements for ground force joint action."[91]

A summit meeting of sorts between Weyland and the new chairman of the Joint Chiefs, Adm. Arthur Radford, took place in late December 1953. They agreed that the existing operational plans for use of nuclear weapons for the Far East were out of date. A number of new plans were therefore required. If hostilities in Korea resumed, there should be a plan employing only those forces already deployed in theater "with some air reinforcement from SAC." Ground forces would withdraw and atomic weapons be employed during that phase. Radford noted that "previous boundaries and restrictions would be removed and that atomic weapons would also be used." Weyland explained that FEAF atomic planners had already worked out counter-air and interdiction plans, and had already started to liaise with army planners for ground support, but it was clear the first two plans were the priority. As for command and control, Radford agreed wholeheartedly that in a resumption of the Korean War, the Far East Command "and inferentially CINCPAC [Commander in Chief Pacific Command] should be responsible for planning atomic ops. SAC should be in a supporting role to CINCFE and that SAC should deliver weapons on targets and in timing sequence as requested by theatre, as opposed to SAC responsibility to JCS for strikes against interior strategic targets." This ran counter to LeMay's assertions that SAC should coordinate all nuclear planning in concert with the worldwide Emergency War Plan, but Weyland communicated Radford's views back to his air force superiors.[92] At the start of 1954, little progress had been made on coordination of nuclear targeting in the Far East compared to Europe.

The problems and issues encountered by SAC in the 1950–53 period resonate and rebound throughout the history of American nuclear targeting. The first relates to targeting priorities. With the Delta, Bravo, and Romeo schema and a limited stockpile, where did the bombs go, and why? The Destruction category was the most straightforward: SAC could now accomplish what its predecessors only dreamed of during World War II. In a war like that one, bomber-delivered kiloton-yield atomic bombs are merely a more efficient means of accomplishing the same task: destruction of the enemy's war-making capacity. The Delta category became the basis of future urban/industrial targeting in the SIOP.

The emergence of the Blunting problem also presaged significant issues in American policy. If the enemy developed the capability of using atomic weapons against the forward-based forces poised to destroy the Delta targets, and the deterrent was based on effective target coverage of those Delta targets, then what percentage of forces needed to be applied to destroy those enemy strike forces, and when? And how did SAC get the civilian leadership to have the AEC release the capsules so they could be deployed forward and assembled in time for the forces to launch and blunt an enemy's preemptive strike? And where did intelligence and early warning fit into this? This problem, it should be pointed out, related to forward-based forces in Western Europe and the Far East and was not strictly a North American–centric defensive problem. SAC's squadrons in the United Kingdom, French Morocco, Canada, Alaska, Greenland, and Japan did not have hours and hours of warning that the Lower Forty-Eight would have.

As for the Romeo targeting problem, the division of labor among SAC, the theater commanders, and the U.S. Navy was problematic and remained so for decades. The blurring of lines between the Delta target set in western Russia and the Romeo target set in Eastern Europe, and which was the priority in an era of atomic scarcity, reverberated well into the 1960s. Similarly in the Far East: Who was responsible for the destruction of submarine support and production facilities? Were they Delta industrial targets? Was it a Blunting mission? A Retardation mission?

When all was said and done, however, the demonstrated ability of SAC's forces to carry out their tasks in spite of these internal debates was not unnoticed by the opposition. The rapid buildup and modernization of the Soviet air defense forces in less than two years is a significant indicator that they recognized the threat. Nikita Khrushchev later reflected, "[Stalin] was afraid of war.... He knew we were weaker that the United States. We had only a handful of nuclear weapons, while the Americans had a large arsenal. . . . Of course in other areas—conventional ground forces and ground forces—we had the advantage. Stalin . . . knew his weakness."[93] Stalin made no further moves on West Berlin or NATO during this period. He shifted to other methods: covert support to Communist forces in Korea, maintaining the ongoing subversion and espionage operations against the West, and overt signaling with nearly daily overflights over northern Japan. When American F-84s pushed back and shot up Soviet La-11 aircraft over Hokkaido, and when the joint RAF-USAF mission demonstrated that B-45 bombers could get at him in Moscow with little or no warning, American reconnaissance aircraft in isolated areas were shot down by Soviet MIGs under ambiguous circumstances. This was followed by the inexplicable attack against the USS *Oriskany*. These were actions of a contained, frustrated animal lashing out because it could not get its own way, not the actions of a mature superpower seeking global stability.

Khrushchev's post hoc jibes notwithstanding, Stalin pursued thermonuclear weapons and prioritized surface-to-air missile development before he died in 1953. According to Robert Conquest, "[He also] told the aeronautics expert Colonel Tokarev that such a weapon [the ballistic missile] would make it easier for us to talk to the great shop-keeper Harry Truman and keep him pinned down where we want him."[94] Sergo Beria noted that acquisition by the Soviets of a nuclear capability convinced Stalin "that everything was henceforth permitted to him and [the USSR] would soon be able to go over to the attack." What gave Stalin temporary pause, however, was the lack of an effective air defense missile system and thermonuclear weapons. These became prioritized Soviet projects, particularly after the first American thermonuclear detonation in 1952. "It was then that the Americans organized a leak and a document describing their plans fell into our hands. It was a warning intended to let us know that any attempt at aggression on our part would unleash a reaction from them."[95]

That signaling likely was combined with demonstrative activity. Under JCS guidance, SAC mounted Operation Big Stick, which involved twenty-seven B-36s from the 92nd Bombardment Wing based in Fairchild AFB "to effect a show of force in the Far East" during negotiations over Korea in the summer of 1953. Some of these aircraft were equipped with nuclear weapons minus their cores. Led by Col. James V. Edmundson, the B-36s rendezvoused over Attu Island in the Aleutians and then separated to simulate their profiles against their EWP targets in eastern Siberia while transiting to Japan, carefully keeping out of Soviet airspace. Some of the B-36s proceeded to Kadena, and according to Edmundson, "We sat on alert on Okinawa for about ten days in all our atomic splendor."[96] The show of force was an unmasking of SAC Outline Emergency War Plan 8-53, effective as of 20 August 1953. This plan provided "for the atomic attack of selected targets in Communist China in the event of a breakdown of the Korean armistice." General Twining ensured that there was also "Headquarters USAF Outline Plan 8-53," a "unilateral Air Force plan" that was "to provide for the atomic attack of selected Chinese Communist targets" for the same contingency but presumably using all USAF assets in the region, that is, Weyland's F-84 force.[97]

After the death of Stalin in 1953, the Soviet leadership would not make a significant Cold War move on the international scene until the Soviet Union possessed both thermonuclear weapons and a surface-to-air missile defense system to protect Moscow.

5

Four Horsemen I

Targeting the Soviet Union, 1954–56

If somebody could tell us exactly how much punishment has to be meted

out to the Russians in order to make them quit, we could come up with

a tailored strategic force designed to precisely that much. . . . But the

answer to the question of exactly how much knocking around the Russian

will stand—what minimum it would take to fix him so he no longer has

the will to wage war—stands unanswered at this time.

—CURTIS LEMAY to Stuart Symington, 11 January 1954

As we have seen, early American strategy revolved around fighting a World War II–style war with an increasing number of kiloton-yield nuclear weapons. The availability of megaton-yield bombs delivered by bombers completely altered this thinking by 1954. The anticipated but nevertheless shocking destructive power of thermonuclear weapons technology unleashed by the Ivy Mike test in 1952 followed by the astonishing Castle test series in 1954 thrust nuclear strategy and targeting onto a whole new plane. The ability to literally erase everything in a one- to two-mile radius, destroy by blast and fire everything out to another ten, twenty, or even thirty miles, and then deposit radioactive fallout hundreds of miles downrange produced a dilemma. Was nuclear targeting going to remain an extrapolation of traditional strategic bombing, or was this something radically different that required a wholly new strategy? Was it possible to reconcile the two positions in an era when the aspirations of the air power theorists of the interwar period and

World War II could now be met in practical terms but then became irrelevant because whole societies would cease to exist and thus the rationale for strategy would too?

The evolution of the SAC Emergency War Plan and the regional commanders in chief's atomic strike plans from 1954 suggests that there remained some debate. In simplistic terms, there was a discernable shift from "warfighting" to "deterrence" during this period, though the distinction is not completely clear-cut. Nuclear weapons had a deterrent effect prior to 1954, and that effect was recognized and accepted in American circles. However, the willingness to employ nuclear weapons in a regional conflict was reduced over time as the distinction between a regional, battlefield weapon and a strategic bombing weapon blurred, and beliefs that belligerents would not necessarily recognize the distinction emerged. That path acquired new definition later and ultimately led to the production and deployment of nuclear weapons at the tactical level by the 1960s and, with them, employment concepts in a NATO context, mostly to offset superior Soviet conventional capabilities and deter or constrain Soviet actions in that theater during Cold War operations.

The other path took strategic nuclear weapons and plans for their use closer to the realm of pure deterrence, where the objective increasingly became to prevent their use because of their unprecedented destructive capabilities. Paradoxically nuclear forces increasingly played an overt role in Cold War crisis diplomacy, particularly in 1956 during the Suez crisis. Credible forces required credible training and credible plans for deterrence purposes and for employment if crisis diplomacy failed. The idea that prompt destruction of the opposition's ability to harm the United States, and in particular its forward-based forces and their bases in allied countries, would ensure the survival of the state was not new but increasingly drove American nuclear strategy during this time, particularly because the Soviets had thermonuclear weapons and aircraft to deliver them. That trajectory led to the SIOP's immediate predecessors, the Emergency War Plan on the one hand, and the commanders in chiefs' regional war plans on the other.

From Castle to Redwing: Thermonuclear Weapons Developments, 1954–56

On 12 April 1954 Gen. Curtis LeMay, accompanied by two of his subordinate commanders, Maj. Gen. Frank Armstrong of the Second Air Force and Maj. Gen. Walter Sweeney of the Fifteenth Air Force, flew to the Pacific Proving Grounds on a classified flight accompanied by Dr. Carroll Zimmerman, the SAC scientific advisor, and three generals from the SAC operations staff.[1] LeMay was particularly concerned about the levels of radiation absorbed by the aircrews involved in the tests, especially after cloud penetration operations, and how well the B-36s were being decontaminated.[2] During the briefings, the SAC leadership learned that the Castle test series, designed to determine which thermonuclear weapons paths would be taken, had been halted. On 1 March, Shot Bravo dramatically exceeded its estimated 6-megaton yield and detonated at 15 megatons, forcing the evacuation of the atoll's test facilities. On 27 March, Shot Romeo, estimated to yield 3 megatons, also exceeded its yield and detonated at 11 megatons. Another test device, Shot Koon, underyielded, at an underwhelming 110 kilotons. Two of the three subsequent shots overyielded: Union (6.9 MT) and Yankee, predicted to yield 8.5 megatons, went off at 13.5 megatons. The final shot, Nectar, was within its design yield at 1.6 megatons.[3] All of the devices used in these tests except the TX-15 used the same Cobra primary, which was a slightly modified 60-kiloton Mk-7 warhead. The TX-15 used the Viper primary, which was based on the 40-kiloton Mk-12 bomb.[4] The problem therefore lay in the scientific calculations in how the material in the secondaries was supposed to behave.

These unexpected events had unanticipated consequences. The fallout from the Bravo test inadvertently dosed the Japanese fishing vessel *Fortunate Dragon* and contaminated inhabited islands. As a result the Castle tests "became a highly visible and divisive" international issue and "the risks of exposure from fallout that spread around the globe developed into a bitterly contested political question and remained a prominent policy issue until the Limited Test Ban Treaty of 1963."[5] This had implications for SAC basing its nuclear-equipped aircraft in certain countries, particularly Japan, and thus could influence the deterrent effects of the SAC Emergency War Plan if targets could not be covered. As we will see, that state of affairs accelerated SAC's increased emphasis on long-distance aerial refueling and conducting strikes from North America.

Another consequence of Castle was yet another divergence of opinion between the U.S. Air Force and the U.S. Navy. There were three different fallout measurement programs at Castle, one from each of the two services and one from the RAND Corporation. The air force's measurements for how widespread the fallout was were lower than the navy's, and the RAND study's numbers were in between. Though the air force study was determined years later to be based on a flawed scaling model, the divergence of opinion had ramifications for targeting.[6] Of more immediate import for SAC, however, the instrumented B-36D and the B-47 bombers survived the five shots and enough data were collected to permit the development of delivery profiles for those aircraft types so they could employ thermonuclear weapons.[7]

In terms of weapons development and deployment, however, Castle gave the green light to move through and beyond the Emergency Capability period. The liquid-fuel TX-16 was canceled once the efficiency of the solid-fuel weapons was demonstrated. The Union shot at 6.9 megatons confirmed that the EC-14 weapon, of which five were already stockpiled, was viable. The Runt device from Romeo was transformed into the Mk-17. Runt II, the Yankee shot, became the Mk-24. Nectar became the basis of the Mk-15 Zombie and went into production in 1955, while the mighty Shrimp from Bravo went into production as the Mk-21 starting in December 1955 (see table 3).[8] The AEC determined that, after some analysis and manipulation of the secondaries, the yields for thermonuclear weapons could be dialed up to double the Castle yields "or to hold the present yield and reduce the weight by 50%."[9] This implies that the Mk-17, for example, could yield 22 megatons or that the Mk-21, based on the Shrimp, could yield nearly 30 megatons. These insights were the likely basis for LeMay's 8 December 1954 request for the development of a 60-megaton weapon.[10] That said, maintenance personnel

FOUR HORSEMEN I

Table 3. U.S. thermonuclear bomb development, 1954–56

Device	Test	Test yield	Nick-name	Derived weapon	Weapon yield	Stockpile dates
TX-14	Castle Union	6.9 MT	Alarm Clock	EC-14 Mk-14	6.9 MT	February–October 1954 (5 built)
TX-15	Castle Nectar	1.69 MT	Zombie	Mk-15	1.8, 3.8 MT	April 1955–April 1966 (1,200 built)
EC-16	(canceled)	Est. 6+ MT	Jughead	Mk-16	6.9 MT	December 1953–April 1954 (5 casings)
TX-17	Castle Romeo	11 MT (preshot est. 3 MT)	Runt	EC-17 Mk-17	15–22 MT?	May 1954–August 1957 (305 Mk-17 and 24 EC-17 built)
TX-21	Castle Bravo	15 MT (preshot est. 6 MT)	Shrimp	Mk-21 mod 0	18 MT	December 1955–July 1956 enters stockpile; withdrawn June–November 1957 and converted to Mk-36Y1 mod 1 (275 built)
TX-24	Castle Yankee	13.5 MT (preshot est. 8.5 MT)	Runt II	EC-24 Mk-24	15–27 MT?	April 1954–October 1956
TX-15 X-1 (stockpile Mk-15 used)	Redwing Cherokee	3.8 MT		Mk-15	Up to 18 MT	
TX-21C	Redwing Navaho	4.5 MT		Mk-21 mod 1 "clean" bomb		Mk-21 mod 1 not produced
Bassoon device	Redwing Zuni Redwing Tewa	3.5 MT 5 MT		First steps to Mk-41 bomb		

were taught that yields for the Mk-17, for example, were generally set at 15 megatons, while the Mk-21 was set for 18 megatons.[11]

As for the Soviet thermonuclear program, after pursuing their indigenous "Layer Cake" design to its 400-kiloton dead end in 1953, the Soviet scientists reached out for help via the extensive Soviet intelligence apparatus in the United States. They got it in the form of Perseus, an agent in the American thermonuclear program. After a crash program consisting of thirteen shots throughout 1954–55, on 6 November 1955 they detonated a 250-kiloton device, likely similar to the Greenhouse George shot.[12] Three weeks later, on 22 November, a TU-16 bomber dropped the first Soviet two-stage thermonuclear weapon, the RDS-37, which yielded 1.6 megatons. The weapon was designed to yield much more but had been "derated," that is, turned into a "clean" weapon for the exercise to reduce fallout.[13] This not only limited the Soviets' exposure to international criticism à la the Bravo event; it also obscured what yields they were actually employing in their weapons. More important, the RDS-37 was not a "device": it was an air-droppable weapon. That said, the first attempt to drop failed when the plane's radar bombing system quit and the TU-16 crew had to land with an armed H-bomb. When the test did take place, the shock wave reflected off an inversion layer, destroying at least one village and generating civilian casualties.[14] Of course, these mishaps could be concealed in a totalitarian society and prevented the same sort of international criticism the Soviets encouraged against the United States after Castle Bravo.

The next American test series, Redwing, should not be seen as a response to the Soviet series: it was a planned follow-on to Castle. During the deliberations LeMay pushed Twining for a full-up B-52 airdrop test of the Mk-21 (based on the Bravo shot's Shrimp) throughout the summer of 1955. His reasoning: "A tremendous effort has been made to develop the B-52 Mk 21 weapon system. In the next few years it will become the most important component of our strike forces. To base our national defense upon such a system without a complete proof test would be unwise." If an airdrop was conducted, "the actual delivery configuration can be used as a basis for operational planning without delay." If a "ground burst and positioned aircraft are tested, it takes many months to interpret whatever useful data is obtained. In the interim, conservative planning factors which penalize the weapons system effectiveness must be used."[15] LeMay was implying that without accurate data, SAC's crews and aircraft would be put at risk because they would have to get closer to their targets. The alternative was to significantly increase the yield of the weapons. That said, LeMay was particularly concerned about B-52 crews escaping the initial radiation burst of a detonation after delivery, and more testing was needed on this.[16] His larger point, however, was that the capability had to be credible for deterrence purposes and, once again, be seen to be credible. LeMay was initially rebuffed and told that the Mk-21 "ha[d] been proven by components" already and that higher-level interest was focused on the TX-15-X-1, a modified Mk-15 Zombie.[17]

It is difficult to set aside the idea that LeMay and SAC were in some ways being carried along by the larger American thermonuclear drama at this time. The main drivers appear to have been the Atomic Energy Commission, the Armed Forces Special Warfare Project, the Joint Committee on Atomic Energy, the competing labs at Berkley (later Livermore) and Los Alamos, plus all of the strong personalities involved who were responding to the Eisenhower administration's national security strategy but paradoxically also driving it. As the physicist Herbert York said at the time, "The United States cannot maintain its qualitative edge without having an aggressive R&D establishment that pushes against the technological frontiers without being asked. That is the inevitable result of our continuing quest for a qualitative edge to offset the other side's quantitative advantages."[18]

The Redwing test series, held from May to July 1956, had two broad purposes. The first was an "open" shot whereby media and allied observers were invited to watch and report to the world in general (and the Soviets in particular) what the United States was capable of. The second involved testing devices for air defense weapons, the warhead for the navy's Regulus cruise missile, and four tests associated with the Mk-28 weapon that would dominate the stockpile in the 1960s. Special emphasis was placed on fallout reduction with the first design of a "clean" bomb, that is, one with reduced fission. This was the Bassoon device, of which two were detonated during Redwing: Zuni in a "clean" and Tewa in a "dirty" configuration. Bassoon became the basis for the extremely high-yield Mk-41, which was stockpiled in the early 1960s.[19] It also led to a quest for the Holy Grail of bomb design: one that would generate the destructive power of a nuclear weapon while reducing fallout effects. The "clean" bomb concept continued during the next two test series, Plumbbob (1957) and Hardtack (1958). Redwing also tested technological advancements like "sealed pit" weapons, external neutron generators, and tritium reservoirs, techniques that eventually facilitated SAC airborne alert operations.

But the star of the show was the presidentially authorized Shot Cherokee. Cherokee was to demonstrate a complete weapons system package, culminating with an airburst at 5,000 feet over a target array simulating an industrial complex. On 21 May 1956 a B-52B named *Barbara Grace* from the non-SAC 4925th Test Group (Atomic) carrying an Mk-15 weapon approached Nam Island at Bikini Atoll at 40,000 feet. Then, due to a crew-based navigation error, they released the weapon early. The Zombie detonated at 3.8 megatons four miles short of the target island, at nearly 5,000 instead of 3,000 feet. It was Crossroads Able all over again, except this time SAC did not have to take the rap. The fireball destroyed target arrays that were instrumented for blast. The fleet of response aircraft awaiting input to their sensors included B-47s and B-52 bombers, B-57 and B-66 light bombers, F-84F and F-101A fighter-bombers, and navy A3D carrier-based bombers. Most were too far away, though subsequent shots in the series, particularly Zuni, were used to get the necessary data later.[20]

None of the public observers knew this at the time, however, and dutifully reported the first successful drop and detonation of an American thermonuclear bomb from a jet bomber—which it was. A month later the "miss" was reported by the *New York Times*, prompting a statement from Secretary of the Air Force Donald Quarles to the effect that the miss "was not great enough to have a serious effect on the success of the experiment."[21]

Of greater import was the fallout assessment. The Redwing planners took great pains after Castle to overinstrument the region and increase resources examining the fallout phenomenon. Their conclusion: "Cherokee produced no fallout.... No detectable ocean area contamination was found.... Similar surveys after Shot Osage, an airburst, confirmed the Cherokee finding that significant fallout does not occur after airbursts."[22] The written research reports did not echo task force commander Rear Adm. B. Hall Hanlon's comments in a classified briefing film; in his view, although there was no fallout over water, it was unclear if an airburst over land would produce the same results.[23] Furthermore, according to B-47 crews who participated in all of the Redwing shots, "a surprising conclusion . . . was that the weapons 'effects' between a one-megaton and fourteen megatons were not significantly different, other than a longer 'flash' period for the larger weapon."[24]

What emerged from Castle and then Redwing were two belief systems. First, thermonuclear weapons could be modified to generate a range of effects. Some of these effects could enhance or augment radioactive contamination; some modifications could reduce it. The second was that thermonuclear weapons could be airburst at optimal heights to reduce if not eliminate fallout. Combining the two beliefs could lead strategists and planners to become less concerned about radioactive fallout and focus on the already well-known and well-studied effects like blast/shock and thermal energy. And in the climate of the 1950s, those public figures who were vocal about fallout and disarmament could easily be marginalized in such circles.

Immediately after Redwing, LeMay reactivated his request for a 60-megaton bomb. His original request, which was in fact based on a USAF HQ study "that such weapons were mandatory to destroy hardened targets," was discarded because "critics saw no useful military purpose in producing it." Though the idea of a 60-megaton bomb seems excessive by today's standards, there was more to LeMay's thinking than he has been given credit for, and the debate provides insight not only into SAC planning in the mid-1950s but also into Soviet thinking in the early 1960s, when they detonated their derated 54-megaton "monster bomb" on 30 October 1961: "The deterrent value of the weapon dictated its development. . . . Six small weapons could destroy more targets than one large weapon, but the six did not have the deterrent value of the largest possible weapon. The value of a weapon which successfully deterred could not be measured in a real war or a paper battle because the assumption would have to be that it had failed to deter."[25]

Strategy: A New Look and a New Approach, 1953–56

The main issues in the American strategy debate during the early Eisenhower administration revolved around the following questions: Would there be war with the Soviet Union, or could the Soviet Union be contained and deterred? What was the nature of the future war that would be fought if war did break out? Would that war start on its own, or would it start after an escalatory situation in the Far East or Europe? What role should nuclear weapons play in such wars? When should nuclear weapons be employed? Finally, and related to the previous two questions, what was the appropriate force structure to handle the overall situation in a cold war (aka "peace") as well as a "shooting war"? And what was the right balance between the American armed services in carrying all of this out? The answers to these questions swung like a pendulum within the JCS and between that body and the National Security Council throughout the 1950s. There was, however, a constant in the flurry of NSC and JCS papers: they all included a variation of one of the following phrases:[26]

> "The United States . . . must develop and maintain an offensive capability, particularly the capability to inflict massive damage on Soviet warmaking capacity, at a level that the Soviets must regard as an unacceptable risk in war."
>
> "Currently the most critical factors in the military aspects of our security are air defense of our Continental U.S. vitals and our ability to retaliate swiftly and powerfully. . . . A capability for swift and powerful retaliation is a deterrent and in the even of hostilities will blunt the enemy offensive and reduce his capabilities."
>
> "Military requirements call for a strong military posture, with emphasis on the capability of inflicting massive retaliatory damage by offensive striking power."

There was no real debate about this: the only question was what percentage of national and military resources should be applied to that task in relationship to the other tasks. The subsequent issue that emerged was how to deter a Soviet attack on Western Europe and the relationship of the response to such an attack to the strategic offensive striking power force. That issue lasted the entire Cold War. In a major shift from Truman-era strategic language, "deterrence" underpinned everything in the Eisenhower-era documents, increasingly so by 1955, after the Castle series; the term "mutual deterrence" was even used in the mid-1950s to describe a situation that might exist in 1960 where the Soviets had as many nuclear weapons as the United States—what in the 1970s was called "parity."[27]

In April, June, and October 1953 the Eisenhower administration laid out its national security policy. The sections relating to nuclear weapons used language employed in Truman-era policy: "We set the following objectives . . . prevent or counter aggression, deter general war, provide the basis for winning a general war if one should be forced upon us," and "develop and maintain an offensive capability, particularly the capability to inflict massive damage on Soviet war-making capacity, at a level that the Soviets must regard as an unacceptable risk in war." Unlike earlier policy, the June 1953 iterations included more specific guidance related to American objectives in a war with the Soviet Union: military operations would generate a situation where U.S. objectives were achieved, but unlike in the Second World War, there was no requirement for unconditional surrender. Conditions would be set to eliminate "Soviet Russian domination in areas outside the borders of any Russian state allowed to exist after the war." "In addition, if any bolshevik regime is left in any part of the Soviet Union, [the United States will ensure] that it does not control enough of the military-industrial potential of the Soviet Union to enable it to wage war on comparable terms with any other regime or regimes which may exist on traditional Russian territory."[28] The October 1953 restatement of the national security policy enhanced the language on nuclear weapons use, specifically: "The security of the United States requires . . . development and maintenance of . . . a strong military posture, with emphasis on the capability of inflicting massive retaliatory damage by offensive striking power." Furthermore, the update recognized that war conducted against the Soviet Union and war conducted against Communist China may be exclusive of one another.[29]

The Eisenhower administration continued to refine its basic national security policy into 1954, specifically in response to intelligence collected from overflights of the Soviet Union and its allies. Without rejecting earlier views on the role of nuclear weapons in American policy, the August 1954 revisions of the policy recognized that the deployment of thermonuclear weapons produced a situation whereby "a total war involving the strategic use by both sides of nuclear weapons would bring about such extensive destruction as to threaten the survival of Western civilization and the Soviet regime."[30] As a result, "this situation could create a condition of mutual deterrence." "The free world powers are becoming increasingly cautious about joining in actions which they believe will enhance the risk of war. Because Soviet action under this situation cannot be accurately predicted, the free world will have to be especially vigilant. . . . [This could] tempt the Soviets into attacking the United States if they believed that initial surprise held a prospect of destroying the U.S. retaliatory power before it could be used."[31] Ultimately, "to ensure Soviet fear that strategic nuclear attacks upon the U.S. would be followed by the nuclear devastation of the USSR and the destruction of the Soviet regime" the United States had to maintain and protect the retaliatory force.[32]

By 1955 the policy remained relatively stable. Additions included an emphasis on countering surprise and technological breakthroughs that might undermine deterrence. Notably, however, the policy specifically rejected "the concept of preventive war" but did not define what preventive war was. The policy also rejected "acts intended to provoke war," while at the same time making clear U.S. "determination to oppose aggression despite risk of general war." "And the United States must make clear its determination to prevail if general war eventuates."[33]

For all intents and purposes the Eisenhower administration created a coherent national policy, established broadly interpretable strategic language at the NSC, and left the JCS to duke it out over the proportion of resources to be applied to meet those objectives. The Truman-era JCS war-planning mechanisms were unable to keep up and were replaced with a new system in 1954 that itself "failed to operate as anticipated."[34] The one-, four-, and five-year plans for this period were not all approved on time and were not simpatico with each other. The one thing that was coherent was their expression of the pattern of war that was likely to be fought. This concept was symbiotic with and influenced by the NATO strategic concept, MC 48. It described a war with the Soviet Union consisting of two phases: an initial phase in which nuclear weapons use would dominate, and a subsequent phase in which one side would run out of nuclear weapons and the war could be concluded on more or less conventional terms. The first phase could last up to a month, while the second would last years.[35]

In practical terms, this meant having NATO forces hold the NATO Area in Western Europe, while naval forces struck the Soviet Union's peripheries and kept the sea lines of communication open with North America. The strategic air offensive would hit the Soviet Union while the air defense forces in North America protected those forces from destruction.[36] What happened in the subsequent phase was something between a land invasion of an irradiated Soviet Union and cleaning up what was left of the United States. More attention was given to the latter as the 1950s progressed.

The JCS debate during this time related to what percentage of resources during "peace time" should be put into the forces earmarked for second-phase operations. The U.S. Air Force's response was: very little. If the strategic striking force was strong in peace time, there would be no war. In the event war broke out, the strategic striking force was the critical element of the first phase anyway, so, given a limited budget, why not invest in it at the expense of forces that might not be needed? Of course the U.S. Army leadership argued that not all wars would start with a bolt from the blue: some would arise from subversion and insurgent situations, while others might arise from escalatory situations. Nuclear weapons use might not be appropriate in all circumstances (this at a time the U.S. Army was preparing to arm itself with everything from intermediate-range ballistic missiles to nuclear hand grenades). That debate continued throughout the Eisenhower administration and eventually became an acrimonious public policy issue as the army fought back against perceived obsolescence while retaining a quasi-conventional capability.[37]

The translation of the JCS-level strategic concepts to functional plans was left to the commanders in chief of the unified and specified commands, as it had during the Truman years. Those plans, however, were increasingly based on nuclear weapons availability and thus required coordination both at the JCS level and between the commanders in chief and SAC. The halting steps toward the latter described in chapter 3 continued into the mid-1950s and are examined later in this chapter. It was one thing to have a strategy on paper; it was another to have delivery systems and the casings. But it was another thing altogether to have access to vital components of the primaries. At the JCS level interservice competition boiled down to who could get more of the scarce cores assigned to their forces, and that meant dealing with the White House and the Atomic Energy Commission.

Once again it is important to understand that at this point, SAC did not own or control complete nuclear weapons. The command had casings assigned to it by the mutual consent of the president and the AEC chairman. The cores were stored in AEC National Stockpile Sites or military Operational Storage Sites that had AEC custodians assigned to them. Cores were not yet stored overseas in non-U.S. territories.

How the unified and specified commands bid with the JCS on the number of cores they wanted to carry out their plans was relatively straightforward. Each command generated an annual Atomic Annex that was examined and approved by the JCS. These were used as the basis for the command-level coordination conferences.[38] Within the JCS an organization on the Joint Staff tallied up the numbers and made recommendations for the number of capsules and weapons that should be allocated; those numbers were examined, approved by the JCS, and issued to the commands. How the JCS interacted with the AEC and the White House after that is obscure. From later years it appears the president approved on an annual basis those JCS numbers, in consultation with the AEC.[39]

What can be determined is that there were a total of 1,703 American nuclear weapons in 1954, 2,422 in 1955, and 3,692 in 1956.[40] In 1955 LeMay complained to Twining that he was two hundred weapons short of the number of aircraft he had to carry out the assigned tasks. SAC possessed nine hundred combat-ready aircraft and trained crews, which suggests that the number of bombs assigned to SAC was seven hundred, or nearly 30 percent of the stockpile.[41] Over in Europe, SACEUR was told he could plan for 125 weapons at this time.[42] It is unclear how many weapons were assigned to the Far East and the naval commands at this time, but CINCLANT conducted around forty strikes in the first two days of a war during command post coordination exercises with SAC.[43]

There was a JCS nuclear weapons reserve that was expressed in number of capsules and thermonuclear weapons. For example, to load out the empty two hundred aircraft, LeMay wanted "all Charlie and Dog capsules, and all TN weapons" that were in the JCS reserve allocated to SAC. He also asked for "an additional 70 Baker capsules," again from the JCS reserve.[44] The president and the JCS were therefore able to exert some control over the unified and specified commands' strategic plans by conferring or limiting the number and types of components and weapons they had access to. Forcing commanders to Darwinistically compete for resources was by no means a traditional way of creating strategy, but then with the capabilities of the thermonuclear weapons demonstrated during Castle, tradition was perhaps of limited value.

SAC in Transition, 1954–55

Gen. Nathan Farragut Twining had, by this point, replaced the ailing Hoyt Vandenberg as U.S. Air Force chief of staff. Like Norstad, Twining served in the Mediterranean and later the Pacific and, similar to Norstad, firmly believed that the world would have been "far less dangerous if our highest political officials had fully recognized and supported the post-war objectives [of limiting Soviet influence] as seen by Sir Winston Churchill."[45] Twining had personal insight into the Soviet Union and its leadership: he and Thomas Power, then at Air Research and Development Command, were part of a delegation that visited the country in the summer of 1956. During a reception at Marshal Georgy Zhukov's house, Premier Nikolai Bulganin and First Secretary Nikita Khrushchev arrived unannounced. Twining said later, "The more blatant assertions of Khrushchev compelled me, in spite of my desire to remain in a strictly military role, to respond with a defense of U.S. posture in world affairs."[46] Power was even more blunt recounting the affair: "I met some of the key men behind the global Communist conspiracy . . . and I was struck with both their cocky self-assurance and brutal frankness. . . . The Soviet leadership is irrevocably committed to . . . the annihilation of the capitalist system and establishment of Communist dictatorship over all nations of the world."[47]

Twining viewed containment as passive and defensive and was uncomfortable with it, especially when Communist aircraft repeatedly shot down American reconnaissance aircraft over international waters. He spent time cogitating over the preventive war issue but eventually concluded it was never going to be official American policy. For him, collective security was the way to go, backed up with SAC, which he characterized as "a force which the Communists can comprehend." Presenting the most credible deterrent force possible was Twining's objective. In his view, the containment system existed "to restrict communism within its existing borders, then let it destroy itself through internal corrosion and decay."[48] Power held identical views.[49]

That said, Twining had to navigate the JCS labyrinth to sustain the deterrent effort. He frequently played good cop to LeMay's bad cop.

Twining chided LeMay in 1955, explaining that the most recent SAC emergency war plan on the JCS books was EWP 1-51 and that SAC planning language had to be brought into line with JCS language. However, SAC developed EWP 1-53 and it was in operation by 1954. Did LeMay simply stop sending the SAC EWP to the Joint Chiefs of Staff because he had gone rogue? Not exactly. He send four copies instead of sixty-five and kept SAC's plan on a need-to-know basis, even within the JCS.[50] Without knowing the specifics, LeMay ascertained, possibly through Maj. Gen. Joseph Carroll, head of the Office of Special Investigations, and Lt. Gen. Pearre Cabell, former USAF head of intelligence and then at the CIA, that there were leaks at very high levels. As we now know, Donald Maclean and Guy Burgess of the Cambridge Five were the most damaging, but there was also the U.S. Army's Lt. Col. William H. Whalen, unmasked in the early 1960s, who worked on the Joint Chiefs of Staff and provided Soviet agents with vast amounts of information "concerning the retaliation plans by the U.S. Strategic Air Command."[51]

In any event, the JCS apparently saw no need to formally approve every SAC EWP for this period. As a result, the EWP 1-49/EWP 1-51/ EWP 1-53 "process" described previously transitioned into, simply, the SAC Emergency War Plan, or just EWP. Everything associated with this "living document" became part of the overall SAC Emergency War Order implementing the war plan when it was activated. Thus every SAC unit had its own Emergency War Order governing the disposition of its forces and resources in response to Emergency War Plan requirements. The categorization of targets by Bravo, Romeo, and Delta categories was dispensed with in mid- to late 1954, as "these were not intended to become world-wide applications of tactical air missions, counter-air as such. Unfortunately, through common usage of such terms, these objectives [had] become recognized as over-all objectives. . . . This misunderstanding would be corrected and new terms applied."[52]

The iteration of the Emergency War Plan in late 1953 to early 1954 appears to have been similar to EWP 1-49 except that the B-47 replaced the B-29s and B-50s and there were three times as many B-36s. The first wave would consist of six B-36 wings launched from the continental United States, two B-47 wings in French Morocco, two B-47 wings in the United Kingdom, and one B-47 wing from Guam. A second B-47 wing would deploy to the Far East and another to Alaska to follow on. Four B-47 wings would then deploy to French Morocco and strike, while twelve B-47 wings would head for the United Kingdom, refuel, and then strike.[53]

The early 1954 EWP targets consisted of "500 industrial targets."[54] As we will recall, the 1950–52 EWP Delta target lists included up to

123 targets, of which there were two hundred weapons in the 40- to 80-kiloton-yield range assigned to destroy them. So what accounted for the fivefold increase in targets? Reexamining the EWP 1-49 target list provides one answer: not all identified industrial targets were necessarily covered by the original two hundred weapons in the first place back in 1950–52. Take, for example, the city of Sverdlovsk, with four primary industrial targets circa 1955: Arms Plant 8, Arms Plant 9, Ball Bearing Plant 6, and a chemical plant. In 1950 no more than two 47-kiloton- or 83-kiloton-yield weapons would have been committed, which would not have destroyed all four targets. Three to four 83-kiloton Mk-6 weapons, however, would ensure the destruction of all four targets.

Once there were more thermonuclear weapons available, however, the calculus changed. For comparative purposes, even a single 13.5-megaton Mk-24 delivered by a B-36 would not have covered all four of the Sverdlovsk targets, given the dispersion of the facilities, but two Mk-24s delivered by two B-36 aircraft would have (assuming all weapons were airbursts). Thermonuclear weapons permitted, to a certain extent, a "savings" in atomic weapons (in this case three to four Mk-6s) to be used against smaller targets, like the problematic power plants that were individually isolated from target complexes and not worth a higher-yield weapon.

The forces to carry out the EWP evolved significantly from 1954 to 1956. The six B-36 wings included a mixture of variants totaling 230 aircraft, though there were fewer than 170 combat-ready crews for them. The B-29 and B-50 medium wings converted to the six-engine B-47B and then the longer-range B-47E jet bombers from three wings in 1951–53 and then a dramatic expansion to include twenty-six wings by 1956. With initially 40 aircraft assigned per wing (45 later), that gave SAC 880 in 1954 and 1,000 by 1955. Again, not all had combat-ready crews.[55] The thermonuclear weapons buildup started in early 1954 with eleven Emergency Capability weapons: six TX-16 and five TX-14s. "Featherweighted" B-36s from the 19th Air Division's 7th and 11th Bombardment Wings at Carswell AFB, Texas, were, in an emergency, to proceed to Kirtland AFB, load the weapons from the AEC's Manzano Base, and ferry them to Thule

Air Base and Nouasseur Air Base in French Morocco, where they would be launched against their targets.[56]

As the Emergency Capability weapons were phased out in early 1955, the first of the huge and heavy Mk-17 and Mk-24 weapons, of which 305 were built, were introduced in 1955 to be delivered exclusively by B-36s. The JCS assigned approximately 700 atomic and thermonuclear weapons to SAC that year; 168 B-36s were available to carry the Mk-17/24s, leaving between 500 and 600 Mk-6 weapons assigned to the B-47 force. LeMay's 1955 request for 200 additional weapons included 90 of the 500-kiloton Mk-18s and 70 "B" cores for Mk-6s, which suggests that 40 more Mk-17/24s were part of that request.[57] The vast majority of SAC bombers were, in 1954–56, carrying Mk-6 atomic bombs with yields ranging from 47 to 83 kilotons, depending on the available core. The first of 275 Mk-21 (4.5 MT) and 1,200 Mk-15 (3.8 MT) thermonuclear weapons destined for B-47 units were deployed in late 1955 and early 1956, respectively, to replace the Mk-6 weapons in frontline use.[58]

By 1955 there was approximately 700 allocated weapons and 500 targets. The reason for the discrepancy in the two numbers is straightforward: not all SAC aircraft would reach their targets, due either to aborts or to enemy action. This margin suggests a 25 to 30 percent loss rate was anticipated. One should not discount the possibility that the JCS reserve would have been released for restriking targets after poststrike reconnaissance runs by RB-36s and RB-47s had been conducted in the intervals between the twelve-hour strike waves.

The permanently manned SAC overseas bomber base complexes during this period included five in the United Kingdom (7th Air Division), three in French Morocco (5th Air Division), and one in Guam (3rd Air Division).[59] Overseas rotational duty during these years regularly brought B-47s and B-36s from "Zone of the Interior" (U.S.) based units forward to these locations. Usually an entire wing would rotate forward.[60] The pattern for this period was a B-47 wing at Sidi Slimane with their tankers at Ben Guerir, French Morocco, and a B-47 wing spread out in the United Kingdom between Greenham Common, Mildenhall, and Fairford in 1954 and at Upper Heyford, Brize Norton, and Lakenheath in 1955. There was a three-month B-36 wing deployment to Guam in 1954, and then an annual month-long deployment of a B-36 wing to UK bases in 1954 and 1955. Eielson AFB in Alaska started B-47 rotations in 1955.[61] Nouasseur saw the rotational visits of a B-36 wing, with space planned for a second wing.[62]

Problems associated with timely availability of nuclear weapons cores were highlighted after the results of Exercise First Base in January 1954. This exercise was designed to test the deployment of a B-47 wing from March AFB in California to the UK base complex in order to support SACEUR's requirement for the destruction of retardation targets. A special B-47 rigged to carry capsules loaded and departed the AEC storage site adjacent to Limestone AFB in Maine to rendezvous with the B-47 wing; it was able to attack ten of the fifteen nominated targets in forty hours.[63]

It was clear, however, that with the introduction of the IL-28 jet bomber into forward bases in Eastern Europe and the successful 1953 demonstration of its nuclear capability, SAC's ability to conduct operations like First Base in an emergency was increasingly problematic. In early 1954 Eisenhower authorized the deployment of complete nuclear weapons, as opposed to components, to sites in Guam, the United Kingdom, and French Morocco. The first cores were moved from U.S. Navy ships to the 30th Depot Squadron in the United Kingdom on 7 May 1954, which in turn distributed them to Sidi Slimane and Nouasseur in Morocco, and Upper Heyford, Fairford, Brize Norton, Lakenheath, and Sculthorpe in the United Kingdom. By 1955 four SAC bases and nine Tactical Air Command bases in the United Kingdom had nuclear weapons. Other sites, like Goose Bay in Canada and Thule in Greenland, retained components with no cores.[64]

But that was not all. Efforts continued to develop suitable runways elsewhere for what was termed poststrike recovery. Of course, any 10,000-foot runway was capable of being used for the opposite purpose. By the 1954–56 period, the SAC UK base network was in full swing, as were the bases in French Morocco, Wheelus AFB in Libya, and Dhahran in Saudi Arabia. Guam started to host a forward-deployed B-47 wing on rotation in 1954.[65] By late 1955 the weight of the fourteen B-47 wings that were supposed to stage or operate out of the United Kingdom shifted to some extent to Morocco. The Moroccan bases were now scheduled, in the EWP, to handle 535 medium bombers, tankers, and fighters, plus up to 75 very heavy bombers. Morocco was also "extremely important in contingency plans wherein the U.S. might be fighting alone."[66]

Efforts to co-opt Turkey, initiated in 1951, started to pay off by 1954. Adana, later Incirlik Air Base, was a priority project, as was the lesser-known Batman Air Base further east. In essence, Incirlik and Batman replaced the Abu Sueir recovery base in Egypt, which had its Seaweed detachment and equipment threatened by nationalist unrest, and Dhahran, which became less important due to "technical developments."[67] Incirlik and Batman, however, became more than just poststrike recovery bases, though they retained that capability and had decontamination facilities. In 1955 Turkey and the United States signed a bilateral nuclear agreement that eventually led the way to classified service-to-service agreements vis-à-vis the stationing of nuclear weapons at Incirlik and even later the provision of nuclear weapons for Turkish strike aircraft.[68] During the Suez Crisis in November 1956, twelve B-36 bombers and six C-124 transports, two of them conducting "classified missions," arrived at Incirlik, where an obscure SAC electronic intelligence (ELINT) reconnaissance operation dubbed Sam Spade and involving RB-47s was operating. Incirlik regularly hosted Big Horn deployments of five B-47s and a pair of KC-97 tankers on rotation from U.S.-based units starting in 1955.[69] This gave SAC the ability to reach targets east of the Urals.

The precariousness of SAC's heavy dependence on bases in French Morocco was highlighted in the summer of 1955, when uprisings against French rule took place throughout the country. The United States quickly determined these were not Communist in origin and even played a mediating role between the rebels and the French administration, leading to independence in 1956.[70] Though SAC retained its bases, LeMay had his staff look for backup sites.

SAC had had its eye on Spain for some time, but the American relationship with the Franco regime was problematic and for a time the USAF was discouraged from having anything official to do with the country. This changed in 1955, possibly because of the situation in Morocco. The first quiet efforts to establish a SAC capability in Spain started in 1955 with the prepositioning of fuel at Parajas, Muntados, and San Pablo.[71] In June 1955 a USAFE requirement for "six operational support bases and one nuclear weapons storage site" was tabled, which unleashed SAC in a competition to acquire basing rights in Spain.[72] By 1956 SAC units in the United Kingdom were conducting monthly exercises to Muntados, San Pablo, and Zaragoza, with five B-47s and a KC-97 each, followed by a deployment of fifteen B-47s to Zaragoza in October. Torrejon was also on the horizon to be "exercised." All bases were incorporated into the Emergency War Plan by 1956, though there was construction slippage well into 1957.[73]

Alerting SAC during this period was very different from alerting the same organization during later decades of the Cold War. It was only after 1957 that the bomber force was fully armed with nuclear weapons on fifteen-minute ground alert, and still later did the B-52 force conduct airborne alert operations. There was no Defense Condition, or DEFCON, system yet. An early 1954 "Alert and Evacuation Test" demonstrated the SAC readiness levels for the period. Out of 1,533 available bombers, 89, or 6 percent, were ready in one hour at Condition Alfa, prepared to load up nuclear weapons and launch. At the third hour, 658 bombers, or 57 percent, were at that level of readiness, with 201 more in lesser stages of preparation (Condition Bravo). At hour five, the numbers were 625 and 371, respectively; this drop-off likely reflected the fact that the B-36s could not be kept on alert for protracted periods because the static weight of a fully fueled B-36 generated undue stress on the nose gear and struts and also resulted in fuel leaks.[74] Indeed, from the seventh hour to the seventeenth, the readiness rate of the Alfa bombers dropped down to 143, with 933 at Condition Bravo. Note that the maximum number of Condition Alfa bombers was 658, which was probably the number of nuclear weapons assigned to SAC in early 1954.[75]

SAC plans between 1954 and 1955 envisioned three to four strikes conducted at twelve-hour intervals twelve hours after being alerted; "180 atomic and thermonuclear strike aircraft" would hit their targets, and at the end of forty-eight hours, a total of 880 aircraft would

FOUR HORSEMEN I

have completed their missions. If SAC had thirty-six hours' warning, "400 aircraft [could] be dispatched in the first wave," followed by "two subsequent waves," for a total of 1,000 aircraft. With four days' warning, 1,000 bombers could participate "in the first simultaneous strike against Soviet objectives."[76]

LeMay remained exceptionally concerned about SAC vulnerability in the early stages of a future crisis. The AEC storage facility adjacent to Loring AFB in Maine was a significant bottleneck; for example, B-47s from distant bases like Lake Charles AFB in Louisiana had to fly there first to load up before carrying out their missions.[77] He explained to Eisenhower, "Our principal limitations now are liability to attack on the ground through insufficient alert time, delays occasioned in obtaining release to us at alert time of weapons not under our custodial responsibility." His suggested solution included authorization "to load weapons at National and [Air Material Command] storage sites beginning with the first indication of an enemy attack or preparation for such attack." He explained, "This will enable my forces to get off the ground fully prepared to attack enemy targets when I am authorized to do so and if early warning of only one or two hours is received." He also wanted the "temporary deployment of complete weapons to overseas locations coincident with the temporary rotation of tactical units."[78]

It is tempting to contextualize this request in light of the domestic American "Bomber Gap" debate, to suggest that there was no credible Soviet bomber threat to North America at this time and therefore LeMay's request was alarmist and based on exaggerated and incomplete information. However, as we have seen, substantial SAC forces were forward-deployed in the United Kingdom, North Africa, and the Far East, and thus vulnerable to the Soviet IL-28 force, and crucial support bases in the north were well within range of TU-4 aircraft. A significant proportion of SAC's first-wave strikes would have come from those bases. This problem played a significant role in altering SAC's approach.

SAC's dependency on North East Air Command bases at Goose Bay and Ernest Harmon greatly concerned planners: a handful of enemy strikes could completely disrupt the Emergency War Plan.

Fourteen B-47 wings concentrated in the United Kingdom, not only for prestrike but for poststrike recovery, made too lucrative a target for forward-based Soviet forces. Furthermore, Gen. Frank Armstrong of Second Air Force reminded LeMay that the Soviets closely observed the route "because it [was] the only one available": "If it is [available], we win. If it is not, we do not go any place—period. . . . To lose Goose Bay would be disastrous."[79]

SAC prioritized the problem and conducted experiments in 1954 and 1955. One of these was Exercise Leap Frog in August 1954. Thirty B-47s departed Hunter AFB in Georgia, refueled from KC-97 tankers based at Kindley AB in Bermuda, and landed at the bases in French Morocco. The next day those aircraft attacked their targets and returned to French Morocco. At the same time fifteen more B-47s departed Hunter, refueled over Kindley and then again over French Morocco, struck targets in France, and landed at Sidi Slimane in French Morocco and at Wheelus in Libya. On the third day, thirty more B-47s departed Hunter, struck their targets, refueled over French Morocco and again over the Azores, and returned home. Exercise Hot Point conducted in 1955 had the seventy-two B-47s from the wings at Hunter AFB and MacDill AFB in Florida deploy to Morocco and Libya and prepare to strike, and then the next day sixty-two B-47s from Hunter and MacDill aerial-refueled, hit their targets, and recovered to Morocco and Libya while the forward-deployed B-47s went in. Leap Frog and Hot Point suggested that, with aerial refueling, dependency on the North East Air Command and UK bases could be creatively reduced.[80]

Armstrong, however, believed, "[Soviet] capability denies us Lages, Iceland, Wheelus, and Sidi Slimane." He wanted to hit Soviet bomber airfields from forward bases to protect the tanker-staging bases. In his view, the forward-based B-47s should be prioritized against those targets, and not the industrial targets.[81]

LeMay, responding to Armstrong, wanted to develop five more bases in Alaska and to approach Canada for additional airfields, all to support the KC-97 tanker force. In this schema, the Midwest-based B-47 wings could launch directly against Soviet targets and return to the United States. He wanted to keep ninety aircraft deployed forward between the United Kingdom and Morocco in austere bases, and then rotate alert bombers to those sites.[82] Looking ahead, LeMay explained to Twining that the Soviets would have an intermediate-range ballistic missile "by 1960" that would put *all* forward bases at risk, including Thule, Keflavik, and Alaska. The solution, he asserted, was the B-52 bomber and KC-135 tanker combination operating from North America, and an alert force that could be launched in under an hour.[83] But that was in the future. As for the world of 1955, LeMay lobbied for a preemption policy:

> I am hopeful that the word "aggression" will be redefined and accepted by the United Nations. The new definition . . . must recognize that we are now living in an age when it can no longer be an issue of morality that a nation must receive the first physical blow before it can respond with force; in fact, the first blow can now signal the end of a conflict rather than a beginning. Therefore, certain enemy actions short of war should constitute sufficient threat to the non-aggressor nation that it would be justified in launching direct attack, at least on enemy strategic air power, to forestall its own disaster. If this new philosophy can be accepted, it might well give us the solution to many of our current problems.[84]

This was the basis for a dramatic shift in SAC targeting in 1956–57. But were the intelligence data even available to support such operations?

SENSINT: Pre–U-2 Aerial Reconnaissance Operations

The traditional narrative of the relationship between aerial reconnaissance and nuclear targeting goes like this: Before the U-2, there was nothing other than some tattered and unreliable interrogation reports and Nazi-era photos. Then in June 1956 the entire world changed as the Iron Curtain and the veil over Curtis LeMay and SAC's eyes were simultaneously thrown back by the genius of Lockheed and the CIA. All was revealed; there was no Bomber Gap. When pressed, some writers grudgingly admit that SAC conducted reconnaissance over-flights before the U-2 but then in the same breath hint darkly that such flights were rogue activities not under the control of a responsible government agency and designed to provoke a nuclear war.[85]

The reality of the situation was more complex. The projected intelligence-targeting-reaction problem was, as we have seen, well-known. In late 1949 LeMay communicated his thoughts on the issue to Vandenberg:

> It would appear economical and logical to adopt the objective of completely avoiding enemy attack against our strategic force by destroying his atomic force before it can attack ours. Assuming that as a democracy we are not prepared to wage a preventive war, this course of action poses two most difficult requirements:
> 1) An intelligence system which can locate the vulnerable elements of the Soviet striking force and forewarn us when attack by that force is imminent, and
> 2) Agreement at top governmental level that when such information is received the Strategic Air command will be directed to attack.
>
> Your background and experience with the CIA should enable you to evaluate more accurately than I the intelligence feasibilities in this regard, should, for example, the CIA be directed to establish a program similar in size, backing, and scope to the Manhattan Project.[86]

This is a far cry from the traditional view that employs third-hand CIA reminiscences to portray LeMay and therefore SAC as backward and reactionary to CIA reconnaissance developments that led to the U-2.[87] Notably, the SAC-CIA liaison arrangements were cordial throughout the early to mid-1950s, particularly when General Cabell, USAF, was deputy director of Central Intelligence, though others suggest that the SAC-CIA relationship deteriorated later.[88]

That said, the USAF and SAC kept their reconnaissance operations close to the chest. When a CIA team was briefed by SAC in December 1957, over a year and a half after the first U-2 overflights of the Soviet bloc, the leader reported, "I was very much surprised that we were given a briefing of SAC's overflight accomplishments. I had no idea that they had covered as much of the Arctic bases as they indicated nor was I aware of the Far Eastern overflights in recent weeks. . . . In view of [USAF intelligence] demands for service in connection with AQUATONE [U-2] photography . . . I feel we are in a position to request reciprocity."[89]

The SAC briefing data were part of the SENSINT security control system (or "compartment," using later terminology), which was eventually closed out and merged in October 1962 with Talent, the CIA's U-2 data control system, and Keyhole, the satellite data control system.[90] SENSINT data came from those USAF overflights conducted from at least 1954 and possibly earlier, like the 1952 Ju-Jitsu mission. It also included attaché aerial photography. As such SENSINT was the basis for SAC targeting in those areas of the Soviet Bloc covered by the flights prior to the advent of U-2 overflights of the Soviet Union in July 1956.

Consequently, Emergency War Plan targeting during this time was to some extent an improvement over EWP 1-49 and EWP 1-51. Several Europe-based projects mounted by the USAFE's 7499th Composite Squadron (later Group) in 1954–55 stand out. Project Hot Pepper and Pretty Girl were the use of special C-54D aircraft equipped with ELINT and cameras flying through the Berlin air corridors to collect on the opposition in East Germany. These operations were augmented with Pie Face, a C-97 transport equipped with a huge camera in the nose. Pie Face was expanded in 1954 to include peripheral slant photography along the Norwegian, Iranian, Greek, and Turkish borders with their Communist neighbors. Operation Sara Jane involved three C-54E VIP "diplomatic" transports modified with concealed cameras for collection over Eastern Europe and the Berlin-Moscow route.[91]

Regular overflights of the Soviet Union, China, and North Korea were conducted between 1954 and 1956. Escalating Soviet activity against American intelligence collection aircraft in the Far East, including engagements against escorted RB-45Cs followed by penetrations of Japanese airspace and the shootdown of a MiG-15 by U.S. forces in response, were the initial indicators. In January 1954, however, FEAF determined that there were indications of possible Communist offensive operations in Korea: codes were changed earlier than usual; there was unusual IL-28 activity; and there was significantly increased MiG activity in North Korea.[92]

The result was Project Haymaker, the modification of a sextet of RF-86F Sabres for reconnaissance missions. Operating above 50,000 feet, the Haymaker essentially photographed every major potential target in the Soviet Far East and China that was within range of Komaki Air Base in Japan or forward bases in South Korea. Haymakers photographed targets in Vladivostok, Port Arthur, Dairen, Shanghai, Mukden, and Khabarovsk. They caught a whole regiment of TU-4 nuclear bombers located at Spassk-Dalniy Airfield.[93]

On 23 April 1954 three RB-45CS in RAF markings with RAF crews lifted off from RAF Sculthorpe to conduct the long-delayed sequel to the 1952 Ju-Jitsu operation. A human intelligence source in the Soviet People's Air Defense Command reported that one RB-45C passed

> unnoticed [by] Soviet warning systems in Austria and Hungary [and] was not detected before reaching the western Ukraine, where the information transmitted by the interception station was incorrect and the aircraft penetrated almost to the Moscow region. The Moscow warning system allegedly intercepted the aircraft on its return flight. . . . The PVO units were unable to intercept the aircraft [and did not do so] until it was landing somewhere in West Germany. Col. Tsipsivadze said that if the aircraft had been carrying atomic and hydrogen bombs it could have destroyed several large Soviet cities and returned unharmed. . . . Marshal Bulganin warned that if enemy aircraft again succeeded in penetrating Soviet territory, all PVO authorities would be sent before a firing squad.[94]

Then on 8 May 1954 three RB-47ES led by Col. Harold Austin lifted off from RAF Fairford, refueled from KC-97s off Norway, and headed for the Kola Peninsula. Two of the RB-47ES turned around outside Soviet airspace to distract the PVO forces, while Austin's RB-47E headed to Murmansk to photograph the airfields in the vicinity. Even though they were intercepted by MIGs, the flight continued to Archangel and photographed airfields there before withdrawing past Leningrad toward Finland while under attack. The take included nine major airfields, plus the knowledge that the new MIG-19s were capable of engaging B-47s at their operational altitude in daylight.[95] By 1955 "foreign radar photography" was employed to create target folders for B-47 units rotating through UK bases.[96]

The solution was to introduce the modified RB-57A Heart Throb variant in 1955. These operations, code-named Sharp Cut, took place throughout 1955; the aircraft overflew the Soviet Union until the introduction of the U-2 in 1956. There is little information available on these missions other than the fact that one of the Heart Throb aircraft conducted an operation called Switch Blade against China in 1956.[97] Aircraft with an even higher ceiling, the RB-57D, were deployed in 1956. The Black Knight penetration operations replaced Haymaker in the Far East and likely the Sharp Cut operations in Europe until December 1956, when the decision was made to rely solely on U-2 aircraft for plausible deniability.[98]

The most spectacular project was Home Run, also known as "the Thule operation," conducted from April to July 1956 by SAC's 55th Strategic Reconnaissance Wing. Detachments deployed to Thule Air Base and, using two squadrons of KC-97 tankers stationed there, conducted photographic and electronic reconnaissance of the Soviet Arctic coastal areas from Murmansk to Anadyr, including Novaya Zemlya and the other Soviet-controlled islands. These missions involved combinations of RB-47E photoreconnaissance, RB-47H electronic reconnaissance, and RB-47K SLAR-equipped aircraft. On 6 May 1956 six aircraft lined up wings abreast penetrated Soviet airspace and photographed eastern Siberia in its entirety. Once the RB-47ES were home, the RB-47H ELINT and signals intelligence (SIGINT) operations continued at a reduced scale and were renamed Rocky Point.[99] As one observer noted, "When HOME RUN was over, the United States had concrete assurances that the northern approaches to the Soviet Union were poorly defended. Our nuclear strategic deterrent could penetrate the northern Soviet border if it had to with little attrition along the way."[100]

One must conclude that SAC had very specific photographic targeting information of important areas of the Soviet Union two years before the advent of the U-2. And none of the aircraft was shot down, though MIGs regularly tried to intercept. It does not appear, however that SAC had up-to-date photographic data on targets between Moscow and the Urals, over the Urals, and into the central Soviet Union. The U-2's importance, when it came on line, lay in its ability to cover that gap.

Back in the USSR: ELINT, COMINT, SIGINT, and the PVO

The tracking of Soviet radar developments was not new: a variety of operations involving monitoring aircraft went back to 1946. However, the combination of the jet bomber, thermonuclear weapons, decreased reaction time for forward-based forces, and the need to demonstrate that the Soviet air defense system could be penetrated led to a revamped campaign to determine the extent and vulnerability of that system by 1954. This was driven by Power at SAC and then at Air Research and Development Command (ARDC) as much as by anybody: he was at the center of the USAF's research-and-development universe, and it was clear to him during its development process that the new B-47 was vulnerable without adequate countermeasures.[101]

The shooting down of numerous American and even Swedish SIGINT ferret aircraft over international waters by Soviet MIGs was not a deterrent to future operations, given the stakes. For the most part collecting peripheral data was not a problem if the ferrets stayed outside of the twelve-mile limit. Gaining data in the interior of the Soviet Union and its satellite powers was a different matter. It is important to note that like the photoreconnaissance operations, this was not just a SAC mission, and the magnitude of the problem led to focusing practically the entire Western intelligence apparatus on it. Once again there remain allegations that probing the Soviet air defense system was deliberately designed by SAC's leadership to provoke a war. There is no evidence to support this. There was a calculated campaign in different theaters by a variety of American and Allied forces, usually British, to collect information on the opposition's systems so that information derived from it could increase the probability of bomber penetration, and thus increase the credibility of the deterrent system as a whole.

It is uneconomical to list every SIGINT or communications intelligence (COMINT) flight or operation here. In effect, American and British aircraft operated around the entire periphery of the Communist world, from the Arctic to the Caspian and Black Seas, from East Germany to the Kamchatka Peninsula. This included RAF B-29s,

U.S. Navy P4MS, Swedish C-47S, USAF RB-50GS, SAC RB-36s, and a variety of other means. The SIGINT-ELINT-COMINT mission was regularized between 1954 and 1956. For example, detachments of the RB-47HS replaced the older Haystack RB-50GS at Mildenhall and Yokota. These Slip Knot detachments flew weekly collection missions on the periphery of the Soviet Bloc. When specialized interception capability was needed to monitor Soviet missile tests from the Black and Caspian Seas, ERB-47s and a highly modified telemetry collection, or "TT," ERB-47 deployed to Turkey for Sam Spade and Vice Squad missions.[102] At the same time, USAFE flew COMINT collection missions on behalf of the National Security Agency in a motley collection of transport aircraft; these were regularized and replaced with the Sun Valley modified C-130 aircraft in the 1950s.[103]

To what extent did the PVO's inability to shoot down the RB-45C and RB-47 overflights reflect its overall ability to intercept a SAC attack circa 1954 to 1956? By this point the SAC force consisted of B-47s and B-36s. The PVO interceptor force for the period had approximately seventy regiments of jet aircraft, which at first glance appears formidable. Eighteen of those regiments were equipped with MIG-15 day fighters. The bulk of the PVO consisted of thirty MIG-17 regiments, an aircraft that was essentially an extrapolation of the MIG-15. There were seven regiments of the improved MIG-17, the afterburner-equipped F model. All in all, these fifty-three regiments were incapable of night or all-weather interception. There were nine regiments of the MIG-17 P or PF model; these had air-intercept radar, as did the five regiments of the twin-engine Yak-25 and Yak-25M interceptors. The first MIG-19 interceptor regiment was also introduced at this time. The fifteen regiments with air-radar-based intercept capability were in key air defense districts like Leningrad, the approaches to Moscow, Kiev, the central Urals, and Khabarovsk; the MIG-17s were in frontline locations in depth from East Germany to Ukraine and Belarus, and the MIG-15s usually in tertiary air defense districts in the central Soviet Union. Generally three regiments of day fighters were associated with a regiment of all-weather interceptors, but some of those all-weather regiments were not at full strength. Overall the PVO's aircraft were capable of handling intruders operating at altitudes up to 54,000 feet but with dramatically less coverage at night.[104] It is unlikely at this point that the Western intelligence apparatus could distinguish which bases contained all-weather interceptor or merely day fighters. What was understood, however, was the Soviets' dependence on ground-controlled intercept (GCI) operations based on radar sites.

One development that generated concern in SAC was the dramatic proliferation of the P-20 or Token radar system. Based on a highly modified copy of the American AN/CPS-6 radar, Token operated on five (later seven) frequencies and was therefore difficult to jam with early 1950s-period ECM jammers: all of the Token's frequencies had to be jammed at once. The existing early warning radars—the Knife Rest, Dumbo, Cross Fork, and Rus systems—picked up incoming aircraft, but the Token handled the GCI portion of the interception by feeding position data to the interceptor controller or the pilot.[105]

In the early 1950s Western SIGINT and COMINT flight data led to the conclusion that high-frequency radio was used for the speech component of the intercept. The countermeasure was to identify and jam those frequencies. However, the Soviets suddenly shifted to very high-frequency radios at this time, a system that had a shorter range and thus could not necessarily be intercepted by ground stations on the periphery of the Soviet Union.[106] The combination of significantly increased numbers of unjammable radars with unknown and thus unjammable voice frequencies led to a crisis in 1953–54. The bomber-protective mechanisms that SAC harbored during Korea were irrelevant by 1954, and there was corresponding concern that SAC would be unable to penetrate the PVO's system. Indeed ELINT intercepts analyzed in 1954 indicated that the MiG-17P had an air-intercept radar, dubbed Scan Odd.[107]

When the CIA conducted a radar study in preparation for the first U-2 operations in 1956, they distilled all of the U.S. Air Force and British information for their purposes; therefore it provides insight into the PVO system that SAC had to be able to penetrate.[108] In a general sense, the Eastern European countries had clusters of early warning radar, but the only height-finding capability was located in East Germany. Hungary was particularly thick with the Knife Rest early warning system. Think of this as early warning in depth, though Token GCI radars were also located in these countries. In the Soviet Union proper, there were all types of early warning radars, but these were paired with Rock Cake and Trespass height finders. Substantial numbers of Token GCI radar were identified along the Baltic Sea and in Poland, Czechoslovakia, Hungary, and Romania. The zone from the Black Sea to Leningrad was thick with all types of current and obsolete early warning radar, plus Token. The system thinned out only near Turkmenistan, but thickened again opposite Afghanistan. The Far East was determined to have spotty coverage by the early warning and GCI radars, except for Vladivostok, whose coverage resembled the western Soviet Union's. China's coverage existed but was poorly distributed and spotty.[109] The CIA assessment for its "vehicle," the U-2, might also have applied to SAC in the 1954–56 period: "It is believed possible to enter the USSR in any other area other than the strip from the Baltic to Rumania with careful planning and have a high probability of avoiding the [Cross Fork]. It is barely possible that one might enter through Czechoslovakia. It is not possible to avoid Knife Rest at any point in the USSR border and one could avoid Tokens only on the northeastern Siberia–Pacific Ocean coast."[110]

With the data pouring in on Soviet air defense developments, several crash programs were implemented by ARDC and then SAC. The 376th Bombardment Wing was reorganized and reequipped to conduct electronic warfare support operations for the bomber force. Their B-47s were modified as Blue Cradle aircraft, their bomb bays loaded with various types of jammers. Each fifteen B-47 cell penetrating enemy airspace in the EWP was to be shadowed by a pair of Blue Cradle B-47s. Their purpose was to interfere with all forms of Soviet radar as well as GCI radio frequencies. In the EWP the jamming aircraft, after penetration, were to orbit Moscow-Leningrad-Kiev and continuously disrupt Soviet defenses. In the first large-scale test, forty B-47 bomb carriers supported by fourteen Blue Cradle B-47s successfully penetrated NORAD radar in a no-warning exercise. All Blue Cradles were eventually "shot down," but all forty bombers got through unscathed.[111]

Herringbone: SAC Responds to a New Threat

SENSINT aerial photographs taken southwest of Moscow in 1955 revealed seven nearly identical herringbone-shaped facilities that were a mile long and half mile wide each.[112] In March 1955 a flight of RB-45Cs from the 19th Tactical Reconnaissance Squadron led by Maj. John B. Anderson departed RAF Sculthorpe and refueled over Denmark in what was to be the third iteration of the 1952 Ju-Jitsu flights. Project Ink Spot, overseen by ARDC, modified these Tactical Air Command RB-45Cs in late 1954 to improve their performance.[113] The three aircraft flew three loops from west to east and back over the western Soviet Union. Flying around 41,000 feet, Anderson's RB-45Cs ingressed after in-flight refueling, photographing several bomber bases on the way to the Soviet capital.[114] Whether one of the RB-45Cs reached the outskirts of the Soviet capital is difficult to determine from available information. The photographs could instead have come from a specially modified USAF C-54E aircraft used for the Moscow embassy run. Code-named Sara Jane, this aircraft had covert cameras and covert controls for them.[115] Vnukovo Airport is in the vicinity, and the shots could have been taken while the C-54E was in the landing pattern.

These "herringbones" had been under British and American attaché observation since they were under construction in July 1953. Then, on a flight from Moscow to Leningrad, American attachés were able to photograph one and later three of them from the air. Soon afterward observers noted the presence of bunkers and a pair of strange devices that, by late 1954, were believed to be a radar system. The sites were added to the USAF's Aeronautical and Information Command Target Complex Chart in 1954.[116] Eisenhower was briefed in December 1954 that they might be part of an air defense missile system.[117]

Ground observers continued to photograph and track the sites' evolution before the March 1955 SENSINT flights. Intense analysis produced a hypothesis of how the radars worked, and by late 1954 "missile-like objects" were spotted at the sites, averaging sixty per site. The radar was designated Yo-Yo, and in time an operational mock-up was constructed to determine its characteristics. The herringbones were laid out in two rings around Moscow, spaced at fifty and ninety kilometers from the Kremlin, which lay at the center. In time a German engineer who worked on the system from 1949 to 1952 was interviewed and confirmed that Yo-Yo's Soviet designation was B-200.[118]

The USAF responded to the discovery of the system in 1954 in parallel with the Token crisis. Though there was knowledge of U.S. Army surface-to-air missile developments, the existence of a Soviet system spurred interest in how SAC would handle it. At this point Power had moved over to command the ARDC, but he kept LeMay apprised on the R&D front. As we have seen, SAC was already looking at using jet fighters with Mk-7 nuclear weapons to destroy radar sites and interceptor bases to clear the way for the bombers. That thinking evolved in parallel with the new missile problem and produced the MX-1601 concept. A conventional "bomber defense guided rocket," under study in 1953, was now changed to incorporate a nuclear warhead.[119] Studies on another system, the MX-2013, were already underway for possible use on the B-47 as a "radar-busting missile," partly in response to the Token crisis. LeMay asked Power to accelerate this program at the end of 1954.[120]

In parallel to these discussions, there was debate over using the B-47 for low-altitude delivery in order to get in under the radar coverage. This started with a requirement for SAC's fighters to use an Immelmann maneuver to deliver an Mk-7 bomb against air defense targets, but LeMay became less interested in this and by late 1954 increasingly interested in examining the possibility in developing "the low altitude capability inherent in aircraft designed for high-altitude operations."[121] In less than a month, ARDC had conducted the B-47 Combat Maneuvers Test, which demonstrated the B-47 could carry out low-level nuclear weapons delivery, though Power told LeMay that he was "apprehensive of the effects of the knowledge that the B-47 [would] perform the Immelmann turns and barrel rolls upon [his] flight safety record" if crews were not specially indoctrinated in the maneuver. This was the basis of the Low-Altitude Bombing System (LABS) capability for the B-47 that came into the system by 1956.[122]

The MX-2013 project paced LABS in early 1955 with speedy development of the SW-7 ("supersonic W-7"), a nuclear warhead capable of delivery by a supersonic aircraft.[123] At this point the project was formally renamed the GAM-67 Crossbow. The Crossbow would be equipped with a W-7–derived W31 warhead yielding 40 kilotons. Specially equipped B-47s with a crew pod in the bomb bay would, in theory, launch and direct up to four Crossbow missiles using radar-detection and -locating equipment.[124] This system, however, still required extensive testing.

The acceleration of the nuclear antiradiation missile and the B-47 LABS capability in early 1955 clearly indicates that SAC was significantly concerned about the emergent surface-to-air missile threat. Project Steve was the icing on the cake. Conducted days after the RB-45C flights, Power ordered a "special mission" using a B-52 from Boeing in Seattle. The aircraft achieved 56,500 feet outside radar cover. (Power ordered it to go as high as it could, but when the engines started flaming out they had to drop to 54,000 feet to restart.) "Simulated bomb release over Seattle was at . . . 56,000 feet." It was critical, however, that radar sites "continuously tracked" the B-52 while it was at 57,000 feet and six F-86Ds without drop tanks scrambled to intercept. One of them reached 51,000 feet and two had radar contact with the B-52 but could not engage.

However, "NIKE radar . . . picked up the B-52 at 150 nautical miles. The B-52 was tracked to the target." NIKE sites classified the mission as "on target, engaged, and theoretical mission accomplished before B-52 reached target."[125]

The possibility that the current SAC bomber force and the certainty that the future SAC bomber force were both vulnerable to the "Herringbone system" was the impetus for a significant acceleration of USAF research-and-development programs associated with bomber penetration in 1955 and 1956. The next projects of significance were the WS 122A and WS 123A decoy systems, initiated in 1955. Initially designed to simulate a B-47, the parameters changed so the missile could be internally carried and then launched by the larger B-52 to confuse enemy radar with maneuvering false targets. These led directly to the deployment of the Quail decoy missile, later carried by the B-52.[126]

But the development of a standoff nuclear missile launched from a bomber was slow. Conceptually the idea was sound, and the GAM-63

Rascal, devised in 1949, was by 1955 being test-launched from B-50 and specially modified DB-36 and DB-47 bombers. However, the air force requirements for the missile imposed too much on the system. For example, it had to be able to carry a biological, chemical, or nuclear warhead. There were issues with the missile's stability and that of the carrier aircraft. It was also a physically large weapon but it only carried a W5 warhead similar to the 83-kiloton Mk-5. In other words, there was not enough bang for the buck with Rascal, so an Mk-27 warhead (with a 3.5- to 5-MT yield) was adapted to the missile later in 1957.[127]

In early 1956 LeMay and Power continued their correspondence on the bomber penetration problem. LeMay reconfirmed in February, "We are rapidly approaching an era wherein SAC aircraft may be required to fight their way to the target through a strong airborne missile defense." As a result, he argued that "the highest priority must be given to the development of other measures of defense: [electronic countermeasures, infrared countermeasures] and especially anti-radiation missiles."[128] In April 1956 there was a note of alarm from LeMay, likely triggered by in-depth analysis of the Herringbone system: "Due to estimated enemy defensive capability, which will seriously challenge the B-47 and B-52 penetrations, it is imperative that the B-52 [air-to-surface missile] reach operational units by 1960." LeMay even considered mounting the U.S. Navy's Regulus II cruise missile on a B-52. However, there were deficiencies with the guidance system and a perceived need for a larger warhead.[129]

To underscore how serious the situation was, the U.S. Air Force issued an emergency requirement to develop a low-altitude laydown version of the Mk-39 thermonuclear bomb, code-named Big Tail.[130] The existing thermonuclear weapons were built around high-altitude delivery—drogue chutes, barometric detonation initiation systems, and so on—so the aircraft could escape the weapons' effects. With the Soviet antibomber missile system and the need for low-level delivery, the bombs themselves now had to change. To permit the aircraft to escape, the yields had to potentially be dialed down, which had a knock-on effect in terms of accuracy. Consequently the requirement for crew proficiency with LABS maneuvers went up, and with that so did the training casualty rate of both humans and aircraft.

The planned intercontinental ballistic missile system even started to figure in the bomber penetration equation, but it was a slow process as the SAC commander viewed the new "Manhattan-type project," Atlas, as a bureaucratic and strategic competitor for SAC's funding.[131] LeMay wrote in July 1955, "There are those who see the solution to this in the intercontinental ballistic missile. I would be inclined to agree, but with reservations concerning time phasing, reliability, accuracy, and weapon yield. Above all I wish to sound a warning against heeding the claims of zealots and fanciers who would prematurely re-organize our forces. . . . I believe that it would be courting national disaster to decimate the conventional proven force and its follow-on of the true manned supersonic bomber before the missile system has proven a progressive replacement."[132]

In LeMay's thinking in 1955, the ballistic missile was useful "against area targets only" and not against "Soviet air power objectives . . . unless it were to be employed in prohibitive numbers." However, he later modified his position: "It appears now that the prime characteristics of the ICBM can be exploited best by using it initially to damage and disrupt the Soviet air offense and defense systems on the ground, holding them down until they can be destroyed by the manned bomber. The ICBM will also be useful in disrupting control centers and their comms and defense network."[133] As we will see, this thinking eventually led to the original concept of operations for the Minuteman ICBM.

We can see the direct impact of the existence and discovery of the B-200 radar and the S-75 surface-to-air missile system in 1954–55 on SAC's 1960 force structure, which eventually consisted of B-52s conducting low-level operations to drop low-altitude lay-down bombs after launching air-to-surface missiles to clear out the air defense system in conjunction with plentiful and cheap ballistic missiles. That said, by late 1956 SAC possessed none of these capabilities except for a handful of DB-47E aircraft whose crews were training to carry and deliver the Rascal with its smaller-yield warhead.[134]

The unasked question in the corridors of American airpower was this: If Moscow was defended by an estimated 3,360 surface-to-air missiles (60 missiles each at fifty-six sites) and could not be threatened with a credible nuclear strike, could the Soviet leadership be deterred? And when exactly would the Herringbone system go online?

The Herringbone system was, in fact, called the S-25 Berkut. After four years of development, test shots took down an unmanned TU-4 bomber on 26 April 1953. Six months later the test system successfully engaged and shot down a pair of unmanned IL-28s. The delivery of the weapons to their "pastures" and the radar equipment to the "vegetable warehouses" started in 1954. This was completed in early 1955. The Politburo then met, and Khrushchev confirmed that the S-25 system should be formally accepted into the PVO. After the first U-2 flight over Moscow in July 1956, the system was "placed on combat duty" on 7 July, and orders were given to the command on 26 July to engage intruding aircraft. None of this was apparently known by the Western intelligence apparatus at the time.[135]

This period was highlighted by dramatic developments in the nuclear bombs that SAC was to deliver, which in turn significantly altered SAC operational planning. At the same time, the first Soviet steps toward a thermonuclear-delivery capability put SAC's forward-based units and thus SAC deterrent plans at risk. Similarly, developments in the Soviet air defense system, which included the progressive deployment of their first surface-to-air missiles, led to dramatically stepped-up intelligence collection so that the bomber force could remain potent. SAC's response was to develop a host of plans involving aerial refueling that could support bomber strikes from North America to supplement the forward-based forces and to pour resources into the means to defeat the Soviet missile systems. Dramatic reconnaissance overflights produced much more detailed information on targets, which served two purposes: demonstrating capability and the production of more granular targeting. However, the combination of a defensive ring of missiles around Moscow and a demonstrated thermonuclear bomber capability led to more aggressive Soviet international behavior, and with that came increased concern over Western Europe and the Far East theaters of operations.

6

Four Horsemen II

Targeting Europe and the Far East, 1954–56

The Chinese people are not to be cowed by U.S. atomic blackmail. Our
country has a population of 600 million and an area of 9,600,000 square
kilometers. The United States cannot annihilate the Chinese nation
with its small stack of atom bombs. Even if the U.S. atom bombs were so
powerful that, when dropped on China, they would make a hole right
through the earth, or even blow it up, that would hardly mean anything
to the universe as a whole, though it might be a major event for the solar
system. We have an expression, millet plus rifles. In the case of the United
States, it is planes plus the A-bomb. However, if the United States with
its planes plus the A-bomb is to launch a war of aggression against China,
then China with its millet plus rifles is sure to emerge the victor. The
people of the whole world will support us.

—MAO ZEDONG, 1955

The Emergency War Plan was SAC's main effort against its
main enemy, the Soviet Union. That said, the ongoing problem of how to handle overlapping targets with NATO forces
in Europe grew in the mid-1950s with the increased need to cover
Soviet forces that could take out SAC's forward bases, the increased
availability of nuclear weapons on aircraft carriers, and the ongoing
debate over the primacy of targeting coordination between SAC and
SACEUR. Nuclear targeting in the Far East too posed complexities,
but of a different sort. If the United States went to war with the Soviet
Union, where did Communist China fit into the schema, let alone

North Korea? These were not analogues to the Soviet-dominated Eastern European satellites, yet the holistic view of global Communism endemic at the time led some to think the Chinese should not receive special treatment, especially after the Korean War went into abeyance in 1953. As a result, the overlap between the SAC EWP and the regional forces of Far East Command remained muddled until the 1954–55 Taiwan Straits crisis. That situation generated a separate plan based on the embryonic targeting established in 1951–53. It also demonstrated that there was more flexibility to American nuclear targeting than has been previously understood for this period.

The European Theater

The relationship between the nuclear forces assigned to SACEUR and SAC's planning evolved significantly from 1954 to 1956, while SACEUR absorbed nuclear forces assigned to support him in his plans.[1] As with SAC EWP planning, SACEUR's plans evolved almost month to month as new and in many cases interim capabilities came on line and were replaced. The emergent problem for SAC and SACEUR related to the convergence of several factors. First, the number of weapons and delivery systems assigned to SACEUR significantly increased. Second, their ranges remained limited compared to the locations of many of the targets necessary to offset a Soviet assault on NATO. As early as 1952 the European-based planners realized that the SAC EWP and any SACEUR nuclear planning "must be looked upon as two parts of a whole rather than as independent and more or less exclusive projects."[2] But as we have seen, in an era of atomic scarcity, LeMay wanted SAC to handle everything. By 1953 the concern over lack off coordination was even more acute, as Lauris Norstad noted: "I am convinced that we must give proper weight to the impact of the SAC offensive on SACEUR's mission in order to make our plans sufficiently realistic to be acceptable." He emphasized, "NATO as well as U.S. interests would be served by establishing the extent to which the SAC effort can reduce the length of time during which we have to sustain various SACEUR defensive operations in Europe."[3]

The unified and specified commanders' Target Coordination Conferences were the primary means to deconflict SAC and SACEUR nuclear strikes at this time. The 1954 conference proceedings resulting in the SAC Atomic Annex were approved by the JCS on 30 March 1955, and the 1955 proceedings were approved on 3 July 1956.[4]

SACEUR's Central Region Emergency Defense Plan in 1954 included two types of targets marked for destruction by air power: "atomic" and "otherwise." There were six hundred Priority Interdiction Targets, including nearly every bridge on every major river from the Rhine in West Germany to the Vistula in Poland. The Counter Air Force Targets included 220 airfields in East Germany, Poland, Czechoslovakia, the Soviet zone in Austria, and Hungary, of which 104 were "suitable for MIG-15 operations." The "Strategic Concept" had two large arrows, one over Norway and Finland aimed at Moscow, and another from Albania, Bulgaria, Romania, and then to Moscow.[5] The initial thinking was to defeat or absorb the first Soviet atomic attack and then massively counterattack every air base the opposition possessed using ground- and sea-based airpower.[6] Preemption, however, was off the table for the time being, according to the chairman of the Joint Chiefs of Staff Adm. Arthur Radford.[7]

The IL-28 problem loomed large in 1954–55. SACEUR Al Gruenther and his air deputy, Norstad, like their predecessors, were concerned that the "greatest present enemy threat [was] atomic capability" from Soviet aircraft and "later missiles" and that "Atomic weapons were indispensable" in dealing with them. Any delay in the initial exchange would be "fatal." In SACEUR's view "preplanning [was] desirable to insure instant retaliation (loaded gun aimed and ready to fire)." Gruenther noted there was a significant limitation "upon preplanning" that precluded the "capability for atomic attacks directed by subordinate commanders as well as SACEUR in accordance with combat developments." Like Ridgway before him, Gruenther wanted the ability to preempt and he wanted to explore how far down that could be delegated. In his view, plans needed to be drawn up that provided "systematic attacks on Soviet air, tactical only, leaving strategic to SAC by continuous close coordination." These were eventually called "scheduled" or "hell or high water" attacks.[8]

Planning by Supreme Headquarters Allied Powers Europe (SHAPE) from 1954 on was conducted under the assumption that

SAC and RAF Bomber Command would emphasize "the earliest possible destruction of the Soviet atomic delivery capability," followed by the "reduction of those elements of the Soviet resources which [would] have the most immediate effect on [NATO's] combat situation" and the "retardation of the advance of Soviet Bloc forces against SACEUR's area."[9]

SHAPE's Atomic Strike Plan was promulgated in 1956. SACEUR was assigned 125 nuclear weapons for planning purposes, and his headquarters deliberated with their subordinate commands on how those would be employed. There were Green weapons assigned to commanders for immediate use and Black weapons held in reserve to await SACEUR's release. Overall release, R-Hour, was governed by SACEUR. Thirty of the 125 weapons were assigned to the Central Region in the Green category, though there was debate between the land and air components as to allocation: 20 were allocated for counter-air operations and 10 for interdiction.[10]

As for SAC-SACEUR coordination, the Atomic Strike Plan specified that "SAC would support ACE [Allied Command Europe] to the extent agreed by CINCSAC and SACEUR or as determined by the U.S. JCS. CINCSAC would retain operational control of his forces supporting ACE." In continued, "While SACEUR's forces would carry out immediate destruction and interdiction of the enemy threat generally in areas outside the USSR proper particularly in Central Europe, strategic Allied operations would attack the Soviet atomic offensive capability based in the USSR proper and, in addition ensure that no further substantial build-up against ACE would emanate from the zone of the interior of the USSR."[11]

This state of affairs led to horse-trading by LeMay, Gruenther, and Norstad. In 1954–55 SAC was assigned to hit thirty-three targets on SACEUR's behalf. In early 1956 Gruenther asked that SAC take on an additional twenty-three targets for a total of fifty-six.[12]

So what would the SAC-SACEUR campaign have looked like? This was completely dependent on available nuclear-capable forces. For the 1954–56 period, there were three types: U.S. Air Forces Europe light bomber and fighter-bomber squadrons; USAFE cruise missile squadrons; and SAC B-47 squadrons. In general terms, SAC B-47 wings in the United States regularly rotated to six bases in the United Kingdom, while elements of the 49th Air Division were based out of six more bases in the United Kingdom. Forward-based elements of the 49th Air Division were located at four bases in France, and two in West Germany. Three Pilotless Bomber Squadrons occupied bases in West Germany; their original locations were to have been Greenham Common and Lakenheath, but this was changed to get them closer to their targets. Nuclear weapons storage capacity was well developed in the United Kingdom, where all twelve bases had depot units. In West Germany the main site was at Hahn Air Base. In France there was a nuclear storage unit at Toul-Rosières Air Base with satellite facilities under construction at three more sites.[13]

The employment of these forces broke down according to the range of the aircraft involved, the effects of hitting their targets, and their reaction times in the event of war. If war occurred in, say, 1956, the first strikes would have been conducted by the 417th Fighter-Bomber Squadron out of Hahn Air Base. Led by Chuck Yeager, this F-86H squadron equipped with Mk-12 bombs yielding 12 to 14 kilotons each was responsible for the destruction of the Soviet radar and air defense communications system across southern East Germany to the Polish border.[14]

The next phase involved the B-61A (later TM-61A) Matador cruise missiles. There were three squadrons west of the Rhine based at Bitburg, Hahn, and Sembach, with twenty-four mobile missiles per squadron composing the 701st Tactical Missile Wing. The Matadors were dispersed from their main bases and directed from mobile command stations located on the high ground from Bremerhaven to the Czech border. As such the missiles could be guided to their targets two hundred miles beyond the stations, assuming the command links were not jammed. Each Matador carried a warhead based on the Mk-5 weapon, which some sources suggest was set to yield between 50 and 60 kilotons, though the Mk-5 could yield at least 83 kilotons depending on core-pit combinations. The Matador force was scheduled to launch twenty-four missiles within eight hours, and another thirty-six missiles within seventy-two hours.[15] The navigation system essentially limited the Matador targets to clearly identi-

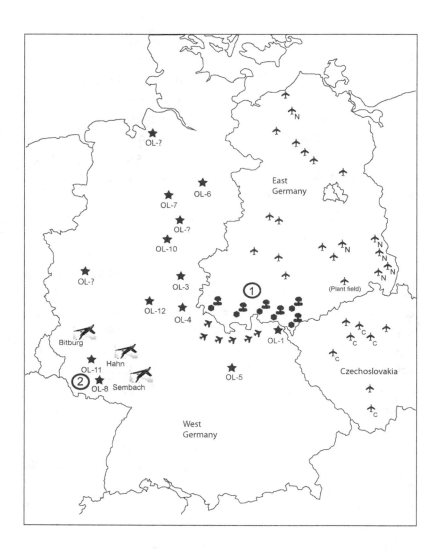

Map 8. Initial strike operations in the event of war in 1956 would have had the 417th Fighter-Bomber Squadron destroy the air defense system in southern East Germany (1). Closely behind them would have been the Matador cruise missiles of the 701st Tactical Missile Wing stationed at twelve deployment sites west of the Rhine (2). The missiles would have been guided to destroy Soviet, National Volkesarmee, and Czech air force MIG bases using the MSQ-1A Matador Automatic Radar Command systems located at several operation locations throughout West Germany to extend guidance range. There is a possibility that the IL-28 Beagle bomber bases in range of the Matadors could have been cross-targeted with B-47s. Courtesy of the author.

fied fixed facilities. There were, in addition to the IL-28 bases, twenty Soviet air bases in East Germany. These were the likely Matador targets, each to be destroyed via airburst. The six communication sites that controlled the MIG fighter and fighter-bomber regiments would have been picked off by F-86HS operating from Hahn.[16]

Following the 417th and the 701st would have been the SAC rotational B-47 wing from Greenham Common. The purpose of the follow-on strikes would likely have been to neutralize any Soviet system capable of disrupting SAC bases in the United Kingdom. U.S.-based B-47s would be deploying over the Atlantic to those six bases to refuel and proceed to their targets in the Soviet Union. In this case, the main threat to that deployment came from seven bases containing the Soviet IL-28 bomber force in East Germany. These bases were conveniently in a straight line paralleling the Polish border. They would have been sequentially destroyed by Mk-5 and/or Mk-6 weapons yielding around 83 kilotons each, with the B-47s egressing north and returning over Denmark to the United Kingdom to re-arm. Another IL-28 base slightly deeper in Poland at Brzheg and an IL-28 base at Hradcany in northern Czechoslovakia in line with the East German IL-28 bases would probably have been hit in the initial strike as well.[17]

Immediately behind the B-47s going after the IL-28 bases would have been another wave of SAC B-47s from Fairford, Brize Norton, Upper Heyford, or Lakenheath. Supported by jamming aircraft, these squadrons would penetrate through the air defense gap in East Germany and then across Poland to the western Soviet Union and destroy bomber bases containing either TU-4 or TU-16 bombers, then egress to the north and return to the United Kingdom via the Baltic.

In behind this force was yet another wave of B-47s, again based in the United Kingdom. It was imperative for SACEUR and his seriously outnumbered forces to completely disrupt the Soviet Union's ability to reinforce and resupply the Group of Soviet Forces Germany and its twenty-six armored and mechanized divisions. The only means by which this could be accomplished was the destruction of bridges and railroad marshalling yards at key nodes. Poland presented a complex problem in this regard. The adjustment of the

Map 9. After the F-86Hs and Matadors disrupted or destroyed the air defense system in East Germany (1) the resultant gap would have been exploited by B-47s from RAF Greenham Common directed against IL-28 Beagle light bomber bases (2). Additional B-47s accompanied by ECM aircraft would penetrate the gap and strike IL-28 and TU-4 bomber bases in the western Soviet Union (3). More B-47s would destroy the logistic system throughout Poland (4). Courtesy of the author.

borders westward in 1945–46 created a situation where there was a dense rail network in what had been Germany and a much thinner one in what remained of Poland after half of that country was ceded to the Soviet Union.

The destruction of some combination of these nodes, perhaps between twenty and twenty-five of them, with Mk-6 weapons would have dramatically impaired Soviet efforts to reinforce East Germany. Penetrating the destroyed air defense network in southern East Germany, four streams of B-47s would have destroyed the logistics nodes along the East German–Polish border, the ones on the Polish-Soviet border; bridges over the Vistula River, and several points in what had been Germany.[18] The B-47s would likely have come in on an angle from the south, destroying the targets from north to south in order, again egressing to the Baltic and back to the United Kingdom. It is likely that the bridges would have been destroyed with groundbursts; note that bridges in Hiroshima and Nagasaki survived 15- and 21-kiloton airbursts. Similarly, tests in Nevada demonstrated

FOUR HORSEMEN II

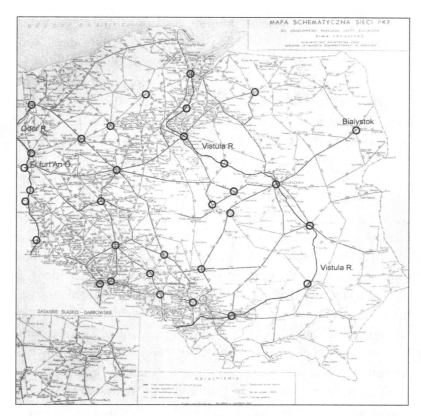

Map 10. The destruction of twenty to twenty-five railway junctions, bridges, and marshalling yards with nuclear weapons in Poland, particularly those on the Vistula and Oder Rivers, would have completely disrupted the Soviet Union's ability to sustain and reinforce any offensive action against NATO's Central Region. These key nodes are superimposed on a contemporary Polish national railway map that clearly portrays the former German rail network and western Polish network that were forced together into a single entity in the wake of World War II. Scan in author's possession.

that precursor waves would knock over rolling stock and destroy the tracks; thus it is also possible that low-altitude bursts would have been used against the marshalling yards.[19]

SACEUR's B-45, F-86H, and F-84G aircraft based in the United Kingdom lacked the range to get at these targets, though the B-45 with an Mk-5 could reach Poland. Their role in the proceedings therefore related to the battle for the Central Region. At this point NATO's Allied Land Forces Central Europe command was only starting to incorporate West Germany into NATO, and as such the defense line lay between the Rhine and the Inner-German Border.[20] 49th Air Division aircraft operating from Sculthorpe, Shepherd's Grove, Bentwaters, Wethersfield, and Woodbridge were positioned to attack targets in western East Germany and points west. Any concentration of enemy forces piling up while crossing rivers in West Germany were likely targets, while the longer-range B-45s could hit relevant interdiction targets in East Germany as required.

Given the range issues, 49th Air Division forces in France and West Germany not committed to support SAC could have been used against targets in western Czechoslovakia. There were numerous air bases west and north of Prague suitable for destruction, like Brno-Turany and Prerov, but it is likely that Matadors would have been employed in this role. Further south, Austria was divided like Germany into occupation zones. The Soviets maintained air bases in their zone until 1955, specifically, Weiner-Neustadt, which hosted IL-28 aircraft. The ranges from this base to the United Kingdom were extreme, so it is possible that the destruction of this formation was relegated to the F-86Fs stationed at Fürstenfeldbruck in Bavaria. This would have been a conventional strike as there were no nuclear weapons stored there, though during an alert some might have deployed forward.[21] There were, however, other options.

SACEUR's Southern Region was not exactly bereft of nuclear support during this period. From 1954 to 1956 the U.S. Navy maintained two attack carriers on a rotational bases in the Mediterranean: one tended to be stationed in the eastern region and the other in the west. Another carrier, usually one equipped with anti-submarine aircraft, was usually present as well.[22] The load-out for each ship varied but usually consisted of AD-4 Skyraiders and F-2H-3B Banshees. A detachment of AJ-2 Savages based in Lyautey, French Morocco, operated from the carriers when they moved past Gibraltar into the Mediterranean. By 1956 the FJ Fury and for a time F-9 Cougar fighters were also available. Fighter aircraft dedicated to nuclear strike carried Mk-7 and Mk-12 weapons.[23]

An indication as to what the western Mediterranean-based carrier targeted is evident in an incident in which a pair of AD-4 Skyraid-

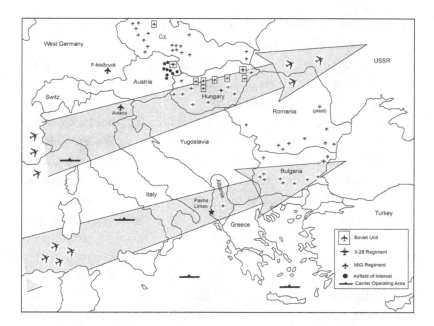

Map 11. The Hungarian-Romanian and Bulgarian corridors. Sixth Fleet aircraft carriers and land-based tactical air would have been used to destroy the Warsaw Pact air defenses so that SAC B-47s could penetrate and hit bomber bases in Ukraine. Defensive targets for the carriers included airfields in occupied Austria and the Soviet submarine base in Albania. Courtesy of the author.

ers from the USS *Hancock* violated Czech airspace and were subsequently engaged by MiG-15s, which inflicted some damage.[24] This suggests that carrier-based air operating off Genoa, Italy, had the ability to destroy the IL-28 base at Wiener-Neustadt, among other targets. A carrier sailing off Genoa or the Tyrrhenian Sea could use its aircraft to reach any target from southern Czechoslovakia, Hungary, eastern Romania, and Albania. Another carrier positioned in the Aegean or Ionian Sea could strike any target in the Balkans or the eastern Ukraine with its combination of aircraft.

As we have seen, there were already a number of Retardation targets in Romania and Bulgaria assigned to the U.S. Navy to forestall a land invasion of Greece and Turkey. Any land force attempting to invade Italy would present targets as it concentrated to force the Alps from Austria or breach through Yugoslavia in the Trieste region. Similarly, any attempt to use Austria as an avenue to turn

NATO's flank in southern West Germany could also be attacked from the sea. Of note, SACEUR assigned a nuclear-capable squadron to be deployed from bases in France or West Germany to the southern flank starting in 1955; it likely would have operated from Aviano Air Base in northern Italy.[25]

The only significant naval threat to the aircraft carrier task forces in the Mediterranean at this time was from four to six Soviet Whiskey-class submarines based in Albania. (The Fifth Eskrada would not appear until the 1960s to challenge the Sixth Fleet.) Rumors of Bloefeldian submarine caves on the island of Sazan abounded starting in 1948, but by 1954 the intelligence apparatus had concluded that they did not exist. Soviet submarines were, however, based in the defended but unprotected docks of Pasha Liman, though an underground base was eventually constructed near Porto Palermo. The Soviet-mentored and -trained Albanian Air Force was small in the mid-1950s, being only a squadron of MiG fighters at the Berat-Kucove Air Base.[26] The destruction of the submarines would have been a priority for the Sixth Fleet and the destruction of Berat-Kucove would have been necessary to facilitate that strike. As for air threats, TU-4 bombers from western Ukraine staging from Crimea were detected conducting exercises against naval targets in 1954.[27]

An important set of targets for Sixth Fleet carriers included elements of the Hungarian and Romanian air defense systems.[28] The most direct route for SAC's B-47s staged from bases in Spain and French Morocco to their targets in the industrialized portions of Ukraine, Moscow, and west of the Urals was over Yugoslavia (and possibly Austria), exploiting what amounted to a geographical funnel superimposed over the Hungarian and Romanian border region, over the Carpathians and into western Ukraine. An attack on this route would also have exploited jurisdictional and coordination complexities of the border area. Destruction of the southern Hungarian radar system plus Sarmellk, Taszar, Fokto, Kecksmet, and Kunmadaras air bases and their Hungarian and Soviet regiments of MiG-15s and MiG-17s would clear the way in Hungary, with bonus damage to the IL-28 units at Kecksmet and Kunmadaras. On the Romanian side, radar in this zone appears to have been limited to the vicinity of Timisoara, Arad, and Oradea-Mare air bases and their Soviet and Romanian MiG-15 and MiG-17 regiments.[29] Notably, detailed information on the Hungarian and Soviet air defense system from radio frequencies to command-and-control structures became readily available in late 1956, during the Hungarian Revolution.[30]

A new weapon became available to the Sixth Fleet in 1956: the Chance-Vought Regulus cruise missile. This missile had a range of five hundred nautical miles and carried a W-5 warhead, a modified Mk-5 bomb. The yield of the W-5 is usually given as 40 to 50 kilotons, but the Mk-5 could yield around 83 kilotons.[31] The carrier USS *Randolph* had Guided Missile Group 2 embarked with four Regulus missiles on her 1956 Mediterranean deployment.[32] The weapons' characteristics suggest that it was optimized for airfield destruction and could conduct a vertical supersonic terminal dive onto its target. The range of the system, if launched from a carrier operating off the Italian coast on a line from Genoa to Florence, could strike any relevant airfield in Hungary as well as the bases in Albania. A combination of Skyraider-delivered Mk-7 bombs against radar sites, and then Regulus missiles followed by Banshee-delivered Mk-7 bombs against airfields would have been enough to clear a path for SAC through the Hungarian-Romanian funnel to western Ukraine.

Finally, there was NATO's northern flank. Information on how nuclear weapons would have been employed during the 1950s in this region is extremely limited. The most likely course of action would have been to attack Soviet naval and air bases on the Kola Peninsula with NATO Striking Fleet Atlantic, which included at least two U.S. Navy aircraft carriers and available information points to the destruction of the naval facilities and, in particular, submarines and their support facilities in the Murmansk area after Soviet air cover had been destroyed.[33] As we have seen, ample targeting information was available by the mid-1950s to undertake this task.

The Far East, 1954–56

The threat situation in the Far East in the 1950s was radically different from the one confronting SAC and NATO forces in Europe. Air force and navy planners had to remain on alert for a possible renewal of hostilities on the Korean Peninsula, especially after the drawdown of UN forces after the Armistice. SAC Emergency War Plan coverage had to be maintained against Soviet targets in the Far East, especially targets housing and supporting strategic bombers that could strike North American targets. Then there was Communist China, which supported North Korea in the north, facilitated the Viet Minh against the French in the south, and was in a de facto war with the Chinese nationalists that decamped to Formosa and engaged in a blockade of the Chinese coast. The number of contingencies involving nuclear weapons use potentially outstripped the forces available on the ground and at sea. Deterrence was a far more difficult proposition to implement in the Far East.

Like the European situation there were also several commands in the Far East that required coordination. There was SAC, with its forward-based medium bombers working under a complicated arrangement with Far East Command; there was the air force's Far East Air Force, which reported to CINCFE's Far East Command in Japan; FEAF's nuclear strike fighter aircraft came under FEC's Japanese Air Defense Force; there was Commander in Chief Pacific Fleet in Hawaii, who "cut" Task Force 77 and its aircraft carriers to FEC but also retained aircraft carriers for employment elsewhere in the Pacific at the behest of the JCS command, CINCPAC. There were attempts to rationalize and coordinate nuclear targeting during the 1954–56 period, but none of them was a satisfactory or long-term solution.

To Far East planners, the Korean War was in temporary abeyance. Still, on 31 December 1953 an RB-45 escorted by fighters was engaged by Communist aircraft over international waters. A similar incident occurred on 22 January 1954, with the escorting F-86s bagging a MiG from a group that attacked the reconnaissance aircraft. In January FEC's intelligence apparatus identified seven threat indicators that led them to believe an air attack might be launched imminently: "Several [enemy] code changes were made out of sequence and earlier than usual; there has been unusual IL-28 night activity, and an increase in MiG activity in North Korea."[34] Back in Washington, analysts ominously suggested that, even after Operation Big Stick, "it [was] unlikely that the Communists would have misunderstood the U.S. warnings, although they might have underestimated U.S. determination to carry them through with atomic weapons." If there were renewed hostilities, and the USAF bombed bases in China with nuclear weapons as part of nuclear strikes against North Korea, there were concerns that the Chinese might target bases in South Korea and Okinawa, possibly with nuclear weapons supplied by the Soviets.[35] Everything was interlinked.

The FEAF strike force expanded significantly by early 1954, due in part to Otto Weyland's concern that the U.S. Navy would dominate targeting responsibilities in the region because they had nuclear-capable aircraft carriers already deployed. The three squadrons of the 49th Fighter-Bomber Wing were now fully equipped with F-84G capable of LABS maneuvers: the 7th Fighter-Bomber Squadron was stationed at Itazuki, the 8th at Misawa, and the 9th at Komaki, for a total of forty-one aircraft. Mk-7 weapons minus their nuclear cores were located at bases in Japan, as they had been in 1953. FEAF had to complete its strikes within forty-eight to seventy-two hours in the event of war. The fighter-bomber forces were supposed to be prepared to conduct operations two hours after the arrival of the cores, with the priority targets consisting of counter-air targets. Transport aircraft belonging to the 315th Air Division were assigned to deliver weapons and nuclear components from Guam with C-124 aircraft, with at least one exercise moving ten training weapons from Guam to Japan.[36]

The problem was the cores, which were not all under USAF custody or control: some were kept in Guam in the custody of the 12th Aviation Field Depot Squadron, but others were aboard U.S. Navy ships. These scarce cores could easily be diverted for other purposes that were inimical to FEAF's objectives by the other commands unless they were firmly earmarked. SAC controlled the 12th Aviation Field Depot Squadron on Guam, but Weyland and FEAF insisted on the construction of a separate FEAF nuclear storage facility.[37] This eventually became the 3rd Aviation Field Depot Squadron based at Kadena Air Base on Okinawa.[38]

On 20 January 1954 SAC was directed by the JCS to coordinate "atomic operations in the event of further hostilities *in* Korea" and to prepare "a plan for the use of atomic weapons in the event of Chinese Communist aggression *outside* Korea." For the "in Korea" part, SAC was to coordinate with CINCFE and CINCPAC, but for outside of Korea SAC could plan on its own and submit plans to the JCS. The coordination of the FEAF atomic force with other forces was discussed in an all–air force dinner in January 1954 that included Weyland, Twining, LeMay, and others; this meeting was prompted by a JCS message to FEC, SAC, and CINCPAC to get on with sorting out coordination arrangements. Here Weyland conveyed his discussions with Gen. Joe Hull, commander Far East Command, who told him that he did not want command or operational control of SAC units. If he needed SAC support, he would go through the JCS channels. With a "substantial number" of nuclear weapons about to be allocated, a coordinating element, the Theater Joint Operations Center, was to be established, with SAC X-Ray observing. A reluctant LeMay "came to the conclusion that he could 'live' with the provisions as stated."[39]

When the focus shifted to what the army might think, all were concerned that they would "have extravagant ideas and make extravagant plans in accordance with their own interpretation" of the new state of affairs. That left the navy. Some feared the navy would want to absorb Far East Command into CINCPAC so it could get control of everything from Kamchatka to Indochina.[40]

The Far East Command plan was supposed to stress "air retaliation as the key element."[41] However, the Far East Command EWP in early 1954 directed that the FEAF atomic strike force "conduct atomic attacks in support of operations of [Eighth Army] and [Naval Forces, Far East] as directed by CINCFE." An exercise akin to Prophecy was then conducted to look at coordination machinery. Dubbed Race Track, this exercise diverged significantly from the earlier FEC plan. With observers from SAC X-Ray and CINCPAC on hand, the Theater Joint Operations Center quickly determined that there was not enough intelligence on the targets of opportunity envisioned by the army planners, and the "concept of gaining air superiority through reducing the aggressor atomic delivery capability" took hold. Only then, in a second phase, were targets of opportunity pursued. But who was the final authority for designation of the weapons? Was it FEAF acting for the theater commander, or the army ground forces?[42]

While Race Track was underway, France's position in Indochina dramatically deteriorated. The French war in Indochina, already supported by the Chinese Communists, was deliberately aggravated and then escalated by Mao after 1953. Captured American artillery from Korea, Chinese military advisors, and even intelligence information on French strategy and plans flowed south to Ho Chi Minh. Mao's objective was "to gain access to embargoed Western technology and equipment. . . . Mao's plan was to make the Vietnamese intensify the war to 'increase the internal problems of France' . . . and then when the French were on the ropes, to step in and broker a settlement."[43]

This demonstration would be made at a place called Dien Bien Phu. The Chinese deployed Gen. Wei Guo-qing to plan the operation, and their intelligence sources passed the French plans to the Viet Minh, who cut off and besieged the French garrison in a dramatic battle in the first half of 1954. What Mao did not count on was that the French might go to the Americans for help. The initial plan, Operation Vulture, called for sixty B-29s to drop conventional bombs escorted by 150 U.S. Navy carrier-based aircraft; these aircraft would come from the thirty-two B-29s with the 98th Bombardment Wing at Yokota, and the 19th and 307th bombardment wings at Kadena, which had sixty-seven B-29s between them.[44] Ultimately, Secretary of State John Foster Dulles rhetorically asked the French, "And if I gave you two A-bombs for Dien Bien Phu?" The delicate issue as to whether nuclear weapons would be used to break the siege coexisted with preparations to do so. The strike would likely have been conducted from U.S. Navy aircraft carriers, probably the USS *Essex*, using AD-1 Skyraider aircraft dropping Mk-7 nuclear weapons: "The day prior to the attack the French were supposed to deepen their trenches by a foot and half. . . . Five minutes before detonation . . . French troops were to hunker down in their trenches. Three weapons were to be used in a triangular pattern, fused for airburst in the hills above the entrenched camp." Another option was to drop two weapons on the border facilities with China that were logistically supporting the Communist Vietnamese effort.[45] The operation was shelved by Eisenhower.

The shift from possible B-29 or B-50 use to U.S. Navy aircraft carriers to support the French suggests that SAC was not keen on contingency operations of this type. The likely reason was the paucity of forces in the Far East at this time. At one point the number of nuclear-capable B-29s and B-50s stationed on Guam dropped to between six and eighteen, and all of them were destined to attack targets in China or Korea if war resumed.[46] In May, however, the commander in chiefs for the Far East, Pacific, and SAC were instructed to revise their earlier plans "in the event of further Chinese Communist aggression in Korea or Indo-China."[47] SAC increased its rotations to Guam, with the B-29-equipped 19th Bombardment Wing returning complete in May, rotating with the 96th and then the 98th throughout 1954. Plans were then made to replace the reciprocating aircraft with a B-47 wing in October, but this force structure changed due to increased tensions in the region. On 1 October 1954 a ninety-day SAC rotation arrived at Guam, but instead of weary B-29s it consisted of the 92nd Bombardment Wing with its gargantuan B-36s.[48]

A complex situation involving the Nationalist Chinese and their attempts to hang on by their fingernails to the offshore islands between mainland China and Formosa escalated in 1954. With success at hand over the French in Indochina, Mao turned to deal with his hated enemies. The only way he could invade Formosa, however, was to cross the Taiwan Straits. The offshore islands were closer, but they still required amphibious forces to take them over. That involved building up enough shipping to do so, but American reconnaissance aircraft patrolled the area regularly to spot any buildup and provide early warning. These aircraft were regularly engaged by Chinese fighters. Nationalist Chinese fighters also locked horns with the Communist Chinese; sixteen Nationalist aircraft were downed between 1950 and 1954.[49]

The U.S. Navy kept a constant eye on the situation, but in August 1954 Zhou Enlai called for the "liberation" of the offshore islands and Formosa. Quemoy Island, just off the coast, was one of twenty-five islands in Nationalist hands. It came under bombardment by Chinese artillery and later aerial attack from nearly one hundred aircraft in January 1955.[50] The calculating Mao wanted to "push the situation to the brink of nuclear confrontation with America, which would face Russia with the possibility of having to retaliate on China's behalf unless it let Mao have the Bomb."[51] Mao asked Khrushchev for nuclear weapons technology, but the Soviet leader told him it was too expensive. Perhaps a nuclear reactor could be provided. Mao upped the ante with more attacks against the offshore islands "[calculating that he could] nudge America into threatening to use nuclear weapons." Which is exactly what Eisenhower did. The Joint Chiefs of Staff examined options to use nuclear weapons against China; these were discussed by Ike and his National Security Council. Public statements by the chief of naval operations Adm. Robert Carney referred to the "destruction of China's military potential."[52] Other material preemptively leaked to the press, to Eisenhower's great annoyance.[53] This likely served to reinforce LeMay's already jaundiced views of the U.S. Navy.

A February 1955 reappraisal of planning coordination revealed a muddle of command-and-control issues:

> CINCPAC operations in defense of Formosa may well lead to operations against targets on the Chinese Mainland and later to expanded hostilities with China. For those operations, CINCPAC plans envisage extensive use of CINCFE's Air Forces as well as his own Naval Forces. On the other hand, CINCFE is required to plan and prepare for hostilities with China if the Korean Armistice breaks down. His plans naturally envisage use of FEAF's Forces and CINCPAC's Naval forces. Targets under the two plans are identical in many instances. We thus have two JCS area commanders planning military operations against a common enemy with the determination as to which commander will be in charge to be made later, depending upon the geographical area in which the initiating incident occurs.[54]

Twining instructed LeMay on 30 March 1955 to prepare a SAC contingency plan that remained separate from these problems. LeMay reported back the next day that SAC had the plans and was "ready for [immediate] execution by use of B-36 [aircraft] based on Guam to deal with any eventuality involving Communist China." There was one B-36 wing on Guam, and SAC had two more "on warning alert" prepared to deploy from the United States. Guam could handle sixty B-36s; "they [would] have immediate capability for combat operations," that is, access to nuclear weapons from the depot on the island, and "target selections [were] made."[55]

In response Twining asked LeMay why B-47s were not to be employed. LeMay explained that "B-36-type aircraft [could not] be used as advantageously against USSR targets as against Communist China targets" and, besides, "all of the B-47s and their crews were busy": "Employment of B-47s against Communist China targets puts us off-balance in case of general war since all B-47s required in this role against the USSR."[56]

Twining demurred—for the time being. He told LeMay that, in his view, SAC had to "be sufficiently flexible to participate in localized operations in that area as well as be prepared to carry out general war responsibilities." He wanted SAC to be able to use B-47s on short-notice operations "against invasion forces, gun positions, troop concentrations, ports, airfields and other support targets."[57]

So what was SAC supposed to hit, and how was it going to hit it? And how did its staff know where those targets were in this pre-U-2 period? On 1 April 1955 the Chinese complained that eighteen reconnaissance aircraft overflew their country in four waves.[58] These were likely a squadron of recently deployed reconnaissance aircraft flown by Nationalist Chinese pilots with USAF support.[59] As it turned out, the availability of targeting data was in some ways better for China than it was for the Soviet Union. There was long-term American involvement in Chinese development going back decades, and of course the United States supported Nationalist China throughout World War II.[60] The bulk of Communist Chinese industry was in Manchuria and based on Japanese plants, so there was substantial information available from Japanese sources. Nationalist Chinese human intelligence of varying quality was available, including material provided through the emergent West German intelligence apparatus as early as 1953.[61] SIGINT came in from the British colony of Hong Kong, "America's watchtower in China," which boasted a plethora of British and Australian units and facilities.[62]

Of equal importance was LeMay himself: he had commanded U.S. Army Air Forces bomber forces in China itself in 1944 and knew some of the targets personally, specifically Hankow, which was incinerated by B-29s during the war.[63] Indeed LeMay's liaison with Mao and his forces during the war afforded him insights into the man and the situation that even the Eurocentric Eisenhower and his advisors lacked.[64] There was one exception: the vice chief of staff USAF and future chief of staff Gen. Thomas D. White had served for four years in China "as a student of the Chinese language" earlier in his career, was awarded a medal from the U.S. Marine Corps aviation contingent in China, and maintained an interest in the culture. (He collected Chinese art.)[65] Both men would have agreed with the historian Hans van de Ven that Mao "was a tough revolutionary, who [was] committed to the use of violence, and perfected its use as he learned from experience, not just for the sake of the revolution and the creation of a New China . . . but to enhance his own personal power."[66]

The SAC plan for the 1955 China operation is unavailable. The existing record suggests that, despite his 1960s-era boast that China would have backed off in Korea if Beijing, Hankow, and Manchuria were struck, LeMay understood the futility of engaging in a land war with Communist China and was less than enthusiastic about the limited nuclear strikes planned in the 1950–53 period. After discussions with LeMay and Weyland in late 1952, White accepted the argument that extending the air war into Manchuria and destroying the Antung Airfield complexes would not by itself achieve anything. The only means they saw to drive Communist China to the table over Korea was to combine strategic air attacks against critical targets like transportation centers with a naval blockade of the Chinese coast.[67] This thinking remained in vogue two years later, during the 1955 Taiwan Straits crisis, but there was a lack of enthusiasm at the higher levels of the U.S. Air Force when it came to going to war with China proper: the Soviet Union was generally seen to be the primary enemy. LeMay held and later expressed the belief that the Communist China–Soviet relationship was not as tight as others believed. Perhaps they would even become antagonists.[68]

That Twining pushed LeMay into preparing to cover what amounted to operational-level targets related to the defense of the offshore islands and Taiwan strongly suggests that the original SAC contingency plan for China in 1955 was based on traditional strategic bombing targets and had to be slightly modified to accommodate operational-level targets.[69] If confronted with a JCS task that instructed SAC to destroy Chinese Communist war-making capacity, what would LeMay's staff have generated? If the planners were limited to targets inside Communist China, and this appears to have been the case, what could be reasonably accomplished? The go-to target sets thus far were petroleum and steel production, aircraft and vehicle factories, anything that could support jet aircraft operations, and naval bases and construction yards. With thirty B-36s on tap in Guam and another sixty available for operations based in the United States, a logical number of targets would come in around ninety, though we should recall that some B-36s were capable of carrying up to four Mk-6 or Mk-18 weapons, while others were optimized to carry one of the large Mk-17 or Mk-24 thermonuclear weapons. We should rule out airfields as targets for the time being (there were around 140 of these identified by 1955) and examine the other categories first.

The destruction of the Chinese land forces would have been impossible due to their size and dispersion, though their logistics establishment in the hinterland supporting invasion preparations, particularly rail junctions, could have been destroyed. The destruction of Communist China's means of projecting power outside of China proper was likely a U.S. Navy task, which we will examine later. This leaves critical industries that China needed to maintain a war footing: steel, oil, and aircraft and vehicle manufacturing.

Destruction of the Chinese Communist steel-making capacity would have required eight nuclear weapons. The Chiu-chuan Iron and Steel Plant was the deepest target facility to the west, in a desolate area south of Mongolia. A B-36 with an accurately delivered Mk-6 or Mk-18 weapon would have been suitable to destroy it. The second-deepest target plant was Chung-ching Iron and Steel Plant No. 1, in the heart of the country. An attack similar to that employed against Jiayuguan is a reasonable assumption given the distances from Guam. Nanjing and Shanghai boasted between two and four facilities associated with steel. The sprawling nature of these targets

FOUR HORSEMEN II

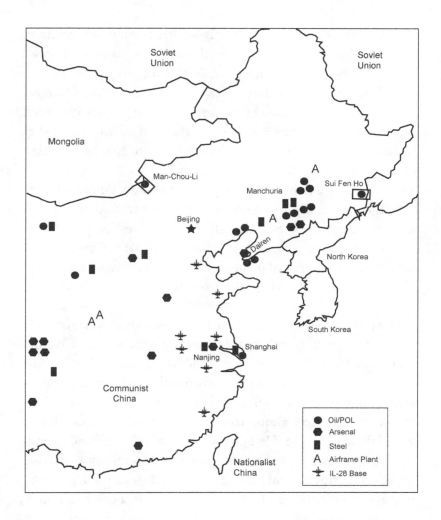

Map 12. Probable SAC targets in Communist China, 1955. The destruction of
Communist China's war-making capacity would have included oil, steel, and
aircraft production facilities, plus identified arsenals and IL-28 Beagle bomber
bases. Of note are the two petroleum transshipment rail nodes at Man-Chou-Li
and Sui-Fen-Ho, which handled 100 percent of petroleum shipments
from the Soviet Union. Courtesy of the author.

and the closer distance to Guam suggest the employment of Mk-17 or Mk-24 thermonuclear weapons. Similarly the plants at Tai-yuan and the Shih-ching-shan Iron and Steel Plant just west of Beijing would have required the larger weapons. The most difficult targets were in MiG-ridden Manchuria: a pair of plants adjacent to each other between Shenyang and Fu-shun. The need for maneuverability in this environment suggests the employment of light Mk-18 weapons with their 500-kiloton yield or even Mk-6s with a 12, 14, 18, 37, 47, or 81–83 yield rather then dragging in a bulky Mk-17 or Mk-24.[70]

Targeting the Chinese Communist oil production system was a more complex task, even though annual Chinese oil production equaled a single day's production in the United States. Consequently, approximately 57 percent of the oil and petroleum products used in Communist China were imported from the Sino-Soviet Bloc.[71] Some components of the Chinese oil industry were more important or more vulnerable than others. There were fifteen primary production facilities, which included principal refineries, synthetic plants, natural crude oilfields, and crude shale oil production plants. Most important, however, analysts found "no evidence that either reciprocating-engine or jet-engine aircraft fuels [were] manufactured in China," although there were announcements that the Lan-chou refinery would do so after 1956.[72] In other words, the ability of the Communist Chinese air force to conduct protracted operations was based on available storage and on imported aviation gasoline from the two Soviet refineries in the Far East. Therefore a combination of extraction, processing, storage, and transportation targets would, if hit, significantly reduce Communist China's war-making capacity.

In order to shut down this industry, SAC had to destroy not only the domestic production facilities but also key routes into China from the Soviet Union. There were only two entry routes for Soviet oil into Communist China. The first was Man-Chou-Li (Manzouli), a desolate rail transshipment point southeast of the Trans-Siberian Railroad waypoint at Chita and then Lanzhou, which was used during World War II by the Soviets to support China against Japan.[73] The other was Sui-fen-ho, in the forested hills west of Pogranichny in the Soviet Union, with its spur to the Trans-Siberian Railroad north of

Vladivostok. Both railyards handled one million tons, that is, 100 percent of China's imported oil and petroleum products, per year.[74] Sui-fen-ho was clearly of interest to SAC: sometime prior to October 1955, a USAF Haymaker SENSINT flight took photos of the facilities, including the petroleum storage tanks and the railroad yards. These pictures augmented photography taken earlier in 1951 by a Far East Air Force reconnaissance run.[75]

Attacking Man-Chou-Li and Sui-fen-ho with nuclear weapons would have been a dicey proposition. Both facilities were about a mile and a half away from the Soviet Union, so a miss would clearly be problematic. This suggests two possibilities. The first would be a run paralleling the border with a lower-kilotonnage-yield weapon, perhaps an Mk-6 with an 8-kiloton yield and the weapon fused for groundburst; an airburst would destroy only what was on the yard at the time, but a groundburst would deny the yard completely and make reconstruction or bypass impossible in the constricted terrain. The destruction radius of an 8-kiloton weapon would neatly cover the town and facilities and deposit minimal fallout (1–10 r/hr) in a remote part of the Soviet Union.[76] The second option would have been to find a railroad node or nodes deeper inside China, perhaps one colocated with another target with war-making capacity.

During this period Communist China was believed to possess meager strategic oil storage capacity. There were two large, very vulnerable sites at Dairen: Ssuerkhou and Kanchingtzu. There was another large site at Yuan-ping-chen, much deeper in near Tai-yuan, southwest of Beijing. Notably the Communist Chinese recognized this deficiency and between 1958 and 1963 constructed twenty-six strategic and regional oil storage facilities, which was increased to thirty-six by 1966.[77] In 1955, however, the expenditure of three weapons, or fewer if the Yuan-ping-chen refinery was taken out collaterally with the steel plant at Tai-yuan by an Mk-17 or Mk-24, would, in combination with the severing of rail links, dramatically reduce Chinese military operations to using limited local stocks. The Dairen sites, on the other hand, were geographically situated in such a way that they could have been hit with airburst weapons to limit fallout onto the Korean Peninsula and Japan.

The complete neutralization of Communist China's petroleum industry required the destruction of fifteen refineries and adjacent facilities. In effect, 75 percent of Communist China's refining capacity was concentrated in Manchuria. Four of these plants were clustered around Fushun, which, as we have seen, was also the location of a major steel plant. The delivery of a pair of Mk-17 or Mk-24 weapons would have taken out all of these facilities. Northeast Petroleum Plants No. 5 and No. 6 were conveniently located across the Bohai Sea from their sister facility, Plant No. 7, and the strategic storage facilities at Dairen; a pair of B-36s carrying multiple weapons could have engaged all five facilities. Plant No. 8 and Plant No. 10 were at Kirin in northern Manchuria, roughly in a straight line on the other side of the mountains west of Sui-fen-ho and its transportation facilities. Plant No. 9 was directly south of Plant 8. A single large weapon on Kirin and a smaller one on Plant 9 would have permanently stopped all production in northern Manchuria.[78]

The other seven refineries were spread out. The refinery located at Shanghai would likely have been destroyed collaterally with the steel works there. Lan-chou (Lanzhou) and its aviation fuel potential would have required special treatment because of its deep location in the center of the country. An attack similar to the Chiu-chuan Iron and Steel Plant strike is a logical assumption. The three primary oilfields were Yumen, Yen-ch'ang, and Wu-su. The Yumen facilities were northwest of the Chiu-chuan Iron and Steel Plant at Jiayaguen and could have been destroyed by the same aircraft targeting the steel plant with a second weapon. Yen-ch'ang was considered "of local importance only" and probably would not have been targeted. Wu-su, which lay on China's westernmost border, was essentially terra incognita. In terms of chemical plants, these were under construction and were not operational until 1959. The limited capacity that did exist appears to have been colocated with petroleum-based industries and would have been collaterally destroyed.[79]

Other targets related to Communist China's war-making capacity included two airframe and three aero-engine plants. Three of these were known quantities based on Japanese facilities and located in Harbin and Mukden in Manchuria, while the other two were in the vicinity of His-an in central China. These were dedicated to MIG fighter and IL-28 production.[80] The Manchurian sites were known and had been overflown by RB-45Cs with photo-radar mapping missions in 1951.[81]

As for weapons production, Communist China was not credited with any factories for the production of armored fighting vehicles, but did have a substantial artillery, heavy weapons, and small arms industry supported by a small number of explosives factories. There were twelve major and fifty-eight minor arsenals identified from World War II and Korean War sources.[82] The destruction of the minor arsenals would have been uneconomical, but the destruction of seventeen airframe plants and munitions factories, many of them adjacent to steel works and petroleum facilities, would have rendered Communist China incapable of projecting modern military power in the region for years, if not decades.

As to the issue of fallout from the strikes in Manchuria, the effects of even a pair of Mk-17s or -24s groundburst at 22 megatons at Shenyang and Fushun would have blanketed northeast Manchuria with radioactive material generating over 1,000 roentgen per hour; 600 was considered a lethal dose in 1955. A shift in the wind would have dusted Vladivostok with about 10 to 100 roentgen per hour.[83] Clearly the use of 83- and 500-kiloton weapons would not have generated this degree of lethality (except locally, of course), so if a decision were made to limit Mk-17/24 use, fallout would not necessarily have been a regional problem.

Of course, China did not necessarily need modern military power to assist its Viet Minh allies with taking down the French Union Forces in Indochina or to launch human wave attacks and push UN forces back in Korea: Communist China in the 1950s was postured for national liberation war in Asia, not National Socialist–like mechanized Blitzkrieg.[84] A number of things impressed LeMay from his experiences in China. He took note of the all-encompassing aspects of the Mao-led "peoples war"; he was impressed by the Long March and that fact that Mao did his time pulling rollers alongside his fighters to build an airfield to support American aircraft.[85] SAC could destroy Communist China's industrial capacity and prevent it from projecting power across the straits onto the offshore islands and Formosa, but could it destroy China's real war-making capacity, which lay in the huge numbers of Chinese and Mao's ability to inspire and mobilize them?

Perhaps it was possible with Project Respondent. During the Korean War, LeMay was instructed to convert one bomber wing into a chemical- and biological-warfare-delivery formation by the end of 1952. This was a Department of Defense (i.e., a Robert A. Lovett) initiative, as Thomas White made clear to LeMay; it was routed through the air force and not something that emerged from air force planning.[86] After LeMay watched the Top Secret indoctrination film *Strategic Employment of Biological and Chemical Weapons* in 1953 he confessed, "The matter of fact manner in which the commentary in this film depicts the results of BW-CW warfare left a bad taste in my mouth." (This coming from LeMay, of all people.) The SAC commander pointed out that the film had "a man in a USAF's Colonel's uniform discussing a plan for killing a million people in Moscow by germ warfare." This was "dangerous" because the film provided "a most powerful psychological weapon if it fell into the wrong hands."[87]

On 8 July 1954 LeMay requested that SAC be relieved of all biological and chemical warfare responsibilities.[88] Not until 1958 did the JCS agree, establishing only "a token retaliatory supply" of chemical weapons for Europe. The air force possessed "a limited offensive biological warfare capability" and was, in the main, uninterested in expanding it during this time.[89] Biological warfare appears to have played no role in targeting Communist China. Nuclear weapons remained in the forefront.

As for the Chinese Communist air defense system, the U.S. Navy was in the lead in developing the radar picture through extensive ferreting operations with P4M-1Q Mercators that spanned the entire Communist Chinese coastline. CIA-facilitated efforts, dubbed Fox Hunt, resulted in the transfer of P4Y-2 Privateer ELINT aircraft from the U.S. Navy to the Nationalist Chinese air force. The so-called Technical Research Group also acquired a B-17 that was appropriately equipped. The Communist Chinese radar setup initially included obsolete Soviet,

Japanese, and U.S. systems, but in 1955 the Soviets provided twenty-three Token systems for the newly established air defense system modeled directly on the Soviet PVO. Importantly, the Communist Chinese lacked height-finding radar, particularly along the coast.[90]

The Communist Chinese air defense forces were considered to be a known quantity by the time SAC set its sights on China. The People's Liberation Army Air Force in 1955 essentially resembled the Soviet air forces circa 1952: MiG-15s that were under the command of ground controllers operating on jammable frequencies, with little or no night intercept capability. Estimates asserted that the Chinese system was "considerably inferior to that attained by the USSR itself."[91] One should not, however, rule out adaptability: Communist forces in Korea did score kills against B-29s at night on a handful of occasions using innovative tactics. Vital points were protected by radar-controlled anti-aircraft artillery and searchlights. Unlike Korean war operations, however, SAC would not have its hands tied behind its back when it came to electronic countermeasures like jamming and chaff.

Indeed individual Chinese pilots may have gained experience against Americans and allies over Korea, but the Communist Chinese air defense system as a whole was relatively untested in 1955.[92] The exceptions were the units operating opposite Taiwan, which were preoccupied with a variety of Nationalist Chinese nocturnal intruders; in some cases they used IL-28s to drop flares so intercepting MiGs could see their targets and press attacks home. Later on in 1958 TU-2 twin-prop bombers were converted into night-fighters, but these would have been unavailable in 1955.[93]

There appears to have been some debate regarding numbers and location, however. The deployment pattern suggests that in 1951, during the Korean War, the bulk of the estimated 590 Chinese Communist MiGs were stationed in Manchuria at eighteen bases, with another nine bases on the Dairen peninsula, three at Tsingtao, and six around Beijing.[94] However, between 1952 and 1954 large numbers of MiGs appeared at nine bases in Canton, Hanzou, and Shanghai.[95] Construction on the Shandong Peninsula increased the number of bases from one to five. The question for SAC planners in 1955 was this: Were the Korean War–era Manchurian bases now empty and their aircraft redeployed to the south, or were there just more Chinese aircraft overall and all bases remained occupied? What was clear was that "along the extreme southern coastal areas the air defense capabilities are less and in the interior areas are non-existent."[96]

The number of targets SAC had to take out to destroy Communist China's war-making capacity included thirteen petroleum refineries, four large oil storage facilities, eight steel and iron plants, five aircraft factories, and twelve major arsenals. If we include seven IL-28 bases but leave the maritime and air base targets adjacent to Taiwan and the offshore islands to the tender mercies of the U.S. Navy, the number of SAC targets comes in at between forty-two and forty-nine. That said, some targets were colocated and could be destroyed with single large weapons. The problem of fallout drifting from strikes in China onto adjacent countries would have been serious, particularly if the Soviet Union remained aloof from the conflict and the United States wanted to keep Japan as an ally. This suggests that the weapons could have been fused for airburst for most targets. In this case, the Mk-18 with its higher but sub-megaton yield would have been ideally suited. One cannot, however, rule out the use of the Mk-17 or Mk-24 airburst over a target complex consisting of two or more facilities. Indeed, as we have seen, there was some debate over how extensive fallout would be after the Castle test series in 1954. In any case, SAC would not have been as concerned about fallout as it would be in later years.

With thirty B-36s forward-deployed on Guam, and another sixty available, what would the plan have looked like? (See map 13.) The location of Guam relative to the targets, the pattern of targets, and air defenses suggest several approaches. The attack would have been conducted at night with maximum use of electronic countermeasures and would be structured and timed to achieve surprise. Seventeen of the targets were in central China with virtually no protection. An end run over Hainan Island, where there was little or no effective radar or ground-controlled intercept capabilities, and then north, attacking Canton on the way, was one likely route. There was increased interest in the intelligence community throughout 1954 in identifying radar in southern China, and most of it was in the Canton area.[97]

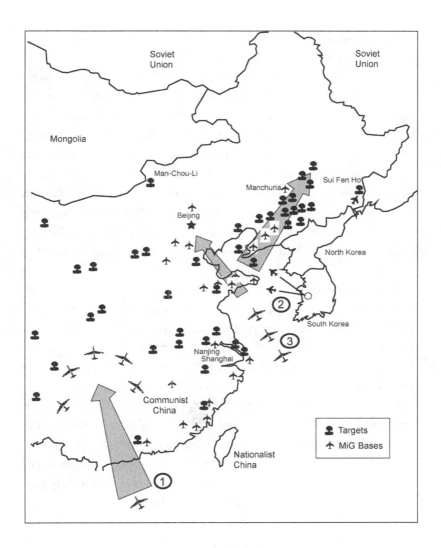

Map 13. Projected routes and phasing of SAC operations against Communist China had the 1955 offshore islands crisis escalated. Using the targets from map 12 as a basis, B-36 bombers from Guam would have bypassed or otherwise penetrated the Communist Chinese air defense system in the south near Canton (1) while FEAF's F-84G fighter-bombers struck air defense bases on the Dairen and Shandong Peninsulas (2). This would have allowed two B-36 streams to take out targets on the way to Beijing and Manchuria (3). Courtesy of the author.

The B-36 bomber stream could then spread out and roll up the target facilities one by one.

A second target cluster could have included the steel plant, arsenal, and two to four IL-28 bases around Shanghai. This target set was protected by nearly 175 MiG-15s, none of which were all-weather capable. The toughest nut to crack, however, was the Beijing-Manchuria-Shandong triangle. To get at Beijing and Manchuria, SAC had to fly over the Yellow Sea, and then the Shandong and Dairen Peninsulas, assuming that SAC did not want to activate a North Korean hornet's nest and overfly the Chinese ally on the way in. The bulk of the Communist Chinese air forces was lodged here, with Beijing in depth protected by another two hundred MiG-15s, again, none of which were all-weather capable.

This was where FEAF's 49th Fighter-Bomber Wing came in. The Wing's forward-based squadron at Taegu, South Korea, was a nuclear-capable unit equipped with Mk-7 nuclear weapons (minus the cores) and with crews who had targets in China.[98] In theory, this would have provided fifteen F-84Gs with LABS capability to go in ahead of SAC at low level and blast the airfields on the Shandong and Dairen Peninsulas. Of note, the Dairen air defense control center was Soviet-controlled and believed to be linked to the PVO in the Far East.[99] The Shanghai air bases were also in range of Taegu or from the squadron based at Komaki, Japan, with recovery at Taegu. Such a strike would have opened the door completely, permitting B-36s to hit fifteen targets in Manchuria and the five petroleum targets in the Jinzhou-Dairen area. Another B-36 cell could then proceed to Beijing. Both groups had the option of proceeding northeast and exfiltrating across the narrowest part of North Korea around Hoerjong-Rason, and then over the Sea of Japan to recover in Japan, where Operation Big Stick had confirmed which airfields could handle B-36s back in 1953.

In a general sense the SAC offensive against Communist China would have been phased and multipronged. The first phase would have been the sweep to the south over Hainan and then Canton, and then into the interior. This move would have generated some alarm and focus on the south right at the time the second phase struck the air defense system on the Shandong and Dairen Peninsulas with F-84Gs. The third phase would see the second group of B-36s penetrate through the area and split up to hit the Beijing and Manchurian target clusters.

That left the east China coast, the offshore islands, and Taiwan. The SAC operations plan was probably separate from the U.S. Navy's operational plans for a number of reasons. There were scenarios whereby limited use of nuclear and conventional weapons were needed, not the outright destruction of the Communist Chinese industrial base. For example, it was believed that the Communist Chinese possessed between fifteen and twenty U.S.-built landing ship tank (LST) vessels as well as thirty smaller amphibious craft. Taiwan or the offshore islands could not have been invaded and held by Communist China without them.[100] In 1954 they were based in Canton, Shanghai, and Dairen. The U.S. Navy did not need to destroy all three cities to destroy this sealift. The lack of a serious Communist Chinese navy in 1954–55 to escort the LSTs at this point would have permitted their destruction at sea by destroyer gunfire or conventional airstrikes from aircraft carriers.

This brings us to the U.S. Navy and their plans for nuclear operations against Communist China. From 1954 to 1956 the U.S. Navy maintained five attack carriers in the Pacific on rotation, a slight drop from seven or eight during the Korean War.[101] By this point almost all *Essex*-class attack carriers had been converted to carry nuclear weapons. The cores were stored in a special compartment in the bow, while a special ammunition storage space reached by a special elevator from the hanger deck was located below and protected by a U.S. Marine guard detachment. The space on each carrier was limited, probably to around ten to twenty Mk-5, -7, -8, or -12 weapons. Aircraft could be kept in strike configuration in the hanger or on the deck as required to increase the numbers.[102]

As with the SAC operations plan, the U.S. Navy operations plan for this period is not available. Information from Exercise Jack Pratt held in late 1955 and other sources suggests that four aircraft carriers would have been involved and that the main targets were Communist Chinese airfields that were in range of the offshore islands.[103]

U.S. naval forces providing cover to Nationalist Chinese forces would have been vulnerable to land-based air strikes. The most economical way to reduce this vulnerability would be to destroy those bases with nuclear weapons.

Aircraft carriers deployed to the region in the first half of 1955 included the USS *Essex*, USS *Wasp*, USS *Oriskany*, and USS *Kearsarge*, with the USS *Boxer*, USS *Bennington*, and USS *Hancock* rotating in later in the year.[104] The types of aircraft based on these ships reveal their capabilities. The USS *Essex* carried F-2H2B Banshees, Skyraiders, and AJ-2 Savages.[105] The Banshee "squadrons' 'banjos' [were] specially configured to deliver atomic weapons. In addition the difficult night fighter duties of the air group [were] performed by these versatile fighters."[106] As for the AJ-2 Savage detachment, "the primary mission of the 'big-'uns' aboard the Essex [was] high altitude precision delivery of special weapons."[107] The USS *Wasp* had nuclear-capable F-2H2B Banshees from Composite Squadron 3 (one of which may have suffered an accident with its weapon attached) that demonstrated the ability to aerial-refuel from U.S. Air Force KB-29s stationed in Japan.[108]

The USS *Oriskany* carried a special Skyraider unit, VC-35 Detachment George, whose "pilots alternated three at a time to [Naval Air Station] Atsugi, Japan where they flew training flights to develop their proficiency in the delivery of other types of weapons."[109] The USS *Kearsarge* retained Banshee, Savage, and Skyraider capabilities during its multiple deployments to the region. VC-35 Det Fox was "composed of four specially configured [Skyraider] aircraft . . . in a ready status around the clock."[110] The *Kearsarge* also participated in an exercise: on the "third day came the Kay's big test—a full scale battle problem climaxed by an atomic attack."[111] The Banshee squadron "ha[d] the dual mission of special weapons delivery and night all weather interception of enemy aircraft."[112]

The USS *Boxer* boasted a VC-35 Skyraider detachment: "In addition the team composed the Special Weapons unit of the Air Group. Certainly any outbreak of hostilities would have found this highly specialized splinter group a constant thorn in the side of the enemy."[113] The USS *Bennington* had Banshees and Savages.[114] The USS *Hancock* arrived late in 1955 with Banshee "special weapons bombers" from VC-3 and a special detachment of aircraft that could guide Regulus cruise missiles: *Hancock* hosted five Regulus launches earlier in 1955, before being deployed.[115]

The predominant nuclear weapons for the carriers at this point were the Mk-7 and Mk-12 bombs with yields between 10 and 20 kilotons. But it appears as though there was a conventional option involving the destruction of the fuel storage facilities at each base.[116] Some of the four primary targets were located in built-up areas: Nan-Tai Airfield, for example, was just outside of Fuzhou's downtown core. Even if Mk-12 Broks were used at 10-kiloton yield, there would have been considerable loss of life, which would not necessarily have been politically palatable in a limited war situation. In the event Eisenhower ordered SAC in to destroy Communist China's war capacity, such restrictions may not have applied.

The mobility of the carrier task forces permitted them to destroy any target within range of their aircraft along Communist China's coast using escorted strike aircraft during the day and single-plane operations at night. With self-contained photoreconnaissance detachments, the carrier air groups could assess and rapidly retarget as required. This suggests that U.S. Navy plans were not coordinated with SAC's for the China operations in 1955. The aircraft carriers' movements would not have been predictable enough to move and blow a hole through the Communist Chinese air defenses at, say, Canton for SAC's B-36s to pour through after departing Guam. Indeed LeMay would not have wanted to count on the U.S. Navy for any critical part of SAC's operations if he did not have to.

The 1955 crisis wound down in April and the Communist Chinese ceased their operations against Nationalist Chinese forces on the offshore islands. Later in 1955 the U.S. Navy conducted Exercise Jack Pratt, designed to "evaluate the readiness of the Seventh Fleet to deliver a major atomic offensive." Four aircraft carriers loaded with nuclear weapons moved into the Taiwan Straits in December 1955.[117] Mao used these moves as leverage with Khrushchev, who caved in and agreed to provide Mao with a cyclotron as well as a nuclear reactor. Chinese scientists departed for Soviet nuclear facilities, presumably at Chelyabinsk, for training.[118] Meanwhile American leaders and analysts congratulated themselves that they had shown resolve; they believed Mao backed down due to the overwhelming military forces brought to bear in the region.

Immediately after the crisis, U.S. Air Force Chief of Staff Twining requested an analysis of the relationship between U.S. Navy aircraft carriers and SAC, a question clearly triggered by the command arrangements for the Taiwan Straits crisis. Twining was told (or reminded) that SAC's "number one task" was the destruction of the Soviet long-range air forces and that these were "the first enemy targets that would have to be destroyed." They were located deep in Soviet territory and had to be taken out quickly, before they could generate damage against American bases. Naval aircraft had a short range, and the weapon load was deemed incapable of handling certain targets: "Our studies of weapons effects convinces us that weapons with yields upwards of 70 KT would have to be used to assure positive destruction of the primary airfields of an enemy. . . . Only the heavy attack bombers of the Navy can carry these higher yield weapons." There were "less than a hundred heavy attack bombers that [could] operate from carriers," and SAC at this point "ha[d] 1590 aircraft capable of delivering high-yield weapons."[119]

In the "size matters" department: "Studies we have made show that one B-52 wing could deliver almost twice as many megatons of bombs, as the whole carrier attack bomber force that the Navy could have in position in the event of war." The JCS allocation of high-yield weapons, Twining's staff noted, was the proof of the pudding: "CINCSAC—93%, CINCLANT and CINCPAC together—only 7%." This same ratio was established for the next two years. And this made sense, even to CNO Adm. Arleigh Burke, who confirmed that the navy targeted "threats which threaten[ed] Navy control of the sea." Those targets included "submarine pens, bases, and airfields from which planes are launched to threaten control of the sea."

If the navy could contribute to the destruction of airfields that could threaten SAC operations, fine; the air force would "never reject such assistance." But the air force wanted "firm, positive plans backed by definite commitments of forces": "This is not just a matter of making forces potentially available. . . . Every one of those targets that have been selected by the Joint Chiefs of Staff must be on the 'destroy list' of a proven crew, fully trained and instantly ready to man their aircraft to perform their assigned mission." The lack of predictability because of the main strength of the aircraft carrier, its mobility, made it less useful to SAC operations.

Both services explored Far East coordination issues well into 1956. The seemingly simple matter of time-control measures emerged as a challenge. CINCPAC, communicating with CINCSAC and CINCFE, wanted to confirm the relationships between the various air force terms. Execution Time, or E-Time, was the launch time for nuclear forces. The terms "Strategic Warning" and "Tactical Warning" were in vogue: Strategic Warning was twenty-four hours' warning, while Tactical Warning was just fifteen minutes. CINCPAC's view: "It is essential that with Tactical Warning there be mutual agreement on a common zero hour for all preparatory action and movement beyond that which is routine in existing peace situation, and with Strategic Warning that there be clear agreement on earliest takeoff time." The JCS should select the time: "Actual war would perhaps result in varying warning times for various forces, consider actual initiation of war subject [to] many possible variations that only acceptable alternative . . . is to assume that time and degrees of tactical warning is the same world-wide."[120]

By the fall of 1956 CINCPAC, CINCFE, and SAC had hammered out a complex solution. There were three plans. The first two were based on Strategic Warning, and the third was based on Tactical Warning. There were "minor conflicts involving the safe separation of [times on targets] and/or [redacted]." That is, SAC did not want to be flying through a mushroom cloud generated by a navy plane attacking an adjacent target. These issues "were resolved to the mutual satisfaction of Commanders concerned." When all three commanders unveiled their plans, it turned out the secondary issues were on how to deconflict electronic countermeasures and the recovery of strike aircraft. The primary issues remain redacted but likely related to duplication of targeting.[121]

Following on to this was the establishment in early 1957 of a Joint Coordination Center similar to the one in Europe. SAC wanted it in Guam, while CINCPAC wanted it in Hawaii at their bunker at Kunia. SAC X-Ray had been moved to Kunia anyway, so the Joint Coordination Center was established in this underground facility. It acted in essentially the same fashion as its counterpart in Europe.[122]

The relationship between SAC and the NATO theater of operations coalesced from its fitful start in the early 1950s but entered a tumultuous period when the prioritization of targets was hotly debated. At the same time, the ability of the Soviet Union to mount a preemptive strike (be it conventional or nuclear) against SAC's forward-based forces increased, leading to the diversion of SAC resources against targets in Eastern Europe while at the same time the command remained focused on target coverage in the Soviet Union vis-à-vis the bomber threat to North America. The emergent U.S. Navy nuclear capability played a larger role in the European effort leading to greater need for coordination. At the same time, SAC and the rest of the U.S. Air Force was confronted with a completely different planning problem in the Far East. The requirement to deal with Communist China as a separate problem injected flexibility into SAC operations, something that has remained obscured historically. The problems of the forward-based nuclear forces and their relationship to the main Emergency War Plan continued into the mid- to late 1950s as SAC solidified its approach against the Soviet Union.

1. (*Left to right*) Gens. Lauris Norstad, Curtis LeMay, and Thomas Power were three of the most influential U.S. Air Force leaders involved with nuclear strategy development from the 1940s well into the 1960s. All were highly suspicious of the intentions of the Communist world prior to the formal inauguration of the Cold War, based on personal experiences. This picture, taken on the morning of 10 March 1945, shows Power's return from leading the air raid that destroyed Tokyo. Norstad and LeMay were on hand for an immediate debrief. The effects of the visitation of air power against Imperial Japan motivated them to ensure the same thing did not happen to the United States. Thomas S. Power Papers, Special Collections Research Center, Syracuse University Libraries.

2. The Boeing B-47 was Strategic Air Command's workhorse throughout the 1950s and into the 1960s. The design, of which nearly 1,200 were built, predated the existence of thermonuclear weapons and was subject to continuous modification during service. Ultimately it was capable of delivering the largest-yield weapon in the American arsenal of the day, the 19-megaton Mk-36. By the mid-1950s B-47s and their nuclear payloads were stationed at forward bases in the United Kingdom, Spain, Morocco, Alaska, and Guam. With aerial refueling, continental U.S.–based B-47s would strike targets throughout the Soviet Union after the first wave had gone in. Courtesy of U.S. Air Force.

3. To ensure target coverage of the Soviet Union and thus establish credible deterrence, continental U.S.–based B-47 wings required tanker bases in Canada. These low-profile bases—Namao and Cold Lake, Alberta; Churchill, Manitoba; and Frobisher Bay, Northwest Territories—housed KC-97 tankers and "mole hole" alert facilities. As the international situation changed, the number of KC-97s at each base could be increased. Infrastructure also existed so that nuclear weapons could be moved forward to some of these bases from the United States so recovering B-47s could conduct restrike operations. Courtesy of Canadian Department of National Defence.

SECRET

FOR OFFICIAL USE ONLY

CARIBOU AIR FORCE STATION

LIMESTONE, MAINE

4. & 5. Our impressions of nuclear weapons are generally formed by the availability of instantly ready weapons like ICBMs. In the early to mid-1950s, however, technical and legal constraints placed on releasing nuclear weapons were considerable. The special nuclear material, the cores (fig. 4), belonged to the Atomic Energy Commission and not the U.S. Air Force. These were stored singly in "birdcages" and only released by AEC custodians who were stationed at a handful of operational and national stockpile sites, such as Maine's North River Depot (also known as Site Easy and later designated Caribou Air Force Station; fig. 5). Once released the cores were inserted into the bomb casings by U.S. Air Force bomber crews while they were on the way to their targets. Photos by the author.

R. R. TRANSLOADING YARD

SUI–FEN–HO, CHINA

44° 24' N–131° 09' E

SCALE 1:9,100

DATE OF PHOTOGRAPHY

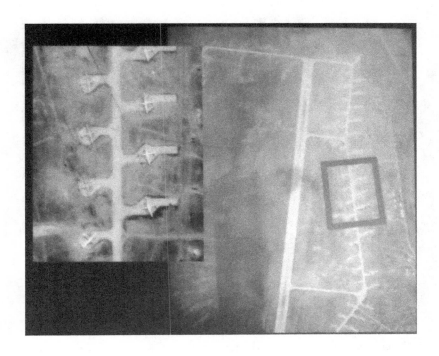

6. & 7. The traditional belief that there was little or no aerial photography of crucial targets in Communist countries prior to the advent of U-2 operations in 1956 is erroneous. The material collected during SENSINT flights, which were conducted with presidential and (when appropriate) prime ministerial approval, developed substantial targeting data. Figure 6, taken by a deep-penetration flight of Sui-Fen-Ho on the Soviet-Chinese border, was used to determine how dependent Communist China was on Soviet aviation gasoline (100 percent), with obvious targeting implications in the event of war. Figure 7 shows Spassk-Dalniy Airfield in the Soviet Union, a base housing TU-4 bombers. The photos were taken in 1955 and 1954, respectively. Courtesy of National Museum of the U.S. Air Force and CIA.

8. The Castle nuclear test series held in March–April 1954 was designed to determine which path should be taken for the development of a deliverable thermonuclear bomb. Though the gargantuan 15-megaton Castle Bravo shot and its aftereffects took center stage, the Union shot's "Alarm Clock" device became the basis for what appears to have been the first stockpiled "dry" thermonuclear weapon, the Mk-14. Seen here loaded onto a B-36 bomber, the Mk-14 was an Emergency Capability weapon that was superseded by three other designs in a matter of months. Courtesy of U.S. Department of Energy.

9. (*oppostie top*) Equipped with F-86H Sabres, the 417th Fighter-Bomber Squadron, led by Lt. Col. Chuck Yeager (*second from left*), was scheduled to destroy the air defense system in southern East Germany with Mk-12 Brok weapons yielding 12 to 14 kilotons each. Once this corridor was open, SAC B-47s based in the United Kingdom were to exploit the gap and destroy any Soviet or Bloc air base housing nuclear-capable IL-28 Beagle bombers. Succeeding waves of B-47s would also use the gap to destroy the Polish railroad system to disrupt Soviet reinforcement and resupply. Courtesy of U.S. Air Force.

10. (*oppostie bottom*) Tactical Air Command's Matador cruise missiles played an important role in supporting Strategic Air Command operations in Europe and the Far East. Optimized for airfield destruction, they could inflict damage on the opposition's air defense system prior to the arrival of SAC's bombers. As their ground-launched cruise missile descendants would later, some Matador deployments were employed to reassure allies as much as to deter adversaries. Courtesy of U.S. Air Force.

11. The Soviet R-5M ballistic missile, known to NATO as the SS-3 Shyster. On 2 February 1956 the Soviet Union conducted Operation Baikal, the successful launch and detonation of an R-5M equipped with a nuclear warhead. By 1959 R-5MS equipped with 300-kiloton warheads were secretly deployed to six sites covering bases in Turkey, Italy, and West Germany. A portable missile system, the R-5MS could hit SAC bases in Spain and the United Kingdom if redeployed westward to presurveyed sites in Warsaw Pact countries. The United States would not launch and detonate a ballistic missile equipped with a nuclear weapon until 1958 and would not deploy such a system before 1960. Author's collection.

12. (*opposite top*) The Soviets' ubiquitous TU-16 Badger was classed as a medium bomber by the Western intelligence agencies and as such casually dismissed as a threat to North America. In reality, some versions were aerial-refuelable and by the late 1950s could carry air-launched missiles equipped with nuclear weapons. Tests conducted in the mid-1950s confirmed that TU-16s could operate from unimproved runways and from ice floes, the latter confirmed by RCAF overflights of Soviet drift ice stations in 1958. This in part forced SAC to examine every possible airfield in the Soviet Union that could be used as a TU-16 operating location, as they threatened SAC's advanced bases. Photo by the author.

13. (*opposite bottom*) Gen. Nathan Twining, chairman of the Joint Chiefs of Staff, flanked by Air Marshal Roy Slemon of the Royal Canadian Air Force and Lauris Norstad, then Supreme Allied Commander Europe. The highly experienced and effective Twining shepherded the U.S. Air Force through a period of unprecedented technological, strategic, and political change. In 1953 he asserted, "In my opinion SAC's deterrent influence on USSR aggressive intentions can only be maintained by an effective force in being, properly manned, equipped, and trained, at the proper time period, and whose combat capability is universally recognized and unquestioned." He held to this philosophy throughout his tenure. In 1955 Twining and Power visited the Soviet Union, and after interacting with senior Soviet leaders, both redoubled their efforts to present the strongest possible deterrent posture. Courtesy of Canadian Department of National Defence.

14. Gen. Thomas Dresser White, chief of staff of the U.S. Air Force in the late 1950s. A low-key officer who had substantial experience living and working inside the Soviet Union and China in the 1930s, he was loath to accept "alternative undertakings" deliberately targeting the Soviet population and instead pushed for preemptive strategies that would limit damage to the United States and its allies: "There is mention of possible U.S. initiative in primary war. Dangerous as that issue is, because of the preventive war anathema, it is properly raised at some point as long as we make it clear that U.S. initiative and preventive war are not synonymous." Courtesy of U.S. Air Force.

15. The Mk-15 thermonuclear bomb, seen here in a maintenance bay in 1956 with its tritium boost system being carefully monitored. Based on the Zombie device detonated during Shot Nectar in the 1954 Castle series, the 3.8-megaton-yield Mk-15 was the most numerous nuclear weapon in the American strategic arsenal, with 1,200 units. A modification of the Mk-15, the Mk-39 mod 2, known as the Big Tail, was an advanced laydown weapon scheduled to be used for low-level delivery against Soviet targets. Seven hundred Mk-39s of all models were built.
Courtesy of U.S. Air Force.

16. The Mk-36 was a modification the Mk-21 bomb, which in turn was based on the Shrimp device detonated as the Castle Bravo shot in 1954. When it inadvertently exceeded its estimated yield by almost three times (6 to 15 megatons), weapons designers learned that the yield of such weapons could be dramatically scaled upward. Modified Mk-21s, called the Mk-36Y1 mod 1, yielded 18 megatons, while the purpose-built Mk-36 mod 0, code-named Last Resort, yielded 19 megatons. Around 940 of both weapons types were built. Photo by the author.

17. Commander of the Pacific Air Forces Gen. Laurence Kuter (*left*), seen here with LeMay, who was visiting Nationalist China as a signal by Eisenhower to Mao during the 1958 Taiwan Straits crisis, was confronted with unique targeting challenges: "Population as such does not appear to be a profitable target system in this area, with 650,000,000 people in China and with the Soviet Far East offering the other extreme of a very low population density representing only a small fraction of the population of the Soviet Union. Nevertheless, there are a few population centers of extreme importance. From these centers stems the immediate direction of the Communist war effort." Courtesy of U.S. Air Force.

18. The guided missile submarine USS *Grayback* and her confreres cross-targeted Soviet bomber bases in the Far East with Regulus cruise missiles carrying W27 warheads that yielded nearly 2 megatons each. Regulus missiles were secretly stored on remote Pacific island bases so that cruise missile submarines could reload, go back in, and strike targets that had been missed in the first waves of the Emergency War Plan. Courtesy of U.S. Navy.

7

Increasing the Deterrent Margin

Strategic Air Command and the Soviet Union, 1956–58

The objective of our national defense policy is deterrence. In the public
mind—both ours and the Soviets'—deterrence is rooted in fear of
nuclear devastation of population centers. However, in the professional
military mind—again both ours and the Soviets'—deterrence is
measured in terms of ability to destroy the enemy's means of long range
delivery of nuclear weapons. This ability—the deterrent margin—is
determined by that margin of combat-ready capability which one side
holds over the other. It cannot be precisely measured. However, unless
our forces are clearly capable of *winning* under operational handicaps of
bad weather and no more than tactical warning, and despite any action
the enemy may take against them, our forces are not a genuine deterrent.
By "*Winning*" is meant achieving a condition wherein the enemy
cannot impose his will on us, but we can impose our will on him.

—GEN. CURTIS LEMAY, Top Secret briefing to the USAF
Scientific Advisory Board, 21 May 1957

The 1956–60 period was marked by dramatic technological and
political changes that had revolutionary impacts on nuclear
targeting. The period started with a new concept, the Air Battle Target System, championed by Curtis LeMay and facilitated by
new information coming in from the U-2 overflights. This shift was
the final move away from the "World War II with nuclear weapons"
strategic concepts that characterized the late 1940s and early 1950s.
Alongside this shift were increased SAC efforts to mount effective

penetration of an ever-changing Soviet air defense system. While SAC was in the process of shifting to and implementing this concept, the Sputnik panic took hold in 1957. This marked yet another shift that had numerous spin-off effects in multiple areas that challenged the American and thus allied deterrent posture. First, the threat changed the tempo of nuclear war from hours to minutes. Second, ballistic missiles were introduced into the American force structure, both in the air force and the navy, a change that had both short-term and long-term effects. Third was the discovery of the effects of high-altitude nuclear detonations uncovered during the Hardtack nuclear test series in 1958. This in turn led to the opening up of space as a theater of operations that had the potential to fundamentally affect SAC operations. Consequently, by 1958 the Air Battle Target System had to be reconciled with these potential and actual changes. By 1959 the whole concept of American nuclear targeting and its coordination itself had to be reassessed, which led directly to the creation of the first SIOP in 1960. At the same time, forward-deployed forces in Europe and the Far East had to adjust to all of these changes and increase their coordination with SAC operations.

To comprehend these multiple, overlapping, and potentially confusing concurrent factors, it is necessary to break them down into digestible sections. Chapter 7 will examine SAC and its evolution up to the Sputnik challenge. Chapter 8 will explore the technological and political changes brought about by these and other challenges from 1957 to 1960 that eventually had a direct bearing on the EWP and its implementation. Chapter 9 looks at the Basic War Plan itself as it evolved from the EWP.

The JCS and Strategy to 1959

The evolution away from named global war plans was completed well before 1956, but in 1957–60 the new system stagnated. The original idea of a family of plans to include a Joint Long-Range Strategic Estimate (four to eight years out), a Joint Strategic Objectives Plan (three years out), and a Joint Strategic Capabilities Plan (next fiscal year) could no longer withstand the weight of technological change. There were efforts to improve the Joint Strategic Objectives

Plan, but only the Joint Strategic Capabilities Plan (JSCP) had any relevance for this period.[1] JCS thinking on how a war might be conducted was situated in the context of the Eisenhower administration's annual reaffirmation of the Basic National Security Policy, to whit: "Our efforts should be directed to: a. Deterring further communist aggression, and preventing the occurrence of total war so far as compatible with U.S. security. . . . This stress on deterrence is dictated by the disastrous character of total nuclear war. . . . The Communist rulers must be convinced that aggression will not serve their interests: that it will not pay. . . . Nuclear weapons will be used in a general war as authorized by the President. Such authorization as may be given in advance will be determined by the president."[2]

Throughout this period, however, there was back-and-forthing in the annual policy statement over the role of nuclear weapons in limited wars, an argument that grew increasingly esoteric and one which the practitioners looked at with bafflement if not skepticism. That said, the JSCP was a direct reflection of NATO strategic concept MC 48 from 1954 and its successors MC 14/2 and MC 14/2 (revised) in 1956–57.[3] The purpose was to deter, and if deterrence failed, to conduct a credible forward defense. If there were a general war, it would be characterized by two phases, the first in which nuclear weapons were employed, lasting up to thirty days where strategic advantage would be obtained. The second would be a period of undetermined duration with a "period of readjustment" and follow-up leading to a cessation of hostilities. The projected length of the first phase got shorter every time the strategic concept was revisited, perhaps proportional to the increasing yields of nuclear weapons at this time. But the underlying purpose—deterrence—remained constant.[4] That said, the JSCP promised, "Offensive opportunities created by the initial exchange [of nuclear weapons] will be exploited."[5]

The evolution of the JSCP appears to have had very little impact on SAC and its planning despite the fact that the JSCP "became the arena for arguing again about whether to retain existing definitions of cold, limited, and general war," and therefore the proportion of resources that should be applied to each.[6] Arguably the 15 March 1956 statement of Basic National Security Policy had greater impact on SAC. That document stated, "The United States is now capable of inflicting massive nuclear damage on the USSR, and will acquire by about mid-1956 the capability to mount a decisive nuclear strike against the USSR." And "decisive" had a specific definition: "For the purpose of this estimate, 'decisive' means damage such that either (1) the ability to strike back is essentially eliminated or (2) civil, political, and cultural life is reduced to a condition of chaos." Another definition was carefully written into the policy: "'Crippling' is used to indicate a degree of destruction, disruption and loss of life that, while not decisive, would raise serious questions as to the ability of the United States to recover and regain its status as a great industrial nation for a considerable period of years."[7]

SAC was supposed to deter, and if deterrence failed, to provide the United States with strategic advantage even after a crippling attack directed against it. However it appeared that SAC had to be capable of carrying out two separate but overlapping tasks, within the constraints of not conducting preventive war. What was a SAC war plan supposed to look like under these conditions? And how was it to be carried out?

Toward a New Targeting Policy:
The Air Power Battle Target System

LeMay and his staff at SAC ascertained in mid-1955 that the strategic balance was shifting under their feet. Over the course of the next year LeMay attempted to influence the president and the JCS into accepting a new SAC employment concept. This campaign started with LeMay proselytizing Nathan Twining in March 1955 after the annual commanders' conference. Reiterating that the U.S. Air Force leadership agreed with "the establishment and maintenance of an intercontinental force as the first priority task" and that "emphasis [should] be primarily placed on the offensive force," it was accepted that "the first requirement [was] to win the battle against Soviet Air Power." "A force capable of winning this air battle would also be capable of performing any other tasks required of it after the air battle had been won; whereas the development of a force based upon the achievement of specialized tasks would not, on the other hand, be of optimum composition to win the air battle." Here LeMay laid the groundwork for the eventual alteration of SAC as well as Tactical Air Command's missions and structure. These seeds bore fruit in the late 1950s.[8]

By the time he briefed Eisenhower and the Joint Chiefs at Quantico in June 1955, LeMay was primarily concerned about a Soviet surprise attack that meant bombers evacuated from SAC bases would be able to deliver only a reduced response against Soviet targets: "This retaliatory effort by the strategic force might be decisive; however by giving the Soviets the initiative it is probable that the outcome of the war would not be favorable to the United States."[9] He listed SAC's "principal limitations" at this time: "Liability to attack on the ground through insufficient alert time; delay in obtaining release to us at the alert time of the weapons not under our custodial responsibilities; [and] lack of advanced North American continental bases for air refueling operations."[10] It is important to understand, in light of the concurrent and historical debate over the veracity of the Bomber Gap, that LeMay's concerns were geared toward forward-based SAC forces, not just SAC bases in North America. Recall that the SAC Emergency War Plan had multiple wings of B-47s operating from bases in the United Kingdom, Spain, North Africa, and in the Pacific.

The Bomber Gap controversy began in 1956, nearly a year after LeMay worked on the Air Power Battle Target System, so it is highly unlikely that the relatively esoteric debate over the exact production numbers of Soviet Mya-4 Bison bombers played a role in influencing SAC's new targeting concepts and plans to any great degree. LeMay, Twining, Radford, and Allen Dulles, director of the CIA, all dutifully went before a subcommittee chaired by former secretary of the air force Stuart Symington, a Democrat taking on the Republican Eisenhower administration in the run-up to the 1957 fiscal year budget.[11] With the Symington subcommittee's excessive emphasis on the numbers of a single aircraft type, the focus on the present and not the possibilities of the future, its employment of outrage and exaggeration for public effect, and its understandably American-centric approach, this public expression of the Bomber Gap amounted to political theater and was completely misleading vis-à-vis the realities of what was really happening when it came to Soviet capability. Memoirs asserting that the CIA flew a U-2 over the Soviet Union in 1956, took a few pictures, and then everybody agreed that there was no Bomber Gap because a handful of Mya-4 Bisons were spotted contribute to a distorted historical understanding of the situation confronting SAC in 1956.[12]

There were, in fact, two Bomber Gaps, but the details of one of them were not discussed in the hearings. The first was the potential gap between the number of Mya-4 Bisons and B-52 Stratofortresses. At the time LeMay testified to the committee that there were more Bisons estimated to be available in early 1956 than there were B-52s. This was not intentionally misleading, as some allege.[13] Full-scale production of the Mya-4 started in 1954, and according to a Russian source, "the Mya-4 achieved initial operating capability . . . when the B-52 was still undergoing trials."[14] It was the extrapolation of an estimated production schedule to the 1960s that was incorrect, and there was, of course, no way that the American intelligence apparatus could have predicted the abrupt Khrushchev-inspired shift away from bombers toward intermediate-range ballistic missiles and intercontinental ballistic missiles, which essentially shut down further Mya-4 production by the late 1950s.

The second Bomber Gap included the IL-28 Beagle light nuclear bombers, as discussed in previous chapters; the 63 TU-4A Bulls still in service; and the TU-16 Badger medium bombers. The TU-16 was built in substantial numbers. For our purposes, however, there were 700 TU-16s of all types available by 1956. In 1957 there were 1,144 TU-16s, of which 224 were capable of in-flight refueling; 263 could carry standoff missiles, of which 44 were capable of inflight refueling. Of these aircraft 453 were TU-16A or atomic bomb carriers; the first of these were deployed in November 1953. The standoff missile carrier, the TU-16k-16 carrying a KSR-2 missile with a 1-megaton-yield warhead, started to deploy in 1957.[15]

The classification of the TU-16 as a medium bomber by CIA analysts simply because of its range is, in retrospect, narrow and indicative of a constrained imagination. Not so with the Soviets. The TU-16 could be used from unpaved runways and was successfully tested in

INCREASING THE DETERRENT MARGIN

this capacity in 1955 or 1956. Later, "operations from sparsely-equipped auxiliary airfields in the tundra and on Arctic ice were made on a regular bases," according to a Russian history of the aircraft.[16] In 1958 Royal Canadian Air Force Lancaster AR aircraft conducting surveillance operation Apex Rocket discovered a damaged TU-16 on an ice runway at Soviet drift ice station NP-6.[17] The implication is that the Soviet TU-16 force could be used creatively in a conflict in ways that CIA analysts did not anticipate. And 264 aircraft of the TU-16 force had the equipment for in-flight refueling in 1957. Again, past assertions that the Soviet bomber force was not relevant in the 1950s because it was not an intercontinental force like one envisioned by American analysts and historians should be discarded.

In terms of Soviet nuclear bombs, the American and allied intelligence apparatus was able to use a variety of methods to detect Soviet nuclear weapons tests. The AFOAT-1 organization (Air Force Office of Atomic Energy) used aerial sampling and seismic detection in combination; this was an allied effort that included specially modified U.S. Air Force U-2s and Royal Canadian Air Force Lancaster ARS and CF-100s. Seismic detection stations at Flin Flon, Manitoba, and Yellowknife, Northwest Territories, among others around the world, cued the "bug flights." Analysis of atmospheric bomb debris left a "finger print" of the materials that went into the design.[18]

AFOAT-1 would have determined that during the period after the first test of a Soviet two-stage thermonuclear weapon on 22 November 1955, the Soviet effort seemed to have plateaued throughout 1956 and early 1957. There were four thermonuclear detonations (in addition to numerous smaller kiloton-yield tests), but none of them exceeded 1 megaton: there were two 900-kiloton tests, a 650-kiloton test, and a 320-kiloton test. It would have been difficult for AFOAT-1 analysts to determine whether or not these tests were derated weapons that in combat service would have a much greater yield. The Soviet designers hit their stride by late 1957 with a 520-kiloton thermonuclear test, followed by two more at 1.6 and 2.9 megatons.[19]

LeMay wanted SAC sorties to "be directed against Soviet air power targets." "The air battle must be won first," he insisted, "and as quickly and decisively as possible." He wanted a better and more responsive alert system, one that "hasten[ed] the decision in the air battle which minimized damage at home" and would provide "maximum immunity for the SAC forces by confusing, saturating, and diluting the enemy defense." If that were possible, then "the force [could] be preserved to continue its air battle, retardation, and enemy war potential objectives." This clearly thrust what used to be called the Blunting target set ahead of Retardation and Destruction, though it appears this terminology was abandoned by 1955. LeMay predicted, also in 1955, "The USSR . . . will continue to develop its war-making industry and war-waging facilities thereby increasing the target system with which we must concern ourselves." Obliquely referencing SENSINT flights, he noted, "Obviously our past intelligence estimates have erred on the low side, as demonstrated by recent fly-overs."[20] Again, LeMay's concerns were clearly about aircraft other than the Mya-4 Bison.

Concerns over the vulnerability of SAC's forward-deployed forces and tanker bases were echoed by LeMay's subordinate commanders (especially Maj. Gen. Frank Armstrong, commanding the Second Air Force) throughout 1955, which accelerated LeMay and his staff's attempts to articulate a solution.[21] LeMay's response indicates that he dropped everything to reexamine these issues. In his evolving view, he firmly established the objective: "I consider victory in the air battle will determine the decision in any future war. All offensive air power must be effectively employed against the air battle objectives to win this victory as quickly and decisively as possible." Most important was this point: "I am concerned about the low level of the theatres' offensive air force potential for contributing to our major tasks of destroying the enemy capability to deliver high yield weapons against the United States *and her allies*. The forces in the advanced areas are also extremely vulnerable to Soviet attack. I consider SAC as a backup force for the limited theatre capability with the probability that SAC will conduct a great majority of the active operations in winning the air battle."[22]

While SAC remained dependent on the B-47 bomber and the KC-97 tanker, forward bases remained of serious concern: "North African bases will be especially vulnerable to attack if ninety B-47s are permanently stationed there."[23] The only real solution at this time appeared to have B-52s and KC-135s operate from bases in the United States, but these aircraft would not be available in quantity for some time.

Between mid-1955 and early 1956, LeMay continued to chip away at getting the "air power battle" accepted not only by the U.S. Air Force but also by the JCS. The U.S. Air Force process produced unsatisfactory (at least to LeMay) force structure proposals. These compromise documents attempted to appease all and, again in LeMay's view, obscure what was really important. In his correspondence with Twining in early 1956, LeMay argued that any force structure policy had to accept the following propositions:

> The paramount aim expressed in the National Security Policy is to deter war, and to prevail should war eventuate. The prime objective of the Air Force must then be to develop and maintain a force structure which will act as a deterrent to war and which will win the air power battle in event of war. . . . Strategic Air Forces provide the greatest single deterrent to war. As such, they hold the key to the security of the Nation. Should the requirements for these forces be compromised in favor of less effective forces, then it follows that the security of the Nation is also compromised.[24]

He believed the ongoing emphasis on theater forces "squander[ed] . . . limited resources on weapons systems that ha[d] very limited capability against air power targets threatening the United States."[25] In effect LeMay was arguing that, unless they could contribute to the destruction of air power targets related to enemy systems that threatened SAC, theater forces were not useful given present budgetary limitations.

LeMay had better luck within the JCS. Twining accepted what LeMay had to say and by early March 1956 was able to convince the other members to endorse the new approach. (Radford needed no convincing.) The new JCS language was "to destroy, as a matter of first priority, the Soviet capability to launch weapons of mass destruction against areas or forces vital to the United States and allied war effort."[26] In a message from the JCS titled "Operational Planning for the Defeat of Communist Air Power in General War," all unified and specified commands were informed that, within the context of the JSCP, "the JCS consider[ed] that the global threat of Communist air capabilities together with the effects of atomic weapons require[d] coordination of the operations of several commanders involved." The commanders were instructed to send representatives to SAC HQ in May 1956 to "develop a modus operandi for the detailed pre-D-Day coordination of the initial offensive operations of all JCS commands against Communist air power." The commanders were to sort out the "timing and weight of the initial effort (QUICK STRIKE capability)" and penetration and withdrawal routes and timing of attacks to avoid or minimize fly-through of atomic clouds and minimize hostile anti-aircraft fire and interception. "Prestrike and poststrike use of our world-wide network of air base facilities preclude saturation or over-concentration of United States forces." The same went for electronic countermeasures. Intelligence was to be shared and coordinated. And there were many other "housekeeping" matters. LeMay was instructed to "prepare and submit to the JCS a summary of the coordination procedures."[27]

The conference was convened in early June, and LeMay was able to get the "modus operandi" for "coordinating the detailed war plans of the various JCS commanders." This included assumptions and definitions. The agreed date on which the hypothetical future war would start was 3 October 1956, which gave everybody several months to carry out their tasks. However, there was no agreement when the coordination would take place. There were three positions: SAC, Commander in Chief Northeast Command, and Commander in Chief Alaska Command "believed that the global and dynamic nature of the air power battle [was] such as to require a simultaneous analysis at a central location of all the JCS commands' plans for the total defeat of Soviet air power." The CINCFE, CINCEUR, and USAFE commanders predictably disagreed: they wanted to have theater coordination first, then global coordination at a central location later. Then there were the U.S. Navy–dominated commands: CINCLANT, CINCPAC, and CINCNELM. They wanted coordination done "at staff level within areas of local theatre interest and much in the same manner as present target coordination [was] accomplished." LeMay asked the various representatives whether this was "personal opinion or whether it reflected guidance they had received from their commanders." CINCPAC, CINCEUR, and CINCLANT representatives told him it came from their bosses. It was clear to LeMay that there would be no movement on the issue and he "had no alternative but to terminate the conference."[28]

The Radford-led JCS was not fazed by this disagreement and approved SAC's new target annex, which reflected LeMay's air battle targeting concepts on 3 July 1956.[29] The JCS then modified its position: CINCEUR, CINCLANT, CINCNELM, and CINCSAC would "effect appropriate coordination." The commanders in chief of Far East, Pacific Command, Alaska Command, and Strategic Air Command would do the same for their areas. When all coordination was complete, a worldwide coordination conference would be held in Washington, not at SAC HQ, and it would be chaired by the JCS.[30] The Far East and Pacific crew had their coordination sorted by the end of September 1956: CINCSAC, CINCFE, and CINCPAC each produced three coordinated plans: two for strategic warning and one for tactical warning.[31] At the end of 1956 SAC reported, "In addition to the development of coordinated target lists, the coordination conferences resulted in the acceptance by all JCS commanders of the primary importance of winning the Air Power Battle."[32] This was debatable, but it was at the very least politically consumable. By May 1957 the Air Power Battle Target System consisted, according to LeMay, "of 1539 Desired Ground Zeroes of which 954 require[d] immediate attack in order to minimize the enemy's capability for initial strike," leaving 585 DGZs for other strikes related to the System.[33]

Reducing the Unknowns: The Advent of the U-2

The growth in the target list is directly attributable to CIA's deployment of the Lockheed U-2 reconnaissance aircraft in mid-1956. That said, the CIA view on the impact of the U-2 predominates in the historical literature and has been transmitted uncritically by aviation aficionados in the technical histories published subsequently. CIA memoirs denigrate the U.S. Air Force, SAC, and in particular

LeMay in a spirit of personal animosity framed against the background of intense interagency competition. Indeed the dominant pro-CIA view is that of the National Photographic Interpretation Center's leading personality who was permitted to write about the U-2 and NPIC.[34]

It is important to note, however, that although the U-2 eventually provided SAC's targeteers with overwhelming amounts of data, it initially supplemented data collected by the earlier SENSINT flights and other sources. (For example, the 303rd Bomb Wing exercised the capability in 1956 to "bomb a northern airfield during winter using target material based on 15–17 year old photography.")[35] Those who labored in obscurity in SAC's Reconnaissance Technical Squadrons prior to the creation of NPIC and those who flew SENSINT missions without getting shot down did not write about their experiences to any great extent; thus the SAC Reconnaissance Technical Squadrons output when compared to NPIC remains equally obscure. The CIA and its NPIC remained for many years unaware of the details of the SENSINT flights until the decision was made to exchange data between the organizations and eliminate the SENSINT compartment. Even a leading NPIC personality stated in his 2010 memoir that that he did not have complete access to the SENSINT information in the 1950s, nor did he know when or where the flights occurred. Processed intelligence was provided by SAC to CIA, something that obviously galled certain CIA personalities who clearly believed themselves to be intellectually superior to military personnel.[36]

The reality was that the U-2 program was supported by the U.S. Air Force as well as by SAC. The air force also received U-2 aircraft of its own, thirty machines for the 4080th Reconnaissance Wing (Light) in 1957. These were also used against Soviet targets.[37] LeMay, his deputy Maj. Gen. Francis "Butch" Griswold, and SAC's four operations, plans, and intelligence generals were actually "witting" of the CIA's Project Aquatone prior to September 1955, so the U-2 project and its capabilities were no surprise to them.[38] Recall that back in 1949 LeMay suggested that CIA create an intelligence "Manhattan Project" for aerial intelligence collection. He remained silent about

SAC reconnaissance operations in his public speaking and his writings. One could make the argument that his over-the-top bellicosity over who controlled aerial reconnaissance was designed to distract CIA from what SAC was up to by keeping those same CIA personalities off-base about SENSINT. In the same vein, is it reasonable to suggest that the commanding general of SAC should *not* have been upset with a civilian agency attempting to seize total control of aerial photographic intelligence gathering?

SAC's Reconnaissance Technical Squadrons played a significant role in converting U-2 photography into usable targeting information. In SAC's case, Eastman Kodak, the CIA contractor in Rochester, New York, provided a duplicate positive of the "take" to the 544th Reconnaissance Technical Squadron at Offutt AFB. This unit of eight hundred men then made four identical negatives of the original film roll. One set stayed at SAC HQ, while the other three were sent to the 8th RTS (Westover AFB), the 2nd RTS (Barksdale AFB), and the 3921st RTS (West Drayton, United Kingdom). These data, code-named Talent, were used by those organizations in the "preparation of dossiers on SAC targets for delivery of atomic weapons." The results were made available to all three SAC numbered air forces, the 7th Air Division in the United Kingdom, plus SAC headquarters.[39]

The CIA had different uses for the imagery, specifically the generation of national intelligence estimates and other materials that contributed to the formulation of national security policy under the Eisenhower administration. The CIA officers working with SAC, however, determined that Talent information interpreted by SAC's RTS personnel had "the effect of altering the priority upward and downward of SAC targets, added some, eliminated some." A CIA interlocuter also noted, "The effect on chart making has not only been substantial but could in a live situation be critical because of changes in certain instances at considerable variances to the past available charts." Another report found that Talent data interpreted by SAC doubled the number of known new Soviet radar installations from 106 to 236.[40] Lt. Gen. Lloyd Leavitt, who flew U-2s in the 1950s and later was deputy SAC commander, wrote in his memoirs that the U-2's importance did not lie in the mire of the "bomber gap" and "missile gap" debates but rather in the "extensive intelligence" collected on the Soviet Bloc air defense system, followed by "the exact location of key industrial targets, transportation facilities, power plants, military bases, seaports, and command centers."[41] Talent sharpened, clarified, and expanded, but the earlier data, going all the way back to Wringer and information from allies and other agencies, such as the NSA, were still used to determine where the U-2s should look.

The Doomsday Armada, 1956–58

In 1956–57 SAC's main effort was on the B-47 force. In round numbers this came in at twenty-six wings of B-47s, with forty-five aircraft per wing. Most of these were the longer-ranged "E" model. The Medium Bombardment Program essentially stabilized at these numbers, increasing slightly by 1960 to twenty-eight for a total of 1,260 aircraft. In the United States they were divided among the three numbered air forces. There were seven bases in the Southwest, one in the Northwest, nine in the Midwest, eight in the South, and three in the Northeast.[42] This was not optimal, as some bases contained two wings of B-47s, that is, ninety bombers each. Twenty-eight nuclear weapons delivered on target, or twenty-eight sabotage teams spreading caltrops on twenty-eight runways, could destroy or immobilize the bulk of the B-47 force based in the United States.[43] Clearly, after the Sputnik events in 1957, SAC's Pearl Harbor–like crowding became cause for concern. There were even reports in late 1955 to early 1956 that nuclear weapons storage areas were overcrowded because there were so many weapons.[44]

Then there was the Heavy Bombardment Program, which was in significant flux throughout the mid- to late 1950s. The eleven wings of the B-36 force, of which there were seven B-36 and four RB-36 wings in 1955, were combined into ten wings and the RB-36s optimized for bombing in 1956; then three of these wings started conversion to the B-52 that same year. By 1957 there were two B-36 wings in the Northwest, three in the Southwest, one in the Midwest, and one in the South. The number of qualified crews dwindled as the program was progressively phased out in favor of the

B-52, of which there were two wings training during 1956 and one operational by the end of the year.[45] The six SAC Fighter Escort Wings, with their F-84FS and F-84GS, were phased out between 1956 and 1957.[46]

As for overseas deployments, the SAC concept of operations had eleven of its twenty-eight U.S.-based B-47 wings rotate overseas on ninety-day deployments (see map 14). This included the UK base complex of six to seven bases, depending on the year; three bases in Spain; and three in Morocco. (The Far East will be examined in chapter 11.) In 1956 Adana Air Base in Turkey had its status change from a staging base to an operating base for peace and war. The occasional Big Horn deployments brought five B-47s and a pair of KC-97s to the base. Classified exercises involving six C-124 transports suggest that B-47s would have been flown forward from one of the other overseas bases and then loaded up with nuclear weapons brought in by C-124s at a given alert level. In 1957 Adana was redesignated Incirlik Air Base.[47] In addition to all of the existing forward bases, four large civilian airports were designated in the SAC Emergency War Plan as recovery airfields: Bandirma and Ankara Esenboga, Turkey; Rabat-Sale, Morocco; and Barcelona, Spain. SAC Mobile Recovery Teams and Air Material Command "B" teams were scheduled to deploy by KC-97 to these locations fifteen hours after E-Hour.[48]

During the 1950s the U.S. government used both military and civilian aid agencies to construct airfields in several countries capable of handling jet aircraft. Usually this required a ten- to twelve-thousand-foot all-weather runway. These airfields could be used to recover SAC bombers after their strikes deep in the Soviet Union east of the Urals. With the appropriate clearances from host nations (or perhaps not), the reverse was also true, in which case something like Big Horn could have been used to get B-47s even closer to Soviet targets. In Turkey there was Diyarbakir, Eskisehir, and Batman, assisted by the U.S. Army Corps of Engineers. In Pakistan, Mauripur, Sargodha, and Peshawar airfields were expanded in 1958 with Corps of Engineer help. (Peshawar was used to support U-2 operations.) Karachi Airport was expanded using funds

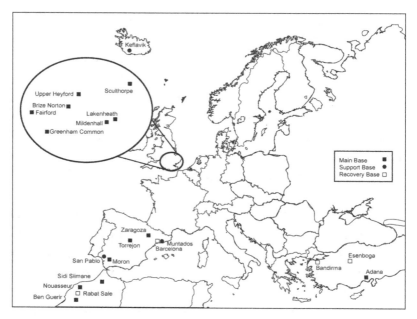

Map 14. SAC overseas base complexes, 1956–58. Courtesy of the author.

from the International Cooperation Administration (a predecessor to the U.S. Agency for International Development). The possibilities in Iran appeared boundless, but progress was slow, in part due to Soviet pressure on the shah. Between 1958 and 1966 Mashhad, Hamadan, and Dezful airports received International Cooperation Administration funding related to civil aviation. Hamadan Airport was renamed Shahrokhi Air Base in 1962, and Mashhad runway was extended again to 14,000 feet in 1965.[49] Certainly American interest in the Baghdad Pact was not purely defensive, nor was American aid totally altruistic. And not to be forgotten was the Kandahar Airport in Afghanistan, also funded by the International Cooperation Administration and under construction in 1958.[50] With these developments SAC interest in Dhahran in Saudi Arabia progressively waned between 1955 and 1958.[51]

Then there were the overseas aerial refueling bases. Each B-47 wing included a KC-97 tanker squadron, colocated with the bombers. By 1956 there were twenty-two KC-97 squadrons, totaling around eight hundred aircraft. The existing staging and refueling base concept during this time involved deploying KC-97 tankers to Lajes, Azores; Thule, Greenland; and Keflavik, Iceland; in addition to Goose Bay, Labrador, and Ernest Harmon in Newfoundland in an emergency. Back in late 1954 LeMay and Maj. Gen. Walter Sweeney brainstormed SAC's future force structure using a thirty-inch-diameter globe and pieces of string to measure B-47 ranges.[52] Sweeney, a LeMay confidant, cut his teeth during the Battle of Midway, where he led B-17 strikes against Japanese ships, and later survived having his B-29 shot down. His introduction to atomic issues was on the Joint War Plans Committee in 1947. He then served as SAC's director of plans before being promoted to command the Fifteenth Air Force.[53]

As the threat to SAC's forward-based forces became more acute, LeMay and Sweeney's deliberations took on greater importance. The main problem, as we have seen, lay in the congestion in the Northeast basing area. Sweeney's analysis was that SAC B-47 wings based west of the Mississippi River could be more readily brought to bear in two ways. The first was to develop bases in Canada for KC-97 tankers. The second was to develop two bases to back up Thule Air Base. In this way, Sweeney argued, he could "re-route units of the 15th Air Force . . . scheduled for strikes against Moscow and Leningrad over the Edmonton-Thule route." Sweeney and LeMay envisioned five routes to carry this out, using some as a "shell game" to confuse the opposition.[54]

This conceptualization was briefed to Twining in January 1955 but was put into abeyance, probably because of the shift to China targeting that dominated events for at least six months. LeMay attempted to get five austere bases in Alaska enlarged so that one KC-97 tanker squadron could be stationed at each in addition to Eielson and Elmendorf, which were deemed to be increasingly vulnerable. There was little enthusiasm for this scheme, probably due to the high cost and harsh climate.[55]

LeMay and Sweeney's 1954 cogitations eventually, after some hard politicking, evolved into facts on the ground starting in 1956. This came in two phases, the first of which is relevant to the 1956–57 period. Bluie West 8 in Greenland, opposite Baffin Island, part

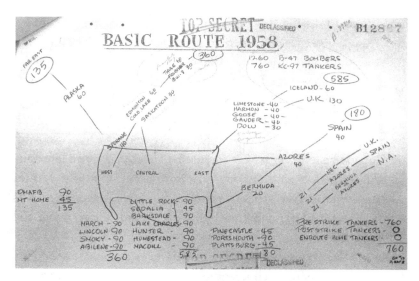

Map 15. Discussions between LeMay and Maj. Gen. Walter Sweeney in 1954 on the future vulnerability of forward bases to Soviet strikes produced the basis for SAC's increased use of aerial tankers to get SAC's B-47 force to targets in the Soviet Union. This vision was implemented, with some modification, by 1958, when Canada agreed to the low-key stationing of tankers at several bases. Courtesy of Library of Congress, LeMay Papers.

of the World War II northeast staging route and already transformed into Sondrestrom Air Base in 1952, was handed over to SAC in 1957 and KC-97s were stationed there on rotation. In 1956 a KC-97 unit, the 303rd Aerial Refueling Squadron, was permanently stationed at Kindley AFB, Bermuda.[56] Thule Air Base, already home to Temporary Duty Assignment KC-97s, had their numbers increased to twenty aircraft rotating in from two squadrons.[57] Similarly Goose Bay and Harmon in Canada and Eielson and Elmendorf in Alaska had their tanker complements increased. Back in the United States, Dow AFB in Maine was transformed in 1955 from a fighter base into a tanker base hosting twenty-two KC-97s from the 4060th Air Refueling Wing.[58] Similarly Malmstrom AFB in Montana received the 4061st Air Refueling Wing.[59] The second part of the plan, however, was delayed until 1958; this was the establishment of four low-profile but high-capacity SAC tanker bases in western and northern Canada.

INCREASING THE DETERRENT MARGIN

It is important to note the existence of the Hairclipper-trained SAC wings at this point. The SA-1 Guild surface-to-air missile system around Moscow led to the development of a variety of technological means to get the bombers through, but these means would not be available for some time. The stop-gap was the introduction of the Low Altitude Bombing System used by F-84 fighter-bombers into select units of the SAC B-47 force. In 1956 SAC designated three wings to develop Hairclipper capabilities, one per numbered air force: the 22nd Bomb Wing (Medium) at March AFB with the Fifteenth Air Force; the 306th at MacDill AFB with the Second Air Force; and the 310th at Schilling and later Forbes AFB with the Eighth Air Force. Experiments recommended a mission profile whereby the B-47 dropped down to 50 to 500 feet, executed the Half Cuban Eight "over the shoulder" toss with the bomb, and accelerated away in the direction the plane approached. The initial LABS system did not employ a drogue retarded bomb, which suggests the Mk-6 and/or a modified Mk-15 were the weapons employed. Hairclipper squadrons were on almost continuous deployment to Nouasseur in Morocco and to Greenham Common in the United Kingdom from 1956 to early 1958.[60]

And then there were the bombs themselves. Up until 1958 the custody, storage, and release of nuclear weapons involved the president, the Atomic Energy Commission, Department of Defense, and the services. This was an evolutionary process. The president authorized "disbursements" from the AEC to the DOD. These weapons and cores initially remained under AEC custody while under DOD control. The dispersement might have an AEC weapon dispersed to Defense under AEC custody but remaining in an AEC National Stockpile Site. It might also mean having an AEC custodian at an Operation Storage Site having custody of the core, but the "shape" was in the custody of the U.S. Air Force. During this period, Eisenhower authorized the transfer of weapons with yields under 600 kilotons along with their cores to overseas storage sites, but he would not permit thermonuclear weapons cores to be deployed. There were other combinations of custody and control, none of them responsive to an imminent threat.[61]

The relationship between the AEC and DOD was known as "split custody." The system required a presidential directive to initiate the Emergency Transfer Plan. This allowed the AEC custodians to insert the cores into the shapes, whether those shapes were under AEC or DOD custody, whether they were in a National Stockpile Site, an Operational Storage Site, or a Special Service Facility (also known as "bombs on base"). Notably, however, Eisenhower did want to speed the process up slightly. In the pre-DEFCON era, the Emergency Transfer Plan could be implemented if a Defense Emergency were declared by any one of the unified or specified commanders. They could also be transferred if Air Defense Readiness Red or Yellow Warning were called by Commander in Chief North American Air Defense. This is an early example of what would be called "pre-delegation." Under these conditions, if LeMay as SAC commander declared a Defense Emergency, the AEC custodians would perform the actions necessary to prepare the bombs for use. This meant inserting the core into the In-Flight Insertion mechanism of the bomb so that when the plane was airborne and the appropriate authentications were received, the crew could activate the IFI mechanism and complete the assembly process. This posed problems for SAC as the shape would have to be unloaded on the ground, the core put in, and the bomb reloaded onto the plane. If SAC wanted to maintain aircraft on alert, a better method or procedure had to be found.[62]

For this period the primary nuclear weapons in SAC's inventory included the Mk-6, Mk-15, Mk-17/24, and the Mk-21. The Mk-36 also entered the stockpile during this time (see table 4). A typical B-36 base included a mix of weapons. For example, the Operational Storage Site How (aka West River Depot, aka Deep Creek Air Force Station) next to Fairchild AFB provided six Mk-6 with C pits, twelve Mk-6 with B pits, six Mk-17 with C pits, and a single Mk-24 with a C pit, for a total of twenty-five weapons to the wing.[63] A typical B-47 base like March AFB had a Special Service Facility that was loaded with Mk-6 mod 6, Mk-15 mod 0, and Mk-21 mod 0 weapons to support the B-47s of the 22nd and 320th Bombardment Wings.[64]

Table 4. SAC thermonuclear weapon availability, 1957–60

Weapon	Yields	Notes	Numbers
Mk-15 mod 0	1.8,[1] 3.8 MT,[2] 4 MT[3]		1,200
Mk-15 mod 2	1.8 MT, 4 MT[4]	Tritium boosted Sealed pit[5] Contact fuse[6]	
Mk-39 mod 0	3.8 MT	Modification of Mk-15, also known as Mk-15/39 Drogue chute for surface burst capability	
Mk-39 mod 1 SP	3.8 MT	Purpose-built Mk-39 with tritium boosted Sealed pit[7]	700
Mk-39 mod 2 SP	3.8 MT	Advanced Laydown weapon Bat and Big Tail low-level modification of the Mk-39 mod 1	
Mk-21	4.5 MT	Modified into Mk-36[8]	
Mk-36 mod 0	19 MT[9]	Purpose-built Mk-36 Code-named Last Resort	665[10]
Mk-36 Y1 mod 1	18 MT[11]	Modified Mk-21 mod 0, also known as Mk-21/36[12] Auto In-Flight Insertion High-altitude release Free fall or retarded	275
Mk-36 Y2 X1 mod 1	6 MT[13]	Reduced fallout "Clean" weapon	6 to ?
Estimated number available			2,846

1. Operation Castle Nectar was a "Zombie" test that yielded 1.69 megatons.

2. Operation Redwing Cherokee, a test of a war reserve Mk-15, yielded 3.8 megatons. FOIA USAF, "History Fifteenth Air Force January through June 1956"; FOIA DOE, SC-M-67-661, "History of the Early Thermonuclear Weapons Mks 14, 15, 16, 17, 24 and 29, June 1967."

3. Malucci, B-47 Stratojet, 118, 133.

4. Malucci, B-47 Stratojet, 221.

5. FOIA USAF, "History of the 93rd Bombardment Wing, November 1958."

6. Chuck Hansen, Swords of Armageddon (disks in author's possession).

7. FOIA USAF, "History of the 93rd Bombardment Wing, November 1958."

8. "AFSWP Special Weapons Refit Order Apr–Jul 57," in Hansen, US Nuclear Weapons, 148.

9. Malucci, B-47 Stratojet, 17, 133. Hansen notes in US Nuclear Weapons (156) that the Mk-36 yield was 9–10 megatons.

10. Hansen notes in *Swords of Armageddon* that 940 Mk-36s of all mods were manufactured, that is, the 275 Mk-21s modified into Mk-36 mod 1 should be included in the total.

11. FOIA USAF, "History Fifteenth Air Force January through June 1956"; FOIA DOE, SC-M-67-661, "History of the Early Thermonuclear Weapons Mks 14, 15, 16, 17, 24 and 29, June 1967."

12. FOIA DOE, "AFSWP Special Weapons Refit Order Apr–Jul 57."

13. See also Hansen, *Swords of Armageddon*, for his estimates of the Y2 numbers where he asserts that there were only six Mk-36Y2 weapons made. Hansen makes reference to "clean" weapons being a fraud in an earlier article, "Beware the Old Story."

The 300 or so Mk-17 and Mk-24 weapons with their huge yields were slowly removed from service between October 1956 and October 1957: the B-52 was unable to deliver them. The Mk-15 and the Mk-21 became the primary thermonuclear weapons in service, capable of delivery by B-47s and B-52s. The Mk-15 came in at two yields, 1.8 and 3.8 megatons, and was the most prolific of the weapons, with an estimated 1,200 deployed starting in April 1955. The Mk-21, of which an estimated 275 were available, was based on the Castle Bravo weapon but was tweaked from 15 to 18 megatons in its service configuration.[65] The 1,100 available Mk-6 weapons by this time had a new series of cores and pits that produced a new set of yields: 8, 26, 80, 154, and 160 kilotons, upgrading the weapon from 12- to 18-, 37-, 57-, and 83-kiloton ranges.[66] The Mk-39 series, including the Big Tail modification of the Mk-15, came into service in 1957 to supplement the Mk-15s: around 700 of these were produced, each yielding 3.8 megatons. The Mod 2 was a special low-level release weapon.[67] Between June and November 1957 the 275 Mk-21s were converted into the Mk-36Y1 mod 1. Around 665 Mk-36s were built in addition to these conversions to total 950 Mk-36s.[68]

The Mk-15 could be dropped free-fall or retarded delivery using a parachute. Its fusing included both barometric and radar proximity "for the near surface burst." The prox fuses "gave good coverage, not only straight ahead of the bomb but to the side. This caused detonation if the Mk 15 dropped close to the side of a building."[69] Because of its high yield, the Mk-21 was dropped retarded. It could airburst or near-surface-burst, but the "near-contact burst" was "the primary option." The surface burst "[acted] as cleanup in the event of a malfunction of the air-burst option."[70] The sixth modification of the Mk-6 retained the six height-of-burst settings of the earlier models but added contact fusing and barometric sensing. Like its larger brothers, if the Mk-6 airburst system failed, it detonated on contact with the ground.[71]

It is important to divert here for more detail on the Mk-36 program, as this had significant implications for targeting throughout the late 1950s. The discovery during the 1954 Castle test series that the effects of thermonuclear weapons could vary depending on the makeup of the secondary stage led to the Navaho shot during the 1956 Redwing test series. Navaho was based on the Castle Bravo device but had certain modifications to reduce fallout. This was called the TX-21C, presumably C for "clean," and it yielded 4.5 megatons compared to Castle Bravo's estimated 15 megatons. (The estimation range for the shot was 3 to 8 megatons.)[72] One difference involved alteration of the secondary on the device to reduce the fission products generated by the fusion process.

The very political and very public fallout and "clean bomb" debates occurred at this time.[73] During this debate the TX-21 transformed into the Mk-36Y1, while the TX-21C evolved through a convoluted process essentially into the Mk-36Y2. This is confusing because all the existing 275 Mk-21 weapons were converted between June and November 1957 into Mk-36Y1s as well. The Mk-36Y1 yielded 19 megatons, while the Mk-36Y2 yielded around 6 megatons but apparently had the fission output of a 250-kiloton weapon while retaining the thermal and blast effects of a 6-megaton weapon. There is some debate over the number of Mk-36Y2s in the stockpile, but there were at least six by August 1958. It is equally unclear how many Mk-36Y2s were deployed.[74] Again, the possibility that fission effects and fallout could be reduced had implications for targeting. Of note, the 32nd Aviation Depot Squadron at Lake Charles AFB was chastised during a 1958 Operational Readiness Inspection for not stenciling the correct yield designation on their Mk-36 weapons.[75]

The SAC Atomic Weapons Requirement Study

At this point it is important to mention the public appearance of a document, "SAC Atomic Weapons Requirement Study for 1959 . . .

SM 129-56," dated 15 June 1956. This document, located at the U.S. National Archives, was partially declassified in 2014 and has subsequently been employed by various entities for sensationalist and activist purposes, many of which assert that this was SAC's nuclear war plan. It consists of a twenty-page introduction, including an explanation of the Air Power Battle Target System, and several hundred sheets with lists of locations in the Sino-Soviet Bloc and elsewhere. The context of this document is, however, perhaps more prosaic. First, it is a study that uses part of the Air Power Battle Target System as its basis. The study's audience was the JCS, as indicated by designation "SM-129-56." SAC was responding to 15 February and 16 March 1956 JCS requests. Therefore this document's context lies in LeMay's already expressed concerns over having SAC preempted overseas, which would undermine SAC's ability to handle target coverage inside the Soviet Union and thus undermine the deterrent. The context also involves his efforts to resolve that conundrum, Twining's interest in the problem, and contemporary discussions within the JCS on how to solve it.

So what was the JCS studying that required a detailed list of possible targets? Was this the actual Emergency War Plan? The clue here is the mention of "types and numbers of weapons" and, most important, "total Oralloy EQ (kg)."[76] This refers to the amount of nuclear material needed for the destruction of all the targets in the study. This study's purpose was likely to make a case for the allocation of scarce nuclear material to SAC by demonstrating in detail two options for its use, which, of course, precluded the material requirements for rival organizations like Tactical Air Command and the U.S. Navy. As we have seen, LeMay previously had argued for the allocation of more cores to SAC in 1955. The requirements study was essentially that argument taken to a higher and more sophisticated level.

Some have used the document to emphasize what they assert to be SAC's amorality and illegality and, by extension, that of the U.S. government, focusing in this case on the direct targeting of populations.[77] From today's standpoint and possibly incorrect assumptions on what this redacted and incomplete document's purpose was, it is easy to see how this aspect could upset those who steep themselves in the principles of twenty-first-century international law, where the use of MQ-1 Predator unmanned aerial vehicles equipped with Hellfire missiles is decried as "indiscriminate." That said, when confronted by RANDists over his planning in other circumstances, LeMay correctly pointed out that it was his job to provide the president with options.[78] As this JCS study was not the EWP, it should not be assumed that directly targeting the Soviet population was explicit in actual plans at this point, even though the Basic National Security Policy document 5602/1 implied that the United States should plan for inflicting "decisive" damage, either by destroying Soviet military strike potential or by reducing Soviet "civil, political, and cultural life . . . to a condition of chaos."[79] Direct and deliberate population destruction was hotly debated in the JCS later in 1958–59.

That said, there is no doubt at all that the execution of the Air Power Battle Target System target set would have generated massive casualties, as would earlier iterations of the EWP. For the men who lived through Pearl Harbor and fried Tokyo, however, the need to protect the U.S. few clearly outweighed the USSR many. After all, deterrence, according to *Dr. Strangelove*, "is the art of producing, in the mind of the enemy, the *fear* to attack." And that remained the basis of the whole exercise, as stated by Eisenhower and his NSC, Radford and Twining in the JCS, and LeMay at SAC. The fact is this study is firmly rooted in the deterrent policy and deterrent strategy of the United States circa 1956. Assessing it outside of this context, as many have done, is ahistorical and perhaps disingenuous.

The "SAC Atomic Weapons Requirement Study for 1959 . . . SM 129-56" appears to have been a case study in overstatement in the context of bureaucratic competition for scarce resources. How much utility does it have in the context of the SAC EWP for the 1956–58 period? There are several strikes against it. First, it was produced before the significantly expanded availability of imagery brought on by the U-2, so the document is possibly more reflective of the Emergency War Plan prior to 1956 and not necessarily the 1958 or 1959 Basic War Plans nor the SIOPs in the 1960s. Second, it reflects the Air Power Battle Target System, one of several target systems that we know existed. The document perhaps reflects what SAC wanted

JCS to follow in the future, not necessarily what the JCS wanted SAC to do in 1956. Existence of this document does not rule out the use of or instructions to use other target sets.

The other information in the study that indicates that it does not exactly reflect the actual Emergency War Plan is that mention is made of weapons systems that did not exist yet and some that would never exist in the numbers assumed by the study for the 1956–59 period. For example, the Crossbow antiradar missile with a nuclear warhead was never deployed operationally. Snark was programmed for four squadrons, but only a single squadron was deployed, and then only for a year. Similarly, the Rascal air-to-surface missile was briefly deployed to a single squadron and then canceled. A generic intermediate-range ballistic missile was included because no decision had been made on Jupiter or Thor missiles. In addition, the study used generic bomb data: all thermonuclear weapons are ground-burst, all kiloton-yield weapons are airburst.[80] In reality, not all targets were created equal and would have required more flexibility than this: some thermonuclear weapons would have been airburst, while some atomic weapons would have been groundburst. LeMay's demonstrated penchant for withholding operational information when it came to the JCS must be recognized again; there was no way he would have permitted too much operational information to flow to the JCS. The "SAC Atomic Weapons Requirement Study for 1959" does not tell us how the plan would have been carried out; it does not tell us what forces were available, what the EWP's limitations were, or anything about how the enemy might counter it. That said, when used with other materials, it can help us understand SAC's Emergency War Plan.

The Air Power Battle Target System
and the Emergency War Plan, 1956–57

Using the 1957 LeMay briefing numbers, of the 1,539 Desired Ground Zeroes, 954 were scheduled for immediate attack, leaving 585 DGZs for follow-on strikes. There were 1,260 B-47s, approximately 420 B-36s, and 90 B-52s (few of which were combat-ready). There were 1,200 Mk-15s, 275 Mk-21s, 700 Mk-39s, and some percentage of the

940 Mk-36s produced, representing a high-end figure of 3,115 out of 5,717 total nuclear weapons in the U.S. stockpile in 1957. One calculation suggests there were approximately 504 of these weapons were in the AEC National Stockpile Sites, 753 in the Operational Storage Sites adjacent to SAC air bases, and 1,641 in the Special Service Facilities located on SAC bases. Some 7 percent of the available thermonuclear weapons, around 218, were not located in any of these facilities. There were approximately 1,100 Mk-6 weapons available as well, for a high-end approximation of 4,215 nuclear bombs that could have been available to SAC in 1957–58. This represented approximately 74 percent of the American stockpile in 1957.[81]

During this period SAC's Emergency War Plan evolved on an annual basis. In a general sense, there were two plans that used the same target system (the Air Power Battle Target System) and the same force structure. The first was the Strategic Warning plan, in which "the United States . . . had decided to take the initiative." SAC had twenty-four hours or more to prepare, then the alert force would launch, and subsequent waves would follow every twelve hours. The second was the Tactical Warning plan, in which the Soviets held the initiative and attacked with little or no warning. For the Strategic Warning plan, the first SAC launches were to occur six hours after E-Hour was declared, and "the entire initial strike would be airborne by E plus 12 hours." The Strategic Warning plan was emphasized from 1956 to 1958.[82]

Strategic Warning and the conditions that generated it were far different from the DEFCON system we are familiar with today; that system did not go into effect until late 1959. Strategic Warning in the 1950s was not necessarily a condition imposed by imminent nuclear attack. Strategic Warning was declared at some point in a crisis, like Suez or Lebanon, where there were substantial moves of Soviet forces, not just nuclear forces. The progressive generation of SAC into a force capable of destroying 1,539 DGZs and, most important, the enemy's ability to see that buildup with his vast intelligence apparatus, constituted the deterrent underpinnings of that process. If the enemy backed off, fine. If he didn't, then he got hit with the full weight of SAC's Emergency War Plan at a time of the president's choosing.

Tactical Warning was a response to an enemy attack, nuclear or conventional, with little or no warning. Presumably the Tactical Warning process saw some form of nuclear or conventional attack against forward-deployed SAC forces, say in the United Kingdom. Such a move would then trigger an immediate SAC response against priority strategic nuclear targets from both forward-deployed units and U.S.-based ones. That is, the Tactical Warning scenario was not quite the same as the more familiar "bolt from the blue" scenario that had first warning coming from the NORAD radar networks, thus triggering the launch of the bombers from their bases in the United States.

Of importance here was that the unified and specified commanders, including LeMay at SAC, had the right to declare Defense Emergency on their own using specific criteria established by the JCS. As we have seen, this permitted the emergency agreement between the AEC and DOD to go into effect and allow the custodians to release the cores for the bombs. Note also that we are dealing with a set of circumstances where the Fail Safe (later Positive Control) program did not yet exist. That said, Eisenhower asserted that nuclear weapons would not be employed without his express permission. The mechanisms for doing so evolved in response to this problem throughout the late 1950s into what is commonly called "pre-delegation."

The Strategic Warning plan presumably employed weapons against the 1,539 DGZs in the Air Power Battle Target System, with 954 in the first wave and 585 in the second. Around half of the first wave would have been launched from forward bases. It should be emphasized that there would have been cross-targeting and attrition factors built into this plan. The 1,539 DGZs were not necessarily 1,539 separate targets. Two or three weapons would have been directed against, say, a bomber airfield, with the possibility of one or two getting through, or roughly a 30 percent attrition rate. If that bomber airfield had a known nuclear weapons storage site fifteen kilometers away, that site would have been a separate target with several DGZs allocated to it, again to ensure its destruction. Some targets, like the Semipalatinsk nuclear weapons testing facility, for example, might have had seven dispersed targets (four test complexes, the airfield, the weapons storage area, and Kurchatov City), each of which may have had two to three weapons allocated to them.

The Tactical Warning plan envisioned the destruction of "210 targets with three weapons per target in order to stop further attacks against the United States."[83] That number of targets, to be destroyed by one-third of the available nuclear weapons, or 630 DGZs, is almost one-third of the Strategic Warning plan's 1,539 DGZs. This plan appears to have assumed that only one-third of SAC would survive a no-notice attack on its bases and penetration through the Soviet air defense system. This suggests that the 585 or so bombers in the United States would have been employed against them, following whatever forward-based forces survived.

This is where 1960s terminology does not work to describe SAC's mid- to late 1950s EWP. To call this a "counterforce" plan, which some Kennedy administration and RAND people later did, is too narrow a description.[84] Certainly there are subtleties that suggest it was not exactly Dulles-like massive retaliation. Yes, the plans attacked Soviet nuclear delivery systems, but they also attacked their air defense system and anything associated with airpower, broadly defined: airframe plants, for example. Note also that embedded in the official language is the phrase "in order to stop further attacks against the United States." Narrowly interpreted, that could mean ensuring that the Soviets' physical capabilities were destroyed. It could also mean their leadership and command and control was to be targeted and destroyed or otherwise compelled to quit. There is no discussion at all of direct population targeting.[85]

That said, "each unit was given a number of targets for recycle or special contingency strikes."[86] Clearly there were some options that were not part of the Strategic or the Tactical Warning plans. And as we have seen, 7 percent of the thermonuclear weapons stockpile was not allocated by the JCS at E-Hour. The three hundred or so obsolete Mk-17/24 weapons that could be employed by aging but not yet retired B-36 bombers against a destroyed or heavily disrupted Soviet air defense system likely constituted this reserve force. Note that these numbers correlate to the numbers of targets in EWP 1-49 and its immediate successor, with a generous margin of combat loss for the strike force.

Consequently American nuclear targeting was perhaps more flexible at this time than is generally understood. Ike had several options. He could, during a crisis scenario, progressively generate SAC so it could implement the Strategic Warning scenario, hoping to deter the Soviets. If necessary he could strike with some 1,500 or more aircraft against a specific target system that also would have generated plenty of bonus damage. If the United States took a hit first, he could strike with some 630 aircraft, or however many survived the first Soviet strikes, against a more restricted target set to limit damage to the United States, and then use whatever forces were left in North America to follow on and destroy a subset of the preemption list. Finally, there appears to have been some form of reserve or contingency capability for both scenarios, with targets unspecified but possibly based on the old EWP 1-49 or 1-53.

The weight of the EWP in its Strategic Warning variant had some 495 bombers, deployed in overseas bases, plus 765 in the United States, of which 243 were scheduled to be in the first wave departing the continent. A second wave consisted of at least 522 aircraft.[87] By extrapolation, the Tactical Warning plan would have consisted of some number of the 495 aircraft of the deployed overseas wings plus the first wave of 243 showing up some time after transit from North America and perhaps a third wave generated from surviving forces to combine to take out the 210 priority targets with 630 weapons.

One can see why LeMay and his commanders were seriously concerned about the heavy emphasis on SAC's forward bases and their vulnerability. If the bulk of the forward-deployed 495 aircraft were destroyed before they could disperse, and it would have taken just 13 well-delivered nuclear bombs or heavy conventional strikes to do just that, this left the 243 bombers on alert in the United States to destroy the 210 priority targets against a non-degraded air defense system with no forward tanker bases, at least until the surviving non-alerted U.S.-based aircraft were brought up to speed. This situation unmasked the glaring necessity for additional tanker bases in northern North America for both scenarios. Again, credible target coverage under all contingencies was deemed crucial for deterrence. Between 210 and 630 aircraft successfully delivering bombs on their targets were considered the bare minimum needed to reduce damage to the United States if deterrence failed.

The unavailability of the Emergency War Plan from this period should not deter us from examining how it was supposed to be implemented. Each of SAC's numbered air forces retained a Reconnaissance Technical Squadron. These produced detailed reports on targets of interest identified by the three numbered air forces as well as by SAC HQ. These reports were pooled and then shared with CIA's NPIC. It is possible to identify what each RTS was interested in and then extrapolate generally what their parent number air force targets were.[88]

Each RTS had a particular geographic area of interest. The 3921st RTS with the 7th Air Division in the United Kingdom focused on East Germany, Poland, Austria, Czechoslovakia, Hungary, and Kaliningrad in the USSR. The 8th RTS was exclusively focused on Murmansk, Leningrad, Moscow, the Baltic States, and Belarus. The 544th and 2nd RTS handled Hungary, Romania, Bulgaria, Albania, Ukraine, the Caucasus, and south-central Soviet Union.[89]

The Strategic Warning Component of the EWP

Let us deal with the Strategic Warning plan first. Part of the Fifteenth Air Force was relegated to handling around 135 targets in the Soviet Far East, and the deeper targets in the west-central Soviet Union and will be handled in chapter 11, so we will first look at the Warsaw Pact and west-central Soviet Union. If after a twenty-four-hour-long SAC buildup the Soviets had not backed off on their course of action and the president decided to preempt, the sequence of events would likely have looked like this in 1957.

The conduct of USAFE operations against East Germany would have resembled that described in chapter 6: F-86s with Mk-12 Broks destroying the air defense system in southern East Germany, while Matador cruise missiles destroying every MIG base they could in East Germany and western Czechoslovakia.

The next wave, from SAC's 7th Air Division in the United Kingdom, had four components operating nearly concurrently. The first

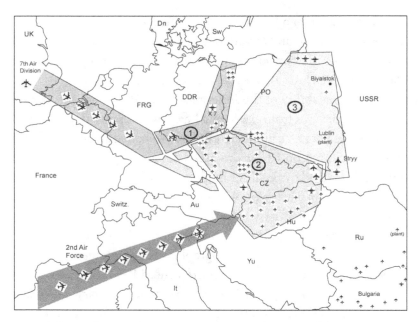

Map 16. 7th Air Division operations, 1956–58. Courtesy of the author.

was the destruction of the IL-28 bases in East Germany, as in earlier plans, plus three MIG bases in southeastern East Germany, thus
opening a corridor into southern Poland. The second was the priority destruction of the IL-28 base at Hradcany, Czechoslovakia, and
strikes against seven Soviet and Czech MIG-17 bases in the western part of the country, six more in the central part of the country,
and five in western Hungary. This served multiple purposes. First,
it preempted any possible quick Soviet strike from forward bases
against SAC's overseas bases in Europe. Second, it opened a corridor
through Czechoslovakia, this for 7th Air Division's third component.
After destroying a pair of MIG bases in eastern Czechoslovakia, the
way was clear for the destruction of the Cherlyany IL-28 base and
the Stryy TU-16 base south of Lviv, both in the westernmost part of
the Soviet Union. Third, it assisted other SAC forces in opening the
Hungarian-Rumanian corridor.

The 7th Air Division kept a close eye on bases in Austria that
were known to be capable of launching IL-28s. A number of scenarios could have put those bases back into Soviet hands very quickly:

INCREASING THE DETERRENT MARGIN

a coup d'état or subversion in the run-up to the war, or perhaps the use of airborne forces to seize them in the initial stages of a war are but two. If there was information that such a move was likely or underway, then these bases would also have been targeted for destruction by 7th Air Division, USAFE, and/or the U.S. Navy if they were in position.

Continuing with 7th Air Division's operations, we shift to Poland and Kaliningrad. While 7th Air Division B-47s were destroying targets in East Germany, Czechoslovakia, and Hungary, a more complex situation presented itself. The agreement between SAC and SACEUR stipulated that SAC would handle around fifty targets on behalf of SACEUR. However, these targets were not all part of the Air Power Battle Target System and their destruction was not necessarily crucial for protecting forward-deployed SAC forces. The priority was getting B-47s onto targets that had the capability of inflicting damage on SAC and on North America. The 7th Air Division's interest in Poland included as a priority the IL-28 base at Brzheg and four other airfields around Wroclaw (Breslau) that they might disperse to, a cluster of MiG bases in northwestern Poland, possibly the runway at the Lublin aircraft plant in southeastern Poland, and then the Polish MiG base at Biata Podlaska. This last base protected the crucial Brest-Litovsk/Bialastok logistics and transportation complexes but could also interfere with penetration into Belarus. The destruction of the Soviet logistics system in Poland, that is, between twenty and twenty-five bridges and marshalling yards, would likely have been handled by B-47s returning to the United Kingdom from the first wave, reloading with Mk-6 bombs, and then going back in later.

The destruction of the four MiG bases in northwest Poland likely was to facilitate strikes against targets in Kaliningrad. These included IL-28 bases at Dunaevka and Chkalovsk and a potentially troublesome interceptor base containing MiG-17P and Yak-25Ps. The 7th Air Division kept an eye on two airfields in Latvia, but for the most part that was Eighth Air Force territory.[90]

The actions of the 7th Air Division were essentially the first phase of the EWP, but given the tight timelines this becomes a bit of an artificiality. The Eighth Air Force components of the EWP overlap to some extent with the 7th Air Division's, and there were at least two. With the timed buildup in the Strategic Warning plan, some Eighth Air Force units would have deployed forward to the United Kingdom, while others were alerted at their bases in the United States. The priorities of the Eighth Air Force were the destruction of bomber aviation and any airfield these aircraft could operate from, the reduction of Leningrad, and the destruction of key targets in and around Moscow. Getting at these targets, however, required some deft preparation. UK-based B-47s could exploit the southern East German corridor created by 7th Air Division, but five MiG bases in southern Poland needed to be destroyed to completely clear the way to the Soviet border. A second route could be blown through by destroying six other MiG bases across northern Poland, again behind 7th Air Division strikes in the Polish northwest.

In the Arctic, SAC SENSINT flights in 1956 detected two possible staging bases on the Franz Josef Land islands. This included the 11,900-foot runway at Gogmana Airfield and the 6,000-foot Nagurskaya Airfield. These were the closest Soviet airfields to North America.[91] Their destruction would have been a priority for Eighth Air Force units.

For the Eighth Air Force wings coming in from New England via aerial refueling and across Norway and Sweden, other corridors were required, most of them through the Baltic States (see map 17). On the way, however, was the Mya-4 long-range bomber base at Siaulai, Latvia; the TU-16 base at Tartu, Estonia; and the IL-28 base at Parnu, Estonia. Siaulai would have received considerable attention, probably the largest weapons in the Eighth Air Force inventory set for groundburst. The excessively large but undermanned and apparently little-used "transport" air base at Pajuostis would have received similar attention. To get into Belarus, however, another corridor was needed, and the Soviet PVO was crafty. The air defense laydown for the Baltics had six MiG bases in Estonia, eight in Latvia, one in Kaliningrad, but none in Lithuania. Lithuania did, however, have five empty but maintained reserve airfields. Each MiG base in Latvia was doubled up with two regiments per airfield, mixed MiG-15, MiG-17, and MiG-19s.[92]

INCREASING THE DETERRENT MARGIN

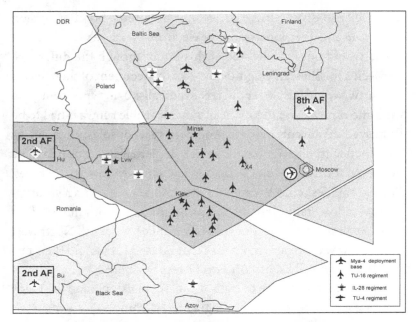

Map 17. Eighth Air Force and Second Air Force operations against Soviet bomber bases in the western Soviet Union, 1956–58. Eighth Air Force units striking from the United Kingdom and after aerial refueling from the United States had some target overlap with Second Air Force B-47s operating from Spain. Similarly, Second Air Force B-47s launched from French Morocco had overlapping target coverage with the Spain-based units. The Moscow strikes could have been launched from the United Kingdom, Spain, or French Morocco.
Courtesy of the author.

The proximity of Lithuania to seven key Soviet bomber bases in Belarus, one on the Latvian-Russian border and two on the Belarus-Russian border, suggests that the Soviets prepared Lithuanian airspace as a bomber surge corridor of their own. Once the Belarusian bombers were launched, the MIGs in Latvia deployed to the reserve bases to cover the gap. Another possibility was that this was some form of trap: make it look in peacetime like there was a possible corridor for SAC to exploit, but then secretly redeploy and massively defend it in wartime.

The Eighth Air Force's next targets were in Belarus and on the Latvian-Russian border. There were five TU-16 bases, a TU-16R base, a TU-16K base, and a TU-4 base, each with a regiment of aircraft.

The ability to distinguish at a distance between a bomber version of a TU-16 and a reconnaissance or electronic warfare version of the TU-16 would not have existed at this point, though the difference between a missile-carrying TU-16K, like the regiment of them based at Ostrov, would have been. In any event, all TU-16 types could use the same runway, and therefore all TU-16-capable runways had to be destroyed to prevent their use. And despite its obsolescence, TU-4s equipped with nuclear weapons were still lethal and thus had to be destroyed too. Adjacent to Belarus in Ukraine were two TU-16 bases, Poltava and Seshcha (Bryansk). Poltava, one of the USAAF's original Operation Frantic bases in 1944, was crammed with three to four TU-16 regiments, at least one of them a tanker regiment. Northwest of Moscow was Migalovo Air Base that housed IL-28s and then TU-16s. These were all Eighth Air Force's responsibility.

Destruction of the five to eight MiG bases in Estonia and the Gdov Air Base gave access to the Leningrad target complex. The main targets were likely Leningrad Airport, with its bomber-capable runway, plus Levashino and Yanino airfields, which could have operated TU-16s. Most of Leningrad's aerial defenses were halfway to Finland, including the more dangerous Yak-25M interceptors, leaving two MiG bases at Gorelovo and Pushkin on the city's perimeter. All in all, Leningrad would have been subjected to at least five weapons.

The Eighth Air Force was also focused on activities in the northern reaches of the Soviet Empire. The geographical proximity of bases in this region to Thule, Keflavik, Goose Bay, and Ernest Harmon was of considerable concern. Two large air bases near Murmansk, Severomorsk-1 and -3, hosted TU-14T jet torpedo bombers and IL-28s until 1956, then TU-16s were deployed in a variety of variants, including air-to-surface missile carriers from 1956 onward. Further south at Lakhta (Katunino) near Arkhangelsk TU-16s started operating around 1957, while the nearby base at Yagodnik divested itself of IL-28s in 1958. The U.S. Navy also covered the Severomorsk bases.[93] Again, maritime aviation bases capable of operating TU-16s were indistinguishable in a targeting sense from ones belonging to long-range aviation. To get through to these bases, it would have been necessary to destroy three PVO airfields and their MiG-

17PF regiments. B-47 units from the American Midwest were lined up on these targets.

Moving to the southwestern approaches and focusing on the Second Air Force, it is evident that the 7th Air Division was set up to clear a path in western Hungary. That said, the U.S. Navy was interested in pretty much every air base in Hungary as well. Though the 1954–55 iteration of the EWP envisioned cooperation in generating a corridor through Hungary, by 1957 it does not appear to have been accomplished. The difference was that by 1957 SAC had more B-47s available, had a greater variety of yields to work with, and had the Spanish bases in play. The U.S. Navy, on the other hand, was increasingly concerned with the nuclear air threat to the fleet and would have been interested in any location from which attacks could be launched against carriers in the Mediterranean. SAC in Omaha was clearly interested in every airfield in Hungary as well, and there was overlap with the 7th Air Division on two of them. Another, Taszar, was the focus of a joint SAC-CIA-USN reconnaissance project, underlining its geographical importance and thus its probable destruction by multiple weapons.[94]

B-47s from SAC's Spanish bases had at most sixteen Soviet, Hungarian, and Romanian MiG bases to contend with before opening another corridor into the Soviet Union proper, in this case Soviet-occupied Ukraine. With the preliminary destruction of the Cherlyany and Stryy bomber bases by the 7th Air Division, the next major targeting problem consisted of nine bomber bases in central Ukraine; one of these was an IL-28 base, while eight housed various versions of the TU-16. There may also have been some targeting overlap between the two SAC air forces with the bases at Poltava and Seshcha.[95]

Moving further south, Second Air Force wings coming in from the United States across the Atlantic to Morocco would have exploited a corridor situated from the southern edge of the Carpathians to the southern border of Bulgaria, after first destroying three MiG bases in Albania. Overflying Yugoslavia, the initial strikes would have included six Romanian and eleven Bulgarian airfields, one of these hosting IL-28s. Almost all bases contained at least one MiG regiment, from all versions of interceptors (MiG-15s to MiG-19s), in some cases two regiments. The Bulgarians did not go in for reserve airfields like their other Warsaw Pact brethren, and the destruction of their main bases would have ended their ability to put up an effective air defense. With the way cleared, priority targets included four TU-16 airfields in Crimea, the nuclear-capable IL-28 base at Karankut, the nuclear weapons training airfield at Baherove and its associated airfield at Feodosia, plus the IL-28 base at Melitopol in southern Ukraine.[96] Of note, the low-profile Big Horn deployment of five B-47s to Adana Air Base in Turkey during the Suez-Hungary crisis in 1956 suggests that the Crimean bases could have been struck even earlier on activation of the EWP.

The possibility that Col. Gamal Abdel Nasser might permit his patrons to use Egyptian air bases to cover SAC's Moroccan and Spanish bases did not escape SAC's notice. Indeed there was substantial Talent reportage on nine Egyptian air bases, some of which was generated by the 7th Air Division and some by SAC HQ.[97] This could have been in support of a possible conventional intervention in a future Arab-Israeli war, or a preemptive strike against forward-deployed Soviet forces, or both. (Some Soviet TU-16s operating from Egypt were known to wear Egyptian Air Force insignia.)[98] Similarly the 7th Air Division generated Talent reports on every air facility in Israel, which suggests that employing that country as a recovery base may have been under consideration if Turkey became untenable.[99]

As for the Soviet atomic weapons production complexes, substantial information on the system was available prior to 1956 and then refined by U-2 coverage in 1957. There were three uranium processing plants: Elektrosal, Glavoz, and Novosibirsk. Large gas diffusion plants were located at Verkh-Neyvinskiy, Tomsk, and Angarsk. Plutonium production was centered on Kyshtym, Tomsk, and Krasnoyarsk. (Information on the presence of three nuclear weapon stockpile sites located near some of these facilities was sporadically available before 1960; in one case there was even Genetrix balloon coverage of the Krasnoyarsk and Dodonovo sites.)[100] These were all large facilities that would have required high-yield airbursts to load the structures and destroy them. Testing and development plants like Sarov and Kasli were known but were smaller in size. Kiloton-

INCREASING THE DETERRENT MARGIN

yield weapons would have sufficed. Some facilities were located near airfields; these were also separately targeted, presumably so that components and weapons could not be flown out and weapons assembled elsewhere. The bulk of the complexes were in the central Soviet Union and likely assigned to Fifteenth Air Force units.[101]

Other special targets would have been on the priority list. There were three major test areas, again with long, bomber-capable runways: the nuclear weapons proving grounds at Semipalatinsk, where weapons were observed in loading pits;[102] the missile test facility at Kapustin Yar; and the missile test facility at Tyuratam. Experimental and test systems that could be used expediently in a conflict had to be destroyed promptly. SAC would have been highly interested in targeting the Aralsk-7 Biological Warfare Research Facility, with its unique starburst-shaped airfield in the Aral Sea, and a cluster of facilities in Tver, north of Moscow: the Lisiy Island test facility and the city of Vyshny Volochyok, just down the road southeast from Migalovo Airfield bomber base.[103] Due to the dispersed nature of all of these facilities, they likely would have required multiple weapons each in order to destroy them. Destruction of the laboratories at these sites and nearby airfields from which biological weapons could be dispersed would have made them priority targets with the highest yield weapons.

The destruction of all Soviet airframe plants was important in the EWP. First and foremost, these plants had runways that bomber-size aircraft could operate and to which nuclear weapons could be dispersed. Second, the criteria of preventing further nuclear attacks on the United States in the Tactical Warning plan was not necessarily limited to hours after the first strikes, as our later concept of nuclear war condition us to think. If an airframe plant could finish off partially built aircraft, those were a threat, particularly if weapons from the undiscovered storage sites were transported to them. An example of this mentality: during the Battle of Stalingrad, a Soviet factory continued to make tanks even while German forces were fighting the defenders in another part of the complex.

At this point there were eighteen airframe plants in the Soviet Union with long runways, not including those in Moscow. These would not necessarily have been priority targets in the Strategic Warning plan, like the bomber airfields, but would probably have been hit from SAC forces based in the United States. The Eighth Air Force would have been responsible for airframe plants at Voronezh and Kharkov in the west in the first wave, and Gorki, Kazan, Molotov/Perm, Kuybyshev, and Saratov in the central trans-Urals region later. Second Air Force bombers coming across the Atlantic and supported from Spain and Morocco would have been responsible for Tbilisi, possibly Chklov. The plants to the east, including Novosibirsk, Omsk, Irkutsk, Ulan-Ude, and Komsomolsk, would have been the responsibility of the Fifteenth Air Force.[104] Mya-4 Bisons had been spotted at Novosibirsk Airfield in 1957.[105]

The number of Talent reports generated by SAC's Reconnaissance Technical Squadrons from 1956 to 1958 include hundreds that describe airfields, landing grounds, and strips. There were several reasons for this. First, the planners wanted to ensure they had not missed some out-of-the-way Soviet air force base or a facility that was disguised as something else. Second, the planners clearly had a list of every facility ever used by the Luftwaffe in the Soviet Union during World War II and wanted to confirm they were no longer employed. Third, and most important, the IL-28 and TU-16 were capable of operating from semi-improved facilities, as demonstrated in 1955–56. Could any of these hundreds of facilities or fields be employed as dispersal sites, even for single aircraft? Or as expedient pickup points for nuclear weapons? Could PVO move MiG interceptors to places not known by the Western intelligence apparatus? Was there evidence of improvement, facilities, or personnel at any of them? Could MiG interceptor bases be expediently improved to host dispersed bombers?

To use Leningrad as an example, Eighth Air Force planners examined sixteen separate aviation facilities in and around the city. They concluded that five were operationally important. Several were forest resupply strips from the war and irrelevant. A couple were weedy flying clubs. One was a dilapidated 1930s-era airport with large but overgrown grass runways. None of these was capable of jet aircraft operation, so they were probably not even added to the target lists.[106]

In effect, anything that could take Soviet bomber aircraft was identified and targeted by SAC, and if it happened to be a PVO station,
so much the better: bonus damage. This helps to account for a proportion of the large numbers of Desired Ground Zeros in the Strategic Warning plan, and the hoovering up of that data by the U-2s
contributed directly to that part of it.

Some PVO MIG interceptor bases would have been destroyed
on the way in by the first wave of strikes from forward bases. Those
remaining would likely have been destroyed during the second wave
to prevent their use by other Soviet forces. Inside the Soviet Union
and occupied Baltic States and Ukraine, there were around sixty
PVO airfields in the late 1950s. All of these appear in Talent reportage between 1956 and 1958.[107]

Note that SAC had what appears to be an inordinate interest in
Soviet seaplane bases at this time. No fewer than fourteen of these
were examined by SAC photo interpreters in 1956–58, including the
Beriev Design Bureau at the Taganrog Airframe Plant Dimitrov 86
west of Rostov-on-Don.[108] At this point the Soviets possessed the
Be-6 Madge patrol seaplane but were working on the Be-10 Mallow,
a jet-propelled amphibious patrol bomber. The Be-10 was conceptually similar to the contemporary U.S. Navy P6M Seamaster amphibious nuclear bomber, an experimental aircraft designed in the 1950s
for the planned Seaplane Strike Force. Obviously an amphibious
nuclear bomber would have generated significant targeting problems for SAC, thus Talent coverage was maintained on both the production facility and on the assorted bases the Mallow could operate
from. Twenty-six Mallows were produced, but in the early 1960s a
turboprop amphibian, the Be-12 Mail, also came into service. As
the U.S. Navy's Martin P5M Marlin was nuclear-capable, it followed
that the Soviet aircraft might be as well: the Be-12SK was in fact the
nuclear-capable version.[109] It would be logical to include these facilities on SAC's target lists.

Targeting Soviet Nuclear Weapons Storage Sites

The most important information imparted by the Talent analysis
next to the specifics of the air defense system was the disposition

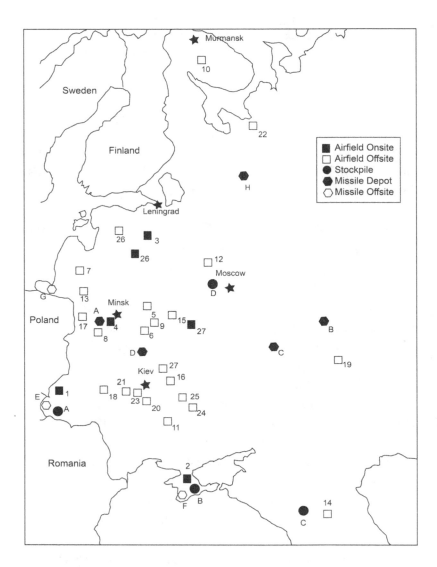

Map 18. Soviet nuclear weapons storage sites, 1949–60. Airfield Onsite:
1: Stryy (TU-4, IL-28, TU-16); 2: Karankut (IL-28); 3: Soltsy (TU-4, TU-16);
4: Machulishche (TU-4, TU-16); 26: Ostrov (Gorokhovka) (TU-16); 27: Seshcha
(Dubrovka) (possible weapon storage area [WSA]) (TU-4, TU-16). Airfield
Offsite: 5: Orsha (TU-4, TU-16); 6: Bobryusk (TU-4, TU-16); 7: Siauliai (Mya-4,
TU-95 support); 8: Baranovici (TU-4, TU-16); 9: Bykhov/Mogliev (TU-4, TU-16);
10: Olenya (TU-16); 11: Kirovograd (Kanatovo, Veselivka) (TU-4, TU-16);
12: Migalovo (Valdy, Tver-9) (IL-28); 13: Kedainiai (possible WSA); 14: Stavropol
(TU-95 support); 15: Pochinok (Shatalovo) (TU-4, TU-16); 16: Priluki (TU-4,
TU-16); 17: Shchuchin (IL-28); 18: Starokonstantinov (IL-28); 19: Engels

(Mya-4); 20: Uzin (Chepelevka) (TU-4, TU-95); 21: Zhitomir (Ozernoye) (TU-4, TU-16); 22: Kholm (Katunino) (IL-28, TU-16); 23: Belya Tserkov (planned WSA) (TU-4, TU-16); 24: Poltava (TU-4, TU-16); 25: Mirgorod (unfinished WSA?) (TU-4, TU-16); 26: Tartu (TU-4, TU-16); 27: Nezhin (possible WSA) (TU-4, TU-16). Off map: Dolon (TU-95); Vozdvizhenka (Voroshilov) (TU-4, TU-16); Ukrainka (Seryshevo) (TU-16, Mya-4); Belaya (Irkutsk) (TU-4, TU-16); Khorol (Zavatinsk) (TU-4, TU-16); Alekseyevskoye (TU-16); Ugolnyy ("bounce" airfield). National Stockpile: A: Delyatin (Ivano-Frankivsk-16); B: Sudak (Feodosiya-13); C: Mozdok (Nalchik-20); D: Mozhaysk (Mozhaysk-10). Off map: Sarov (Arzamas-16); Yuryuzan (Zlatoust-30); Nizhnaya (Sverdlovsk-16); Dodonovo (Krasnoyarsk-26); Malaya Sazanka (Svobodnyy 21); Korfovskiy (Khabarovsk 47); Kurchatov (Semipalatinsk Test Site); Golovchino (Belgorod-22); Berezovka (Saratov-63). Missile Support Depot: A: Novaya Mezinovka (R-5A/SS-3); B: Surovatikha (1960: R-12/SS-4); C: Tambov (R-5A/SS-3); D: Gomel-30 (R-5A/SS-3, also support to Pribytki Air Base TU-4, TU-16); H: Nyandoma (Kargopol-2) (R-7/SS-6 support to Pletsetsk). Missile Offsite Storage: E: Mukachevo (SS-3/R-5M warhead storage); F: Crimea (SS-3/R-5M warhead storage); G: Gvardeysk (SS-3/R-5M warhead storage).
Courtesy of the author.

of the Soviet nuclear weapons storage system. Based on available information, it appears as though the United States had had progressive insight into the Soviet system throughout the 1950s. Indeed there was understandable confusion among the analysts in the early days as they struggled to categorize the structures in the facilities and compare them to their American equivalents. The American system had national stockpile sites, operational storage sites, and special service facilities at the SAC bases. The Soviet system wasn't organized in the same way: one site labeled by American analysts as a national stockpile site had one-third of the storage capacity of several others of the same designation, and half of the capacity of a site supporting a bomber airfield.[110]

The main problem in examining this issue historically is the probability that the USAF had imagery of some of the storage sites from the 1952 to 1956 SENSINT flights and only selectively passed this information on to the CIA or other agencies before the 1960s.[111] Thus, when the U-2 flights started in 1956, their existence and location only slowly emerged in the CIA's analytical world in 1957–58 and were fully confirmed in the 1960s with the advent of the reconnaissance satellites. Therefore it is perhaps best to reconstruct the

Soviet system and then compare it to what was known by SAC and the CIA in 1956–58.

It was generally confirmed by Keyhole and other analysis that by 1970 the Soviets had twelve "national stockpile sites," two storage sites at Arctic Staging Bases, and ten or eleven facilities associated with nuclear storage called "sensitive operations complexes." These SOCs and the Arctic Staging Base facilities were built starting in 1959–62, so these can be eliminated from consideration for the 1950s.[112] The number of storage facilities near airfields during the 1950s, something akin to the Special Service Facilities at SAC bases, is more difficult to determine. There were one IL-28, one TU-16, and five TU-4 bases with on-site storage by 1955, but as the decade progressed and the TU-4 gave way to the TU-16, at least twenty-three off-site storage facilities supporting air bases were built. Five missile support depots were also constructed, the first completed in 1956, as were three missile warhead storage sites colocated with R-5D / SS-3 ballistic missiles.[113]

Using the available information, presumably U-2 information, the USAF and CIA produced competing documents: "Special Weapons Areas, November 1956" and "Special Weapons Storage Installations, Probable, USSR, 12 December 1956." Some disagreement over an installation at Mozhaysk west of Moscow led to a protracted debate in February 1957. Mozhaysk appears to have been initially photographed during a SENSINT flight and rephotographed by a U-2 in 1956. USAF intelligence informed the JCS that Mozhaysk was similar to an installation at Valdai, thus implying there was imagery of both prior to the U-2 overflight. In reality, "Valdai" was a site code-named Tver-9 and it was 13.4 kilometers from Migalovo Air Base, home of the IL-28s of the 56th HBAD. "Mozhaysk" was actually Mozhaysk-10, a national stockpile site employing the same standardized storage bunker type.[114] The main USAF Talent-based report, "Soviet Airfields: Special Weapons and Storage," came out in February 1957. Spin-off analysis suggests that, at a minimum, twelve sites in addition to these two were analyzed in it, most of them supporting bomber operations at airfields: Bobriusk, Bykhov, Kirov, Machulishchi, Migalovo, Ostrov, Siauliai, Stryy, Khabarovsk, and Ukrainka. A 1959 U-2 overflight also observed special weapons storage and loading areas at Engels Airfield, initial home of the Mya-4 bomber regiments.[115]

There were, however, several national stockpile sites that remained undiscovered by the American intelligence apparatus at this time. Delyatin (Ivano-Franovsk-16) was hidden in a Carpathian valley 135 kilometers from the Romanian border and nowhere near an airfield. It boasted a large helipad which, by its dimensions, suggests that the huge Mi-6 Hook transport helicopter coming into service in 1957 would have been used to move the weapons. It had been identified as a stockpile site by 1960, but first identification is unclear.[116] Then there was Sudak (Feodosiya-13) in Crimea. It was completely different in layout from Delyatin and appears to have been almost a copy of Manzano Base at Albuquerque or Clarksville Base in Tennessee, with portals driven under the mountain and the weapon components stored separately and assembled in galleries. Sudak was over an hour from the Feodosiya Airfield, but its proximity to Baherove Air Base near Kerch is also interesting: Baherove was the Soviet functional equivalent of Kirtland AFB, where the Armed Forces Special Weapons Project worked on modifying aircraft, the creation of safety procedures, and the crafting of delivery profiles for nuclear weapons. SAC and the CIA knew about Baherove but did not appear to know about Feodosiya-13 until the 1960s.[117]

There was intense interest by all American parties in the Mozdok Airfield and any ancillary facilities located around it in North Ossetia. Though no bomber units were permanently based there, the large and well-maintained facility was clearly established behind the Caucasus as a forward base for strikes into the Mediterranean, Turkey, Iran, and the Middle East. Certainly some of the Ukraine-based TU-16s could have been designated to deploy to Mozdok and load up there. The Nalchik-20 national storage site was believed by CIA to be among the first built in the early 1950s. Another valley-based facility like Ivano-Franovsk-16 and also equipped with a Hook-size helipad, Nalchik-20, was 135 kilometers from Mozdok Airfield and would have escaped a strike directed at the bomber deployment base. Its location was probably unknown to American targeteers in the 1950s.[118]

Three other sites were located next to but some distance away from nuclear weapons fabrications facilities deep in the forests around Chelyabinsk: Karabash (Chelyabinsk 115), Yurazan (Zlatoust-30), and Nizhnaya (Sverlovsk-16). Each was three hours by road from major airfields and population centers and all were uncovered using satellite imagery only around 1962.[119]

The Soviet doctrine of locating operational nuclear storage sites eight to fifteen kilometers upwind from the bomber bases is in contrast to the SAC airfields, with their Special Service Facilities' Weapons Storage Areas located on base. The Soviet mania for security clearly played a role here in that the 12th GUMO custodial organization did not belong to long-range aviation or any other Soviet air force organization. When it came to targeting, however, this dispersion posed a problem. A 19-megaton groundburst from, say, an Mk-15 or Mk-36Y1 would have produced a 4-kilometer-wide crater that, if centered on the runway, would have generated only 5 psi overpressure 12.2 kilometers away. This would not have been enough to destroy the storage bunkers. Indeed, with the recognized Soviet policy of using forced laborers and disposing of them later, the stored weapons could have been recovered as the radioactive contamination would have reached only 10 roentgens per hour at that distance, depending on the winds, and the weapons transported elsewhere for use. This would have posed SAC targeteers some issues. Assuming an airfield and its storage facility were known, it was perhaps better to employ two Mk-15s, each yielding 3.8 to 4 megatons, one against the airfield and another against the storage site, rather than a singular and large 19-megaton weapon directed only at the airfield hoping to incapacitate the storage site. This case would have likely been applied only to targets where the storage facility was clearly identified. The disruptive effects of 19 megatons in the vicinity of a bomber base should not be underestimated and would have been the second-best alternative if there was a suspected storage area that was unlocated.

Targeting Moscow

Moscow remained a central target in both the Strategic Warning and the Tactical Warning plans. The Moscow area was not only the

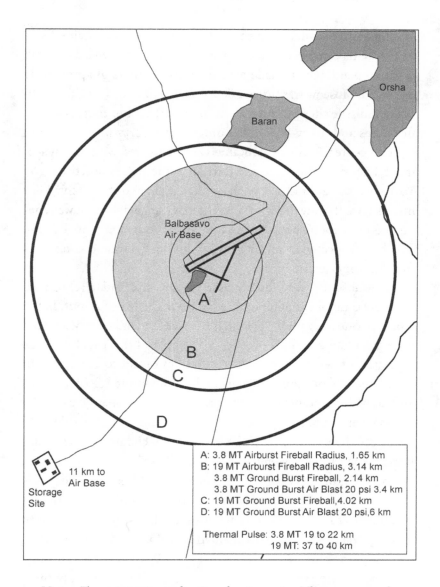

Map 19. The comparative application of a 3.8-megaton Mk-39 weapon and a 19-megaton Mk-36 weapon against two regiments of TU-16 bombers at Balbasavo Air Base and the nuclear storage site supporting them. The most economical option would have been to employ optimal targeting against both using a single groundburst Mk-36 weapon dropped in between the two sites, if the location of the storage site were known, rather than use two Mk-39 weapons. Lethal fallout effects from the 19-megaton groundburst could have extended along a three-hundred-kilometer or longer hot line, depending on wind conditions.
Courtesy of the author.

administrative center of the Soviet Empire; it also contained several airfields capable of handling large jet aircraft as well as the Fili airframe plant, which made Mya-4 Bison bombers. As previously discussed, Moscow was surrounded with two rings of SA-1 Guild anti-aircraft missile sites, twenty-two of them in the inner ring at twenty-five miles and thirty-four in the outer ring at forty-five miles from the city center. Each site contained sixty missiles, with an engagement range of between ten and thirty-five kilometers, and the B-200 Yo-Yo fire-control radar at each site had a range of thirty-five kilometers (twenty-one miles).[120] Overall long-range detection was conducted by A-100B short-range radar and A-100D long-range radar, which were located in another ring about three hundred kilometers from the city center.[121]

In the absence of standoff missile systems SAC had to rely on the specially trained Hairclipper units to crack the Moscow nut. In the words of one B-47 pilot, "[Hairclipper was] the only way we would have got bombs in on Moscow."[122] The bulk of this capability was regularly rotated to Nouasseur Air Base in Morocco. After the 7th Air Division from the United Kingdom preempted Soviet IL-28s and hit western Hungarian air bases, and after the Spain-based B-47 wings cleared a path through the Hungary-Romania corridor and destroyed the PVO and TU-16 bases in central Ukraine, the Hairclipper crews in Morocco would launch and follow through behind them.

The most likely engagement scenario for Moscow in 1957 was this. There was substantial aerial photography on the southwest quadrant of the Moscow SA-1 defenses: the line from Nouasseur to Moscow via the Hungary-Romanian corridor is a direct one when using a globe and string to measure it.[123] To clear a path through the first SA-1 ring required the destruction, at a minimum, of three sites. The Yo-Yo fire control radar was directional: it sent a three-dimensional pie-shaped fan of energy out, not a 360-degree one. These fans overlapped with adjacent sites. Destroying three sites in the first ring and four in the second, where the overlap was greater, rendered the rest of the system useless as it was unable to conduct engagements behind itself. B-47 crews conducting LABS maneuvers like those employed by Hairclipper had a circular error probable training standard of five thousand feet, or nearly a mile (1.5 kilometers).[124] Hairclipper crews would probably have employed the unretarded Mk-15 with a yield of 3.8 megatons. The SA-1 sites were large: the launcher "herringbone" was half a mile wide by a mile long. The alert launchers were not hardened but the storage and Yo-Yo site were, so a groundburst would have been needed in order to fully kill the site. A miss by one mile or the use of an airburst still would have rendered the site inoperable, with the thermal effects destroying the exposed missiles.

The gaping hole in the SA-1 defenses would have had five to seven pillars of radioactive material ascending and then being deposited to the east. The Eighth Air Force was scheduled to handle Moscow targets and would have arrived some time after it attacked the bomber bases in the Baltics, Belarus, Leningrad, and Murmansk.[125] The effects of the attack on the SA-1 system, specifically those that might interfere with flight operations, would have dissipated by the time the assault on the other targets started, perhaps an hour or so later.

The Moscow targets themselves are interesting (see map 22). One B-47 pilot recalled that his target was "a military field on the edge of the Soviet capital" and it was going to be hit with "the biggest and dirtiest weapon in the inventory."[126] This was either the Mk-21 with an 18-megaton yield or the Mk-36Y1 at 19 megatons, and the target was likely Tushino Airfield. In keeping with the Air Power Battle Target System, there were several large airfields and one airframe plant identified within the central Moscow area. And, importantly, airfields were more likely to appear on bomb-nav radar than any other target type, with the exception of the distinctive, irregularly shaped Kremlin complex. The application of three groundburst 18- or 19-megaton-yield bombs on almost any geometric combination of these targets, each weapon gouging out a four-kilometer-wide crater, would have rendered Moscow uninhabitable. That said, the Kremlin was at the time 3.6 nautical miles south of Airframe Plant 30 at Moscow Central Airfield and 4.5 nautical miles east of Airframe Plant Fili 23, with its Bison production line. By adding a fourth DGZ to the east at a readily identifiable rail confluence, the destruction of the Kremlin was ensured if only one of the four easternmost strikes

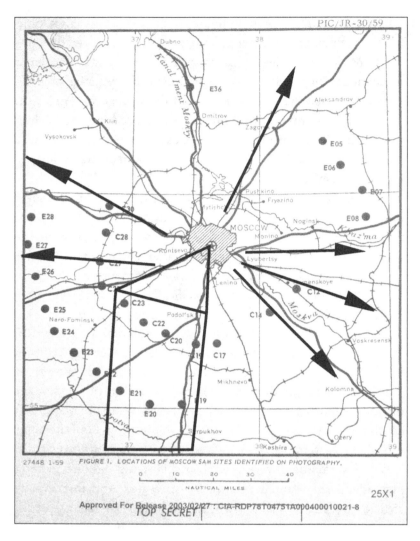

27448 1-59   FIGURE 1. LOCATIONS OF MOSCOW SAM SITES IDENTIFIED ON PHOTOGRAPHY.

0   10   20   30   40

NAUTICAL MILES

25X1

Maps 20. & 21. Getting through the SA-1 Guild missile defenses was a sine qua non for the destruction of Moscow. Map 20 is a CIA facilities map. The superimposed arrows depict B-47 ingress and egress routes. The fact that the missile defenses consisted of two full circles around the city was understood. For targeting purposes, however, SAC would probably have gone with known locations, and given the shortest flight time to bases in Spain and Morocco, SA-1 sites in the southwestern quadrant would have been prioritized for the Hairclipper-trained units. Map 21 portrays analysis derived from pre–U-2 USAF SENSINT photography. One can discern the Herringbone SA-1 sites. These were photographed by the Sara Jane C-54E diplomatic mail plane using concealed cameras. Courtesy of CIA.

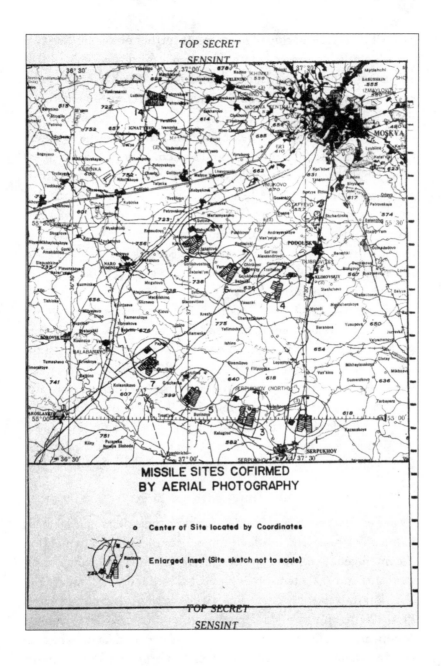

MISSILE SITES COFIRMED
BY AERIAL PHOTOGRAPHY

o   **Center of Site located by Coordinates**

Enlarged Inset (Site sketch not to scale)

made it in. A second ring of four targets further out, including two large identifiable power plants, and then a third ring beyond that consisting of an identified nuclear storage site (Mozhaysk) and three large airfields would have required additional strikes. The Eighth Air Force was also interested in the Sosonio (E-02) and Starozheltikovo (C-02) SA-1 sites in the northeast quadrant. These were likely egress routes for the aircraft striking central Moscow. The southeast egress route would have been over sites C-14 (Khlynovo)/E-15 (Zevalovo) and C-12 (Volodino)/E-13 (Staroye). The western route included SA-1 sites to the west: C-27 (Pestovo), E-27 (Strygino), C-28 (Yershovo), and C-23 (Zverevo). There was a northwest egress route over Kostrovo (E-31), Istria (C-30), and Narynka (E-32) The Elektrosal nuclear facility and nearby SA-1 site E-08 (Fedorova) were also scheduled for destruction.[127]

The generation of "bonus" damage to Moscow using the Air Power Battle Target system would have been understood by the targeting staffs templating out three to nine 18- or 19-megaton-yield weapons and was probably intentional. It followed the established precedent with the earlier EWPs vis-à-vis Moscow targeting. Intrawar bargaining concepts generated by theoreticians, like city withholding, were simply not relevant in this environment. There was no "Hot Line" yet. The EWP in 1957 was a fight to the finish and was the furthest thing from World War II–with-atomic-bombs imaginable at the time.

Getting Through to the Target

As in earlier years, the penetration problem remained a central focus of the USAF research-and-development commands, not to mention the intelligence community. SAC knew that PVO had over a thousand MiG and Yak interceptors supported by hundreds of radar sites. They knew the Soviet system, like NORAD's, was constantly evolving. Ferret flights and ground intercept stations on the Soviet periphery, American and allied, poured a constant stream of data in to be analyzed and converted into mission-specific information for B-47 crews. Radar frequencies were constantly collected and assessed, a science that took on new dimensions in 1957, when a U.S. Navy earth-moon-earth communications test station at Chesapeake Beach, Maryland,

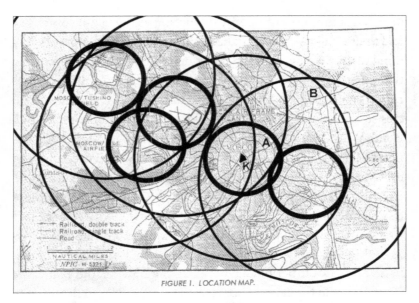

FIGURE 1. LOCATION MAP.

Map 22. Central Moscow targets. This map is superimposed on a contemporary CIA facilities location map for Moscow. After penetrating the city's defenses, B-47s would have delivered their 18- to 19-megaton-yield Mk-36 bombs on several airfield targets in the Moscow area selected for their radar reflectability. The Kremlin, due to its size and shape, would also have been visible to radar and likely have been target number 1. A fifth weapon was aimed at a prominent railroad confluence. Groundbursts would have ensured the collapse of underground facilities. The "A" rings represent 4-kilometer-wide fireballs, while the "B" rings represent 12.2-kilometer blast radii at 5 PSI. Note that the Kremlin is within the "B" ring for Moscow Airframe Plant 30 and Moscow Fili Airfield, and the Tushino and Fili strikes would collaterally destroy the Bison airframe plant. The map does not depict the thermal pulse radius, which would have extended more than 30 kilometers from each Desired Ground Zero. Six other DGZs in a ring outside of the core and then three airfields on the periphery of the city were targets for follow-on strikes leading to the complete destruction of the city. Courtesy of CIA.

intercepted some very powerful signals originating from the Soviet Union bouncing off the moon. This was PVO's new P-14 Tall King early warning radar, and steps were taken to plot their locations.[128]

In an abrupt move, however, in 1956 PVO changed its ground-controlled intercept equipment from high-frequency radio to very high-frequency radio. The PVO system was for the most part dependent on GCI; even the Scan Odd–equipped MiG-17P interceptors were to be vectored by controllers to their "boxes." SAC's planning involved jamming or otherwise disrupting PVO ground controllers and their tenuous links with their MIG or Yak charges, not just jamming their radar systems. The introduction of VHF radio reduced the range the GCI signals propagated, and thus the ground intercept stations were no longer capable of cataloguing these frequencies so they could be programmed into the jammers of the 376th Bomb Wing's EW B-47s. There were several remedies: the U-2s carried ELINT collection equipment, and the U.S. Air Force and NSA deployed ten Sun Valley C-130 COMINT intercept aircraft in peripheral areas. One Sun Valley C-130 was shot down in September 1958 during one operation. The Royal Air Force, whose RB-50G ELINT aircraft were the first to identify Scan Odd, deployed Comet R Mk-2s to Bodo, Norway; Cyprus; and Habbinaya, Iraq, to gather intelligence on Soviet peripheral areas like the Barents, the Baltic, the Black Sea, and the Iranian border.[129] The PVO used a related set of standardized frequencies that could be blanked out.

The PVO in 1957 was a potpourri of aircraft types. There were three models of MIG-17s: the P model with Scan Odd air intercept radar; the PF, which had afterburners; and the PFU, a limited-run collection of forty aircraft modified to carry very early RS-1-U (AA-1 Alkali to NATO) beam-riding air-to-air missiles. The second was the MIG-19 series with the SV high-altitude interception model and the P version with GRANAT radar. The Yak-25M dual-seat, dual-engine radar-carrying interceptor was also in service in limited numbers.[130]

Despite the fact that there were nearly two thousand interceptor aircraft in the PVO inventory and they exhibited tremendous technological innovation, there were significant vulnerabilities. The primary one was that PVO pilots were slaves to their jammable GCI system. The other problems were aircraft-specific. The Yak-25M had trouble reaching the B-47 service ceiling; it was optimized for low-level intercept but had no "look-down–shoot-down" capability because its radar pointed forward in the direction of flight. As for the MIG-19P, it could match the B-47, but there were not enough trained crews available and the type suffered from repeated radar malfunctions and poor reliability. The MIG-17s other than the P had no radar, "which made using them against the Stratojets pointless."

The P model "had radar but lacked the speed and altitude performance required to oppose the Stratojet."[131]

SAC, on the other hand, invested heavily in electronic countermeasures. The Blue Cradle B-47s of the 376th and 301st Bombardment Wings stood alert alongside their nuclear-armed brethren overseas, prepared to deploy a pair of ECM planes for each fifteen-plane B-47 cell penetrating PVO radar cover. Constant exercises against surrogate Soviet radars and NORAD honed the capability: "The way we did it, we had the fourteen BLUE CRADLE planes spread apart in tier at high altitude, There was a lot of jamming, power all over the place. Behind them came forty bombers each with a couple of jammers One by one the B-47 bombers would go silent, drop out of the formation and go to low level, 1,000 feet, skirt across the country, pop up, "bomb" the city, go back to low level and return to base."[132] "The B-47E bomber itself carried chaff, jammers, and an electronic warfare detection system of its own."[133]

If the SAC EWP had been executed at night or under poor weather conditions, the bulk of PVO would have been unable to intercept the B-47 force. During the daytime, a mass scramble would probably have generated some attrition, but the GCI links would have been jammed and it would have been visual flight rules all the way for the interceptors. There was little or no low-level intercept capability. Indeed, after initial penetration, the SAC plan involved orbiting the Blue Cradle B-47s over Belarus, Moscow, and Ukraine while different waves came in. Anti-aircraft artillery, of which the Soviets had plenty, did not have the ability to kill a B-47 conducting a LABS run even if it were detected.

As for the B-47 force, navigation skills had to be at a premium for the EWP to succeed. In a significant improvement over the earlier "K" systems, the B-47E model carried the MA-7 Bombing Navigation System, with the AN/APS-64 radar with a range of 240 miles and a low-level capability that gave returns 35 miles ahead of the aircraft. But most important, the AN/APS-64 had characteristics of what would later be called Terrain Following Radar, which permitted low-level operations not seen previously.[134] New information from U-2 flights dramatically contributed to B-47 force accuracy: there were new charts, and target study time was further reduced through the progressive reduction in "no show" targets. In the past crews knew generally where a target was, they flew there, acquired nearby terrain features on radar, computed an offset and bomb run, and released their weapon. Now, with better information, the crews could visualize their targets in advance and could get there more expeditiously. One unknown, however, was the possibility that the Soviets might have a means to jam the radar on the bomb-nav system either on the way in and throw off navigation, or have point jammers near possible targets to interfere with the final bomb run. SAC tactical doctrine was established for this specific eventuality.

The Tactical Warning Plan Component of the EWP

But what if SAC was in retaliatory mode? What if the Soviets struck first? SAC anticipated that it would lose all of its overseas bases, including Thule, Keflavik, Goose Bay, and Harmon, in such a move. With the UK, Spanish, and Moroccan bases out of action, or politically neutralized during a crisis, what could reasonably be accomplished? This had implications in peacetime as well as war. SAC had to have the ability to "prevent further attacks against the United States" in order to present a credible deterrent. The Tactical Warning target set was a subset of the Strategic Warning target set but in a truncated and different sequence. The number of retaliatory targets was set at 210, with three bombers assigned to hit each target, anticipating that one would get through a prepared and possibly more coherent air defense system. Soviet bombers may have already been employed or even dispersed. This meant that all of the IL-28 and some of the TU-16 bases that would have employed their bombers in a preemptive or other strike would no longer be part of that Tactical Warning list. It likely assumed that the 7th Air Division had been destroyed or neutralized. What would prevent further damage? Once again, we need to move beyond the thirty-minute war we have been conditioned to understand as the norm for a nuclear war.

The obvious targets were the Soviets' atomic energy complexes and their airfields to prevent more nuclear weapons from being made and deployed. Another probable target grouping would have been the air bases around Murmansk and the Kamchatka Peninsula, given their proximity to North America and their role as "bounce" air bases for long-range aviation. Another possibility was Soviet airframe plants, again with their airfields, to prevent more bombers from being constructed. SAC bombers operating from the Midwest and using aerial refueling were the likely candidates to hit those, combined with anything that got off the ground in the Far East. SAC's Far East bases assumed a greater importance in the Tactical Warning plan, which probably accounts for the deployment of Hairclipper-capable squadrons to Andersen AFB in Guam.

Destruction of the Mya-4 base at Siauliai and the "transport" airfield at Kedainai in the Baltic states were crucial to prevent "bounce" operations from forces stationed deeper inside the Soviet Union. Another targeting possibility included any bases in East Germany that could handle large bombers; with the United Kingdom destroyed or neutralized, use of the airfields around Berlin brought long-range bombers geographically closer to North America, significantly closer than those based around Murmansk, for example.

If SAC was unable to suppress the seven bases in Belarus, nine in central-east Ukraine, and four in western Russia, the aircraft based there could have been employed through the Baltics or Germany against their targets. Any identified nuclear weapons storage area in those regions would also have been targeted to prevent reloading or dispersal. The Crimean bases would have been a problem, but a shuttle raid with recovery in Turkey, Cyprus, Iran, or Israel was a possibility.

The weight of a retaliatory attack could not have excluded the Moscow target complex. The loss of Hairclipper units would have posed significant problems for such a strike, although there were some squadrons with this capability based in the American Midwest. An attack patterned on the Strategic Warning plan portion dealing with Moscow would have been possible, with the assault against the SA-1 complexes in the northwest quadrant the likely target instead of those in the southwest. At least three large-yield weapons on Moscow targets would have made the point.

The best SAC option would have been a night attack avoiding known portions of the Soviet air defense system with maximum electronic countermeasures in play. Any retaliatory plan would have been to some extent dependent on the availability of B-47 jammer aircraft. Those were mostly located at Lockbourne AFB, and the Soviets' ability to reach that base and destroy it would have been problematic given the NORAD air defense system of the period. SAC's dispersal plans would have decreased the probability of such an attack. On the down side, several of the Soviet national stockpile sites remained unidentified at this point. SAC would have to destroy delivery means and airfields to reduce the possibility of those weapons' use.

The United States maintained a reserve in the form of the unallocated weapons and B-36 aircraft. SAC's ability to conduct post-strike reconnaissance, either post-Soviet or post-SAC, would have been crucial here. A B-47 training unit at McConnell AFB in Kansas contained nineteen RB-47s in addition to sixty-nine other B-47s and appears to have had a damage assessment role in their Emergency War Plan.[135] CIA and SAC U-2s would have had to deploy forward, probably to bases in the Central Treaty Organization area and the Far East to collect the information required for an assessment of SAC strikes under conditions of Tactical Warning. Only then could the reserve have been employed with any hope of effectiveness. The destruction of the Soviet atomic energy production complexes east of the Urals would have been a probable course of action. Again there are no data that support the idea that "city-busting" and deliberate population targeting were part of the plan. That said, the unallocated reserve force would have given the president that option if he chose to employ it, whether the dust from the "smoking, radiating" ruins was still setting or afterward. At the very least the destruction of Soviet industrial capacity would have been assured even with tactical warning.

The Air Power Battle Target System moved to the forefront of the SAC deterrent effort, particularly after new and better information was developed on the totality of Soviet capabilities. Earlier SAC analysis of the implications was borne out, and forward thinking from 1954 to 1955 was implemented, specifically, tanker-supported strikes against targets throughout the Soviet Union from North American bases and the development of a low-level thermonuclear weapon delivery capability against Moscow. Most important, however, was the implementation of complementary plans, the Strategic Warning and Tactical Warning plans coupled with a graduated buildup system. These developments provided options to the national political leadership, particularly during the increased number of international crises that the Soviets and Communist Chinese leadership initiated. While SAC was in the process of implementing these plans, dramatic technological changes forced a series of midcourse corrections that threatened to undermine the evolving deterrent system.

8

Prosteishiy Sputnik

Midcourse Corrections, 1957–59

My personal belief is that we really know too little of the Soviets' total
military capabilities and exact intentions to arrive at a conclusive
judgement on which to base a well-defined and rigid deterrent strategy
for the future. . . . I am convinced that we can devise and indefinitely
maintain an effective deterrent against any kind of aggression, at
acceptable cost and risk. But this deterrent must be based on a
continuous and factual assessment of the threat and must be
designed for no other purpose than to meet the threat.

—GEN. THOMAS S. POWER, 1958

The 1957–59 period was unprecedented in the complexity, scope, and rapidity of technological change as it affected nuclear targeting and deterrence. As with the Manhattan Project, there were multiple concurrent processes in the U.S. national security apparatus dedicated to responding to existing as well as anticipated Soviet threats. War planners were forced to carry out their work with an ever-changing force structure as well as demanding political imperatives, particularly with regard to basing and alliance relationships, not to mention the impact of three international crises that had nuclear weapons use implications. This tremendous across-the-board acceleration was absorbed by American military leaders and translated into facts on the ground in order to maintain the deterrent margin. At the same time there was a plethora of challenges related to Soviet attempts to limit or otherwise offset American and allied plans and capabilities. These concurrent problems and their solutions had deep ramifications for the creation of the Single Integrated Operational Plan as it emerged in 1960, but also over the long term as the SIOP evolved. Some weapons systems envisioned in the 1957–60 period were deployed in the 1960s and their descendants remained in service well into the 1980s. Some concepts for their employment and the context for this lay in the late 1950s. This chapter corrals these processes and sets the stage for the shift from the Emergency War Plan to the Basic War Plan of 1958, which itself was the predecessor to the SIOP.

Changing of the Guard

Equally critical to the process were the military leaders who were forced by circumstances to handle these adjustments. In what can only be described as an alignment of the planets, the U.S. Air Force leadership at this time coalesced with the right people, at the right time, in the right positions. Curtis LeMay, who was in the public forefront from 1948 to 1957, was the odds-on favorite to replace Nathan Twining as chief of staff of the air force. Yet this did not happen. LeMay was moved, almost laterally, from Offutt to Washington to become the vice chief of staff. It appears at first glance that he languished there during the period before ascending to the chief of staff position in 1961, but he did exert influence in subtle and important ways.[1]

The intense and unrelenting Thomas Power took command of SAC in 1957. This was an astute move. Power commanded Air Research and Development Command in Baltimore after he left as SAC's vice chief of staff in 1954. His last posting, generated by LeMay at the time, positioned Power to observe, influence, and, most important, learn about the upcoming technologies and bureaucratic processes that produced significant technological changes, like Mach-speed bombers and ballistic and cruise missiles. While in this position Power regularly fed LeMay detailed summations of technological developments that affected not only SAC but the entire air force while he was head of ARDC. When Power took over SAC, he was intellectually, technologically, and bureaucratically positioned to take full advantage of the situation.

When it came to the threat, Power was simpatico with the wise, gray-haired, incongruously black-eyebrowed Twining. In 1956 Twining, Power, and others visited the Soviet Union as part of a controversial air force delegation, and both men dealt point blank with the Soviet leadership, including Khrushchev.[2] Twining was at this point the air force chief of staff, having replaced the ailing Hoyt Vandenberg. Both Power and Twining stalked the golf circuit, which gave them ample opportunities to have an informal meeting of minds.[3] Twining, in the role of vice chief of staff and then the chief, was the man who discretely handled every aerial incident in which U.S. Air Force aircraft were shot up or shot down by Communist bloc forces in the 1950s.[4] As the chief of staff, Twining was also in the forefront of dealing with the interservice command-and-control problems with the U.S. Navy when it came to targeting. He was then elevated to chairman of the Joint Chiefs of Staff in 1957, having labored in that arena with his predecessor, Adm. Arthur Radford.

Twining's replacement was the enigmatic but highly experienced Thomas Dresser White. The rectangular-faced White had extensive flying experience throughout China, having been posted there in the 1920s to learn the language. He was then posted to be the air attaché in Moscow, flying Ambassador William Bullitt around the Soviet Union at the height of the Stalin purges in the 1930s. Aligned with George Kenney in the Pacific War, White was displaced to the Joint Strategic Survey Committee in the late 1940s, after Kenney was removed, where he was involved in the war-planning activities described in chapter 2. White possessed crucial diplomatic and bureaucratic credentials for the Pentagon environment and appears to have left the pick and shovel work to LeMay.[5]

Rounding out the guard were the "two Larrys": the smooth, charismatic Lauris Norstad, now the Supreme Allied Commander Europe, and the intense Laurence Kuter, Commander in Chief Far East. Norstad was involved, as we have seen, in nuclear planning starting in 1945, and then he was in deep in European affairs as NATO's Commander in Chief Allied Air Forces Central Europe as the struggles between SACEUR and SAC were sorted out in the early 1950s. Kuter's strategic bombing pedigree went back to the Pacific War, but he also attended the Yalta Conference in 1945. And of course there was the pipe-smoking "Opie" Weyland, who moved in to clean up Tactical Air Command.

It is crucial to point out that, unlike their military counterparts, all of these men had direct experiences with the Communist world and, to a certain extent, its leadership. Those experiences continued to play a role in their assessment of what was needed to deter the opposition during this dangerous time. Of equal importance, all of these men maintained a professional interest in changing technologies, and many of them witnessed nuclear tests in the 1940s and 1950s; that is, they had direct experiences with the weapons they might have to employ or that might be used against the United States. Nuclear warfare was not a theoretical or academic exercise to them.

Red Moon: Sputnik's Impact

The psychological impact of Sputnik I on the U.S. population should be classed in the league of the Pearl Harbor and 9/11 attacks. The realignment of national priorities and financial resources was as profound. Would the existence of this new Soviet capability undermine NATO unity? What did it mean to the confidence of the national military establishment, not to mention the presidency? How did the demonstrated technology affect the precarious deterrent margin? These and related questions have been examined historically and are important ones.[6] But there was substantially more context to the Sputnik achievement and its impact on SAC and the Emergency War Plan.

The American and allied intelligence apparatus kept a close eye on missile and nuclear weapons developments through its networks of sensors. Throughout 1956 the Soviets conducted nine nuclear weapons tests. The most pertinent of these was Operation Baikal, conducted on 2 February 1956. This was the full-on launch of an R-5M ballistic missile (SS-3 Shyster, in NATO parlance) and the detonation of a modified RDS-4-based warhead.[7] With a 1,200-kilometer range, it could hit targets throughout Western Europe with a 300-kiloton-yield warhead, though these details were not available at the time to American intelligence analysts, nor the fact that the R-5M was an operational system projected for deployment by 1957. Of equal importance were a pair of 900-kiloton thermonuclear tests that suggested a possible yield for the R-5M and any future missiles to any analysts looking at seismic data from, say, Air Force Technical Applications Center.[8]

What American intelligence did not and could not discern was Khrushchev's personal interest in the R-5M and its successors. After the R-5M test, Khrushchev and the Presidium were briefed by Chief Designer Sergei Korolev on the system. Khrushchev wanted to know "how many warheads would be needed to destroy England," as she was "America's closest ally." He was told by Minister of Defense Industry (later Minister of Defense) Dimitri Ustinov that five would accomplish that task, with another seven or nine against France. These would be enough "to crush defenses and disrupt communications and transportation, not to mention the destruction of major cities."[9]

In 1957 there were thirteen Soviet nuclear tests. Of these a 1.6-megaton shot on 24 September and a 2.9-megaton shot on 2 October are notable. The significance of the proximity of the 2 October shot to Sputnik should not be discarded, nor should the launch of Sputnik II on 3 November, after the second megaton-yield nuclear test. It is highly likely this constituted active signaling by the Soviets; for example, back in the summer of 1957 the Soviet propaganda apparatus had announced to the global ham radio community what frequencies Sputnik would be transmitting on.[10] They knew about American and allied national technical means and played to them.

The Sputnik "panic" in the United States itself was in fact the result of cumulative information compiled and distributed by the American media, not just the fact that Sputnik was orbiting over the country unhindered. U.S. Air Force media analysis provided to General White and Secretary of the Air Force James H. Douglas noted this culmination in some detail, including summations of discussions and concerns in the press over several related subjects: a recent Soviet "super long-range ballistic missile" test; the first Earth satellite; a Soviet "announcement . . . that an extremely high altitude thermonuclear explosion had taken place"; plus open warnings by Khrushchev relayed through American reporters and his public assertions that ballistic missiles made manned bombers obsolete.[11]

Under LeMay, however, SAC had been wargaming its future force structure throughout 1957 for an ICBM threat environment set in 1961–62. In one set of exercises, SAC destroyed only 39 percent of its targets in the initial strike. A "maximized" force structure destroyed 77 percent of its targets. SAC assumed only fifteen minutes of warning (RAND analysts said there would be none at all) and worked out methods of dispersal and alert involving home and satellite bases. Simply put, the alert process had to be sped up if SAC was going to reduce a ballistic missile threat. In June 1957 LeMay told White, "For three years now, I have counseled more B-52s, more KC-135s and a maximized alert force, well dispersed. Every thoughtful analysis of the future that I have seen has confirmed my conviction. Only if we have such a force can we be reasonably assured that war will be avoided on our terms in the critical 1960–65 time period."[12] LeMay's staff were coming up with novel methods of dispersing forces and were still trying to gain tanker bases in Canada to give SAC more flexibility. An early test of what would become the Reflex Action deployments took place in July 1957.[13]

On 14 October White, almost with a sigh, told Power that most studies on the SAC deterrent problem were now obsolete and asked him to reexamine the situation.[14] Their communications focused initially on the alerting and release procedures, with Power pushing to reduce the alert period from the one hour previously established under LeMay to fifteen minutes. An air force paper titled "Instructions for the Expenditure of Nuclear Weapons under Special Circumstances" had already been circulated to the JCS by White. There was debate but no agreement among the members. Gen. Maxwell Taylor "agreed that authority to order retaliatory attack may be exercised by CINCSAC if time or circumstances would not permit a decision by the President." The chief of naval operations, Adm. Arleigh Burke, "was reluctant to go this far," but White believed that "there might be a possibility of securing their agreement ultimately." White had pressed the chiefs on delegating authority down to SAC's numbered air force commanders but "ran into stiff resistance and . . . finally went along with stopping with [Power's] headquarters." However, White told Power, "Your plans provide for [the] assumption of authority by your Air Force commanders under specified circumstances. This can be construed as at least an element of the delegation we would prefer. . . . We still consider that the President's instructions would permit specific delegation to your Air Force commanders."[15]

As it turned out, it wasn't just the threat of an ICBM attack that had White and Power concerned. Both were significantly concerned about an emergent Soviet submarine threat. White discussed the problem with Burke; he "consider[ed] the threat to [SAC] facilities overseas to be of such a magnitude as to warrant immediate investigation." Using U.S. Navy intelligence analysis that credited the Soviets with 450 submarines, White explained that his primary concern was SAC bases on islands, particularly Guam.[16] Power also talked to Burke and expressed concern that the "threat encompasse[d] at least 50 percent of the SAC bases."[17] At this point the Soviets did not have missile submarines deployed, so this was anticipatory and prescient on White and Power's part, though they may have been aware of the Soviet R-11FM missile system, first tested in 1955 for insertion into the Zulu-class ballistic missile submarines, which then came into service in 1958. On 10 October 1957, right after the Soviet 2.9-megaton test at Novaya Zemlya, the Soviets conducted a live test of the T-5 nuclear torpedo. Fired from the diesel-propelled Whiskey-class submarine S-144, the weapon yielded 10 kilotons, which would have had some effect if it were fired against SAC bases located close to shore.[18] To what extent the American intelligence apparatus knew about the T-5 test at the time remains unclear.

Power's concurrent concern was the complete lack of early warning of a missile attack of any kind, be it directed against SAC's forward bases or against those in the continental United States. He told White he would place SAC on thirty-minute reaction time as of 7 January 1958.[19] White poured coal into the Air Research and Development Command engine to get moving on an existing project, specifically emphasizing that this was "not a new task, for [they] knew it would come to this eventually, but an immediate task of protecting the United States from surveillance or attack from space."[20] The result would be the Ballistic Missile Early Warning System and the

Missile Defense Alarm System satellite constellations, but these would not be deployed until the early 1960s.

The early Sputniks, which included Sputnik III, launched on 15 May 1958, were not mere propaganda stunts or pure scientific studies. They were crucial steps toward achieving an ICBM capability. Knowledge of the space environment and how it affected ballistic missiles provided a strategic advantage. Additionally, understanding planet Earth was the key to accuracy. Sputnik III was equipped to collect geodetic information, including the effects of gravity in this regard. By 1958 Soviet submarines were collecting undersea gravitational data between the Soviet Union and North America so that Soviet data (which was unavailable to the United States) could be linked with the open-source data collected from Western sources on gravitational measurements. This potentially increased the accuracy of their ballistic missiles over those of the United States, whose forces had no such data for the Soviet Union and had yet to start gathering undersea gravity data for an ICBM force that did not yet exist. In 1958 a Soviet Zulu IV ballistic missile submarine was forced to the surface off Greenland by the U.S. Navy; it was in a position to take out Goose Bay, Ernest Harmon, Thule, Sondrestrom, or Keflavik, all bases that, as we have seen, were crucial to the execution of the existing Emergency War Plan.[21]

SAC Responds to Sputnik

Brig. Gen. Bonner Fellers, U.S. Army Retired and late of Douglas MacArthur's staff in 1945, wrote in a magazine piece published soon after Sputnik, "The amazing Soviet satellite, as it circled the globe, ushered in a rash of desperate demands for a wild defense spending orgy." He went on, "For those who believe America's salvation lies in spending our way out of every difficulty and danger, the Red moon came as manna from Heaven."[22] Thomas White in many ways agreed with Fellers and established new but limited USAF priorities in response to Sputnik while he struggled to unravel the Gordian knot of ballistic missile programs that had been foisted on him by a variety of circumstances, most of them political.[23] He was smart enough to leave it to the resource-conscious LeMay to handle their implementation: "Any bottlenecks encountered should be promptly brought to your attention and taken to [the secretary of defense] or wherever required to cut them loose." These high-priority items were of no surprise to LeMay as he had pressed for them throughout 1957: SAC dispersal, northern tanker bases in Canada, and increased alert facilities for nuclear weapons.[24] Seven days later, the U.S. Air Force's Strategic Plan of Operations was amended thus: "The concept of maintaining one-third of SAC's strike force on constant alert is approved."[25] This, of course, made Power at SAC less unhappy and gave Twining (or at least his staff) more work shuffling cash to cover the costs.

There were several large programs that altered SAC's concept of operations, though it is crucial to note that these existed in SAC planning shops and some thought had been given to implementing them over time. The potential Soviet capability of a no-notice strike and the compressed time lines led to all three being implemented simultaneously.

The first and most profound was SAC's dispersal concept. This was a complete realignment of how SAC handled its basing system and with it the vital logistics and maintenance systems, and more important, the organization culture that had to accompany these changes. In the earlier concept, several bombardment wings occupied a single base, and those wings rotated to forward bases for three-month periods. Given the pattern of the earlier EWPs, there was no need to disperse the B-36s and B-47s from their state-side bases to other locations except to move them forward to stage for strikes. In the forward areas, dispersal sites existed to handle both the staging forces and forces returning after the first strikes. With the increased Soviet capabilities, however, all this had to change. At the same time, SAC was introducing B-52 bombers and KC-135 tankers. Just sending them to former B-36 bases and replacing one heavy bomber with another was not going to work.[26]

The initial idea was to have three B-52 squadrons (fifteen aircraft per) and their tankers (ten aircraft per) at one base and then in an emergency send two of the squadrons and their associated tankers to two other airfields. There were going to be eleven B-52 bases, so that meant twenty-two dispersal bases for a total of thirty-three. The B-47s were still going to be crowded on their existing bases. What was to be done with them? This was a huge problem, given that there were more than two thousand aircraft involved. What about maintenance? And how about the nuclear weapons? How would those be handled in dispersal bases? These problems occupied SAC throughout 1958.[27]

That was the "peacetime" posture problem. But what about now, today, if the Soviets struck? Working closely with their Canadian counterparts in the RCAF, SAC formulated SAC OPLAN 10-59, the Hostile Action Evacuation Plan. In an emergency, the most vulnerable continental U.S. bases "flushed" their bombers and tankers as quickly as possible to orbit areas over Canada. Each orbit area was associated with an air base or airport for emergency recovery. In this case, Loring, Westover, Plattsburg, and Pease air force bases surged their aircraft over Gander, Newfoundland; Summerside, Prince Edward Island; Greenwood, Nova Scotia; Chatham, New Brunswick; and Torbay, Newfoundland. These moves obviously had to be carefully coordinated with NORAD. OPLAN 10-59 was a pure survival tool to preserve as much of the force as possible.[28] More detailed thinking was required, especially when it came to the vital B-52s, and those argumentations contributed to the acceptance of Airborne Alert.

Related to this was the decision to implement Fail Safe, its name changed to Positive Control in May 1958. Positive Control was a key mechanism linking the ground alert force with the Airborne Alert Force and the Reflex forces overseas. At various levels of alert, CINC-SAC could launch his forces but not commit them for attacks against the Soviet Union without presidential authority. This posed problems in a crisis: what if the launch order was received and there were no tankers present to refuel the orbiting bombers?[29]

When it came to the B-47 force, ideas expressed in 1957 evolved into the SAC Alert Concept. It was clear before Sputnik that the forward bases were vulnerable. At the same time the cost of maintaining entire forty-five-plane B-47s wings forward was gargantuan, especially when it came to maintenance manpower. Out of this came Reflex Action. In effect, the wing-size rotations were replaced with detachments of B-47s and crews for weekly rotations. The nuclear weapons remained at the forward bases; the rotating B-47s came from North America. The planes landed, were loaded, and were placed on fifteen-minute alert. The size of the detachment varied depending on whether the Reflex forces were located in the United Kingdom, Spain, Morocco, Alaska, or Guam (Reflex was called Air Mail on Guam). Reflex also took place inside the United States; the original southern-southwestern base concept was now obsolete, so B-47 units located there Reflex'd to bases in the northeastern United States. Reflex Action was in full effect by early 1958.[30]

But what to do with all of the other B-47s being brought back to the United States, aircraft that were now dangerously concentrated in the older base system? Two solutions were in the offing. The first was the use of civilian airports for bomber force dispersal. In conjunction with other government agencies, a National Airport Plan was produced in 1958 and then continually updated. This plan listed and categorized every airfield, airport, and air base in the United States by runway length and wheel loading as well as possible organizational use. For example, out of twelve classes, Class 1, and thus priority of interest, was Air Force Heavy Bomber, while Class 2 was Air Force Medium Bomber and Heavy Troop Carrier. There were only four Class 1 civilian facilities in the United States, something that gave momentum to solving the B-52/KC-135 base problem, but there were forty-seven Class 2 facilities, more than enough for the B-47 force.[31]

Another crucial change was the implementation of the Northern Tanker Force concept. As we have seen, this went back to 1955–56, when LeMay and his staff brainstormed on how to reduce SAC dependency on the Northeast Air Command bases and to extend the reach of the projected B-52 force and contacted their Canadian counterparts to explore a solution.[32] This chugged along until Sputnik, but that event shook up the Canadian government, which accelerated the survey process and reaffirmed the provision of four bases for modification to take SAC aircraft.[33]

The post-Sputnik difference was that SAC tankers were to be at these bases in peacetime. In the previous concept, on an alert KC-

97s deployed to these bases, which reduced the vulnerability of the entire force as the B-47s did not have to wait hours for the tankers to fly to their refueling points before departing for the rendezvous. In the new concept, the tankers and bombers took off at the same time, more or less, and rendezvoused over northern Canada: "Under the new alert concept there would be no time to deploy the tankers to forward bases due to the decreased warning time." In its final version, there were four bases: Frobisher Bay, Northwest Territories; Namao, Alberta; Cold Lake, Alberta; and Churchill, Manitoba. Six KC-97s were kept on Reflex alert, with parking space and fuel for fourteen more in the event of an international crisis. There was a "mole hole" alert facility, and the aircraft and crews rotated from the United States every week.[34] If war broke out, "these twenty aircraft [would] yo-yo operate and fly a maximum of five (5) sorties per aircraft within a minimum of 72 hours to a maximum of 15 days."[35] The most important effect was that this permitted the repatriated B-47s from Europe now based in the U.S. Midwest and Southwest to be advantageously deployed against the Soviet Union from multiple routes, thus generating increased stress on Soviet resources in peacetime as well as wartime.

The most dramatic and ultimately public response to Sputnik was the Airborne Alert concept, immortalized in the film *Dr. Strangelove*. Originally suggested in 1956, the idea of keeping a proportion of the SAC bomber force in the air at all times so that it was invulnerable to attack gained credence with Power, who implemented testing under the Curtain Raiser project in December 1957. Over the years the evolution of Airborne Alert has been confused with its depiction in popular culture. Throughout the late 1950s, it was envisioned as a temporary measure until a reliable ballistic missile warning system was in place, but in the 1960s it evolved into a Cold War signaling tool. Curtain Raiser led to several other tests, including Head Start I and II, Big Sickle, and others. However, at some point the tests morphed into an unacknowledged Airborne Alert. And this related to the dispositions of the nuclear weapons carried by the force and presidential authorization for their dispersal to it.[36] That in turn related to the issue of dispersing nuclear weapons to SAC forces beyond the existing DOD-AEC agreement.

In early 1958 SAC was "authorized to maneuver on its own authority only atomic weapons," and "hydrogen (TN) weapons" could only be maneuvered "with Presidential authority." By June 1958 "SAC had yet to receive the authority to maneuver TN weapons."[37] This was granted in October 1958 by Eisenhower, who demanded monthly reports on the status of the "maneuver," including number of weapons types, aircraft, and units. In this case aircraft commanders assumed "temporary custody of AEC weapons."[38] The situation was complicated by the need to reexamine the nuclear weapon overflight arrangements with Canada, as well as the need to demonstrate to Eisenhower personally that the safety mechanisms were effective. The Steel Trap "airborne alert indoctrination flights" became a de facto Airborne Alert Force at least by late 1958. The 1960s version, which differed from its predecessors for a variety of reasons, was formalized and code-named Chrome Dome.[39] For the six-month period of July to December 1959, for example, eight B-52 units contributed to generating twenty to twenty-three sorties per day, maneuvering a total of 4,230 Mk-15, Mk-36, and Mk-39 thermonuclear weapons.[40]

New Weapons, New Threats: Operation Hardtack

Operation Hardtack, conducted from April to August 1958, consisted of thirty-five atmospheric tests at Eniwetok and Bikini atolls. There were several groups of tests, including an underwater series and a high-altitude series; the majority were dumped into a "weapons development" category. As with previous test series, there are substantial discrepancies in the partially declassified data as to which test shot correlated to which experimental device or weapon. Leaving aside the underwater and high-altitude tests, of primary interest here for SAC operations are the four processes during Hardtack that produced the next generation of SAC nuclear bombs. These included the Mk-43 bomb (B-58 Hustler), Mk-28 (B-52 bombs, Hound Dog cruise missiles, and the basis for the W49 intermediate-range ballistic missile warhead), the Mk-41 bomb (B-47s and B-52s), and the Mk-53 bomb/B-53 weapon (B-52 and B-58 bombers, Titan II ICBMs).

LeMay's requested feasibility study on a 60-megaton bomb was completed by April 1957, but Eisenhower limited the Hardtack test series to weapons up to 15 megatons and those with an emphasis on "clean" configurations. Once Power was commanding SAC, he reiterated the requirement for the 60-megaton bomb and placed priorities on normally configured bombs as opposed to reduced-fallout "clean" configurations.[41]

The available information suggests that two sets of progressive tests were conducted during Hardtack that eventually resulted in the Mk-41 bomb and its successor, the Mk-53. Building on Redwing shots Zuni and Tewa (3.5 MT clean and 5 MT dirty), shots Sycamore, Poplar, and Pine appear to have been tests of how to tailor an Mk-41's effects. Sycamore was supposed to yield 5 megatons but went off at 92 kilotons. When the test was repeated for Poplar, it was supposed to yield either 5 or 10 megatons; it yielded 9.3. Pine, an attempt at a "clean" Mk-41, was supposed to yield 4 or 6 megatons but went off at 2.[42]

Building on the Navaho TX-21 shot in Redwing, plans were made to generate a 10-megaton version. The Butternut primary test detonated and yielded 81 kilotons instead of 105. Yellowwood, a full-up "clean" test that was supposed to yield 2.5 megatons fizzled at 330 kilotons. With their noses firmly to the grindstone, the engineers and scientists recocked and detonated Oak at 8.9 megatons (versus an estimated yield of 7.5 MT).[43] These tests were the basis of the Mk-53 bomb/B-53 weapon.

Two months after the test series, the University of California Radiation Laboratory analyzed the Hardtack data and concluded that modifications could be made to an existing design to provide additional yields in two versions: a 45-megaton weapon and a 60-megaton weapon.[44] Whether the basis for them was the Mk-41 or the Mk-53 is unclear, but the fact that "the United States, without further testing, [could] develop a warhead of 50–60 MT for B-52 delivery" was confirmed years later.[45]

The eventual mainstay of the B-47 and B-52 force in the 1960s, the Mk-28 bomb and warhead, was also tested during Hardtack. The progressive test of Mk-28 components had already taken place during

Redwing. Of the Hardtack shots, the most heavily redacted material on specific weapons effects from the documents by far relates to Shot Walnut (1.45 MT), though Koa and Fir are very close in yield and all three clouds rose to 60,000 feet. The 1.37-megaton Koa, for example, left a crater that was so radioactive it could not be assessed until 1959. Certain instruments from the Koa shot could not be recovered for three days, compared to one day for another test. However, unlike the other tests, Koa overloaded concrete underground test structures.[46] This suggests that it may have been a competitor or a version of the Mk-28.[47] Koa was detonated the day after Fir, but its sampling was contaminated by Fir fallout. An examination of the subsequent sample separation process suggests that Fir and Koa had different outputs but were of the same design.[48] The torpedo-shaped Mk-28-Y1 went into production in early 1959, and there were at least five different versions with different yields.[49] These gave SAC bombers an expanded low-level delivery capability and eventually reduced reliance on the Hairclipper-trained units and their stressed-out B-47s.

A B-52D equipped with long-range external fuel tanks from Wright Patterson was present for these shots; unlike previous test B-52s that focused on "a symmetrical tail-on position," this one was designed to record "asymmetrical" stresses to nuclear weapons detonations.[50] That is, SAC wanted information on new delivery profiles and effects related to these new weapons, particularly before the projected atmospheric test moratorium went into effect. The U.S. Navy deployed the new A-4D Skyhawk and FJ-4 Fury on other Hardtack shots for similar purposes.

The idea that a nuclear detonation generated an electrical signal went right back to the Trinity test in 1945. Numerous American and British researchers, working independently between 1951 and 1955, refined this thinking. A team at Edgerton, Germeshausen, and Grier Inc. developed shielding to prevent electrical detonators on the nuclear devices from going off in lightning storms; these were built into every device tested by the AEC throughout the period. During their tests in Australia the British found their instrumentation fried by an electrical pulse before it could record data, an effect dubbed "radioflash." In 1954 Los Alamos scientists determined that gamma rays triggered the effect.[51] Using later terminology these effects were called groundburst electromagnetic pulses.

British scientists then noticed a double pulse in their thermonuclear tests (later called E-1 and E-2: a third pulse, E-3, was uncovered subsequently); after some examination they believed it could be used to detect and determine the yield of such weapons. Further investigation, however, led to the suspicion that energy from one warhead detonating in proximity to another could have two effects: the neutrons would contaminate the target warhead at an atomic level and cause it to fizzle, and electrical energy generated by various particles would destabilize the electrical systems on the target warhead and/or its missile.[52] This was, in effect, the conceptual basis for the antiballistic missile. The collaboration of the American and British scientists on electromagnetic pulse (EMP) started around 1956, but the details remain classified. In 1958 there were extensive and highly classified U.S.-UK discussions centered on determining how vulnerable systems were to EMP.[53]

The result appears to have been a joint project code-named Floral. Its objective was to collect data on high-altitude nuclear detonations to support development of antiballistic missiles and develop protective measures. Project Floral had several components embedded within the Hardtack series; these included three high-altitude nuclear detonation shots, Yucca, Teak, and Orange. Another component included covert monitoring facilities established by the United Kingdom and the United States in South Africa in support of a three-shot high-altitude series code-named Argus. Argus had other, concurrent purposes in this case to test theories related to activating the Van Allen Belts with nuclear weapons as a possible antiballistic missile measure. U.S. Navy monitoring ships deployed to stations in the Atlantic and Pacific oceans to collect data while RAF and USAF aircraft did the same. Explorer IV, one of the first American satellites, was also involved.[54]

The results of the six tests were significant. A preliminary report to General White described "maximum blackout effects" from a detonation at 125,000 feet (23 miles). Antiballistic missile systems, radar, and data processing would be dysfunctional for two to thirty minutes. Ballistic Missile Early Warning System radar "may be degraded, depending on the relative position of the burst, target, and radar."[55] The effects on radio communications were the most noticeable and pronounced. The gamma radiation bursts from the Teak and Orange shots, conducted at Johnson Island, "were the sources of serious communications blackouts in the South Pacific." Simply put, high-frequency communications were shut down for hours and in some places days because the medium they needed to bounce off of, the ionosphere, was severely disturbed by the 3.8-megaton-yield detonations conducted at 76 kilometers (47 miles) and 43 kilometers (27 miles). More surprising, there were concerns raised whether the two shots might "burn a hole into the natural ozone layer" with their "ultraviolet emissions." Fortunately they did not.[56]

The three Argus shots employed w-25 warheads (usually optimized for X-ray output: they were Mk-28 thermonuclear bomb primaries and were also used in the MB-1 rocket), which yielded 1.7 kilotons. No detrimental effects were noted during Argus, but apparently it was quite a light show as the bombs triggered artificial aurorae in the Van Allen Belts.

The main takeaway from Project Floral was that high-altitude nuclear detonations could seriously degrade strategic communications and damage electrical systems. And SAC and the presidential communications systems were heavily invested in single-side band high-frequency communications, which depended on ionospheric propagation. Floral had also been unable to explore the issue of component damage; requests to delay the Hardtack roll-up and conduct another Teak-like shot were denied by Department of Defense and the Atomic Energy Commission.[57] That work emerged after Boeing looked at the alarming possibility that groundburst EMP from large nuclear weapon detonations could "couple" to the underground cables associated with ICBM silos and possibly fry their electronics.[58]

Less than two months after the Floral shots, an extraordinary meeting took place in Las Vegas of eleven contractors and government labs involved in the production of strategic weapons systems. There was near-unanimous agreement "that a serious problem existed that directly affected the probable wartime success of the ICBM program": "Some effort has been made toward protection from these [electromagnetic forces, but] it appears that our efforts are inadequate and based on assumptions that may very well be erroneous."[59] The implications of EMP were profound: a ballistic missile attack with no warning using a small number of optimally detonated weapons could wreak utter havoc and undermine the American deterrent. On the other hand, it could be a potential war-winner for the United States but only if the president chose to go first.

The Better Mousetrap: B-52s, KC-135s, and Air-to-Surface Missiles

Lt. Gen. Ennis Whitehead, a retired friend of Thomas White's who regularly provided him with substantial amounts of unsolicited advice, opined in 1956, "The B-52 is currently a fine bomber. It will be a very old bomber in ten or fifteen more years. *We must replace the B-52s in time.*"[60] SAC's heavy bomber force based on the "six turnin' and four burnin'" B-36 was by 1958–59 completely superseded by the jet-engine B-52, which remains in service as there words are written in 2018. By 1958, however, SAC conceptualized the B-52 as a system that included the KC-135 tanker aircraft. Previously the ratio of one KC-97 tanker squadron per B-47 wing held sway, but new basing, range, targeting, and consumption requirements resulted in the projected need for two of the new jet-engine KC-135s for every three B-52s.[61] When LeMay was CINCSAC back in 1955 he called for 1,900 B-52s and 1,300 KC-135s to handle any "increases in the Russian air power target system."[62] In the final measure, the U.S. Air Force acquired 744 B-52s and 732 KC-135s.[63]

After Sputnik, the generation of the Strategic Wing concept progressively took place as the B-52s and KC-135s came into service. In this scheme, one B-52 squadron (fifteen aircraft) and one KC-135 squadron (ten aircraft) would occupy a single base and constitute, with its maintenance and logistics units, a singular formation. The need to get the B-52s as close as possible to Soviet targets while still achieving a dispersed posture based in the continental United States resulted in a complete reorganization of bases and the construction of seven more to support the EWP, this in addition to the existing B-47/KC-97 force laydown.[64]

Some B-36 units converted to B-52s and remained in place, and the Strategic Wing dispersion would not be fully completed until 1961 or 1962. Indeed the activation of a Strategic Wing did not necessarily mean that bombardment and air refueling squadrons were assigned at the time of activation. The B-52 wing buildup progressed from five wings in 1957 to nine in early 1959 and eleven by 1960, for a total of thirty-three squadrons at eighteen bases, with intent to progress to twenty-seven bases by 1960. Of this force, 268 B-52s were on fifteen-minute ground alert as of 30 June 1959.[65] In terms of raw numbers, there were 495 B-52s and 1,245 B-47s.[66]

It was all well and good at the JCS level to use raw numbers of bombers on the charts and graphs they passed to the secretary of defense. However, these forces were dependent on tanker support. And that was a problem. The first KC-135s entered SAC's inventory in mid-1957, but like the B-52s these were progressively entered into service as production and training permitted. There were several hundred KC-97s used to refuel the B-47s and that could also refuel B-52s in a pinch, but the production of the necessary KC-135s slowed down in 1958, affecting SAC's ability to implement the EWP. B-47 units based in the southern United States required two tankings by KC-97s so they could get at their targets; thus the need for the Canadian bases. Estimates based on Operation Power Flite in 1957 determined that two KC-97s were needed to fuel one B-52; thus it would take four KC-97s to handle one B-52 on a refueled mission against the Soviet Union. Consequently the lack of KC-135s detracted from that capability and thus target coverage.[67]

Added to this was the constant shuffling and reshuffling of SAC's refueling assets like so many cards in a poker game. For example, the 4060th Air Refueling Wing at Dow AFB in Maine complained in 1958 that there was no firm directive for setting up refueling wings; there were too many changes and not enough time to develop firm policies.[68] By October 1959, however, a dispersal exercise dubbed Fast Move had 70 KC-135s and 86 KC-97s successfully deploy to support 29 B-52s and 164 B-47s, which essentially constituted the Alert Force.[69]

B-52 survival matters were not limited to basing and warning: what was the best means to ensure that the bombers got through an increasingly dense Soviet air defense system? SAC understood that eventually the SA-1s around Moscow, or their successors, would be deployed elsewhere. Relying on specialized units might not be the way forward. Indeed the 6th Air Division's Hairclipper units reported in March 1958 that B-47 upgrading and "personnel withdrawals severely limited the ability of the wing to accomplish productive Hairclipper training. Sufficient sorties were not available," leaving the wing based at MacDill AFB in Tampa, Florida, with 20 percent of the necessary training sorties completed.[70] In any event, structural problems with the B-47s moved Power to cease Hairclipper training in 1958. After a fleet-wide aircraft modification program, the Hairclipper maneuver was replaced with a "pop-up" delivery profile that reduced stress on the airframes but increased to some extent the vulnerability of the delivery aircraft.[71]

Substantial U.S. Air Force staff and technological efforts were already, by 1957, being poured into acquiring an air-to-surface missile for SAC's bombers. These included the B-47/Rascal combination and the GAM-67 Crossbow nuclear antiradar missile, among other feasibility studies. There was also a concept employing the Snark intercontinental cruise missile in combination with a decoy-dispensing cruise missile dubbed Goose. Even LeMay appeared overwhelmed, writing to White in astonishment, "There are 12 proposals on the air-to-surface missile in the hands of ARDC."[72] White noted "the usual optimism of long-range program estimates" and wanted to cut costs. He proposed dropping the Snark requirement from four to two squadrons, reexamining Goose, and "eliminat[ing] the RASCAL program." He was loath to drop Rascal because of the "valuable training" it provided and because "it was the only system of its kind in existence": "It creates a threat against which no known air defense system is effective and it can have a significant effect on Soviet air defense planning."[73] But after sixty-four of sixty-five GAM-63 launch failures, the Rascal squadron at Pinecastle AFB was shut down and the project canceled.[74] Crossbow, it turned out, "had less range than the Soviet radar" it was supposed to destroy, and it was too slow.[75] White finally came to the same conclusion in early 1958 that LeMay had back in November 1955.[76]

Two proposals were most promising, The first was an air-launched ballistic missile. The second was a proposal by North American Aviation for a cruise missile launched from a B-52. Back in late 1955, after conferring with Power at ARDC, LeMay had determined, "By 1962 an air-to-surface missile for the B-52 can be operational which can be launched 400 or more miles from the target, with as much as 10 megatons yield and with an accuracy of one nautical mile."[77] This proposal was expedited by White after Sputnik and after LeMay recommended it.[78] The North American project, now called the GAM-77 Hound Dog, could be introduced into the upcoming B-52G aircraft, and by April 1958 the JCS established a warhead requirement for the GAM-77: "It is desired that the Mk-28 warhead, which is already developed, be adapted to satisfy this requirement."[79] LeMay's staff also examined Goose but were curious about a cheaper decoy missile called Quail that could be carried by B-52s.[80] Goose could not, as it turned out, simulate a penetrating B-52 effectively and so was canceled.[81] Quail and Hound Dog became priority projects; the air-launched ballistic missile project would continue, with the idea that it would be employed by the Airborne Alert Force when available. Could either be adapted to the B-47? This "might save the government millions" and "extend the value of the B-47 for years to come."[82] White canceled Rascal on 16 October 1958.[83] And Goose was not far behind, once it was evaluated against Quail.[84]

The USAF Weapons Board advising White and LeMay agreed, and grouped Snark, Rascal, and other systems as hedges "against premature dependence on a new system" that would "[result] in 'too little, too late.'" White was confronted with three parallel force structure paths. There was the bomber force, regarding which the Board pointed out that officers were pilots and were comfortable with aircraft, but less so with ballistic missiles. There was space warfare, an up-and-coming field of battle. The Board also pointed out, "The need for funding both types of weapons systems [ballistic missiles and bombers] until sufficient confidence is gained in missiles to reduce our investment in aircraft is causing chaos in planning, programming, and development." Their recommendation was that SAC be "composed of weapon systems which [would] discourage a would-be aggressor from overt attack. Failing this, it should be capable of destroying his capacity and will to continue the conflict."[85]

In their view, the B-52 had to be modified for low-level operations, carry Hound Dog or an air-launched ballistic missile, and carry Quail. The B-47 force needed to be modified to include a low-altitude Doppler navigating radar and a multiple-bomb clip. (This was for the upcoming Mk-28 weapon, of which four could be carried, thus increasing target coverage per aircraft.) The B-58, which was not yet in service, should be acquired for only two wings, modified for low-level operations, and have air-to-surface missile capability as well as improved countermeasures. Strategic missiles were still in the "hedge" stage, but Titan and Atlas should continue, as should Minuteman, including a mobile version. An advanced ICBM "[leading] to a space capability" should be explored.[86] That became Titan II.

This is approximately the force structure that emerged to implement the SIOP in the 1960s. For SAC it streamlined programs and affected savings in many venues so that EWP planning could progress with less uncertainty. That said, the last versions of the EWP in the 1950s could not take advantage of these programs and remained dependent on not only the Hairclipper-trained B-47 crews for specific low-level operations but, paradoxically, Tactical Air Command and the U.S. Navy. On the plus side, Tommy Power identified a higher strategic rationale for the entire force structure:

> Presently, a large proportion of the total Soviet military effort and manpower is devoted to their air defense. . . . [This] is in direct response to our current strategic threat. This effort cannot fail to result in a decrease in their strategic offensive capability. In the future, our possession of a multi-threat force will compel the Soviets to expand this defensive force tremendously. The Soviets must be capable of defense against low level attack, supersonic high altitude attack, and against attack with ballistic missiles. The fact [is] that each of these three threats will require a separate and distinct defensive system. . . . If the Soviets should fail to take adequate measures against each of our threats, then they must accept the fact that they have been deterred—unless they believe that they can destroy our offensive forces with their initial attack.[87]

The Main Ally of the Main Adversary: The Royal Air Force

The details of the United Kingdom's struggle to develop a nuclear capability are beyond the scope of this work, though there is a rich history exposing most of the elements involved in that process.[88] For our purposes, however, the Royal Air Force Bomber Command's V-Force enters our story with its attainment of a nuclear capability in 1958 and the subsequent formal arrangements with SAC regarding target coordination. The conditions for this were set with a reexamination of the restrictive Atomic Energy Act, which was amended in 1958 to permit customized country-to-country nuclear information-sharing agreements. Prior to this, Bomber Command had four nuclear bomber types in service: the Canberra B(I)8 light bomber and three medium bombers: the straight-wing Vickers Valiant, the crescent-wing Handley-Page Victor, and the futuristic delta-wing Vulcan. These last three constituted V-Force. At the end of 1958 there were twelve squadrons of V-bombers: 54 Valiants, 18 Vulcans, and 10 Victors, and more aircraft concurrently pumped out at the factories with an objective of attaining 144 of all three types in total. Four squadrons of Canberra B(I)8s were available, but the large Blue Danube nuclear weapons could be carried only by V-Force.[89]

The RAF had its own weapons. There were approximately fifty-eight of the 16-kiloton Blue Danube bombs. Though it entered service in 1953, it had to wait until the Valiants came on line in 1955 to deliver it. This weapon had been tested in the Australian desert and was a known quantity. That could not be said about the sketchy Violet Club, the "interim megaton weapon," of which there were five. The Violet Club was replaced later in 1958 with twenty-nine Yellow Sun Mk-1s. The yield ranges for these two weapons have been deliberately obscured over the years and remain so. Estimates suggest that both weapons used a Green Glass primary and apparently yielded somewhere between 330 and 500 kilotons.[90] That said, thermonuclear weapons tests at Christmas Island in 1957 and 1958 involved Valiants air-dropping larger weapons: Orange Herald, a 700- to 800-kiloton boosted fission weapon; the Short Granite 300-kiloton two-stage thermonuclear weapon; the Grapple X test at 1.8 megatons; and

Grapple Y at 3 megatons. The Flagpole shot of Grapple Z yielded 1.21 megatons.[91] The British demonstrated that they were capable of producing and detonating thermonuclear weapons, but it would take time to introduce them into the force structure.

This brings up an important point. The purpose of the British nuclear deterrent was to give Britain "a capability to independently inflict an unacceptable level of damage upon the Soviet Union" exclusive of its arrangements with the United States, NATO, or whomever.[92] This purpose had to exist in parallel with the British-NATO relationship and again in parallel with what SAC was going to do, or not going to do. In effect, the RAF developed three overlapping nuclear forces nested in two.

The RAF had been communicating with its American counterparts since 1954 on how to have some form of atomic cooperation. Twining and LeMay, through his 7th Air Division commander, were the primary drivers here; Twining was amenable to helping the RAF prepare to modify its aircraft to deliver the Mk-7 weapon and sketched out draft procedures to release nuclear weapons to British aircraft that were so modified. LeMay was always concerned about coordination issues, and if Bomber Command arrived on scene, as it surely would, it would be better to be in on the ground floor.[93] Indeed Bomber Command was already operating four squadrons of B-29s, called "Washingtons," in British service.[94] There is no available information as to what the status of these aircraft were vis-à-vis nuclear capability while they were in British service. The Canberra light jet bombers had some modifications for carrying the American Mk-7, should it become available, and their crews were being trained in LABS profiles by their counterparts in NATO's 4th Allied Tactical Air Force by at least 1956.[95]

The concept of information exchange and weapon availability was approved by Eisenhower and then by both countries in March 1957, pending modification of the Atomic Energy Act, which took place in 1958. Project E was "technically effective from 1 October 1958." Seventy-two V-Force bombers were to be modified and provided with American Mk-5 weapons. Approximately one hundred Mk-5s were stored in three British Special Storage Areas under the custody of the U.S. Air Force 99th Air Depot Squadron; the British nuclear weapons at those sites were moved to the other nine British Special Storage Areas. These Mk-5s apparently were half the yield that the RAF was expecting, that is, either 47 kilotons instead of 92, or 18 kilotons instead of 47. In any event, they were an improvement over the Blue Danube's 16-kiloton yield.[96] Forty two V-bombers had been modified for Mk-5 delivery by the end of 1958, and the rest completed by March 1959.[97] In parallel to this was the Canberra force. The four squadrons based in West Germany were allocated to SACEUR in the event of war; they got approximately ninety-six Mk-7 weapons, again under American custodial control.[98] That reduced the NATO target coverage load on SAC just as its B-47 wings were repatriating to the United States and replaced with Reflex Action deployments. The Canberra force in the United Kingdom may have received or been allocated Project E Mk-7 weapons, but the details remain obscure.

When it came time to coordinate their forces, however, discrepancies arose between Bomber Command, SAC, and SACEUR. The primary one was that Project E weapons for V-Force could not be released unilaterally by the United Kingdom; they had to be released with the concurrence of the United States. Project E weapons for the RAF assigned to NATO could be released only by SACEUR. That left the fifty-eight Blue Danubes and up to twenty-nine Yellow Sun Mk-1s for unilateral British action against the Soviet Union (or others, say in the Middle or Far East) if that were deemed necessary. The express intent with regard to the Soviet adversary was to deliver "(a) 35 bombs on 15 cities with populations in excess of 600,000; (b) 25 bombs on 25 cities mostly with a population in excess of 400,000."[99] Contrast this with consistent 1940s and 1950s American objectives of destroying the Soviet Union's war-making capacity if deterrence failed.

Needless to say, the logistics, let alone the politics, of responding to three masters was difficult. Details of the Mk-15/39 weapon had been passed to the British in 1957, and by 1958 the Americans were prepared to provide them under Project E.[100] Whether it was the technical issues inherent in modifying V-Force to deliver them, the future possibilities of British devices tested during Grapple, or sovereignty-based control and release issues that put paid to this idea is unclear.

Norstad was happy to have any nuclear forces under command and not SAC-controlled, and he welcomed the addition of the Canberra force to NATO's 2nd Allied Tactical Air Force. Power was very enthusiastic to have the RAF as a nuclear partner and ensured this was widely publicized to include a high-profile visit of RAF Vulcans to Offutt AFB. Then it came down to the brass tacks of SAC–Bomber Command coordination. After two meetings between the two entities "examination of separate [Bomber Command] and SAC plans had shown that every Bomber Command target was also on SAC's list and that both Commands had doubled-up strikes on their selected targets to ensure success."[101] Clearly the prospect of four weapons allocated per target was not economical and required revision. However, the issue of readiness came to the fore: Bomber Command did not have the same system as SAC, that is, something like Reflex, and it would take time to determine how that would work. Consequently, for 1958 SAC planners asserted that "the deterrent potential of the V-Force, without a quick reaction capability, was little or no greater than an equal number of [USAF] TAC bombers in the UK. In addition SAC would continue to plan for unilateral action and cover all first priority targets, regardless of the RAF capability. Thus the RAF capability would not influence the overall SAC force or targeting requirements."[102]

It was recognized, however, that this situation would change when V-Force received thermonuclear weapons and their alert program was implemented. With its borrowed American kiloton-yield bombs V-Force was a shaky backup to SAC's Reflex forces, at least for the time being. Even when the British deployed and assigned their thermonuclear weapons to targets, it was clear there were limits to coordination and cooperation: "Neither [SAC] nor Bomber Command were prepared to reveal, even to each other, the nuclear yield allotted to each target under the coordinated plan. [Air Marshal Kenneth Cross] said that the nominal figure for planning purposes was one megaton but this varies between kiloton-range yield in the case of our Blue Danube to multi-megaton bombs in the SAC armoury.... In this area alone there is a barrier to coordination and duplication and wastage is inevitable until American legislation is altered."[103]

Left unsaid in the SAC–Bomber Command discussions was concern in some American quarters that a British government might, perhaps, opt out of a conflict or might not commit forces in time to hit SAC's priority targets. This may be one reason why the B-47 Hairclipper units, with their special capabilities and targets, were stationed in Morocco and Spain as well as in the United Kingdom.

Going Ballistic: Intermediate-Range Ballistic Missiles

Ballistic missiles were not going to be a panacea to the bomber penetration problem in the late 1950s, despite what missile enthusiasts claimed. The exceedingly complex nature of the Manhattan Project–like concurrent development of U.S. Air Force ballistic missiles is more than adequately handled in other works.[104] The compressed narrative is this: In the early to mid-1950s the U.S. Air Force and the aviation industry had a symbiotic relationship that generated concurrent research and development on several ballistic and cruise missiles, which then competed for funding. There were conflicting requirements within the USAF that changed constantly in relationship to nuclear weapons developments. At the same time there were "roles and missions" debates with the other services. The key USAF players were Thomas White, who played a significant role in achieving a rapprochement between the services in 1952, and Nathan Twining, who was able to forestall transfer of the Atlas ICBM program to the Office of the Secretary of Defense, which considered having the ICBMs controlled by a super-agency. White and Twining empowered Power at ARDC, who then created an internal ICBM "super agency," the Western Development Division commanded by Maj. Gen. Bernard Schriever, which had its own special links to the AEC for warhead development.[105]

The Atlas ICBM was on track after 1951, when the decision was made to produce the backup ICBM design, the Titan, in parallel. At the same time, there was a confluence of three factors that led to the development of an intermediate-range ballistic missile (IRBM).

North American Aviation suggested making a small ICBM first and then upscaling it if the other two projects did not work out. The Air Staff considered the possibility of a "tactical ballistic missile," while at the same time the British were considering whether to produce their own IRBM and ICBM or "buy American." The USAF Scientific Advisory Committee pushed such a missile in response to the Killian Report. Schriever opposed the IRBM, but in the immortal words of historian Jacob Neufeld, "although Headquarters USAF was not yet certain what to do with this shorter-ranged missile it took several positive steps."[106] The U.S. Army was working the Redstone and Jupiter missiles, and they could not go unchallenged. The U.S. Navy too was up to something, something to do with solid fuels. White and Twining were able to convince the JCS to endorse the idea that "IRBM 1," or Thor, would be a USAF project, and "IRBM 2," Jupiter, would be a joint U.S. Army–U.S. Navy project. The compromise, however, was that both would have the same priority as Atlas and Titan.[107] To confuse matters even further, Col. Edward Hall at the Western Development Division (and brother of Ted Hall, a Soviet atomic spy) figured out how to produce large solid-fuel rocket engines, thus reducing the size and cost of ICBMs. This led to Weapons System Q, later the Minuteman ICBM program, and then Minuteman itself became a concurrent priority project by 1959.[108]

Throughout the early to mid-1950s senior USAF leadership's views on ballistic missiles ranged from the messianic (Gen. Earle Partridge) and the visionary (White, Schriever) to the wary (LeMay) and operationally and politically realistic (Power and Twining). LeMay's supposedly antimissile stance has been highlighted by innumerable critics over the years. His actual view as stated to Twining in late 1955: "I consider an intercontinental ballistic missile with a capability of instantaneous launch and with acceptable reliability, accuracy, and yield to be the ultimate weapon in the strategic inventory. During the interim, and until these capabilities are proven, we must establish internal objectives and utilize demonstrably effective weapons systems. . . . As far as the intermediate range ballistic missile is concerned, I feel this is a step backward and in my opinion this program should never have been started."[109]

PROSTEISHIY SPUTNIK

Power, coming out of ARDC, was a ballistic missile enthusiast but fully cognizant of the plethora of teething troubles of getting several systems into service simultaneously. He was correctly positioned by the time he became CINCSAC to appreciate what ballistic missiles could do and not do, and when they did come on line in the 1960s he was better prepared to accept them, limitations and all, than LeMay was in 1955–56.

That said, one close observer noted in 1957, "In an atmosphere of urgency and indecision . . . these programs are being played off against each other because a) It is easier to procrastinate than make a decision; b) There appears to be a desire to treat both services equally and c) There are strong political implications in a decision for either system."[110] White himself was annoyed. The IRBMs were being pushed by the civilian leadership: "I must object strongly to the Air Force being given a mission and then constrained to do it in a specified manner. I consider the decision to produce and deploy both Jupiter and Thor to be primarily the result of the publicity given to the Jupiter system."[111] After all was said and done, the USAF was assigned both the army's Jupitar IRBM and the upcoming Thor IRBM.[112]

The question for SAC's EWP planners was this: Where were ballistic missiles going to fit into the program? How did IRBMs and ICBMs positively contribute to target coverage? Could they even hit targets? How reliable were the missiles? Would the warheads detonate? And the all-important question: Who controlled ballistic missiles? SAC? SACEUR? The other commanders in chief? RAF Bomber Command? Ballistic missiles posed new problems for target coordination even before they were operationally deployed.

It his 1956 maneuverings to retain control over the future IRBMs (assumed to have a 1,000- to 1,500-nautical-mile range, an accuracy of 2 miles CEP, and 1-MT warhead), Twining consulted with senior USAF leadership and informed the secretary of defense, "The IRBM appears to be primarily suited to the functions of strategic air warfare and interdiction of enemy land power and communications. . . . [This] requires that the U.S. Air Force operate the land-based IRBMs to ensure proper coordination with the manned bomber forces operating in the same general areas [and] minimize the period when U.S. and allied forces will be exposed to attacks with mass destruction weapons."[113]

Twining also noted that the U.S. Navy could have sea-launched IRBMs in the future. And therein lay the deep origins of the debate over interservice coordination that would in part lead to the first SIOP in 1960. The potential problem of theater-level coordination also emerged early on: "Possible locations for the IRBM system are in England, Germany, Libya, Turkey, Formosa, Korea, Philippine Islands, and Japan. Location of the IRBM in these countries would provide coverage for a large percentage of the strategic targets in Russia and the Soviet Bloc countries. In addition, such deployment would ensure 100% coverage of current and anticipated theater targets for both general and local war conditions."[114]

More detailed analysis suggested that the IRBM was useful as a war deterrent "and an effective operational weapon if its use [was] required." As for its targets, the IRBM's "most attractive features" made it suitable for employment against "the enemy's airfields and missile sites from which atomic attacks against the United States or its allies [could] be launched. Other targets for the IRBM would be the enemy's defensive air forces, both aircraft and missiles; tactical air forces; enemy land power and communications; and industrial targets."[115]

British interest in an IRBM was raised in parallel with other nuclear sharing endeavors, and after 1957 they were on track to develop a cooperative arrangement involving Thor. This process was complicated by Atomic Energy Act strictures prohibiting warhead transfer, and as a result the Thor deployment to the United Kingdom in 1959 developed release and targeting complexities.[116] At the same time, SACEUR Lauris Norstad wanted an IRBM for NATO forces and USAF HQ explored replacing manned aircraft squadrons with IRBM squadrons on a one-to-one basis to save money.[117] LeMay was probably laughing up his sleeve when the USAFE staff argued back that manned aircraft could not be replaced by missiles, at least not yet. The unstated concern in the halls of USAFE was perhaps that SAC would control those IRBMs and not USAFE, leading back to the SAC-SACEUR command and coordination problems of the early 1950s.[118]

The intercommand arrangements for IRBM targeting coordination were not straightforward, and neither were the diplomatic arrangements. LeMay fielded questions from Norstad and Power, and then went to a frustrated White, who told him to get guidance from the secretary of defense, implying that, since this was Defense's idea in the first place, they had the answers.[119] That proved to be a futile exercise, so White consulted with LeMay, Power, and Norstad and came up with this statement: "Actions with regard to the IRBM program will be based on the concept that these are strategic weapons; as such from a military point of view they [will] be under single direction; political considerations will not permit achieving this at this time; it remains essential, however, that CINCSAC coordinate the targeting of the entire IRBM force."[120]

In his conversations with Power, White explained that "the underlying principle from the beginning was to place IRBM's under the command and control of CINCSAC in adherence to the objective of having the overall strategic offensive under a single commander." NATO IRBMs "present[ed] a special problem": "Political considerations have dictated that IRBM's allocated to NATO countries be placed under the operational control of SACEUR." The weapons were offered to NATO countries with this understanding. "I realize the problem that this arrangement presents in respect to targeting," White said. After talking to Norstad he told Power, "He is in complete agreement that NATO IRBM's must be targeted to complement the strategic offensive and he has agreed to coordinate targeting with you." USAFE was to be the point of contact for USAF negotiations with NATO.[121]

Then the JCS expressed their position in April 1958 that IRBMs had been "offered to and [would] be deployed within NATO countries and put at the disposal of SACEUR." This meant the Jupiters that were going to be based in Italy and Turkey. USCINCEUR, the U.S. national commander "[would] not exercise control over IRBM squadrons of allied nations," that is, the RAF-USAF Thor force. Furthermore, the new state of affairs did "not require any alteration of the missions of USCINCEUR, SACEUR, or CINCSAC."[122] Which was as clear as mud and echoed the problems LeMay and Norstad encountered in the early 1950s.

And then there were practical problems inconveniently raised by the technical staff. After tests and recalculations, IRBM accuracy was now estimated to be two miles CEP, not one mile. According to the staff, "[This] largely negates its usefulness in the counter atomic/counter air task which is the primary job for USAFE (SACEUR's [Atomic Strike Plan]) and [Pacific Air Forces]. Such a CEP creates many problems in gaining agreed targeting concepts for the IRBM in an NATO environment where weapons restraints and psychological factors play an important role in operational planning." They added, "In the NATO area, command and control arrangements that will allow a quick reaction from NATO's IRBMs are far from realization."[123]

Why? The Herter-Caccia arrangement that established the UK Thor program had language in it that had to be adhered to. The W49 warheads remained in the custody and control of the 99th Aviation Depot Squadron.[124] "[But] the decision to launch these missiles will be a matter for joint decision by the two Governments. Any such joint decision will be made in the light of the circumstances at the time and having regard to the understanding that the two Governments have assumed in Article 5 of the North Atlantic Treaty."[125]

The British delayed making the Thor system operational in 1958. U.S. Air Force observers with the 7th Air Division pointed out that the system could have been ready in early 1958, but the British refused to mate the warheads. It would take six hours to mate each warhead and then prepare the launcher, and the W49s were in an American storage area that was some distance from the Thors. The 7th Air Division believed that the British government was sensitized to antinuclear sentiment and would delay mating until after their October 1958 election.[126] It wasn't until May 1960 that this process was completed.[127] Ballistic missiles had promise and they would deliver. But not yet. The deterrent remained firmly based on the bomber forces and the forward-deployed tactical forces until the 1960s.

All of these changes had significant effects on the Emergency War Plan, to the point that it was replaced with the Basic War Plan. It is clear that Sputnik and associated events had a significant impact on American deterrent operations. It is equally clear, however, that the probability that ballistic missiles would be deployed by the Soviet Union had been anticipated by LeMay and SAC's staff years before. As a result, when he took over as CINCSAC, Power could reach into the SAC golf bag and pull out the appropriate clubs and drivers after October 1957: dispersal, northern tanker bases, Reflex Action, and increased ground alert. The planned B-52/KC-135 force that would augment and then replace the B-47/KC-97 force, however, took some time to deploy. Power pressed for an Airborne Alert Force in the face of a no-warning ballistic missile threat to both SAC's forward-deployed forces and those in the continental United States. He also had to confront a new threat that LeMay had not: the potential debilitating effects of high-altitude nuclear detonations delivered by ballistic missile, as dramatically demonstrated during the Hardtack test series.

A key weakness at this juncture was the lack of an effective air-to-surface missile for the bomber force, coupled with the decreased B-47 capability to conduct LABS delivery profiles, which reduced SAC's ability to take out targets around Moscow. IRBMs were problematic at this time as well, mostly for political reasons, while RAF Bomber Command, even in its advanced bases, was essentially an adjunct to SAC's capabilities in such a war until its readiness and its weapons could improve. Again, the key issue for Power and LeMay was target coverage. Deterrence was dependent on having trained, equipped, and capable forces. The 1958 Middle East Crisis appeared to validate SAC's concept of operations, particularly during the buildup period, which the Soviets could see. The question remained: Could SAC carry out effective operations under conditions of Strategic Warning and Tactical Warning in the late 1950s?

9

Coming Together

The Basic War Plan, 1958–60

It seems to me that there has been too much irresponsible talk about
the number of Russian cities we would have to destroy in order to win a
nuclear war. After all, the primary objective of our military effort is not to
destroy cities and kill people but to protect *our* cities and *our* people by
deterring aggression and thereby preventing nuclear war from happening
in the first place. To achieve this objective, our offensive forces must meet
two specific requirements. First, they must possess the unquestionable
capability to win a decisive military victory, that is, to destroy the enemy's
fighting capacity. Second, they must be configured to insure the survival
of sufficient strike capability even under the most unfavorable
condition, namely, a massive surprise attack.

—GEN. THOMAS S. POWER, 1959

As we have seen, a multitude of factors influenced how SAC
and the other deterrent forces carried out their primary mission after Sputnik in October 1957. The strategy itself evolved,
however, between 1958 and 1959. "Emergency War Plan" remained
the term generally employed by practitioners and operators, but new
factors led to substantial changes in the application of deterrent and
retaliatory force. This was, as before, partially driven by technological changes and as perceptions of the threat itself evolved. Interservice competition for scarce budgetary resources and competing
visions of how a war might begin, or even the type of war that might
be fought, played a significant role, especially the emergence of what

came to be called "minimum deterrence." The Emergency War Plan was eventually renamed to accommodate these and other changes and became the Basic War Plan (BWP), which at first glance was an evolution of the EWP. In reality, however, the changes were profound and led its further evolution into the Single Integrated Operational Plan in 1960.[1]

The Other Missile Gaps and the Early Warning Problem

After 1957 Tommy Power was forced to assume that a no-warning attack was the worst-case scenario SAC had to plan for. Those who recall the Cold War are familiar with NORAD and its early warning systems: the Ballistic Missile Early Warning System radars in the Arctic and United Kingdom and the Missile Defense Alarm System infrared detection satellites. In the world of the 1980s, these systems were assumed to provide warning of an ICBM launch and predicted impact areas, with about thirty minutes between launch and impact. However, we are dealing with a time in which those systems were conceptualized but not yet deployed.

Like the so-called Bomber Gap, the very public Missile Gap debate that emerged after Sputnik and gathered momentum during the 1960 American elections focused on whether there was or was not a missile threat to North America at the time.[2] At first glance the actual deployment dates of Soviet ICBMs suggest that there was not: the R-7 and R-7A (SS-6 Sapwood) ICBMs went on combat duty in June and September 1960 and were deployed in limited numbers (two in 1960, and four more in 1961). The R-16 (SS-7 Saddler) made its first appearance in 1961 (six deployed), followed by twenty-eight more in 1962.[3] The U.S. Air Force, the intelligence community, and the Washington DC political arena had a lively debate on the matter, one that got increasingly heated the more the credibility of its participants and their budgets appeared to be on the line. Nothing, however, was said publicly about the submarine missile launching threat: the Soviets had six Zulu IV and V submarines (two 1-MT-yield R-11FM missiles each) by 1958 and then seven Golf submarines (three R-13 missiles each) by 1959. Seven more Golfs were deployed by 1960.[4]

And again, paralleling the Bomber Gap debate, there was no open discussion of intermediate-range ballistic missiles that could strike SAC's forward-based forces in Europe and Asia, or from the sea. Power was increasingly aware of the submarine missile threat in 1957 and 1958, and frequently pointed it out internally. The USAF explored the possibility that Airborne Early Warning aircraft had a chance of detecting the missiles after launch and that the nuclear-tipped BOMARC missiles deployed on the East Coast might have a chance at intercepting them. There was no coverage on the Pacific coast.[5] But then there was Europe. What was to be done there?

The nature of early warning intelligence itself in the 1950s shifted because of the speeded-up nature of a potential attack. Photographic intelligence could identify preparations for a war as the enemy massed or prepared his logistics system. Examples of this include Operation Apex Rocket and Operation Air Brake, which were regular Royal Canadian Air Force and USAF missions designed to "maintain surveillance of Soviet operations in the Arctic in order to detect any build up of radar or airfield capability."[6] A human intelligence source deep inside the enemy's structure could provide warning of decision-making processes. But up against totalitarian states with closed airspaces, these methods were too slow. And U-2s had their limitations, most of them related to political will. Signals and communications intelligence were the only methods that might provide that fifteen minutes necessary for Tactical Warning, especially for the forward-based forces. It is not a coincidence that by 1958 over 54 percent of the National Security Agency's efforts were directed against the Soviet Union itself, let alone against the Warsaw Pact satellites and Communist China, especially when in 1956 the NSA was taken over by USAF lieutenant general John Samford.[7]

Most SIGINT and COMINT was at this time collected by a vast network of ground stations. Under the Canadian-UK-U.S. SIGINT sharing arrangements, the network stretched from Alert, Northwest Territories, Canada, to Hong Kong; from Peshawar to Habbinaya, Iraq; and from Sinop, Turkey, to Sembach, West Germany, and Kirknewton, Scotland. There were nearly 250 American, British, Canadian, Australian, and New Zealand ground stations.[8]

Not all stations were created equal, however. Geographical locations was crucial for certain interception operations. Sometimes specially trained teams arrived for a given task and departed. The U.S. Air Force Security Service (USAFSS) possessed two unique SIGINT units: the 6901st Special Communications Group at the Zweibrücken Communications Annex in West Germany and the 6902nd Special Communications Group located at Shiroi Air Base, Japan. These units conducted what was termed "continuous" or "blow-by-blow" reporting on Soviet attempts to intercept U-2 (and presumably other) missions over the USSR. They also had the ability to send priority SIGINT directly to SAC headquarters at Offutt AFB on a special SAC COMINT channel.[9] It is likely that all overseas USAFSS stations had a special SAC COMINT channel. How the SAC intelligence apparatus handled the material and conveyed it to Power and his deputy Butch Griswold for early warning purposes is unclear. What is clear is that in the late 1950s USAFSS units had the ability to extensively intercept and process Soviet Morse, radio traffic, and even facsimile communications.[10]

The organizations that conceptualized and developed the Ballistic Missile Early Warning System radars, Lincoln Laboratories and General Electric, had a space tracking radar test bed operational in 1956 at Millstone Hill, Massachusetts. Millstone "successfully detected Sputnik I" on 5 October 1957. Two similar radars were constructed, one on the island of Trinidad and the other at Prince Albert, Saskatchewan, Canada. The Trinidad site tracked ICBMs undergoing testing at Patrick AFB in Florida. These were space surveillance systems, however, and not purpose-built warning systems. It is unclear whether communication links existed between them and NORAD or SAC in the 1950s, though the Trinidad site was used for surveillance in the 1960s because of its proximity to Cuba.[11]

There was another system, however, that perhaps had some utility. In 1955 the U.S. Air Force and General Electric established an AN/FPS-17 radar site near Diyarbakir Air Station in southern Turkey. This gargantuan radar, the prototype of the ones that would be used in the Ballistic Missile Early Warning System, was employed to gather data on launches from the Soviet's Kapustin Yar ballistic missile test site. A second radar was added in 1958.[12] With the arrival of the new radar, the nomenclature of the units stationed at Diyarbakir changed: Turkey–United States Logistic Detachments 8 and 9 at Air Force Station Diyarbakir became USAF Security Service Detachment 8. A new secure compound was established, along with stricter security.[13] In addition to its regular peacetime collection activities, the probability exists that SAC could have received early warning data from Diyarbakir.

It is easy to see that the early warning problem was acute, especially under conditions of Tactical Warning. This had spin-off effects on the number of aircraft Power wanted on ground and later Airborne Alert on a day-to-day basis. It also highlights the vulnerability of the forward-based forces in light of their reaction capabilities. The IL-28 Beagle problem and the increased number of TU-16 Badgers was augmented in the late 1950s by the deployment of the R-5M ballistic missile system (SS-3 Shyster). The first R-5Ms were deployed between 1956 and 1958 to several locations; the sites at Simferopol in Crimea achieved combat duty status with their 300-kiloton nuclear warheads in May 1959. These were closely followed by a second set of sites at Gvardeysk near Kaliningrad and a third set of sites at Mukachevo in western Ukraine.[14] Each site had four launchers and twelve nuclear-tipped missiles. There was a fourth set of sites established near Fürstenberg in East Germany in late 1958 which achieved operational capability in May 1959, but they were later withdrawn. By 1960 there were R-5M units in Kaliningrad and in the Far East. Other planned sites included Vlore in Albania and "starting positions" in Romania and Bulgaria. With a range of 1,200 kilometers (647 nautical miles), the R-5Ms at Gvardeysk could hit any target in northern West Germany and the Netherlands, while the Simferopol and Mukachevo sites could hit targets in Turkey, Greece, southern Italy, and, critically, Cyprus. The Fürstenberg/Vokel deployments put London and some of SAC's UK bases in range.[15] The possibility that R-5M missiles from Mukachevo could have been quietly moved forward by road or rail into Hungary to pre-surveyed sites to increase their reach cannot be ruled out.[16]

The possibility that some of these missiles could have been used to generate electromagnetic effects over target areas also cannot be

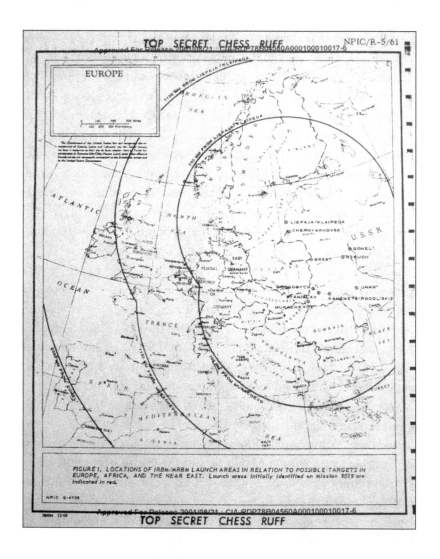

FIGURE 1. LOCATIONS OF IRBM/MRBM LAUNCH AREAS IN RELATION TO POSSIBLE TARGETS IN EUROPE, AFRICA, AND THE NEAR EAST. Launch areas initially identified on Mission 9019 are indicated in red.

Map 23. The covert Soviet deployments of the R-5M (SS-3 Shyster) ballistic missile system facilitated Khrushchev's belligerent behavior in the late 1950s. CIA had HUMINT on the Ukraine-based sites but appears to have had no firm photography prior to 1961 and did not know for sure whether the sites contained R-5M or R-12 missiles prior to the mid-1960s. Of greatest concern were the sites at Mukachevo, west of the Carpathian Mountains. The R-5Ms there put the Jupiter sites and other bases in Italy at risk while they were under construction, but if they had been R-12s instead, all of SAC's UK bases would have been covered. SAC anticipated this state of affairs, which contributed to the establishment of Reflex Action. Courtesy of CIA.

ruled out; the Soviets closely followed the Hardtack and Argus-series high-altitude shots in 1958, and their scientific specialists assessed these effects in their own literature as early as December 1958. Indeed three of their own high-altitude tests in 1962 were conducted with 300-kiloton-yield detonations using missile-delivered warheads from R-5Ms. It is entirely possible they had a rudimentary capability, albeit untested because of the moratorium, as early as 1959.[17] Combined with the significant numbers of Soviet light and medium nuclear bombers, these weapons could have had a decisive affect on SAC's and SACEUR's forces in Western Europe. Clearly the replacement of forward-deployed B-47 wings with Reflex deployments was a prudent move.

The Thor and Jupiter deployments to the United Kingdom, Italy, and Turkey appear less provocative in retrospect, and the R-5M deployments cast a new light on Khrushchev's bluster about being "forced" to respond in Cuba because he was "targeted" by NATO IRBMs that were deployed long after his R-5M force was. It also provides added context to the 1962 Cuban Missile Crisis Jupiter trade-off undertaken by the Kennedy administration. Indeed the R-5M deployment itself presages the secret Cuban deployment of IRBMs and MRBMs in 1962.[18]

Khrushchev precipitously pulled out the Fürstenberg missiles in August 1959 for reasons that remain obscure but may have been due to the imminent deployment of the longer-range R-12. It appears that the CIA had HUMINT on the Simferopol and Mukachevo sites in June 1958 that could not be confirmed. A retrospective analysis of HUMINT data conducted in April 1961 turned up 1958 data on the Fürstenberg deployment as well as the Gvardeysk and Mukachevo deployments. At some point in 1961 the Gvardeysk and Mukachevo sites became priority reconnaissance targets and were finally identified by satellite that year. The Simferopol sites were tentatively identified in a Talent report between 1956 and 1958, tentatively after a satellite pass in 1961, suspected in 1962, but not confirmed until 1964.[19] It is unclear whether SAC, USAFE, or SACEUR knew where the Simferapol sites were before 1961. Peripheral slant photography could have located the Simferopol sites, but the Gvardeysk sites were well inland. Also of note, the R-5M missile support facility at Novaya Mezinovka was detected by U-2 photography in 1958, but CIA analysts missed its relationship to the deployed R-5M forces.[20] Soviet missile units did employ high-frequency radio, so it is possible that they were identified through SIGINT efforts. Whether SAC, USAFE, or SACEUR would have conducted nuclear "spec fire" on suspected MRBM sites and facilities is unclear but cannot be ruled out. Mukachevo certainly would have been destroyed as rapidly as possible.

Attaining Victor Alert: The European Components

By the late 1950s there were five different commands involved in the targeting coordination problem in and around Europe. SAC had its Reflex Action aircraft in the United Kingdom, Spain, and Morocco, with the ability to deploy forces to Turkey under certain conditions. There was RAF Bomber Command with its forces in the United Kingdom. U.S. CINCLANT, who was "double-hatted" as NATO SACLANT, was a player. Then there was NATO SACEUR, who was double-hatted as U.S. CINCEUR. The U.S. Navy's Sixth Fleet was committed to support SACEUR. Finally, there was U.S. Air Forces Europe, which had a convoluted relationship with practically everybody else.

The relationships among these commands depended on the situation, and there were potentially four of these. First, if the planets aligned, NATO could act promptly in a unified manner. Second, the United States and the United Kingdom could act on their own if NATO could not make up its mind on a timely course of action. Third, the United States could act alone if NATO could not or would not and the United Kingdom changed its mind at the last minute. And fourth, the United Kingdom could act alone. In terms of planning, NATO SACEUR had his Atomic Strike Plan (ASP) that was dependent on American weapons being released to him and delivered by American and British delivery systems, but on a combination of presidential assent and NATO assent. The United Kingdom had a national plan for its V-Bombers, with British-made weapons. Notably, the types of sorties SAC crews prepared for are suggested by their names. Some SAC bomber crews had an alert sortie, a crew assigned sortie, a subsequent assigned sortie, and a nomad sortie.[21]

This is where the anomaly of USAFE came in. It was an American national command reporting to U.S. CINCEUR that provided forces to NATO SACEUR's commands "upon the assumption of operational control by SACEUR," but not all of its forces were so committed.[22] Some were structured to assist SAC's Reflex and follow-on forces to get through the Soviet and Bloc air defenses. In this case, U.S. CINCEUR, who happened to be NATO SACEUR, was a JCS commander who, like the other commanders in chief, had various levels of discretion to release American nuclear weapons under specific circumstances. It is probable that the combination of the SAC Basic War Plan and these forward-based TAC elements launched under CINCEUR OPLAN 100-1 and coordinated with the SAC effectively constituted the U.S.-only plan. As such, the BWP and OPLAN 100-1 could be activated without reference to SACEUR's ASP (and vice versa, for that matter). But then what about RAF Bomber Command? In all likelihood the V-bombers equipped with American Mk-5s were integrated into the BWP, while those equipped with British bombs could be used as part of the BWP or held for the British national plan.

In the last years of the 1950s, the number of nuclear forces stationed in Western Europe was substantially larger and with a greater variety of systems than earlier in the decade. The importance of the United Kingdom as an "unsinkable aircraft carrier" is clear in map 24. There were ten V-bomber bases, with a mix of Victor, Valiant, and Vulcan squadrons, and six SAC Reflex bases. TAC had six bases containing F-101A, B-66, and F-100 strike aircraft. On the continent were four RAF Canberra bases and four USAF F-100 bases in West Germany, plus the Matador cruise missile units and their deployment sites. The upheaval in the Franco-American relationship limited nuclear strike aircraft to one base with an F-100 squadron and then only until 1959; the other F-100 squadrons had to take off from their French bases, land at the West German bases, load with nuclear weapons, and launch.[23] Working around the Mediterranean, SAC retained Reflex deployments at three bases in Spain and three in Morocco. There were one or two rotational TAC squadrons of 18 F-100s each at Aviano Air Base, Italy, and another at Incirlik, Turkey. The overall number of U.S. Air Force and RAF nuclear strike aircraft

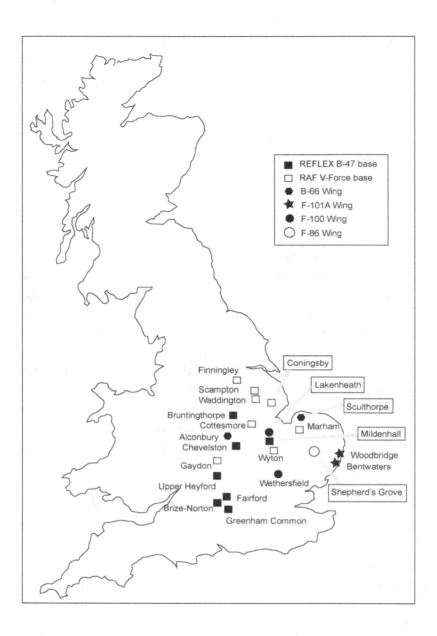

Map 24. The Unsinkable Aircraft Carrier, 1958–59. The United Kingdom hosted twenty-two nuclear-capable American and British strike bases during this period, with SAC B-47s rotating in from the United States to the Reflex Action bases in detachments of six. Courtesy of the author.

available in the NATO area in late 1959 was 724, with nuclear weapons available at all bases except the ones in France, and 225 F-100 aircraft rendered vulnerable by the unfavorable political situation.[24]

The first West German nuclear-capable units came on line in 1959. There was a Matador cruise squadron, Flugkörpergruppe 11, located at Kaufbeuren Air Base in southern Bavaria.[25] In addition there was a Luftwaffe F-84F squadron at Norvenich Air Base "which [the USAF] had trained and which had stockpile facilities at the site, but as yet had no weapons. There was also an American custodial unit at that site." Norstad was prepared to move the weapons in and wait for the bilateral agreement to be signed.[26]

JCS-SACEUR correspondence in 1958 noted that Norstad could base his plans on the assumption that 2,500 kiloton-yield and 50 megaton-yield weapons were available, though the 2,500 figure included artillery shells and tactical surface-to-surface missiles as well as gravity bombs and cruise missile warheads. For comparative purposes, SACLANT had 400 nuclear anti-submarine weapons, 400 kiloton-yield gravity bombs, and 100 megaton-yield gravity bombs for planning purposes.[27]

SACEUR's Atomic Strike Plan had three "programs." The Scheduled program was "directed against the enemy atomic delivery capability within SACEUR's area of responsibility." The Counter Radar program consisted "of automatic attacks against certain radar and control centers." The Interdiction program had "targets whose destruction [was] likely to have a major impact on the movements of enemy forces."[28]

The development of the Victor Alert capability by 1958 allowed certain American and British forces committed to the ASP, OPLAN 100-1, and the BWP to be launched within fifteen minutes of an alert. Victor Alert facilities, similar to SAC's Alert Facilities, were established at all strike bases in the United Kingdom, West Germany, Italy, and Turkey and had the crews colocated with their nuclear-armed aircraft in designated compounds ready to go at a moment's notice.[29] Between 1958 and 1960 aircraft on Victor Alert could launch around seventy-six weapons in fifteen minutes, or approximately 10 percent of the available aircraft and missiles allocated to the plans.[30] It appears that prior to the 1960s and under certain conditions TAC's Victor

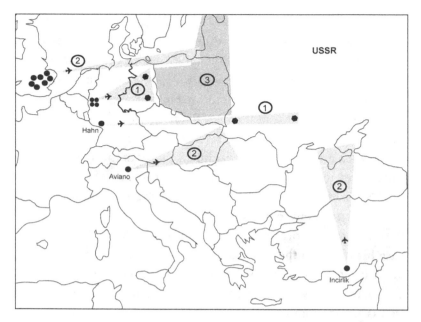

Map 25. Victor Alert strikes, 1958–60, showing special F-100 deep strikes against air defense control centers in western USSR and RAF Canberra strikes against East Germany (1). F-100s from the United Kingdom would destroy air defense bases (2), opening routes for F-101A and B-66 strikes against targets in Poland and western USSR (3). These actions would facilitate penetration of Reflex Action B-47s in the United Kingdom. Simultaneous strikes would be conducted against air defense bases in the Hungary-Romanian corridor to open up routes for Reflex Action B-47s in Spain and Morocco, while F-100s at Incirlik in Turkey would strike air defense targets in Crimea to open routes for follow-on B-47 strikes. Other Victor Alert forces would destroy fighter and bomber bases throughout the Warsaw Pact. Courtesy of the author.

Alert aircraft could be launched like SAC's Alert Force and held in a loiter pattern until a go-code was issued.[31] This later changed, and alert aircraft could not even be powered up unless the preliminary part of the release order was issued.[32]

East Germany and the Group of Soviet Forces Germany, with their massive concentrations of airpower and associated facilities, dictated how the ASP unfolded and thus influenced the BWP as well. The primary problem remained, as we have seen, the IL-28 force and its bases, from which the Soviets and their allies could preempt SAC and SACEUR action. The probability that jet fighter-bombers equipped with nuclear weapons would soon come onto the scene merely increased the number of possible targets. The destruction of those bases was dependent on the neutralization of the radar system, which consisted of both Soviet and East German systems. Similarly, American and British forces outbound to strike targets in the Soviet Union could be subject to interference by Soviet, East German, Polish, and Czech fighter aircraft as the bombers circumvented the East German land mass to the north and south.

Taking on this formidable system was no easy task, and its defeat lay in the proper sequencing of several diverse forces. The East German air defenses were split into Air Defense Division 3 (LVD-3) in the north and LVD-1 in the south. Superimposed on this were the air forces of the Group of Soviet Forces Germany's 16th Air Army with its own radars and fighter capabilities.[33] Thus SACEUR's ASP generally had British and American (and later West German) forces allocated to NATO 2nd Allied Tactical Air Force (2 ATAF) going after the north and American and French forces going after the south. In all probability the Victor Alert aircraft from RAF Germany, four Canberras, were targeted against the LVD-3 air defense command post located at Cölpin, and the cluster of "soft" higher air defense command and communication facilities in the Eggersdorf-Strausberg area, east-northeast of Berlin, which included Nachrichtenregiments 14 and 17 and the associated command post; and the Soviet command centers at protected facilities located at Wittstock and Merseburg.[34] The RAF Canberra crews were trained in LABS delivery and the aircraft carried a Mk-7 weapon. This version of the Canberra, the B(I)8, was specially equipped for intruder operations at night and low level.[35] Destruction of the highly centralized air defense command system would have been somewhat discombobulating for the opposition. Follow-on strikes by Canberras would also have been employed against the radar sites in the 2 ATAF area of operations, thus opening up enemy airspace for strikes against fighter airfields in northern East Germany.[36] The Group of Soviet Forces Germany complex at Zossen-Wünsdorf, which also included the headquarters of the 16th Air Army, was in all likelihood a priority target, having been identified and kept under observation since 1952. The National

Socialist–era bunkers were not rehabilitated until 1960–61, so the complex was "soft."[37]

A similar strike against the LVD-1 control facility at Kolkwitz by low-level F-100s from Hahn would have had a disruptive effect, echoing the Yeager F-86H strike plans from earlier in the decade. The Matador cruise missile could "pass under minimum radar detection ranges [in order to] compound the enemy's air defense problem" but had a larger warhead more suited to airfield destruction and probably was not scheduled to take out radar sites.[38] This task went to the F-100 pilots trained for LABS delivery of the Mk-7 weapon after an approach at 200 feet.[39] There were twelve radar sites arrayed in a "C" along the southwestern border of East Germany, with four more in depth, all within minutes of the F-100s stationed at the four bases on the western side of the Rhine.[40] The F-100s "carried just a small nuke, but [their] target [was] the big air defense complex on the other side of the Fulda Gap. Small, but more than enough to vaporize all their radar antennas and fry the electronics."[41]

The destruction of the four stations along the East German–Czech border plus Kolkwitz would permit NATO 4th Allied Tactical Air Force (4 ATAF) the freedom to go after the IL-28 bases along the East German–Polish border, Poland, and northern Czechoslovakia probably with F-100s as they now had a significant range improvement over the F-86Hs they replaced. They also could carry Mk-7 or Mk-28 weapons, depending on the F-100 version that was available.[42] Employment of the Matadors must remain speculative. Six of these missiles were on Victor Alert and could have been used against the identified IL-28 bases right after the air defense system was neutralized. It is also a strong possibility that F-100s and Matadors were cross-targeted on those bases. The rest of the Matadors were ideally suited, once alerted, to undertake the systematic destruction of the remaining air bases in East Germany and western Czechoslovakia. Twenty-four missiles were scheduled to be launched within eight hours of an alert, in addition to the six Victor Alert missiles, and thirty-six more within seventy-two hours.[43] With the air defenses over East Germany in complete disarray, the application of Matadors against fixed interdiction targets like bridges and rail junctions also appears to be a reasonable assumption.

Some USAFE units on Victor Alert had specialized tasks directly related to SAC's BWP. For F-100s based in West Germany, there were four PVO air defense command centers in western Ukraine, as described by one fighter pilot, Warren Kerzon:

> Our wing's primary mission was to train for and be ready to launch nuclear strikes against the Soviet bloc air defense system. . . . The success of knocking out the concentration of enemy airfields to the East would depend on the skill, proficiency and determination of a few dozen junior officers like me launching from our bases in western Europe. Every target that I was responsible for was part of the Eastern bloc air defense system. Our job focused on knocking out with tactical-size nucs the Mig interceptor bases that would be launched against our strategic bomber force coming across from the States behind us. It was our job to eliminate this enemy fighter threat in advance of their arrival over their strategic targets. However, in addition to the enemy fighter bases that were targeted, the command structure . . . decided that a vital target was the central command and control location for the western Soviet air defense system. This target was a close equivalent to [NORAD HQ]. . . . Knock this type of target out and you cause a major disruption in the coordination and control of the entire enemy air defense elements.[44]

This critical target was near Lviv and involved a "1.1 megaton fusion device," likely an Mk-28.[45] Another was a similar air defense control bunker, between Popilnya and Vasilkov, to be struck by Victor alert units from Ramstein Air Base:

> Targets closer than 450 nautical miles (518 miles) from home base did offer a potential round-trip mission. These short-range targets also allowed up to 20 minutes of loiter time in the target vicinity, while the National Command Center awaited a presidential order declaring H hour (weapon delivery time). Still, a delay in declaring H hour while the fighters were en route meant a one-way mission. Yet, the pilots accepted this as part of the job. . . . Some targets were more than 1,000 miles away. One of the more distant targets was a Soviet air defense center located about 60 miles southwest of Kiev,

Ukraine. Part of the attack route was to be flown at high altitude to Vienna; once inbound to the target the pilot was to turn at a large Danube River bridge and descend to 50 feet for a low-level dash to deliver the weapon.[46]

These special missions were briefed to Secretary of Defense Thomas S. Gates:

> As you know, [the missions include] only a few targets in the Western USSR. I told the Secretary that we do not deliberately pre-plan one-way missions, and he replied that we might be asked to do so. [Secretary Gates] stated his impression that our strike forces should be directed towards general war targets such as USSR control centers in the even of an attack on the United States, rather than dilute our forces within the existing mix of interdiction, counter air, and control center targets. The Secretary felt that the attack of USSR control centers by our forces would justify the assignment of targets beyond the maximum radius of action of USAFE aircraft.[47]

The other two air defense control centers were at Mukachevo, forward of the Carpathians, and one at Kolmayya on the western side.[48] These strikes plus strikes conducted by other forces (discussed later) opened up a corridor for SAC's Reflex forces in Spain and Morocco into central Ukraine with its bomber bases, and then the southwestern approaches to the Moscow air defenses. A squadron of eighteen rotational F-100s which had four aircraft on Victor Alert at Incirlik Air Base in Turkey was positioned to strike Soviet bases in the Crimea and the air defense system around the Black Sea.[49] This would likely have included the TU-16 bases in Crimea to pre-empt any attack against NATO, and the air defense bases to open up a corridor for SAC. Another rotational squadron of eighteen F-100s at Aviano likely had the task of destroying air bases in Czechoslovakia and Hungary, thus replacing the coverage of some of the SAC B-47s that were repatriated to the United States when Reflex came into effect. These F-100 aircraft were on two minutes' alert.[50]

This brings us to the UK-based nuclear strike units. The F-100 wing stationed at RAF Woodbridge handled the northern East German radars and air bases with low-level strikes. For example, future chief of staff USAF Merrill "Tony" McPeak's "first Victor Alert target was the airfield at Peenemunde [a] home station for an East German fighter regiment":[51]

> Our targets changed every six months or so, so I didn't always stay on Peenemunde. And it wasn't always me who was responsible for Peenemunde. I would pull alert with that as my target, and I'd be relieved by another pilot who would come in and have it as his target. Also, Peenemunde was a fairly important target; therefore it's likely that people in other squadrons away from my base were assigned to attack it also. Peenemunde probably had three or four aircraft assigned to attack it, which is good because not all three or four were going to get through, believe me.[52]

The F-100s at RAF Lakenheath were scheduled against targets in East Germany, possibly Poland, and, with KB-50 refueling, the westernmost Soviet Union.[53] One deficiency of the F-100 force in Western Europe was that the aircraft at that time "had no all-weather capability except MSQ," the ground-based navigation system similar to that used for the Matador.[54] Behind them, however, were the longer-range F-101As launched from RAF Bentwaters, which took on targeting responsibilities in the eastern Baltic States in 1959.[55] They were equipped with radar navigation and had "limited adverse weather bombing capability."[56] Their primary weapon was also the Mk-7, though the Mk-28 came into service later in 1959.[57] The F-101A force was scheduled to go in low, between 50 and 100 feet, against its targets:

> The Wing had a set number of specific targets. Each pilot had one specific target they were responsible for. Pilot rotation on alert was organized to make sure that all of the Wing's targets would be covered by the pilots selected for the alert period. The pilots did occasionally receive a new target responsibility, but they only had one target to "work on" at a time. All of the pilots understood, but were not briefed, that other strategic "assets" would also be targeted on their specific target. The Wing's targets were varied, but usually were Warsaw Pact airfields.[58]

These airfields were in northern East Germany, northern Poland, and the Baltic States, with the IL-28 and TU-16 bases taken out after the air defense system was compromised. Some targets appear to have been interdiction targets in Poland. Others were in the Soviet Union proper. The F-101A crews assigned to them had to refuel from KB-50 tankers over the North Sea to get back to their bases, but some were skeptical about the feasibility of this part of the plan.[59] Behind them were the even longer-range B-66s based at RAF Alconbury and RAF Sculthorpe. These twin-jet bombers were capable of carrying one Mk-7 and then, in 1959, two Mk-28s. The B-66 had different attack profiles:

> We got the Mark 28 weapon. . . . [I'd] punch in the Y-settings, one through four, which determined the yield. If it called for Y-1, that was the greatest yield, 1.1 megatons. . . . The target would call for a certain yield level, and we'd program the weapon accordingly. At that setting there was no safe fly-over of the target. At 38,000 feet the bomb would blow us out of the sky. So the procedure was to drop, break hard left or right into a 135 degree turn, and go as fast as you could to get away.[60]

The B-66 squadrons handled the Baltic States and Poland because of their longer range and payload: "[One] target was a Russian naval headquarters on one of the Baltic states. The damn thing sat about a quarter of a mile up in the city. We would have killed everybody just to get the Russian naval headquarters. Then I would have broken away and headed for Katowicz airfield to drop my second bomb."[61]

The destruction of the ASP's priority targets (radar and control sites, IL-28 bases, and fighter airfields) with both Victor Alert and immediate follow-on forces now gave SACEUR's remaining forces and SAC's Reflex as well as main efforts greater room to maneuver. Even if SACEUR was on the receiving end of surprise enemy attack and only the Victor Alert force got off the ground and hit its targets, the destruction of those targets would have contributed to assisting SAC's strike from the surviving Reflex forces and the follow-on forces from North America.

Once the ASP's priority targets were destroyed, SACEUR's forces would have seamlessly shifted their targeting to the interdiction program. By the late 1950s SACEUR had enough aircraft and ones with greater range to replace some of the SAC B-47s that were previously targeted against the enemy's logistics and transport system. For example, RAF Germany had ninety-six Canberra B(I)8s available, four of those dedicated to Victor Alert and a portion to the counter-radar plan. The four RAF Germany bases contained one Mk-7 bomb (later an Mk-28 set for 70 kt) per aircraft.[62] In an ideal situation, after the destruction of the alert targets and the fifteen radar stations in the 2 ATAF area of operations in East Germany, that left between seventy and seventy-five Mk-7 weapons for employment against interdiction targets from East Germany to the Polish-Soviet border. There were six east-to-west railway lines that the Soviets could employ to move their forces forward from the Soviet Union and continue to support the Group of Soviet Forces Germany, and a seventh in Czechoslovakia. Twenty to twenty-five of the Mk-7 weapons delivered against the rail network (bridges, other defiles, and marshalling yards) in Poland, plus the Soviet-Polish and Polish–East German transshipment rail yards would have effectively forced the Group of Soviet Forces Germany to fight with what it had on hand and without timely reinforcement. Destruction of key bridges in East Germany would have generated huge traffic jams of attacking Soviet armored vehicles, thus making them profitable targets for nuclear weapons employment.

A similar state of affairs awaited Warsaw Pact forces in Czechoslovakia and Hungary at the hands of over a hundred 4 ATAF F-100s. In addition "there was a provision in the war plan for nuke-loaded fighters to fly along suspected invasion routes in East Europe looking for targets of a particular type and size—targets of opportunity. . . . One criterion was [a] formation of at least 500 enemy troops."[63]

From the Sea: U.S. Navy Carrier Strike Operations

The evolution of U.S. Navy carrier strike capability was significant between 1957 and 1960. The earlier strike groups consisting of detachments of AJ-2 Savage propeller bombers, F-2H2B Banshee strike fighters, and prop-driven AD Skyraiders gave way to combinations of squadrons of twin-jet A3D Skywarriors, the delta-wing jet A4D Skyhawks, and several improved versions of the AD Skyraider. The *Essex*-class and *Midway*-class carriers had already completed their upgrades, just as the huge USS *Forrestal*–class came on line. The U.S. Navy assigned two types of carriers to the Sixth Fleet in the Mediterranean. The first were ships of the *Essex*-class, usually carrying two A4D Skyhawk squadrons and a AD Skyraider squadron, both types optimized for nuclear strike. The *Midways* and *Forrestals*, on the other hand, carried a squadron of A3D Skywarriors, two A4D Skyhawk squadrons, and one or two AD Skyraider squadrons, again optimized for nuclear strike. From 1957 to 1960 rotations brought the total of carriers in the Mediterranean at any one time to two *Essexes* and usually one *Midway* and one *Forrestal* or two *Forrestals*.[64] It is unclear exactly how many carriers were committed to the Second Fleet in the North Atlantic at this time, but NATO Striking Fleet Atlantic planned for two British and four U.S. carriers in wartime, so at least two in peacetime was a likely day-to-day capability, with loadouts similar to those ship types assigned to the Mediterranean.[65]

In terms of deliverable nuclear weapons, the FJ Fury jet fighter, three marks of the AD Skyraider, and the A4D Skyhawk carried the Mk-7 weapon with variable yields between 8 and 61 kilotons. The AD-5/5N, AD-6 and AD-7 Skyraiders also could carry the BOAR, a rocket-assisted Mk-7; this gave the propeller-driven Skyraider precious seconds to escape the weapons effects. The AD-4, -5, and -6 could also carry the Mk-8 gun-assembly penetrating weapon, while the AD-7 could carry its replacement, the Mk-91; both weapons yielded between 20 and 30 kilotons. The AD-7 Skyraider and the A4D-1 Skyhawk could carry the Mk-91, but both could also could deliver the Mk-12 Brok, its yield increased from the earlier 12 to 14 kilotons to 20. As for the A3D Skywarrior, the A3D-1 version could deliver the Mk-15 mod 0 and mod 1 thermonuclear weapons with a 3.8-megaton yield; the Mk-39 mod 0, with a similar yield; and the Mk-27, which yielded 2 megatons.[66] One squadron of A4Ds embarked on the USS *Saratoga* deployed in 1959 was equipped with Bullpup standoff missiles. One version of the Bullpup, the B model, carried a W54 nuclear warhead that yielded several kilotons, but it is unclear whether these were available in 1959.[67]

The U.S. Navy has not released its targeting plans for this period, but an approximation is possible with available data. Navy areas of interest in Europe, according to processed Talent information, fell into seven regions: four associated with Sixth Fleet operations in the Mediterranean and three associated with Second Fleet operations in the Norwegian and North Seas.[68] These areas of interest correspond to probable carrier operating areas, the ranges of their embarked aircraft, exercises, and available nuclear weapons types.

Generally the aircraft carriers in the Mediterranean had six areas from which timely strikes against Warsaw Pact and Soviet targets could be launched effectively: off Genoa, the Tyrrhenian Sea, the Ionian Sea, around Crete, the Aegean, and around Cyprus. The *Essex*-type carriers mostly operated in the first three, and the *Midways* and *Forrestals* used the other three, with overlap in the Ionian Sea.[69]

Those carriers carrying AD Skyraider and A4D Skyhawk squadrons "were responsible for neutralizing [Warsaw Pact] air defense bases with nuclear weapons" as part of what was called the Rollback Campaign to open up routes for SAC's aircraft.[70] As in previous plans, the U.S. Navy used Talent data to keep track of 127 airfields and airstrips in Czechoslovakia, Hungary, Romania, and Bulgaria. Of these, forty-three were part of the air defense system either as primary bases or dispersal strips: fifteen in Czechoslovakia, eleven in Hungary, seven in Romania, and ten in Bulgaria. As in the past, there were two possible corridors to be taken out: one up to the Czech-Hungary-Romania-Ukraine border region, and the sector south of the Carpathians in Romania and Bulgaria. Some airfields in southwestern Poland were also scrutinized. Airfields capable of jet aircraft operations in Austria remained under surveillance as well in case of a forward deployment of enemy forces. Attacks on the Warsaw Pact airfields and radar sites would have been conducted by AD Skyraiders and A4D Skyhawks at low level delivering Mk-7s and Mk-12s. The priority targets would have been handled by the Skyhawks given their speed relative to the slower ADs, which would have been employed against dispersal airfields and fixed sites. In the

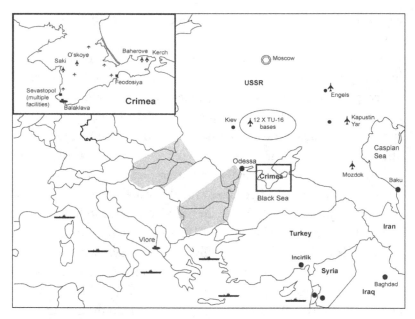

Map 26. Sixth Fleet operating areas in the Mediterranean in relationship to targets in the Warsaw Pact countries, Crimea, and the Caucasus for the 1958–60 period. Courtesy of the author.

case of strikes against Bulgaria and Romania, returning strike aircraft would have refueled from AJ-2 tankers over Bari, Italy. Similarly, a PVO air defense base at Artsyz west of Odessa hosting the MIGs of the 90th Fighter Aviation Regiment fit within the range parameters of carrier-based aircraft and would have contributed to rollback.[71]

The only sea threat to the Sixth Fleet carriers came from four Whiskey-class Soviet submarines supported by an Atrek-class submarine tender based out of Vlone Bay, Albania, and that base was protected by five airfields. This was a priority reconnaissance target endorsed by the commander of the Sixth Fleet, CINCNELM, and the chief of naval operations as the Berlin Crisis of 1959 spun up, and likely was a priority set of targets for destruction in the event of war.[72]

The destruction of air bases in the Warsaw Pact countries also served another purpose: it could preempt the forward deployment of the TU-16s and IL-28s from bases in central Ukraine, some of which were equipped with standoff cruise missiles that would put the carriers at risk. The possibility of dispersion and forward deployment

COMING TOGETHER

of the TU-16s and IL-28s likely was the basis for the Sixth Fleet's interest in the Caucasus, Syria, and Iraq. The enigma of Mozdok Airfield remained, with the U.S. Navy mistaking a cluster of structures at the airfield as a possible nuclear weapons storage site and missing the actual site completely. Mozdok was a likely staging base for any TU-16 attack on the carriers in the eastern Mediterranean and certainly would have been destroyed as soon as possible. U.S. Navy analysis of Talent imagery produced reports on four airfields in Syria, nine in Iraq, three in Lebanon, and one in western Iran. With the pro-Soviet tilt in Syria and Iraq, the possibility of forward basing by Soviet bombers either in peacetime or during a crisis had to be anticipated and covered off.[73] All of these sites were vulnerable to AD and A4D operations.

Moving in closer to the Soviet Union, an area of particular complexity was Crimea. SAC's focus was on Saki and Oktobroskoye TU-16 airfields, which could pose threats to SAC bases in Spain and Morocco. There was intense interest in Bagerovo Airfield and associated facilities because of their relationship to the Soviet nuclear weapons program. The U.S. Navy, however, was interested in the torpedo boat pens, submarine bases, and shipyards in and around Sevastopol and Balaklava, as well as the air defense airfields and seaplane bases in their vicinity, for a total of eleven targets. To the east was Feodosiya Naval Base, repair yards, and port, plus three airfields. Crimea would have been handled by SAC, TAC, and the U.S. Navy. Some of the F-100s stationed at Incirlik would likely have been first directed at the 62nd Fighter Aviation Regiment's MIG-15s and MIG-19s at Belbek Air Base and the 326th Kerchenskiy Twice Red Banner Fighter Aviation Regiment MIGs at Kirovskoye Air Base. Depending on the situation, SAC would have dealt with the two TU-16 airfields and the Bagerovo facility, though the U.S. Navy was also interested in the TU-16 bases, so the possibility of multiple weapons directed against them was high: these bases were out of the A4D's range, so A3Ds with Mk-15 or Mk-27 weapons would have been used if they were time-sensitive targets. Later, after a five-hour flight from their carriers, the AD Skyraiders would have struck the naval bases and facilities around Sevastopol and Feodosiya.[74] The underground submarine base near Balaklava would have been targeted with an Mk-91 penetrating weapon.[75] How all of this was coordinated and deconflicted is unclear, but it was probably done during the Worldwide Coordination Conferences. Whether the SS-3 sites were identified and targeted at this time is also unclear, but they probably were not.

Targets for the A3D Skywarrior squadrons from Mediterranean-based carriers remain obscure. U.S. Navy Talent analysis suggests interest in the oil facilities and port at Baku; several facilities around Novosibirsk, including the airframe plant and airfields; the airfields near the atomic energy facility at Tomsk; Semipalatinsk Airfield and complex; Omsk Airfield, plant, and complex; Kapustin Yar missile launch facility; and the Tyura Tam ICBM testing facility. Most of these lay outside of the A3D's range, however, even if they were launched from a carrier sailing off Cyprus with recovery in Turkey. All of the Caucasus targets, however, were viable. Similarly, there was Talent analysis of some but not all of the TU-16 and IL-28 bases in the Ukraine and Belarus. Generally the ones closer to the West were of interest. Only one possible special weapons storage area was noted, and it was nowhere near a real site.[76]

It is probable that the U.S. Navy also targeted Moscow. It was within A3D range if the carrier launched from the Aegean or the Norwegian Sea and the aircraft used evasive routing around the Soviet air defense system with recovery in Scandinavia or Sinop, Turkey (with the plane on fumes). Navy planners focused on different SA-1 Guild sites than SAC's planners did. Using Mk-15 or Mk-27 weapons delivered in toss-bombing fashion from aircraft coming in at 500 feet, A3Ds could have taken out the SA-1 site near Naro-Fominsk and the Kubinka air defense airfield to open a narrow corridor from west to southwest so that follow-on aircraft could target the city using some of the six airfields scattered around the city as aim points; the U.S. Navy produced its own assessment of the same airfields targeted by SAC. Another two SA-1 sites, one near Aleksandrov in the northeast quadrant of the outer Guild ring and another near Lyubertsky in the inner ring, appears to have been an alternative corridor for a navy strike.[77] The largest-yield weapon available was the 3.8-megaton Mk-15. For the navy to achieve the same level of damage against Mos-

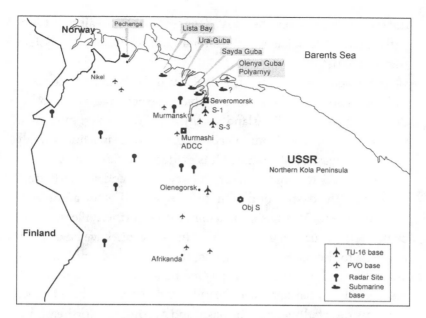

Map 27. Projected targets on the Kola Peninsula. Courtesy of the author.

cow as SAC would have been difficult: six Mk-15s yielded under 24 megatons, while a single Mk-36 could yield 19 megatons.

On the northern front, the U.S. Navy's primary targets were the plethora of naval and air facilities on the Kola Peninsula (see map 27). SAC overflights and Talent coverage provided targeteers in the Second Fleet with extreme detail on the dispersed facilities scattered among the hand-shaped rocky coves. Operations against the Kola area bases would have been complex and plans would have differed depending on how many carriers were on station in the Norwegian Sea. How an attack on the Kola bases would have been phased in the late 1950s must remain speculative.

That said, PVO's 21st Air Defence Corps was centralized on three bases, each housing a fighter aviation regiment: Kilp-Yavr, near Murmask; Afrikanda, near Olenegorsk; and Monchegorsk further south. These regiments were equipped with a combination of MiG-19PS, MiG-19PMS, MiG-17S, and MiG-17PFS, all of which required ground-controlled intercept and none of which possessed look-down–shoot-down capabilities. The PM version of the MiG-19, with its air-to-air missiles, was probably the most dangerous of these aircraft types with regard to U.S. Navy strike aircraft, but its fire control system was problematic.[78]

There were a pair of forward dispersal airfields and a sector control center south of the submarine base at Pechenga, and another dispersal base on Kildin Island northwest of Kola Inlet. PVO radar stations were arrayed from the Norwegian border in a line roughly to the southeast of Murmansk; it is evident the PVO expected the weight of attack to come from the Norwegian Sea and not north from the Arctic. The destruction of these bases as well as the air defense control center at Murmashi and a joint PVO–Northern Fleet control center at the Murmansk Northeast Airfield would have been a prerequisite to the main attacks against the fifteen-odd naval, marine, and other aviation targets.[79] A4Ds led by A3Ds acting as pathfinders would likely have handled the radar and forward air base targets, the A3Ds directed against Murmashi and Murmansk Northeast Airfield. The attack profiles would have consisted of a low-level attack under 500 feet, with LABS used to permit the delivery aircraft to escape. Using Mk-7 or Mk-12 weapons, the height of burst would have been between 1,100 and 2,000 feet and would have destroyed the radar sites and fighter airfields. To ensure the destruction of the underground control center in Murmashi, an Mk-15 or Mk-27 would have been required.[80]

The number and types of targets were substantial, including submarines, surface ships, oil tank farms, command and control, and repair facilities. Command and control would have been prioritized, so the headquarters of the Red Banner Northern Fleet at Severomorsk would have been destroyed more or less immediately. Also included in this strike would have been the large jet bomber-capable airfields, Severomorsk-1 and -3 and two other airfields near Murmansk to prevent TU-16s, some equipped with standoff missiles, from getting airborne. The jet bomber base at Olenegorsk and its associated nuclear weapons storage facility, Olenegorsk-2, would have been hit as a matter of priority.[81] In this case A3Ds with Mk-15s or Mk-27s would have been appropriate, but how this would have been deconflicted with SAC strikes against the same targets remains obscure.

The Soviet northern submarine force would have had a higher targeting priority than the surface fleet as the submarines would have to be destroyed before they could disperse and hide in the depths. There were five submarine bases, working west to east. Pechenga had Whiskey-class attack submarines and a tender situated in a protected cove. Next was Litsa Bay, which was under construction to support the upcoming Echo-class cruise missile submarines, but eventually it also had a submarine tender located there. Then there was Ura Bay, also with a submarine tender and a probable dispersal site. Sayda Bay was the home base of the Golf-class ballistic missile submarines. Olenya Bay too hosted Golf-class submarines and was later categorized as a dispersal site.[82] All these locations would have been susceptible to Mk-27 weapons airburst to generate maximum overpressure on support facilities and docked submarines. Polyarny, however, was an altogether different targeting problem. These facilities were spread out on uneven ground, which suggests that a pair of Mk-27s airburst over the center of the base would have been required.

In behind these strikes would have been the AD Skyraiders directed against less time-sensitive and fixed targets. Skyraiders with Mk-91s could have been employed against two suspected submarine pens near Polyarny and a third in a cove halfway to Kilden Island. The destruction of the seaplane base west of Severomorsk was a likely strike, depending on how seriously the U.S. Navy took the threat from nuclear-armed seaplanes. Reconnaissance aircraft launched in behind the main strikes to determine bomb damage assessments for restrikes was also likely.[83]

A carrier operating from the North Sea or southern Norwegian Sea could have been directed at naval targets like the bases at Vysotsk and Kronstadt west of Leningrad, and the Baltic Fleet facilities in the Baltic States, like Tallinn, Riga, Haapsalu, and Leipaja naval bases. There were also seven shipyards in Leningrad. These would likely have been lower priority targets.[84]

Burning Down the House: SAC versus the Soviet Union

The assault on the Soviet Union, had it occurred between 1958 to 1960, would have followed the TAC and U.S. Navy operations dedicated to opening corridors into the Soviet Union proper. There would have been five waves after this. The first would have been the forward-based Reflex Action B-47s, closely followed by part of RAF Bomber Command's V-Force. The Airborne Alert B-52s would have been next, followed by the ground alert bombers based in the United States. Finally, the unalerted SAC bombers in the United States would have constituted the fifth wave after reconnaissance operations had taken place to determine what was left and worth destroying in the context of American war plans.

The Reflex B-47s were stationed in groups of six at five bases in the United Kingdom, three in Spain, and three in Morocco, for a total of sixty-six aircraft. The weapons allocation at each base provides clues to how the Reflex forces would have been employed. Three of the bases had the Mk-39 mod o bombs: Greenham Common, Mildenhall, and Zaragoza. All the others had Mk-36 mod 1s.[85] As we have seen, the Mk-39s were a derivative of the Mk-15 and geared toward a low-level delivery by Hairclipper-trained crews. This low-level capability was designed to open gaps in the SA-1 Guild missile defenses surrounding Moscow. Similarly, an estimated 60 megatons was needed to completely destroy the Moscow targets in the center of the defenses; three Mk-36s set at 19 megatons meets this criteria. With one weapon per aircraft, a minimum of six aircraft with Mk-39s, three per SA-1 line, and three equipped with Mk-36s would have been needed to undertake this task, and this assumes no losses. Deploying two or even three of these packages appears reasonable for SAC to ensure Moscow's destruction and assumes redundancy in the face of mechanical trouble, navigation errors, and the effects of the air defense system. The fact that only three bases had the Mk-39s, two in the United Kingdom and one in Spain, aligns with this. The northern route from the United Kingdom would have exploited the effects of TAC strikes on the East German, Polish, and Baltic air defenses. By exploiting the gaps over Lithuania, the western quadrants of the Moscow defenses could have been struck. From Spain the strike group would have exploited the Hungarian corridor, by then cleared by TAC and the U.S. Navy, through Ukraine, and then to the southwest quadrant of the Moscow defenses. The destruction of the air defense command centers at Lviv and southwest of Kiev by the special TAC strikes launched from West Germany would have added to the PVO's confusion in trying to react to this package. Even if Soviet SS-3s or aggressive political activity disrupted Reflex operations from the United Kingdom, there were still bases in anti-Communist Spain from which to mount the Moscow action.

That accounts for approximately twenty-seven of the sixty-six Reflex B-47s, leaving thirty-nine equipped with Mk-36 weapons. The priority targets were emphasized repeatedly by White during the debate over minimum deterrence:

> In the case . . . of tactical or strategic warning, there would be 3 tasks; one, to destroy the enemy's capability to destroy us—that will be the first priority; next, would be to blunt the enemy attack on our deployed military forces and other forces in Europe and Asia; and, third, systematically destroy the Soviet Union's ability to wage war. In the case of surprise attack, the mission would be to do the greatest possible damage to the Soviet Union as a whole with attention to applying that destruction in such a way as to do as much damage as possible to their residual military strike force.[86]

The bulk of the Soviet long-range air forces and their nuclear storage sites lay within the reach of the Reflex B-47s (see map 28). Broadly, there were seven targets in the Baltic states and Kaliningrad, nine in Belarus, six west of Moscow, thirteen in Ukraine proper, and four in Crimea. There was also the large heavy bomber base, Engels, and the production plant and runways at Saratov, as well as the Kapustin Yar missile test site near Volgograd. These last would probably have been handled by a combination of the F-100s at Incirlik supporting a strike by a Big Horn B-47 deployment to that base. Whether this would have been a detachment from Morocco or Spain or would have been brought in during a crisis buildup is unclear. Again exploiting the Baltic approach and the Hungarian corridor, Reflex B-47s from the United Kingdom would have also hit the Baltic-Belarusian bomber base grouping and the Ukrainian grouping with Mk-36 weapons.

This takes us to RAF Bomber Command's V-Force, which consisted of 92 aircraft by October 1958 and then 108 by mid-1959, half

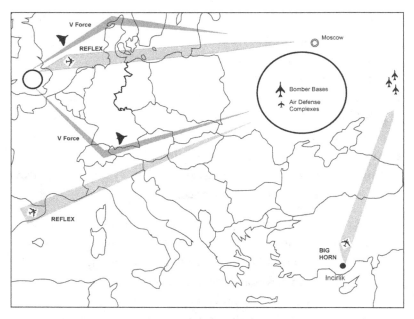

Map 28. Reflex and V-Force routing, 1959. Courtesy of the author.

of which were Valiants, the rest Victors and Vulcans. Seventy-two of these aircraft were modified to carry the Mk-5 weapon under Project E, and three of the ten V-Force airfields were serviced by U.S. custodial detachments. Essentially 50 percent of the force was able to launch with the Mk-5s at this time.[87] Importantly, V-Force had not yet attained the same levels of high alert that Reflex B-47s had. Valiants and Victors, for example, took thirty minutes to prepare for launch.[88]

The existence of different plans provides us with insight into where the V-bombers fit into the Basic War Plan. After eighteen months of work, a combined SAC–Bomber Command understanding emerged. According to British sources, and repeated in numerous secondary sources, V-Force was "assigned" 108 targets broken down into 69 cities "which [were] centres of government or of other military significance," 17 long-range air force airfields, and 20 elements of the air defense system.[89] The sources do not, however, situate these numbers and targets within the context of the Tactical or Strategic Warning components of the plan.

COMING TOGETHER

The Project E weapons were American weapons delivered by British aircraft but only within the context of the Basic War Plan, not the British national plan. Fifty percent of V-Force was postured to do so, that is, forty-five to fifty aircraft. This implies that the twenty air defense targets and seventeen bomber airfield targets would be hit with this component of the force (with, of course, some attrition). The British retained half of their force equipped with British-made nuclear weapons, presumably so that their national plan against forty-five cities could be implemented if necessary and without American interference. Alternatively, these forces would be used against some of the sixty-nine cities that were "centers of government" or "militarily important." But those were not the priority targets.

The destruction of the next layers of the Soviet air defense system was crucial for the SAC bombers coming in from North America. There were fifteen identified air defense control centers from Kaliningrad to Leningrad. There were three more behind them in Belarus (Minsk, Baranovici, and Babruysk) and five behind them in an arc covering forward of the northwest and southwest quadrants of the Moscow defense system. In addition to the four air defense control centers in western Ukraine that were going to be hit with TAC F-100s, there were three centers in eastern Ukraine, at Kharkov, Dnepropetrovsk, and Stalino (Donetsk).[90]

First, that air defense layer lay out of range of the TAC forces in Western Europe. Second, the Reflex B-47s were optimized for low-level operations to evade that system, but the B-52s and B-47s that were incoming from North America were not. A proportion were optimized for high-level delivery, though this was changing by 1959.[91] Redundant targeting of the Soviet bomber bases in the Baltics, Belarus, and Ukraine by V-Force was probably designed to ensure that anything the Reflex forces missed or, say, the IL-28 bases that posed no threat to North America and were not hit by the B-47s, were mopped up.

V-Force operations in 1958–60 were focused on two penetration routes: the French-Swiss corridor and the Norway-Sweden corridor. Operating in cells of six aircraft, "routes through Sweden and Switzerland gave the longest tracks through non-combat zones."[92] The

V-bombers on the southern route, like the Reflex forces preceding them, would have exploited the gaps blown through Hungary and western Ukraine, while the forces on the northern route would have avoided East German and Polish air defenses altogether in order to concentrate on targets in the Baltic States and then penetrate into Belarus. The Mk-5 weapon, even at the 40- to 50-kiloton yield, was adequate for these targets.

This brings us to SAC's Airborne Alert Force. In March 1958 Canada approved SAC Airborne Alert overflights, and in July Eisenhower approved Airborne Alert indoctrination flights. After the Head Start and Big Sickle tests later that year, the first Steel Trap flights started in 1959. These consisted of ten to twelve B-52 sorties per day, each equipped with two thermonuclear weapons. The predominant weapon types were the Mk-15 and Mk-39, and occasionally the Mk-36.[93]

Airborne Alert has been epitomized in the films *Fail Safe* and *Dr. Strangelove*, and the bulk of the literature and other discussions focus on the Chrome Dome Airborne Alert operations of the 1960s. The earlier operations of Steel Trap and its successors Down Field and High Trip were different. Power originally wanted an Airborne Alert Force of sixty B-52s to offset SAC vulnerability to ballistic missile attack. LeMay and White talked him out of this costly approach, with LeMay suggesting that the number of bombers in the air might increase to correspond to the evolution of a crisis in order to increase the American deterrent capacity during such affairs.[94] In other words, the Airborne Alert Force was a signaling tool on one level, but it was also a combat force that was not vulnerable to a preemptive Soviet attack. Along these lines, Power used the existence of the Airborne Alert Force to signal Khrushchev that he was personally targeted in Moscow, but the probability is high that the B-52s assigned to Steel Trap were targeted elsewhere.[95] The Steel Trap forces quite neatly drew attention away from the Reflex forces that would take down Moscow at low level by refocusing Soviet attention to the north instead of the southwest.

The question then becomes: What did SAC do with ten to twelve B-52s carrying twenty to twenty-four nuclear weapons that were

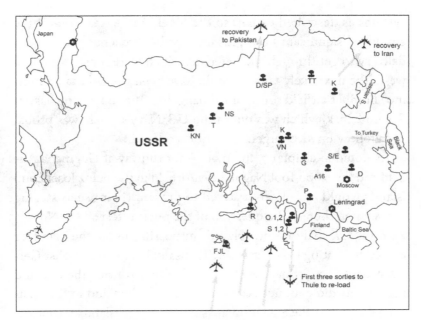

Map 29. Projected Steel Trap Airborne Alert Force targets, 1958–59. S: Severomorsk-1 and -2. O: Olenegorsk-1 and -2. R: Rogochevo Airfield. FJL: Franz Josef Land. P: Plesetsk ICBM sites. D: Dyaglievo Bison air base. S/E: Saratov/ Engels Bison complex. TT: Tyura Tam missile complex. K: Kantubek biological warfare complex. D/SP: Dolon/Semipalatinsk complex. NS: Novosibirsk atomic energy plant. T: Tomsk atomic energy plant. VN: Verkh-Neyvinskiy atomic energy plant. K: Kyshtym atomic energy plant. KN: Krasnoyarsk atomic energy plant. G: Glazov atomic energy plant. A16: Azramas-16 a tomic energy plant. Courtesy of the author.

moving north over Newfoundland, Manitoba, and British Columbia, refueling from KC-135 tankers, and returning to their bases in the American Southwest on a daily basis? The most logical employment of these aircraft and their weapons was to strike targets that could not be hit by Reflex B-47s or Bomber Command's V-bombers. There was also the priority of hitting targets that were a threat to North America. This suggests several possibilities.

The most straightforward targets for B-52s coming over the Pole would have been the large Severomorsk-1 and -3 air bases near Murmansk, and then the Olenegorsk Airfield and Olenegorsk-2 nuclear storage site. The probability is low that SAC planners would have relied on the U.S. Navy being in position and taking out the air defense systems as described earlier, so the Steel Trap B-52s would have employed significant ECM plus low-level approaches and pop-up delivery to get through the defenses, which were mostly oriented west. The next likely targets would have been the Lakhta (Katunino) bomber airfield south of Arkhangelsk. The submarine base at Severodvinsk, which was out of the U.S. Navy's reach, was probably a follow-on SAC target.

As noted in chapter 7, the 11,900-foot runway at Gogmana Airfield and the 6,000-foot Nagurskaya Airfield in the Franz Josef Land islands would have been cratered to prevent their use as staging bases. Then there is the question of the nuclear test site at Novaya Zemlya. CIA analysis downplayed any possible use of the island for air activity, citing harsh weather. That said, National Socialist Germany based six U-Boats at a base on the island during the war, and the Soviets did conduct aviation operations then and in the postwar period.[96] As the Soviets increasingly used the island as a nuclear test range, more and more facilities emerged, many of them identified during SENSINT flights.[97] These included the large Belushya Guba (Rogochevo) Airfield, which hosted the Polyarny Aviation Division with its MiG-17FS.[98] The probability is high that it would be targeted early by B-52s because of the size of the airfield and its location relative to North America, its relationship to the nuclear test site, and because constant surveillance of it was difficult given the climatic conditions. Of note, the storage of Mk-36 weapons at Thule, six of them, afforded the initial Airborne Alert B-52s striking these northerly targets the ability to refuel, reload with large-yield weapons, and then go in deep to the southern-most targets in the south-central Soviet Union.

Another complex that was likely marked for early destruction was the facilities around Plesetsk. HUMINT in 1958 suggested there was substantial construction of a missile facility, but U-2 imagery was blurry and could not confirm the details before 1960. The site was nonetheless designated an ICBM complex. In reality the SS-6 ICBMs were initially deployed at three closely spaced "soft" launch sites in 1959 but were not combat-ready for some time. By 1961–62 six launch areas and a fourth launch point were built and were by then under observation by satellite reconnaissance missions.[99] The probability is high that an Airborne Alert B-52 was targeted on the suspected initial launch points even though SAC did not have detailed knowledge of the sites. Bomber bases west and east of the Urals would also have been prioritized. The most important were Dyagelivo near Ryazan and Engels near Saratov, both with Mya-4 Bison units. There was Dolon with its TU-95 Bears, east of the Semi-palatinsk nuclear test ranges, which boasted a bomber-capable air-field and a nuclear weapons storage area under construction.[100] Two other priority target complexes would have been the space launch facilities and ICBM sites at Tyura Tam (Baikonur) and the Aralsk-7 biological warfare research center and its star-shaped airfield at Kan-tubek on Vozrozhdeniya Island in the Aral Sea.

Airborne Alert B-52s were ideally positioned to destroy the Soviet nuclear weapons production complexes east of the Urals. By the late 1950s these included the well-documented uranium-processing plants at Glazov and Novosibirsk; the gas diffusion plants at Verkh-Neyvinskiy, Tomsk, and Angarsk; and plutonium production at Kyshtym, Tomsk, and Krasnoyarsk.[101] Extensive analysis of the elec-tric power production and transmission system in the Urals was con-ducted starting in 1958. It is difficult to determine whether this was for the purposes of estimating the power requirements for, say, the gaseous diffusion plant at Verkh-Neyvinskiy so that production could be estimated, or for identifying critical power nodes that lay outside of the Soviet air defense umbrella, such as the Zlatoustinskaya sub-station. Possibly it was undertaken for both reasons.[102] For compar-ative purposes, this would have been the equivalent of destroying the Norris Dam in Tennessee so that the three uranium-enrichment plants at Oak Ridge would be forced to cease production.

Six B-52s with two weapons each could have destroyed these tar-gets: the first bomb from each plane could destroy the nuclear mate-rial plants, thereby reducing weight and increasing range and thus permitting the use of second bombs against the deeper targets Aral-sk-7, Tyura Tam, Dolon, and Semiplatinsk. The Tyura Tam facili-ties would have required several weapons given the dispersion of the launch sites. Recovery in Iran, possibly at Masshad; Kabul, Afghanistan; Peshawar, Pakistan; or Rajauri, Kashmir, would have been challenging and the aircraft would have been on fumes provided they evaded PVO's southern defenses.[103]

Under conditions of Tactical Warning, then, SAC could hit sixty-six targets with the Reflex Alert Force in Western Europe and twenty-four targets with the Airborne Alert Force, for a total of ninety targets in the western and central Soviet Union. Fifteen Air Mail B-47s in Guam and six Reflex B-47s in Alaska would hit twenty-one targets in the Far East. This leaves the Alert Force at bases in the United States on fifteen minutes' alert. SAC had 146 bombers on ground alert in 1958, 169 in 1959, and 349 by 1960. The limiting factor was the number of tankers on alert and their locations. For example, in 1959 all 169 alert aircraft in the United States had a tanker in support, but in 1960 the 349 alert bombers had only 237 alert tankers to support them.[104] This, of course, would change under conditions of Strategic Warning. In a scenario where SAC had to go under Tactical Warning, then, 111 forward-based bombers added to the ground alert bombers gave SAC the ability to launch 245 bombers in 1958, 268 in 1959, and 448 in 1960.

The number of targets covered, however, depended upon the ratio of B-47s to B-52s. In approximate numbers, there was a 1:4 ratio of alert B-52s to alert B-47s in 1958, which increased to two B-52s for every three alert B-47s by late 1960.[105] This would fluctuate on a daily basis, so a Heisenberg view of the ground alert force in the United States in early 1960 would have had 140 B-52s and 210 B-47s on alert for a total of 349 aircraft. Again in approximate terms, this would have allowed for the coverage of around 490 Desired Ground Zeros. Combined with overseas alert forces armed with 111 weapons, this gave SAC the ability to cover approximately 601 Desired Ground Zeros with its Alert Force by 1959–60.

So what were the U.S.-based alert forces going to hit after the Reflex, V-Force, and Airborne Alert forces went in and why? The most probable course of action was to restrike those targets in case these forces were unable to complete their missions for whatever reason, be it enemy action, navigational error, or other mishap. For example, during an Operational Readiness Inspection at the 96th

Bomb Wing in October 1959, erroneous data were discovered in five Combat Mission Folders that would have negatively affected the execution of those missions.[106] And targeteers weren't perfect: a SAC analysis of what they determined to be Kostroma Airfield was in fact a parallel pair of wide roads.[107] Soviet submarines with nuclear torpedoes or cruise missiles could attrit U.S. Air Force bases on the eastern seaboard and reduce the weight of their strikes.

Even if the Soviets had flushed their aircraft in the interim, vital logistics and support capabilities inherent to the bases, as well as the runways themselves, needed to be destroyed to prevent their use. The Eighth Air Force with the alert forces from eight B-47 and five B-52 wings was postured to do so, supported by the tanker bases in eastern Canada and Greenland, which were programmed to refuel fifty-four B-47s from three wings.[108] These were supposed to penetrate Swedish airspace and then exploit the destroyed or otherwise disrupted air defense system in the Baltic States and Belarus, then into Ukraine. Any large airfield from Leningrad to Crimea not taken out in the initial strikes by Reflex or V-Force forces would have been obliterated to ensure that any remaining Soviet bombers could not stage from the central or far east and attack North America or NATO countries from the western Soviet Union. The predominant weapons were the Mk-15 and Mk-39 (both mods) delivered with low-level pop-up maneuvers.[109]

The possibility of enemy action from submarines affecting Second Air Force operations was nonexistent at this time. With nine wings of B-52s and five of B-47s, the Second Air Force was postured to handle targets deeper inside the Soviet Union via the new tanker bases established at Royal Canadian Air Force stations Namao, Cold Lake, Churchill, and Frobisher Bay.[110] Second Air Force also boasted two strategic wings which had a squadron of B-52s colocated with a squadron of KC-135s.[111] The strategic wings had a 1:1 bomber-tanker ratio, permitting deep penetration even from bases in Texas and Oklahoma. Other strategic wings were being established at K. I. Sawyer, Kinchloe, and Wurtsmith air force bases in Michigan, but these were not available until 1961–62. Part of the Fifteenth Air Force, with five B-52/KC-135 strategic wings and seven B-47/KC-97 wings, was also

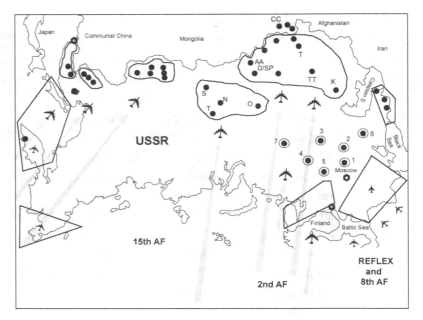

Map 30. Basic War Plan target complexes, 1959. 1: Dyaglievo Air Base. 2: Engels Air Base, Saratov plants. 3: Kuybyshev complex. 4: Kazan complex. 5: Nizhniy Novgorod. 6: Kapustin Yar complex. 7: Sverlovsk complexes. TT: Tyrua Tam. K: Kantubek. T: Tashkent. AA: Alma Ata. CC: CHICOM airfields. D/SP: Dolon/Semipalatinsk complex. O: Omsk. N: Novosibirsk. T: Tomsk. S: Stalinsk. Courtesy of the author.

assigned to missions in the south-central USSR, while others were dedicated to Far East and Chinese targets (see chapter 10). The most important of these were the strategic wings at Grand Forks AFB and Minot AFB, North Dakota. They were capable of reaching any target in the south-central Soviet Union.

Alert targets in the Caucasus would have prioritized the Mozdok facilities; Tbilisi, with its airframe plant and three large airfields; and Yerevan, with two large airfields. They were protected by the 14th Air Division's three MiG regiments at three other PVO airfields.[112] The major oil production center at Baku was protected by the 15th Air Defence Corps with five MiG regiments, but the Baku area itself had eleven airfields. Half of these could handle bomber aircraft.[113] Some air defense suppression would have been required before the arrival of bombers, likely provided by F-100s stationed

COMING TOGETHER

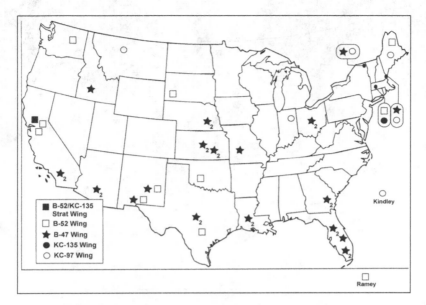

Map 31. This 1958 SAC "Zone of the Interior" (United States) basing map highlights Gen. Thomas Power's primary concerns regarding vulnerability after the Sputnik event. In some cases two four-squadron B-47 wings occupied a single base after implementation of the overseas Reflex Action deployments, which were themselves undertaken to reduce vulnerability of the forward-based SAC forces. Courtesy of the author.

in Turkey or from Sixth Fleet aircraft carriers, or both. The numerous oil facilities in and around Baku would likely have been hit by Eighth Air Force forces that were not part of the Alert Force later on or by Sixth Fleet carriers. The phasing of strikes in the Caucasus is unclear. A plausible route was from the eastern United States–United Kingdom–Hungary-Romania, over the Black Sea and then in from the west, hours after the initial USAFE and U.S. Navy strikes would have cleared out the air defense system.

The next cluster of targets belonged to the Second Air Force: these lay between the Urals and Moscow. The Dyagilevo bomber airfield northwest of Ryazan had Mya-4 Bisons. The destruction of the Mya-4 Engels bomber base, plus the two large airfields in Saratov, one next to the airframe plant, was also crucial. Again, if the Airborne Alert B-52s were unable to complete their missions against Engels or Dyagilevo, then the follow on missions would have. The

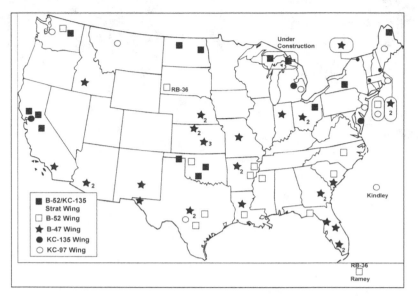

Map 32. By 1960 the expansion of the B-52 force produced the "strategic wing" concept, each with a B-25 squadron and a KC-135 squadron, and the construction of the northern tier bases was well underway. This plus the expansion of B-52 bases in California and Washington allowed SAC to reach targets deep in the Soviet Union without depending on Thule, Keflavik, and Eielson as it had during the B-36 era. Courtesy of the author.

Kuybyshev complex to the east, with two airfields and an airframe plant, was of particular interest to SAC. There were four MiG bases at almost cardinal points to the city to protect the facilities.[114] North of Kuybyshev were the Kazan airframe plants and two large airfields. Northwest of Kazan lay Nizhniy Novgorod, with three large airfields. Restriking the spread-out missile launch and testing facilities plus the airfield at Kapustin Yar was also likely in this wave.

Moving east, Second Air Force and Fifteenth Air Force targets were clustered in three geographic areas. The closest was the Sverdlovsk target complex, including the nuclear weapons production facilities at Verkh-Neyvinskiy and Kyshtym, and the large airfield to the south of Sverdlovsk itself. Once again Tyura Tam and Kantubek would have been hit on the way to the next cluster, essentially from Tashkent to Alma Ata. An examination of Soviet dispositions in this region suggests a redoubt in the mountains of the south,

COMING TOGETHER

remote from the rest of the country. Both Tashkent and Alma Ata had airframe plants and two large airfields. There were twenty-one other airfields that interested SAC. Almost all of these were large enough for TU-16 bombers. Additionally there was the missile test site at Sary Shagan, which also had a very large airfield.[115] In a general sense each main city was protected with MIG regiments forming an Air Defence Division or Corps located at three airfields, with the city at the center. Other targets under SAC's observation were the Zang Keruval, Tihua, and Tacheng airfields in western China. They were likely grouped with the central Soviet targets because of their remoteness from eastern China and proximity to other strikes to the north.[116]

The last geographic cluster was handled by Fifteenth Air Force. The Dolon and Semipalatinsk facilities would have been hit on restrike. The airframe plant and two large airfields at Omsk, the airframe plant and its associated large airfield at Novosibirsk, and the nearby and overly large commercial airport built in 1957 would have been targeted, likely in the alert wave. To the northeast of Novosibirsk was Tomsk, with its nuclear weapons production facilities and airfield.[117]

The penetration capability of the SAC Alert Force differed from earlier years with the introduction of the B-52. The B-47 force depended on dedicated ECM aircraft and the destruction of air defense control centers and radar to achieve penetration into the heavily defended Baltics, Belarus, Ukraine, and Moscow regions. The B-52s, however, depended on evasive routing around the Talent-identified Soviet air defense system and densely populated areas, which was easier done the further east the targets were, and on low-level delivery profiles. Indeed each B-52 was essentially its own ECM aircraft Though the ECM fit differed from squadron to squadron and wing to wing, the basis for it included fourteen jammers of four different types set to different frequencies collected by the ELINT aircraft, three warning receivers of three different types, and eight chaff dispensers.[118]

As for low-level operations, each aircraft crew in the SAC training system aspired to be the functional equivalent of the earlier specialized Hairclipper-trained crew, though with somewhat different delivery parameters. Throughout the 1958–60 period there were basically two primary nuclear weapons in different variants. There was the Mk-15 and its derivative, the Mk-39 (Big Tail), which yielded 3.8 megatons. The Mk-21 and its derivative, the Mk-36 (Last Resort), could yield 18 to 19 megatons. In a general sense, the alert B-47s carried dialed-up Mk-36s and the alert B-52s carried Mk-15s and Mk-39s. For follow-on strikes, however, some B-52 units deeper in the delivery schedule, like the 4130th Strategic Wing at Bergstrom AFB, carried Mk-36s. The Mk-36 tended to be a war reserve weapon for other U.S.-based B-52 units while their alert aircraft carried Mk-15s and Mk-39s.[119]

The threat from surface-to-air missiles was understood long before Francis Gary Powers was shot down on May Day 1960, so SAC Tactical Doctrine adjusted accordingly even before the SA-2 Guidelines were deployed starting in 1959. After the LABS maneuver was disposed of, SAC bombers had two low-level delivery profiles, the Short Look and the Long Look, sometimes known as the Bat technique. After a 400-nautical-mile ingress flight at under 500 feet, the bomber started an abrupt climb to an established altitude (3,700 for B-47s, 4,300 for B-52s), then leveled for 5 to 15 seconds (120 seconds under certain conditions). The bomb was released over the target, then the bomber dove to 100 feet and climbed after detonation to cruise altitude for egress. If the weapon was parachute-retarded, this gave the bomber more time to escape. The Large Charge involved the delivery of two bombs on two targets ten to fifteen miles apart, for example, the nuclear facilities north of Tomsk and the Tomsk Airfield, and could be a Short Look or a Long Look depending on conditions.[120]

The height of burst varied depending on the target and was not standardized. As one SAC B-47 crew member explained, "These little fellows worked best if they exploded above ground. There was no sense wasting all that devastation digging a bigger hole. Spread the goodies over [a] nice big area."[121]

Finally, the non-alert bombers in the United States, or at least those that could be generated under conditions of Strategic Warning, have to be accounted for. An examination of Talent report lists and their producers strongly suggests that, despite the debate over alternative undertaking discussed in the next chapter, the BWP remained geared to the destruction of the Soviets' means to deliver and produce nuclear weapons. The destruction of Moscow was integral to the plan. It was only in the summer of 1960, that is, in the shift from the BWP to the SIOP, that U.S. Air Force targeteers used Talent data to revisit and update target data on what would henceforth be classified as urban/industrial targets. For example, among the new Talent reports, facilities like the Uralmash Heavy Equipment Plant at Sverdlovsk, Stalingrad's heavy metal industry, Kharkov's Tank and Locomotive Plant 75, and the Railroad Car Manufacturing Plant in Nizhniy Tagil were reexamined. Aviation industrial facilities not colocated with large airfields were added, like the Aircraft Engine Plant 154 at Voronezh.[122]

Consequently we need to look again at White's statements to determine what those targets would likely have been. He referred specifically to the destruction of the Soviet "residual military strike force"—not industry, not population. Presumably this encompassed any system the Soviets had to project aerospace power outside of the Soviet Union: fighters, fighter-bombers, light bombers, medium bombers, heavy bombers, submarines, missiles, and space systems. After all of the other waves had gone in, the only way to determine what needed to be struck next was by aerial reconnaissance, SIGINT/ELINT, and the seismic detection systems. This suggests some form of pause after the U.S.-based Alert Force had gone in to determine what was left to destroy, then assigning forces, and carrying out strikes. It remains unclear exactly how conflict termination would have been carried out; instead of psychologically stressed voices over red telephones negotiating a cease-fire, it may have simply been the wind blowing the charred, radioactive remains of the Soviet Union into the atmosphere and into the dustbin of history.

The primary challenges to the SAC deterrent system included Soviet ballistic missiles and the consequent reduction in reaction time. This put the forward-based forces at even greater risk of preemption, which in turn generated adjustments to them, including the Reflex Alert and Airborne Alert deployments. At the same time, a significant increase in non-SAC nuclear capabilities, both U.S. Air Force and U.S. Navy, relieved SAC of certain target sets and permitted a greater focus on the Soviet Union proper. The possibility that SAC would be dependent on those forces to gain access to the western Soviet Union existed. However, SAC was joined by a new nuclear-capable ally: the Royal Air Force Bomber Command's V-Force. Yet the sheer cost of these endeavor led to debate over the best form of deterrence: the Emergency War Plan with its Air Power Battle Target System, or a new concept obliquely referred to as the "alternative undertaking."

10

Megadeath Musings

Alternative Undertaking and Deterrence, 1958–60

The advocates of the "minimum deterrent" are also inferring that they can
state fairly precisely the maximum number of weapons systems required
to support this concept because the targets would be population and
industrial centers. It would appear that the Air Force has contributed, to
a certain degree, in the generation of this concept through an over-use of
the term "retaliation" and many people have come to associate the present
national concept of deterrence with retaliation capability alone. The
necessity for being prepared to take the initiative in the event of strategic
warning has not been emphasized enough. Should a decision be made to
settle for a minimum deterrent, i.e., one which would have the capability
to destroy only industrial and population centers, then this Nation will
have lost forever the capability to react militarily to strategic warning
and take the initiative in eliminating military targets.

—GEN. THOMAS WHITE, 1959

The low-key Thomas Dresser White was the fulcrum in the
balancing act that was the U.S. Air Force's nuclear strategy
debate up until 1960.[1] White did not have the same high public profile as, say, LeMay or Power, and was not one to accept past
practices as the template for the future. Yet at the same time he was
dealing with formidable personalities like the former and current
SAC commanders with their established pedigree, on one hand, and
Otto Weyland, the commander of Tactical Air Command, and Earle
Partridge, the commander of Air Defense Command and NORAD,

on the other. SACEUR Lauris Norstad was in a category all on his own. The air force was more than just SAC, but how would other perspectives be accommodated in the face of budgetary realities and the climate of interservice competition? This process, which went into high gear in the summer of 1957, played a significant role in shifting nuclear targeting emphasis by 1959.

White had a handful of people he relied on for outside perspectives. There was retired general Ennis C. Whitehead ("In the event of a Soviet surprise attack, the safest place for SAC's airplanes is en route to or over Red targets").[2] His special assistant, Col. Leo Paul, offered more thoughtful ruminations on the works of the RAF marshal Sir John Slessor.[3] When in a public report William Kaufman from the International Study Group at Princeton slammed Massive Retaliation (or rather, what he thought it to be) as a dangerous "all or nothing" strategy, Paul passed it to White, noting, "Kaufman's contentions are well written and will be persuasive to readers who, like him, are only partially informed. . . . His analysis of the military deterrents the U.S. has, and can exploit, does not do justice to the flexibility of air power."[4]

In the summer of 1957 White was well aware that the budget ax was going to fall. At the same time the main argument making the rounds of the air force was that, in order to prevent the all-or-nothingness of Massive Retaliation, the United States needed the ability to deter and fight "local wars" and thus needed to reexamine its force structure. This discussion was influenced by a larger debate, not only within the defense establishment but in the public domain, over what strategy was appropriate for the United States under the prevailing circumstances. Was there going to be a "nuclear stalemate" resulting in "mutual deterrence"? What was the lowest level of nuclear forces required under those conditions? This led to theorizing about "minimal deterrence." Donald Quarles, secretary of the air force, ruminated about "sufficiency."[5]

The clear implication for White was that this would lead to an intermural fight for resources not only at the service level but also within the air force itself. Weyland was the first out of the gate: "With the advent of the small high yield nuclear weapons and the capability of the smaller more economical tactical aircraft to deliver these . . . the most economical weapons system for the 'counter-air' and 'retardation' job is now the all weather tactical system." These weapons could be used in limited as well as general war, and, by implication, SAC could be reduced.[6] If White did not handle this adroitly, the U.S. Air Force was going to be a house divided against itself when it went up against the other services, which were now openly pushing for variants of minimal deterrence.

White anticipated the inevitable "SAC is too big" argument by priming Quarles:

> The highest priority military task set forth in national policy is the maintenance of a secure and effective deterrent and retaliatory force. . . . The deterrent and retaliatory posture of the United States lies almost wholly in [SAC]. These circumstances demand that [SAC] be kept, quantitatively and qualitatively, in such a state as to ensure successful penetration of enemy defenses and to act as a positive deterrent to Soviet aggression. . . . The size and the quality of [SAC] from a military viewpoint, must always be viewed in the light of the increasing number of targets in the growing Soviet Long Range Air Army and the certainty of increased attrition of our forces as a result of improving Soviet air defense systems. The extent of the target system imposes rigid quantitative minimums.[7]

That is, SAC had to be big, and there were legitimate reasons for this to be so. White then shifted fire to gain buy-in from the USAF fiefdoms. To do so he established a study to look at what the 1960–70 U.S. Air Force should look like, and at the same time instructed LeMay to form a panel to examine the air force in the face of the upcoming budgetary realities. White probably anticipated that LeMay would stack the deck; it was clear that with Maj. Gen. John P. McConnell in the lead it was a SAC-dominated exercise.[8]

Key points from the report included these concerns: "Following U.S. tradition, existing policy is largely reactive in nature and is inadequate in cold war. It may prove inadequate in Secondary War, and is setting the stage ('absorb the first blow') for disaster in Primary War." The United States was saddled with "World War II concepts, with a veneer of nuclear air power philosophy, [that] have largely influenced [NSC] policy," and nothing would change until at least 1963. A prime competitor was the U.S. Navy, which argued that SAC would be destroyed on the ground, leaving only USAF forces to respond. This argument was increasingly wedded to Adm. Arleigh Burke's assertion pointing to "the danger of preparing for only all-out nuclear war with the observation that we could be conceivably forced into a position of choosing between capitulating on local problems or accepting all-out nuclear war."[9]

The counter to these arguments, for the panel, was to base strategy on several concepts. First, "the highest priority mission of the National Military Establishment [was] to deter Primary War on terms acceptable to the United States." Second was the possibility of taking the initiative and having the ability to "gain a decision favorable to the United States should Primary War occur": "The United States must prepare to destroy the enemy homeland if necessary to enforce our will on the enemy nation. . . . Enforcing our will is defined as facilitating in obtaining diplomatic and political objectives."[10]

This required a new target system, "the destruction of which [was] possible in the event of initiation of the war by the U.S. or after Soviet surprise attack; and the elimination of which [would] accomplish the purposes set forth above." Forces beyond those necessary to carry this out were important because after the first phase of the war, "the remainder of the nuclear strike forces [would] maintain air surveillance of the Soviet Bloc and destroy residual nuclear capability." TAC's role was noted: "In the larger sense SAC is already charged with the destruction of enemy air power targets. The diversification essential to optimum effectiveness requires TAC to attack such targets well behind the periphery of the USSR."[11] There was more, much more, including unsolicited recommendations on reorganizing the whole Unified Command Plan.

The McConnell Report, when it was tabled in August 1957, was immediately passed by White to an unnamed interlocutor, probably retired general James Doolittle. This individual noted that is was "an accurate reflection of the views of a sizeable segment of the thinking Air Force": "It has the vitality, drive, and impatience characteristic of both the 'young Turk' and the seasoned operator who despair of progress by evolution. . . . [However,] the report is not responsive to reality. The concept is too absolute, even though it may be pure and correct in military logic."

> Concept for operations for primary war: there is an emphasis on surprise attack as the only (not merely the most likely or most dangerous) source of primary war. This is weak, in that it eliminated an obvious contingency which can not and will not be dismissed outside the Air Force with anything like the dispatch of the Board Report. There is mention of possible U.S. initiative in primary war. Dangerous as that issue is, because of the preventive war anathema, it is properly raised at some point as long as we make it clear that U.S. initiative and preventive war are not synonymous. Seeking means to avoid suffering the first blow in other than surprise attack, is not equivalent to preventive war and should be explored with great care. . . . [The reports lacks] an appreciation of the U.S. and Free World political assets and limitations which are in essence the foundation of Western Civilization.[12]

However, there were valuable items that White could extract and use, or that others would extract and use later.[13]

In the November 1957 USAF Commander's Conference, White took the participants, who included Secretary of the Air Force James Douglas, "Tooey" Spaatz, and Edward Teller, through the McConnell Report and the 1960–70 force structure study. The numbers of bombers constituted a main discussion point. Power's presentation noted two extremes: if he had an alert force of 585 bombers, 380 tankers, and 51 missiles, he could destroy 37 percent of the 439 Desired Ground Zeros, while TAC and the other forces would destroy 16 percent of the targets, for a total of 53 percent target coverage of the Tactical Warning target set. The overall number of aircraft needed to maintain that alert force was 2,089 bombers and 950 tankers. With an additional 45 B-52s, 173 tankers, 66 air-to-surface missiles, and 45 ICBMs added to the alert force, Power believed SAC could destroy 71 percent of the critical DGZs (which would increase in number to 466 by 1962). The argument predictably devolved: "SAC must be large enough but no one agrees on *how* large precisely." Then Partridge piped up: "SAC is too big: [what if] we do some other things, [like] attack cities?" Then SAC could be reduced in size. Unfortunately, neither Power's nor LeMay's response was recorded by the stenographer.[14] The conference was inconclusive: "the 'radical' view [was] unacceptable" and "the 'conservative' view [was] too conservative." Thus the argument emerged: "SAC may be too large. The key to this issue is the target system. There is a chance that counter-air targeting is counter-productive."[15] Power, however, reminded White that target coverage was everything in the deterrence game.[16]

Something had to give: the air force needed both SAC and TAC. Reexamination of SAC targeting took place against this backdrop.

White was conflicted and unhappy in the conference's wake. His views coalesced in early 1958 as he was increasingly concerned about language and perception in policymaking and public circles. He told Weyland, "No small portion of this is the growing belief that the military establishment has no capability less than all-out nuclear retaliation. [Massive Retaliation] is not mandatory in response to limited aggressions in underdeveloped areas. . . . The tone of our presentations must be one of restraint, with stress on the freedom of choice, from the standpoint of political decision, available to the U.S., as a result of *existing* flexible and selective capability."[17]

At a classified speech at Quantico, White pointed out that his biggest concerns were the "attacks on SAC's budget": "Insurance is often considered a burden until the accident it is intended to cover actually occurs." Clearly annoyed, he continued:

> The Communists capitalize on *our* humanitarian standards, on *our* doubts and fears—as they have done in the case of nuclear weapons. I am disturbed at the Communist success in this particular area. It is symbolized in my mind by a U.S. tendency to consider seriously self-restraints in nuclear weapons planning in the face of sure knowledge that no such restraints will be applied by the enemy. I am amazed that symptoms of this appear in military thinking as well as in the newspapers. Our preoccupation with niceties in nuclear warfare, particularly in *retaliatory* attack would, I am sure, delight the Kremlin.[18]

MEGADEATH MUSINGS

The arguments for minimum deterrence put forward by political scientist and Weapons Systems Evaluation Group member George Rathjens in a June 1958 *Bulletin of Atomic Scientists* article were of some concern to White. This was a clear-cut case for nuclear submarines and Polaris missiles as a cost-saving initiative. White's staff cogently and, to some extent, ironically responded, "This is merely a repetition of the same situation indulged in by the British Bomber Command during World War II when for lack of a daylight survival capability they claimed that massive bombing of the workers was more effective than pinpoint bombing of industry in accomplishing the same agreed objective." Alarmed, however, they stated, "If we allow this concept of deterrence and retaliation to gain momentum on the one hand, while the Army's Limited War concept as the priority threat takes hold, we may find ourselves in a very difficult position with respect to the justification of Air Force policies, forces, and programs."[19]

Power, ever the operator, was concerned that the Polaris system would interfere with SAC bomber and missile operations and therefore concluded, "Since CINCSAC must have the authority over planning, target assignment, timing and readiness of all elements of the force, the Polaris weapons system must be under his command and control. The resulting structure would comprise a Unified Command," which Power would presumably take charge of.[20] After clashing with LeMay over force structure costs in the fall of 1958, Power mended fences and proceeded with White and Twining to brief Secretary of Defense Neil McElroy on SAC's needs, which now included B-58 medium bombers and the Titan ICBMs. McElroy was annoyed at the briefing and told the group that "all services say the same thing about their weapons systems, but the problem was to find systems whose contribution was marginal or overlapping and eliminate them" to save money. This led to a discussion over "how much was enough to deter and 'knock out' the U.S. or the USSR." White opined that at first he thought "General Power was arguing too much to be helpful": "But later on I revised this impression and feel, on balance, that it was valuable to have had him present." McElroy turned on Twining "and commented on the failure of the JCS to come up with the proper composition of the retaliatory forces."[21]

Minimum deterrence would not go away. There was now open discussion about "soft" versus "counterforce" targets in the media, which led White to issue instructions to the air force not to discuss the issue publicly.[22] White sounded out LeMay, who responded:

> There is no easy solution to war, no simple target system that will win. Wars can be won by airpower, but only if you have the capability to drive through the defenses and destroy a substantial portion of the [enemy's] war making capacity and in so doing demonstrate that the remainder will be destroyed rapidly. It follows that you have no deterrent unless the enemy is convinced before hand that this is so. A force designed to destroy a small number of targets (200 according to the Army) lends itself to destruction by surprise attack. . . . The real danger, however, is a force of this size has no chance of defeating enemy forces. Therefore, we face destruction even though we destroy 200 targets. In that case, in the battle of deterrents, I think we lose because we value human life and our resources more than the Soviets, therefore *they* have the deterrent.[23]

In early 1958 a concept referred to as "Alternative Undertaking" emerged in JCS deliberations over nuclear targeting. Whether or not its title was intended to be ironic, in its original form this concept explored how the United States would react to a "general war initiated under disadvantageous conditions." If so, each commander in chief was to "select from his target list those high priority targets which would be attacked under the assumption that only 25 percent of his atomic delivery forces would be available," and they were to focus on "destruction of government controls and population centers within the USSR to the extent necessary to neutralize the capabilities of the USSR to carry on the war."[24]

On the last day of 1958 Norstad queried White on the implications of Alternative Undertaking: he was concerned, as was Larry Kuter in the Pacific Air Forces, about the practical aspects of having to implement it if it were made policy. White responded, "[My position] is in direct opposition to the Army and Navy Chiefs whose current proposals would not only give greatly increased stature to the 'Alternative Undertaking' targeting concept, but would in fact

MEGADEATH MUSINGS

make the 'Alternative Undertaking' tantamount to the sole objective of nuclear offensive forces and the basis for establishing the nation's deterrent posture."[25] White's written response to the JCS reiterated his belief that deterrence was based on "an established and recognized U.S. capability to neutralize that military strength which is a threat to the U.S." under conditions of strategic warning. "Even after an attack with little or no warning, [the force structure also had] to destroy any remaining Soviet offensive strength and basic national strengths which allow for further concerted Soviet effort." White asserted to the JCS:

> These forces must also deter attacks against our allies. There must be an established U.S. capability—recognized by both the Soviets and our allies—to react positively to any aggression against U.S. allies. . . . It must be evident to the Soviets that the U.S. has, in fact, a credible option of responding to any such aggression by an attack against the fundamental military strength of the Soviet Union itself. To achieve this credibility the U.S. must have the capability to destroy a critical portion of the Soviet atomic delivery capability, particularly that which can be brought to bear against the United States.[26]

The Polaris force could not do all of this. White penciled elsewhere, "Polaris Operational Concept: 156 cities" and the notation "130 x 40 equalling 5200 MT."[27] (The proposed Polaris force was forty submarines, later increased to forty-one, of which there would have been ten on patrol at any one time for a total of 160 available warheads.) White told Norstad, "Certain areas of ambiguity in the present Joint Chiefs of Staff guidance preclude a prompt resolution of your immediate problems." He was, however, going to recommend to the JCS that a "single target list" be developed to resolve what would essentially be two different force structures to implement two different targeting concepts. This list would "allow some degree of operational flexibility in order to adjust for a degraded capability" if the enemy struck first, while at the same time it would "reflect full recognition of the requirement to destroy those targets which pose the greatest threat" to the United States and allies.[28]

The pressure was on White to figure out how to respond to Alternative Undertaking. He wanted to know about "a possible application of a small surviving B-52 force" and asked Power to conduct a study. He asked about the application of chemical and biological weapons for such a force. Lt. Gen. Francis Griswold, Power's second in command, told White that bugs and gas "were not adaptable to small force applications because they [were] designed to produce casualties rather than fatalities." What about TAC's theater forces? "It is concluded that a small short range force with tactical weapons has limited effectiveness against enemy population." What about SAC? "It is concluded that a small airborne alert force with high-yield weapons can threaten annihilation to a significant fraction of the enemy population. The calculated fatalities from an attack by sixty (60) B-52s effective at the target area is [redacted]. . . . High-yield thermonuclear weapons delivered by long-range bombers provide the greatest small force potential against enemy population." "Salted" nuclear weapons should be ruled out:

> When salting agents are substituted for active material in a normal weapon, there is a loss of weapon yield of one-third to one-half, with consequent decreases in blast and thermal effects as well as reduced fission product fallout. If the proper salting agent is selected, the total fallout effects of the salted weapons can be increased over the effects of the normal weapon at late times and low dose rates, but only slight increases are realized early enough to contribute to the desired high fatality rates. In general, salting a weapon causes a net loss in the military effectiveness of the weapon.[29]

Interestingly, Griswold's figure of sixty B-52s lines up closely with Norstad's original 1945 estimate and is just slightly more than the United Kingdom's assessment for their national plan. Later, during deliberations over Thor in the JCS, the reality emerged that the British had their own population-destruction plan and wanted it coordinated with the nonexistent American population destruction plan so they could fit the Thors into combined targeting plans. This generated problems. White had to do some tap dancing via his staff:

MEGADEATH MUSINGS

How could the U.S. Air Force support British Alternative Undertaking while railing against it in the JCS?

> It will be pointed out to us as an example of SAC (and Bomber Command) agreement with the Army and Navy concept . . . there is a specific proposal as to "city" destruction . . . and suggests primary and alternative undertakings, with "city" destruction being the primary . . . [other verbiage] suggests two target lists and two targeting concepts, something we are fighting strongly. . . . Last year's JSCP . . . established alternative undertakings, [and] is a good part responsible for this entire situation. The alternative undertakings concept is clearly a source of difficulty, particularly because it seems to possess a theoretical validity which has been twisted and misinterpreted badly in practical use.[30]

White also had to caution Power in his dry run briefing to the JCS in May 1959. SAC looked at identifying two target categories, Military Strength Targets and National Control Targets, and two conditions under which they would be hit, Tactical and Strategic Warning, "with reversed priority under the two different situations." To White, this was acceptable "if SAC sustained a substantial Soviet attack before launch," but it "would appear to the layman to be too rigid and over simplified." The net effect would be "to create unfavorable implications outside the Air Force, which are potentially dangerous to national security"; specifically, it established "control targets as a separate category unrelated to military targets." Control Targets were, in reality, "crucial elements of military strength." To delineate in such a fashion appeared to endorse the validity of army-navy "soft or city strategy proposals."[31]

"This would lead to the conclusions therefore that attacking 'cities' constitutes the most important segment of the strategic effort," thus playing into the hands of those who wanted to reduce SAC. "I think," White added,

> the remainder of the solution lies in recognizing that we do not necessary plan to hit "cities" per se, under conditions of last resort; instead we will hit the most critical and lucrative complexes of the enemy's

military strength within our available capability, even under those extreme circumstances. In essence, this would probably be the enemy's military control system. This system could include or equate to the Soviet communications, governmental (and industrial for that matter) control systems. Many of these centers would be in cities, but this does not alter the need for directing our highest priority efforts toward countering Soviet ability to deliver nuclear weapons. This priority would provide the basis for determining which complexes should be attacked and how they should be attacked with different levels of force available under the various circumstances of warning, intelligence and reconnaissance which could exist. In turn the target list would reflect these factors.[32]

SAC's targeteers were not in any position to implement radical course corrections, however. In 1958 SAC's "emphasis was still on strategic warning" with the Alert Force targets, including "airfields (bomber bases and primary defense bases), industrial complexes, and missile sites." However, by 1959 strike plans "emphasized primarily the tactical warning situation to take advantage of the alert force. Although this force was a fairly small one when spread over the enemy target system, it did give SAC early retaliatory capability." If there was more warning time, it would be augmented. "If the U.S. retaliated to a Soviet surprise attack, the Alert Force was targeted to destroy the [enemy's] capability to continue to deliver weapons of mass destruction, and his capacity to exploit any success he may have achieved in an initial attack."[33] Minimum deterrence targeting against population targets was evidently not part of the SAC war plan before 1960, but Alternative Undertaking later led to a discussion of Alternative Retaliatory Efforts, which ultimately became one of the underpinnings of the 1960s Single Integrated Operational Plan.[34]

The Feasibility of Minimum Deterrence

Specific information on how Alternative Undertaking planning was carried out remains sketchy, although some extrapolation is possible. White's 1959 request to SAC regarding the minimum number of targets necessary for the "annihilation of a significant fraction of the enemy population" resulted in an estimate of sixty B-52s "effective at the target area" using "high-yield thermonuclear bombs," presumably the Mk-36 mod 1 set to yield 19 megatons. This suggests targeting the sixty largest Soviet cities and rules out any damage that could be caused by forward-deployed TAC, a force regarded as not viable for this kind of operation.[35]

The policy for the United Kingdom's national plan, established in December 1957 and updated in 1958, focused the V-Force effort on 131 Soviet cities with a population greater than 100,000; 98 of these were within 2,100 kilometers from bases in the United Kingdom.[36] The British national plan at this point, however, was limited by the size of the V-Force and the number of available national weapons. In December 1958 there were forty-five Valiants, eighteen Vulcans, and ten Victors for a total of sixty-eight delivery aircraft.[37] In 1958 there were fifty-eight Blue Danubes (16 kt) and five Violet Clubs interim thermonuclear weapons (330 to 500 kt), and in 1959 there were still fifty-eight Blue Danubes and now thirteen Yellow Sun 1s (500 kt), for a total of sixty-three and seventy-one weapons, respectively.[38] Forty-two of the sixty-eight V-Force bombers available in 1958–59 were modified to carry the "E" weapons, the American Mk-5s, which likely would not be available for the national plan.

The British Joint Intelligence Board listed 130 Soviet cities with a population greater than 100,000, of which 54 were deemed "targets of major importance." Ten of those cities lay outside the V-Force range. This suggests that in mid-1958 there were forty-four or so targets on the British national plan list. Further information suggests that two weapons were assigned to each target, and probably extra weapons for Moscow and Leningrad.[39]

With SAC looking at an estimated sixty cities for possible annihilation if instructed to do so under Alternative Undertaking, and Bomber Command looking at forty-four to fifty-four, and with both forces using the same parameters, cities of 100,000 people or greater, what would the target lists have looked like?

A 1960 CIA study, "Population Concentration in the Soviet Union," is probably the closest we can get to those lists, barring the release of more information. The study surveyed cities larger than 50,000 people, of which there were 299. Approximately 33 percent of the Soviet population—at that time 208.8 million—lived within ten miles of the centers of those cities. Thirty cities had populations greater than 500,000, and there were 121 cities with populations ranging from 100,000 to 500,000 (see appendix B).[40]

Bomber Command could reach Moscow from its bases in the United Kingdom, so any target that lay in the Baltic SSRs, Belarus, or Ukraine was likely on the list. Bomber Command's interest in establishing a Supplementary Storage Area at Akrotiri, Cyprus, suggests that that coverage could be extended to the Caucasus and to cities east of the Urals.[41] SAC, of course, had the ability to reach any of the cities on the target list. For SAC, the detonation of a 19-megaton-yield weapon on any of these targets would have annihilated the population, assuming it had not been evacuated. Moscow and Leningrad would have taken three and two weapons, respectively. An informal CIA analysis of SAC suggested that three aircraft would have to have been assigned to each Desired Ground Zero to ensure target destruction.[42] In the context of the Griswold study for White, 180 B-52s would be required to achieve the destruction of the sixty largest Soviet cities and kill something substantially less than 33 percent of the Soviet population. For those advocates of minimum deterrence in the JCS who thought 150 to 200 cities would be enough, the numbers required would be 450 to 600 bombers, assuming again a two-thirds loss rate on the way in. None of this would have any effect whatsoever on Soviet nuclear forces striking the United States and its allies.

As for Bomber Command, the 16-kiloton-yield Blue Danubes could have caused Hiroshima-like damage if effectively and optimally delivered onto their targets, but this would probably not have been enough to completely destroy the population as desired. Yellow Sun 1, with 330 to 500 kilotons, was more likely to do so, but there were only thirteen of them in 1959, and almost half of them would probably have been expended on Moscow and Leningrad. In other words, the British national plan was reminiscent of the very early SAC EWP's.

One can see that the minimum deterrence proponents had a seductive case: 156 missiles fired from the sea appeared to be more cost-effective. There was, however, little discussion of Soviet civil defense measures, city evacuation, or other passive defense approaches. Those in the USAF who were familiar with the Soviet Union (or China, for that matter) and who were involved in targeting during the late 1940s knew that the Soviets could move mountains with forced labor and an ideologically coercive social system: witness the evacuation of industry east of the Urals in 1941 and the removal of "unreliable" ethnic groups in their entirety to Siberia. There was a resilience that the Soviet peoples possessed in spite of the horrors visited upon them by the predations of both the National Socialist regime and the Soviet socialist regime. Threatening to potentially kill 33 percent of them from an intangible system like Polaris in the late 1950s was a questionable method of deterring their leadership. These were men like Khrushchev and Mao, who were responsible for murdering millions of their own people by decree and demonstrably thought nothing of the mass expenditure of life in the event of war. A deterrent had to be seen and be seen to be effective so they could be reminded that it was real, particularly during a crisis situation.

The Four Rs: Reconstitution, Recapitulation, Residual Forces, and Recycling

One argument against minimum deterrence was the requirement to retain forces to continue the war against the Soviet Union after the first blows had been struck and to deter other players from exploiting damage and disruption generated by a Soviet attack on the United States. There were optimists and pessimists in every walk of life in the 1950s on the matter of whether a war would continue after the first day, and the dedication of resources to the "subsequent period" remained under debate. The JCS view, as expressed by Adm. Arthur Radford, was that "the ultimate strategy would depend largely on the relative advantage achieved in the initial phase": "It would include follow-up offensive operations to achieve victory and attain Allied war objectives. We would need, in this second phase, at least a residual atomic capability in addition to ready forces of all Services."[43]

Going back to the 1940s, SAC had detailed plans for bomber recovery to forward bases and for reloading them for subsequent strikes after reconnaissance operations identified what had been hit or not hit. These continued into the late 1950s and were designated "reconstitution" operations. For example, the 4379th Refueling Wing based at Randolph, Texas, was to deploy twenty-four KC-97s to "airlift mobile recovery teams." They were also to pick up teams from Kelly AFB, a nuclear maintenance and storage depot. At Execution Hour plus fifteen, they were to depart for sixteen locations: the Canadian bases in the northeast, plus the UK, Spanish, and Moroccan bases. Notably teams were assigned to airfields at Barcelona, Spain, and Bandirma and Esenboga in Turkey.[44]

In some overseas locations storing nuclear weapons, adaption kits for B-47s were prepositioned. These were designed so that a B-47 delivering an Mk-15 weapon, say, could land and have its bomb bay reconfigured to carry the Mk-6 weapon. This was called "recycling."[45] Practically every SAC base contained Mk-6 mod 6 weapons by 1958, in addition to multimegaton weapons.[46] It took 51 minutes to load an Mk-6 weapon, one hour 39 minutes to load an Mk-15 or Mk-39, and one hour 51 minutes to load an Mk-36.[47]

The nuclear storage site at Goose Bay in Labrador contained Mk-6s but without their cores.[48] These were to be used for restrike purposes. The use of this site was subject to substantial political debate after its construction in 1951 and its use caught in the gears of ongoing bilateral Canadian-American nuclear weapons negotiations in the late 1950s.[49] A second restrike site existed at RCAF Station Namao, near Edmonton, Alberta. A portion of the ammunition storage site for this base was segregated and guarded for USAF use, and a number of the empty storage igloos were modified to handle tritium maintenance. No weapons were apparently stored here, but B-47s recovering from their initial strikes could have reloaded with weapons flown up from the depot at Site How, aka West River Depot aka Deep Creek Air Force Station, adjacent to Fairchild AFB in Washington State.[50] The third restrike storage site was at Thule Air Base: it contained Mk-6 mod 6 and Mk-36 mod 1 weapons.[51] Another possible site was Kindley AFB in Bermuda, which retained nuclear storage but without the weapons in residence.[52]

From a command-and-control point of view, Power had to intervene when a vague directive was issued permitting theater com-manders to commandeer any aircraft in their geographical area of responsibility in wartime. Power was vehement that SAC retain its recycle capability and took the matter to a high level to resolve the dispute.[53]

If the Reflex forces at forward bases were destroyed, there were still the SAC forces in the continental United States. There were at least twenty-five medium bomber wings on eighteen bases in the south-central United States that could not be reached by Soviet systems. And of course there were more than enough nuclear weapons for SAC to deliver: 946 Mk-36s, 1,200 Mk-15s, 700 Mk-39s, and 1,100 Mk-6s, totaling 3,946 weapons.[54]

Among them were the units of 55th Strategic Reconnaissance Wing, which included fifteen RB-47H ELINT aircraft and ten RB-47K weather reconnaissance aircraft. These would deploy either after American forces had absorbed a strike or after the first wave of the Alert Force had gone in to its targets. Staging teams in C-124 transports would deploy to forward bases, possibly Wheelus in Libya, Ernest Harmon, and a base in Alaska to conduct reconnaissance operations.[55] The importance of weather reconnaissance is self-evident in nuclear warfare, when weapon delivery speed and fallout prediction were the order of the day.

The 4347th Combat Crew Training Wing (Medium) at McConnell AFB in Kansas had twenty-three B-47s, forty-six TB-47s, nineteen RB-47s, and twenty Combat Mission Folders assigned to it. Seven of these folders were studied by three crews each, and the remaining thirteen were studied by one crew each, suggesting that the RB-47s played a role in poststrike reconnaissance either of the Soviet Union or to conduct bomb damage assessments on the United States, or both.[56] Similarly the SAC U-2 unit, the 4080th Strategic Reconnaissance Wing (Light), was prepared to conduct poststrike reconnaissance, and plans were made to incorporate CIA U-2s.[57] SAC also retained a squadron of twenty-seven RB-52Bs of the 22nd Bombardment Wing at March AFB.[58]

Another organization that played a role in residual targeting was Atomic Energy Detection System's Long Range Detection unit, the

1009th Special Weapons Squadron.[59] This unit operated subsurface arrays at detachments around the world designed to collect seismic data as part of the peacetime intelligence collection effort against the Soviets' nuclear weapons testing program.[60] The 1009th had three wartime functions: "a. Support the post-strike reconnaissance effort of the Strategic Air Command nuclear offensive by recording and reporting the nuclear explosions that occur on the European-Asian land mass. b. Provide data to support a continuing estimate of enemy nuclear weapons capability. c. Provide data, if facilities permit, to requesting military and civil agencies on environmental radioactive contamination."[61]

The importance of having these resources on hand is straightforward: SAC had the ability to mount a major reconnaissance effort to determine what had been hit if the United States and its forces were attacked first, or after the decision was made to preempt. Of equal importance was the existence of recycle and recapitulation operations and the fact they were exercised regularly.

But that was not all. There was Tactical Air Command, with over four hundred nuclear-capable fighter-bombers based in the United States. On Strategic Warning, TAC was to be "dispersed with the [continental United States] as a residual reserve for required deployment after the outbreak of hostilities."[62] This thinking was progressively clarified after 1958, when TAC's mission directive was interpreted thus: "Provide residual forces following a nuclear exchange between the USSR and the U.S., which can survive, be reconstituted and deployed to carry on the war."[63] As the TAC leadership noted, "This force in general war, supported by an appropriate number of troopcarrier aircraft, could well make a substantial difference in our national posture after the main nuclear offensive has been laid down by SAC and forces overseas. Hence, the survival of a significant portion of this force after a nuclear exchange is of major strategical importance. . . . Historically, the nation with the greatest strength in uncommitted reserves available after the first shock of battle prevails."[64]

All World War II–era aircraft, such as the C-47s and B-25s, that were in use at USAF bases were to be evacuated and concentrated at non-SAC airports and formed into Provisional Transport Squadrons. Air routes that avoided SAC bases were plotted for them.[65]

SAC and TAC's "residual capacity" was significant in numbers, exercised its capability, and likely constrained Soviet freedom of action in that it limited their options under both Cold War and hot war conditions. The overt use of military force, at least outside of the Soviet Bloc, could be countered at varying degrees and levels of effectiveness, but the deployed American and then British forces were equipped with nuclear weapons which may or may not be used. Creative employment of the Soviet IL-28, TU-16, and SS-3 forces might have carried the day over Berlin or Western Europe. The Soviet submarine missile force and submarine-fired nuclear torpedoes augmented with the existing Long Range Air Force bombers could have seriously disrupted SAC operations in eastern Canada and the U.S. East Coast. Destruction of SAC bases in the United Kingdom, Spain, and Morocco from airpower when combined with those moves, however, would only have delayed the inevitable riposte, with the Airborne Alert Force in the lead. And once again there was no Hot Line to negotiate anything over. If it was on, it was on.

Attempts by the Soviets to alter the "correlation of forces" with moves like the Fürstenberg R-5M deployment to East Germany coupled with Soviet influence activities in the United Kingdom make sense retrospectively in this context, as does the 1961 breaking of the nuclear test moratorium and the acceleration of the SS-7 ICBM program. The deployment of forty-two R-12 (SS-4 Sandal) and twenty-four R-14 (SS-5 Skean) ballistic missiles to Cuba in 1962 also takes on a whole new dimension historically. The deployment of these missiles placed the SAC bases that were otherwise uncoverable by Soviet forces at risk, thereby limiting retaliatory options under either Strategic Warning or Tactical Warning conditions. Consequently the Soviet Far East dispositions took on an increased importance, particularly the secret deployment of SS-5s to Anadyr in the early 1960s.

As for the United States, reverting to a minimum deterrence force structure at this point would have been the wrong move at the wrong time. That said, what amounts to a navalized version of SAC's 1950s modus operandi (targeting philosophy, mass, credible demonstrable capability, forward deployment, actively engaging with the adversary on the psychological plane in peacetime) was employed by the U.S. Navy in the 1980s. Its proponents assert their strategy ended the Cold War.[66]

Implementing an explicit population destruction strategy as a basis of deterrence was seductive from a cost-benefit analysis in American circles and from the limits of an emergent capability among the British. The American deterrent system was clearly a massive and costly endeavor. The unwillingness of the U.S. Air Force leadership to accept the argument that the Soviet and American nuclear systems canceled each other out and thus war would not occur under any circumstances was based on direct experiences with Soviet leaders and behavior. To them the risk was simply too great to hedge bets on a minimum deterrent. The U.S. Air Force leadership was, however, increasingly pushed into a corner by the other services, whose arguments were supported more and more by nonmilitary analysts from academia, think-tanks, and the media debates driven by their arguments. The inability to quantify the deterrent system in the Organization Man age in the face of ongoing periodic nuclear crisis with Communist China and the Soviet Union also played a role. That said, the fact that Khrushchev backed off over Berlin in the face of SAC exercises coupled with the knowledge that even if he defeated the forward-based SAC bombers the Soviet Union would be utterly destroyed has to be set against the Alternative Undertaking debate. But what about Mao and Communist China? How was the deterrent system supposed to work against a country that could shrug off Alternative Undertaking–type damage?

11

The Acme of Skill

The Basic War Plan, the General Emergency Operations Plan,
and the Far East, 1957–60

I'm not afraid of nuclear war. There are 2.7 billion people in the world;

it doesn't matter if some are killed. China has a population of 600 million;

even if half of them are killed, there are still 300 million people left.

I'm not afraid of anyone.

——MAO ZEDONG, 1957

The Far East, as we have seen, was a separate theater of war with significantly different strategic problems than those encountered by NATO, USAFE, and SAC in Europe. First there was the critical need to neutralize the threat against North America posed by Soviet long-range air operations stationed in the Soviet Far East. Second was the requirement to destroy Soviet naval capabilities that threatened the entire region in a general war. Alongside this was the requirement to destroy Soviet war-making capacity in the region, capacity that was not necessarily dependent on Soviet activities in the West. The United States was also committed to the defense of South Korea and Japan in the event of a general war or renewed hostilities with North Korea. The United States was also committed to the defense of Taiwan, with the possibility that hostilities in that situation might be expanded to the Communist-controlled Chinese mainland. Forces committed to the region may also be required in a general war. There were other, more limited contingencies in the region that might demand nuclear weapons use, possibly in conjunction with British forces. The geographical spread of these operations and the multiple planning variations, which included the U.S. Navy and its forceful personalities in the region, demanded an agile U.S. Air Force deployment and particularly an agile command structure.

Command and Control in the Far East: Harmonious Entities?

U.S. military commands in the Far East and the Pacific were reorganized in 1958. Far East Command ceased to exist, as did Far East Air Forces, while Pacific Command expanded to handle the region and FEAF was folded into Pacific Air Forces (PACAF), located at Hickam Air Force Base in Hawaii. Pacific Command was commanded by CINCPAC Adm. Felix Stump, who handed off to Adm. Harry Felt in 1958. Gen. Larry Kuter took over FEAF in 1955 and seamlessly transitioned that command into PACAF before relinquishing it to Gen. Emmett "Rosie" O'Donnell in late 1959. For the most part, however, Felt, Kuter, and CINCSAC Gen. Thomas Power constituted the "connective tissue" throughout this period when it came to coordinating the Basic War Plan and CINCPAC's planning.

The combat-hardened Felix Stump had "almost a maniacal fixation on communism" and did not want to give the Communists one inch in the Pacific. His replacement, the equally combat-hardened, "blunt, tough, demanding taskmaster" Harry Felt, was of like mind: he was considered "a rabid anti-Communist."[1] Stump's ships had been regularly shot up off North Korea, incurring casualties and damage long after the 1953 Armistice.[2] Felt had served with the U.S. Military Mission in Moscow throughout 1944 and was intimately familiar with Stalin's modus operandi, especially during the Frantic affair. His negative experiences there clearly played a role in formulating his beliefs. When Felt commanded Carrier Division 3 on the USS *Essex* in 1954, a British civilian airliner en route to Saigon was shot down off Hainan by the Communists. Felt "set a trap," and AD-4 Skyraiders from the USS *Philippine Sea* shot down two Communist La-7 or -11 fighters.[3]

Kuter also had a jaundiced eye when it came to Communism. Standing in for "Hap" Arnold at the Yalta Conference in 1945, one of Kuter's tasks was to gain coordination of the combined bombing offensive with the Soviets and to obtain "basing rights in Siberia

THE ACME OF SKILL

for the B-29s."[4] He pushed to base four B-29 wings near Vladivostok for operations against Japan, and, when agreement to that was not forthcoming, in the Amur region. After tiresome negotiations produced an initial agreement, it was overturned by the Soviets, and "American planners found it was impossible to attain any practicable agreement with the Russians." Kuter later noted that Alger Hiss, a Soviet agent, was part of the American delegation, but Kuter refrained from connecting the dots in the public domain. He did, however, record the frustrations inherent in the Soviets' "continuous obstruction" and the Soviet policy that "Red troops and Soviet citizens should not come in direct contact with American men or patently American material."[5] Kuter was not a fan of the Soviet Union nor its approach to international relations, but he was not as vocal about it as his counterparts.

Kuter was then involved with the early iterations of Lauris Norstad's 1945 postwar force structure exercise regarding a possible strategic air campaign against the Soviet Union.[6] After Orvil Anderson was removed from the Air University for intemperate remarks related to preventive war, Kuter was brought in and attempted to expand the air force's intellectual horizons. He believed that Secretary of State John Foster Dulles's involvement in the new annual Air University symposium played a role in Dulles's assertion that American policy should be based on Massive Retaliation.[7]

The primary problem that Kuter and his naval counterparts were dealing with in the Pacific between 1957 and 1959 was the allocation of scarce resources to handle the multitude of contingencies in their region, and then to what extent these plans could involve the use of nuclear weapons. All contingencies had to be undertaken against the possibility of a larger war with the Soviet Union that might start in another region. As a result, there was a tug of war between the CINCPAC admirals and Kuter over resources, where they were allocated, and who would handle what tasks. Kuter opined:

> The real danger in a nuclear war appears to me to be the very real possibility of the various Commanders of the Joint Chiefs of Staff acting independently and motivated by understandable and inevita-

ble self-interest. . . . The present unified command system simply is not compatible with the thermo-nuclear type war we now envisage. There certainly will be no large World War II ground type campaigns, supported by air and naval forces, and commanded by a single commander in the field. General nuclear war will be extremely short in duration and will be worldwide in scope and activity. The only beneficial coordination possible in this type of war with be at the level of the Service Chiefs themselves, who can in turn direct their respective forces worldwide. For Limited War operations, the expenditure of nuclear weapons will unquestionably be very closely controlled by the President . . . through the Joint Chiefs.[8]

Read one way, it appears Kuter did not trust the CINCPAC admirals on some level and believed that they might adopt a posture in the Pacific region that would not be able to fulfill the primary global objective, which was to provide mutually supporting efforts with PACAF's wartime requirements and, by extension, SAC's. Another possibility was that Kuter believed CINCPAC would spread resources too thin in an attempt to cover every anti-Communist contingency. He and Twining ran into this problem with Stump in 1957. Stump had insisted, "Non-Communist countries need assurances that nuclear weapons will be used to defend them." After visits to South Vietnam and Taiwan, Stump reported to the JCS, "[Ngo Dinh] Diem and Chiang [Kai-shek] . . . have insisted that the United States must use its atomic weapon capability, but they have both expressed disturbing doubts about our willingness to do so." Twining was told, presumably by Radford, "Our actions should clearly evidence our capability and determination to resist Communist aggression with all necessary force, including the use of nuclear weapons as appropriate."[9]

Kuter concurred, up to a point:

These people insist that the actual presence of our combat-ready aircraft in their countries is a greater deterrent to the CHICOMS [Chinese Communists], the North Koreans, and the Communist forces in Manchuria and Siberia than the wing of B-47 in Guam backed up by all our H-bombs and bombers on the far side of the world. It is certain that military minds on both sides of the iron and bamboo

THE ACME OF SKILL

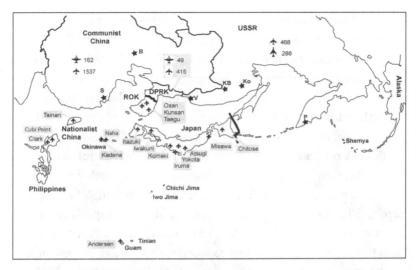

Map 33. Pacific Air Forces basing and threat, 1959. Courtesy of the author.

curtains can weigh and appreciate the tangible and positive visual effect of century series fighters. . . . Precipitous or premature withdrawal on an extensive scale . . . might lead some nations in the Far East to neutralism and possible surrender to Communism.[10]

In essence, Kuter was forced to maldeploy PACAF's nuclear forces in order to compromise on Cold War and hot war requirements imposed by CINCPAC, a state of affairs that was aggravated by the Japan problem (see map 33). Nuclear weapons could not be based in Japan, at least not assembled weapons, and with the pending Security Treaty, possibly not even weapons components.[11] A complicated debate involving air base crowding in Japan, the requirement to be seen to prop up South Korea's president Syngman Rhee, and intermural interservice issues forced Kuter to deploy nuclear-capable F-100Ds to the execrable K-55 air base in South Korea, where those forces promptly had a nuclear accident with an Mk-7 weapon and an F-100D.[12] There was pressure to send an entire wing to the K-55 base, but Kuter was able to reduce it to a "token force" and had B-57s based in Japan "in evidence by frequently overflying Seoul."[13]

Similarly, Kuter was pressured to overextend his forces to Taiwan. Stump had pledged Matador cruise missiles to Taiwan. Kuter wanted them instead in Chitose, Japan, presumably so they could cover the Vladivostok air base complexes. The CINCPAC war plan then demanded twenty Matadors on Taiwan. Therefore an initial token force was arranged.[14] Kuter was, however, supportive of Matadors in South Korea: "I intend to plan for an eventual deployment of a Matador unit to Korea as soon as possible. If necessary, I can deploy a token force earlier, as we have done in Taiwan."[15]

But the nuclear agreement with South Korea was not yet signed: "We are currently considering reprogramming the 588th Tactical Missile Group (or a portion thereof) currently scheduled for Chitose, Japan, to Korea. The decision to introduce nuclear weapons into Korea has not yet been made. . . . An increased rotation of PACAF forces into Korea, in addition to the proposed MATADOR deployment may prove an acceptable commitment of USAF forces in Korea."[16] Some of Tommy White's advisors were enthusiastic about this idea, believing, "The Matador in Korea could be a potential Korean Strategic Retaliatory Strike Force. Should Korea be threatened by CHICOM, the U.S. could turn over to ROK [Republic of Korea] the Matadors with nuclear weapons and thus enable ROK to announce that an attack on ROK would result in ROK attack upon industrial centers of China with nuclear weapons."[17]

The Military Assistance Advisory Group Taiwan got carried away and "proposed that an atomic delivery capability be provided to [Chinese Nationalist] F-86F aircraft." Kuter's staff suggested that F-84Gs be substituted. Even Stump recoiled from this proposed project, asserting that "the probability that once the [Nationalist Chinese air force] has LABS, it [would] be only a step to the time when they would want to put it to use."[18] Kuter was just as enthusiastic as Stump and saw such a move as a drain on scarce nuclear logistics capabilities.

As part of an attempt to figure its way out of the Far East muddle, U.S. Air Force wargaming in early 1958 overseen by LeMay examined six different local war campaigns from three vantage points: conventional war only, nuclear weapons use by the United States, and nuclear weapons use by both sides. Notably, "the possible extension of local wars following an atomic exchange by the United States and China was not considered." The results were a series of disconnected points that reinforced the existing view that, given the state of the force structure in the region, nuclear weapons had to be used in almost all scenarios: "If there are locals wars and China is involved with modern weapons, U.S. will have to use atomic weapons." Some scenarios "demand[ed] immediate response—others [did] not." Taiwan was one. Other wars would be prolonged "even with the use of atomic weapons." There was another conclusion: "Atomic weapons should be used early in the campaign. The commitment of atomic weapons in a bi-lateral atomic war should be made as early as possible. A 'wait-and-see' policy would be a distinct disadvantage." For Korea, presumably, "early deep atomic interdiction [was] invaluable . . . due to long lines of communication involved in this area and the desire to prevent build-up of forward supplies by enemy ground forces." Existing forces were vulnerably positioned: "A joint sanctuary would prove to the advantage of the United States. Lacking such understanding, the destruction of our Far East air base structure by the [Chinese Communist Air Force] would require us to mount B-52 strikes from the distant bases in Alaska, Hawaii, and the Middle East."[19] This exercise merely reinforced general USAF views on regional nuclear weapons use and proved less than useful in sorting out what should be done about the situation.

Application of American nuclear forces in the Far East was further complicated by the insertion of Alternative Undertaking targeting guidance by the JCS, just as it was cause for concern at SAC and by SACEUR. Kuter cogently summed up the problem for White in December 1958, which in turn highlighted the nature and extent of practical targeting problems in PACAF's peculiar circumstances. Kuter was especially concerned that there be "assurance that our initial atomic operations are directed against those targets which insure the greatest payoff" and that there be "the greatest assurance of successful attack against those targets." His interpretation of JCS guidance: "primary undertakings in which our efforts are devoted to essentially military targets" and "alternative undertakings, in which our efforts are devoted first to population and concurrently, with remaining available means, to the neutralization of the enemy's atomic delivery capabilities." When CINCPAC applied these concepts to targeting, the result was "two complete separate target lists for PACAF—one for our quick strike force (alternative undertakings) and one for the GEOP [General Emergency Operations Plan] operations (primary undertakings)." Primary Undertakings assumed strategic warning; Alternative Undertakings did not.[20]

The problem for Kuter and PACAF was this: "This duality of targeting means that targets high on the priority list for alternative undertakings may be in a low priority, or not even appear, on the target list for primary undertakings and vice-versa." When the same target did appear on both lists, "the target elements selected for destruction, DGZ, and weapon assignment need not necessarily be the same." Most important for Kuter, because of the mere existence of Communist China:

> Population as such does not appear to be a profitable target system in this area, with 650,000,000 people in China and with the Soviet Far East offering the other extreme of a very low population density representing only a small fraction of the population of the Soviet Union. Nevertheless, there are a few population centers of extreme importance. From these centers stems the immediate direction of the Communist war effort as well as the means for long-term political, industrial and economic control of the resources of the Communist Far East; they contain a very high proportion of the total managerial and skilled labor forces; and they are essential communications links for both military and political operations. It appears to me that we *must* insure the destruction of these centers under any condition.
>
> There are also in the Communist Far East a number of offensive bases which *must* be destroyed if we are to survive and continue to fight. I believe it essential that our guidance require the destruction of these targets as a first effort, again regardless of the circumstances. A single target list, applicable whether our full forces or only the quick strike force is available, would insure that our initial effort includes all of these essential targets of both categories.[21]

For crews, there were practical problems:

> Present duality of targeting requires that quick strike crews revert to their GEOP targets, if not launched against quick strike targets. This

means that at a time when we are momentarily expecting a directive to attack, we are switching our ready crews from what were the highest priority targets, to other targets requiring different weapons. This introduces at best an element of confusion at the most critical time, and may result at any given moment in some at least of the higher priority GEOP targets being left uncovered. Clearly, our chances of hitting the highest priority targets will be improved if these targets remain assigned to the quick strike force even after we have received the initial warning, with additional strike aircraft, as generated, taking on additional but lower priority targets.[22]

The solution, for Kuter, was to have a single target list for all commands to work from: "We have made some progress in bringing CINCPAC guidance more into line with our needs and concepts."[23] But for Kuter the most basic question of how to provide enough target coverage to ensure the destruction of the Chinese Communist population in order to deter their leadership remained unanswered by the JCS. And as LeMay determined earlier in the 1950s, such alternative undertaking was really not a viable strategy, especially when it came to Communist China.

There were also issues associated with releasing nuclear weapons. There were the practical problems of having nuclear-equipped aircraft in forward areas, like K-55: "Assuming though that our quick-strike aircraft did manage to take off, with only the tactical warning provided by radar, the chances are slim that a Presidential decision for expenditure of their weapons could reach the pilots before they aborted for fuel. In the final analysis, when we have nine squadrons of supersonic fighters capable of megaton deliveries against high priority targets, we will be remiss in shooting at less than 100% effectiveness. A greater round the clock all weather bombing capability, coupled with decentralized expenditure authority for high yield weapons, are absolute 'musts.'"[24]

So he pushed White to devolve release authority to him for USAF units. White responded in the same vague way he responded to Power on similar issues: "I must also advise you that except for certain special conditions de-centralization of expenditure authority for nuclear weapons is not anticipated in the foreseeable future. However, I am positive you will not permit the failure to obtain these two 'musts' to stand in the way of maximizing the effectiveness of your combat units within the limitations of the equipment of U.S. policy."[25]

How exactly Kuter interpreted this is unclear.

In 1960, however, Pacific Command clarified its missions and tasks.[26] The command's stated mission was to "conduct a strategic defense by exploiting offensive capabilities in order to defend the Western Hemisphere" and "protect resources, areas, bases and locations." There were ten tasks, in order of priority. Task number one was to "defend the United States against attack through the Pacific, by maintaining a forward strategy on the periphery of the Sino-Soviet Bloc." This was handled in late 1960 by the SIOP, and its activation was dependent upon "military forces of the U.S. and USSR" being "overtly engaged." In earlier iterations this contingency was likely handled by CINCPAC's General Emergency Operations Plan, or GEOP.[27] There was also a plan for the defense of Taiwan and the Penghu Islands, one for defending the Philippines, and another for the defense of Korea. A separate plan existed to blockade the Chinese coast, and another for a strategic mine-laying campaign in the entire region. There were several plans for noncombatant evacuation operations and to support internal uprisings in Communist countries, should they occur. The Cold War Plan involved supporting and promoting "U.S. interests and deter Communist aggression." Another was the Defense of Mainland Southeast Asia, to "counter Communist aggression or insurgency."[28]

SAC's Basic War Plan at this time did not involve North Korea, nor did it involve Communist China; these were separate plans to be covered by separate forces under the CINCPAC GEOP, while at the same time some GEOP targets were in the Soviet Union.[29] Kuter at PACAF had to cover all of these contingencies and at the same time coordinate with SAC. SAC was eventually assigned contingency strike plans in the Pacific area that were not necessarily part of the BWP either. SAC already had forces deployed to the region, in this case fifteen B-47s stationed on Guam at Andersen AFB, of which ten were on continuous alert, some of which were associated with the BWP.

THE ACME OF SKILL

Fifteen B-52s from two SAC strategic wings were then assigned by the JCS to "maintain a capability to support CINCPAC contingency operations with [U.S.]-launched strikes."[30] Power, Kuter, and Stump met to coordinate SAC operations with CINCPAC; this served as the basis for Kuter-Felt coordination when Felt took over.[31]

Knowing the Enemy: Intelligence in the Far East

The available intelligence on the force dispositions of all three potential antagonists was, in retrospect, very good and built on data that went all the way back to World War II. As before, the data were compartmentalized, but as the 1950s drew to a close there was significantly more cooperation among those conducting the collection. Working through the geographical areas, the Chukotska Peninsula and the Northern Siberian coast had received attention from SENSINT flights earlier in the 1950s. This coverage was upgraded in late 1959 with the deployment of three USAF U-2s to Eielson AFB in Alaska. The Congo Maiden detachment's purpose was to "[find] soft spots in Siberia's air defense network" as this " was a vital aspect of SAC planning." Operating just outside of three nautical miles of the Soviet coasts, the Congo Maiden flights collected ELINT as well as photographs. The operations were also extended to the Kamchatka Peninsula.[32] The sextet of Black Knight RB-57Ds that overflew Vladivostok in 1956 remained active for some time, but their usefulness waned in the wake of U-2 deployments.[33]

CIA U-2s overflew Communist China starting in 1958. Operating from Naha Air Base on Okinawa, at least three missions were conducted in January, April, and September 1958. The first went as far as Beijing; the tracks of the other two missions do not appear to be available.[34] That said, there were Talent reports generated for numerous installations throughout Communist China and, notably, around Khabarovsk and Komsomolsk-on-Amur in the Soviet Union.[35] These can be attributed to a U-2 overflight of those cities on 1 March 1958.[36]

The special relationship between the United States and the Chinese Nationalists, who had by this point consolidated on the island of Formosa, led to extensive intelligence collection activities directed against Communist China. A trio of ex-USAF B-17s and trio of B-26s flown by Nationalist Chinese pilots ramped up operations in 1956. (Several C-46 "Old Bull" COMINT aircraft were added later.) Both aircraft types delivered propaganda leaflets and collected ELINT on risky deep-penetration operations, some of which were staged from the K-8 air base in South Korea (Kusan). The sheer number of missions is illustrative of the breadth and depth of the activities: in 1956 there were twenty-nine B-17 and twenty-three B-26 missions; in 1957 there were sixty-one and forty-five, respectively. A CHINAT B-17 reached Beijing on one operation. Operational losses, including two of the B-17s, led to Project Cherry, the USAF modification of five surplus U.S. Navy P2V-7 for the CIA to be flown by Chinese pilots; these aircraft took their place in the inky night blackness over Red China. The take suggested that Communist Chinese radar coverage was "fair to good" but that they had a "shortage of adequate [Ground Controlled Intercept] radar." Attempts to intercept the penetrating aircraft suggested that the Communist Chinese had "inadequate experience in night and all-weather flying." As the Soviets provided more technology to the Mao regime, the ELINT flights determined that their "radar was still having difficulty in detecting aircraft at low altitude." Significantly for SAC planners, "the Communist Chinese had dramatic coordination issues, particularly in fusing early warning radar, height-finding radar, GCI communications, and interceptor direction."[37]

The full extent of the North Korean overflight program remains obscure. There was a specially equipped RB-57A from either the 6021st Tactical Reconnaissance Squadron or its sister unit, the 6091st, both of which operated from Yokota Air Base in Japan. This aircraft was code-named Switch Blade and was responsible for operations over both China and North Korea.[38] There is no indication that USAF or CIA U-2s were used over North Korea at this time, and the extent of South Korean air operations over the North also remains obscure. There was, however, extensive and detailed HUMINT and defector information available on the North Korean Air Force, including air order of battle, radar operation, and tactical doctrine.[39] The U.S. Navy continued to fly P4M-1Q Mercators along all of the Commu-

THE ACME OF SKILL

nist coasts to collect ELINT; one of these was attacked by a pair of MIGs from North Korea in 1959.[40]

Ground stations feeding the NSA and GCHQ proliferated in the region. One of the most important became Soya Point on the northernmost coast of Hokkaido. This station was able to collect extensive data on Soviet systems like Scan Odd and Scan Fix airborne intercept radars; the Bee Hind warning radar on Soviet bombers; Mushroom, the Soviet bomber navigation system; and the Fire Can and Sun Vision coastal defense radars.[41]

In overall numbers, American and allied forces confronted 1,537 observed MIG fighters and 162 observed IL-28 bomber aircraft operating from eighty-one bases in Communist China.[42] Soviet TU-4 bombers in regimental strength had also been transferred to the People's Liberation Army Air Force, providing Communist China with a long-range bombing capability.[43] There were an estimated 415 to 469 MIG fighters and 49 IL-28s operating from eleven bases in North Korea.[44] As for the Soviets, there were nine PVO MIG regiments in Primorsky and Khabarovsk Krais, and four more on Kamchatka-Chukota and associated islands, for approximately 468 MIG-type aircraft.[45] In terms of regional strike forces, the Soviets retained around eight regiments of TU-16 aircraft on four bases, or 288 aircraft.[46]

Knowing Yourself: Order of Battle in the Far East

There was a plethora of American nuclear forces assigned to targets in the Far East. PACAF retained the 8th Fighter Wing stationed at Itazuki Air Base in Japan, equipped with F-100Ds and "personnel . . . trained in the employment of atomic weapons."[47] Also stationed in Japan was the 3rd Bomber Wing, equipped with B-57 twin-engine light bombers located at Johnson Air Base (later Iruma Air Base). The 18th Tactical Fighter Wing, also with F-100s, operated out of Kadena Air Base in Okinawa.[48] Prior to this, FEAF nuclear-capable units were located at Itazuki and Komaki Air Bases; Mk-7 weapons for their F-84Gs without their cores were based there, with the cores to be flown in from Kadena once they were alerted. With the arrival of new aircraft and with the deliberations over the U.S.-Japan Security Treaty after 1957, the logistics arrangements changed. The 7th

Tactical Depot Squadron at Kadena managed assembled Mk-7s for the 18th Tactical Fighter Wing, but "shapes" without cores remained at some bases on mainland Japan, including Misawa Air Base. Alert forces could not operate from Japan with fully assembled weapons, however, so F-100s and B-57s rotating in from Japan and from Okinawa stood alert in South Korea at Osan Air Base, Kusan Air Base, and on at least one occasion at Taegu Air Base. The weapons were handled by Detachment 1, 7th Air Depot Squadron. Detachment 1 was in fact almost as large as its parent unit: 307 personnel for the 7th Air Depot Squadron, and 203 for Detachment 1.[49]

Iwakuni Air Base, converted to a Marine Corps Air Station in 1958, had nuclear weapons stored on a U.S. Navy landing ship tank, the USS *San Joaquin County*. Stationed just off the Japanese coast, this ship was disguised as an electronic repair depot ship.[50] Nuclear weapons were also stored aboard other U.S. Navy ships that were home-ported at Okinawa but stationed off other American bases in Japan. One of these was the seaplane tender USS *Salisbury Sound*, the flagship of the Taiwan Patrol Force.[51] For the most part, other U.S. Navy "Service Force ammunition ships had been modified to transport bombs but not nuclear capsules and their crews were not trained to assemble nuclear weapons."[52] The seaplane tender USS *Curtiss*, used as the AEC support vessel in the various Pacific Proving Ground test series, also had nuclear weapons storage and assembly capacity.[53]

Due to the vulnerability of PACAF's air bases relative to the threat, a storage facility and a portion of Detachment 1 were located in depth on what was referred to in documents as "the Volcano Islands," that is, Iwo Jima. A site north of Central Field was identified. Though authorized in either 1956 or 1957, complete weapons were apparently not stored prior to 1960.[54]

PACAF also controlled Matador cruise missile units. The first of these, the 310th Tactical Missile Squadron, deployed to South Korea in July 1958 and included "both the missiles and corresponding nuclear capsules."[55] It consisted of three flights of twenty missiles each, stationed at Osan, Kimpo, and Chichon-Ni, with Guidance and Control detachments along the DMZ and on the embattled island of Paengnyung Do off the North Korean west coast. At the same time, the 868th Tactical Missile Squadron deployed to Tainan Air Station in Taiwan, acquiring its first Quick Strike commitment in January 1959. The 868th maintained one missile at 15 minutes' readiness, the next one available within 40 minutes of an alert.[56] Plans to station a Matador squadron at Chitose in Japan were shelved due to the 1958 security agreement with Japan.

SAC forces related to the region came from three sources. The first was the Reflex sextet of B-47s at Eielson AFB in Alaska supported by the 14th Aviation Depot Squadron with Mk-36 mod 1, Mk-15/39, and Mk-6 weapons.[57] The second was the rotational B-47 force at Andersen AFB on Guam from the 96th Bomb Wing (Medium) based at Dyess AFB.[58] This unit increased its Air Mail alert force from fifteen to seventeen aircraft, of which twelve were on continuous alert. They were supplied by the 3rd Aviation Depot Squadron that managed Mk-36, Mk-39, and Mk-6 bombs for Air Mail and any augmentee units. SAC also maintained the 12th Aviation Depot Squadron at Kadena Air Base on Okinawa; it contained Mk-6 and Mk-39 weapons, presumably for restrike operations.[59] The airfields on Tinian were maintained to some extent into the 1950s and likely served as an alternate or fallback position in the western Pacific.

In addition to the Air Mail and Reflex commitments to the region, SAC was instructed by the JCS to "maintain a capability to support CINCPAC contingency operations" using units based in the United States.[60] Units assigned to these tasks included 95th Bomb Wing (Heavy) from Biggs AFB, Texas, with eight of its B-52Bs, and the 4134th Strategic Wing at Mather AFB, California, with fifteen B-52Fs. The Biggs-based unit was assigned a Glass Brick tasking, that is, the forward deployment of eight B-52s and tankers when a specified alert condition was achieved. The 4134th B-52s were not supported with KC-135 tankers and thus would have conducted un-refueled strikes from California and then recovered at a forward base, reloaded, and struck again.[61] Of note, aircraft from the 93rd Bomb Wing later assigned to Glass Brick carried Mk-6 mod 6 and Mk-15 mod 2 weapons for reduced fallout purposes.[62]

For the most part, however, the Pacific was the realm of the U.S. Navy, and the primary nuclear delivery mechanism was the aircraft carrier. Between 1957 and 1960 the U.S. Navy retained no fewer than six carriers in the region. Generally four of these were forward-deployed, with two in transit for rotation. In 1958 and 1959, however, these numbers increased to eight, but dropped back to six in 1960. Nine of these carriers were upgraded *Essex*-class ships, but two were the larger USS *Midway* and larger and newer USS *Ranger*.[63]

Each aircraft carrier's delivery capability varied depending on the year and the types of available aircraft. Notably, the carrier load-outs differed from carriers deployed to the Mediterranean. By 1958 carriers on Pacific cruises carried short-range attack jets like the FJ-4B Fury and the A-4 Skyhawk, and the long-range twin jet A3D Skywarrior. The Furies and the Skyhawks replaced several aircraft types, while the twin-propeller AJ-2 Savage was replaced by the A3D. The most prevalent system, however, was the long-range propeller-driven AD Skyraider series, which served into the 1960s.[64]

Under the "neither confirm nor deny" policies related to Japan and for legitimate operational security purposes, the number of nuclear-capable units and the presence of nuclear weapons on the ships were kept obscure. The low-profile "W" Division personnel maintained the weapons aboard ship. That said, U.S. Navy squadrons openly stated the capability, and all Fury, Skyhawk, Skyraider, and Skywarrior units in the Pacific Fleet were trained and equipped for nuclear weapons delivery.[65] For example, for the four A3DS embarked on USS *Ticonderoga*, "the mission of the detachment [was] to provide carrier based, long range, high speed nuclear weapon delivery capability to the Seventh Fleet."[66] VA-192, embarked on the USS *Bon Homme Richard* and whose patch featured a dragon entwined with a mushroom cloud, was "equipped with the FJ-4B Fury fighter-bomber": "The squadron is a part of America's first line defense in the Western Pacific. The pilots fly long hours to maintain their capability for delivering an atomic punch. If Communist aggression should bring war to the Far East, among the first to deal destruction to the Enemy would be . . . Golden Dragons."[67] AD Skyraiders of VA-215 on the USS *Lexington* in 1960 had as their mission "to conduct both conventional and nuclear offensive attack operations with emphasis on specially assigned tasks": "a. Conduct strikes against enemy installations b. destroy enemy naval units and shipping at sea, c. Provide support for amphibious or land operations. d. Maintain capability to operations from aircraft carriers during darkness and low visibility."[68] For VA 55 on the USS *Hancock* "special weapons delivery [was] the squadron's primary mission. . . . Several special types of weapons delivery [were] practiced, including the famous 'idiot loop,' which starts at 50 feet of altitude."[69] One A-4 unit sported a cartoon with a huge bomb labeled "Mushroom Seeds."[70] Marine Attack Squadron 214, the first U.S. Marine Corps squadron certified for nuclear weapons delivery, embarked on the USS *Hancock* in 1957 with its F-2H2B Banshees and later was deployed to Iwakuni Marine Corps Air Station, Japan.[71]

The U.S. Navy's delivery capability was directly related to how many weapons were on each ship and how many weapons could be moved to forward areas in an emergency. Exact numbers are not available, but as of 1960 the *Essex*-class USS *Ticonderoga* had its "weapons inventory . . . increased to 62 weapons."[72] The *Midway*-class carriers could carry two hundred nuclear weapons.[73] Prior to a six-month Pacific deployment, ships home-ported at Bremerton, Washington, sailed for California, where nuclear weapons were loaded from Naval Air Station Alameda and/or Naval Supply Center Oakland after having been moved by rail from Naval Ammunition Depot at Hawthorne, Nevada. Other loading points were Naval Weapons Station Seal Beach, California, and Naval Air Station North Island, presumably for the San Diego–based ships.[74] In the forward areas, there was Naval Air Station Barber's Point and Naval Ammunition Depot Waikele Beach on Oahu, and Naval Air Station Agana and Naval Magazine on Guam. Naval Air Station Cubi Point and the Naval Magazine Subic Bay hosted units and weapons. For example, during the 1958 crisis, excess A3DS and ADS, some from the USS *Ticonderoga*, were shore-based at Cubi Point. Naval Air Facility Naha on Okinawa also retained a nuclear weapons maintenance unit.[75]

Some carriers were also equipped with Regulus cruise missiles armed with the W27 warhead yielding close to 2 megatons. During 1957 USS *Lexington* embarked Guided Missile Group 1, detachment G: "Working in close cooperation with the missile cruisers and submarines of the Seventh Fleet, the GMGRU team has demonstrated its ability to convey an atomic payload to a target at near sonic speed, with pin point accuracy. Notable among the successful operations that have been conducted was the 270 mile strike of a REGULUS fired from the cruiser HELENA. Taking over guidance 180 miles out, the FJ-6 Fury piloted by Lt. R. P. Blount shepherded the bird to a point directly over the target island, where the charge was fired by remote control."[76]

Detachment C was embarked on the USS *Shangri La* in 1958; it worked with the submarine USS *Tunny* and FJ-6 Fury guidance and control aircraft to deliver simulated nuclear strikes using Regulus.[77]

The U.S. Navy deployed conventionally propelled guided missile-launching submarines on deterrent patrols starting in 1958. These vessels carried the Regulus I cruise missile, with a range of five hundred nautical miles, carrying a W27 warhead that yielded close to 2 megatons. There were four submarines of two types: USS *Tunny* and USS *Barbero* each carried two missiles, while the USS *Grayback* and USS *Growler* each carried four. In 1958 and 1959 the USS *Tunny* was employed, with her two missiles, but rotations between the four submarines ensured that six missiles were available for launch in the event of war. The submarines loaded their missiles at the West Loch nuclear storage facility on Oahu. After refueling at Adak, Alaska, the submarines proceeded to their patrol areas, which were off the Arctic coast of the Soviet Union or, later, the North Pacific.[78] After the weapons had been launched, the submarines would proceed to a nuclear weapons storage facility on the island of Chichi Jima, reload with prepositioned Regulus missiles and W27 warheads, and then were to be assigned further targets. Regulus missiles and warheads were also stored on Guam.[79]

Attack by Fire: The Far East and the BWP

If the SAC Basic War Plan had been activated in either its Strategic or Tactical Warning modes, the immediate Quick Strike action would have been to launch the Reflex B-47s stationed at Eielson AFB in Alaska. The first targets to go would have been the airfield at Lavrentiya, the closest Soviet airfield to North America, followed by the

THE ACME OF SKILL

destruction of the PVO airfield at Provodeniya. The next pair of Reflex force targets included the "bounce" bomber airfield at Mys Shmidta on the Arctic coast and the target complex at Ugolnyy, near Anadyr. Ugolnyy included a "bounce" airfield, a PVO air defense control center, and a heavy radar site. There was a large underground nuclear storage facility under construction nearby which was likely detected during Project Home Run in 1956.[80] In any event, like other Soviet nuclear storage facilities, it was some fifteen kilometers away from the airfield. A potential Eielson Reflex tasking was the staging airfield at Tiksi, also on the Arctic coast. Though it was some distance away, a risky tanker-supported B-47 strike was possible. Uel'kal was seen to host IL-28s; thus its destruction was likely. Similarly IL-28s were detected operating from Wrangel Island as early as 1954. The relatively short duration of the Eielson Reflex missions suggests that they would have returned to base, rearmed, and conducted further strikes.[81] Initially Mk-36 weapons were loaded on the Reflex B-47s, but this was changed to the lower-yield Mk-39 mod 2 in mid-1959, that is, the low-level release version of the Mk-39 weapon. The Mk-36s were kept at Eielson for follow-on strikes, presumably to reduce fallout on Alaska.[82]

The importance of Soviet Arctic airfields to American targeteers is highlighted by the allocation of a U.S. Navy Regulus-carrying submarine to operate near the Arctic Circle. During the Lebanon Crisis in 1958, the USS *Tunny* sailed with its two missiles to take up patrol positions off of what was likely the Mys Shmidta airfield.[83] Given the five-hundred-mile range of the missile, the *Tunny* could have taken out Ugolnyy from this launching position as well. The application of U.S. Air Force and U.S. Navy cross-targeting strongly suggests their targets' importance. Incapacitation of Eielson's Reflex forces would not have stopped the destruction of Ugolnyy and Mys Shmidta. Destruction of the airfields with megaton-yield weapons, even if Soviet bombers were not present, would have completely denied their use against North America and opened the door for SAC to pour through the gap.

After the Reflex forces and submarine-launched missiles opened the gates, the Irkutsk strikes would have followed. An important col-

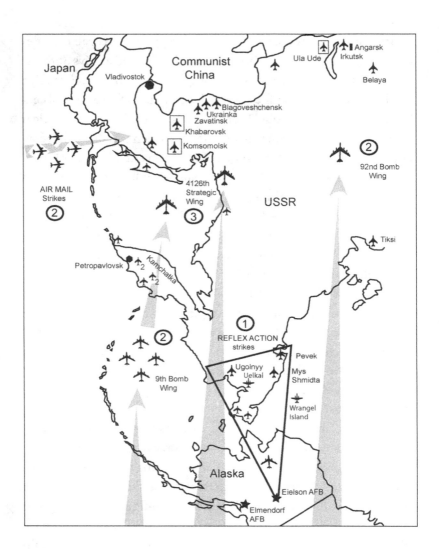

Map 34. By 1959 SAC's Basic War Plan for the Far East involved the destruction of air bases closest to Alaska with Reflex Action forces stationed at Eielson AFB (1). The destruction of the air defense system on Kamchatka and Sakhalin and deep strikes against bomber bases on the Amur were next (2), followed by strikes against the Mya-4 Bison and other bases around Ukrainka (3).
Courtesy of the author.

lection of targets lay deep in the Soviet interior, reachable only by B-52s. There was the Angarsk nuclear weapons production facility, geographically situated between the TU-16 bomber base at Belaya and Airframe Plant No. 39, with its large runway. Another large airfield lay southeast of the city. Across Lake Baikal was Ulan-Ude, with Airframe Plant No. 99 and its runway. Another likely target was the isolated large airfield west of Borzya. The Fairchild AFB-based 92nd Bombardment Wing was best positioned geographically to handle these targets, with a rather dangerous recovery to Okinawa (or Adak). Nine B-52s from this unit were on a special alert code-named Fireball.[84]

Simultaneously, the destruction of Soviet facilities on the Kamchatka Peninsula would have been underway. The organization tasked with these strikes was the 9th Bombardment Wing at Mountain Home AFB in Idaho. After tanking up from KC-97s forward-based at RCAF Station Namao and then from the tanker task force at Eielson, the B-47s from this formation were in a position to destroy the 6th Kurilskaya Air Defence Division. This included PVO control centers and airfields at Kruterberegovo, Yelizovo, and Vasilev Bay, plus the airfields at Lenino, Kozyrevsk, and Klyuchi and ten radar sites. (Kozyrevsk was hazily identified as a bomber base by the CIA in 1957 but was in fact an old PVO dispersal field.) The second line of PVO defenses protecting the approaches to the Soviet Far East Vladivostok bastion from the north were located on Sakhalin Island, which retained seven radar sites and two PVO airfields, Sokol and Smirnykh.[85]

These B-47 strikes opened up a path to the crucial Soviet long-range air force bases on the Amur River. B-52s from the 4126th Strategic Wing at Beale AFB, again geographically proximate to the targets, would have gone in to destroy the large Mya-4 Bison and TU-16 Badger base at Ukrainka and the TU-16 base at Zavatinsk, after penetrating the air defense system at low level. The identified nuclear storage site four miles northeast of Ukrainka would have been struck separately from the main base if a 3.8-megaton Mk-39 were not deemed enough to destroy it. The older TU-4 base west of Blagoveshchensk and the PVO airfield east of Belogorsk were other likely targets to ensure they could not be used for other purposes. Again, even if the alert Mya-4s flew the coop, destruction of their support facilities to prevent restrike or to prevent aircraft under maintenance from being brought online dictated destruction of the facilities with ground-burst multimegaton-yield weapons.[86] The possibility that Air Mail B-47s from Guam were also targeted against these airfields cannot be ruled out; they were closer and could have reached these bases first, with recovery to northern Japan. Ukrainka's importance suggests that it was likely targeted by both forces, with a B-47 strike arriving first, followed by a B-52 strike later.

There were other numerous important facilities in and around Komsomolsk-on-Amur and Khabarovsk. It is unclear whether they would have been targeted by California-based B-52s from the 4126th Strategic Wing at Beale, by the Guam-based Air Mail B-47s, or both. On the coast opposite Sakhalin Island near Mongokhto was a Naval Aviation TU-16 base with a protective PVO base at Vanino; again, any TU-16 base could be used by long-range aviation for bounce strikes. Komsomolsk-on-Amur was home to Airframe Plants 126 and 130, with associated airfields, plus a large seaplane base. To the east was the Komsomolsk-on-Amur 31 nuclear storage depot, not yet discovered by the intelligence apparatus. SAC was also interested in the Komsomolsk seaplane base. Deeper in was Khabarovsk, containing a very large airfield at Aircraft Plant No. 83 that served as the primary repair facility and depot for the entire Soviet Far East. Two PVO airfields protected the city. The Khabarovsk-47 nuclear storage depot was eventually constructed several miles southwest of the city, but it is unclear whether SAC knew of its existence at this time. Of note, the destruction of the urban-based targets would have collaterally destroyed key railroad nodes linking the Soviet Far East with the rest of the Soviet Union.[87] Similarly the destruction of the refineries at Khabarovsk and Komsomolsk-on-Amur would have completely crippled Soviet petroleum production in the Far East.[88]

CINCPAC's GEOP targeting differed from SAC's BWP targeting elsewhere. Backtracking slightly, the extensive Soviet Pacific Fleet facilities in and around Petropavlovsk would have been handled by CINCPAC's GEOP, though one should not rule out the possibility

THE ACME OF SKILL

of a SAC follow-on attack later in the BWP program, probably from 9th Bombardment Wing at Mountain Home AFB. The U.S. Navy retained an aircraft carrier in the northern Pacific in part to handle Petropavlovsk target coverage. There were multiple targets whose destruction would have dramatically canceled the Soviet navy's capabilities in the Pacific. There was Petropavlovsk Naval Base Tarya Bay, the primary Soviet submarine base ten kilometers across the bay from Petropavlovsk-Kamchatskiy city itself; it included ballistic missile–launching submarines in its inventory. Adjacent to it was a large oil tank farm. To the east lay a large supply and ammunition depot and to the southeast a seaplane base. Across another bay was Petropavlovsk Naval Base Seldevaya Bay, a major repair facility. To its north was a suspected missile-loading area, eventually designated the Viliuchinsk nuclear storage site.[89] SAC's follow-on targeting involved the detonation of three weapons on or under the bodies of water between the facilities.[90]

There were extensive naval facilities in and around Komsomolsk-on-Amur and Khabarovsk that would not necessarily have been prioritized by SAC targeteers. The submarine construction facilities at Shipyard Amur 199 in Komsomolsk and the naval repair facilities at both locations are two examples. These were likely handled by carrier-based strike aircraft from the northern Pacific–based carrier. The Naval Aviation base near Mongokhto with its TU-16s was probably cross-targeted by U.S. Navy carrier-based aircraft and SAC. However, there were at least ten naval facilities grouped around Sovetska Gavan, including a submarine base, Shipyard 263, storage depots, and two major petroleum storage facilities. These were likely targets for an aircraft carrier operating in the northern Pacific and probably not initial SAC targets.[91]

Interestingly, the Mya-4 bomber base at Ukrainka was a Talent target for the U.S. Navy, indicating it was targeted for destruction, perhaps using A3D Skywarriors for this long-range mission.[92] The variety of carrier-based aircraft with differing ranges and weapons loads permitted fairly flexible targeting. Smaller aircraft like the FJ-4B and the A-4 could "buddy refuel" using a partner aircraft of the same type. A3Ds could act as pathfinders and refuelers due to their superior navigation capabilities. The movement of the aircraft carrier itself toward a target after launch could extend the range of strike aircraft.[93]

Moving south we come to the complexities surrounding the finger-shaped Vladivostok area. In the late 1950s forty-seven radar stations of every conceivable type in Soviet service at the time were located on the perimeter of Soviet territory here; ten of those were opposite Communist China, stretching all the way up to Khabarovsk. The ones around Vladivostok were controlled by the 23rd Air Defence Corps, with its headquarters at the 119th Communications Center in Vladivostok itself. The 23rd Air Defence Corps controlled four fighter-aviation regiments, one with Yak-35M, another with MiG-17PF, and two MiG-17 interceptor regiments situated on four bases, two near Vladivostok and the coast, and two in depth.[94] Sector headquarters were likely situated at those airfields.

The CINCPAC GEOP governed the assault on Primorsky Krai. Unlike the SAC Basic War Plan, the CINCPAC plan was fragile specifically because of the Pacific Air Forces' maldeployment. If the Tactical Warning variant was in play, it is possible that the forces assigned to the initial phases of the missions would have been destroyed on the ground at K-55/Osan and K-8/Kunsan air bases in South Korea by the Soviet TU-16 force, as would have the other air units based in Japan. The F-100s on alert might have flushed, but the fragile command-and-control process would likely have failed and the aircraft that did get off the ground would not have received the orders to go in before they burned off the fuel needed to get to their targets. Indeed, depending on the international situation, the cores for the U.S. Air Force weapons stored in Japan might not have arrived in time.[95] In that event CINCPAC's aircraft carriers and the low-profile U.S. Marine Corps units at Iwakuni might have had to conduct the initial assault.

If the Strategic Warning variant was in play and the decision was made to go in, some of the alert F-100s would have focused on the dense Soviet air defense system. Aircraft would have come in low from the Sea of Japan to avoid the radar system as well as a handful of radar picket ships, and the first target to go would have been the air defense communications center in Vladivostok, followed by several radar sites west of the city extending to North Korea. The Soviet ground-controlled intercept site located at Chongjin in North Korea would likely have been bypassed if North Korea had not moved against South Korea. Then the three PVO air bases at Uglovoye, Shtykovo, and Novorossiya would have been struck. The colocated direction centers at these stations would have been destroyed or disrupted by those attacks. A single F-100 operating at extreme range would have been required to destroy the PVO air base at Dolina.

These strikes would have opened up a gap to be exploited by some of the alert B-57 light bombers stationed at K-8/Kunsan. Their targets would have included the TU-16 bases at Ussuriysk, Khorol, and Spassk-Dalniy to preempt conventional or nuclear bomber operations against Japan and South Korea and to prevent further use of the airfields and facilities by bombers based in the interior or any stray survivors from the SAC strikes. PVO fighters colocated at Ussuriysk would have been collaterally destroyed. The destruction of the PVO airfield west of Stepnoye would have been included to ensure that any interceptor direction was disrupted. If the staged B-57s or F-100s at Misawa received the cores for their weapons in time, these forces could have been used to open up gaps in the PVO systems in the Kuriles, Sakhalin, or the coastal radars in Primorsky Krai so that B-47s from Guam or B-52s from the United States could hit targets in Khabarovsk or the Ukrainka-Zavatinsk bomber base complexes.

The U.S. Navy aircraft carrier or carriers operating in the Sea of Japan had two options. They could restrike the PVO system around Vladivostok in case the F-100s were unable to carry out their tasks first, and then go after targets of naval significance, or assume the PVO system was down and carry out their primary undertakings. The former was the probable course of action. There were at least twelve target complexes spread out in the Vladivostok area, each requiring different targeting tactics because of the terrain. Assuming the air defense system was disrupted, any naval commander's first concern would be to destroy any forces capable of striking the carrier itself. There were two Naval Aviation TU-16 bases, Artem and Romonovka;

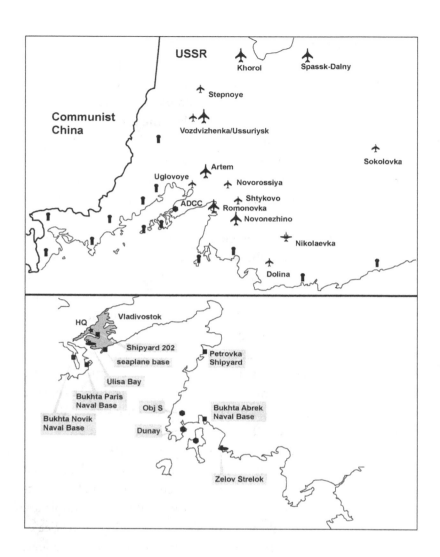

Map 35. EWP and GEOP targets, Vladivostok, Soviet Far East, 1959.
Courtesy of the author.

another airfield at Novonezhino hosting a variety of Naval Aviation units; and an IL-28 base at Nikolaevka. These would be destroyed as quickly as possible with the fastest naval aircraft available, the FJ-4B Fury and A-4 Skyhawk. Similarly, the Soviet Pacific Fleet Headquarters in Vladivostok, if it had not already been disrupted by the F-100 strike at the PVO communications center, would have been taken out quickly to disrupt regional command and control.

Once the carrier task force was comparatively secure from aerial attack, the AD Skyraiders or even Regulus missiles launched from aircraft carriers or accompanying cruisers could pick off the other facilities at their leisure. The submarine bases would likely have been prioritized; there was one at Ulisa Bay (with collateral destruction of the adjacent torpedo boat base and maintenance facilities) and another at Zalev Strelok. Another was under construction at Dunay, with a missile-handing area. None apparently had underground facilities, though there was a massive cavern-like submarine pen with canals under construction at Pavlovsk Bay, Zalev Strelok.[96] Berthing areas for in-port combatants would have been next. These tended to group Soviet vessels by type; for example, Bukhta Abrek Naval Base was home to cruisers and destroyers, while Bukhta Novik Naval Base hosted cruisers, destroyers, and amphibious shipping. Bukhta Paris was the home of the mine warfare squadrons. U.S. Navy targeteers also expressed interest in the seaplane station. There were two large shipyards: Shipyard 202 in the heart of Vladivostok, and Petrovka Shipyard on the eastern shore of Ussuriyskiy Bay. The existence of the Shkotovo-22 nuclear storage facility north of Dunay may or may not have been known to the targeteers. The destruction of the Dunay Naval Storage Depot and magazines on Putyatin Island could have been accomplished with the detonation of a nuclear weapon in the bay between the two. Further down the coast at Nakhodka lay a ship repair yard and a large petroleum storage facility. The Soviet Pacific Fleet and its facilities, with the exception of ships at sea, could have been rendered nonexistent in under two hours. And if these strikes were somehow ineffective, the B-52s from the 4128th Strategic Wing from Amarillo AFB were scheduled to destroy targets around Vladivostok on their way to Beijing.[97]

The East Is Red: Communist China and North Korea

RAND analyst Daniel Ellsberg reported that there was no border between the Soviet Union and Communist China on CINCPAC GEOP targeting plots that he saw in the late 1950s. Both countries would be treated as one if there were a war.[98] In retrospect, this looks short-sighted and dangerous, seen through the backward lens of the Sino-Soviet split. However, on 17 July 1958 Mao ordered his forces to readiness in preparation to attack Taiwan while simultaneously threatening to send troops to the Middle East to support Soviet interests if the crisis in that region escalated. On 31 August 1958, during the Taiwan Straits Crisis, the Soviet Union announced that "any threat against the [People's Republic of China] would be considered a threat to the USSR."[99] As early as 1952 the Soviet and Chinese air defense systems were believed to be integrated.[100] And, as we have seen, Communist China was dependent on aviation fuel from the Soviet Far East refineries. There was a logic underlying Harry Felt's CINCPAC GEOP.

We are also confronted with the CINCPAC interpretation of the 1960 SIOP as a plan to be activated in the event of overt hostile activities related to the Soviet Union, with no mention of Communist China. This probably reflected the earlier BWP. There were, additionally, a number of smaller-scale CINCPAC contingencies dealing with Communist China, Taiwan, and the offshore islands.[101] Lacking more detailed historical information, it is probable that CINCPAC planning assumptions were based on the view "An attack against one is an attack against all": that if the United States was at war with the Soviet Union, the Communist Chinese had a mutual defense pact that obligated them to participate in some fashion and thus it too should be struck by U.S. forces. However, if Communist China engaged in unilateral action against, say, the offshore islands, the assumption appears to have been that the Soviet Union was not necessarily obligated to reciprocate, thus the nature of CINCPAC contingency planning. Similarly, if North Korea attacked South Korea, it would have likely been handled as a unilateral act and the response by CINCPAC would have been limited to North Korea until such

THE ACME OF SKILL

time as Communist China or the Soviet Union overtly involved themselves in the conflict, and then the GEOP would be activated.

Neither North Korea nor Communist China had at this time the ability to attack North America. Both countries did, however, possess forces that could have had a decisive effect on American operations in the region; thus these would have to be covered and destroyed quickly under whatever circumstances prevailed at the time. What would PACAF's objectives be at this point if ordered to strike under conditions of Strategic Warning? The priority would have been the destruction of any Communist Chinese forces that could hit the handful of American bases in the region. In effect, a mixture of Matadors, F-100s, and B-57s on alert in South Korea, plus F-100s at Kadena, were available for immediate use, while the Itazuki- and Iruma-based forces in Japan had to await the arrival of their weapons' cores. Kuter had to assume these would not be available or at the very least held back to deal with any contingency that developed regarding North Korea. If, for example, the Matadors were taken out (they were in a "soft" configuration on pads and not in bunkers), he had the marines available at Iwakuni within hours to conduct strikes across the 38th Parallel.

For PACAF, the key weapon systems to deal with Communist China and North Korea were Matador cruise missiles. The squadron on Taiwan could cover the handful of Communist Chinese airfields on the mainland opposite Chiang Kai-shek's stronghold. South Korea's central geographic position meant that all three Communist countries could be rapidly struck under any contingency. There were sixty Matadors at three sites: one north of Seoul, another at K-55/Osan Air Base, and a third near Chungju. With a seven-hundred-mile range and optimized for airfield attack, the Matadors could handle most of PACAF's pressing problems. For example, all eight identified Communist Chinese IL-28 bomber bases were in range, including two near Beijing, and all twelve North Korean military airfields, including two IL-28 bases, were in range. The location of the Matador ground control station on Baegyeong-do Island clearly played a role in extending the control range of the missiles into Chinese territory. Follow-on or concurrent strikes using the alert B-57s at K-8/

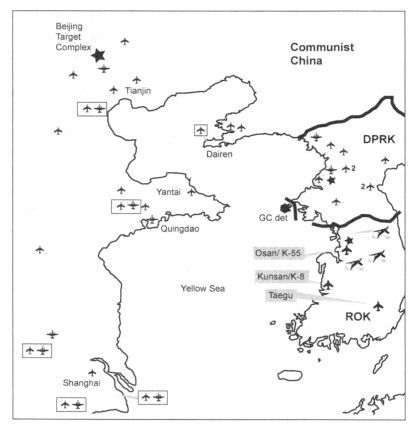

Map 36. Pacific Air Forces GEOP targets, 1959. Courtesy of the author.

Kunsan against the Communist Chinese IL-28 bases in case Matadors malfunctioned were likely. The aircraft had the range and were geographically positioned to do so.

The Chungju missile site may have supported the initial assault against the Primorsky Krai air defense system: the F-100s were not all-weather aircraft, but the Matadors were.[102] Having three sites and three enemies simplified targeting and sequencing: if the war was on with North Korea and not the other belligerents, one-third of the missiles remained available to handle targets north of the 38th Parallel. That said, the CIA reported, "The pilots of the regiment that is charged with the defense of Pyongyang have volunteered to fly their airplanes into any matador missiles launched at Pyongyang."[103]

THE ACME OF SKILL

Under conditions of both Tactical and Strategic Warning, the alert forces also had the task of destroying the Chinese Communist air forces in order to gain air superiority over the Yellow and East China Seas. This was necessary for two reasons: aircraft carrier task groups would be operating in both zones, and the air defense system had to be rolled back in anticipation of SAC's B-47s and B-52s striking their targets in the Chinese interior. There were four clusters of Communist Chinese air defense forces: Dairen covering the path to Manchuria; Tianjin, protecting the approaches to Beijing; Yantai-Quingdao; and Shanghai-Ningbo-Hangzou-Suzhou. In some cases IL-28s and MIGs were colocated. Abandoned airfields were also regularly examined to determine whether they could be used for dispersal; at this point they generally were not.[104] The F-100 force at Kadena was directed against MIG bases opposite them, while the Itazuki F-100 forces could be directed at both the Shanghai and Quindao areas once they received their cores. Alert F-100s at K-55/Osan were likely directed against Dairen and Yantai-Quingdao MIG bases.

Generally, SAC operations against Communist China were to be conducted by B-52s assigned to CINCPAC on a contingency basis. These included the 95th Bombardment Wing at Biggs AFB, which had eight aircraft equipped with Mk-15 and Mk-39 weapons. At some point in the alert process, these aircraft were to stage to Kadena Air Base on a mission designated Glass Brick.[105] The 4134th Strategic Wing at Mather AFB in California had fifteen B-52s equipped with Mk-39s reserved for contingency strikes that were to be assigned to crews three hours before departure. The 4134th was also to deploy a mobile recovery team to Kadena, implying that surviving aircraft would be rearmed and sent back in after their initial missions.[106]

There appears have been a change in targeting in 1959, probably in response to Kuter's concerns that the PACAF was not prepared to shift to urban-industrial targeting, with its vulnerable forward-deployed forces (see table 5). In April–May 1959 the CIA's National Photographic Interpretation Center appears to have been asked to generate hasty analysis of eight Communist Chinese urban areas.

Examination of the analysis suggests they were selected for common reasons. Five were provincial capitals; all possessed large railroad marshalling yards, and all were geographically proximate. Their destruction not only collaterally wiped out a substantial percentage of Communist Chinese war-making capacity but also cut off northeast China from the rest of the county. That made it more difficult to support North Korea if it were engaged in a conflict, but this course of action also isolated the Manchurian industrial complexes.[107]

The Beijing urban area was also reexamined by the National Photographic Interpretation Center in 1959.[108] Like Moscow and Berlin, Beijing was a center for research, development, and industry as well as the administrative hub for the country. Consequently, the city was spread out, with numerous targets interspersed among the population (which was between 5 and 7 million people). SAC bombers had at least nine facilities to hit, in addition to the city center. These included the IL-28 base at the Nanyuan Airfield, which was adjacent to a large airframe plant; the Lian-Tuen Airfield to the west, and Changping Airfield with seventy-seven MiG fighters to the north. Capitol Airport to the northwest was jet-capable with long runways. The Peiping Reactor atomic energy facility to the southwest was identified by National Photographic Interpretation Center analysts. Also to the southwest was possibly the largest example of potential "bonus damage" in Communist China: the Chang-hsintien Missile Development Center was surrounded by two division-size army barracks, an armored school, an ammo depot, a locomotive plant, a thermal power plant, and a large petroleum storage area. To the west of the city lay the gargantuan Shih-ching-shan Iron and Steel Works, surrounded by three thermal power plants. These facilities had been photographed by Nationalist Chinese pilots over the course of the 1950s and correlated with HUMINT and were on U.S. Air Force target charts and mosaics.[109] At least ten Mk-15 or Mk-39 weapons would have been required to ensure the destruction of these dispersed targets. Unlike Moscow, Beijing had no surface-to-air missile system at this point and minimal if any significant night intercept capability.

Table 5. Chinese urban area targets, 1959

Urban area	Estimated population	Complexes
Cheng-Hsien, Henan Province (capital, Zhengzhou)	770,000	Thermal power plants Locomotive repair plant Chemical manufacturing Small steel plant Tractor plant
Tsinan, Shandong Province	700,000	Iron and steel plant Locomotive and automotive Rubber factory Explosives plant Thermal power plant Arsenal
Xi'an, Shaanxi Province	1.5 million	Atomic research center Munitions plants Iron and steel plants Aircraft repair and assembly Locomotive and automotive
Luoyang, Henan Province	500,000	Ferrous metal processing Heavy machine works Ball-bearing plant Phosphate plant Munitions works Thermal power plant
Qingdao, Shandong Province	850,000	Petroleum storage Ammunition plants Iron plant Rubber production Submarine repair base Naval base Metal fabrication plants
Taiyuan, Shanxi Province	830,000	Chemical works and phosphate Ore processing Iron and steel Locomotive and automotive 3 thermal power plants
Tianjin, Hebei Province	?	Airfields Ports
Wuhan, Hebei Province	?	Shipbuilding Submarine construction Ore processing Airfields Bridges over the Han River

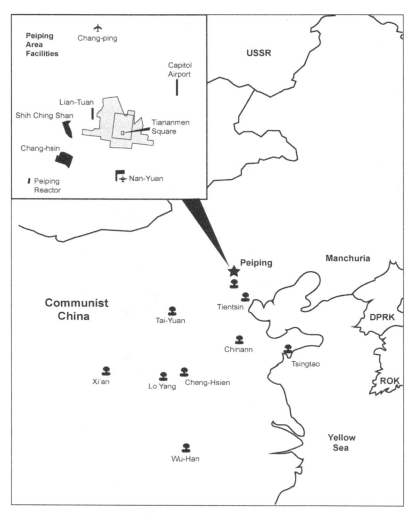

Map 37. Chinese urban area targets, 1959. Courtesy of the author.

The role of the Air Mail B-47 force on Guam is ambiguous. Ellsberg states that alert aircraft on Okinawa were targeted against both the Soviet Union and Communist China as part of the CINCPAC GEOP.[110] Discussions between Kuter, Felt, and LeMay in August 1958 suggest something much more nuanced. If Mao attacked the offshore islands and Eisenhower authorized a response using nuclear weapons, fighter aircraft would respond if the weather was clear and it was daylight. SAC would follow up at night (or if the weather was

THE ACME OF SKILL

bad) "against those airfields requiring re-strikes." The response differed yet again if the authorization came at night:

> The intent of our concept is to have SAC aircraft make the first strike against bases. . . . This assumes we can get the necessary high level decision. This would be done before [Pacific Command] forces become actively engaged in the hope that the CHICOMs would then realize U.S. intent . . . and cease further operations. If the CHICOMs do not cease operations, we visualize Phase II of CINCPAC Operation Plan 22-58 would be ordered implemented and augmented by SAC as necessary. . . . If SAC strikes made under our concept do not deter the CHICOMs then we agree that [IL-28] Beagles must be hit wherever they are.[111]

There were eight IL-28 target bases in Communist China that would have required half of the Air Mail alert force to destroy them. However, if the Guam B-47s had to be used against the five Fujian air bases, there was a problem. Destruction of these targets using multimegaton Mk-36 mod 1 and Mk-39 mod 0 weapons would have generated significant fallout onto Taiwan. Fortunately, the 3rd Aviation Depot Squadron on Guam had Mk-6 kiloton-yield weapons on hand. The possibility that the small number of Mk-36Y2 "clean" weapons could have been employed in this contingency also existed; there were at least six of these and there were five targets. Mk-36Y2 delivery against certain Chinese targets upwind of Japan might also have been desirable.

The U.S. Navy's GEOP targets of interest in Communist China appear to have had three groupings (see map 38). The northern-most one included naval units and air bases that could interfere with an aircraft carrier's freedom of movement in the Yellow Sea, and even the Gulf of Chihli. Submarine bases were prioritized. The possibility that the U.S. Navy was even prepared to launch A3Ds against targets in and around Beijing on a Doolittle-like raid from these zones cannot be ruled out.

The central grouping included Shanghai, with its Kiangnan Submarine Base and numerous other naval facilities, plus the cluster of naval bases to the southeast: Hou-so Ching Submarine Base and the

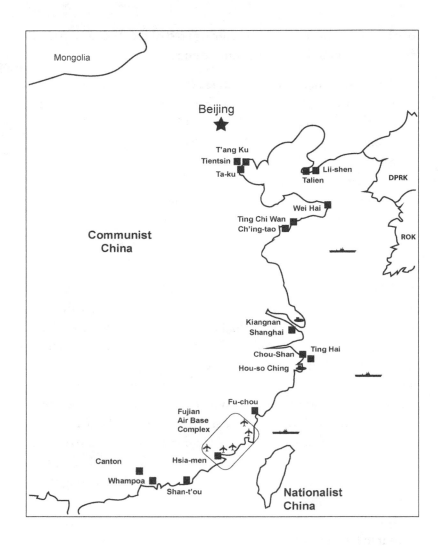

Map 38. Projected U.S. Navy GEOP targets in Communist China, 1958–60.
Courtesy of the author.

Chou-Shan and Ting Hai bases, where amphibious shipping was located. The third grouping contained the three naval bases opposite Taiwan from which amphibious operations could be launched, and finally Whampoa and Canton north of Hong Kong.[112] The number of air bases equipped with every MIG type available at the time, from Dairen to Canton, was dramatic. These would have to be destroyed first before the destruction of the Communist Chinese fleet and its facilities was undertaken. This amounted to fifty bases, over a thousand aircraft, and four hundred radar sites supporting them.[113] The task—three or four aircraft carriers taking this on against an aroused foe and succeeding—would have required substantial guile and would likely have to have been undertaken at night. The destruction of the eastern-most Chinese Communist air defenses by PACAF would have substantially contributed to the northern-most component of the plan.

Conclusion

Its not what the American people think of SAC. . . . It's what Khrushchev
thinks of SAC that counts. If he thought he could render us helpless,
he might be willing to try. Just what is the deterrent point is
the question. Even I do not know.

—GEN. THOMAS POWER, 1959

In building our nuclear force, nobody can tell you exactly when enough
has been done. My philosophy has been to have overwhelming strength
so it makes no difference if you are off by a couple of decimal points. . . .
This is a vicious arms race and you can't play for higher stakes.
The question is whether you can win this highly competitive
race without really going all out.

—GEN. THOMAS POWER, 1964

The truism that no plan survives contact with the enemy applies
to nuclear warfare as much as it does to other forms of organized violence. The Emergency War Plan and its variants, we
must remember, were initially extensions of planning for a World
War II–style war that then transformed into deterrent mechanisms
that would have been the basis for a nuclear war had it occurred. The
plans did not have to be perfect; they had to be credible enough to
generate uncertainty and inhibition among the leaders of the Communist world. Indeed the pace of technological change from a small
number of propeller-driven bombers and kiloton-yield bombs to

large numbers of jet bombers, ballistic missiles, and megaton-yield weapons in less than ten years was staggering. The ability of U.S. Air Force leadership to manage these challenges and do so effectively under the pressures placed on it should be recognized for the astounding achievement it was. There is truly no comparative situation in human history. These men held the world in their hands, their motives underpinned by a universal suspicion of the Soviet Union, a suspicion based on direct experiences with a malevolent Communist system. Nuclear deterrence in the 1950s was no rogue operation, and its many facets had the sanction of the commander in chief, President Dwight D. Eisenhower.

American nuclear strategy in the 1950s has for decades been described—and dismissed—as Massive Retaliation. Perhaps instead of "overkill" it was really a period of "massive deterrence." The key underpinning of the strategy, as expressed through the Emergency War Plan, was that American deterrence rested on credible target coverage, that is, the demonstrable ability to get through to targets and destroy them if it became necessary. Simply having nuclear weapons and the ability to deliver them was not enough. Crews had to be trained, be proficient and motivated, and seen by the opposition to be so. Targets had to be identified; realistic plans had to be made. Those aspects could remain in the shadows. But the existence of bomber and tanker bases and, most important, their location proximate to their targets until longer-range delivery systems became available was also part of the deterrent equation. Indeed basing was in some ways integral to how the Cold War itself played out in other areas, such as influence operations and foreign aid.

There was a demand to adapt and adjust these factors on a regular basis so that credibility in the system could be maintained. Targeting forward-based enemy forces as a priority instead of hitting industrial or interdiction targets is one example. Equally important was the need to constantly review the survivability of the forces that would undertake wartime tasks and thus their ability to cover targets; this was a common theme throughout the 1950s. Again, it was necessary that the opposition see this adaptation take place, up to a point.

Crucial aspects of massive deterrence included the observable reliability of the deterrent force's nuclear weapons and their delivery aircraft. Nuclear weapons testing was not merely about determining whether the devices would go off; the plethora of scientific activities relating to aircraft and crew exposure and delivery profiles was as much a part of the tests as measurement of the gross effects. The fact that a B-52 dropped a thermonuclear weapon that detonated over a target array and survived is as important as the fact that a particular configuration of materials led to a multimegaton detonation.

Knowing what to hit and perhaps letting the opposition know that there was enough knowledge of a variety of targets to do so was yet another factor in massive deterrence. Previously held assumptions and beliefs that there was little knowledge of Soviet targets prior to the first U-2 overflights in 1956 were really a cigar-generated smokescreen to protect the fact that there was substantial U.S. Air Force overhead imagery of the Soviet Union and China. We may quibble about how much was enough at any given time, but the fact remains that the conduct of reconnaissance operations directly contributed to deterrence. This was particularly evident to the Soviets, Stalin in particular, when RB-45Cs could reach Moscow unhindered, coupled with the knowledge that their B-45 relations could carry a nearly 100-kiloton-yield bomb and deliver it onto the Soviet capital. No matter what was said in the arenas of interservice and interagency rivalry, SAC had better targeting information than has been previously understood.

One of the most important issues of the day was the question of what the most appropriate target set was to achieve deterrence functions in peacetime while at the same time satisfying strategic success criteria in wartime. And what was the most economic deterrent force structure to be maintained in peacetime? In the 1940s nuclear weapons were an extension of World War II–style strategic bombing designed to support a World War II–style war with a similar tempo; thus industrial targets were appropriate. As nuclear weapons became more destructive and the realization set in that national culture could be destroyed, the destruction of any Soviet target that could generate damage to the United States and its allies moved to the fore: bases, airfields, bomber production, and atomic weapons production. Who cared if steel production was reduced under these circumstances? The war would last only a week at most.

Targeting Moscow remained a constant as the centrality of the Soviet leadership to the Communist enterprise was correctly ascertained. But then, to save money and to reduce the U.S. Air Force budget for redistribution elsewhere, the concept of deliberate systematic population destruction was formally introduced by the U.S. Army and U.S. Navy due to the seduction of cost-effectiveness and the possibility of larger slices of the budgetary pie. And the new nuclear ally, Great Britain, with its smaller nuclear force, was pursuing a similar Alternative Undertaking. The U.S. Air Force was forced to compromise.

Many have assumed the 1950s Emergency War Plans were inflexible or, in analyst Herman Kahn's words, a "Wargasm." Even the adoption of the term "flexible response" in the 1960s suggests that this was believed to be the case, and a new strategy with a new name was required. But was the Emergency War Plan really inflexible? For the early war plans in the 1940s and 1950s, the point was moot: there was a general war plan, and the EWP fit into it, and there was no comparative time constraint on carrying out the strategic bombing task. It was flexible enough for the circumstances of the day. Soon afterward nuclear weapons augmented forward-deployed American forces to deter the crushing numbers of Soviet conventional forces based in Eastern Europe. With the increased concern over preemption of SAC's forces by forward-based enemy forces equipped with nuclear weapons, however, that changed. Challenging and thus undermining the probability of an American nuclear response to Soviet adventurism opened up Pandora's box and forced flexibility on the EWP. Some forces had to be available to counter possible preemption. Others had to be prepared to interdict the enemy advance. Getting through to targets in the Soviet Union required navy assistance to open corridors through the air defense system.

The problem of targeting in the Far East, with the three-headed hydra of North Korea, the Soviet Union, and Communist China, required special handling. There were various subplans for dealing with these adversaries, ones that did not necessarily require unleashing the EWP. In this respect there was a level of flexibility. And there had to be: deterring Mao was perhaps a different prospect from deterring Khrushchev and required a different methodology. The same went for Kim Il-sung, who was likely self-deterred while he rebuilt what was left of North Korea after a war that did not involve the detonation of nuclear weapons.

But most important there had to be enough American nuclear capability available to ensure that targets in the Soviet Union were covered, no matter what the outcome of these other aspects of the campaign. Thus the EWP developed into two plans: a preemption option and a retaliatory option. And, in terms of readiness to carry out these options, SAC developed a graduated buildup schedule that was adaptable to any situation the United States found itself in in order to carry out either option. The graduated buildup itself was part of the deterrent system. It was not a matter of unleashing American nuclear forces over whatever level the Soviets chose to operate at. It was a matter of signaling concern or resolve by alerting SAC and giving the president the option to preempt or retaliate or even conduct limited strikes against Communist China. Those moves themselves and the demonstrable capability to carry them out was an umbrella under which conventional forces could be maneuvered by the policymakers as chess pieces to address the circumstances of whatever crisis was in play, from Berlin to the Middle East and the Taiwan Straits. The EWP was never an all-or-nothing proposition, as its critics asserted; they were just not briefed on all aspects of the plan. And why should they have been?

A key theme that emerges from this study includes the oft-discussed competition between SAC and TAC, and the U.S. Air Force and the U.S. Navy, over who had the highest proportion of resources to carry out the deterrent task and thus who was on the top of the pyramid in the Pentagon. The compromise solution at the planning level, to include theater coordination mechanisms and an annual global deconfliction conference at the JCS level, was appropriate as the commands felt their way through this challenging period. With the increase in tempo brought on by the ballistic missile and the proliferation of targets brought on by better intelligence, however, this had to change, and in late 1960 it did. At the JCS level, the competition morphed into the debate over Alternative Undertakings and associated force structures, with moral and military imperatives set ostensibly against a cost-benefit analysis. Again, a compromise was reached by late 1960. The convergence of these challenges produced the Joint Strategic Target Planning Staff, the National Strategic Target List, and the Single Integrated Operational Plan, a system that would operate for the next thirty years, until the end of the Cold War.

Finally, we should examine the role that the EWP played in the Cold War generally. If we accept the view that the Cold War was a combined military-political-economic competition for the domination of the world, and that constantly adjusting military force structures played a significant role in the give-and-take dynamic of the conflict, where does the American deterrent system of the 1950s fit into that?

Soviet objectives were never benign or isolationist, no matter what their propaganda output claimed or what their Western sympathizers in media, academia, and culture asserted. The Soviet Union of the 1950s was an organism bent on expansion and competition using a variety of overlapping methods. It posed a political, conventional, and nuclear threat to Western Europe; it attempted to undermine Western influence in the strategically vital Middle East; and it assisted its Communist allies while they conducted open warfare in Asia.

The Soviet Union was clearly constrained in its worldwide activities on some level in the 1950s that it was not by the 1970s. Their back-channel negotiating points during the "surprise attack" discussions in November and December 1958 reflected Soviet concerns and the specific forces that were generating those conditions: "The Russians still maintain the line that they are willing to discuss certain technical matters provided these matters are in conjunction with (a) Ban the bomb (b) Withdrawal from overseas bases (c) reduction by ⅓ of the forces in Europe (d) no nuclear weapons in Germany (e) No flights of long range bombers with nuclear weapons over international waters or over foreign countries."[1]

If they could not prohibit outright the nuclear weapons offsetting their massive conventional forces, they wanted SAC withdrawn from overseas bases, a reduction of forces in Europe, West Germany turned into a nuclear-free zone, and no airborne alert. It is not a coincidence that only one of these capabilities was removed from the chess board during the course of the Cold War. The U.S. Air Force deployed F-111 strike aircraft with appropriate nuclear weapons to the United Kingdom in 1971 to 1993, a deployment analogous to the Reflex B-47s. Forces assigned to NATO were constantly upgraded, and there were more nuclear weapons in West Germany than any other American ally, right until the 1990s. Only airborne alert was curtailed in 1968, and that was due to a cost-benefit process.

Attempts by the Soviets to circumvent the deterrent system and regain some form of strategic initiative in the Cold War included "soft" measures like influence operations and arms control, support to wars of national liberation, and "hard" measures like the mass deployment of ballistic missiles in 1961 to the occupied Baltic States, Ukraine, and later Cuba. The Cuban episode failed because the Soviets could not fully offset SAC's retaliatory capabilities and confront the U.S. Navy's conventional forces on the quarantine line. Wars of national liberation required support that was implicitly protected by a nuclear umbrella and a conventional lifeline. The result was a dramatic increase by the end of the 1960s in Soviet naval capabilities, the permanent stationing of Yankee-class ballistic missile submarines off North America with more nuclear weapons on board than were stationed in Cuba in 1962, and the pursuit of superiority in Strategic Rocket Forces to offset SAC. It was not a coincidence that Soviet adventurism in Africa, Afghanistan, the Middle East, and Latin America in the 1970s dramatically expanded after parity was achieved and the American deterrent system was held in check.

In the 1950s the Soviets were limited to making bellicose threats and crushing opposition inside Eastern Europe. When confronted during his blatant attempts to expand Soviet influence, Khrushchev backed down every time. He was deterrable. Even when he secretly deployed SS-3 ballistic missiles in 1958–59, which had limited deterrent value because their presence was unknown to the West, he withdrew them. His repeated climb-downs during international crises had a negative impact on the Soviet Union's relationship with Communist China, with subsequent long-term effects on the Cold War itself as the Soviets lost credibility with their allies. Whether Mao was deterred is more difficult to determine, as his objectives were related to his relationship with the Soviet Union; the United States was merely a pawn in the larger Mao game with Khrushchev.

The existence of SAC's capabilities had a measurable effect on Khrushchev and thus Soviet actions throughout the 1950s, which in turn had an impact in the wider course of the Cold War. The reduction of SAC and the acceptance of a minimum deterrence force structure in the 1950s would have produced an entirely different state of affairs, and perhaps our world would not be the same as it is today. In a discussion with the media over Pat Frank's 1959 postapocalyptic best seller *Alas, Babylon*, Thomas Power endorsed the book's scenario, stating, "There are no winners, only losers to varying degrees."[2]

APPENDIX A

SAC Emergency War Plan 1-49 and 1-51 Targets

Methodology

The complete SAC Emergency War Plans 1-49 and 1-51 and their associated plans are not available at this time, so this appendix is a close approximation of their targets. Working through this process is crucial to understanding the evolution of American nuclear war planning as the EWP 1-49 and EWP 1-51 target lists provide the basis for the urban/industrial component of the SIOP in the 1960s. British nuclear strategy focused on many of the same targets.

Using the JCS criteria as a starting point, it is possible to identify likely industrial targets in the categories of oil, aluminum, steel, and electrical power generation. There is a 1950 EWP 1-49 map available that is derived from the plan, but its locations are imprecise. The initial list here builds on the 1947 JCS list of twenty-four targets, cross-indexed with Broiler and Halfmoon's target list of seventy cities. These names were then cross-indexed with Dropshot's control center targets, and then compared with the map in the 1945 Norstad document. This was the basis for named locations. The locations were grouped using what would have been the regional complex grouping methodology used in 1952.

The locations on this list were checked against Wringer and other HUMINT and OSINT (open-source intelligence) material from 1946 to 1953. They were then compared with 1960s-era Talent-Keyhole data. This allowed the evolution of the targets in each named site from 1947 to 1970 to emerge and to filter out targets constructed or modified after 1953. The criteria for inclusion in the final list was that it was something that was known by the USAF and CIA from 1946 to 1953 and could be demonstrated that it was known at that time. Reverse-engineering Talent-Keyhole information clearly would not work. For example, some TU-4 bases were closed by 1957 and were not transformed into TU-16, TU-95, or MYA-4 bases. Other facilities, particularly some involved in Soviet atomic weapons production, had not yet been built. Consequently this appendix depicts SAC EWP 1-49 and EWP 1-51 targets as they evolved from 1950 to 1953.

Table 6. SAC Emergency War Plan 1-49 and 1-51 targets

Target region/ complex	Sites	Sources	Remarks
LENINGRAD			
Leningrad	Red October Works No. 466	OSINT	Wasserfall guidance
	Kirov Tank Plant No. 117	HUMINT	
	Trust 54 Iron and Steel Works		
	Aircraft accessories plant		
	Multiple electronics plants		
	Ports of Leningrad and Kronstadt		
Volkhov	Volkhovastroi and Kirov aluminum plants	OSINT	
MOSCOW			
Moscow	Ramenskoye Airfield	German	R&D
	Aviation Engine Plant 45	HUMINT 1948+	V-weapons
	Moscow-Khimki Airfield	USAF SENSINT	Beagle production
	Moscow Central Airfield/Airframe Plant No. 30		Later Bison factory
	Moscow Fili		
	Airfield and Moscow Fili Airframe Plant No. 23		
	Mikulin Aircraft Plant 300		
	3 power plants		

Target region/ complex	Sites	Sources	Remarks
Gorki	Gorki Heavy Equipment Plant	HUMINT 1948–52	
	Gorki Airframe Plant Ordzhonikidze No. 21	PHOTOINT 1953	
	Gorki Tank Works No. 112		
	Nitrogen plant		
	Gorki Igumnovo Airfield		
	Gorki Metals Factory		
	Gorki Milling Machine Works No 113		
	Gorki Chemical Combine		
	Stalin Armaments Plant No. 92		
	Molotov Auto Works (tank plant)		
	Refinery		
	Yava Chemical Plant		
	Power plant		
Ivanovo	Baturin Chemical Plant	German	
		PHOTOINT 1956	
Kazan	Kazan Airframe Plant No. 387	German	
	Kazan Airframe Plant Gorbunov No. 22	HUMINT 1947–55	
	Kazan Aircraft Engine Plant No. 16	USAF 1953	
	Zavod 40 Ammunitions Plant		
	Power plant		
Molotov (Perm)	Stalin and/or Molotov Aircraft Plan No. 19	HUMINT 1949+	
	Tank Plant No. 148	USAF	
	Armament Combine No. 172/Molotov Artillery Works No. 172		

Location	Facility	Source
Tula	Synthetic fuel plant, from Magdeburg "Kalinin" Plants 535, 536	PHOTOINT 1954 HUMINT 1947+
Ukhta	Ukhta refinery	HUMINT 1952
Vitebsk	Petroleum storage Marshalling yard, bridge, logistics bottleneck Biological warfare research?	OSINT HUMINT 1949+
Yaroslavl	Rubber factory Tank production Chemical warfare factory Refinery Shipyard 2 power plants	HUMINT 1948+
DONETS BASIN		
Debaltsevo	Debaltsevo Steel Foundry	OSINT HUMINT
Dneprodzerzhinsk	Dneprodzerzhinsk Metallurgical Plant 2 coke plants	OSINT HUMINT
Dnepropetlovsk	Petrovski Metallurgical Plant Karl Libknecht Metallurgical Plant Komintern Steel Kombine Missile development and production center Machine building plant Chemical factory Pipe rolling mill	USAF 1950 HUMINT 1952 USAF 1953 ss-1b, ss-3, missile production hidden next to auto and refrigerator production (Plants 186D and 192)

Target region/ complex	Sites	Sources	Remarks
Gorlovka	Kirov Machine Plant	OSINT	
	Coke plant	HUMINT	
Kerch	Kerch Metallurgical Plant	OSINT	
		HUMINT	
Kharkov	Kharkov Airframe Plant No. 135	German	
	Power Station No. 1	HUMINT 1949+	
	Kharkov Tank Factory	USAF	
	The Stalin Factory		
Konstantinovka	Konstantinovka Coke Plant	OSINT	
	Konstantinovka Metallurgical Plant	HUMINT	
Kramatorsk	Kramatorsk Metallurgical Plant	HUMINT	
	Khartsyzsk Pipe Plant	OSINT	
	2 machinery building plants		
	Power plant		
Krivoy Rog	Krivoy Rog Metallurgical Plant	OSINT	
		HUMINT	
Nikitovka	Nikitovka Coke Plant	OSINT	
		HUMINT	
Nikopol	Nikopol Pipe and Tube	OSINT	
		HUMINT	
Nikolayev	Tractor plant	OSINT	
	Shipbuilding Yard 444	HUMINT	

Location	Facility	Source
Novomoskvosk	Novomoskvosk Sheet Mill	OSINT HUMINT
Odessa	Rolling mill	
	Pervomayask Metallurgical Plant	HUMINT 1952+
	Refinery	OSINT
	6 railroad shops	
	Port	
Stalino (Donetsk)	Stalino Iron and Steel Works	German
	Karpova Nitrogen Plant	OSINT
	Makeyevka Metal Works	HUMINT 1947+
	Munitions factory	
	4 coke plants	
Toretsk	Machinery factory	OSINT
Voronezh	Voronezh Aircraft Engine Plant No. 154	German
	Voronezh Aircraft Assembly Plant No. 64	HUMINT 1949+
	Power plant	
Voroshilovgrad (Luhansk)	Almanazaya Iron Works	OSINT
	4 coke plants	HUMINT
	October Revolution Locomotive Factory	
	Parkhomenko Heavy Machine Plant	
	Pipe rolling mill	
	Voroshalivgrad Metallurgical Works	
	Power plant	
Yenakiyevo	Yenakiyevo Metallurgical Plant	OSINT

Target region/ complex	Sites	Sources	Remarks
Zaporozhye	Aircraft Engine Plant No. 478	German	
	"Magnesium Plant" Denprovskiy Titanium-Magnesium Factory	HUMINT	
	Zaprozhtal Iron Works	OSINT	
		USAF 1952	
Zhdanov	Azovstal Metallurgical Plant	OSINT	
	Il'ich Steel Plant	HUMINT	
VOLGA			
Kuybyshev	Kuybyshev Metallurgical Plant	German	Sole producer of Bear
	Kuybyshev Aircraft Engine Plant No. 24	HUMINT 1951+	Lend-lease refinery
	"Zavod 2" (cover was Kuybyshev No. 2)	TK 1960+	
	Airframe Plant 1		
	Airframe Plant 18		
	Petroleum refinery		
Penza	Penza Machinery Plant	HUMINT 1948+	
Saratov	Saratov Airframe Plant 292	German	
	Third State Antifriction Bearing Plant	HUMINT 1947+	
	Refinery	USAF 1951+	
	Airplane Parts Factory 306		
	Power plant		

Stalingrad	Aluminumstroy No. 2 Rolling Mill	German	
	Red October Steel Plant	HUMINT 1946+	
	Stalingrad Tractor Factory		
	Red Barricades Ordnance Plant No. 221		
	Dzerzhinski Tractor Factory		
	Stalingrad Iron Works		
	Lazur Chemical Works		
	2 power plants		
Syzran	Petroleum refinery	OSINT	
	Aircraft Accessories Plant No. 481	HUMINT 1952+	

CAUCASUS

Astrakhan	Oil shipments via the port	HUMINT 1949+	
	Kirov Shipyards		
Baku	Nov Baku Refinery	German	Largest petroleum refineries in the USSR are in Baku
	Baku Naval Base complex	OSINT	
	Dzhaparidze Petroleum Refinery	HUMINT 1953	
	Budenny Petroleum Refinery		
	Andreyev Petroleum Refinery		
	Stalin Petroleum Refinery		
	Port of Baku		
	Karayev Petroleum Refinery		
	Vano Sturua Petroleum Refinery		
	Oil fields of the Buzovny Oil Trust		
	2 power plants		

Target region/complex	Sites	Sources	Remarks
Batumi	Batumi Petroleum Refinery	OSINT 1949	
	Port of Batumi Harbour	HUMINT 1950	
	Petroleum shipping docks		
Grozny	Grozny Oil Wells	German	
	Refinery No. 3	HUMINT 1948+	
Gurev	Bolshoi Pershnoi Island Oil Plant No. 441		Lend-lease refinery
Krasnador/Maikop	Oil production	German 1943–45	
		OSINT 1953	
Mokhach Kala	Artillery factory	HUMINT 1953	
	Oil refinery	OSINT 1947	
Neftadag	Oil fields	OSINT	
		HUMINT 1952+	
Tbilisi	Aircraft Plant No. 3	HUMINT 1950+	
	Nitrogen factory		
	Tank training and storage		
Yerevan	Aluminum Factory 216	OSINT	
URALS			
Chelyabinsk	Kirov Tractor Works Tank Factory, aka Kirov Tank and Tractor Plant	HUMINT 1947–51	
	Metallurgical plant		
	Power plant		

Location	Facility	Source
Chkalov	Airplane Factory Zavod 47	HUMINT 1947–51
	Kirov Plant for Tractor and Tank Parts	
	Airfield	
	Foundry for locomotive parts	
Kamensk	Kamensk-Uralskiy Aluminum Combine	HUMINT 1949+
	Aircraft Parts Plant 268	
Magnitogorsk	Stalin Steel Combine	HUMINT 1949+
	Power plant	PHOTOINT 1957
Nizhny Tagil	Kaganovich Tank and Railroad Car Plant No. 183	HUMINT 1949+
	Nizhny Tagil Metallurgical Combine	
	Tagil Stroi Metal Plant	
	Dzerzhinsky Railway Car Factory	
Orsk	Orsk Refinery	HUMINT 1950+
	Wiener Neustadt aircraft plant transferred here	Lend-lease refinery
Krasnoturinsk/ Serov	Aluminum factories	OSINT
Sterlitamak	Sterlitamak Explosives Plant 850	Germany
Sverdlovsk	"Ural Engineering Works" Arms Plant No. 8	HUMINT 1950+
	"Uralmash Machine Plant" Arms Plant No. 9	USAF 1955
	Bearing Plant No. 6	
	Radio Technical Manufacturing Zavod 659	
	V weapons electrical testing and production	
	Power plant	

Target region/complex	Sites	Sources	Remarks
Ufa	Motornyi, aka "Ufa Engine Plant 26"	HUMINT 1949+	Largest engine plant in USSR
	Petroleum:	OSINT	Shell Oil
	Ufa Novo Ufimskiy		
	Staro Ufimskiy		
	Ufa Novo Chernikovsk		
	Ufa synthetic alcohol plant		
	Cracking refinery delivered		
Zlatoust	Zlatoust Armament Plant No. 66	OSINT	
		HUMINT 1947	
		German	
CENTRAL ASIA			
Alma Ata	Atomic power research	HUMINT 1953	
	Tractor plant		
	Tashkent Mechanical Plant		
	Large military airfield		
	Alma Ata Bearing Repair Works		
Chimkent	Lead combine (Kalinin Lead Plant)		
	Tractor factory/tank factory		
Tashkent	Aluminum factory	OSINT	

KUZNETSK BASIN			
Kemerovo	Kemerovo Chemical Combine	OSINT	
	Nitrate fertilizer plant	HUMINT 1952	
	Power plant		
Novosibirsk	Novosibirsk Airframe Plant Chkalov No 153	HUMINT 1947+	
	Steel Fabricating and Munitions Combine, Novosibirsk Combine No. 179		
	Ammunition Plant		
Stalinsk	Stalinsk (Kuznetski?) Metallurgical Combine	OSINT 1946+	
	Aluminum Combine Stalin and Stalinsk Heat and Power Plant	HUMINT 1946+	
	Smelter	USAF 1955	
IRKUTSK			
Irkutsk	Airframe Plant 39 and airfield	HUMINT 1948	
	Kuibyshev Metallurgical Works, Irkutsk		
Ulan-Ude	Airframe Plant No. 99	Wringer 1950+	
	3 power plants		
FAR EAST			
Komsomolsk	Komsomolsk Airframe Plant 126 and 130	Wringer	Fitter, Fagot, Beagle
	Amur Shipyard 199	USAF 1952	Main sub construction yard in
	Refinery No. 409	USAF 1953	Far East
	Chemical Plant No. 39	HUMINT 1954	

Target region/ complex	Sites	Sources	Remarks
Khabarovsk	Osipovskiy Kirov Shipyard 368	HUMINT 1949	"One of two major refineries in
	Refinery 419	HUMINT 1951	the Far East"
	Ussuri South Shipyard	HUMINT 1952	TU-4 training for China
	Armament and Machinery Plant Rembaza Kaganovich 105	USAF 1956	
	Khabarovsk Airfield		
	El'ban Explosive Plant 637		
	Aircraft Plant No. 83		
Vladivostok	Vladivostok Submarine Base, Ulisa Bay	HUMINT 1947	
	Vladivostok Naval Base and Shipyard 202	HUMINT 1948	
	Bystry Shipyard	USAF 1954	
		PHOTOINT 1955	
INDIVIDUAL TARGETS			
Bialystok	Marshalling yard, bridge, logistics bottleneck		
Brest Litovsk	Marshalling yard, bridge, logistics bottleneck	HUMINT 1951+	
Frankfurt an den Oder	Marshalling yard, bridge, logistics bottleneck		
Murmansk Arkhangelsk	Multiple naval bases and airfields		Removed from EWP after 1950
Kaliningrad	Submarine components	HUMINT 1950+	

Omsk	Omsk Aircraft Plant Stalin 166	HUMINT 1950
	Omsk Aircraft Engine Plant Baranova 29	USAF 1952+
	Omsk Tank Plant Voroshilov 174	
	Omsk Petroleum Refinery	
	Rubber products plant	
Ploesti refineries	Astra Romana, Romano Americana, Vega, Dacia, Orion, Colombia, Redeventza, Xenia	AAF World War II
Sosnovets	Aluminum plant	OSINT

POWER PLANTS

Shatura, Dubrovka, Kashira, Shterovska, Zuyevka, White Russian GRES, Berezniki, Solikamsk, Kuznetsk, Stalinogorsk, Novorossiysk, Elektrogorsk, Artem, Mironovskaya, Slavyansk, Cherepet'	OSINT HUMINT

Target region/ complex	Sites	Sources	Remarks
BRAVO TARGETS			
Balbasavo, Kazan, Poltava, Priluki, Bobriusk, Blagoveshchensk, Dyagilevo, Lebedin, Bykhov, Baranovich, Tartu, Sol'tsy, Belaya, Tsurkov, Konotop	TU-4 operating bases	HUMINT SIGINT	
ATOMIC PRODUCTION			
Elektrosal	Metallurgical facility	OSINT	
Krasnoyarsk-45	Uranium enrichment	HUMINT	
Sverdlovsk-44	Uranium enrichment	PHOTOINT	
Sukhami	Heavy water		
Kyshtym	Plutonium separation, weapons fabrication		

Source code: These do not line up with the locations but are a compilation of source types and dates for the target area. German: World War II aerial imagery; HUMINT or Wringer: human intelligence; OSINT: open-source intelligence; PHOTOINT: ground photography intelligence or non-Talent-Keyhole aerial photography intelligence; USAF: USAF sources.

Soviet Cities and Population, 1960 Estimates

Soviet Cities of 500,000 or More Population (28)

Yerevan

Baku

Minsk

Tbilisi

Karaganda

Riga

Krasnoyarsk

Chelyabinsk

Gorki

Ivanovo

Kuybyshev

Leningrad

Moscow

Novosibirsk

Omsk

Perm (Molotov)

Rostov

Saratov

Stalingrad/Volograd

Sverlovsk

Ufa

Dnepropetrovsk

Kharkov

Kiev

Odessa

Stalino

Tashkent

Kazan

Soviet Cities of 400,000 to 500,000 Population (5)

Alma Ata

Voronezh

Yaroslavl

Lvov

Zaporozhye

Soviet Cities of 300,000 to 400,000 Population (9)

Barnaul

Krasnodar

Magnitogorsk

Irkutsk

Stalinsk

Tula

Khabrovsk

Nizhny Tagil

Makyevka

Soviet Cities of 200,000 to 300,000 Population (27)

Tallin

Frunze

Vilnius

Kaunas

Kishinev

Vladivostok

Arkhangelsk

Astrakhan

Bryansk

Kaliningrad

Kalinin

Keremovo

Prokop'yevek

Kirov

Kursk

Orenberg

Penza

Taganrod

Ryazan

Tomsk

Ulynovsk

Grozny

Izhevsk

Luganak

Nikolayev

Gorlovka

Zhdanov

Soviet Cities of 100,000 to 200,000 Population (76)

Leninikan

Kirovbad

Gomel

Mogilev

Vitebsk

Kutaisi

Akmolinsk

Semipalatinsk

Petropovlovsk

Ust-Kamenogarsk

Chimkent

Uralsk

Komsomolsk Amure

Rubtovsk

Biysk

Armavir

Noril'sk

Ussuriysk

Stavropol

Kopeyak

Zlatoust

Chita

Dzerzinsk

Angarsk

Cheremkhovo

Kaluga

Anzhero-Sudzhensk

Leninsk-Kuzenetski

Belovo

Kiselevsk

Kostromo

Kurgan

Syzran

Lipetsk

Babushkin

Kolomna

Kuntsevo

Orekhovo-Zuyevo

Perovo

Podolsk

Serpukhov

Orsk

Orel

Chusovoy

Shakhty

Novoshatinsk

Smolensk

Kamesnsk-Uralskiy

Tambov

Stalinogorsk

Tyumen

Vladimir

Kovrov

Vologda

Rybinsk

Sterlitimak

Ulan-Ude

Makhachkala

Petrozavosk

Ordshonikidze

Ashkhabad

Chernovtay

Dneprodzerhinsk

Kherson

Kirovgrad

Simferopol

Sevastopol

Kadiyevka

Poltava

Kramatorsk

Vinnitsa

Zhitomir
Andizhan
Kokand
Namangan
Samarakand

NOTES

Introduction

1. U.S. National Archives and Records Administration (USNARA), RG 218, CCS 354.2 U.S. (4-12-57), "Results Obtained from Ex DODEP, 12 April 1957," 22 April 1957; telex 12 April 1957; memo JCS to chief of naval operations (CNO), "Alert Ex 31 May 1957," 27 May 1957; memo Chief CP Cops to secretary of defense (SECDEF) and JCS, "Report of May Exercise of JCS Emergency Conference," 24 June 1957.

2. USNARA, RG 218, CCS 354.2 U.S. (4-12-57), "Results Obtained from Ex DODEP, 12 April 1957," 22 April 1957.

3. U.S. Navy Operational Archive (USNOA), Strategic Plans Division, box 315, file A-5, Op ALERT message traffic.

4. Kahan, *Security in the Nuclear Age*, 149.

5. Allison et al., *Hawks, Doves, and Owls*, ch. 3.

6. Sagan, *Moving Targets*, 11.

7. See Gaddis, *Strategies of Containment*.

8. Bruce Kuklick's *Blind Oracles* is but one example.

9. Rhodes, *Dark Sun*, 225.

10. Jervis, *The Illogic of American Nuclear Strategy*, 65.

11. This mantra was frequently employed when I was a graduate student in the early 1990s.

12. A proponent of the "irrelevance" argument is Mueller, *Retreat from Doomsday*.

13. See, for example, Anne Applebaum's trilogy *Gulag: A History*, *Iron Curtain: The Crushing of Eastern Europe 1944–1956*, and *Red Famine: Stalin's War on Ukraine*. See also Getty and Naumov, *The Road to Terror*; Amis, *Koba the Dread*; Conquest, *Reflections on a Ravaged Century*; Courtois et al., *The Black Book of Communism*.

14. Evans, *Blacklisted by History*; Hornblum, *The Invisible Harry Gold*; Rossiter, *The Spy Who Changed the World*; Carr, *Operation Whisper*; Albright and Kunstel, *Bombshell*.

15. As detailed in Andrew and Mitrokhin, *The Mitrokhin Archive II*; Haynes and Klehr, *In Denial*; Koch, *Double Lives*.

16. See Sarin and Dvoretsky, *Alien Wars*; Katz, *The Third World in Soviet Military Thought*; Patman, *The Soviet Union in the Horn of Africa*; Kaplan, *The Third World in Soviet Military Thought*.

17. See Fravel, *Active Defense*, chs. 3 and 4.

1. *Kami no itte*

1. Kenji Hall, "Japan's A-Bomb Goal Still a Long Way Off in '45," *Japan News,* 7 March 2003; "Wartime Documents Shed Light on Japan's Secret A-Bomb Program," *Asahi Shimbun,* 29 June 2015; Weiner, "Retroactive Saber Rattling?" See also Frank, *Downfall,* 253.

2. Gordin, *Five Days in August,* 10.

3. Norris, *Racing for the Bomb,* 380.

4. Overy, *The Bombers and the Bombed,* ch. 1.

5. Giangreco, *Hell to Pay,* 161; Frank, *Downfall,* ch. 6.

6. Norris, *Racing for the Bomb,* 381–85.

7. Thomas and Witts, *Ruin from the Air,* 75, 149; Norris, *Racing for the Bomb,* 381–88; Giangreco, *Hell to Pay,* 142.

8. Norris, *Racing for the Bomb,* 394.

9. Gordin, *Five Days in August,* 95–99.

10. Hoddeson et al., *Critical Assembly,* 126.

11. Szasz, *The Day the Sun Rose Twice,* 62–66, chs. 4 and 6. See also Defense Nuclear Agency Nuclear Test Personnel Review, Defense Nuclear Agency (DNA) 6028F, "Project TRINITY 1945–1946."

12. Though I do recognize that that debate's origins were an extension of the Second World War debate over the use of strategic bombing aircraft in support of nonstrategic objectives. Operation Cobra in Normandy in 1944 comes to mind, for example.

13. Giangreco, *Hell to Pay,* 142–43, 286–87; Gordin, *Five Days in August,* 101; Frank, *Downfall,* 313.

14. Harry H. Hubbell Jr. et al., ABCC Technical Report 3-69, "The Epicenters of the Atomic Bombs," and Shunzo Okajima et al., RERF Technical Report 12-75, "Effects of the Radioactive Fallout of the Nagasaki Atomic Bomb." Both available at Radiation Effects Research Foundation, https://www.rerf.or.jp/en/library/list-e/.

15. The latest assessment of the numbers can be found in Giangreco, *Hell to Pay.*

16. Frank, *Downfall,* 84.

17. As discussed in Reed and Stillman, *The Nuclear Express,* ch. 8.

18. See, for example, Steiner, *Bernard Brodie and the Foundations of American Nuclear Strategy,* ch. 1.

19. LeMay and Kantor, *Mission with LeMay,* 389.

20. Power and Arnhym, *Design for Survival,* 11–12.

21. Beria, *Beria My Father,* 112–13, 118–19. See also Kevin Kennedy, "Here Comes the D-Day Myth Again," History News Network, 6 June 2019, https://historynewsnetwork .org/article/172164.

2. Per Ardua ad Atomica

1. Wolk, *The Struggle for Air Force Independence,* 131.

2. Jordan, *Norstad,* 37.

3. Meilinger, *Hoyt S. Vandenberg,* 37–40. For a historiographical take on Frantic, see Brad Miller, "The Great Experiment: Remembering Operation Frantic, 1944–1945," Lviv Polytechnic Electronic Scientific Archive, 2012, http://ena.lp.edu.ua:8080/bitstream/ntb /27854/1/020-103-111.pdf.

4. Library of Congress Manuscript Division (LCMD), Vandenberg Papers, box 63. See the entire folder titled "Special Secret Activities: A Personal Report to the Commanding General, 14 April 1945." The enclosed material spills over into 1946.

5. Wolk, *The Struggle for Air Force Independence*, 131–32.

6. This document is cited in Ham, *Hiroshima Nagasaki*, 488–89, but it is decontextualized and then distorted by Ham's overblown language (e.g., "the Pentagon had written the death sentence of America's next enemy"). The full document, derived from USNARA RG 77 microfilm dealing with the Manhattan Engineering District, is available on Alex Wallerstein's blog, "The First Stockpile Requirements (September 1945)," 9 May 2012, http://blog.nuclearsecrecy.com/2012/05/09/weekly-document-the-first-atomic-stockpile-requirements-september-1945/, where Wallerstein graciously stitched together the Photostatted pieces of the map for our viewing.

7. Ham, *Hiroshima Nagasaki*, 488–89.

8. The document has been employed over the years by American journalists and activists in a decontextualized way to "prove" that the United States was planning a first strike. The document is currently employed in Russian influence operations, in some cases alongside decontextualized depictions of the Dropshot study, to "prove" the United States was planning a first strike in order to justify current Russian behavior. An example of this distortion is the short film *Watch the US Nuclear Strike on 66 Soviet Cities*, which shows up on YouTube, youtube.com/watch?v=yRBgb89jZtk (in Russian), and its Russian equivalents: diana-mihailova.livejournal.com/1408607.html. The War Chronicle website, as well as Topwar.ru, Newsrambler.ru, and countless other Russian military and news platforms proliferate this specific material.

9. LCMD, Vandenberg Papers, box 63, "Presentation Given to President by Major General Lauris Norstad on 29 October 1946."

10. LCMD, Vandenberg Papers, box 63, "Presentation Given to President by Major General Lauris Norstad on 29 October 1946."

11. LCMD, Vandenberg Papers, box 63, "Presentation Given to President by Major General Lauris Norstad on 29 October 1946."

12. Four overlapping Pincher documents were consulted for this book: Joint War Plans Committee, "Strategic Study of Western Europe, 15 May 1947"; Joint Strategic Plans, "Concept of Operations for PINCHER, 2 March 1946"; Staff Studies, "Problems Derived from Concept of Operations for PINCHER, 13 April 1946"; and JWPC, "Joint Basic Outline Plan Short Title: PINCHER, 27 April 1946." These can be found in the University Press of America microfilm collection, Records of the Joint Chiefs of Staff, Part 2, 1945–53: US and USSR.

13. Rosenberg, "US Nuclear Stockpile."

14. As discussed in Barlow, *Revolt of the Admirals*, ch. 3. See Weisgall, *Operation Crossroads*.

15. Wolk, *The Struggle for Air Force Independence*, 131.

16. LeMay and Kantor, *Mission with LeMay*, 335.

17. Morrison, *Point of No Return*, 115–16.

18. LeMay and Kantor, *Mission with LeMay*, 397; Coffey, *Iron Eagle*, ch. 15. On RAND, see Collins, *Cold War Laboratory*, ch. 2.

19. Kozak, *LeMay*, 272–73.

20. LeMay and Kantor spend ten pages on the "Utah affair" in *Mission with LeMay*, 142–52; on Guam, 340. On leaks, see Giangreco, *Hell to Pay*, 125; Coffey, *Iron Eagle*, 254.

21. Lapp, *Kill and Overkill*, 56.

22. James P. Delgado et al., "Assessment of the Deep Sea Wreck USS *Independence*," Frontiers in Marine Science, 12 July 2016, https://www.frontiersin.org/articles/10.3389/fmars.2016.00080/full.

23. FOIA USAF, "A History of the Air Force Atomic Energy Program 1943–1953 Introduction and Chapter 1: Project SILVERPLATE, 1943–1946," 299–314. See also DNA 6032F, "Operation CROSSROADS 1946" for the missing data.

24. FOIA USAF, "A History of the Air Force Atomic Energy Program 1943–1953 Introduction and Chapter 1: Project SILVERPLATE, 1943–1946," 351.

25. FOIA USAF, "A History of the Air Force Atomic Energy Program 1943–1953 Introduction and Chapter 1: Project SILVERPLATE, 1943–1946," 363–65.

26. Wolk, *The Struggle for Air Force Independence*, 132–33; FOIA USAF, "A History of the Air Force Atomic Energy Program 1943–1953 Introduction and Chapter 1: Project SILVERPLATE, 1943–1946," 371.

27. Garbinski, *North River Depot*, 11–21; On the Mk-3, see Furman, *Sandia National Laboratories*, 267–71. Rosenberg, "US Nuclear Stockpile."

28. See Meilinger, *Bomber*; Borowski, *A Hollow Threat*; Kaplan, *To Kill Nations*; Rosenberg, "Origins of Overkill"; Curatola, *Bigger Bombs for a Brighter Tomorrow*.

29. See Grynkewich, "Advisable in the National Interest." Note that Grynkewich goes into detail on the personality issues surrounding Kenney. I agree that this was a major contributor to his relief, but there is not enough space to go into this fascinating subject here.

30. Grynkewich, "Advisable in the National Interest." See also LeMay and Kantor, *Mission with LeMay*, 431.

31. As quoted in Grynkewich, "Advisable in the National Interest," 5.

32. Ross, *American War Plans*, ch. 3; FOIA (USAF) Robert D. Little, "A History of the Air Force Atomic Energy Program 1943–1953 Vol. 3 Building an Atomic Air Force 1949–1953," 143.

33. Ross, *American War Plans*, 56–57.

34. Thanks to Harald Rabeder for his extensive knowledge of Luftwaffe Aufklarungs operations. In his extensive Luftwaffe aerial photo archive at www.wwii-photos-maps .com, which unfortunately is no longer operative, one could see the high quality of the images. Some images had English wording placed over the German, indicating their reuse by the USAF.

35. FOIA USAF, "Interview with Colonel Robert Work, Prepared by The History Office HQ Air Intelligence Agency, 30 July 1999."

36. FOIA CIA, Information Report, "Cracking Refinery at Ufa, 10 March 1952."

37. FOIA CIA, Information Report, "UAZ Aluminum Plant near Kamensk," 28 November 1952.

38. This little-known organization was a mini intelligence agency in its own right. FOIA CIA, memo for DCI, "Additional Air Force Requirements for the Anders Collection," 14 February 1951; see also FOIA CIA, "Research Aid: The Air Information Division of the Library of Congress," 30 April 1956.

39. Cloud, "American Cartographic Transformations during the Cold War." See also FOIA CIA, M-12 study "Mil-Geo: The Geographic Service of the German Army," September 1951.

40. Meilinger, *Hoyt S. Vandenberg*, 35–39.

41. Luftwaffe imagery of Saratov airframe plant was available at www.wwii-photos -maps.com, but the site is no longer active. See FOIA CIA, Central Intelligence Group (CIG) Intelligence Report, "Industrial Information: Aircraft Factory at Saratov, 20 August 1947"; Information Report, "Aircraft Observed over Saratov, 25 October 1949"; Information Report, "Construction of a New Aircraft Plant in Saratov, 31 March 50"; Information Report, "Jet Fighter Observed at the Factory Field of Airframe Plant No. 292 in Saratov, 15 December 50" (includes the accurate sketch of a MiG 15); Information Report, "Industrial Installations I Southwest Saratov, 5 June 51"; Information Report, "Aircraft Plant No. 292 at Saratov, 13 March 52"; Office of Research and Reports (ORR), "A Limited Analysis of the Saratov Aircraft Engine Plant No. 292, 26 September 1956"; ORR, "Estimated Floorspace of Saratov Aircraft Plant No. 292, 23 July 1957"; Information Report, "Airframe Plant No. 292 in Saratov, 8 January 1959"; Photographic Intelligence Center, "Airframe Plant 292 and South Airfield, Saratov, USSR, July 1960"; Photographic Intelligence Committee (PIC), "Saratov Airframe Plant No. 292 Saratov USSR, October 1964"; National Photo Interpretation Center (NPIC), "Saratov Airframe Plant 292, July 1969."

42. I cross-indexed all twenty-four cities on the JWPC 486/7 list with historic USAF and CIA analysis. The original target data from Luftwaffe and intelligence sources from the 1940s remained viable and accurate for all twenty-four cities as their industrial apparatus evolved throughout the Cold War.

43. FOIA CIA, NPIC, "Kazan Airframe Plant Gorbu, November 22, September 1980"; FOIA CIA, NPIC, "BLINDER in Flight, Kazan Area, USSR, 20 November 64"; FOIA CIA, NPIC, "BEAR H Probably in Production, 23 March 1984"; FOIA CIA, NPIC, "Moscow Fili Airframe Plant No. 23, 1965"; FOIA CIA, NPIC, "New Generation Delta-Wing Aircraft at Novosibirsk Airfield West USSR, July 1966."

44. FOIA CIA, Information Report, "Aircraft Observed over Kazan, 29 December 49." Note the sketch of the TU-4 attached. See also FOIA CIA, Information Report, "Production of TU-4 Aircraft at Aircraft Plant No. 22 Kazan, 10 March 1952."

45. FOIA CIA, Photographic Interpretation Report (PIR), "Aircraft Engine Plant No. 45, Moscow USSR, May 1965"; PIR, memo, "Moscow Airframe Plant #30, 26 June 1956"; Information Report, "V-2 Experiments at Moscow/Khimki and Plants Nos. 301 and 456, 20 February 52"; PIR, "Moscow Tushino Plants No. 82 and No. 500, June 1964"; PIR, "Index of Aerospace Installations in the Moscow Area, February 1968."

46. Ross, *American War Plans*, 68–69.

47. Barlow, *Revolt of the Admirals*, 115–16.

48. Miller, *Nuclear Weapons and Aircraft Carriers*, 81–87.

49. LeMay and Kantor, *Mission with LeMay*, 440.

50. FOIA USAF, "A History of the Air Force Atomic Energy Program 1943–1953 Introduction and Chapter 1: Project SILVERPLATE, 1943–1946," 372.

51. FOIA USAF, "A History of the Air Force Atomic Energy Program 1943–1953 Introduction and Chapter 1: Project SILVERPLATE, 1943–1946," 393–97.

52. Sean Maloney, "SAC and Canada," unpublished paper, 2015.

53. Maloney, "SAC and Canada."

54. FOIA USAF, "A History of the Air Force Atomic Energy Program 1943–1953 Introduction and Chapter 1: Project SILVERPLATE, 1943–1946," 393–405. See also Lloyd, *A Cold War Legacy*, 103.

55. LCMD, Vandenberg Papers, box 38; see Vandenberg's 16 March 1948 "Blitz Book."

56. Maloney, "SAC and Canada."

57. Records of the JCS, reel 5, JCS and the Soviet Union frames 0092–0117 (6 May 1948), JCS, "Brief of Short-Range Emergency War Plan DOUBLESTAR/FLEETWOOD/HALFMOON."

58. LCMD, Vandenberg Papers, box 38, "Blitz Book."

59. Rosenberg, "Origins of Overkill," 16; Ross, American War Plans, 83–84.

60. LCMD, Vandenberg Papers, box 38, "Blitz Book."

61. See Anne Fitzpatrick, "Igniting the Light Elements: The Los Alamos Thermonuclear Weapon Project, 1942–1952," Thesis LA-13577-T, Los Alamos National Laboratory, July 1999, 248.

62. Miller, To Save a City, 24. See also FOIA USAF, "7th Air Division, Strategic Air Command, January–June 1952." U.S. ambassador Lewin Douglas made a verbal but enduring agreement with Bevin on the use of four British bases by the USAF: Upper Heyford, Fairford, Brize Norton, and Greenham Common.

63. LeMay and Kantor, Mission with LeMay, 411–12; Lloyd, A Cold War Legacy, 107.

64. Lloyd, A Cold War Legacy, 107–8; Polmar, Strategic Air Command, 15–16.

65. Polmar also notes in Strategic Air Command that in 1946 six B-29s deployed to Rhein-Main air base and flew along the Yugoslav border in response to the shoot-down of a pair of American transports by Yugoslav fighters and that this was the first instance of "signaling" using B-29s. The specifics of how this was ordered and by whom require more research.

66. LeMay and Kantor, Mission with LeMay, 431.

67. FOIA OSD, Ernest May et al., "History of the Strategic Arms Competition 1945–1972 Part I, March 1981," 40.

68. FOIA (USAF) Robert D. Little, "A History of the Air Force Atomic Energy Program 1943–1953 Vol. III Building an Atomic Air Force 1949–1953," 143; Ross, American War Plans, 97.

69. Special Collections Research Center (SCRC), Power Papers, box 2, letter from Hackett to Power, 27 December 1948.

70. "Strength Keeps Peace: LeMay," Nebraska State Journal, 15 February 1949.

71. Lloyd, A Cold War Legacy, 136; "B-50 Circles World Non-Stop," Lubbock Evening Journal, 2 March 1949; "Tucson B-50 Circles Globe in 4-Day Nonstop Flight," Tucson Daily Citizen, 2 March 1949.

72. Cold War–era literature completely downplays the B-29 deployment from the Soviet view, which is interesting as these writers did not have access to Soviet sources. Examples include Taubman, Stalin's American Policy, chs. 7 and 8; Ulam, Expansion and Coexistence, 454; George and Smoke, Deterrence in American Foreign Policy, ch. 5.

73. Andrew and Mitrokhin, The Mitrokhin Archive, ch. 9.

74. Volkogonov, Stalin, 537.

75. Djilas, Rise and Fall, 155, 169.

76. Beria, Beria My Father, 206.

77. Beria, Beria My Father, 206.

3. Imminence of War I

1. Chang and Halliday, Mao, 354.

2. Scholarship from the 1980s and 1990s arguing that the United States provoked the Korean War has been decisively refuted by material that has emerged from Russian and

Chinese archives. See Chang and Halliday, *Mao*, chs. 34 and 35; Jian, *Mao's China and the Cold War*, ch. 3; Dikoetter, *The Tragedy of Liberation*, ch. 7; see particularly Zhang, *Red Wings over the Yalu*.

3. FOIA (USAF) Robert D. Little, "A History of the Air Force Atomic Energy Program 1943–1953 Vol. III Building an Atomic Air Force 1949–1953," 143–45.

4. FOIA (USAF) Robert D. Little, "A History of the Air Force Atomic Energy Program 1943–1953 Vol. III Building an Atomic Air Force 1949–1953"; Ross, *American War Plans*, 86–97.

5. FOIA OSD, Memorandum for the Joint Chiefs of Staff, "Report on Evaluation of the Effectiveness of Strategic Air Operations, 8 February 1950."

6. Brown, DROPSHOT, 194–206.

7. LCMD, Twining Papers, box 94, "Strategic Air Command Progress Analysis 1 November 1948–31 December 1956"; LCMD, LeMay Papers, box B-193, memo Sallanger to Montgomery, "Comments on the Initial Atomic Strike Capability of SAC," 12 September 1950; FOIA OSD, Memorandum for the Joint Chiefs of Staff, "Report on Evaluation of the Effectiveness of Strategic Air Operations, 8 February 1950."

8. LCMD, LeMay Papers, box B-60, letter Twining to LeMay, 9 June 1955.

9. FOIA OSD, Memorandum for the Joint Chiefs of Staff, "Report on Evaluation of the Effectiveness of Strategic Air Operations, 8 February 1950."

10. Poole, *The Joint Chiefs of Staff and National Policy*, 85.

11. Which itself was influenced by Operation Chastise, the RAF "Dambusters" raid. Speer, *Inside the Third Reich*, 365–69.

12. The definitive work on the TU-4 is Gordon et al., *Tupolev TU-4*. See also Zaloga, *The Kremlin's Nuclear Sword*, ch. 1; FOIA CIA, SNIE 11-7A-54, "Soviet Gross Capabilities for Attacks on the US and Key Overseas Installations through 1 July 1957," 14 September 1954; FOIA CIA, "Current Intelligence Bulletin," 17 July 1952; FOIA CIA, "Current Intelligence Bulletin," 18 June 1954, where analysts believe that aerial refueling exercises were conducted in the interior "for some time" before they were first detected elsewhere in 1954.

13. FOIA CIA, "Current Intelligence Bulletin," 27 February 1953.

14. FOIA CIA, "Current Intelligence Bulletin," 26 March 1954; FOIA CIA, "Current Intelligence Bulletin," 1 July 1954.

15. LCMD, LeMay Papers, box B-192, memo LeMay to Findletter, 23 March 1950.

16. LCMD, LeMay Papers, box B-192, memo Vandenberg to LeMay, 1 April 1950.

17. LCMD, LeMay Papers, box B-193, "Topical Study Monographs: Maneuver of June 1950."

18. LCMD, LeMay Papers, box B-193, "Topical Study Monographs: Maneuver of June 1950," 81; Rosenberg, "Origins of Overkill."

19. LCMD, LeMay Papers, box B-192, memo LeMay to Dops and Plans, "Priority for the Atomic Offensive," 27 June 1950.

20. LCMD, LeMay Papers, box B-194, "Minutes of the Third Meeting of the Target Panel, 7 March 1951."

21. LCMD, LeMay Papers, box B-194, "Minutes of the Third Meeting of the Target Panel: Briefing to the Target Panel."

22. SCRC, Power Papers, box 2, letter Power to Schlatter, 22 November 1948.

23. LCMD, LeMay Papers, box B-51, letter Cabell to LeMay, 7 January 1949.

24. Morrison, *Point of No Return*, 91.

25. LCMD, LeMay Papers, box B-194, "Minutes of the Third Meeting of the Target Panel, 7 March 1951."

26. LCMD, LeMay Papers, box B-194, "Minutes of the Third Meeting of the Target Panel, 7 March 1951"; LCMD, LeMay Papers, box B-194, letter LeMay to Moore, 3 March 1951; LCMD, LeMay Papers, box B-194, letter Cabell to LeMay, 5 April 1951; LCMD, Twining Papers, box 54, memo DCS/Ops, 18 April 1951. There was an overlapping debate over Circular Error Probable that is too detailed to get into here that had a direct bearing on Weapons Systems Evaluation Group (WSEG), AEC, JCS, and weapons requirements. Again, because SAC had its act together, could speak with a unified voice with compelling data, and was prepared to do so, it eventually got all of the goodies it wanted.

27. LCMD, LeMay Papers, box B-195, letter White to LeMay, 9 October 1951.

28. LCMD, LeMay Papers, box B-195, letter White to LeMay, 9 October 1951; LCMD, LeMay Papers, box B-194, letter LeMay to Moore, 3 March 1951; LCMD, LeMay Papers, box B-194, letter Cabell to LeMay, 5 April 1951; LCMD, Twining Papers, box 54, memo DCS/Ops, 18 April 1951.

29. Rosenberg, "Origins of Overkill"; Poole, *The Joint Chiefs of Staff and National Policy*, 85–86.

30. LCMD, LeMay Papers, box B-196, Briefing deck, 4 January 1952.

31. LCMD, Twining Papers, box 94, "Strategic Air Command Progress Analysis 1 November 1948–31 December 1956." Note that a wing of B-47s was available by the end of 1953, but teething problems prevented it from being considered fully combat ready.

32. LCMD, LeMay Papers, box B-194, message LeMay to Vandenberg, 15 January 1951; LCMD, LeMay Papers, box B-195, LeMay to Vandenberg, 9 August 1951; LCMD, LeMay Papers, box B-199, LeMay to Vandenberg, 5 December 1952.

33. U.S. Department of Energy (DOE), RDD-7, "Restricted Data Declassification Decisions 1946 to Present," 1 January 2001.

34. FOIA USAF, "History of the 44th Bombardment Wing (M), January–June 1954."

35. The terms "core" and "pit" are sometimes used interchangeably. An example of this is the congressional research study by Jonathan E. Medalia, "US Nuclear Weapon Pit Production: Options for Congress," 21 February 2014. In the 1940s and 1950s they were two separate things.

36. Letter to the author from Vice Adm. John T. Hayward, 9 July 1991. See also Fitzpatrick, "Igniting the Light Elements."

37. Hansen, *US Nuclear Weapons*, 148.

38. LCMD, LeMay Papers, box B-199, "SAC Commander's Conference, 19 January 1953."

39. LCMD, LeMay Papers, box B-196, LeMay address to Air War College, 9 June 1952.

40. See Coffey, *Decision over Schweinfurt*, 3–20, 69–91, 143–44.

41. Power was deputy commander of the 304th Bombardment Wing from January to April 1944. The 304th Bombardment Wing conducted repeated missions against aircraft factories in Austria and against Ploesti during this time. Power flew B-24s on these missions.

42. LCMD, LeMay Papers, box B-194, letter Cabell to LeMay, 5 April 1951.

43. Indeed the draconian secrecy imposed today by the Department of Energy on release of 1950s nuclear weapons requirements and capability information to researchers is directly related to the now obsolete need to keep production and stockpile figures from the same period secret.

44. LCMD, LeMay Papers, box B-196, LeMay address to Air War College, 9 June 1952.

45. Author's discussions with personnel who served in the Joint Strategic Target Planning Staff. The JCS definition was very general: "a geographical area, complex, or installation planned for capture or destruction by military forces." U.S. Department of Defense, *Dictionary of Military Terms*, 352.

46. The retroactive debate over blast and fire effects is handled in detail in Eden, *The Whole World on Fire*. Johnstone defends the focus on blast effects in *From Mad to Madness*, 86–88.

47. In the absence of access to the actual EWP 1-49 planning documents, this depiction is based on WSEG-1 in 1950; the SAC briefing to JCS in 1951, as discussed in Poole, *The Joint Chiefs of Staff and National Policy*; 1952 SAC data used for establishing future bomber requirements in LCMD, LeMay Papers, box B-54, Consolidated Aviation, "MX-1964 Supplement to Basic Proposal." Note the map depicting the "top ten industrial target areas." Extensive analysis of Wringer and CIA data on the targets for the 1950–53 period conforms to these areas on a year-by-year basis and confirms the 1950–52 target evolution.

48. LCMD, LeMay Papers, box B-193, memo for Secretary of the Air Force from Anderson, 15 August 50. Note that these subplans were given titles like EWP 2-50 and EWP 1-53 but were not necessarily accepted as replacements for EWP 1-49 by the JCS. Instead EWP 1-49 remained the overall accepted concept, and these other plans were dubbed "Alternate Emergency War Plans." See LCMD, LeMay Papers, box 193, letter LeMay to Norstad, 2 September 1950. See also box B-199, SAC Commander's Conference, 20 November 1952. Note that the JCS was revising its own planning processes during this time as well.

49. Jackson, *Strike Force*, ch. 2.

50. Lloyd, *A Cold War Legacy*, 232–33.

51. LCMD, LeMay Papers, box B-194, message Edwards to LeMay, 26 February 1951.

52. LCMD, LeMay Papers, box B-193, memo for Secretary of the Air Force from Anderson, 15 August 1950. See also LCMD, LeMay Papers, box B-196, basing map, 4 January 1952.

53. LCMD, LeMay Papers, box B-196, Briefing deck, 4 January 1952 E+1 to E+5 deployment slides.

54. LCMD, LeMay Papers, box 200, "Field Representative Europe Report on Ex PROPHECY, Part II, 3 March 53."

55. FOIA CIA, Information Report, "Red October Steel Plant in Stalingrad," 28 April 1954; FOIA CIA, Information Report, "Red Barricade Ordnance Plant No. 221," 5 December 1952; FOIA CIA, Information Report, "Lazur Chemical Factory in Stalingrad," 15 March 1952; FOIA CIA, Information Report, "Dzerzhinsky Tractor Factory in Stalingrad," 10 May 1954; FOIA CIA, Information Report, "Construction of a New Aluminum Plant Near Stalingrad," 28 April 1955.

56. LCMD, LeMay Papers, box 54, letter Johnson to LeMay, 1 July 1949; USNARA via National Security Archive, "Presentation by the Strategic Air Command, Commander's Conference United States Air Force, Ramey Air Force Base, 25-26-27 April 1950."

57. Gellately, *Stalin's Curse*, 62.

58. USNARA via National Security Archive, "Presentation by the Strategic Air Command, Commander's Conference United States Air Force, Ramey Air Force Base, 25-26-27 April 1950."

59. FOIA USAF, "Supplement to the 11th Bombardment Wing (H) History, 19th Air Division, June 52"; LCMD, LeMay Papers, box B-194, USAF Inspector General, "Report on

Strategic Air Command Capabilities to Initiate and Sustain Combat Operations," 19 March 1951; LCMD, LeMay Papers, box 200, message 14 February 1953; LCMD, LeMay Papers, box 200, "Briefing Notes on Change of Status of Command Since General LeMay's last Visit: Operations," 14 February 1953.

60. LCMD, LeMay Papers, box 193, letter Sallanger to Montgomery, "Comments on Initial Atomic Strike Capability of SAC," 12 September 1950. See also USAF Inspector General, "Report on Strategic Air Command Capabilities to Initiate and Sustain Combat Operations," 19 March 1951; LCMD, LeMay Papers, box 193, letter Atkinson to LeMay, 21 August 1950.

61. USNARA via National Security Archive, "Presentation by the Strategic Air Command, Commander's Conference United States Air Force, Ramey Air Force Base, 25-26-27 April 1950."

62. LCMD, LeMay Papers, box 193, "Topical Study Monographs, 1950: June 1950 Exercise"; LCMD, LeMay Papers, box B-193, message Old to LeMay, 30 August 1950; LCMD, LeMay Papers, box B-199, letter Old to LeMay, 21 November 1952.

63. Dwight D. Eisenhower Presidential Library (DDEL), memo Dulles to Eisenhower, 3 March 1953, https://www.eisenhowerlibrary.gov/sites/default/files/research/online-documents/declassified/fy-2012/1953-03-03.pdf; LCMD, LeMay Papers, box B-199, message McConnell to LeMay, 5 December 1952; LCMD, LeMay Papers, box B-195, letter Anderson to LeMay, 6 June 1951. See also LCMD, LeMay Papers, box B-199, message 7 Air Division to SAC, 6 December 1952, where the Special Duty Flight RB-45Cs and their KB-29 tankers were allegedly in Norwegian airspace, causing a diplomatic "flap."

64. LCMD, LeMay Papers, box B-202, letter Musgrave to LeMay, 16 September 1954.

65. See LCMD, Twining Papers, box 55, memo to Twining, "Briefing on Yugoslavian Personnel whom you will meet Monday at 0900," 8 June 1951. It is not clear what was discussed exactly beyond the Mutal Defense Aid Plan. In FRUS 1951, vol. 4, part 2, memo Burns to Harriman, 26 January 1951, baldly states that Yugoslavia was to be treated with a "priority equal to that of the NATO countries." It is unlikely that status came without a quid pro quo. See also FOIA CIA, "Current Intelligence Bulletin, 30 September 1951." The context of the situation is aptly provided by Péter Vukman, "'The War of Nerves': The Role of the United Kingdom in Military Assistance to Yugoslavia during the Soviet-Yugoslav Conflict, 1948–1953," Cold War History Research Center, Budapest, December 2010, http://www.coldwar.hu/publications/Publication_Vukman_2010.pdf. Compared to Sweden, this one is harder to pin down, and SAC overflight arrangements may have gone unrecorded because of their sensitivity.

66. LCMD, LeMay Papers, box B-196, Bull briefing, operating and staging map.

67. LCMD, LeMay Papers, box B-198, "SAC Commander's Conference, 25 August 52"; LCMD, LeMay Papers, box B-200, message FEAFBC to LeMay, 26 July 1953; LCMD, LeMay Papers, box B-195, "Post Strike Staging of SAC Aircraft," 6 June 1951; LCMD, LeMay Papers, box B-197, "SAC Commander's Conference, 2 June 1952"; LCMD, LeMay Papers, box B-199, message SAC to Alaska Command, 24 December 1952. Torbay, Newfoundland, was originally considered but was abandoned in favor of Keflavik.

68. LCMD, LeMay Papers, box B-195, "Post Strike Staging of SAC Aircraft," 6 June 1951; LCMD, LeMay Papers, box B-199, letter Old to LeMay, 21 November 1952.

69. LDMD, LeMay Papers, box B-199, letter Old to LeMay, 21 November 1952.

70. Davis, "USAF War Readiness Materiel."

71. Range data for the B-36 variants and models is from Knaack, *Post–World War II Bombers*, 54–55. See FOIA USAF, SAC "Final Report: Operation BIG STICK, 19 Aug–4 September 53." See also Edmundson, "Six Churnin' and Four Burnin.'"

72. FOIA CIA, National Intelligence Estimate (NIE), "NIE 11-2A-63: The Soviet Atomic Energy Program," 2 July 1963; FOIA CIA, memo Chief of Station Karlsruhe to distribution list, "REDSOX/CARCASS Project: Operational Requirements in Support of CARCASS Missions," 9 January 1952; FOIA CIA, Henry S. Lowenhaupt, "On the Soviet Nuclear Scent," CIA Historical Review Program, 2 July 1996.

73. See the following FOIA CIA Information Reports: "War Plant at Tura in the Urals," 22 December 1948; "Atom Bomb Plant in Armenia," 20 July 1950; "Atomic City in 'Soviet Ruhr' Employs 62,000 Specialists," 24 July 1950; "The Atomic Bomb Potential of the USSR," 23 July 1951; "Max Vollmer, German Scientist in the USSR," 22 September 1952; "Five Atomic Centers in USSR," 7 October 1952; "German Scientists in the USSR," 11 June 1953; "Soviet Atom Plants," 23 November 1953; "Transportation and Security Information on Chelyabinsk, Kyshtym, Kasali Area," 6 December 1954. Note particularly the presence of disinformation or fabrication, particularly in the open-source intelligence, related to the facilities in Armenia. Note also that the USAF was targeting the Glazov plant at least by 1954, probably earlier: NPIC Photographic Intelligence Board (PIB), "Uranium Metals Plant, Glazov, USSR," August 1961.

74. For a detailed examination of the evolution of the Soviet atomic bomb enterprise by facility, see Yury A. Yudin, "Manuscript on the History of the Soviet Nuclear Weapons and Nuclear Infrastructure, Technical Report on Tasks A-1 and A-2," DocPlayer, n.d., https:// docplayer.net/19674840-Manuscript-on-the-history-of-the-soviet-nuclear-weapons-and -nuclear-infrastructure.html.

75. Scrivner, "Pioneer into Space," 351.

76. See Yudin, "Manuscript on the History of the Soviet Nuclear Weapons and Nuclear Infrastructure," for facilities by location; FOIA CIA, memo for Project Director, Ad Hoc Requirements Committee, "Review of Requirements," 24 October 1957.

77. LCMD, LeMay Papers, box B-195, letter White to LeMay, 9 October 1951.

78. LCMD, LeMay Papers, box B-196, address to Air War College, "Essential Considerations in the Conduct of Strategic Air Operations," 9 January 1952.

79. LCMD, LeMay Papers, box B-196, memo LeMay to Vandenberg, 4 January 1952. See also SAC to HQ USAF, "Report of Deficiencies Affecting Combat Capability," 15 November 1951.

80. It is interesting to note the yield of this test, 42 kilotons, is similar to Sandstone X-Ray and Yoke (37 and 49 kt). Klaus Fuchs provided the levitated pit and composite core technologies to the Soviets in 1948, and they were able to implement them in under two years. The Soviets were able to reduce the diameter of their weapons using this technology. See Yudin, "Manuscript on the History of the Soviet Nuclear Weapons and Nuclear Infrastructure."

81. FOIA CIA, Information Reports: "Enlargement of Tartu Airfield," 29 September 1948; "Tartu Airfield," 8 June 1954 (see sketch of Tartu Airfield); "Tartu Airfield," 16 October 1950; "Konotop Airfield," 6 February 1952; "Bobriusk Airfield," 5 May 1950; multiple reports, 13 February 1950 (see sketch of Bobriusk Airfield).

82. Gordon et al., *Tupolev TU-4*, ch. 6.

83. FOIA CIA, Information Report, "Production of TU-4 Aircraft at Aircraft Plant No. 22 in Kazan," 10 March 1952.

84. FOIA CIA, Information Reports: "Production of TU-4 Aircraft at Aircraft Plant No. 22 in Kazan," 10 March 1952; "Enlargement of Tartu Airfield," 29 September 1948; "Tartu Airfield," 8 June 1954; "Tartu Airfield," 16 October 1950; "Konotop Airfield," 6 February 1952; "Bobriusk Airfield," 5 May 1950; multiple reports, 13 February 1950.

85. LCMD, LeMay Papers, box B-196, address to Air War College, "Essential Considerations in the Conduct of Strategic Air Operations," 9 January 1952.

86. Gordon et al., *Tupolev TU-4*, ch. 7.

87. LCMD, LeMay Papers, box B-195, message 8AF to LeMay, 31 October 1951; LCMD, LeMay Papers, box B-195, study, "Vulnerability of North East Airbases," 8 October 1951; LCMD, LeMay Papers, box B-195, letter LeMay to Anderson, 23 November 1951.

88. Aldrich, GCHQ, 119.

89. FOIA CIA, Information Report, "Survey of TU-4 Operational Airfields in East Germany," 8 February 1952. See also LCMD, Twining Papers, box 120, "Briefing for Secretary Finletter: The Mission of the Alaskan Command and Problems Entailed in Its Accomplishment, 15 December 1950." The bases in East Germany and Poland are closer by air to North America than comparable facilities in the Leningrad-Moscow area.

90. FOIA CIA, "Current Intelligence Bulletin," 31 October 1953.

91. E.L., "Secret History: How Close Were Finnish-American Relations during the Cold War," *Economist*, December 1, 2011, https://www.economist.com/eastern-approaches/2011/12/01/secret-history. For Finnish bases, see "Finland: Air Bases during the Cold War," Military Airfield Directory, https://www.mil-airfields.de/fi-finnland/flugplaetze.html.

92. LCMD, LeMay Papers, message McConnell to LeMay, 8 July 1952.

93. Hall, "The Truth about Overflights." See Sqn. Ldr. John Crampton's reminiscences on his participation in the operation in Royal Air Force Historical Society, *Journal No. 23*, 97–99, and Royal Air Force Historical Society, *Air Intelligence Symposium Bracknell Paper No. 7*.

94. The best estimate based on geographical grouping is that the Baltic penetration collected on Tartu and Solsti; the Belarusian penetration got material on Baranovichi, Bobruisk, Bykhov, and Dyagilevo; while the Ukrainian penetration got Balbasavo, Poltava, Priluki, Belaya Tserkov, and Lebedin. At least one aircraft penetrated as far as Moscow to collect on Dyagilevo, which lay slightly southeast of the city.

95. LCMD, LeMay Papers, box B-196, letter LeMay to Vandenberg, 2 January 1952; LCMD, LeMay Papers, box 200, message LeMay to Twining, 24 March 1953.

96. FOIA CIA, Information Report, "Soviet Airfields in the Northern Area," 5 March 1954.

97. FOIA CIA, "Soviet Long-Range Aircraft Capability: Western USSR," 11 February 1957.

98. Solsti, Bykhov, Poltava, and Belaya. FOIA CIA, "BACKFIRE Deployment, USSR," map, 1977.

99. See DNA 6020F, United States Atmospheric Nuclear Weapons Tests Nuclear Test Personal Review, "Shots ABLE, BAKER, CHARLIE and DOG: The First Tests of the TUMBLER-SNAPPER Series 1 April–1 May 1952."

100. Zimmerman, *Insider at SAC*, 53.

101. FOIA CIA, Information Reports: "Moscow-Fili Aircraft Engine Plant," 7 February 1950; "V-2 Experiments at Moscow/Khimki ad Plants Nos. 301 and 456," 20 February 1952; "Military Aircraft Armaments Plants at Moscow-Khimki Airfield," 3 May 1950; "Aircraft

Engine Plant No. 500 in Moscow-Tushino," 11 May 1950; "Aircraft Engine Plant No. 45 in Moscow," 23 May 1950; "Aircraft at Moscow-Khimki Airfield," 7 February 1952; "Installations and V-Weapon Launchings at Moscow/Khimki Airfield," 20 February 1952; "Industrial Plants in Moscow Region," 16 April 1952; "EF-Type Aircraft Development at Zavod No. 1, Observations at Moscow/Ramenskoye," 6 February 1953; NPIC, "Moscow Tushino Plants No. 82 and No. 500, USSR, June 1964"; NPIC, "Moscow Airframe Plant Fili No. 23, USSR December 1964"; NPIC, "Aircraft Engine Plant No. 45, Moscow USSR, May 1965"; NPIC, "Moscow Central Airfield, June 1981."

102. USAF, Air Information Division Structural Engineering Section, Library of Congress, "Thermal Electric Power Plants of the USSR: Report No. 92 Volume II, September 1957."

103. Zimmerman, *Insider at SAC*, 55.

104. Zimmerman, *Insider at SAC*, 56.

105. FOIA CIA, Information Report, "Locations of Military and Other Important Offices in Moscow," 29 June 1962. I recognize that this map dates from 1962, but the information would have been available in 1950 from embassy and other sources.

106. FOIA CIA, Information Report, "Depth of the Moscow Subway System," 8 May 1950.

107. See Bunker-42 on Taganka, "History 'Bunker 42,'" http://bunker42.com/eng /nasha-istoriya.php. The 47-kiloton assessment is mine.

108. In "Origins of Overkill" Rosenberg quotes Bernard Brodie as having been present when such machinations were undertaken. See also Zimmerman, *Insider at SAC*, 53.

109. Radzinsky, *Stalin*, 556.

110. FOIA CIA, Air Intelligence Information Report, "AA Positions: Moscow Area," 1953. I superimposed the SA-1 Guild deployment map onto the map attached to this intelligence-derived product and found a clear positional relationship to later anti-aircraft defenses, with the weight of the defenses to the southwest and northwest.

111. Djilas, *Rise and Fall*, 276.

112. These data are distilled from the PVO order of battle at WW2, http://www.ww2.dk /new/pvo/pvo.htm and augmented with Gordon and Kommissarov, *Soviet Air Defence Aviation*.

113. For the B-29, B-50, and B-36 ceilings, see Knaack, *Post–World War II Bombers*, 54, 200, 480. For the La-7, see Angelucci and Matricardi, *World War II Warplanes*, 244. For the MiG-9: "Mikoyan-Gurevich MiG-9," Wikipedia, https://en.wikipedia.org/w/index .php?title=Mikoyan-Gurevich_MiG-9&oldid=812195414. For the Yak-15: "Yakovlev Yak-15," Wikipedia, https://en.wikipedia.org/w/index.php?title=Yakovlev_Yak-15&oldid= 788514690. For the P-63: "Bell P-63 Kingcobra," Wikipedia, https://en.wikipedia.org/w /index.php?title=Bell_P-63_Kingcobra&oldid=813277436. For the Spitfire IX: "British Aircraft in Russian Service," Soviet Hammer, 16 March 2015, http://soviethammer .blogspot.com/2015/03/british-aircraft-in-russian-service.html; "Spitfire Mk. IX" (in Russian), www.AirPages.ru.

114. See McGill, *Black Tuesday over Namsi*, for the definitive account of the Namsi operation; Zhang, *Red Wings over the Yalu*, 129–32.

115. Lloyd, *A Cold War Legacy*, 181.

116. Zhang, *Red Wings over the Yalu*, 129–32.

117. Lloyd, *A Cold War Legacy*, 186.

118. LCMD, LeMay Papers, box B-196, attachment to LeMay letter, 27 December 1951.

119. LCMD, LeMay Papers, box B-196, LeMay to Kelly, 29 December 1951.

120. LCMD, LeMay Papers, box B-196, Kelly to LeMay, 9 January 1952.

121. LCMD, LeMay Papers, box B-199, "SAC Commander's Conference, 19 January 1953"; McLaren, *Republic F-84*, 56–68.

122. These data are distilled from the PVO order of battle at WW2, http://www.ww2.dk/new /pvo/pvo.htm and augmented with Gordon and Kommissarov, *Soviet Air Defence Aviation*.

123. FOIA CIA, CIG Intelligence Report, "Soviet Air Force Units in Bulgaria," 14 December 1947; FOIA CIA, Information Reports: "MiG 15 Aircraft in Bulgaria," 24 September 1951; "Soviet Military Bases in Bulgaria," 28 September 1953; "Location and Strength of Soviet Aircraft in Hungary," 22 April 1954; "Hungarian Air Defense System," 28 February 1957; "The 21 Soviet Jet Fighter Squadron," 28 April 1953; "Soviet Air Order of Battle in Rumania," 30 April 1953; "Soviet Air Force in Rumanian," 4 December 1953.

124. FOIA CIA, USAF Directorate of Intelligence, "USAF Contribution to NIE-64 (Part 1): Soviet Bloc Capabilities through Mid-1953," 28 April 1952.

125. FOIA CIA, Information Report, "Fighter Tactics against B-36D Aircraft," 2 August 1954. See particularly the sketches.

126. LCMD, LeMay Papers, box B-196, letter LeMay to Kelly, 29 December 1951.

127. As discussed in detail in Farquahar, *A Need to Know* and in Aldrich, GCHQ.

128. FOIA National Nuclear Security Administration (NNSA), Frederick C. Alexander Jr. "SC WD 68-334: Early Thermonuclear Weapons Development: The Origins of the Hydrogen Bomb," May 1969.

129. Yudin, "Manuscript on the History of the Soviet Nuclear Weapons and Nuclear Infrastructure."

130. FOIA USAF, "A History of the Air Force Atomic Energy Program 1943–1953 Volume V: Atomic Delivery Systems."

131. See Fitzpatrick, "Igniting the Light Elements."

132. FOIA USAF, "A History of the Air Force Atomic Energy Program 1943–1953 Volume V: Atomic Delivery Systems."

133. Letter from Vice Adm. John T. Hayward to author, 13 November 1990.

134. LCMD, LeMay Papers, box B-192, letter LeMay to Vandenberg, 30 June 1950.

135. LCMD, LeMay Papers, box B-197, memo for the record, LeMay to HQ USAF, 8 April 1952.

136. DNA 6019F, "Operation TUMBLER-SNAPPER 1952."

137. FOIA NNNS, SC-M-67-661, "History of the Early Thermonuclear Weapons Mks 14, 15, 16, 17, 24 and 29," June 1967.

138. FOIA NNNS, SC-M-67-661, "History of the Early Thermonuclear Weapons Mks 14, 15, 16, 17, 24 and 29," June 1967.

139. DNA 6036F, United States Atmospheric Nuclear Weapons Tests Nuclear Test Personal Review, "Operation IVY 1952."

140. DNA Joint Task Force Seven, "Operation IVY: Final Report Joint Task Force 132, 1952," 9 January 1953; FOIA USAF, "Technical Report, Air Force Weapons Task Group 132.4 Op IVY Jan–December 1952." The USAF report wasn't sure about the yield and postulated it could be as high as 20 megatons. The JTF-7 report has the 6- to 12-megaton estimate.

141. Armed Forces Special Weapons Project, WT-750, "Operation UPSHOT-KNOTHOLE: Project 5.3: Blast Effects on B-36 Type Aircraft in Flight, March–June 1953"; DNA 6036F,

United States Atmospheric Nuclear Weapons Tests Nuclear Test Personal Review, "Operation IVY 1952."

142. Armed Forces Special Weapons Project, WT-750, "Operation UPSHOT-KNOTHOLE: Project 5.3: Blast Effects on B-36 Type Aircraft in Flight, March–June 1953"; DNA 6036F, United States Atmospheric Nuclear Weapons Tests Nuclear Test Personal Review, "Operation IVY 1952."

143. U.S. Naval Radiological Defense Laboratory, W. B. Heidt et al., WT-615, "Report to the Scientific Director: Nature, Intensity, and Distribution of Fall-Out from Mike Shot," April 1953.

144. LCMD, LeMay Papers, box 200, letter LeMay to Mills, 7 February 1953; LCMD, LeMay Papers, box 200, letter Mills to LeMay, 19 February 1953; FOIA USAF, "A History of the Air Force Atomic Energy Program 1943–1953 Volume V: Atomic Delivery Systems."

145. LCMD, LeMay Papers, box B-104, Commander's Journal, "Concept of Operation for Use of Thermonuclear Weapons," 10 June 1953.

146. Hansen, *US Nuclear Weapons*, 61–68.

147. FOIA USAF, Special Weapons Division to Air Research and Development Command (ARDC), "Summary-Nuclear Weapons Development," 11 August 1954; FOIA USAF, Special Weapons Division to Santa Fe Operations Office ASEC, "Development of USAF Electrolytic Units," 18 March 1954; FOIA USAF, "A History of the Air Force Atomic Energy Program 1943–1953 Volume V: Atomic Delivery Systems"; FOIA Armed Forces Special Weapons Project (AFSWC), R+D Reading File 1954 February–August, letter AFSWC to Los Alamos Scientific Laboratory, "Termination of Contractor Support for TX-16 Operations, April 1954"; FOIA USAF, Special Weapons Division to ARDC, "Operations Planning for TX-16 Weapons Support and Delivery," 25 March 1954.

148. FOIA DOE, "Minutes of the Thirty-fifth Meeting of the General Advisory Committee to the US Atomic Energy Commission, May 14, 15 and 16, 1953."

149. LCMD, LeMay Papers, box 201, "Air War College Strategic Stockpile," 6 December 1953.

150. LCMD, LeMay Papers, box B-104, Commander's Journal, "Concept of Operation for Use of Thermonuclear Weapons," 10 June 1953.

151. FOIA DOE, B. F. Murphy to S. C. Knight, "Surface Bursts," 13 April 1953.

152. On the EC/TX series weapons and yields, see Jacobsen et al., *Convair B-36*, ch. 11. On Exercise Prophecy and its use of thermonuclear weapons, see LCMD, LeMay Papers, box 200, "Field Representative Europe Report on Ex PROPHECY, Part II, 3 March 53."

153. FOIA CIA, Information Report, "Air Defense System (PVO) of the Soviet Union," 17 July 1950.

154. FOIA CIA, IAC drafts, "Implications of Soviet Nuclear Weapons Tests During 1953," 26 October 1953. The final version was circulated to Allied intelligence agencies. Note that the drafts revise the future yield estimate from 1 million tons to hundreds of thousands of tons of TNT. See also FOIA CIA, "Current Intelligence Bulletin, 21 August 1953."

155. LCMD, LeMay Papers, box B-200, message LeMay to Twining, 22 May 1953.

4. Imminence of War II

1. Barlow, *Revolt of the Admirals*, 115–17.

2. LCMD, Vandenberg Papers, box 83, letter Bush to Bradley, 13 April 1950.

3. LCMD, Vandenberg Papers, box 83, letter Landon to Vandenberg, 13 June 1950.

4. LCMD, Vandenberg Papers, box 83, letter Landon to Vandenberg, 13 June 1950.

5. LCMD, LeMay Papers, box B-51, letter Bunker to LeMay, 15 October 1951.

6. LCMD, Vandenberg Papers, box 86, letter Norstad to Vandenberg, 8 October 1951.

7. LCMD, Vandenberg Papers, box 84, letter Norstad to Vandenberg, 15 February 1951.

8. LCMD, Vandenberg Papers, box 84, letter Vandenberg to Norstad, 3 May 1951.

9. LCMD, Vandenberg Papers, box 84, letter Vandenberg to Norstad, 3 May 1951.

10. LCMD, Vandenberg Papers, box 84, letter Vandenberg to Norstad, 30 April 1951.

11. LCMD, LeMay Papers, box B-194, letter LeMay to White, 7 May 1951.

12. LCMD, LeMay Papers, box B-194, letter LeMay to White, 7 May 1951.

13. This classic case of interservice rivalry over budgets and their relationship to capabilities, roles, and missions is handled best by Barlow in *Revolt of the Admirals*. In essence, pro-navy elements called into question the efficacy and reliability of the B-36, which got the air force's back up and led to acrimonious public hearings over airpower and the viability of the B-36 relative to navy plans to use aircraft carriers for nuclear strike operations. When the dust cleared the air force got the B-36, and the navy got a nuclear capability for its aircraft carriers.

14. USNOA, "CNO Report to the Secretary of the Navy, 1951" and "CNO Report to the Secretary of the Navy, 1952"; Miller, *Nuclear Weapons and Aircraft Carriers*, 87, 98, 122–24.

15. Barlow, *Revolt of the Admirals*, 116.

16. Barlow, *Revolt of the Admirals*, 116.

17. FOIA CIA, "Current Intelligence Bulletin, 8 May 1952."

18. Letter to the author from Vice Adm. John T. Hayward, 8 July 1991.

19. Miller, *Nuclear Weapons and Aircraft Carriers*, 98.

20. FOIA DOE, "Minutes of the Thirty-fifth Meeting of the General Advisory Committee to the US Atomic Energy Commission, May 14, 15 and 16, 1953."

21. LCMD, LeMay Papers, box B-54, Johnson folder, "Final Report of 2nd Bomb Group: Operations and Training," 30 June 1950; McLaren, *Republic F-84*, 56–68; USNARA via National Security Archive, "Presentation by the Strategic Air Command, Commander's Conference United States Air Force, Ramey Air Force Base, 25-26-27 April 1950."

22. The author served as the historian for Canadian NATO forces in Germany and has extensive knowledge of the ground in question. See also DDEL, Norstad Papers, Command Structure 1954 folder, chart designated "Priority Interdiction Targets."

23. FOIA CIA, "Fuel Shipments between the USSR and the Soviet Zone of Germany during the Period from 1 March to 6 May 1951"; FOIA CIA, "Rail Freight Traffic via Frankfurt/Oder Border Crossing Point," 30 August 1951; FOIA CIA, Information Report, "Reorganization of Soviet Transit Traffic Through Poland," 12 November 1954; FOIA CIA, Information Report, "Survey of Rail Fuel Shipments via Frankfurt/Oder," 5 April 1951; FOIA CIA, Information Report, "Road and Railroads in the Bialystok-Grajevo Areas," 12 April 1954. See also USNARA via National Security Archive, "Presentation by the Strategic Air Command, Commander's Conference United States Air Force, Ramey Air Force Base, 25-26-27 April 1950." The Frankfurt an den Oder–Brest Litovsk rail lines were the key supply routes for the Group of Soviet Forces Germany.

24. LCMD, Vandenberg Papers, box 84, letter Vandenberg to Norstad, 16 July 1951.

25. See Maloney, *Securing Command of the Sea*, for a full account of the SACLANT controversy. See also LCMD, Vandenberg Papers, box 84, Sweeney to Vandenberg, "Relationship of Strategic Air Command to the North Atlantic Treaty Organization."

26. LCMD, LeMay Papers, box B-195, letter LeMay to White, 18 August 1951.

27. LCMD, LeMay Papers, box B-195, letter LeMay to White, "Arrangements with CINCUSAFE and SACEUR for Conduct of Retardation Operations," 21 August 1951; LCMD, Vandenberg Papers, box 85, memo to Vandenberg, 28 August 1951.

28. LCMD, Vandenberg Papers, box 86, Norstad to Vandenberg and LeMay, 27 September 1951.

29. LCMD, Vandenberg Papers, box 86, message CINCAAFCE to COSUSAF, 7 December 1951; LCMD, LeMay Papers, box B-196, letter LeMay to White, 19 December 1951.

30. LCMD, Vandenberg Papers, box 87, message CINCUSAFE to COSUSAF, 24 March 1952.

31. LCMD, Vandenberg Papers, box 87, message Vandenberg to Norstad, 28 March 1952.

32. LCMD, Vandenberg Papers, box 87, message CINCAAFCE to COSUSAF, 3 May 1952.

33. LCMD, LeMay Papers, box B-198, message LeMay to White, 16 July 1952; LCMD, LeMay Papers, box B-198, message White to LeMay, 11 August 1952.

34. LCMD, Twining Papers, box 57, Daily Log, 31 July 1952.

35. LCMD, Vandenberg Papers, box 87, message CINCAAFCE to COSAF, 2 August 1952.

36. LCMD, Vandenberg Papers, box 87, message CINCAAFCE to COSAF, 2 August 1952.

37. LCMD, LeMay Papers, box B-198, letter LeMay to Norstad, 9 July 1952.

38. LCMD, LeMay Papers, box B-197, message, 15 March 1952; LCMD, Twining Papers, box 201, message Tunner to Twining (date obscured); McLaren, *Republic F-84*, 70.

39. LCMD, LeMay Papers, box B-198, message CG 7th Air Division to CG SAC, 15 July 1952 and 16 July 1952.

40. LCMD, LeMay Papers, box B-199, "SAC Commander's Conference, 20 November 52."

41. LCMD, LeMay Papers, box B-201, "The Strategic Air Command," briefing by Gen. Curtis LeMay, National War College, 28 January 1954.

42. LCMD, LeMay Papers, box 200, "Field Representative Europe Report on Ex PROPHECY, Part II, 3 March 53."

43. LCMD, LeMay Papers, box 200, "Field Representative Europe Report on Ex PROPHECY, Part II, 3 March 53."

44. LCMD, LeMay Papers, box B-201, message Selser to LeMay, "Exercise WORLD SERIES," 6 August 1953.

45. FOIA CIA, "Current Intelligence Bulletin, 31 October 1953."

46. FOIA CIA, Information Reports: "Soviet Aircraft: USSR/Austria," 23 July 1951; "Technical Information on Soviet Aircraft," 8 August 1951; "IL-28 Aircraft," 22 June 1951; "IL-298 Aircraft," 5 July 1951; "IL-28," 20 September 1951.

47. LCMD, LeMay Papers, box B-198, letter McConnell to LeMay, 12 September 1952; LCMD, Twining Papers, note from Weyland to Twining, 30 December 1952.

48. These data are derived from nine FOIA CIA IRs dated 4 November to 29 December 1952 covering Jüterbog, Brand, and Werneuchen airfields. It is clear from close examination that CIA IRs on this subject were not derived from Wringer and involved technically and militarily knowledgeable personnel. On the British Commanders in Chief Mission to the Soviet Forces in Germany (BRIXMIS), see Geraghty, *Beyond the Front Line*, chs. 1 and 2.

49. These data are derived from fifty-one FOIA CIA IRs dated 3 January 1953 to 17 December 1954 covering Wiener-Neustadt, Jüterbog, Briesen-Brand, Werneuchen, Welzow, Finsterwalde, Bad Voeslau, Oranienburg, and Gross Doelln airfields.

50. See Gordon and Kommissarov, *Ilyushin Il-28 Beagle Light Attack Bomber*, for excruciating detail on the number and variants of this fascinating aircraft.

51. Milberry, *Canadair Sabre*, 254–84; Meilinger, *Hoyt S. Vandenberg*, 199; "306th Bombardment Wing," Strategic Air Command, http://www.strategic-air-command.com/wings /0306bw.htm.

52. FOIA CIA IR, "Soviet Troop Movement from East Germany to Poland," 6 July 1953; FOIA CIA IR, "Soviet Evacuate Four Air Bases in East Germany," 13 November 1953.

53. Gordon and Kommissarov, *Ilyushin Il-28 Beagle Light Attack Bomber*, 40; Podvig, *Russian Strategic Nuclear Forces*, 485; FOIA CIA, "Implications of Soviet Nuclear Weapons Tests During 1953," 8 October 1953; "Nuclear Airbombs" (in Russian), http://www .militaryparitet.com/nomen/russia/aviabomb/data/ic_nomenrussiaaviabomb/3/.

54. Gordon and Kommissarov, *Ilyushin Il-28 Beagle Light Attack Bomber*, 81–83. See also FOIA CIA IRs for Chernyakhovsk: 15 November 1949, 11 March 1952; and Stryy: 3 October 1952, 15 July 1953, and 3 December 1953.

55. LCMD, LeMay Papers, box B-192, message JCS to SAC, 2 August 1950.

56. McGill, *Black Tuesday over Namsi*, 44.

57. Brands, *The General vs. the President*, 81.

58. LeMay and Kantor, *Mission with LeMay*, 464.

59. LCMD, Vandenberg Papers, box 86, message Vandenberg to Stratemeyer, 28 November 1950.

60. Foot, *The Wrong War*, 114–15.

61. LCMD, Vandenberg Papers, box 86, message LeMay to Vandenberg, n.d.

62. FOIA OSD, "Notes on visit with General Curtis E. LeMay, Newport Beach, California, December 30, 1984."

63. Anders, *Forging the Atomic Shield*, 127–28.

64. Maloney, "Flying the Mukden Gauntlet."

65. LCMD, LeMay Papers, box B-194, message LeMay to Stratemeyer, 21 May 1951. See Fletcher, *Air Force Bases*, 64.

66. LCMD, LeMay Papers, box B-194, message Briggs to Weyland, 14 February 1951.

67. LCMD, LeMay Papers, box B-194, message Briggs to Weyland, 14 February 1951.

68. LCMD, LeMay Papers, box B-194, letter LeMay to Briggs, 28 February 1951.

69. LCMD, LeMay Papers, box B-194, message LeMay to JCS, 16 April 1951.

70. LCMD, LeMay Papers, box B-194, message CG SAC to COMGEN FEAF, 30 April 1951.

71. LCMD, Vandenberg Papers, box 85, Current HOLD HERE for Gen. Vandenberg file, "Possible Effects of Bombing in Manchuria."

72. LCMD, Vandenberg Papers, box 85, Current HOLD HERE for Gen. Vandenberg file, "Possible Effects of Bombing in Manchuria." See note on chart, "Buildup of Communist Air Strength Against Korea."

73. DNA 6020F, "Shots ABLE, BAKER, CHARLIE, and DOG: The First Tests of the TUMBLER-SNAPPER Series 1 April–1 May 1952"; DNA 6021F, "Shots EASY, FOX, GEORGE, and HOW: The Final Tests of the TUMBLER-SNAPPER Series 7 May–5 June 1952"; DNA 6019F, "Operation TUMBLER-SNAPPER."

74. FOIA USAF, "History of the Far East Air Force Participation in the Atomic Energy Program 1 July 1952–30 June 1953."

75. FOIA USAF, "History of the Far East Air Force Participation in the Atomic Energy Program 1 July 1952–30 June 1953"; Leavitt, *Following the Flag*, 123–32; LCMD, Twining Papers, box 55, note Twining to Burns, 30 July 1951.

76. FOIA USAF, "History of the Far East Air Force Participation in the Atomic Energy Program 1 July 1952–30 June 1953"; Leavitt, *Following the Flag*, 123–32. See also FOIA USAF, "History of the Far East Air Force Participation in the Atomic Energy Program 1 July 1953–30 June 1954." The bulk of the targets in the 1951 Weyland list line up with the ranges of the F-84G aircraft from the 9th FBS deployment airfields. The inclusion of the tanker detachment permitted the Komaki group to launch, hit Vladivostok, and refuel over the Sea of Japan about two-thirds of the way to Japan.

77. LCMD, LeMay Papers, box B-200, memo LeMay to Carmichael, 22 July 1953.

78. Edmundson, "Six Churnin' and Four Burnin'"; FOIA USAF SAC, "Final Report: Operation BIG STICK, 19 Aug–4 September 53."

79. FOIA USAF SAC, "Final Report: Operation BIG STICK, 19 Aug–4 September 53." See also FOIA USAF, "A History of the Air Force Atomic Energy Program 1943–1953 Vol. V Atomic Weapon Delivery Systems," ch. 1 on Mk-6 weapon.

80. FOIA CIA, Information Report, "Komsomolsk Area," 12 March 1954; NPIC PIR, "Airframe Plants 126 and 130 and Komsomolsk Airfield, March 1961"; NPIC PIR, "Petroleum Refinery No. 409, June 1959"; FOIA CIA, Information Report, "Ship Construction in Komsomolsk," 1 June 1954.

81. FOIA CIA, Intelligence Report, "Germans Arrive in Khabarovsk," 19 November 1946; FOIA CIA, Intelligence Report, "Soviet Factories in Khabarovsk," 29 January 1947; FOIA CIA, Information Report, "Khabarovsk Airfields," 3 March 1952; FOIA CIA, Information Report, "Aircraft Plant No. 83 and Airfield in Khabarovsk," 27 February 1952 (see also sketch); NPIC PIR, "Ussuri South Shipyard December 1958"; NPIC PIR, "Armament and Machinery Plant Rembaza Kagonovich 105, July 1959"; NPIC PIR, "Khbarovsk Petroleum refinery Ordzhonikidze 419, USSR August 1959."

82. FOIA CIA, Information Report, "Air Information on Siberia and the Far East," 6 June 1949; FOIA CIA, Information Report, "Soviet Long Range Aircraft Capability Western USSR," 11 February 1957; NPIC PIR, "Aircraft Plant No. 116: Arsenyev USSR, May 1964"; NPIC, "Khorol Airfield East," 27 December 1966.

83. Edmundson, "Six Churnin' and Four Burnin'."

84. FOIA USAF SAC, "Final Report: Operation BIG STICK, 19 Aug–4 September 53."

85. FOIA, "COMFEAF Memos for the Record: Volume V, 1 August 1953 to 4 April 1954," entries 16 September 1953 and 14 October 1953.

86. USNOA, "Chief of Naval Operations Report to the Secretary of the Navy, 1951"; USNOA, "Chief of Naval Operations Report to the Secretary of the Navy, 1952."

87. FOIA, "COMFEAF Memos for the Record: Volume V, 1 August 1953 to 4 April 1954," Weyland entry, 15 November 1953.

88. Cagle and Manson, *The Sea War in Korea*, 469–74; Gordon and Kommissarov, *Soviet Air Defence Aviation*, 30–31. This, incidentally, was the historical basis for the climactic scene in the film *Top Gun*.

89. FOIA CIA, CIG Intelligence Report, "Construction of Soviet Airport in Vladivostok Area," 30 October 1946; FOIA CIA, CIG Intelligence Report, "Soviet Units in the

Vladivostok Area," 1947; FOIA CIA, Information Report, "Air Information: Soviet Heavy Bomber Non-stop Training Flights between Moscow and Vladivostok," 17 August 1948; FOIA CIA, sensitive intelligence (SENSINT) Photo Intelligence Memorandum, "Vladivostok Shipyards, 25 March 1955"; NPIC, "Vladivostok Naval Bases, Ulisa Bay," March 1964.

90. FOIA, "COMFEAF Memos for the Record: Volume V, 1 August 1953 to 4 April 1954," entry 17 November 1953.

91. FOIA, "COMFEAF Memos for the Record: Volume V, 1 August 1953 to 4 April 1954," entry 16 December 1953.

92. FOIA, "COMFEAF Memos for the Record: Volume V, 1 August 1953 to 4 April 1954," entry 23 December 1953.

93. Schecter and Luchkov, *Khrushchev Remembers*, 100–101.

94. Conquest, *Stalin*, 281.

95. Beria, *Beria My Father*, 223, 226.

96. FOIA USAF SAC, "Final Report: Operation BIG STICK, 19 Aug–4 September 53"; Edmundson, "Six Churnin' and Four Burnin.'" See also LCMD, LeMay Papers, box 200, message HQ USAF to COMSAC, 5 August 1953.

97. LCMD, Twining Papers, box 120, memo Director Plans to Deputy Chief of Staff, Operations, "Summary of Existing Plans, 19 October 53."

5. Four Horsemen I

1. LCMD, LeMay Papers, box B-184: "Official Observer List"; "MATS SAM Flight Washington to Eniwetok"; "Information Sheet for Official Observers."

2. FOIA USAF, AFSWC R+D Reading File 1954 February–August, letter Houghton to Chief, Human Factors Division, HQ ARDC, May 1954.

3. U.S. Naval Radiological Defense Laboratory, WT-934, "Operation CASTLE: Summary Report of the Commander, Task Unit 13 Military Effects Programs 1–9," 30 January 1959; U.S. Naval Radiological Defense Laboratory, WT-915, "Operation CASTLE Project 2.5a: Distribution and Intensity of Fallout, January 1956." See also LCMD, LeMay Papers, booklet "Joint Task Force Seven, Operation CASTLE." Note that the maps in this document have pen markings showing the detonation locations and are marked to conform to the laboratory device names used in the tests: Shrimp, Runt, Morgenstern, Ramrod, Alarm Clock, Jughead, and Zombie.

4. FOIA USAF, AFSWC R+D Reading File 1954 February–August, "Summary—Nuclear Weapons Developments," 12 August 1954.

5. Walker, *Permissible Dose*, 19.

6. See Thomas Kunkle's and Byron Ristvey's 2013 Defense Threat Reduction Study, DTRIAC SR-12-001, "Castle Bravo: Fifty Years of Legend and Lore. A Guide to Off-Site Radiation Exposures," Defense Threat Reduction Agency (DTRA), January 2013, https://apps.dtic.mil/dtic/tr/fulltext/u2/a572278.pdf.

7. U.S. Naval Radiological Defense Laboratory, WT-934 "Operation CASTLE: Summary Report of the Commander, Task Unit 13 Military Effects Programs 1–9," 30 January 1959.

8. FOIA NNNS, SC-M-67-661, "History of the Early Thermonuclear Weapons Mks 14, 15, 16, 17, 24 and 29," June 1967; DTRA Fact Sheet, "Operation CASTLE," July 2007.

9. FOIA USAF, AFSWC R+D Reading File 1954 February–August, "Information Relative to the Third ARDC Atomic Weapons Symposium," 27 May 1954.

10. FOIA USAF, "History of Strategic Air Command 1 January 58–30 June 58 Volume I."

11. Gabbard, *Adventures of an H-Bomb Mechanic*, 72; FOIA USAF, "History Fifteenth Air Force, January through June 1956."

12. Podvig, *Russian Strategic Nuclear Forces*, 486–87.

13. Reed and Stillman, *The Nuclear Express*, 34–43. Some sources assert that the rated yield was 3 megatons. See "22 November 1955: RDS-37," Comprehensive Nuclear-Test-Ban Treaty Organization, https://www.ctbto.org/specials/testing-times/22-november-1955-rds-37.

14. See "22 November 1955: RDS-37," Comprehensive Nuclear-Test-Ban Treaty Organization, https://www.ctbto.org/specials/testing-times/22-november-1955-rds-37; "22 November 1955," This Day in Aviation, https://www.thisdayinaviation.com/22-november-1955/.

15. LCMD, LeMay Papers, box B-60, letter LeMay to Twining, 9 August 1955.

16. FOIA USAF, AFSWC R+D Reading File 1954 February–August, "B-52 Delivery Conference."

17. LCMD, Twining Papers, box 81, letter Twining to LeMay, 3 October 1955.

18. York, *Making Weapons, Talking Peace*, 77.

19. DTRA Fact Sheet, "Operation REDWING," July 2007; Hansen, *US Nuclear Weapons*, 69–75; "Operation REDWING 1956: Eniwetok and Bikini Atolls, Marshall Islands," Nuclear Weapon Archive, 22 October 1997, http://nuclearweaponarchive.org/Usa/Tests /Redwing.html. The information on this site appears to have been derived from data produced by Los Alamos National Laboratory that were removed from the internet after 9/11.

20. U.S. Naval Radiological Defense Laboratory, WT-1359 (Prelim.), "Report of the Commander, Task Group 7.1 Operation REDWING," August 1956; U.S. Naval Radiological Defense Laboratory, WT-1344 (EX), "Operation REDWING Technical Summary of Military effects, Programs 1–9," 25 April 1961.

21. "Air Force Admits Miss with H-Bomb," *New York Times*, 17 June 1956.

22. U.S. Naval Radiological Defense Laboratory, WT-1344 (EX), "Operation REDWING Technical Summary of Military effects, Programs 1–9," 25 April 1961.

23. Nuclear Vault, "Operation Redwing: Nuclear Test Film (1956)," YouTube, 7 June 2010, https://www.youtube.com/watch?v=pbVzUXO8a6E.

24. Natola, *Boeing B-47 Stratojet*, 104.

25. FOIA USAF, "History of Strategic Air Command 1 January 58–30 June 58 Volume I."

26. See Watson, *History of the Joint Chiefs of Staff*, chs. 1 and 2.

27. Watson, *History of the Joint Chiefs of Staff*, chs. 1 and 2, p. 47. See also Condit, *History of the Joint Chiefs of Staff*, 6, 20.

28. NSC 153/1, "Report to the National Security Council by the Executive Secretary (Lay)," 10 June 53, in *FRUS 1952–54*, https://history.state.gov/historicaldocuments/frus1952 -54v02p1/d74.

29. NSC 162/2, "Statement of Policy by the National Security Council," 30 October 1953, in *FRUS 1952–54*, https://history.state.gov/historicaldocuments/frus1952-54v02p1/d101.

30. NSC, "Guidelines for NSC 162/2," 7 August 1954, reproduced in Trachtenberg, *The Development of American Strategic Thought*, 35–66.

31. NSC, "Guidelines for NSC 162/2," 7 August 1954, reproduced in Trachtenberg, *The Development of American Strategic Thought*, 35–66.

32. NSC, "Guidelines for NSC 162/2," 7 August 1954, reproduced in Trachtenberg, *The Development of American Strategic Thought*, 35–66.

33. "NSC 5501: Basic National Security Policy," 6 January 1955, reproduced in Trachtenberg, *The Development of American Strategic Thought*, 91–116.

34. Condit, *History of the Joint Chiefs of Staff*, 24.

35. Maloney, *Learning to Love the Bomb*, ch. 2.

36. Condit, *History of the Joint Chiefs of Staff*, 30.

37. As cogently discussed in Bacevich, *The Pentomic Era*.

38. LCMD, Twining Papers, box 94, "Strategic Air Command Progress Analysis 1 November 1948–31 December 1956."

39. The Twining Papers have numerous removed files related to nuclear weapons "allocations" and, to use a later term, "dispersions."

40. DOE, "Restricted Data Declassification Decisions 1946 to Present (RDD-7), January 1, 2001," appendix D.

41. LCMD, LeMay Papers, box B-202, letter LeMay to Twining, 6 June 1955; see also 15 July 1955 classified LeMay address at Quantico. LCMD, Twining Papers, box 94, "Strategic Air Command Progress Analysis 1 November 1948–31 December 1956." The actual numbers for the end of 1955 are 966 combat-ready aircraft and crews, but because LeMay was communicating with Twining in mid-1955, I rounded down. The number of combat-ready aircraft and crews was derived from the SAC Progress Report cross-indexed with the number of wings deployed for the 1955 EWP found in George F. Lemmer, "The Air Force and Strategic Deterrence 1951–1960," USAF Historical Division Liaison Office, December 1967.

42. NATO, "History Supreme Headquarters Allied Powers Europe: The New Approach, 1953–1956."

43. DDRS, 201358-iL-7, memo CINCLANT to Commander, SAC, "Report of Exercise COULEE," 2 December 1953.

44. LCMD, LeMay Papers, box B-202, letter LeMay to Twining, 6 June 1955.

45. Twining, *Neither Liberty nor Safety*, 4, 5–7.

46. LCMD, Twining Papers, box 90. See folder "1956 Russia-Trip to the USSR" for the detailed report by Twining to Eisenhower.

47. Power and Arnhym, *Design for Survival*, 26–27.

48. Twining, *Neither Liberty nor Safety*, 59.

49. As expressed in Power and Arnhym, *Design for Survival*.

50. LCMD, Twining Papers, box 76, letter LeMay to Twining, (18 June 1955); LeMay and Kantor, *Mission with LeMay*, 482.

51. Hunt, *Secret Agenda*, 214.

52. DDRS, document 210628.ii-26, JCS CM-98-54 memo to JCS, "Evaluation of the Atomic Offensive," 10 June 1954.

53. Polmar, *Strategic Air Command*, 36; FOIA USAF, George F. Lemmer, "The Air Force and Strategic Deterrence 1951–1960."

54. FOIA USAF, George F. Lemmer, "The Air Force and Strategic Deterrence 1951–1960."

55. Lloyd, *B-47 Stratojet*, 60–68; LCMD, Twining Papers, box 94, "Strategic Air Command Progress Analysis 1 November 1948–31 December 1956."

56. LCMD, LeMay Papers, box B-201, "Strategic Air Command Commander's Conference, 6 April 1954." The number of EC weapons is distilled from Hansen, *US Nuclear Weapons*.

57. These calculations are based on the data in LeMay's 1955 request cross-indexed with the number of available crews and aircraft derived from the 1956 Strategic Air Command

Progress Analysis data from 1955 and an estimate of the available weapons types for 1955 distilled from AEC weapons histories for that period.

58. FOIA NNSA, SC-M-67-661, "History of the Early Thermonuclear Weapons Mks 14, 15, 16, 17, 24 and 29" and SC-M-67-662, "Mks 21, 22, 26 and 36 Weapons Systems." See also FOIA USAF, "History of the Fifteenth Air Force, July through December 1955" and "History of the Fifteenth Air Force, January through June 1956."

59. Lloyd, *A Cold War Legacy*, 236.

60. Directorate of History and Heritage, Department of National Defence, Canada (DHH), file 73/1223 Series 2 File 1085, memo CplansI to DASP, "Briefing on SAC Tanker Base Requirements in Canada," 11 June 1956.

61. These rotational data are derived from Lloyd, *A Cold War Legacy*.

62. FOIA USAF, "History of the Fifth Air Division, 1 January to 31 December 1955 Volume II—Appendix."

63. LCMD, LeMay Papers, box B-201, letter 7 AD to CINCSAC, 20 February 1954.

64. This information is derived from an unpublished study of USAF nuclear logistics.

65. LCMD, Twining Papers, box 105, "Rotation of SAC Wing on Guam," 7 February 1958.

66. LCMD, Twining Papers, box 100, message Tunner to White, 14 October 1955.

67. LCMD, LeMay Papers, box B-104 D/Plans, "Reprogramming Adana, Turkey to Replace Abu Sueir," 16 June 1953; LCMD, Twining Papers, box 81, "US Position on Saudi Arabia," 24 March 1955. See particularly Grathwol and Moorhus, *Bricks, Sand, and Marble*, chs. 1 and 3.

68. The 1955 "Agreement for Cooperation concerning Civil Uses of Atomic Energy between the Government of the United States and the Government of the Turkish Republic, June 10 1955" does not preclude the transfer of weapons or their stationing in Turkey as long as restricted data are not transmitted. The government-to-government agreement on nuclear weapons and the specific service-to-service agreements are not in the public domain, but the pattern of a civil agreement, followed by government and service agreements related to nuclear weapons, was the basis for all American agreements of this sort with NATO allies after the Atomic Energy Act was amended and Turkey signed in May 1959. See LCMD, Twining Papers, box 110, JCS to SECDEF, "Status of National Security Programs," 2 October 1959.

69. FOIA USAF, "History of TUSLOG Det 10, 7216th Air Base Squadron, July to December 1956"; FOIA USAF, "History of TUSLOG Det 10, 7216th Air Base Squadron, December 1956 to July 1957." See also Fletcher, *Air Force Bases*, 50.

70. FOIA USAF, "History of the Fifth Aviation Division, 1 January to 31 December 1955 Volume II—Appendix"; LCMD, Twining Papers, message Tunner to Twining, 29 August 1955; LCMD, Twining Papers, OPIMEDIATE msg to COSUSAF, 17 August 1955.

71. FOIA USAF, "History of the Fifth Aviation Division, 1 January to 31 December 1955 Volume II—Appendix."

72. LCMD, Twining Papers, box 81, memo for COS USAF from Department of the Air Force, "USAFE Facility Requirement in Spain," 3 June 1955.

73. LCMD, LeMay Papers, box B-104, "Items of Interest for the CinC," September 1956. See also Twining Papers, "Strategic Air Command Progress Analysis 1 November 1948–31 December 1956."

74. FOIA USAF, "History of the 95th Bombardment Wing (H) 1–31 October 1957."

75. LCMD, LeMay Papers, box B-104, Commander's Diary, May 1954, "Alert and Evacuation Test Operations Order 10-53."

76. LCMD, LeMay Papers, box B-202, "Remarks by General Curtis LeMay at Quantico," 15 July 1955. It appears President Eisenhower was present for this briefing.

77. FOIA USAF, "History of the 44th Bombardment Wing (M), January–June 1955."

78. LCMD, LeMay Papers, box B-202, "Remarks by General Curtis LeMay at Quantico," 15 July 1955.

79. LCMD, LeMay Papers, box B-202, letter Armstrong to LeMay, 18 July 1955.

80. LCMD, LeMay Papers, box B-201, "General LeMay's Staff Visit, 12 July 1954"; LCMD, LeMay Papers, box B-104, "Notes for the Commander in Chief, November 1955"; FOIA USAF, "History of the Fifth Aviation Division, 1 January to 31 December 1955 Volume II—Appendix."

81. LCMD, LeMay Papers, box B-202, letter Armstrong to LeMay, 18 July 1955.

82. LCMD, LeMay Papers, box B-202, letter LeMay to Armstrong, 26 July 1955.

83. LCMD, LeMay Papers, box B-202, letter LeMay to Twining, 26 July 1955; LCMD, Twining Papers, box 100, message LeMay to Twining, 15 January 1955.

84. LCMD, LeMay Papers, box B-202, letter LeMay to Armstrong, 26 July 1955.

85. Pocock, *The U-2 Spyplane*, chs. 2 and 3; Lashmar, *Spy Flights of the Cold War*, introduction. Dino Brugioni refutes these assertions in *Eyes in the Sky*, 70–71.

86. LCMD, LeMay Papers, box 192, letter LeMay to Vandenberg, 12 December 1949.

87. See particularly Pocock, *The U-2 Spyplane*, 14.

88. LCMD, LeMay Papers, box B-51, letter Cabell to LeMay, 3 November 1953, LeMay to Cabell, 25 November 1953. See Brugioni, *Eyes in the Sky*, ch. 4.

89. FOIA CIA, memo for Project Director, "Visit to Strategic Air Command," 12 December 1957.

90. FOIA CIA, memo, "Retirement of the SENSINT Control System," 16 October 1962.

91. Grimes, *The History of BIG SAFARI*, 10–12, 17–22.

92. FOIA USAF, "COMFEAF Memos for the Record, General O. P. Weyland, USAF Vol V: 1 August 53–4 April 54," entries 31 December 1953, 5 January 1954, 22 January 1954.

93. See Hall and Laurie, *Early Cold War Overflights*, 115–27, and the National Museum of the USAF display of a Haymaker RF-86F and blow-ups of the aerial photography of Spassk-Dalniy Airfield and its TU-4s. Note also that SENSINT material passed to the CIA for analysis in later years was derived from these and other USAF flights. See, for example, FOIA CIA, "Vladivostok Naval Base and Ship Yard 202, 12 November 57"; "Aircraft Assembly Plant No. 116, Semenovka, USSR, 31 December 57"; "Railroad Station, Yards and Shops Spassk-Dal'niy, USSR, July 1959."

94. FOIA CIA, Information Report, "Soviet Early Warning Systems," 9 November 1954.

95. Reed, *At The Abyss*, 44–46; Natola, *Boeing B-47 Stratojet*, 85–89; Samuel, *I Always Wanted to Fly*, 199–213.

96. FOIA USAF, "History of the 303rd Bombardment Wing (Medium) April 1955."

97. Grimes, *The History of BIG SAFARI*, 25–26; Mikesh, *Martin B-57 Canberra*, 137.

98. Grimes, *The History of BIG SAFARI*, 32–34; Mikesh, *Martin B-57 Canberra*, ch. 22. See also LCMD, LeMay Papers, box B-202, letter LeMay to Twining, 22 December 1955.

99. FOIA USAF, "History of the 55th Strategic Reconnaissance Wing, April–September 1956." See also Hall, "The Truth about Overflights." Hall states that the Home Run flights

ended in May 1956, but the 55th Strategic Reconnaissance Wing history reports that Home Run operations were still going by the summer. It is possible these were deployed to Thule but were in some form of "standby" mode.

100. Reed, *At the Abyss*, 50–51.

101. Kuehl, "The Radar Eye Blinded," 207–8. Power was actually ahead of the curve: his concerns dated from 1951.

102. FOIA USAF, "History of the 55th Strategic Reconnaissance Wing, April–September 1956." See also Tegler, *B-47 Stratojet*, ch. 9.

103. Grimes, *The History of BIG SAFARI*, 115–17.

104. The PVO force structure data are distilled from "Air Defence Forces (PVO)," which has a database down to the squadron level at WW2, http://www.ww2.dk/new/pvo/pvo .htm. See also Gordon and Kommissarov, *Soviet Air Defence Aviation*, 237–39, 308.

105. Price, *A History of US Electronic Warfare*, 114; FOIA CIA, "Foreign Radar Recognition Guide, 1 Sept 59."

106. Price, *A History of US Electronic Warfare*, 139.

107. Price, *A History of US Electronic Warfare*, 138.

108. FOIA CIA, "Soviet Air Defense Intercept Capability by the Use of Radars" and "Distribution of Ground Radars in the USSR and Its Satellites," both undated but clearly representing 1956 when compared with information in the "Foreign Radar Recognition Guide, 1 Sept 59."

109. FOIA CIA, "Soviet Air Defense Intercept Capability by the Use of Radars" and "Distribution of Ground Radars in the USSR and Its Satellites."

110. FOIA CIA, "Soviet Air Defense Intercept Capability by the Use of Radars" and "Distribution of Ground Radars in the USSR and Its Satellites."

111. Price, *A History of US Electronic Warfare*, 140–43, 297.

112. This is based on an analysis of FOIA CIA PIR, "Missile Facilities in the Moscow Area," 12 April 1956. The characteristics of the RB-45C aircraft is from Knaack, *Post–World War II Bombers*; and the notations on CIA PIR, "Herringbone Surface to Air Missile Site C-33," 23 November 1960, plus some collaborative brainstorming with Larissa Reise, Brett Davenport, and Dr. Billy Allen. Comparison of the SENSINT imagery in the 12 April 1956 report with the locations on Google Earth and the camera characteristics suggest the approximate altitude at which the photos were taken.

113. See Samuel, *In Defense of Freedom*; Samuel, *Coming to Colorado*, 244; LCMD, LeMay Papers, box B-58, memo LeMay to Power, 27 September 1954; LCMD, LeMay Papers, box B-58, letter Israel to Schleeh, 10 September 1954.

114. Samuel, *I Always Wanted to Fly*, 189–95.

115. Grimes, *The History of BIG SAFARI*, 21–22.

116. FOIA CIA, Charles R. Ahern, "The YO-YO-Story: An Electronics Analysis Case History," *Studies in Intelligence* 5, no. 1 (Winter 1961): 11–23; CIA PIR, "Herringbone Surface to Air Missile Site C-32," 31 October 1960.

117. FOIA CIA, "Current Intelligence Bulletin, 16 December 1954."

118. FOIA CIA, Charles R. Ahern, "The YO-YO-Story: An Electronics Analysis Case History," *Studies in Intelligence* 5, no. 1 (Winter 1961): 11–23; CIA PIR, "Herringbone Surface to Air Missile Site C-32," 31 October 1960.

119. LCMD, LeMay Papers, box B-58, Wright Air Development Center, "Weekly Information Report for the Period Ending 28 May 1954."

120. LCMD, LeMay Papers, box B-58, letter LeMay to Power, 13 December 1954.

121. LCMD, LeMay Papers, box B-58, letter Power to LeMay, 21 December 1954.

122. LCMD, LeMay Papers, box B-58, letter Power to LeMay, 31 January 1955. See also McGill, *Jet Age Man*, 51–53.

123. LCMD, LeMay Papers, box B-58, letter Power to LeMay, 13 January 1955.

124. LCMD, LeMay Papers, box B-58, letter Power to LeMay, 1 February 1955; LCMD, LeMay Papers, box B-58, letter Old to Power, 11 February 1955; Hansen, *US Nuclear Weapons*, 182–83.

125. LCMD, LeMay Papers, box B-58, letter Power to LeMay, 27 March 1955.

126. LCMD, LeMay Papers, box B-58, letter Power to LeMay, 27 July 1955.

127. LCMD, LeMay Papers, box B-58, letter Power to LeMay, 4 April 1955 and 27 July 1955. Power noted that changes to the program "will probably include the cancellation of the [biological warfare] and [chemical warfare] warhead requirements." See also Hansen, *US Nuclear Weapons*, 179–80.

128. LCMD, LeMay Papers, box B-58, letter LeMay to Power, 28 February 1956.

129. LCMD, LeMay Papers, box B-58, letter LeMay to Power, 3 April 56; Power to LeMay, 11 June 1956.

130. FOIA NNSA, SC-M-67-671, "History of the Mk 39 Weapon," January 1968.

131. LCMD, LeMay Papers, box B-58, letter LeMay to Power, 12 June 1954.

132. LCMD, LeMay Papers, box B-202, "Remarks by General Curtis E. LeMay at Quantico," 15 July 1955.

133. LCMD, LeMay Papers, box B-203, "Remarks by General Curtis E. LeMay to the USAF Scientific Advisory Board at Patrick Air Force Base Florida 21 May 1957."

134. Tegler, *B-47 Stratojet*, 65.

135. This is drawn from Zbigniew Przezak's exceptionally detailed and fully illustrated website based on Soviet primary sources depicting the historical evolution and operations of the S-25 BERKUT: http://infowsparcie.net/wria/o_autorze/pzr_s25berkut.html.

6. Four Horsemen II

1. I am fully aware that SACEUR was Al Gruenther's "NATO hat" and CINCEUR his "American hat" vis-à-vis U.S. forces and nuclear release responsibilities. For stylistic purposes, he will be referred to as SACEUR here.

2. DDEL, Norstad Papers, folder 1 January thru 31 August 1952, message CINCAAFCE to COSUSAF.

3. DDEL, Norstad Papers, folder 2 July thru 31 December 1953, message Air Deputy to COSUSAF.

4. LCMD, Twining Papers, box 94, "Strategic Air Command Progress Analysis 1 November 1948–31 December 1956."

5. DDEL, Norstad Papers, folder Command Structure 1954. See maps "Priority Interdiction Targets," "Counter Air Force Targets," and "Strategic Concept."

6. Morris Honick and Edd M. Carter, "The New Approach July 1953–November 1956," SHAPE Historical Section.

7. Jordan, *Norstad*, 93.

8. DDRS, document 3092431-4, memo Gruenther from Morse, 3 June 1955. See also Honick and Carter, "The New Approach July 1953–November 1956."

9. Honick and Carter, "The New Approach July 1953–November 1956."

10. Honick and Carter, "The New Approach July 1953–November 1956."

11. Honick and Carter, "The New Approach July 1953–November 1956."

12. LCMD, LeMay Papers, box B-202, "Commander's Conference, Wright-Patterson, January 1956."

13. These data are derived from the detailed air base studies in Fletcher, *Air Force Bases*; Jackson, *Strike Force*, 51–87; Jim Oskins, "Early Air Force Special Weapons Career Field History," 2007, http://www.oocities.org/usaf463/earlycareerfieldhistory.html; McAuliffe, "The USAF in France"; Jean-Pierre Hoehn, "Chambley Air Base," Chambley Air Base France, n.d., http://chambleyab.com/images/Bob%20ferguson/Chambley%20information/Article%20from%20air%20fan%201991%20translation.pdf; LCMD, LeMay Papers, box B-200, "Briefing Notes on Change of Status of Command since General LeMay's Last Visit," 14 February 1953.

14. Yeager, *Yeager*, 304–6.

15. Mindling and Bolton, *US Air Force Tactical Missiles*, 100–116.

16. See the 16th Air Army order of battle at WW2, http://www.ww2.dk/new/air%20force/army/16va.htm.

17. This is speculation based on Yeager's remarks as well as the SAC-SACEUR agreement that SAC would take out strategic systems while SACEUR would take out tactical targets, "strategic" defined as any system that could attack SAC bases.

18. A similar operation, the conventional destruction of key logistic bridges in Poland by FB-111s and Tornados, is depicted in Hackett, *Third World War*, 192–96.

19. This is my extrapolation of the existing data. See also Nuclear Vault, "Operation Upshot Knothole (1953)," YouTube, 7 July 2009, https://www.youtube.com/watch?v=PZSjZfAyYB4.

20. Maloney, *War without Battles*, chs. 2 and 3.

21. For the order of battle of Soviet air forces in Austria, see "59th Red Banner Air Army," WW2, http://www.ww2.dk/new/air%20force/army/59va.htm. See also FOIA CIA, Information Report, "Soviet Occupation Forces I Lower Austria and North Burgenland," 6 April 1951; FOIA CIA, Information Report, "Wiener Neustadt Airfield and Military Post," 10 February 1953 and 3 June 1953. See also Beer, "The Soviet Occupation of Austria."

22. These deployment data were derived from an examination of aircraft carrier cruise books at Unofficial US Navy Site, https://www.navysite.de/cruisebooks/.

23. Miller, *Nuclear Weapons and Aircraft Carriers*, ch. 5.

24. LCMD, Twining Papers, box 102, message CINCUSAFE to COS USAF, 31 January 1952. See also references to other incidents in 1954 in the USS *Randolph* Mediterranean Cruise Book 1954 at Unofficial US Navy Site, https://www.navysite.de/cruisebooks/cv15-54/100.htm and https://www.navysite.de/cruisebooks/cv15-54/106.htm.

25. Fletcher, *Air Force Bases*, 13.

26. FOIA CIA, Information Reports: "Saseno Island Naval Installations, Submarine Galleries," 30 November 1950; "Report of Submarine off Albanian Coast," 29 August 1951; "Submarine Shelters at Porto Palermo," 21 December 1951; "Development of Soviet Submarine Bases in the Bay of Vlone and on the Island of Saseno," 28 February 1953; "Soviet Submarine in Albanian Waters," 10 January 1952; "Order of Battle," 26 March 1954; "Submarine Bases in the Vlone Area," 7 October 1954; "Guided Missile Launching Site at Berat/

Kocove Airport," 3 November 1954; "Order of Battle," 18 May 1955; "Mission Coverage Summary Mission 1309 of 19 October 1956." See also FOIA CIA, PIM, "Airfield Activity in the USSR and Satellites, 2 October 1957"; FOIA CIA, JPIB, "Pasha Liman Submarine Base," 25 February 1959; FOIA CIA, JPIB, "Mission 4114, Date of Information, 14 April 1959," 15 April 1959; FOIA CIA, PIC, "Joint Mission Coverage Summary Mission B4122," 18 June 1959; FOIA CIA, OCI, "Current Intelligence Staff Study Soviet-Albanian Relations, 1940–1960 (ESAU XIX-62)," 22 June 1962; O'Donnell, *A Coming of Age*, ch. 4.

27. FOIA CIA, "Roundup 62-133, 6 July 1962."

28. Hungarian airfield targets are discussed in Miller, *Nuclear Weapons and Aircraft Carriers*, 132; Malaika Byng, "Sazan Island: Communist Albania's most Secretive Military Base Open to Tourists," Spaces, n.d., https://thespaces.com/sazan-island-communist-albanias-most-secretive-military-base-opens-to-tourists/.

29. On Hungary: FOIA CIA, Information Reports: "Radar Installations in Hungary," 4 June 1952; "The Airfield at Taszar," 16 June 1952; "Sarmallek Airfield," 4 April 1954; "Location and Strength of Soviet Aircraft in Hungary," 22 April 1954; "Tapolca Airfield," 28 October 1954; "Hungary: Early Warning Radar Stations, Soviet P-3, P-8, and P-20 Radar," October 1956; "Hungary: Radar and Air Defense System in Hungary," 15 February 1957; and "36th Air Army," WW2, http://www.ww2.dk/new/air%20force/army/36va.htm. On Romania: "17th Red Banner Air Army," WW2, http://www.ww2.dk/new/air%20force/army/17va.htm; FOIA CIA, Information Reports: "Wave Lengths of Rumanian Radar Stations," 21 November 1952; "Rumania: Radar and Antiarcraft Defense Information," 15 June 1952; "Rumania: Radar Equipment at Arad," 23 October 1952; "Soviet Air Force in Rumania: Equipment, Personalities," 20 February 1953; "Soviet Air Force in Rumania," 4 December 1953; "Airfields in Rumania," 7 October 1954; "Turda Military Airfield," 10 November 1954; "Soviet Air Force in Rumania," 14 January 1955; "Soviet Control of the Rumanian Armed Forces; Soviet-Rumanian Air Intercept Exercises," 8 December 1955; "Taszar Airfield," 26 March 1957. Note that the contemporary 2 October 1957 Photographic Intelligence Memorandum, "Airfield Activity in the USSR and Satellites," is significantly incomplete and should be used only with other collaborating information.

30. FOIA CIA, Information Report, "Radar and Air Defense System in Hungary," 15 February 1957.

31. Stumpf, *Regulus*, is the definitive history on Regulus. Hansen, *US Nuclear Weapons*, suggests 40 to 50 kilotons, and Stumpf echoes him (p. 58). That said, as we have seen in chapter 3, yields could vary depending on the pit and core combination.

32. Note the presence of the Regulus missile at Unofficial US Navy Site, https://www.navysite.de/cruisebooks/cv15-56/039.htm. On the presence of GM GRU 2, see the USS *Randolph* Mediterranean cruise book at Unofficial US Navy Site, https://www.navysite.de/cruisebooks/cv15-56/162.htm.

33. Maloney, *Securing Command of the Sea*, ch. 4. See also letter to the author from Vice Adm. John T. Hayward, 8 July 1991.

34. FOIA, "COMFEAF Memos for the Record: Volume V, 1 August 1953 to 4 April 1954," entry 5 January 1954.

35. FOIA CIA, SNIE 100-2-54, "Probable Reactions of Communist China, The USSR, and the Free World to Certain US Courses of Action in Korea, 8 March 1954." See also LCMD, Twining Papers, box 102, message COMFEAF to COFS USAF, 12 March 1954.

36. FOIA USAF, "History of the Far East Air Forces Participation in the Atomic Energy Program, 1 July 1953–30 June 1954." See also Leavitt, *Following the Flag*, 127–32.

37. For clarity, the 3rd Aviation Field Depot Squadron deployed from Kirtland AFB to Andersen AFB on Guam on 21 May 1951 to support the B-29 deployment. In 1953 this unit moved to Kadena Air Base, Okinawa, while the 12th Aviation Field Depot Squadron replaced it at Andersen. See FOIA USAF, "History of the Atomic Energy Program in San Antonio Air Material Area, Kelly Air Force Base, Texas, 1 January 1953 to 30 June 1953"; FOIA USAF, "7th Air Division History 1 January–30 June 1952"; LCMD, White Papers, box 12, letter to White, 18 December 1958; Oskins, "Early Air Force Special Weapons Career Field History."

38. FOIA, "COMFEAF Memos for the Record: Volume V, 1 August 1953 to 4 April 1954," entry 4 February 1954, 18 February 1954.

39. LCMD, LeMay Papers, box B-104, message 17 May 1954.

40. FOIA, "COMFEAF Memos for the Record: Volume V, 1 August 1953 to 4 April 1954," entry 8 January 1953, 24 January 1954, 25 January 1954; FOIA USAF, "History of the Far East Air Forces Participation in the Atomic Energy Program, 1 July 1953–30 June 1954."

41. FOIA USAF, "COMFEAF Memos for the Record: Volume V, 1 August 1953 to 4 April 1954," entry 12 March 1954.

42. FOIA USAF, "History of the Far East Air Forces Participation in the Atomic Energy Program, 1 July 1953–30 June 1954."

43. Chang and Halliday, *Mao*, 561.

44. FOIA CIA, Frank Futrell, "The United States Air Force in Southeast Asia: The Advisory Years, 1950–1965," 31–34.

45. Prados, *Operation VULTURE*, 212.

46. Wells, *The Life and Career*, 86.

47. LCMD, LeMay Papers, box B-104, message 17 May 1954.

48. LCMD, LeMay Papers, box B-104, Commander Diary 6, entry 13 May 1954.

49. "ROCAF Combat Losses since 1950," at TaiwanAirPower.org/history/shootdowns.html.

50. FOIA Bendix Corporation, "The Navy and Sub-Limited Conflicts: Final Report, 30 September 1966," A-14.

51. Chang and Halliday, *Mao*, 389.

52. Elleman, *High Seas Buffer*, 38–42.

53. Chang, "To the Nuclear Brink: Eisenhower, Dulles, and the Quesmoy-Matsu Crisis," in Lynn-Jones et al., *Nuclear Diplomacy and Crisis Management*, 200–227.

54. LCMD, Twining Papers, box 100, message Smart to Everest, 9 February 1955.

55. LCMD, Twining Papers, box 100, message LeMay to Twining, 31 March 1955.

56. LCMD, Twining Papers, box 100, message LeMay to Twining, 31 March 1955.

57. LCMD, Twining Papers, message Twining to LeMay, 4 April 1955.

58. Chang, "To the Nuclear Brink."

59. Pocock and Fu, *The Black Bats*, 23.

60. As cogently described in Pompfret, *The Beautiful Country and the Middle Kingdom*.

61. Chern Chen, "The Intelligence Connection between West Germany and Taiwan: An Unknown Chapter of the Cold War," Academia Sinica (in Chinese), http://newsletter.sinica.edu.tw/file/file/121/12117.pdf.

62. Aldrich, *GCHQ*, ch. 8.

63. Morrison, *Point of No Return*, 112–13.

64. LeMay and Kantor, *Mission with LeMay*, 335–38; Coffey, *Iron Eagle*, 124–25; Kozak, *LeMay*, 183–88.

65. SCRC, White Papers, box 10, White bio file, "Lieutenant General Thomas Dresser White biography"; "General Thomas Dresser White," U.S. Air Force, https://www.af .mil/About-Us/Biographies/Display/Article/105243/general-thomas-dresser-white/.

66. Van de Ven, *China at War*, 134.

67. LCMD, LeMay Papers, box B-198, message White to LeMay, 12 October 1952.

68. Brooks, *Bull in a China Shop?*, 22.

69. Johnstone writes, "In our air targeting studies we regularly assumed that economic resources in satellite states should get the same bombing treatment [as the Soviet Union]" (*From Mad to Madness*, 82).

70. The steel and iron plant data are derived from a cross-examination of the following documents: FOIA CIA: CIG, "Iron and Steel Plants in North China, 1946"; IR, "Manchurian Sources of Timber Steel, and Cement," 26 February 1951; IR, "China Economic-Industry Iron, Steel," 22 May 1953; IR, "China Economic-Industry, Production, Iron, Steel, Rubber," 5 March 1954; DOI, "Basic Imagery Interpretation Report: Selected Iron and Steel Plans, China, June 1969"; DOI, "Basic Imagery Interpretation Report: Selected Iron and Steel Plans, China, June 1971." Material from the 1960s was used to eliminate those facilities built later than 1955.

71. FOIA CIA, Economic Intelligence Report, "Intra-Sino-Soviet Bloc Trade in Petroleum 1952–1956, 20 March 1958"; FOIA CIA, Provisional Intelligence Report, "Petroleum in Communist China, 30 July 1956."

72. FOIA CIA, Provisional Intelligence Report, "Petroleum in Communist China, 30 July 1956."

73. Van de Ven, *China at War*, 124.

74. FOIA CIA, Economic Intelligence Report, "Railroad Transportation in Communist China, 1950–54, 28 May 1956."

75. FOIA CIA, Photographic Intelligence Brief, "Petroleum Storage Sui-fen-ho, Manchuria," 2 December 1957; FOIA CIA, "Sui-fen-ho, China and Grodenkovo, USSR Railroad Transloading Yards," 1957. Of interest, Eisenhower was briefed on Soviet petroleum transfers to Communist China in November 1953. FOIA CIA, "Current Intelligence Review," 21 November 1953.

76. Computed using Nukemap but using roentgens instead of rads for dose measurement.

77. FOIA CIA, IR, "Chinese Communist Oil Storage Depots, Dairen," 21 December 1950; FOIA CIA, IR, "Petroleum Reserves and Production in China, 1953"; FOIA CIA, PIR, "Regional Petroleum Storage Installations in Communist China, November 1956"; FOIA CIA, PIR, "Strategic Petroleum Reserve Storage System in Communist China, May 1966"; FOIA CIA, PIR, "The Regional Petroleum Storage of China, June 1967"; FOIA CIA, BIIR, "Refineries and Shale Oil Plants, China, May 1970." As before, material from the 1960s was used to eliminate those facilities built later than 1955.

78. FOIA CIA, Provisional Intelligence Report, "Petroleum in Communist China, 30 July 1956."

79. FOIA CIA, Economic Intelligence Report, "Significant Developments in the Chemical Industries of the Sino-Soviet Bloc 1959," October 1960. An example is Lan-chou, which

had a fertilizer plant adjacent to the refinery. See FOIA CIA, Imagery Analysis Report, "Lan-chou Chemical Industries, China, August 1967."

80. FOIA CIA: "Airframe Plant and Airfield, Ch'eng-Tu, China," 1961; "Airfield North and Airframe Plant 112 Shen-Yang, China," 11 December 1964; "Cheng-Tu Airframe Plant," 5 January 1965; "Activity Review: Chinese Airframe and Aircraft Engine Plants, 1971"; BIIR, "Nan-chang Aircraft Plant 320, October 1968." As before, material from the 1960s was used to eliminate those facilities built later than 1955.

81. Maloney, "Flying the Mukden Gauntlet."

82. FOIA CIA, Information Report, "Nationalist Arsenal Production before Communist Capture and Known Communist Arsenals," 9 March 1950; FOIA CIA, Provisional Intelligence Report, "The Munitions Industry of Communist China, 30 December 1955."

83. Computed using Nukemap but using roentgens instead of rads for dose measurement.

84. See the introduction to van de Ven, *China at War*, for a discussion of Clausewitzian war versus national liberation war vis-à-vis China.

85. LeMay and Kantor, *Mission With LeMay*, 335–37.

86. LCMD, LeMay Papers, box 198, letter LeMay to White, 17 June 1952 and 30 June 1952; LCMD, Twining Papers, box 56, letter Twining to Dl, "BW-CW Testing Program," 15 January 1952.

87. LCMD, LeMay Papers, box 199, letter LeMay to White, 3 January 1953. See also LCMD, LeMay Papers, box B-200, White to LeMay, 21 January 1953.

88. LCMD, LeMay Papers, box B-104, "Staff Items for the Command, 12–27 July 1954."

89. LCMD, Twining Papers, box 106, JCS memo for SECDEF, "Chemical and Biological Warfare," 25 July 1958. The USAF capabilities are discussed in Regis, *The Biology of Doom*; they involved B-50 aircraft delivering the brucella disease using cluster munitions. The material required refrigeration, and the USAF had special refrigerator vehicles capable of being loaded on C-124 transport aircraft to move the agent to SAC's forward-operating locations.

90. FOIA USAF, "COMFEAF Memos for the Record: Volume V, 1 August 1953 to 4 April 1954," entry 22 December 1953; Pocock and Fu, *The Black Bats*, 24–25; FOIA CIA, "Formosa Straits Situation," 13 May 1955.

91. FOIA CIA, NIE 11-5-55, "Air Defense of the Sino-Soviet Bloc, 1955–1960," 12 July 1955.

92. Zhang, *Red Wings over the Yalu*, ch. 9.

93. See Pockock and Fu, *The Black Bats*, for details of these and other innovations.

94. LCMD, Vandenberg Papers, box 85, Air operations versus China folder; see maps. See also Zhang, *Red Wings over the Yalu*, appendixes for order of battle and locations.

95. FOIA CIA, "Airfields of the China Coast," 3 August 1954; compare with PIC, "Airfield and Aircraft Summary, 1959: Communist China." See also ORR, "Photo Intelligence Memorandum: POL Storage Southeast China Airfields, 27 July 1955"; ORR, "Communist China's Air Defense Capabilities," 9 January 1952.

96. FOIA CIA, NIE 11-5-55, "Air Defense of the Sino-Soviet Bloc, 1955–1960," 12 July 1955.

97. FOIA CIA, IR, "Radar Installations, Canton," 13 June 1951, 10 May 1954, 1 June 1954.

98. See Gushee, *52-Charlie*, 131.

99. FOIA CIA, "Current Intelligence Bulletin, 19 July 1952."

100. FOIA CIA, NIE 100-4-55, "Communist Capabilities and Intentions with Respect to the Offshore Islands and Taiwan through 1955, and Communist and Non-Communist Reactions with Respect to the Defense of Taiwan, 16 March 1955."

101. The rotational data are derived from an analysis of the overseas cruise books of each U.S. Navy aircraft carrier deployed to the Pacific from 1954 to 1956. These cruise books have been scanned in their entirety and are available at Unofficial US Navy Site, https://www.navysite.de/cruisebooks/index.html.

102. Author's analysis aboard the USS *Yorktown*, now a museum ship at Charleston, South Carolina. The ship's role changed to anti-submarine carrier by the 1960s, but the special ammunition storage spaces retained their original 1950s dimensions.

103. Elleman, *High Seas Buffer*, 40–41.

104. Unofficial US Navy Site, https://www.navysite.de/cruisebooks/index.html.

105. See USS *Essex* cruise book for 1954–55, Unofficial US Navy Site, https://www.navysite.de/cruisebooks/cv9-55/170.htm.

106. USS *Essex* cruise book for 1956, Unofficial US Navy Site, https://www.navysite.de/cruisebooks/cv9-56/223.htm.

107. USS *Essex* cruise book for 1956, Unofficial US Navy Site, https://www.navysite.de/cruisebooks/cv9-56/008.htm; https://www.navysite.de/cruisebooks/cv9-56/035.htm; https://www.navysite.de/cruisebooks/cv9-56/235.htm.

108. See USS *Wasp* cruise book, 1954–55, Unofficial US Navy Site, https://www.navysite.de/cruisebooks/cv18-55/124.htm.

109. See USS *Oriskany* cruise book, 1954–55, Unofficial US Navy Site, https://www.navysite.de/cruisebooks/cv34-52/134.htm.

110. USS *Kearsarge* cruise book, 1954–55, Unofficial US Navy Site, https://www.navysite.de/cruisebooks/cv33-52/239.htm.

111. Unofficial US Navy Site, https://www.navysite.de/cruisebooks/cv33-52/030.htm.

112. USS *Kearsarge* cruise book, 1954–55, Unofficial US Navy Site, https://www.navysite.de/cruisebooks/cv33-56/240.htm.

113. USS *Boxer* cruise book, 1955, Unofficial US Navy Site, https://www.navysite.de/cruisebooks/cv21-54/152.htm.

114. USS *Bennington* cruise book, 1955, Unofficial US Navy Site, https://www.navysite.de/cruisebooks/cv20-55/094.htm.

115. USS *Hancock* cruise book, 1955–56, Unofficial US Navy Site, https://www.navysite.de/cruisebooks/cv19-56/250.htm.

116. This is suggested by the existence of a CIA Photo Intelligence Memorandum, "POL Storage Southeast China Airfields, 27 July 1955." This document has detailed sketches of the storage in relationship to each base. A nuclear weapon employed against storage areas would obliterate the base, and the airfield is a better identifiable target visually and to radar.

117. Elleman, *High Seas Buffer*, 40.

118. Chang and Halliday, *Mao*, 390. See also Zubok and Pleshakov, *Inside the Kremlin's Cold War*, 217.

119. LCMD, Twining Papers, box 92, "Memorandum for General Twining on the Ability of Aircraft Carriers to Contribute to the SAC Offensive," 6 June 1955.

120. LCMD, LeMay Papers, box 203, message CINCPAC, 25 July 1956.

121. LCMD, LeMay Papers, box 23, message CINCPAC to JCS, 28 September 1956.

122. LCMD, Twining Papers, box 102, message COMFEAF to COFSUSAF, 14 January 1957.

7. Increasing the Deterrent Margin

1. Fairchild and Poole, *The Joint Chiefs of Staff and National Policy*, 7–10.

2. NSC 5602/1, "Basic National Security Policy, March 15, 1956," reproduced in Trachtenberg, *The Development of American Strategic Thought*, 117–56.

3. Fairchild and Poole, *The Joint Chiefs of Staff and National Policy*, 17.

4. Maloney, *Learning to Love the Bomb*, 38–50.

5. Fairchild and Poole, *The Joint Chiefs of Staff and National Policy*, 28.

6. Fairchild and Poole, *The Joint Chiefs of Staff and National Policy*, 29.

7. NSC, "Basic National Security Policy NSC 5602/1," 13 March 1956.

8. LCMD, Twining Papers, box 81, letter LeMay to Twining, 21 March 1955.

9. LCMD, LeMay Papers, box 202, "Remarks by General Curtis E. LeMay at Quantico 15 July 1955."

10. LCMD, LeMay Papers, box 202, "Remarks by General Curtis E. LeMay at Quantico 15 July 1955."

11. Prados, *The Soviet Estimate*, ch. 4.

12. Brugioni, *Eyes in the Sky*, 159–62.

13. FOIA CIA, memo to DCI, "Soviet Heavy Bomber Production," 2 July 1956.

14. Gordon, *Myasishchev M-4 and 3M*, 33.

15. Gordon et al., *Tupolev TU-16*, chs. 3 and 4.

16. Gordon et al., *Tupolev TU-16*, 317.

17. Maloney, "Arctic Sky Spies." Gordon et al. in *Tupolev TU-16* describe the situation from the Soviet perspective and claim that landing operations on ice fields were never repeated. This of course does not mean that this methodology would not have been attempted as a wartime expedient.

18. Maloney, "Arctic Sky Spies." See particularly Romney, *Detecting the Bomb*, ch. 1.

19. Podvig, *Russian Strategic Nuclear Forces*, 485–93.

20. LCMD, LeMay Papers, box 202, "Remarks by General Curtis E. LeMay at Quantico 15 July 1955."

21. See, for example, LCMD, LeMay Papers, box 202, letter Armstrong to LeMay, 18 July 1955.

22. LCMD, LeMay Papers, box 202, letter LeMay to Armstrong, 26 July 1955, emphasis added.

23. LCMD, LeMay Papers, box 202, letter LeMay to Armstrong, 26 July 1955.

24. LCMD, Twining Papers, box 92, letter LeMay to Twining, 3 March 1956.

25. LCMD, Twining Papers, box 92, letter LeMay to Twining, 3 March 1956.

26. LCMD, LeMay Papers, box B-203, "The Operational Side of Air Offense: Remarks by General Curtis E. LeMay to the USAF Scientific Advisory Board at Patrick Air Force Base, Florida, 21 May 1957."

27. LCMD, LeMay Papers, box B-202, message JCS to Distribution List, 6 May 1956.

28. LCMD, Le May Papers, box 203, letter LeMay to Twining, "Report of Conference," 2 June 1956.

29. LCMD, Twining Papers, box 94, "Strategic Air Command Progress Analysis 1 Nov 1948–31 Dec 1956."

30. LCMD, LeMay Papers, box 203, message JCS, 9 July 1956.

31. LCMD, LeMay Papers, box 203, message CINCPAC to JCS, 28 September 1956.

32. LCMD, Twining Papers, box 94, "Strategic Air Command Progress Analysis 1 Nov 1948–31 Dec 1956."

33. LCMD, LeMay Papers, box B-203, "The Operational Side of Air Offense: Remarks by General Curtis E. LeMay to the USAF Scientific Advisory Board at Patrick Air Force Base, Florida, 21 May 1957."

34. Specifically, Dino Brugioni, who wrote *Eyeball to Eyeball* and *Eyes in the Sky*, and Chris Pocock, *The U-2 Spyplane*. See Lt. Gen. Lloyd Leavitt's commentary on Pocock and the personality issue in *Following the Flag*, 229.

35. FOIA USAF, "History of the 303rd Bombardment Wing, January 1956."

36. Brugioni, *Eyes in the Sky*, 68. Despite Brugioni's assertions that he could not find SENSINT data in certain locations while he was researching *Eyes in the Sky*, I was readily able to acquire some of it from CIA sources through FOIA and use it in this book. See also FOIA CIA, memo for Project Director, "Visit to Strategic Air Command," 12 December 1957.

37. Leavitt, *Following the Flag*, ch. 5.

38. FOIA CIA, memo, "SAC Officials Witting of Project AQUATONE," 20 September 1955.

39. FOIA CIA, memo for Project Director, "Visit to Strategic Air Command," 12 December 1957; FOIA CIA, "Strategic Air Command Use of TALENT Materials," 14 February 1958; FOIA CIA, USIB, "US Organizations Involved in Photographic Intelligence," 9 June 1959.

40. FOIA CIA, memo, "Strategic Air Command Use of TALENT Materials," 14 February 1958.

41. Leavitt, *Following the Flag*, 227.

42. LCMD, Twining Papers, box 94, "Strategic Air Command Progress Analysis 1 Nov 1948–31 Dec 1956."

43. Carroll, *House of War*, 216–18.

44. See inspection remarks in FOIA USAF, "History Fifteenth Air Force July through December 1955" and "History Fifteenth Air Force January through June 1956."

45. LCMD, Twining Papers, box 94, "Strategic Air Command Progress Analysis 1 Nov 1948–31 Dec 1956."

46. McLaren, *Republic F-84*, 59–69.

47. FOIA USAF, "History of TUSLOG Det 10 July to December 1956" and "History of TUSLOG Det 10 December 1956 to July 1957."

48. FOIA USAF, "History of the 4397th Refueling Wing, May 1960."

49. Grathwol and Moorhuse, *Bricks, Sand, and Marble*, 19–29, 102, 152–53, 195.

50. See Aloys Arthur Michel, *The Kabul, Kunduz, and Helmand Valleys and the National Economy of Afghanistan*, https://apps.dtic.mil/sti/pdfs/AD0225909.pdf, a 1959 study that was funded by the Office of Naval Research.

51. LCMD, Twining Papers, box 81, memo, "US Position on Saudi Arabia," 24 March 1955.

52. LCMD, LeMay Papers, box 202. The envelopes containing the flight distance pictures, back notations, and string are in this box. The envelope containing the string is labeled Top Secret.

53. "General Walter C. Sweeney, Jr.," U.S. Air Force, http://www.af.mil/About-Us/Biographies/Display/Article/105473/general-walter-c-sweeney-jr/.

54. LCMD, LeMay Papers, box 202, memo Sweeney to LeMay, "EWP Concept," 2 September 1954.

55. LCMD, Twining Papers, box 76, memo LeMay to Twining, 4 January 1955; LCMD, LeMay Papers, box 202, memo SAC HQ to CoS USAF, "Alaskan KC-97 Tanker Bases," 27 June 1955. The projected SAC Alaskan tanker bases were Kenai, Big Delta, Homer, King Almon, and Clear, future home of the Ballistic Missile Early Warning System.

56. "303rd Aerial Refueling Squadron," Wikipedia, https://en.wikipedia.org/wiki/303d _Air_Refueling_Squadron.

57. Tom Hildreth, "Chronology of the 4050th Air Refueling Wing (AREFWG) October 1955–April 1957," http://users.vermontel.net//~tomh/AIRCRAFT/UNITS/4050ARW /4050_AREFWG_5557.html.

58. FOIA USAF, "History of the 4060th Air Refueling Wing, Jan–Feb 1958."

59. "Photos," Malmstrom Air Force Base, http://www.malmstrom.af.mil/News/Photos /igphoto/2000541985/.

60. FOIA USAF, "History of the 22nd Bombardment Wing (Medium) Mar–Aug 57"; Natola, Boeing B-47 StratoJet, 77–78, 131–35, 163; Tegler, B-47 Stratojet, 10, 103, 107, 112; Malucci, B-47 Stratojet, 88, 133, 134.

61. FOIA OSD, "History of the Custody and Deployment of Nuclear Weapons July 1945 through September 1977."

62. FOIA OSD, "History of the Custody and Deployment of Nuclear Weapons July 1945 through September 1977." See also Loeber, Building the Bombs, ch. 8.

63. FOIA USAF, "History of the 92nd Bombardment Wing (Heavy) September 1956."

64. FOIA USAF, "History Fifteenth Air Force January through June 1956"; FOIA DOE, SC-M-67-661, "History of the Early Thermonuclear Weapons Mks 14, 15, 16, 17, 24 and 29, June 1967."

65. FOIA USAF, "History Fifteenth Air Force January through June 1956"; FOIA DOE, SC-M-67-661, "History of the Early Thermonuclear Weapons Mks 14, 15, 16, 17, 24 and 29, June 1967." The numbers of weapons are estimates from Hansen's works.

66. These data are derived from Chuck Hansen, Swords of Armageddon (disks in author's possession), and Hansen, US Nuclear Weapons.

67. FOIA USAF, "History of the 93rd Bombardment Wing, November 1958"; FOIA DOE, SC-M-67-671, "History of the Mk 39 Weapon."

68. The numbers of weapons are from Cochran et al., Nuclear Weapons Databook, 10–11. Hansen notes in Swords of Armageddon that 940 Mk-36s of all mods were manufactured; that is, the 275 Mk-21s modified into Mk-36 mod 1 should be included in the total.

69. FOIA DOE, SC-M-67-661, "History of the Early Thermonuclear Weapons Mks 14, 15, 16, 17, 24 and 29, June 1967."

70. FOIA DOE, SC-M-67-622, "[Redacted] Mks 21, 22, 26 and 36, September 1967."

71. FOIA DOE, SC-M-67-726, "History of the Mk 6 Bomb (Including the TX/WX-13, Mk 18 ad TX-20), November 1967."

72. DTRA Fact Sheet, "Operation REDWING," September 2017; FOIA DOE, AEC, "Release of Atomic Information to UK-Canadian Observers (Proposed Talk by Dr. Ogle)," 20 June 1956(?).

73. See Higuchi, "'Clean' Bombs."

74. FOIA DOE, SC-M-67-992, "[Redacted] Mks 21, 22, 26 and 36 Weapons Systems, September 1967." See also Hansen, Swords of Armageddon, for his estimates of the Y2 numbers, where he implies there were only six Mk-36Y2 weapons made. Hansen makes refer-

ence to "clean" weapons being a fraud in an earlier article, "Beware the Old Story." It is not clear exactly how many Mk-36Y2s were made. An analysis of available AEC information on Mk-36 development suggests that there was some confusion as to Y1 and Y2 yields and their relationship to the Mk-15 and Mk-36 weapons. An attempt by the AEC authorities to sort out the nomenclature that makes reference to Mk-36Y2 instead of TX-36Y2-X1 suggests that the Y2 was in production by the summer of 1957. See also FOIA DOE, "Atomic Energy Commission Meeting No. 1308," 22 October 1957, where the commissioners confirm a "clean" weapon has already been tested, which presumably was during Redwing in 1956.

75. FOIA USAF, "History of the 806th Air Division, July 1958."

76. Strategic Air Command, "Atomic Weapons Requirements Study for 1959: SM 129-56," National Security Archive, 15 June 1956, https://nsarchive2.gwu.edu/nukevault/ebb538 -Cold-War-Nuclear-Target-List-Declassified-First-Ever/documents/section1.pdf.

77. Bill Burr, "US Cold War Target Lists Declassified for the First Time," National Security Archive, update 4 April 2016, https://nsarchive2.gwu.edu/nukevault/ebb538-Cold -War-Nuclear-Target-List-Declassified-First-Ever/#update; Wayne Madsen, "Declassi- fied Documents Reveal Pentagon's 1950s Planned Nuclear Holocaust: 'Systemic Destruc- tion' and Annihilation of Prague, Warsaw, Budapest, Moscow, Beijing . . . More Than 1000 Cities," Global Research, 27 December 2015, https://www.globalresearch.ca/declassified -documents-reveal-pentagons-planned-nuclear-holocaust-systemic-destruction-and -annihilation-of-prague-warsaw-budapest-moscow-beijing/5498130, which was derived from the National Security Archive information. The Madsen article was further recycled by pro-Soviet elements as part of an anti-Ukraine, anti-NATO influence operations cam- paign: see Free Ukraine Now website, https://freeukrainenow.org.

78. "War and Peace in the Nuclear Age: Bigger Bang for the Buck. Interview with Jerome Wiesner," Open Vault from WGBH, 27 March 1986, http://openvault.wgbh.org/catalog/V _DD3A084107E94632B6AD7D428A966304.

79. NSC, "Basic National Security Policy NSC 5602/1," 13 March 1956.

80. Strategic Air Command, "Atomic Weapons Requirements Study for 1959."

81. The numbers of weapons are from Cochran et al., *Nuclear Weapons Databook*, 10–11; the percentages are from FOIA OSD, "History of the Custody and Deployment of Nuclear Weapons July 1945 through September 1977." Note that around two hundred Mk-17s were being retired at this time, and the full production of Mk-36s was not completely deployed, so these figures should be taken as very approximately representing 1957 into 1958.

82. ISCAP, "History of the Strategic Air Command Historical Study #73A: SAC Tar- geting Concepts," (April 1959?).

83. ISCAP, "History of the Strategic Air Command Historical Study #73A: SAC Tar- geting Concepts," (April 1959?).

84. As discussed in Kaufman, *The McNamara Strategy*, chs. 1 and 2; Bundy, *Danger and Survival*, ch. 12.

85. ISCAP, "History of the Strategic Air Command Historical Study #73A: SAC Tar- geting Concepts," (April 1959?).

86. ISCAP, "History of the Strategic Air Command Historical Study #73A: SAC Tar- geting Concepts," (April 1959?).

87. These numbers are extrapolated from a classified 1956 briefing given to the Royal Canadian Air Force during negotiations for tanker bases in Canada. It is one rare occasion

when LeMay permitted operational details to be transferred, but then SAC needed those bases. See DHH, Raymont Papers, file 1085, memo CAS to CCOS, "USAF Requirement for SAC Tanker Bases in Canada," 15 June 1956. The operational detail was retained by the Royal Canadian Air Force and not passed on to the Cabinet Defence Committee during deliberations.

88. For this analysis I used FOIA CIA, CPIC, "Listing of TALENT Reports 1956 through 1958," and FOIA CIA, OCR, "Listing of TALENT Reports, 1957." These two documents present the information in different ways, and by linking the interested organization with the appropriate SAC RTS, a significant portion of the SAC EWP target list can be extracted. It is also possible to determine what was known in 1956 and what was known in 1957. There are 185 redacted pages in the 1956–58 document; these were likely lists of radar stations and communications complexes, collectively called "control centers." In what is probably a coincidence, the number of RTS targeting reports from 1956–58 corresponds closely to the number of B-47s assigned to each numbered air force.

89. FOIA CIA, CPIC, "Listing of TALENT Reports 1956 through 1958"; FOIA CIA, OCR, "Listing of TALENT Reports, 1957."

90. FOIA CIA, CPIC, "Listing of TALENT Reports 1956 through 1958"; FOIA CIA, OCR, "Listing of TALENT Reports, 1957." See also Bert Kondruss's extensive compilation of Warsaw Pact airfield and order of battle data at http://www.mil-airfields.de/flugplaetze.html.

91. FOIA CIA, PIM, "Franz Josef Land," 15 August 1958.

92. This may have been an early example of the Soviet Reflexive Control concept applied to PVO. Reflexive Control was a form of deception whereby the enemy detects a void in the defenses that he believes affords him an advantage when in fact it becomes a manned position in wartime and a trap. See Clifford Reid, "Reflexive Control in Soviet Military Planning," in Dailey and Parker, *Soviet Strategic Deception*, ch. 14.

93. FOIA CIA, CPIC, "Listing of TALENT Reports 1956 through 1958"; FOIA CIA, OCR, "Listing of TALENT Reports, 1957." See also Michael Holm's Soviet air order of battle data at "Soviet Armed Forces 1945–1991," WW2, http://www.ww2.dk/new/newindex.htm.

94. FOIA CIA, IR, "Hungary: Taszar Airfield, 22 Mar 57."

95. Soviet air ORBAT data compiled by Michael Holm, "Soviet Armed Forces 1945–1991," WW2, http://www.ww2.dk/new/newindex.htm; FOIA CIA, CPIC, "Listing of TALENT Reports 1956 through 1958"; FOIA CIA, OCR, "Listing of TALENT Reports, 1957."

96. Michael Holm, "Soviet Armed Forces 1945–1991," WW2, http://www.ww2.dk/new/newindex.htm; FOIA CIA, CPIC, "Listing of TALENT Reports 1956 through 1958"; FOIA CIA, OCR, "Listing of TALENT Reports, 1957." See also Bert Kondruss data at http://www.mil-airfields.de/flugplaetze.html.

97. FOIA CIA, CPIC, "Listing of TALENT Reports 1956 through 1958"; FOIA CIA, OCR, "Listing of TALENT Reports, 1957."

98. Gordon et al., *Tupolev TU-16*, 430.

99. FOIA CIA, CPIC, "Listing of TALENT Reports 1956 through 1958"; FOIA CIA, OCR, "Listing of TALENT Reports, 1957." Though it is recognized that CIA wanted coverage of Israel for a variety of other purposes, especially its nuclear weapons program.

100. FOIA CIA, PIM, "Genetrix Photography," 12 April 1956; FOIA CIA, PIM, "PID Orientation Briefing Outline," 1965. See also Lowenhaupt, "Mission to Birch Woods."

101. FOIA CIA, NIE 11-2A-63, "The Soviet Atomic Energy Program, 2 July 1963." See also FOIA CIA, CPIC, "Listing of TALENT Reports 1956 through 1958"; FOIA CIA, OCR, "List-

ing of TALENT Reports, 1957." The 1963 document provides what was known and how that knowledge evolved throughout the 1950s. See also FOIA CIA, "ODE 4045," 29 August 1957.

102. FOIA CIA, "ODE 4045," 29 August 1957.

103. FOIA CIA, SIRA, "The Soviet BW Program," 24 April 1961; Department of the Army, memo for Chairman, Ad Hoc Requirements Committee, "Army Priority Targets," 27 June 1957. An undated CIA document fragment makes reference to the Stassen overflight proposals and the Lisey Island facilities. The biological warfare sites appear on the Talent report lists under SAC RTSs indicating they understood what they were for and that they were targeted. See also FOIA CIA, "ODE-B 4035," 5 August 1957.

104. Michael Holm, "Soviet Armed Forces 1945–1991," WW2, http://www.ww2.dk/new /newindex.htm; FOIA CIA, CPIC, "Listing of TALENT Reports 1956 through 1958"; FOIA CIA, OCR, "Listing of TALENT Reports, 1957."

105. FOIA CIA, "ODE-4045 (Supplemental No. 1)," 21 August 1957.

106. These data are based on cross-indexing Michael Holm's data for the 18th Red Banner Air Defense Corps with Google Earth and FOIA CIA, CPIC, "Listing of TALENT Reports 1956 through 1958" and FOIA CIA, OCR, "Listing of TALENT Reports, 1957."

107. Michael Holm, "Soviet Armed Forces 1945–1991," WW2, http://www.ww2.dk/new /newindex.htm; FOIA CIA, CPIC, "Listing of TALENT Reports 1956 through 1958"; FOIA CIA, OCR, "Listing of TALENT Reports, 1957."

108. FOIA CIA, CPIC, "Listing of TALENT Reports 1956 through 1958"; FOIA CIA, OCR, "Listing of TALENT Reports, 1957."

109. Winchester, *Concept Aircraft*, 48–49, 146–47; Friedman, *The Postwar Naval Revolution*, 43–46; FOIA CIA, PIR, "Evaluation of Seaplane Activity at Donuslav Lake Seaplane Station and Taganrog Airframe Plant, USSR March 1963"; FOIA CIA, NPIC, "New Developments at Taganrog Airframe Plant Dimitrob 86, April 1974"; FOIA CIA, NIE 11-14-65, "Capabilities of Soviet General Purpose Forces, 21 October 1965." See also Gordon et al., *Beriev's Jet Flying Boats*.

110. This is what CIA analysts referred to as the Delyatin site, aka "Ivano-Frankovsk-16," the site located in the Carpathians. See Holm data on the 12th GUMO sites cross-indexed with Google Earth data and ISCAP, CIA STIR, "The Major Function of the Soviet Sensitive Operations Complexes, March 1970."

111. For example, an undated CIA document, "Western USSR Target List," lists all of the TU-16 bases in central Ukraine, yet there are no Talent reports generated for them in 1956–58, which suggests the data were already collected by SENSINT flights, analyzed, and a sanitized list forwarded to the CIA; these bases have an asterisk next to them. Several SENSINT flights overflew this area prior to the U-2 flights in 1956–57. CIA photo analysis of these bases appears to start in the 1960s with the new Keyhole data, yet we know they were overflown earlier as the latitude and longitude in the "Western USSR Target List" document match exactly the location of the bases on Google Earth.

112. ISCAP, CIA STIR, "The Major Function of the Soviet Sensitive Operations Complexes, March 1970."

113. These data were generated by cross-indexing Michael Holm's Soviet air order of battle data with Gordon's base location data from his books on the TU-4 and IL-28; Google Earth search data; an undated imagery document from the CIA depicting analysis of nuclear storage areas with their latitudes and longitudes but otherwise redacted; CPIC's

"Listing of TALENT Reports 1956 through 1958"; and OCR, "Listing of TALENT Reports, 1957." This shows when the IL-28 and TU-4 units first deployed, the location of their bases and when, and where the storage areas were near those bases.

114. FOIA CIA, AFCIN, "Briefing Paper for the Joint Chiefs of Staff," 26 August 1957; FOIA CIA, "Briefing on the Installation at Mozhaysk," 14 January 1957; FOIA CIA, "Unidentified Soviet Construction Complex Near Mozhaysk," January 1957; Michael Holm's data on Soviet air order of battle and the 12th GUMO sites. The CIA was exploring the possibility that Mozhaysk had something to do with guided missiles and even had the U.S. Army compare it to the Fort Churchill rocket launch site in Manitoba. There is no mention of the Valdai-Migalovo comparison in the CIA material, only in the AFCIN briefing, again suggesting not everything was passed on to CIA. For a list of Talent-based report names, organizations, and dates related to these data, see CPIC's "Listing of TALENT Reports 1956 through 1958"; OCR, "Listing of TALENT Reports, 1957."

115. FOIA CIA, "ODE 8005," 6 December 1959.

116. FOIA CIA, GMAIC, "Soviet Surface-to-Surface Missile Deployment," 1 September 1960.

117. See "Feodosia-13: Former Nuclear Weapons Storage," Russian Urban Exploration, https://rusue.com/feodosia-13-former-nuclear-weapons-storage/; "Russia's Plans for Nuclear Weapons in Crimea," Inform Napalm, 26 September 2016, https://informnapalm .org/en/russia-s-plans-nuclear-weapons-crimea/.

118. ISCAP, CIA S&TIR, "The Major Function of the Soviet Sensitive Operations Complexes, 23 March 1970"; Google Earth analysis of terrain.

119. FOIA CIA, Publications Division, "Status Report, 23 Mar 1962" and "Status Report, 18 May 1962"; ISCAP, CIA S&TIR, "The Major Function of the Soviet Sensitive Operations Complexes, 23 March 1970"; Michael Holm 12th GUMO data; Google Earth analysis of terrain.

120. See Zbigniew Przęzak's SA-1 history (in Polish), http://infowsparcie.net/wria/o _autorze/pzr_s25berkut.html, 1.

121. See map "Layout of the Moscow Anti-Aircraft Defense System Assets," from "The Official Illustrated Guide to Moscow Anti-Aircraft Defense System, 1955," All World Wars, http://www.allworldwars.com/Official-Illustrated-Guide-to-Moscow-Anti-Aircraft-Defense -System-1955.html.

122. Tegler, B-47 Stratojet, 10.

123. Which I did. See also FOIA CIA, JPIC, "Precise Locations of Herringbone SAM Sites in the Moscow Area, December 1959."

124. Malucci, B-47 Stratojet, 88; Price, A History of US Electronic Warfare, 186.

125. FOIA CIA, CPIC, "Listing of TALENT Reports 1956 through 1958"; FOIA CIA, OCR, "Listing of TALENT Reports, 1957."

126. Natola, Boeing B-47 Stratojet, 159.

127. FOIA CIA, CPIC, "Listing of TALENT Reports 1956 through 1958"; FOIA CIA, OCR, "Listing of TALENT Reports, 1957." Examination of the Moscow DGZs in the SM 129-56 document in light of these and other materials is the basis of these projected DGZs. The egress corridors appear to have been dependent on the destruction of the SA-1 sites by the planned ballistic missiles, Snark, and/or standoff air-launched missiles. In the absence of those systems B-47s would have had to rely on speed and electronic countermeasures to escape.

128. Price, *A History of US Electronic Warfare*, 161.

129. Price, *A History of US Electronic Warfare*, 165–66; Clark, *From Hitler's U-Boats to Khrushchev's Spyflights*, 219–22. There was advanced warning in 1952 that this shift would take place. See FOIA CIA, "Central Intelligence Bulletin, 17 September 1952."

130. Gordon et al., *Soviet Air Defence Aviation*, 237–40, 248, 308.

131. Gordon et al., *Soviet Air Defence Aviation*, 57.

132. Price, *A History of US Electronic Warfare*, 143.

133. Tegler, B-47 *Stratojet*, 85.

134. Tegler, B-47 *Stratojet*, 90–92.

135. FOIA USAF, "History of the 4347th Combat Crew Training Wing (Medium Bombardment) July 1958."

8. Prosteishiy Sputnik

1. LeMay's papers have no files for the period after he left SAC to the point where he was promoted to chief of staff of the air force in 1961.

2. The Moscow trip is covered in detail in LCMD, Twining Papers, box 90, and SCRC, Power Papers, oversize box 4.

3. This is suggested in Twining's daily diaries at LCDM for this period.

4. Twining handled investigations and reportage of these incidents. See LCMD, Twining Papers, box 102, Redline files.

5. This is based on a survey of the Thomas White Papers at LCMD. LeMay's communications with White suggest this.

6. See Divine, *The Sputnik Challenge*; Brzezinski, *Red Moon Rising*; Dickson, *Sputnik*.

7. There is some debate in the Russian literature as to the yield and parameters of the 2 February 1956 test. Most sources assert 80 kilotons, but a 2008 paper delivered by A. I. Aydin, S. A. Zelentsov, and A. M. Matuschenko titled "Warming Up the Nuclear Forge for Forging a Nuclear Sword" convincingly argues that the yield was actually a 0.3-kiloton groundburst 160 kilometers north of Aralsk and that the inflation of the yield was "purely populist action." The paper is archived on the ruzhany@narod.ru website.

8. Podvig, *Russian Strategic Nuclear Forces*, 487–89. Indeed the R-5M warhead later came in 300-kiloton and 1-megaton variants.

9. Brzezinski, *Red Moon Rising*, 35–36.

10. Dickson, *Sputnik*, 129.

11. LCMD, White Papers, box 7, memo for COSUSAF, 9 October 1957.

12. LCMD, White Papers, box 7, letter LeMay to White, 24 June 1957.

13. FOIA USAF, "History of the Strategic Air Command 1 January 1958–30 June 1958: Historical Study No. 19 Vol. I."

14. LCMD, White Papers, box 4, letter White to Power, 14 October 1957.

15. LCMD, White Papers, box 7, letter White to Power, 22 November 1957.

16. LCMD, White Papers, box 7, letter White to Burke, 26 November 1957.

17. LCMD, White Papers, box 7, letter Power to White, 23 December 1957.

18. See Podvig, *Russian Strategic Nuclear Forces*, 487–97; Nikolaev, "Submarine Participation in 1955–1961 Nuclear Tests" (in Russian), www.deepstorm.ru; see also the "53-61/53-61M" and "T-5/T-V/53-58" torpedoes at the Military Russian website (in Russian), www.militaryrussia.ru; Weir and Boyne, *Rising Tide*, 78–80.

19. LCMD, White Papers, box 7, letter Power to White, 23 December 1957.

20. LCMD, White Papers, box 16, letter White to Anderson, 5 June 1958.

21. As discussed in Maloney, *Deconstructing* Dr. Strangelove, ch. 9.

22. LCMD, White Papers, box 7, Fellers article and note: "How to Have the ICBM and a Better Defense and Still Cut the Budget $10 Billion."

23. LCMD, White Papers, box 7, memo White to SECAF, 6 December 1957.

24. LCMD, White Papers, box 5, memo White to LeMay, 2 December 1957.

25. LCMD, White Papers, box 5, USAF "Amendment to 20/7, Dated 6 March 1956," 9 December 1957.

26. FOIA USAF, "History of the Strategic Air Command 1 January 1958–30 June 1958: Historical Study No. 19 Vol. I."

27. FOIA USAF, "History of the Strategic Air Command 1 January 1958–30 June 1958: Historical Study No. 19 Vol. I."

28. Public Archives of Canada (PAC), RG 24, vol. 549, file 096103.v3: USAF CCS-Canada, letter CAS, 20 October 1958; memo CplansI to VCAS, "SAC Hostile Action Evacuation Plan," 10 February 1959; message Commander NNR to DI, "Orbit and Dispersal of SAC Aircraft," 16 May 1959.

29. LCMD, Twining Papers, box 106, memo JCS to SECDEF, "Positive Control Presentation to the NSC," 13 May 1958.

30. FOIA USAF, "History of the Strategic Air Command 1 January 1958–30 June 1958: Historical Study No. 19 Vol. I."

31. LCMD, Twining Papers, box 112, memo JCS to SECDEF, "Military Requirements for Civil Airports for Integration into the National Airport Plan," 1 February 1960. See also earlier memo, 8 January 1959.

32. DHH, Raymont Papers, 73/1223, Series 2, file 1085, memo CAS to CCOS, "USAF Requirements for SAC Tanker Bases in Canada," 15 June 1956.

33. DHH, Raymont Papers, 73/1223, Series 2, file 1085, memo CCOS to MND, "USAF Requirement for Refuelling Facilities in Canada," 20 November 1957.

34. DHH, Raymont Papers, 73/1223, Series 2, file 1085, CCOS to DI, "US Requirements for Refuelling Bases," 5 May 1958.

35. DHH, Raymont Papers, 73/1223, Series 2, file 1085, letter Tunner to CAS, "Aerial Refueling Base Requirements," 14 May 1958. For the possible tanker flight profiles, see Cox, "Operation LEAPFROG."

36. See FOIA USAF, "History of the Strategic Air Command 1 January 1958–30 June 1958: Historical Study No. 19 Vol. I," for the origins and initial testing of the Airborne Alert Force. The details of its evolution from there are in Maloney, *Deconstructing* Dr. Strangelove, ch. 7.

37. FOIA USAF, "History of the Strategic Air Command 1 January 1958–30 June 1958: Historical Study No. 19 Vol. I."

38. FOIA USAF, "History of the 307th Bombardment Wing, September 1958."

39. As discussed in Maloney, *Deconstructing* Dr. Strangelove, ch. 7, and *Learning to Love the Bomb*, ch. 8.

40. LCMD, Twining Papers, memo JCS to SECDEF, "SAC Exercise," 4 August 1959.

41. FOIA USAF, "History of the Strategic Air Command 1 January 1958–30 June 1958: Historical Study No. 19 Vol. I."

42. Hansen, *Swords of Armageddon*, TX 41/Mk 41 section.

43. Hansen, *Swords of Armageddon*, TX 46/Mk 53 section.

44. FOIA USAF, "History of the Strategic Air Command 1 January 1958–30 June 1958: Historical Study No. 19 Vol. I."

45. Hansen states in *Swords of Armageddon* that a 25-megaton weapon was stockpiled in 1960, based on a vague reference to an AEC press release he does not cite. He concludes it was the Mk-41 because the Mk-53 was not yet in service. There is no other corroborating source. The 25-megaton figure has been used uncritically in internet sources. A DOE declassification decision dated 20 November 2014 establishes that generally the B53/W53 yield was 9 megatons. The DOE declassification guide for 2002 repeats the 50- to 60-megaton figure and states that the W53 for the Titan II could be increased to 35 megatons.

46. DNA 6038F, "Operation HARDTACK I." See also three differently redacted FOIA versions of "WT-125: Operation HARDTACK Project 2.8, August 1959."

47. See "Operation Hardtack I," Wikipedia, https://en.wikipedia.org/wiki/Operation _Hardtack_I; Hansen, *US Nuclear Weapons*, 193–94. Other material argues that Koa was the XW-35 ballistic missile warhead prototype, except that the XW-35 was already on the rocks before Hardtack started as its yield was not large enough to make up for potential missile inaccuracy.

48. See the three differently redacted FOIA versions of "WT-125: Operation HARD-TACK Project 2.8, August 1959."

49. FOIA DOE, "Quarterly Progress Report Part III: Weapons July–September 1959."

50. FOIA DOE, "Final Report Task Group 7.4, Operation HARDTACK 1957–1958."

51. Baum, "Reminiscences of High-Power Electromagnetics"; Szasz, *The Day the Sun Rose Twice*, 81.

52. American Institute of Physics, Oral History Interviews, J. B. Taylor, interviewed by Kai-Henrik Barth, Wallingford, UK, 3 February 2007, https://www.aip.org/history -programs/niels-bohr-library/oral-histories/33073-1.

53. In part because both sides were likely violating the Atomic Energy Act of 1954. The following files remain closed at the UK National Archives: ES 1/669, "Radioflash from Atomic Explosives 1 January 1856–31 December 1956"; ES 4/361, "Theory of Radioflash Part 1: Early Phase of Radioflash; Part 2 Overall Picture of Radioflash, 1959." See also Baum, "Reminiscences of High-Power Electromagnetics."

54. Documentation declassified by the Eisenhower Library and provided to the DDRS, document 76/238D, briefing items for the president, "Project FLORAL Shot 6, 6 September 1958," 9 September 1958. By my estimation Floral consisted of the three Argus shots (27 and 30 August and 6 September 1958) and three concurrent shots from Hardtack: Yucca (28 April 1958), Teak (31 July 1958), and Orange (11 August 1958). On the covert facilities in South Africa, see USNARA, RG 59, box 2879, message State to Capetown, 19 March 1953 and 23 March 1959.

55. LCMD, White Papers, box 11, folder ACCS Reading File, September 1958, memo to White, "Preliminary Results of High Altitude Tests," 26 September 1958.

56. Herman Hoerlin, "United States High-Altitude Test Experiences: A Review Emphasizing the Impact on the Environment," monograph, Los Alamos National Laboratory, October 1976.

57. LCMD, White Papers, box 11, folder ACCS Reading File, August 1958, memo to White, "Possible Repeat of the TEAK Shot," 15 August 1958.

58. Baum, "Reminiscences of High-Power Electromagnetics."

59. LCMD, LeMay Papers, box B-134, folder Airborne Command Posts, SAC to HQ USAF, 28 December 1960.

60. LCMD, White Papers, box 1, letter Whitehead to White, 15 November 1956.

61. LCMD, White Papers, box 22, memo for CoS, "Tanker Requirements/Program Data," 1 July 1959.

62. LCMD, Twining Papers, box 76, memo LeMay to Twining, "SAC Position on Missiles," 26 November 1955.

63. Smith, *75 Years of Inflight Refueling*, 45.

64. LCMD, Twining Papers, box 105, memo JCS to SECDEF, 13 March 1958; FOIA USAF, "History of the Strategic Air Command June 1958–July 1959: Historical Study No. 79 Vol. I."

65. LCMD, Twining Papers, box 110, memo JCS to SECDEF, "Status of National Security Programs on 30 June 1959."

66. LCMD, Twining Papers, box 107, memo JCS to SECDEF, "Weapons Systems for Strategic Delivery," 20 January 1959.

67. LCMD, White Papers, box 16, letter Power to White, 5 February 1958. On Power Flite, see Smith, *75 Years of Inflight Refueling*, 44.

68. FOIA USAF, "History of the 4060th Air Refueling Wing, Jan–February 1958."

69. Hopkins, *The Boeing KC-135 Stratotanker*, 72.

70. FOIA USAF, "History of the 6th Air Division and 809th Air Base Group, 1–31 March 1958."

71. Knaack, *Post–World War II Bombers*, 138–39.

72. LCMD, White Papers, box 3, memo LeMay to White, 18 July 1957.

73. LCMD, White Papers, box 7, memo White to SECAF, "Defense against Possible Guided Missiles Program Reduction."

74. Knaack, *Post–World War II Bombers*, 128–30.

75. Werrell, *The Evolution of the Cruise Missile*, 120–21.

76. LCMD, Twining Papers, box 76, memo LeMay to Twining, "SAC Position on Missiles," 26 November 1955.

77. LCMD, Twining Papers, box 76, memo LeMay to Twining, "SAC Position on Missiles," 26 November 1955.

78. LCMD, White Papers, box 4, memo AVCOS for COSUSAF, "B-52 Air-to-Surface Missile," 20 August 1957; LCMD, White Papers, box 5, AVCOS to COSUSAF, "Review and Evaluation of the B-58 Program," 31 December 1957.

79. LCMD, Twining Papers, box 106, memo JCS to SECDEF, "Requirements for Warhead for GAM-77," 26 April 1958.

80. LCMD, White Papers, box 5, AVCOS to White, "Status of Goose and Quail Programs," 19 May 1958; LCMD, White Papers, box 14, memo LeMay to White, "Status of Goose and Quail Programs," 6 May 1958.

81. Werrell, *The Evolution of the Cruise Missile*, 124–25.

82. LCMD, White Papers, box 15, memo for Chairman, Aircraft and Weapons Board, "Requirement for an Advanced ASM," 1 July 1958; LCMD, White Papers, box 15, memo for COSUSAF, "Requirement for Advanced ASM," 9 July 1958; LCMD, White Papers, box 15, memo White to LeMay, 10 January 1958.

83. LCMD, White Papers, box 15, memo White to DCOSOPS, 16 October 1958.

84. LCMD, White Papers, box 16, memo AFCCS, "Penetration Aids," n.d.

85. LCMD, White Papers, box 21, memo for Program Panel, Weapon Board, "Guidance for Review of FY 60 Program," 10 April 1959.

86. LCMD, White Papers, box 21, memo for Program Panel, Weapon Board, "Guidance for Review of FY 60 Program," 10 April 1959.

87. LDMC, White Papers, box 27, letter Power to White, 11 August 1959.

88. See Wynn, RAF Nuclear Deterrent Forces; Hennessy, The Secret State (both editions); Moore, Nuclear Illusion, Nuclear Reality; Twigge and Scott, Planning Armageddon; Jones, The Official History of the UK Strategic Nuclear Deterrent.

89. Wynn, RAF Nuclear Deterrent Forces, 123–28, 256; Brookes, RAF Canberra Units of the Cold War, 57–61, 79.

90. The exact yields remain obscured, and there has been a lot of fancy footwork on the part of Her Majesty's government to keep it that way. For example, a Ministry of Defence Fact Sheet states that Yellow Sun Mk-2 was the first operational British thermonuclear weapon, which suggests that Violet Club and Yellow Sun Mk-1 were not thermonuclear in configuration. Similarly, the British categorization of a "megaton range" weapon as a weapon that is 500 kilotons or more in yield strains credulity. Wynn and Hely in Royal Air Force Historical Society, Journal No. 26, 77, note that Yellow Sun Mk-2, using the Red Snow Mk-28 derivative, was the first deployed "hydrogen warhead" and had tritium as a booster. Yellow Sun Mk-1 used a Green Glass, pure fission warhead that yielded 500 kilotons. Violet Club also used Green Glass but had a highly rudimentary safety system that used ball bearings. At least one source asserts that Violet Club yielded only 330 kilotons. Therefore it is legitimate to state that, in terms of deployable weapons in 1958, Britain lacked a megaton-yield thermonuclear weapon. Such a device had been tested during Grapple X, yielding 1.8 megatons in November 1957, but it would have taken time to weaponize. See also McIntyre, "The Development of Britain's Megaton Warheads," especially 58.

91. See Arnold, Britain and the H-Bomb, chs. 10–12.

92. Twigge and Scott, Planning Armageddon, 51.

93. Wynn, RAF Nuclear Deterrent Forces, 252–53.

94. Ashworth, RAF Bomber Command, 148 and appendix IX.

95. Wynn, RAF Nuclear Deterrent Forces, 123–28, 256; Brookes, RAF Canberra Units of the Cold War, 60–61.

96. Wynn, RAF Nuclear Deterrent Forces, refers to the half-yield issue, merely stating that the weapons were half of what was expected, while Moore, Nuclear Illusion, Nuclear Reality, states the the yields were 100 and 50 kilotons. See also FOIA USAF, "History of the Strategic Air Command 1 January 1958–30 June 1958: Historical Study No. 19 Vol. I."

97. FOIA USAF, "History of the Strategic Air Command 1 January 1958–30 June 1958: Historical Study No. 19 Vol. I."

98. Brookes, RAF Canberra Units of the Cold War, 60–61.

99. Hennessy, The Secret State: Whitehall and the Cold War, 187.

100. FOIA USAF, "History of the Strategic Air Command 1 January 1958–30 June 1958: Historical Study No. 19 Vol. I."

101. Wynn, RAF Nuclear Deterrent Forces, 261.

102. FOIA USAF, "History of the Strategic Air Command 1 January 1958–30 June 1958: Historical Study No. 19 Vol. I."

103. Wynn, RAF *Nuclear Deterrent Forces*, 279.

104. Specifically, Neufeld, *Ballistic Missiles in the United States Air Force*; Walker, *Atlas*; Stumpf, *Titan II*; Sheehan, *A Firey Peace in the Cold War*; Stine, ICBM; Boyes, *Thor Ballistic Missile*.

105. Neufeld, *Ballistic Missiles in the United States Air Force*, chs. 3 and 4.

106. Neufeld, *Ballistic Missiles in the United States Air Force*, 115.

107. Neufeld, *Ballistic Missiles in the United States Air Force*, 122.

108. See Heefner, *The Missile Next Door*, chs. 1 and 2.

109. LCMD, Twining Papers, box 76, memo LeMay to Twining, "SAC Position on Missiles," 26 November 1955.

110. LCMD, White Papers, box 5, letter McCorkle to White, 22 November 1957.

111. LCMD, White Papers, box 7, memo White to SECAF, "Thor/Jupiter Decision," 6 December 1957.

112. LCMD, White Papers, box 1, message AM to White, 18 December 1957.

113. LCMD, Twining Papers, box 92, memo Twining for SECDEF, "Operational Employment of the Land-Based Intermediate Range Ballistic Missiles (IRBM)," 1 March 1956.

114. LCMD, Twining Papers, box 92, memo Twining for SECDEF, "Operational Employment of the Land-Based Intermediate Range Ballistic Missiles (IRBM)," 1 March 1956.

115. LCMD, Twining Papers, box 92, memo AFCC to the JCS and service secretaries, "Assignment of Responsibility for Operational Employment of the Intermediate Range Ballistic Missile."

116. For details, see Wynn, RAF *Nuclear Deterrent Forces*; and Boyes, *Thor Ballistic Missile*.

117. The complexities of the NATO IRBM issue are adeptly handled by Nash in *The Other Missiles of October*.

118. LCMD, White Papers, box 12, message LeMay to Everest, 6 May 1958.

119. LCMD, White Papers, box 15, memo White to LeMay, 18 January 1958.

120. LCMD, White Papers, box 19, memo DCOSOPS to White, "Command and Control of the IRBM," 21 January 1958.

121. LCMD, White Papers, box 19, letter White to Power, 4 February 1958.

122. LCMD, Twining Papers, box 106, memo Twining to SECDEF, "Operational Responsibilities of SACEUR/USCINCEUR."

123. LCMD, White Papers, box 12, memo from DCOSOPS to COSUSAF, "Requirement for TM-76 Mace," 14 November 1958.

124. Wynn, RAF *Strategic Deterrent Forces*, 345.

125. LCMD, White Papers, box 22, Herter-Caccia agreement, 27 February 1958.

126. LCMD, White Papers, box 22, memo Runyon to Allison, "Thor Operational Status in the UK," 17 September 1959.

127. Wynn, RAF *Nuclear Deterrent Forces*, 353.

9. Coming Together

1. There appears to be no date in the available information that clearly delineates when the EWP becomes the BWP; one study uses the term as early as 1955. That said, practitioners continued to use "EWP" after the BWP was established, probably because they were used to it and it meant the same thing to them. Twining referred to the SAC Basic War Plan during the 1960 deliberations of what would become the SIOP. The SAC BWP was catego-

rized as an "Operations Plan" as opposed to guidance like the Joint Strategic Capabilities Plan. See LCMD, Twining Papers, box 113, memo CJCS to SECDEF, "Target Coordination and Associated Problems," 29 June 1960.

2. Prados, *The Soviet Estimate*, chs. 6, 7 and 8.

3. Podvig, *Russian Strategic Nuclear Forces*, 121–22, 136.

4. Podvig, *Russian Strategic Nuclear Forces*, 246.

5. LCMD, White Papers, box 7, letter Power to White, 23 December 1957; LCMD, White Papers, box 12, message Atkinson to LeMay, 21 May 1958.

6. See Maloney, "Arctic Sky Spies"; FOIA USAF, "History of the 14th Air Division, 1–30 April 58."

7. Aid, *The Secret Sentry*, 50–51.

8. Aldrich, GCHQ, frontispiece maps; "USAFSS/ESC/AIA Units," 6901st Special Communications Group, http://www.6901st.org/list.htm.

9. FOIA CIA, "Memorandum for the Record: Meeting in SA/PD/DCI office, Room 319 Administration Building on Thursday, 13 November 1958, at 9:00 am regarding Continuous or Blow by Blow Reporting [redacted]"; FOIA CIA, memo for SADPD, "Blow by Blow reporting to SAC," 12 November 58; FOIA CIA, memo for SARPC, "The Attached Papers (SC-06731/58)," 14 November 1958. See also David Ullian Larson, "Zweibrucken, Germany: 6901st Spec Comm Group 1963–1965," https://www.6901st.org/links/Links .htm (link expired; hardcopy in author's possession); Kivett, *Intelligence Failures and Decent Intervals*, 53.

10. As noted in Shackelford, "On the Wings of the Wind," which examines the activities of the RAF Kirknewton intercept station in the late 1950s.

11. Stone and Banner, "Radars for the Detection and Tracking of Ballistic Missiles, Satellites, and Planets."

12. FOIA CIA, Zabetakis and Peterson, "The Diyarbakir Radar"; Stone and Banner, "Radars for the Detection and Tracking of Ballistic Missiles, Satellites, and Planets."

13. See Bruce Barrett, "My Diyarbakir, Turkey, Experience 1958," Merhaba US Military, 2003, http://bocknights.com/1BARRETTBindex.html; "TUSLOG Detachments in Turkey," Merhaba US Military, 2003, http://bocknights.com/TUSLOGdetachments .html; "USAFSS/ESC/AIA Units," 6901st Special Communications Group, http://www .6901st.org/list.htm.

14. FOIA CIA, Chief, Productions Staff, ORR, "Release of Information as SECRET/ NOFORN," 10 January 1962; FOIA CIA, PIR, "Mukachevo MRBM Complex, USSR," January 1964; FOIA CIA, NPIC, "Mukachevo Propellant Handling and Storage Facility," November 1968. See also Strategic Missile Forces Directory, Missile Systems, "Medium Range Ballistic Missile R-5, R-5M (8A62, 8K51)" at (in Russian) ruzhany@narod.ru.

15. Rueger, "Kennedy, Adenauer, and the Making of the Berlin Wall," 37–38. A Russian member of the 72nd Engineer Brigade says that the unit was "alerted for combat use," that is, capable of conducting operations as opposed to imminent launch, in May 1959, one month after the warheads were mounted. The order to depart East Germany and return to the USSR came in August 1959. See the reminisces of A. A. Gulyaev in *Journal of Military History*, no. 10 (2013) (in Russian), republished at ruzhany@narod.ru. See also Smirnov, *Missile Systems of the Strategic Missile Forces from R-1 to TOPOLY-M, 1946–2006* (in Russian), archived at ruzhany@narod.ru.

16. FOIA CIA, "Status of Hungarian and Soviet Military Forces," 9 February 1959. I surveyed the former SS-3 sites near Mukachevo in summer 2019.

17. Pfeffer and Shaeffer, "A Russian Assessment of Several USSR and US HEMP Tests"; "EMP Articles That Shaped the Army HEMP Program"; Jerry Emanuelson, "Soviet Test 184," Futurescience, 7 July 2019, http://www.futurescience.com/emp/test184.html.

18. Nash in *The Other Missiles of October*, 67, writes, "Neither on the road nor in his private conferences with Eisenhower at Camp David (25–27 September) did he broach the IRBM issue. One can only speculate." This is likely because Soviet IRBMs were already deployed, and Khrushchev's accusatory propaganda campaign against "NATO aggression" would have deflated had it become known they deployed first.

19. FOIA CIA: IR, "Air Bases and Guided Missile Launching Site in Crimea," 29 June 1958; PIC, "Joint Photographic Intelligence Report," 17 December 1960; "Medium Range Ballistic Missile Deployment in East Germany, 20 April 1961"; PIL, "Talent/Keyhole Reports June-November 1961," December 1961; NPIC, PIOR, 8 September 1961; NPIC, PIOR, 15 September 1961; NPIC, "Photographic Interpretation OAK Report," 18 October 1961; PIR, "Current Summary of Soviet MRBM Launch Areas Identified on Keyhole Photography," January 1962; Publications Staff to [redacted], "Release of Information as SECRET/NOFORN," 23 January 1962; NPIC, "OAK Part III: Mission 9040, 28–31 July 1962," August 1962; PIR, "Construction Timing of Soviet Deployed MRBM Launch Sites," August 1962; PIR, "Gvardeysk MRBM Launch Complex, USSR," November 1963; PIR, "Simferopol MRBM Complex," February 1964; PIR, "Gvardeysk MRBM Complex, USSR Fixed Field Sites No 1 and 2," February 1965; COMOR, Working Group, "Revised list of [redacted]," 18 June 1964. The U.S. Navy generated a Talent report, "Feodosiya Area GM Launch Site, Poss," between 1956 and 1958; the grid reference puts the site in the Black Sea, but it does line up with the SS-3 sites on land. Whether this was an error or a report was generated or not cannot be determined with available information.

20. FOIA CIA, JPIM, "Novaya Mezinovka Storage Installation," 1 August 1958.

21. FOIA USAF, "History of the 819th Air Division, 1–31 October 59."

22. LCMD, Twining Papers, box 106, memo Twining to SECDEF, 9 April 1959.

23. DDEL, Norstad Papers, Country files, France 1955–59 (6), "Status of Atomic Strike Forces in France," n.d.

24. LCMD, Twining Papers, box 112, memo for SECDEF, "Analysis of United States Retaliatory Posture," 1 April 1960; DDEL, Norstad Papers, Country files, France 1955–59 (6), "Status of Atomic Strike Forces in France," n.d.

25. Mindling and Bolton, *US Air Force Tactical Missiles*, 199–201.

26. FOIA State, memcon Norstad Meeting, 4 February 1959.

27. FOIA JCS, memo JCS to US rep NATO SG, "Planning Assumptions on Atomic Weapons," 22 September 1958.

28. NA (UK) DEFE 6/26, COSC JPS, "SACEUR's Emergency Defence Plan-1958."

29. Vizcarra, *Hun Pilot*, 14, 20, 53; Downer, *Victor Alert*, 11, 12; Kerzon, *Throw a Nickel on the Grass*, 27–29; Samuel, *Glory Days*, ch. 5.

30. The approximation of seventy-six weapons is based on four Victor Alert aircraft per F-100 wing; twelve alert aircraft total for the F-101A wings; four alert aircraft total for the B-66 wings; six Matadors on alert; and one alert aircraft per Canberra base, for a total of four. The Aviano F-100 force sometimes had six or more aircraft on alert, and later on the B-66s could carry two Mk-28s each.

31. John Lowery, "The One-Way Nuclear Mission," *Air Force*, 29 August 2017, http://www.airforcemag.com/MagazineArchive/Pages/2017/October%202017/The-One-Way-Nuclear-Mission.aspx.

32. Kerson, *Throw a Nickel on the Grass*, 27–29.

33. See Die FUTT der NVA, www.nva-futt.de, an extensive website in German dealing with all aspects of the Communist air defense systems in East Germany, maintained by veterans of those systems. See Kersten et al., *Garnisonen der NVA und GSTD* for a detailed examination of NVA facilities.

34. See NR-14, http://home.snafu.de/veith/nr-14.htm; "FUTT in the Western Group of Forces," Die FUTT der NVA, www.nva-futt.de; see entries on Merseberg and Wittstock at "Sperrgebiet: Bunker abd Militaeranlangen dokumentiert," http://www.sachsenschiene.net/. All sites are in German. These protected facilities were believed to have been constructed in 1958.

35. Brookes, RAF *Canberra Units of the Cold War*, 78–84; Jackson, *Canberra*, ch. 5.

36. Jackson, *Canberra*, 41.

37. Kampe, *The Underground Military Command Bunkers of Zossen, Germany*, 35–37; Royal Air Force Historical Society, *Journal No. 23*, 38. In the 1950s BRIXMIS also got into Soviet bunkers while they were under construction prior to occupation, including air defense bunkers. See also FOIA CIA, "Current Intelligence Bulletin, 3 June 1952."

38. LCMD, Twining Papers, box 11, memo JCS to SECDEF, "MACE (TH 76-B) Program," 16 October 1959.

39. On delivery techniques, see Vizcarra, *Hun Pilot*, 20, 24–25.

40. "Geographical Coordinates of the FUTT" and "FUTT in the Western Group of the Soviet Armed Forces" (both in German), Die FUTT der NVA, www.nva-futt.de. I have adjusted the number of sites and locations to reflect the late 1950s.

41. Downer, *Victor Alert*, 29.

42. Knaack, *Post–World War II Fighters*, 133.

43. Mindling and Bolton, *US Air Force Tactical Missiles*, 115–16.

44. Kerzon, *Throw a Nickel on the Grass*, 25, 29–30.

45. Kerzon, *Throw a Nickel on the Grass*, 30.

46. Lowery, "The One-Way Nuclear Mission."

47. LCMD, White Papers, box 1, message Smith to White, 24 March 1960.

48. FOIA CIA, Office of Scientific Intelligence (OSI), "Electronic Aspects of the Soviet Air Defense System," 3 March 1958. See also "1st Radio-Technical Brigade," WW2, http://www.ww2.dk/new/pvo/radar/1rtbr.htm; "19th Air Defence Division," WW2, http://www.ww2.dk/new/pvo/19dpvo.htm.

49. LCMD, Twining Papers, box 112, memo for SECDEF, "Analysis of United States Retaliatory Posture," 1 April 1960; Miller, "The Ups and Downs of an F-100 Super Sabre Pilot."

50. LCMD, Twining Papers, box 112, memo for SECDEF, "Analysis of United States Retaliatory Posture," 1 April 1960; "Robert Gonzalez," Honoring Our Marin Veterans, http://honoringmarinveterans.org/robert-gonzalez/.

51. Mark Thompson, "Air Force Capt. Tony McPeak, over Vietnam," *Time*, 14 June 2012, http://nation.time.com/2012/06/14/capt-tony-mcpeak-over-vietnam/.

52. Thompson, "Air Force Capt. Tony McPeak, over Vietnam."

53. See Vito Tomasino, *Close Calls and Other Neat Stories,* ch. 7, https://www.kracek.com/close-calls.html.

54. LCMD, White Papers, box 12, memo DCOS to COS, "Requirements for TM-76 MACE," 14 November 1958.

55. Sherwood, *Fast Movers,* 14.

56. LCMD, White Papers, box 12, memo DCOS to COS, "Requirements for TM-76 MACE," 14 November 1958.

57. Walpole, *Voodoo Warriors,* 124.

58. "F-101A/C Voodoo," Aviation Forum, https://www.key.aero/forum/historic-aviation/91689-f-101a-c-voodoo?page=4. See also Keith Snyder's commentary, "Robin Olds and the Nuclear Voodoos," *Tails through Time,* 12 September 2010, http://aviationtrivia.blogspot.com/2010/09/robin-olds-and-nuclear-voodoos.html.

59. Snyder, "Robin Olds and the Nuclear Voodoos."

60. Samuel, *Glory Days,* 63.

61. Samuel, *Glory Days,* 64.

62. Brookes, RAF *Canberra Units of the Cold War,* 60–61.

63. Downer, *Victor Alert,* 38.

64. These data were extracted by a thorough examination of the Mediterranean cruise books for USS *Essex,* USS *Intrepid,* USS *Randolph,* USS *Franklin Delano Roosevelt,* USS *Forrestal,* and USS *Saratoga* for the years 1957 to 1960 located at Unofficial US Navy Site, https://www.navysite.de/.

65. Maloney, *Securing Command of the Sea,* 156.

66. Hansen, *US Nuclear Weapons,* 137, 142, 146; Hansen, *Swords of Armageddon,* entries for Mk-8, Mk-27; Little, *Brotherhood of Doom,* 34–38; Maggelet and Oskins, *Broken Arrow,* 27–31; Richard Lundy, "Idiot's Loop: The Day I Nuked Los Angeles," *Flight Journal,* June 2014, https://www.flightjournal.com/wp-content/uploads/2014/06/idiots-loop.pdf?746277.

67. "The Blue Blasters are the only deployed squadron in the Atlantic using the Martin Bullpup air to ground missile. Half way through the cruise their Skyhawks had fired approximately sixteen of these new weapons with amazing accuracy." Unofficial US Navy Site, https://www.navysite.de/cruisebooks/cv60–59/219.htm. See also Hansen, *US Nuclear Weapons,* 184, 187.

68. This was derived from an analysis of the U.S. Navy sections of FOIA CIA, CPIC, "Listing of TALENT Reports 1956 through 1958," and FOIA CIA, OCR, "Listing of TALENT Reports, 1957."

69. See USNOA, Adm. George Anderson oral history; Holloway, *Aircraft Carriers at War,* ch. 7. Author Daniel Ford collected the reminiscences of former AD Skyraider personnel engaged in nuclear operations in Ford et al., *Carrying a Nuke to Sevastopol.*

70. Holloway, *Aircraft Carriers at War,* ch. 7. See also LCMD, Twining Papers, box 107, memo Twining for SECDEF, "Weapons Systems for Strategic Delivery," 20 January 1959.

71. Derived from an analysis of the U.S. Navy sections of FOIA CIA, CPIC, "Listing of TALENT Reports 1956 through 1958," and FOIA CIA, OCR, "Listing of TALENT Reports, 1957"; Holloway, *Aircraft Carriers at War,* ch. 7; Miller, *Nuclear Weapons and Aircraft Carriers,* 98, 132. As discussed in detail in Ford et al., *Carrying a Nuke to Sevastopol;* 90th Independent Assault Aviation Regiment, http://www.ww2.dk/new/air%20force/regiment/shap/90oshap.htm.

72. FOIA CIA, memo Navy Member AdHoc Requirements Committee to Chairman AdHoc Requirements Committee, "Vlone Bay, TALENT Coverage of," 13 March 1959. See also FOIA CIA, Jpint Photographic Intelligence Brief, "Pasha-Liman Submarine Base," 25 February 1959.

73. Derived from an analysis of the U.S. Navy sections of FOIA CIA, CPIC, "Listing of TALENT Reports 1956 through 1958," and FOIA CIA, OCR, "Listing of TALENT Reports, 1957."

74. Derived from an analysis of the U.S. Navy sections of FOIA CIA, CPIC, "Listing of TALENT Reports 1956 through 1958," and FOIA CIA, OCR, "Listing of TALENT Reports, 1957."

75. FOIA CIA, IR, "Submarine Base in Balaklava," 13 December 1949; FOIA CIA, IR, imagery, "Probable Submarine Pen, Balaklava Submarine Base USSR," n.d.; FOIA CIA, IR, "Balaklava Submarine Base," 24 September 1984 (redacted); FOIA CIA, NPIC, "Probable Popup Test Preparations Balaklava Submarine Base and Ship Repair Yard, USSR, 1982." See also Yulia Samarina, "The Cold War Museum in Balaklava," Perekop, 29 April 2012 (in Russian), http://www.perekop.info/balaklava-military-navy-museum/.

76. Derived from an analysis of the U.S. Navy sections of FOIA CIA, CPIC, "Listing of TALENT Reports 1956 through 1958," and FOIA CIA, OCR, "Listing of TALENT Reports, 1957."

77. Derived from an analysis of the U.S. Navy sections of FOIA CIA, CPIC, "Listing of TALENT Reports 1956 through 1958," and FOIA CIA, OCR, "Listing of TALENT Reports, 1957." See J. P. Santiago, "The Bomber Career of the Douglas A-3 Skywarrior, 1955–1968," *Tails through Time*, 18 January 2016, http://aviationtrivia.blogspot.com/2016/01/the-bomber-career-of-douglas-3.html; Miller, *Nuclear Weapons and Aircraft Carriers*, ch. 6.

78. "21st Air Defence Corps," WW2, http://www.ww2.dk/new/pvo/21kpvo.htm; Gordon and Kommissarov, *Soviet Air Defence Aviation*, 238, 247.

79. "21st Air Defence Corps," WW2, http://www.ww2.dk/new/pvo/21kpvo.htm; FOIA CIA, OSI, "Electronic Aspects of the Soviet Air Defense System," 3 March 1958.

80. "21st Air Defence Corps," WW2, http://www.ww2.dk/new/pvo/21kpvo.htm; FOIA CIA, OSI, "Electronic Aspects of the Soviet Air Defense System," 3 March 1958; FOIA CIA, PIC, "Listing of TALENT Reports 1956 through February 1960," April 1960; FOIA CIA, PIC, "Listing of TALENT Reports, March 1959"; FOIA CIA, NSA, "Soviet Air Defense Installations of Advanced Design Located at Krasnovodsk, Murmashi, and Orisk in the USSR," 2 October 1959.

81. FOIA CIA, CPIC, "Listing of TALENT Reports 1956 through 1958"; FOIA CIA, OCR, "Listing of TALENT Reports, 1957." CIA PIR, "Communications Facility, Olenegorsk, USSR," January 1965, has the entire Olenegorsk-2 site blanked out, but it is clear that the site was under observation some time prior to this report: it was constructed in 1954. See also Rusian Ustrakhanov, "Scandinavia's Nuclear Threat: Olenegorsk-2—The Frightening Nuclear Fairy Tale of the Kola Peninsula," *European Dialogue*, 16 September 2013, http://eurodialogue.org/Scandinavia-Nuclear-Threat-Olenegorsk-2; "12th GUMO," WW2, http://www.ww2.dk/new/rvsn/12gumo.htm.

82. FOIA CIA, "The Soviet Northern Fleet," 9 July 1968 (redacted). I have employed the data that were active and available in the late 1950s in this depiction. See also FOIA CIA, "ODE 2040," 13 October 1957.

83. Derived from an analysis of the U.S. Navy sections of FOIA CIA, CPIC, "Listing of TALENT Reports 1956 through 1958," and FOIA CIA, OCR, "Listing of TALENT Reports, 1957."

84. FOIA CIA, PIB, "Soviet Naval Bases and Shipyards: Baltic Sea Fleet," March 1968.

85. FOIA USAF, "History of the Strategic Air Command 1 January 1958–30 June 1958: Historical Study No. 19 Vol. I."

86. LCMD, White Papers, box 26, "Quotes from Testimony in front of the House Appropriations Committee, 28 May 1958."

87. Wynne, RAF Deterrent Forces, 261–63, 272.

88. Brookes, Valiant Squadrons of the Cold War, 75; Brookes, Victor Squadrons of the Cold War, 17.

89. Wynne, RAF Deterrent Forces, 274; Moore, Nuclear Illusion, Nuclear Reality, 101; Brookes, Valiant Squadrons of the Cold War, 75.

90. FOIA CIA, OSI, "Electronic Aspects of the Soviet Air Defense System," 3 March 1958.

91. ISCAP, "History of the Strategic Air Command Historical Study #73A: SAC Targeting Concepts," (April 1959?).

92. Secondary sources tend to focus on V-Force in the 1960s, and there are elaborate discussions of the northern route but little on the southern route. See Brookes, RAF V-Force 1955–69 Operations Manual, 119–23. Former V-Force aircrew have discussed the existence of the southern route prior to its elimination by 1960. See the forums at Professional Pilots Rumour Network, https://www.pprune.org/aviation-history-nostalgia/111797-did-you-fly-vulcan-merged-91.html and https://www.pprune.org/aviation-history-nostalgia/111797-did-you-fly-vulcan-merged-22.html.

93. LCMD, Twining Papers, box 109, memo JCS to SECDEF, "Strategic Air Command Exercise," 4 August 1959; LCMD, Twining Papers, box 11, memo JCS to SECDEF, "July Report on Strategic Air Command Exercise," 1 September 1959.

94. LCMD, White Papers, box 21, memo LeMay to Power, "Airborne Alert Concept."

95. Maloney, Deconstructing Dr. Strangelove, ch. 7.

96. FOIA CIA, GIR, "Noyaya Zemlya, January 1958."

97. See, for example, FOIA CIA, PIB, "Mys Zhelaniya, December 1957."

98. "991st Fighter Aviation Regiment PVO," WW2, http://www.ww2.dk/new/air%20force/regiment/iap/991iap.htm; "4th Air Defence Division," WW2, http://www.ww2.dk/new/pvo/4dpvo.htm.

99. FOIA CIA, memo from Chief, Publications Staff ORR to Chief [redacted], "Release of Information as SECRET/NOFOR to [redacted]," 10 January 1962; FOIA CIA, PIC, "Preliminary OAK 9013," 17 December 1960; FOIA CIA, PIC, memo for COMOR, "USSR and Satellite Targets for Aerial Reconnaissance (CHESS)," 12 September 1961; FOIA CIA, NPIC, "Probable Launch Sites Plesetsk ICBM Complex USSR," 3 June 1966; FOIA CIA, PIC, "ICBM Launch Complex Plesetsk, USSR February 1963."

100. FOIA CIA, "ODE 4155," 9 April 1960.

101. FOIA CIA, NIE 11-2A-63, "The Soviet Atomic Energy Program, 2 July 1963." See also FOIA CIA, CPIC, "Listing of TALENT Reports 1956 through 1958," and FOIA CIA, OCR, "Listing of TALENT Reports, 1957." The 1963 document provides what was known and how that knowledge evolved throughout the 1950s.

102. FOIA CIA, JPIR, "Electric Power in the Ural Region, USSR, July 1961." An earlier version of this report generated from Talent data was available in early 1959.

103. SAC also had Talent reportage on Pooch (Punch) airfield in Kashmir, but the probability of a B-52 taking off again from it if it landed successfully was almost nil.

Pakistan, however, had been approached in 1954 and was "receptive" to the possibility of providing access to B-47-capable airfields. FOIA CIA, "Current Intelligence Bulletin, 29 October 1954."

104. Derived from FOIA USAF, "History of the Strategic Air Command June 1958–July 1959: Historical Study No. 76 Vol. I"; LCMD, Twining Papers, box 110, memo to SECDEF, "Status of National Security Programs," 2 October 1959; LCMD, Twining Papers, box 115, memo to SECDEF, "Status of National Security Programs," 18 July 1960.

105. The alert figures per aircraft per wing per base were derived from an analysis of twenty-eight B-47 and B-52 wings from 1958 to 1960 supplemented with information from Twining Papers memoranda to SECDEF on the "Status of National Security Programs" for 1959 and 1960. At the low end it was four B-52s per wing, and at the high end nine per wing. B-47 units at the high end had fifteen B-47s on alert for a four-squadron wing, but this fluctuated in relationship to Reflex and Air Mail deployments.

106. FOIA USAF, "History of the 819th Air Division, 1–31 October 1959."

107. FOIA CIA, PIC, "Listing of Talent Reports, March 1959." I compared the Talent listing's latitude and longitude with Google Earth imagery and cross-indexed it with Soviet PVO order of battle data and concluded this was probably not a functional airfield associated with military activity.

108. FOIA USAF, "History of the 4081st Strategic Wing, 1–30 April 58."

109. On Eighth Air Force structure, see Lloyd, *A Cold War Legacy*, 301. My assumption, based on an analysis of Talent reports, is that Eighth Air Force essentially picked up the 7th Air Division targeting when that force was reduced to Reflex operations and added them to their existing area of operations. For the available weapons, see FOIA USAF: "History of the 100th Bombardment Wing, 1 Sep–31 October 59"; "History of the 4135th Strategic Wing, 1–30 September 60"; "History of the 817th Air Division, October 1960"; "History of the 4039th Strategic Wing, 1–31 October 1960."

110. See Sean Maloney, "First Steps to Atomic Partnership: Canadian Support to Strategic Air Command in the Early Cold War: 1946–1952," unpublished paper, 2015.

111. Lloyd, *A Cold War Legacy*, 301.

112. "14th Air Defence Corps," ww2, http://www.ww2.dk/new/pvo/14kpvo.htm. See also FOIA CIA, CPIC, "Listing of TALENT Reports 1956 through 1958"; FOIA CIA, OCR, "Listing of TALENT Reports, 1957." See also the updates of March 1959, April 1960, May 1960, June 1960, July 1960, August 1960, and November 1960.

113. "15th Lvovskiy Red Banner Air Defence Corps," ww2, http://www.ww2.dk/new/pvo/15kpvo.htm. See also FOIA CIA, CPIC, "Listing of TALENT Reports 1956 through 1958"; FOIA CIA, OCR, "Listing of TALENT Reports, 1957." See also the updates of March 1959, April 1960, May 1960, June 1960, July 1960, August 1960, and November 1960.

114. Probably containing units of the 28th Air Division. See "28th Air Defence Division," ww2, http://www.ww2.dk/new/pvo/28dpvo.htm.

115. FOIA CIA, CPIC, "Listing of TALENT Reports 1956 through 1958"; FOIA CIA, OCR, "Listing of TALENT Reports, 1957." See also the updates of March 1959, April 1960, May 1960, June 1960, July 1960, August 1960, and November 1960.

116. FOIA CIA, CPIC, "Listing of TALENT Reports 1956 through 1958"; FOIA CIA, OCR, "Listing of TALENT Reports, 1957."

117. FOIA CIA, CPIC, "Listing of TALENT Reports 1956 through 1958"; FOIA CIA, OCR, "Listing of TALENT Reports, 1957." See also the updates of March 1959, April 1960, May 1960, June 1960, July 1960, August 1960, and November 1960.

118. Price, *A History of US Electronic Warfare*, 242–44; FOIA USAF, "History of the 4134th Strategic Wing, 1 May 59–31 July 59."

119. FOIA USAF: "History of the 57th Air Division November 58"; "History of the 93rd Bombardment Wing November 58"; "History of the 96th Bombardment Wing, 1–28 February 59"; "History of the 100th Bombardment Wing, 1 Sep–31 October 59"; "History of the 100th Bombardment Wing, 1–30 September 60"; "History of the 4128th Strategic Wing, January 59–March 60"; "History of the 4130th Strategic Wing, 1–30 April 60"; "History of the 4134th Strategic Wing, 1 May 59–31 July 59"; "History of the 802nd Air Division, 1–30 November 59"; "History of the 4135th Strategic Wing, 1–30 September 60"; "History of the 4039th Strategic Wing, 1–31 October 60"; "History of the 817th Air Division October 1960."

120. FOIA USAF: "History of the 96th Bombardment Wing 1–28 February 59"; "History of the 100th Bombardment Wing, 1–30 September 60"; "History of the 4126th Strategic Wing, 1–31 December 59"; "History of the 4130th Strategic Wing 1–30 April 60"; "History of the 4134th Strategic Wing, 1 May 59–31 July 59"; "History of the 4228th Strategic Wing, 1–31 October 60."

121. Malucci, B-47 *Stratojet*, 135.

122. FOIA CIA, PIC, "Listing of TALENT Reports, June 1960," and "Listing of TALENT Reports, July 1960." See also the updates of March 1959, April 1960, May 1960, June 1960, July 1960, August 1960, and November 1960.

10. Megadeath Musings

1. Rather than rely on the existing secondary literature discussing the 1950s debate over "finite deterrence," I have chosen to depict the debate through White's perspective, as this receives little or no examination elsewhere.

2. LCMD, White Papers, box 1, letter Whitehead to White, 18 December 1954.

3. LCMD, White Papers, box 1, memo Paul to White, "Summary of Sir John Slessor's new book, Strategy for the West," n.d.

4. LCMD, White Papers, box 1, memo Paul to White, "Princeton Report on Massive Retaliation," n.d.

5. FOIA USAF, USAF Historical Division Liaison Office, George F. Lemmer, "The Air Force and Strategic Deterrence, 1951–1960," December 1967.

6. LCMD, White Papers, box 6, letter Weyland to White, 16 July 1957.

7. LCMD, White Papers, box 7, memo White to SECAF, 16 July 1957.

8. It was led by LeMay's eventual 1965 replacement as chief of staff, Maj. Gen. John McConnell, former 7th Air Division commander, a planner at SAC HQ, and commander of the Second Air Force. Panel members were Maj. Gen. Walter Sweeney, the Eighth Air Force commander; Brig. Gen. William "Spike" Momyer, director of plans, representing TAC; and Brig. Gen. Howell Estes, representing the air transport community. Col. John C. Meyer, future CINCSAC, was the Air Defense Command rep.

9. LCMD, White Papers, box 6, folder "The McConnell Report."

10. LCMD, White Papers, box 6, folder "The McConnell Report."

11. LCMD, White Papers, box 6, folder "The McConnell Report."

12. LCMD, White Papers, box 6, folder "The McConnell Report."

13. LCMD, White Papers, box 6, folder Commander's Conference, 4 November 1957. See transcribed notes.

14. LCMD, White Papers, box 6, folder Commander's Conference, 4 November 1957. See transcribed notes.

15. LCMD, White Papers, box 6, letter Dixon to White, 6 November 1957.

16. LCMD, White Papers, box 16, note Power to White, 18 December 1957.

17. LCMD, White Papers, box 17, letter White to Weyland, 12 May 1958.

18. LCMD, White Papers, box 19, White address, "Military Requirements and Resources for FY 60–62, 21 June 58."

19. LCMD, White Papers, box 11, memo Richardson to Gerhardt, 18 July 1958.

20. LCMD, White Papers, box 16, letter Power to White, 20 July 1958.

21. LCMD, White Papers, box 15, notes on White, LeMay, Power, and Twining meeting with McElroy, 23 November 1958.

22. LCMD, White Papers, box 26, memo Baer to Director of Information Services, 3 February 1959.

23. LCMD, White Papers, box 21, AFCCS Reading file, undated note from LeMay.

24. As quoted in Rosenberg, "Origins of Overkill."

25. LCMD, White Papers, box 29, letter White to Norstad, 3 March 1959.

26. LCMD, White Papers, box 29, letter White to Norstad, 3 March 1959.

27. LCMD, White Papers, box 28, folder Commander's Conference, foolscap notes.

28. LCMD, White Papers, box 29, letter White to Norstad, 3 March 1959.

29. LCMD, White Papers, box 27, letter Griswold to White, 1 May 1959.

30. LCMD, White Papers, box 27, letter Wheless to Westover, 12 May 1959.

31. LCMD, White Papers, box 29, letter White to Power, 11 May 1959.

32. LCMD, White Papers, box 29, letter White to Power, 11 May 1959.

33. ISCAP, "History of the Strategic Air Command Historical Study #73A: SAC Targeting Concepts."

34. LCMD, Twining Papers, box 116, memo Twining to Eisenhower, "Alternative Retaliatory Efforts," 13 January 1960.

35. LCMD, White Papers, box 27, letter Griswold to White, 1 May 1959.

36. Wynn, *RAF Deterrent Forces*, 276.

37. Wynn, *RAF Deterrent Forces*, 278.

38. Moore, *Nuclear Illusion, Nuclear Reality*, 256.

39. Twigge and Scott, *Planning Armageddon*, 71.

40. FOIA CIA, "Population Concentrations in the Soviet Union," 22 August 1960.

41. Wynn, *RAF Deterrent Forces*, 128.

42. FOIA CIA, (redacted) to (redacted) Memorandum for the Board, "Some Animadversions regarding the Matter of the 'Missile Gap,'" 21 December 1959. This interesting document should be contextualized as a senior CIA person's opinion on SAC capability during the Missile Gap debate and not as a detailed analysis of the Soviet air defense system. It is used here for computational simplicity.

43. LCMD, LeMay Papers, box B-203, letter Radford to LeMay and attached speech, 27 June 1956.

44. FOIA USAF, "History of the 4397th Refuelling Wing, May 1960."

45. FOIA USAF, "History of the 40th Bombardment Wing, May–June 1958."

46. FOIA USAF, "History of the Strategic Air Command 1 January 1958–30 June 1958: Historical Study No. 19 Vol. I."

47. FOIA USAF, "History of the 340th Bombardment Wing (Medium) August 1958."

48. FOIA USAF, "History of the Strategic Air Command 1 January 1958–30 June 1958: Historical Study No. 19 Vol. I."

49. As discussed in detail in Maloney, *Learning to Love the Bomb*.

50. My assessment of CFB Edmonton ammunition storage area.

51. FOIA USAF, "History of the Strategic Air Command 1 January 1958–30 June 1958: Historical Study No. 19 Vol. I."

52. LCMD, Twining Papers, box 105, has a note on a removed document dated 13 December 1957 relating to the storage of nuclear weapons in Cuba (Guantanamo Bay) and Bermuda. Gitmo stored nuclear depth bombs for the U.S. Navy but without critical nuclear components, while Kindley was a SAC refueling base. At the former Kindley Air Force Base, Bermuda, GoogleEarth imagery shows three overgrown igloos in what was clearly a secure compound on a small isthmus south of the runways, but it is not known when they were constructed. There appears to have been no assigned Air Depot Squadron. There was considerable speculation in the 1980s that this was a U.S. Navy maritime patrol aircraft wartime weapons storage area related to Yankee Box coverage in the 1970s and 1980s. Kevin Stevenson, "U.S. Asked to Explain Report about A-Bombs on Bermuda," UPI, 7 January 1985, https://www.upi.com/Archives /1985/01/07/US-asked-to-explain-report-about-A-bombs-on-Bermuda/4273350209704/.

53. LCMD, White Papers, box 27, letter Power to White, 2 June 1959.

54. Cochran et al., *Nuclear Weapons Databook*, 10–11.

55. FOIA USAF, "History of the 55th Strategic Reconnaissance Wing, Apr–September 56."

56. FOIA USAF, "History of the 4347th Combat Crew Training Wing (Medium Bombardment), July 1958."

57. FOIA CIA, memo Bissell for Dougherty, "Joint Agreement," 18 July 1958; FOIA CIA, memo to Special Assistant and Director, "Subject: [redacted]," 25 July 1958. See also Leavitt, *Following the Flag*, ch. 5.

58. Yenne, *B-52 Stratofortress*, 39, 41, 49, 54.

59. The 1009th was apparently absorbed into the 1035th USAF Field Activities Group on 7 July 1959, changed to the 1035th USAF Field Activities Group, which evolved into the Air Force Technical Applications Center. Information derived from AFTAC *Alumini Association Newsletter*, no. 1 (June 1985), which, unfortunately, is no longer available online.

60. Welch, "From the Beginning."

61. LCMD, White Papers, box 18, memo SAFUS for White, "Incorporation of the Long Range Detection Portion of the Atomic Energy Detection System into an International Test Moratorium Organization," 13 November 1958.

62. LCMD, White Papers, box 14, letter LeMay to White, "Tactical Air Objectives (1960–1970)."

63. LCMD, LeMay Papers, box B-144, letter Sweeney to LeMay, 3 October 1961.

64. LCMD, LeMay Papers, box B-144, letter Sweeney to LeMay, 3 October 1961.

65. FOIA USAF, "History of the 3902nd Air Base Wing, 1–31 January 60."

66. As detailed in Lehman, *Oceans Ventured*.

11. The Acme of Skill

1. Isenberg, *Shield of the Republic*, 644, 772; Galantin, *Submarine Admiral*, 189.

2. United States Pacific Fleet, Headquarters of the Commander in Chief, annual report, 19 July 1954, https://nautilus.org/wp-content/uploads/2012/09/CINCPACFLT-Annual-Report-1954.pdf.

3. "Reminiscences of Admiral Harry Donald Felt Volume I," U.S. Naval Institute, 1974; FOIA CIA, NSC Brief, "China Coast Incidents," 29 July 1954.

4. Laslie, *Architect of Air Power*, 114.

5. For details, see Kuter's blow-by-blow account, *Airman at Yalta*.

6. Laslie, *Architect of Air Power*, 116–17.

7. Laslie, *Architect of Air Power*, 142.

8. LCMD, White Papers, box 16, letter Kuter to White, 12 February 1958.

9. LCMD, Twining Papers, box 105, memo for SECDEF, "US Atomic Support of Non-Communist Countries," 27 December 1957.

10. LCMD, White Papers, box 4, message Kuter to White, 12 September 1957.

11. LCMD, Twining Papers, box 106, memo for SECDEF, "Security Treaty: Japan," 11 September 1958.

12. LCMD, White Papers, box 26, memo to White, 19 January 1958: "A Mk 7 bomb burned at K-55. There was no nuclear core in the bomb. The bomb was on a QUICK STRIKE aircraft and when the pilot allegedly hit the starter button both wing tanks fell off and caught fire." A follow-up memo from White to Kuter scolded, "Your reply . . . did not mention the conditions which existed at Osan-Ni (K-55)." LCMD, White Papers, box 12, message HQ USAF to CINCPACAF, 21 February 1958.

13. LCMD, White Papers, box 7, memo White to DCOS Ops, 26 August 1957; LCMD, White Papers, box 7, memo White to DCS/Plans and Programs, 13 August 1957; LCMD, White Papers, box 4, message Kuter to Smart, 24 September 1957, 26 September 1957.

14. LCMD, White Papers, box 2, message Koon to Berquist, n.d.; LCMD, White Papers, box 4, letter Kuter to Smart, 3 October 1957.

15. LCMD, White Papers, box 4, message Kuter to Smart, 3 October 1957.

16. LCMD, White Papers, box 6, memo Preston for White, "Considerations Involving 58th Fighter-Bomber Wing, 1st Marine Air Wing, and Naha Air Base, Okinawa," 11 September 1957.

17. LCMD, White Papers, box 6, memo Preston for White, "Considerations Involving 58th Fighter-Bomber Wing, 1st Marine Air Wing, and Naha Air Base, Okinawa," 11 September 1957. See Gearhart minute.

18. LCMD, White Papers, box 4, message Wetzel to Smart, 13 December 1957.

19. LCMD, White Papers, box 14, memo LeMay to COS, "RAND Presentation on Project SIERRA," 22 March 1958.

20. LCMD, White Papers, box 29, letter Kuter to White, 31 December 1958.

21. LCMD, White Papers, box 29, letter Kuter to White, 31 December 1958.

22. LCMD, White Papers, box 29, letter Kuter to White, 31 December 1958.

23. LCMD, White Papers, box 29, letter Kuter to White, 31 December 1958.

24. LCMD, White Papers, box 19, memo Kuter to White, 27 June 1958.

25. LCMD, White Papers, box 19, memo White to Kuter, "No Notice Operational Readiness Inspections of PACAF F-100 Units," 14 July 1958 and 21 July 1958.

26. How it did so requires substantially more research. The availability of information on Pacific Command missions and tasks prior to 1960 is limited. The CINCPAC annual history for 1960 likely reflects the same missions and tasks that were in play during 1958–59. See "CINCPAC Command History 1960," Nautilus Institute, 4 May 1961, https://nautilus .org/wp-content/uploads/2012/01/c_sixty.pdf.

27. Ellsberg, *The Doomsday Machine*, 72.

28. "CINCPAC Command History 1960."

29. RAND analyst Daniel Ellsberg states that when he was working with CINCPAC in the late 1950s Communist China and the USSR were treated as the same target set by CINCPAC for the GEOP and that this was based on guidance provided by Eisenhower. Even Ellsberg, after having access to CINCPAC planning at the time, was unsure of the exact relationship between the GEOP and SAC's BWP. Ellsberg, *The Doomsday Machine*, 87–88.

30. LCMD, Twining Papers, box 113, memo for SECDEF, "SAC Contingency Operations, Far East," 24 May 1960.

31. LCMD, White Papers, box 16, memo Kuter to White, 12 February 1958.

32. Leavitt, *Following the Flag*, 211–14.

33. Grimes, *The History of BIG SAFARI*, 32.

34. Pocock, *The U-2 Spyplane*, 126–28.

35. FOIA CIA, PIC: "Listing of TALENT Reports, September 1958"; "Listing of TALENT Reports, June 1958"; "Listing of TALENT Reports, November 1958"; "Listing of TALENT Reports, December 1958."

36. FOIA CIA, "ODE-6011," 8 March 1958.

37. Pocock and Fu, *Black Bats*, 31–36, 42–44.

38. Mikesh, *Martin B-57 Canberra*, 52. An internal CIA memorandum dated 10 October 1962 asserted, "There has been no real photographic coverage for almost ten years," which suggests that SENSINT or something like it was not exchanged until the dissolution of the SENSINT compartment. FOIA CIA, memo for COMOR, "Coverage of North Korea," 10 October 1962.

39. FOIA CIA, IR, "The North Korean Air Force," 15 November 1960 (x2), 28 March 1961.

40. Price, *A History of US Electronic Warfare*, 167.

41. Price, *A History of US Electronic Warfare*, 286. See also Waldron, *Site 18*, 115, 126–27.

42. FOIA CIA, PIR, "Airfield and Aircraft Summary, 1959 Communist China," April 1960. There were 250 IL-28s provided to Communist China by the Soviet Union in the early 1950s.

43. FOIA CIA, "Current Intelligence Bulletin, 31 March 1954."

44. FOIA CIA, IR, "The North Korean Air Force," 15 November 1960. This was up from 310 MIGs and down from 65 IL-28s in the 1956 NIE; see NIE 42.2-56, "Probable Developments in North Korea over the Next Few Years," 3 July 1956.

45. Calculated at an average of thirty-six MIGs per regiment. The number of regiments circa 1959 is drawn from "Air Defence Force (PVO)," WW2, http://www.ww2.dk/new /pvo/pvo.htm.

46. Calculated at twelve bombers per squadron and three squadrons per regiment. This number omits the Naval Aviation strike TU-16 regiments.

47. LCMD, White Papers, box 6, memo Preston to White, "Considerations involving 58th Fighter-Bomber Wing, 1st Marine Air Wing, and Naha Air Base, Okinawa," 11 September 1957.

48. Mikesh, *Martin B-57 Canberra*, 66–67.

49. LCMD, White Papers, box 12, memo Smith to White, "Comparison of Depot Squadrons at Kadena Air Base, Okinawa," 18 December 1958; LCMD, Twining Papers, box 106, memo for SECDEF, "Security Treaty-Japan," 11 September 1958: "The 'atom bomb' in any context still remains in Japan a matter of the utmost emotional intensity. Until such time as this feeling moderates to manageable proportions it would be altogether unrealistic to expect to obtain Japanese agreement for the introduction of nuclear components into Japan." Thus implying nonnuclear components of the weapons were already stored there. See also Paul Carpenter, "Nuclear Arms Work Leads to Wife and New Career," *Morning Call*, 8 August 1995.

50. Ellsberg, *The Doomsday Machine*, 80.

51. Holloway, *Aircraft Carriers at War*, ch. 8. It should be noted that some of the nuclear weapons in the *Salisbury Sound* magazine would have been anti-submarine warfare weapons for the P5M patrol aircraft tended by the ship. *Salisbury Sound*'s sister ship, USS *Norton Sound*, was used for the Argus tests in 1958. USS *Currituck*, another sister ship, rotated with *Salisbury Sound* in the Taiwan Patrol Force flag capacity.

52. Palmer, "My Most Interesting Tour of Duty."

53. John. E. Riggins, "History of Marine Detachments and USS *Curtiss*, 1951–1957," OO Cites, http://www.oocities.org/pentagon/barracks/9528/history.html; "USS *Curtiss*," CurtissWay, http://curtissway.com/uss_curtiss.html, and see links to "Atomic Marines."

54. LCMD, Twining Papers, box 115, "Status of U.S. National Security Programs," 18 July 1960.

55. LCMD, Twining Papers, box 105, memo for SECDEF, "Deployment of a Tactical Missile Group to Korea," 7 January 1958.

56. Mindling and Bolton, *US Air Force Tactical Missiles*, 104–6, 143–50.

57. FOIA USAF, "History of the 14th Aviation Depot Squadron, 1–31 May 59."

58. FOIA USAF, "History of the 96th Bombardment Wing, 1–28 February 59"; FOIA USAF, "History of the 96th Bombardment Wing, 1–31 December 59."

59. LCMD, Twining Papers, box 113, memo for SECDEF, "SAC Contingency Operations, Far East," 24 May 1960; FOIA USAF, "History of the Strategic Air Command 1 January 1958–30 June 1958"; LCMD, White Papers, box 12, memo Smith to White, "Comparison of Depot Squadrons at Kadena Air Base, Okinawa," 18 December 1958.

60. LCMD, Twining Papers, box 113, memo for SECDEF, "Contingency Operations, Far East," 24 May 1960.

61. FOIA USAF, "4134th Strategic Wing History 1 May 59–31 July 59."

62. FOIA USAF, "93rd Bombardment Wing (H) History, June 1960."

63. These data were derived from the 1957–60 cruise books for the aircraft carriers *Yorktown, Hornet, Ticonderoga, Lexington, Hancock, Bennington, Bon Homme Richard, Kearsarge, Shangri La, Midway*, and *Ranger*, http://www.navysite.de/cruisebooks.

64. These data were derived from the 1957–60 cruise books for the aircraft carriers *Yorktown, Hornet, Ticonderoga, Lexington, Hancock, Bennington, Bon Homme Richard, Kearsarge, Shangri La, Midway*, and *Ranger*, http://www.navysite.de/cruisebooks.

65. These data were derived from the 1957–60 cruise books for the aircraft carriers *Yorktown, Hornet, Ticonderoga, Lexington, Hancock, Bennington, Bon Homme Richard, Kearsarge, Shangri La, Midway*, and *Ranger*, http://www.navysite.de/cruisebooks.

66. USS *Ticonderoga*, 1958–59 cruise book, https://www.navysite.de/cruisebooks/cv14-59/274.htm.

67. USS *Bon Homme Richard*, 1958–59 cruise book, https://www.navysite.de/cruisebooks/cv31-58/162.htm.

68. USS *Lexington*, 1960 cruise book, https://www.navysite.de/cruisebooks/cv16-60/261.htm.

69. USS *Hancock*, 1957 cruise book, https://www.navysite.de/cruisebooks/cv19-57/257.htm.

70. USS *Hancock*, 1960–61 cruise book, https://www.navysite.de/cruisebooks/cv19-60/225.htm.

71. "Marine Attack Squadron 214," Wayback Machine, https://web.archive.org/web/20080403103800/http://www.3maw.usmc.mil/mag13/vma214/history.asp. See also USS *Hancock*, 1957 cruise book, "Baa Baa Black Sheep Banshees in the Sky," https://www.navysite.de/cruisebooks/cv19-57/265.htm; "High and Low Altitude Special Weapons Drops," https://www.navysite.de/cruisebooks/cv19-57/266.htm.

72. "CINCPAC Command History 1960," Nautilus Institute, 4 May 1961, https://nautilus.org/wp-content/uploads/2012/01/c_sixty.pdf.

73. Miller, *Nuclear Weapons and Aircraft Carriers*, 203.

74. This is a deduction on my part based on the USS *Midway* 1958 cruise book, https://www.navysite.de/cruisebooks/cv41-59/235.htm, plus the naval nuclear shore station Orbat, "Patches and Placques [*sic*]," Navy Nuclear Weapons Association, https://www.navynucweps.com/patches.htm.

75. USS *Ticonderoga*, 1957–58 cruise book, https://www.navysite.de/cruisebooks/cv14-58/index.html. See also "Patches and Placques [*sic*]," Navy Nuclear Weapons Association, https://www.navynucweps.com/patches.htm; William Cole, "Old Post, Revisited," *Honolulu Advertiser*, 3 May 2007.

76. USS *Lexington*, 1958 cruise book, https://www.navysite.de/cruisebooks/cv16-58/index.html.

77. USS *Shangri La*, 1958 cruise book, https://www.navysite.de/cruisebooks/cv38-58/index.html.

78. Stumpf, *Regulus*, 180–81, 117–20, 129–42, 180; Polmar and Moore, *Cold War Submarines*, 92–93.

79. Stumpf, *Regulus*, 129; FOIA OSD, "History of the Custody and Deployment of Nuclear Weapons July 1945 through September 1977." On nuclear weapons storage at Chichijima, see Palmer, "My Most Interesting Tour of Duty."

80. FOIA CIA, GMAIC, "Soviet Surface-to-Surface Missile Deployment," 1 September 1960. The bunker complex portals are on the north side of the hills and could be seen only with slant photography from the north, that is, inside Soviet airspace.

81. FOIA CIA, GIR, "The Soviet Arctic, July 1959"; FOIA CIA, GIR, "The Chukotsk Peninsula (n/d)"; FOIA CIA, OSI, "Electronic Aspects of the Soviet Air Defense System," 3 March 1958; FOIA CIA, OCI, "Current Intelligence Bulletin," 18 March 1954, 10 April 1954, 20 April 1954.

82. FOIA USAF, "History of the 14th Aviation Depot Squadron, 1–31 May 59."

83. Polmar and Moore, *Cold War Submarines*, 92–93.

84. FOIA CIA, CPIC, "Listing of TALENT Reports 1956 through 1958"; FOIA CIA, OCR, "Listing of TALENT Reports, 1957"; FOIA USAF, "History of the 92nd Bombardment Wing (Heavy), October 1958." Exercise Hot Strike V simulated the EWP.

85. FOIA USAF, "History of the 9th Bombardment Wing, Feb–March 1960"; Exercise Play Ball simulated the EWP with airbursts and retarded drop missions. See also FOIA CIA, OSI, "Electronic Aspects of the Soviet Air Defense System," 3 March 1958; FOIA CIA, memo from Chief, Project HTAUTOMAT to DD(I), "Possible Soviet Super Air Base Complexes," 16 December 1957.

86. FOIA USAF, "History of the 4126th Strategic Wing, 1–31 December 59"; FOIA CIA, CPIC, "Listing of TALENT Reports 1956 through 1958"; FOIA CIA, OCR, "Listing of TALENT Reports, 1957"; FOIA CIA, PIC, "Listing of Talent Reports December 1958"; FOIA CIA, "ODE-6011," 8 March 1958.

87. FOIA CIA, CPIC, "Listing of TALENT Reports 1956 through 1958"; FOIA CIA, OCR, "Listing of TALENT Reports, 1957"; FOIA CIA, OSI, "Electronic Aspects of the Soviet Air Defense System," 3 March 1958; FOIA CIA, PIC, "Listing of Talent Reports December 1958"; FOIA CIA, PIC, "Listing of Talent Reports March 1959."

88. FOIA CIA, EIR, "The Supply of Petroleum in the Far East," 29 August 1958; FOIA CIA, PIC, "Listing of Talent Reports June 1959."

89. FOIA CIA, NPIC/R-193/64, "Petropavlovsk Naval Base Tarya Bay, Petropavlovsk Kamchatskiy, USSR"; FOIA CIA, PIM, "Photographic Analysis of Petropavlovsk and Its Environs, 6 August 1956."

90. This is depicted in "1st City List Complete," National Security Archive, Nuclear Vault, 1964, https://nsarchive2.gwu.edu/nukevault/ebb538-Cold-War-Nuclear-Target -List-Declassified-First-Ever/documents/1st%20city%20list%20complete.pdf.

91. FOIA CIA, PIR, "Soviet Naval Bases and Shipyards: Pacific Ocean Fleet, Part I, March 1968." The data employed were current for the late 1950s.

92. FOIA CIA, PIC, "Listing of Talent Reports March 1959."

93. Little, *Brotherhood of Doom*, 82–83; Holloway, *Aircraft Carriers at War*, ch. 7; Miller, *Nuclear Weapons and Aircraft Carriers*, ch. 5.

94. FOIA CIA, CINCPACFLEET Intelligence Center, "Sino-Soviet Air Defenses Far East, 27 September 63." The data have been adjusted for the 1958–60 period.

95. Ellsberg, *The Doomsday Machine*, chs. 2 and 3.

96. Kelly McLaughlin, "Frozen in Time," *Daily Mail*, 22 March 2017, https://www .dailymail.co.uk/news/article-4338186/The-Soviet-submarine-hideout-revived.html.

97. While a young airman serving with the 4128th Strategic Wing, author John Palcewski created the navigational and target overlays used by the B-52 crews. See "John Palcewski's Journal," Live Journal, http://forioscribe.livejournal.com/.

98. Ellsberg, *The Doomsday Machine*, chs. 2 and 3.

99. Luethi, *The Sino-Soviet Split*, 95–97.

100. FOIA CIA, "Current Intelligence Bulletin, 4 September 1952."

101. "CINCPAC Command History 1960," Nautilus Institute, 4 May 1961, https://nautilus .org/wp-content/uploads/2012/01/c_sixty.pdf.

102. LCMD, White Papers, box 9, message White to Kuter, "No Notice Operational Readiness Inspections of PACAF F-100 Units," 14 July 1958 and 21 July 1958; LCMD, White Papers, box 12, memo for COS, "Requirement for TM-76 Mace," 14 November 1958.

103. FOIA CIA, IR, "The North Korean Air Force," 15 November 1960.

104. FOIA CIA, PCI, "Airfield and Aircraft Summary, 1959: Communist China," April 1960.

105. FOIA USAF, "History of the 95th Bombardment Wing (Heavy), 1–31 October 59"; FOIA USAF, "History of the Strategic Air Command 1 January 1958–30 June 1958: Historical Study No. 19 Vol. I."

106. FOIA USAF, "History of the 4134th Strategic Wing, May–July 1959."

107. FOIA CIA, PIC: "Cheng-hsien (Cheng-chou) Urban Area," 20 May 1959; "Chinan (Tsinan) Urban Area," 20 May 1959; "His-an (Sian) Urban Area," 20 May 1959; "Lo-yang Urban Area," 20 May 1959; "Tai-Yuan Urban Area," 27 August 1959; "Tientsin (Tien-ching) Urban Area," 27 August 1959; "Tsingta (Ching-tao) Urban Area," 20 May 1959; "Wu-han Urban Area," 1 September 1959.

108. FOIA CIA, PIC, "Peiping Urban Area."

109. FOIA CIA, JPIB, "Probable Site of Peiping Reactor," 23 February 1960; FOIA CIA, NPIC, "Airframe Plant Peiping, China," 24 February 1966; FOIA CIA, PIR, "Installations in the Vicinity of the Missile and Propulsion Test Complex Near Peiping, China," July 1963; FOIA CIA, PIR, "Order of Battle," July 1965; FOIA CIA, PIC, "Airfield and Aircraft Summary, 1959: Communist China"; FOIA CIA, IM, "Communist China: Expansion of the Iron and Steel Industry 1966–71," December 1971; FOIA CIA, IM, memo for Chief Resources Division from NPIC, "Three Pei-ping Power Plants," 13 August 1963; FOIA CIA, PIR, "The Chang-Hsin-Tien Missile Development Center Near Peiping, China," August 1965. Information known in the 1958–60 time frame was extracted from these sources.

110. Ellsberg, *The Doomsday Machine*, 88.

111. LCMD, White Papers, box 13, message LeMay to Kuter, 20 August 1958.

112. FOIA CIA, memo DNI to CIA, "Highest Priority Targets in CHICOM," 25 September 1958; FOIA CIA, "Naval Base and Shipyard Kiangnan, Shang-Hai, China," 3 December 1964; FOIA CIA, EIR, "The Shipbuilding Industry of Communist China," 27 August 1952; FOIA CIA, JPIR, "Shipyard and Naval Base, Ting-Hai, China," October 1959; FOIA CIA, PIB, "Hou-So-Cheng Submarine Base, China," October 1963; FOIA CIA, PIB, "Chou-Shan Naval Base and Shipyard," 9 September 1965; FOIA CIA, Mission K-4226, "Submarine Order of Battle," 23 October 1965. Information known in the 1958–60 time frame was extracted from these sources.

113. FOIA CIA, CINCPACFLEET Intelligence Center, "Sino-Soviet Air Defenses Far East, 27 September 63." The data have been adjusted for the 1958–60 period.

Conclusion

1. SCRC, Power Papers, box 4, letter Griswold to Power, 3 December 1958.

2. Warren Burkett, "In Nuclear War, Nobody Wins," *Abilene Reporter News*, 15 January 1959.

BIBLIOGRAPHY

Archives

This work relies heavily on declassified primary sources, many of them acquired through the Freedom of Information Act (FOIA), others through a variety of means. The proliferation of primary sources in singular document form on the internet has generated substantial decontextualization. I have attempted to identify the origins of such documents in the notes. During the course of this project the CIA established the CIA Records Search Tool (CREST) mechanism in conjunction with the U.S. National Archives and Records Administration. Materials requested by me under FOIA are now in the CREST system, therefore all CIA documents used here have been grouped as "FOIA CIA" in the notes and should be accessible in the CREST system. The following are the main repositories employed in this book:

CIA: Central Intelligence Agency
DDEL: Dwight D. Eisenhower Presidential Library, Abilene, Kansas
DDRS: Declassified Documents Reference System, electronic copies of documents from presidential libraries
DHH: Directorate of History and Heritage, Department of National Defence, Canada
DNA: Defense Nuclear Agency
DOE: Department of Energy
FRUS: *Foreign Relations of the United States*, series, Office of the Historian, U.S. Department of State
ISCAP: Interagency Security Classification Review Panel, online
JCS: Joint Chiefs of Staff
LCMD: Library of Congress Manuscript Division
NNSA: National Nuclear Security Administration
OSD: Office of the Secretary of Defense

PAC: Public Archives of Canada

SCRC: Special Collections Research Center, Syracuse University

USAF: U.S. Air Force

USNARA: U.S. National Archives and Records Administration

USNOA: U.S. Navy Operational Archive

Published Works

Aid, Matthew M. *The Secret Sentry: The Untold Story of the National Security Agency.* London: Bloomsbury Press, 2009.

Albright, Joseph, and Marcia Kunstel. *Bombshell: The Secret Story of America's Unknown Atomic Spy Conspiracy.* New York: Times Books, 1997.

Aldrich, Richard J. GCHQ: *The Uncensored Story of Britain's Most Secret Intelligence Agency.* London: Harper Press, 2010.

Allison, Graham, et al. *Hawks, Doves, and Owls: An Agenda for Avoiding Nuclear War.* New York: W. W. Norton, 1985.

Amis, Martin. *Koba the Dread: Laughter and the Twenty Million.* Toronto: Knopf, 2002.

Anders, Roger M., ed. *Forging the Atomic Shield: Excerpts from the Office Diary of Gordon E. Dean.* Chapel Hill: University of North Carolina Press, 1987.

Andrew, Christopher, and Vasili Mitrokhin. *The Mitrokhin Archive.* New York: Penguin Books, 1999.

———. *The Mitrokhin Archive II.* New York: Penguin Books, 2005.

Angelucci, Enzo, and Paolo Matricardi. *World War II Warplanes.* Vol. 2. New York: Rand McNally, 1977.

Applebaum, Anne. *Gulag: A History.* New York: Anchor Books, 2003.

———. *Iron Curtain: The Crushing of Eastern Europe 1944–1956.* Toronto: McClelland and Stewart, 2012.

———. *Red Famine: Stalin's War on Ukraine.* Toronto: McClelland and Stewart, 2017.

Arnold, Lorna. *Britain and the H-Bomb.* London: Palgrave Macmillan, 2001.

Ashworth, Chris. RAF *Bomber Command 1936–1968.* London: Patrick Stephens, 1995.

Bacevich, A. J. *The Pentomic Era: The US Army between Korea and Vietnam.* Washington DC: NDU Press, 1986.

Badash, Lawrence. *A Nuclear Winter's Tale: Science and Politics in the 1980s.* Cambridge MA: MIT Press, 2009.

Barlow, Jeffrey G. *Revolt of the Admirals: The Fight for Naval Aviation, 1945–1950.* Washington DC: Naval Historical Center, 1996.

Baum, Carl E. "Reminiscences of High-Power Electromagnetics." IEEE *Transactions on Electromagnetic Compatibility* 49, no. 2 (May 2007): 211–18.

Beer, Sigfried. "The Soviet Occupation of Austria, 1945–1955." *Akadeemia* 1 (2006): 1–15.

Beria, Sergo. *Beria My Father: Inside Stalin's Kremlin.* London: Duckworth, 2001.

Borowski, Harry. *A Hollow Threat: Strategic Air Power and Containment before Korea.* New York: Praeger Reprint Edition, 1982.

Bowyer, Michael J. F. *Force for Freedom: The USAF in the UK since 1948.* London: Patrick Stephens, 1994.

Boyes, John. *Thor Ballistic Missile: The United States and the United Kingdom in Partnership.* Croyden, UK: Fonthill Media, 2015.

Brands, H. W. *The General vs. the President: Macarthur and Truman at the Brink of Nuclear War*. New York: Doubleday, 2016.

Brookes, Andrew. RAF *Canberra Units of the Cold War*. Oxford: Osprey, 2014.

————. RAF *V-Force 1955–69 Operations Manual*. Sparkford, UK: Haynes, 2015.

————. *Valiant Squadrons of the Cold War*. Oxford: Osprey, 2012.

————. *Victor Squadrons of the Cold War*. Oxford: Osprey, 2011.

————. *Vulcan Squadrons of the Cold War*. Oxford: Osprey, 2009.

Brooks, Matthew R. *Bull in a China Shop? General Curtis E. LeMay's Military Advice to the President During the Cuban Missile Crisis*. Maxwell AL: School of Advanced Air and Space Studies, 2009.

Brown, Anthony Cave. DROPSHOT: *The American Plan for World War III against Russia in 1957*. New York: Dial Press, 1978.

Brugioni, Dina A. *Eyeball to Eyeball: The Cuban Missile Crisis*. New York: Random House, 1990.

————. *Eyes in the Sky: Eisenhower, the CIA, and Cold War Aerial Espionage*. Annapolis MD: Naval Institute Press, 2010.

Brzezinski, Matthew. *Red Moon Rising: Sputnik and the Hidden Rivalries That Ignited the Space Age*. New York: Times Books, 2007.

Bundy, McGeorge. *Danger and Survival: Choices about the Bomb in the First Fifty Years*. New York: Vintage Books, 1988.

Cagle, Malcom W., and Frank A. Manson. *The Sea War in Korea*. Annapolis MD: U.S. Naval Institute, 1957.

Carr, Barnes. *Operation Whisper: The Capture of Soviet Spies Morris and Lona Cohen*. Lebanon NH: University Press of New England, 2016.

Carroll, James. *House of War: The Pentagon and the Disastrous Rise of American Power*. New York: Houghton Mifflin, 2006.

Chang, Jung, and Jon Halliday. *Mao: The Unknown Story*. New York: Anchor Books, 2005.

Clark, Chris. *From Hitler's U-Boats to Khrushchev's Spyflights*. Barnsley, UK: Pen and Sword Aviation, 2013.

Cloud, John. "American Cartographic Transformations during the Cold War." *Cartographic and Geographic Information Science* 29, no. 3 (2002): 261–82.

Cochran, Thomas B., William M. Arkin, Robert S. Norris, and Milton M. Hoenig. *Nuclear Weapons Databook*. Vol. 2: *U.S. Nuclear Warhead Production*. Cambridge MA: Ballinger, 1987.

Coffey, Thomas M. *Decision over Schweinfurt: The US 9th Air Force Battle for Daylight Bombing*. New York: David Mackay, 1977.

————. *Iron Eagle: The Turbulent Life of General Curtis LeMay*. New York: Avon Books, 1986.

Collins, Martin J. *Cold War Laboratory: RAND, the Air Force, and the American State 1945–1950*. Washington DC: Smithsonian Institution Press, 2002.

Condit, Kenneth W. *History of the Joint Chiefs of Staff*. Vol. 5: *The Joint Chiefs of Staff and National Policy 1955–1956*. Washington DC: Office of the Joint Chiefs of Staff, 1994.

Conquest, Robert. *Reflections on a Ravaged Century*. London: John Murray, 1999.

————. *Stalin: Breaker of Nations*. New York: Penguin Books, 1991.

Courtois, Stéphane, et al. *The Black Book of Communism: Crimes, Terror, Repression*. Cambridge MA: Harvard University Press, 1999.

Cox, Donald W. "Operation LEAPFROG." *Airpower* 4, no 4 (July 1957): 288–93.

Curatola, John M. *Bigger Bombs for a Brighter Tomorrow: The Strategic Air Command and American War Plans at the Dawn of the Atomic Age, 1945–1950.* Jefferson NC: McFarland, 2016.

Dailey, Brian D., and Patrick J. Parker, *Soviet Strategic Deception.* Lanham MD: Lexington Books, 1987.

Davis, Shadrach E. "USAF War Readiness Materiel, 1946–1966." *Airpower,* July–August 1967, 1–7.

Dickson, Paul. *Sputnik: Shock of the Century.* New York: Berkeley, 2001.

Dikoetter, Frank. *The Tragedy of Liberation: The History of the Chinese Revolution, 1945–1957.* New York: Bloomsbury, 2013.

Divine, Robert A. *The Sputnik Challenge: Eisenhower's Response to the Soviet Satellite.* New York: Oxford University Press, 2003.

Djilas, Milovan. *Rise and Fall.* New York: Macmillan, 1985.

Downer, Lee. *Victor Alert: 15 Minutes to Armageddon.* Lexington MA: Self-published.

Dragnich, George S. *The Lebanon Operation of 1958: A Study of the Crisis Role of the Sixth Fleet.* Alexandria VA: Center for Naval Analyses, 1970.

Eden, Lynn. *The Whole World on Fire: Organizations, Knowledge, and Nuclear Weapons Devastation.* Ithaca NY: Cornell University Press, 2004.

Edmundson, James V. "Six Churnin' and Four Burnin'. Part II." *Klaxon* 3, no. 4 (n.d.): 6–7.

Eisenhower, Dwight D. *Waging Peace: The White House Years 1956–1961.* New York: Doubleday, 1965.

Elleman, Bruce A. *High Seas Buffer: The Taiwan Patrol Force, 1950–1979.* Newport RI: U.S. Naval War College, 2012.

Ellsberg, Daniel. *The Doomsday Machine: Confessions of a Nuclear War Planner.* New York: Bloomsbury Books, 2017.

"EMP Articles That Shaped the Army HEMP Program." *NBC Report,* Fall–Winter 2004, 47–54.

Evans, M. Stanton. *Blacklisted by History: The Untold Story of Senator Joe McCarthy and His Fight against America's Enemies.* New York: Three Rivers Press, 2007.

Everett, Hugh, III, and George E. Pugh. "The Distribution and Effects of Fallout in Large Nuclear-Weapon Campaigns." *Operations Research* 7, no. 2 (1959): 145–273.

Fairchild, Byron R., and Walter Poole. *The Joint Chiefs of Staff and National Policy.* Vol. 7: *1957–1960.* Washington DC: Office of the Chairman, Joint Chiefs of Staff, 2000.

Farquahar, John T. *A Need to Know: The Role of Air Force Reconnaissance in War Planning, 1945–1953.* Maxwell AFB: Air University Press, 2004.

Fletcher, Harry R. *Air Force Bases.* Vol. 2: *Air Bases Outside of the United States of America.* Washington DC: Center for Air Force History, 1993.

Foot, Rosemary. *The Wrong War: American Policy and the Dimensions of the Korean Conflict, 1950–1953.* Ithaca NY: Cornell University Press, 1985.

Ford, Daniel, et al. *Carrying a Nuke to Sevastopol: One Pilot, One Engine, and One Plutonium Bomb.* Warbird Books, 2014. ebook.

Frank, Richard B. *Downfall: The End of the Imperial Japanese Empire.* New York: Penguin Books, 1999.

Fravel, M. Taylor. *Active Defense: China's Military Strategy since 1949.* Princeton NJ: Princeton University Press, 2019.

Friedman, Norman. *The Postwar Naval Revolution*. Annapolis MD: Naval Institute Press, 1986.

Furman, Necah Stewart. *Sandia National Laboratories: The Postwar Decade*. Albuquerque: University of New Mexico Press, 1990.

Fursenko, Aleksandr, and Timothy Naftali. *Khrushchev's Cold War*. New York: W. W. Norton, 2006.

Gabbard, Alex. *Adventures of an H-Bomb Mechanic: The Story of a Top Boomer*. Knoxville TN: GPP Press, 2005.

Gaddis, John Lewis. *Strategies of Containment: A Critical Appraisal of Postwar American National Security Policy*. Oxford: Oxford University Press, 1982.

Galantin, I. J. *Submarine Admiral: From Battlewagons to Ballistic Missiles*. Urbana: University of Illinois Press, 1995.

Garbinski, John C. *North River Depot: A Novel about the United States First Operational Nuclear Weapons Storage Site*. Morrisville NC: LuLu, 2011.

Gellately, Robert. *Stalin's Curse: Battling for Communism in War and Cold War*. New York: Vintage Books, 2013.

George, Alexander L., and Richard Smoke. *Deterrence in American Foreign Policy: Theory and Practice*. London: Columbia University Press, 1974.

Geraghty, Tony. *Beyond the Front Line: The Untold Exploits of Britain's Most Daring Cold War Spy Mission*. London: Harper Collins, 1996.

Getty, J. Arch, and Oleg V. Naumov. *The Road to Terror: Stalin and the Self-Destruction of the Bolsheviks, 1932–1939*. London: Yale University Press, 1999.

Giangreco, D. M. *Hell to Pay: Operation Downfall and the Invasion of Japan (Updated and Expanded)*. Annapolis MD: Naval Institute Press, 2018.

Gordin, Michael D. *Five Days in August: How World War II Became a Nuclear War*. Princeton NJ: Princeton University Press, 2007.

Gordon, Yefim. *Myasishchev M-4 and 3M: The First Soviet Strategic Jet Bomber*. Hinckley, UK: Midland, 2003.

———. *Soviet Strategic Aviation in the Cold War*. Manchester, UK: Hikoki, 2013.

Gordon, Yefim, and Dmitriy Kommissarov. *Ilyushin Il-28 Beagle Light Attack Bomber*. Shrewsbury, UK: Airlife, 2002.

———. *Soviet Air Defence Aviation 1945–1991*. Manchester, UK: Hikoki, 2012.

Gordon, Yefim, Andrey Sal'nikov, and Alexandr Zablotskiy. *Beriev's Jet Flying Boats*. Hinckley, UK: Midland, 2006.

Gordon, Yefim, Dmitriy Kommissarov, and Vladimir Rigmant. *Tupolev TU-4: The First Soviet Strategic Bomber*. Atglen PA: Schiffer, 2014.

———. *Tupolev TU-16: Versatile Cold War Bomber*. Atglen PA: Schiffer, 2017.

Grathwol, Robert P., and Donita M. Moorhus. *Bricks, Sand, and Marble: The US Army Corps of Engineers Construction in the Mediterranean and the Middle East, 1947–1991*. Washington DC: Center for Military History, 2009.

Grimes, Bill. *The History of BIG SAFARI*. Bloomington IN: Archway, 2014.

Grynkewich, Alexus Gregory. "Advisable in the National Interest: The Relief of General George C. Kenney." MA thesis, University of Georgia, 1994.

Gushee, Edward T. *52-Charlie: Members of a Legendary Pilot Training Class Share Their Stories about Combat in Korea and Vietnam*. Tucson AZ: Wheatmark, 2009.

Hackett, John. *Third World War: The Untold Story*. London: Sidgwick and Jackson, 1982.

Hall, R. Cargill. "The Truth about Overflights." *Military History Quarterly* 9, no. 3 (Spring 1997): 24–39.

Hall, R. Cargill, and Clayton D. Laurie. *Early Cold War Overflights 1950–1956 Symposium Proceedings*. Vol. 1: *Memoirs*. Washington DC: Office of the Historian, National Reconnaissance Office, 2002.

Ham, Paul. *Hiroshima Nagasaki: The Real Story of the Atomic Bombings and Their Aftermath*. New York: St. Martin's Press, 2014.

Hansen, Chuck. "Beware the Old Story." *Bulletin of the Atomic Scientists* 57, no. 2 (March–April 2001): 52–55.

———. *US Nuclear Weapons: The Secret History*. New York: Orion Books, 1988.

Haynes, John Earl, and Harvey Klehr. *In Denial: Historians, Communism and Espionage*. San Francisco: Encounter Books, 2003.

Heefner, Gretchen. *The Missile Next Door: The Minuteman in the American Heartland*. London: Harvard University Press, 2012.

Hennessy, Peter. *The Secret State: Preparing for the Worst 1945–2010*. New York: Penguin, 2010.

———. *The Secret State: Whitehall and the Cold War*. London: Allan Lane, 2002.

Higuchi, Toshihiro. "'Clean' Bombs: Nuclear Technology and Nuclear Strategy in the 1950s." *Journal of Strategic Studies* 29, no. 1 (2006): 83–116.

Hoddeson, Lillian, et al. *Critical Assembly: A Technical History of Los Alamos during the Oppenheimer Years, 1943–1945*. Cambridge, UK: Cambridge University Press, 1993.

Holloway, James L., III. *Aircraft Carriers at War: A Personal Retrospective of Korea, Vietnam, and the Soviet Confrontation*. Annapolis MD: Naval Institute Press, 2007.

Hopkins, Robert Smith, III. *The Boeing KC-135 Stratotanker: More Than Just a Tanker*. Revised and updated edition. Manchester, UK: Crecy, 2017.

Hornblum, Allen M. *The Invisible Harry Gold: The Man Who Gave the Soviets the Atom Bomb*. New Haven CT: Yale University Press, 2010.

Hunt, Linda. *Secret Agenda: The United States Government and Project Paperclip 1945 to 1990*. New York: St. Martin's Press, 1991.

Isenberg, Michael T. *Shield of the Republic: The United States Navy in an Era of Cold War and Violent Peace, 1945–1962*. New York: St. Martin's Press, 1993.

Jackson, Robert. *Canberra: The Operational Record*. Washington DC: Smithsonian Institution Press, 1989.

———. *Strike Force: The USAF in Britain since 1948*. London: Robson Books, 1986.

Jacobsen, Meyers K., et al. *Convair B-36: A Comprehensive History of American's "Big Stick."* Atglen PA: Schiffer Military/Aviation History, 1997.

Jervis, Robert. *The Illogic of American Nuclear Strategy*. Ithaca NY: Cornell University Press, 1984.

Jian, Chen. *Mao's China and the Cold War*. Chapel Hill: University of North Carolina Press, 2001.

Johnstone, Paul H. *From Mad to Madness: Inside Pentagon Nuclear War Planning*. Atlanta GA: Clarity Press, 2017.

Jones, Matthew. *The Official History of the UK Strategic Nuclear Deterrent*. Vol. 1. London: Routledge, 2017.

Jordan, Robert S. *Norstad: Cold War Supreme Commander*. New York: St. Martin's Press, 2000.

Kahan, Jerome H. *Security in the Nuclear Age: Developing U.S. Strategic Arms Policy*. Washington DC: Brookings Institution, 1975.

Kampe, Hans George. *The Underground Military Command Bunkers of Zossen, Germany*. Atglen PA: Schiffer, 1996.

Kaplan, Edward. *To Kill Nations: American Strategy in the Air-Atomic Age and the Rise of Mutually Assured Destruction*. Ithaca NY: Cornell University Press, 2015.

Kaplan, Stephen S. *Diplomacy of Power: Soviet Armed Forces as a Political Instrument*. Washington DC: Brookings Institution, 1981.

Katz, Mark N. *The Third World in Soviet Military Thought*. Baltimore MD: Johns Hopkins University Press, 1982.

Kaufmann, William W. *The McNamara Strategy*. New York: Harper and Row, 1964.

Kersten, Olaf, et al. *Garnisonen der NVA und GSTD*. Berlin: Verlag Dr. Koester, 2011.

Kerzon, Warren J. *Throw a Nickel on the Grass: A Fighter Pilot's Life Narrative*. Raleigh NC: LuLu, 2016.

Kivett, Philip. *Intelligence Failures and Decent Intervals*. Bloomington IN: AuthorHouse, 2006.

Knaack, Marcelle Size. *Post–World War II Bombers*. Washington DC: Office of Air Force History, 1988.

———. *Post–World War II Fighters*. Washington DC: Office of Air Force History, 1986.

Koch, Stephen. *Double Lives: Spies and Writers in the Secret Soviet War of Ideas against the West*. New York: Free Press, 1994.

Kozak, Warren. *LeMay: The Life and Wars of General Curtis LeMay*. Washington DC: Regnery, 2009.

Kuehl, Daniel Timothy. "The Radar Eye Blinded: The USAF and Electronic Warfare, 1945–1955." PhD dissertation, Duke University, 1992.

Kuklick, Bruce. *Blind Oracles: Intellectuals and War from Kennan to Kissinger*. Princeton NJ: Princeton University Press, 2006.

Kuter, Lawrence S. *Airman at Yalta*. New York: Duell, Sloan and Pearce, 1955.

Lapp, Ralph E. *Kill and Overkill: The Strategy of Annihilation*. New York: Basic Books, 1962.

Lashmar, Paul. *Spy Flights of the Cold War*. Annapolis MD: Naval Institute Press, 1996.

Laslie, Brian D. *Architect of Air Power: General Lawrence S. Kuter and the Birth of the US Air Force*. Lexington: University Press of Kentucky, 2017.

Leavitt, Lloyd R. *Following the Flag*. Maxwell AFB: Air University Press, 2010.

Lehman, John F. *Oceans Ventured: Winning the Cold War at Sea*. New York: W. W. Norton, 2018.

LeMay, Curtis E., with MacKinlay Kantor. *Mission with LeMay: My Story*. New York: Doubleday, 1965.

Little, Jim. *Brotherhood of Doom: Memoirs of a Nava Nuclear Weaponsman*. St. Petersburg FL: BookLocker, 2008.

Lloyd, Alwyn T. *B-47 Stratojet*. Fallbrook CA: Aero Publishers, Inc., 1986.

———. *A Cold War Legacy: A Tribute to Strategic Air Command 1946–1992*. Missoula MT: Pictorial Histories, 1999.

Loeber, Charles R. *Building the Bombs: A History of the Nuclear Weapons Complex*. Albuquerque NM: Sandia National Laboratories, 2005.

Lowenhaupt, Henry S. "Mission to Birch Woods." *Studies in Intelligence* 12, no. 4 (Fall 1968): 1–12.

Luethi, Lorentz. *The Sino-Soviet Split: Cold War in the Communist World*. Princeton NJ: Princeton University Press, 2008.

Lynn-Jones, Sean M., et al. *Nuclear Diplomacy and Crisis Management*. Cambridge MA: MIT Press, 1990.

Maggelet, Michael H., and James C. Oskins. *Broken Arrow*. Vol. 2. Raleigh NC: LuLu, 2010.

Maloney, Sean. "Arctic Sky Spies: The Director's Cut." *Canadian Military Journal* 9, no. 1 (August 2008). Online.

———. Deconstructing Dr. Strangelove: *The Secret History of Nuclear War Films*. Lincoln NE: Potomac Books, 2019.

———. "Flying the Mukden Gauntlet." *Friend's Journal of the* MUSAF 40, no. 1 (Spring 2017): 10–13.

———. *Learning to Love the Bomb: Canada's Cold War Strategy and Nuclear Weapons 1951–1970*. Dulles VA: Potomac Books, 2009.

———. *Securing Command of the Sea:* NATO *Naval Planning 1948–1954*. Annapolis MD: Naval Institute Press, 1995.

———. *War without Battles: Canada's* NATO *Brigade in Germany 1951–1993*. Toronto: McGraw-Hill Ryerson Press, 1997.

Malucci, Louis. B*-47 Stratojet*. N.p.: Self-published, 2007.

McAuliffe, Jerome J. "The USAF in France 1950–1967." NMUSA *Friend's Journal* 24, no. 4 (n.d.). Online.

McGill, Earl. *Black Tuesday over Namsi:* B*-29s vs.* MIG*s—The Forgotten Air Battle*. Warwick, UK: Helion, 2013.

———. *Jet Age Man:* SAC B*-47 and* B*-52 Operations in the Early Cold War*. Warwick, UK: Helion, 2012.

McIntyre, Donald. "The Development of Britain's Megaton Warheads." MA thesis, University of Chester, 2006.

McLaren, David R. *Republic* F*-84: A Photo Chronicle*. Atglen PA: Schiffer, 1998.

Meilinger, Phillip S. *Bomber: The Formation and Early Years of Strategic Air Command*. Maxwell AFB: Air University Press, 2012.

———. *Hoyt S. Vandenberg: The Life of A General*. Bloomington: University of Indiana Press, 1989.

Mikesh, Robert C. *Martin* B*-57 Canberra: The Complete Record*. Atglen PA: Schiffer, 1995.

Milberry, Larry. *Canadair Sabre*. Toronto: CANAV Books, 1986.

Miller, Glen. "The Ups and Downs of an F-100 Super Sabre Pilot." DD*-214 Chronicle* 5, no. 3 (March–April 2015). http://dd214chronicle.com/wp-content/uploads/dd214MarchApril2015.pdf.

Miller, Jerry. *Nuclear Weapons and Aircraft Carriers: How the Bomb Saved Naval Aviation*. Washington DC: Smithsonian Institution Press, 2001.

———. *Stockpile: The Story behind 10,000 Strategic Weapons*. Annapolis MD: Naval Institute Press, 2010.

Miller, Roger G. *To Save a City: The Berlin Airlift 1948–1949*. Washington DC: U.S. Air Force History and Museums Program, n.d.

Mindling, George, and Robert Bolton. *US Air Force Tactical Missiles 1949–1969*. Morrisville NC: LuLu, 2011.

Moore, Richard. *Nuclear Illusion, Nuclear Reality: Britain, the United States and Nuclear Weapons, 1958–64.* New York: Palgrave Macmillan, 2010.

Morrison, Wilbur H. *Point of No Return: The Story of the Twentieth Air Force.* New York: Times Books, 1979.

Mueller, John. *Retreat from Doomsday: The Obsolescence of Major War.* New York: Basic Books, 1989.

Nash, Philip. *The Other Missiles of October: Eisenhower, Kennedy, and the Jupiters, 1957–1963.* Chapel Hill: University of North Carolina Press, 1997.

Natola, Mark, ed. *Boeing B-47 Stratojet: True Stories of the Cold War in the Air.* Atglen PA: Schiffer, 2002.

Neufeld, Jacob. *Ballistic Missiles in the United States Air Force 1945–1960.* Washington DC: Office of Air Force History, 1990.

Norris, Robert S. *Racing for the Bomb: The True Story of General Leslie R. Groves, the Man behind the Birth of the Atomic Age.* New York: Skyhorse, 2002.

O'Donnell, James S. *A Coming of Age: Albania under Enver Hoxha.* New York: Columbia University Press, 1999.

Olds, Robin. *Fighter Pilot: The Memoirs of Legendary Ace Robin Olds.* New York: St. Martin's Press, 2011.

Overy, Richard. *The Bombers and the Bombed: Allied Air War over Europe, 1940–1945.* Toronto: Penguin Books, 2013.

———. *Why the Allies Won.* New York: W. W. Norton, 1995.

Palmer, H. Barr. "My Most Interesting Tour of Duty, the Real Weapons Business." *Fireball!* 14, no. 2 (Spring 2005). https://www.ozbourn.org/fireball/FIREBALLVOL14 _2005/April2005.pdf.

Patman, Robert G. *The Soviet Union in the Horn of Africa: The Diplomacy of Intervention and Disengagement.* New York: Cambridge University Press, 1990.

Pfeffer, Robert, and D. Lynn Shaeffer. "A Russian Assessment of Several USSR and US HEMP Tests." *Combating WMD Journal*, no. 3 (2007): 33–36.

Pocock, Chris. *The U-2 Spyplane: A New History of the Early Years.* Atglen PA: Schiffer, 2000.

Pocock, Chris, and Clarence Fu. *The Black Bats: CIA Spy Flights over China from Taiwan 1951–1969.* Atglen PA: Schiffer, 2010.

Podvig, Pavel. *Russian Strategic Nuclear Forces.* Cambridge MA: MIT Press, 2001.

Polmar, Norman. *Strategic Air Command: People, Aircraft, and Missiles.* Annapolis MD: Nautical and Aviation Publishing, 1979.

Polmar, Norman, and K. J. Moore. *Cold War Submarines: The Design and Construction of US and Soviet Submarines 1945–2001.* Dulles VA: Potomac Books, 2003.

Pompfret, John. *The Beautiful Country and the Middle Kingdom: America and China, 1776 to the Present.* New York: Picador Books, 2016.

Poole, Walter. *The Joint Chiefs of Staff and National Policy.* Vol. 4: *1950–52.* Washington DC: Office of the Joint Chiefs of Staff, 1979.

Power, Thomas S., with Albert A. Arnhym. *Design for Survival: A General's Urgent Report to the American People.* New York: Pocket Books, 1965.

Prados, John. *Operation VULTURE.* New York: Simon and Shuster, 2003.

————. *The Soviet Estimate: US Intelligence Analysis and Soviet Strategic Forces*. Princeton NJ: Princeton University Press, 1986.

Price, Alfred. *A History of US Electronic Warfare*. Vol. 2. Baltimore MD: Port City Press, 1989.

Radzinsky, Edvard. *Stalin*. New York: Anchor Books, 1996.

Reed, Thomas C. *At the Abyss: An Insider's History of the Cold War*. New York: Ballantine Books, 2004.

Reed, Thomas C., and Danny B. Stillman. *The Nuclear Express: A Political History of the Bomb and Its Proliferation*. Minneapolis MN: Zenith Press, 2009.

Regis, Ed. *The Biology of Doom: The History of America's Secret Germ Warfare Project*. New York: Henry Holt, 1999.

Rhodes, Richard. *Dark Sun: The Making of the Hydrogen Bomb*. New York: Simon and Schuster, 1995.

Romney, Carl. *Detecting the Bomb: The Role of Seismology in the Cold War*. Washington DC: New Academia, 2009.

Rosenberg, David Alan. "Origins of Overkill: Nuclear Weapons and American Strategy, 1945–1960." *International Security* 7, no. 4 (Spring 1983): 3–71.

————. "US Nuclear Stockpile, 1945 to 1950." *Bulletin of the Atomic Scientists* 38, no. 5 (1982): 25–31.

Ross, Stephen T. *American War Plans 1945–1950*. New York: Garland, 1988.

Rossiter, Mike. *The Spy Who Changed the World: Klaus Fuchs and the Secrets of the Nuclear Bomb*. London: Headline, 2014.

Royal Air Force Historical Society. *Air Intelligence Symposium Bracknell Paper No. 7*. Brighton, UK: Air Force Historical Society, 1997.

————. *Journal No. 23: Cold War Intelligence Gathering*. Oxford: Creative Associates, 2001.

————. *Journal No. 26*. Oxford: Creative Associates, 2001.

Rueger, Fabian. "Kennedy, Adenauer and the Making of the Berlin Wall, 1958–1961." PhD dissertation, Stanford University, 2011.

Sagan, Scott D. *Moving Targets: Nuclear Strategy and National Security*. Princeton NJ: Princeton University Press, 1989.

Samuel, Wolfgang E. *Coming to Colorado*. Jackson: University Press of Mississippi, 2006.

————. *Glory Days: The Untold Story of the Men Who Flew the B-66 Destroyer in the Face of Fear*. Atglen PA: Schiffer Books, 2008.

————. *I Always Wanted to Fly: America's Cold War Airmen*. Jackson: University Press of Mississippi, 2001.

————. *In Defense of Freedom*. Jackson: University Press of Mississippi, 2015.

Sarin, Oleg, and Lev Dvoretsky. *Alien Wars: The Soviet Union's Aggressions against the World, 1919 to 1989*. Novato CA: Presidio Press, 1996.

Schecter, Jerold, and Vyacheslav V. Luchkov. *Khrushchev Remembers: The Glasnost Tapes*. London: Little, Brown, 1990.

Scrivner, John H. "Pioneer into Space: A Biography of Major General Orvil Arson Anderson." PhD dissertation, University of Oklahoma, 1971.

Shackelford, Philip C. "On the Wings of the Wind: The US Air Force Security Service and Its Impact on Signals Intelligence in the Cold War." Honors thesis, Kent State University, 2014.

Sheehan, Neil. *A Fiery Peace in the Cold War: Bernard Schriever and the Ultimate Weapon*. New York: Vintage Books, 2009.

Shemesh, Haim. *Soviet-Iraqi Relations, 1968–1988*. London: Lynne Rienner, 1991.

Sherwood, John. *Fast Movers: Jet Pilots and the Vietnam Experience*. New York: Free Press, 1999.

Slane, Robert M. *Journey to Freedom and Beyond*. Bloomington IN: Trafford, 2004.

Smirnov, G. I. *Missile Systems of the Strategic Missile Forces from R-1 to TOPOLY-M, 1946–2006*. Smolensk: Self-published, 2001.

Smith, Richard K. *75 Years of Inflight Refueling*. Washington DC: Air Force History and Museums Program, 1998.

Speer, Albert. *Inside the Third Reich*. New York: Avon Books, 1970.

Steiner, Barry. *Bernard Brodie and the Foundations of American Nuclear Strategy*. Lawrence: University Press of Kansas, 1991.

Stine, G. Harry. *ICBM: The Making of the Weapon That Changed the World*. New York: Orion Books, 1991.

Stone, Melvin L., and Gerald P. Banner. "Radars for the Detection and Tracking of Ballistic Missiles, Satellites, and Planets." *Lincoln Laboratory Journal* 12, no. 2 (2000): 217–25.

Stumpf, David K. *Regulus: The Forgotten Weapon*. Paducah KY: Turner, 1996.

———. *Titan II: A History of a Cold War Missile Program*. Fayetteville: University of Arkansas Press, 2000.

Szasz, Ferenc Morton. *The Day the Sun Rose Twice: The Story of the Trinity Site Nuclear Explosion, July 16 1945*. Albuquerque: University of Mexico Press, 1984.

Taubman, William. *Stalin's American Policy: From Entente to Detent to Cold War*. New York: W. W. Norton, 1982.

Tegler, Jan. *B-47 Stratojet: Boeing's Brilliant Bomber*. New York: McGraw-Hill, 2000.

Thomas, Gordon, and Max Morgan Witts. *Ruin from the Air: The Enola Gay's Atomic Mission to Hiroshima*. Chelsea, UK: Scarborough House, 1977.

Trachtenberg, Mark, ed. *The Development of American Strategic Thought: Basic Documents from the Eisenhower and Kennedy Periods 1953 to 1959*. New York: Articles-Garlan, 1988.

Twigge, Stephen, and Len Scott. *Planning Armageddon: Britain, the United States and the Command of Western Nuclear Forces 1945–1964*. New York: Routledge, 2014.

Twining, Nathan. *Neither Liberty nor Safety: A Hard Look at US Military Policy and Strategy*. New York: Holt Rinehart and Winston, 1966.

Ulam, Adam B. *Expansion and Coexistence: Soviet Foreign Policy 1917–73*. 2nd ed. New York: Praeger Books, 1974.

U.S. Department of Defense. *Dictionary of Military Terms*. New York: ARCO, 1988.

van de Ven, Hans. *China at War: Triumph and Tragedy in the Emergence of the New China*. Cambridge MA: Harvard University Press, 2018.

Vizcarra, Victor. *Hun Pilot: A Pilot's Account of the First USAF Supersonic Fighter*. N.p.: Thud Pilot Productions, 2017.

Volkogonov, Dimitri. *Stalin: Triumph and Tragedy*. New York: Grove Weidenfeld, 1988.

Waldron, Richard L. *Site 18*. Quincy MA: Squantum, 2005.

Walker, Chuck. *Atlas: The Ultimate Weapon*. Burlington VT: Apogee Books, 2005.

Walker, J. Samuel. *Permissible Dose: A History of Radiation Protection in the Twentieth Century*. Berkeley: University of California Press, 2000.

Walpole, Nigel. *Voodoo Warriors: The Story of the McDonnell Voodoo Fast Jets*. Barnsley, UK: Pen and Sword Aviation, 2006.

Watson, Robert J. *History of the Joint Chiefs of Staff*. Vol. 5: *The Joint Chiefs of Staff and National Policy 1953–1954*. Washington DC: Historical Division, Joint Chiefs of Staff, 1986.

Weiner, Charles. "Retroactive Saber Rattling?" *Bulletin of the Atomic Scientists*, April 1978, 10–12.

Weir, Gary E., and Walter J. Boyne. *Rising Tide: The Untold Story of the Russian Submarines That Fought the Cold War*. New York: Basic Books, 2003.

Weisgall, Jonathan M. *Operation Crossroads: The Atomic Tests at Bikini Atoll*. Annapolis MD: Naval Institute Press, 1994.

Welch, Mary. "From the Beginning." *Post Monitor* 4, no. 4 (December 1996): 1–6.

Wells, Selmon. *The Life and Career of Lt. General Selmon "Sundown" Wells in His Own Words*. Amherst MA: Modern Memoirs Press, 2005.

Werrell, Kenneth P. *The Evolution of the Cruise Missile*. Maxwell AFB: Air University Press, 1985.

Winchester, John, ed. *Concept Aircraft: Prototypes, X-Planes, and Experimental Aircraft*. New York: Amber Books, 2005.

Wolk, Herman S. *The Struggle for Air Force Independence 1943–1947*. Washington DC: Air Force History and Museums Program, 1997.

Wynn, Humphrey. *RAF Nuclear Deterrent Forces*. London: HMSO, 1994.

Yeager, Chuck, and Leo Janos. *Yeager*. New York: Ballantine Books, 1985.

Yenne, Bill. *B-52 Stratofortress: The Complete History of the World's Longest Serving and Best Known Bomber*. Minneapolis MN: Zenith, 2012.

York, Herbert F. *Making Weapons, Talking Peace: A Physicist's Odyssey from Hiroshima to Geneva*. New York: Basic Books, 1987.

Zaloga, Steven J. *The Kremlin's Nuclear Sword: The Rise and Fall of Russia's Strategic Nuclear Forces 1945–2000*. Washington DC: Smithsonian Institution Press, 2002.

Zhang, Xiaoming. *Red Wings over the Yalu: China, the Soviet Union, and the Air War in Korea*. College Station: Texas A&M University Press, 2003.

Zimmerman, Carroll L. *Insider at SAC: Operations Analysis under General LeMay*. Manhattan KS: Sunflower University Press, 1988.

Zubok, Vladislav, and Constantine Pleshakov. *Inside the Kremlin's Cold War: From Stalin to Khrushchev*. Cambridge MA: Harvard University Press, 1997.

INDEX

Be-6 Madge patrol aircraft, 229
Be-10 Mallow patrol bomber, 229
Be-12 Mail patrol aircraft, 229
Beach, Edward (Ned), 2
"Beagle problem," 95–97, 153. *See also* IL-28
    bomber
Beale AFB, 367
Bee Hind radar, 359, 380
Beijing targets, 378
Bergstrom AFB, 72
Beria, Lavrentiy, 16, 37, 69, 73
Beria, Sergo, 16, 37, 108
Berlin air corridors and intelligence collec-
    tion, 137
Berlin airports, 245
Berlin Crisis (1948–49), 3, 19, 20, 28, 32, 34–
    35, 37
Berlin Crisis (1959–60), 1, 9, 304
Betts, Richard K., 5
Bevin, Ernest, 35
Biggs AFB, 361, 377
Big Horn B-47 deployments, 131, 203, 226, 311
Big Tail, 147, 210, 324
Bikini Atoll, 16, 25, 118, 261
biological warfare and facilities, 147, 178,
    227, 336
Bitburg Air Base, 155
"Black Thursday" (Korean War), 71
Blunting (Bravo) target category, 44–45, 47,
    63–66, 82, 106, 107, 127, 196
BMEWS (Ballistic Missile Early Warning Sys-
    tem), 255–56, 265, 284, 286
"bolt from the blue" scenario, 216
BOMARC (IM-99, CIM-10) surface-to-air mis-
    sile system, 285
Bomber Gap debate, 43, 96, 133, 135, 193–94,
    202, 284, 285
bombing encyclopedia, 49
bomb-loading pits, 13
bonus damage concept, 15, 240, 378
Bossier Base, 94
"bounce" air bases, 245, 364–65
Bradley, Omar N., 82
"breakaway" maneuver, 77
Brodie, Bernard, 15, 47
"bug flights." *See* cloud sampling operations
Bulganin, Nikolai, 126, 138
Bullitt, William, 251
Bunker, Howard, 83

Burgess, Guy, 127
Burke, Arleigh, 186, 255, 330
Bush, Vannevar, 82–83
BWP (Basic War Plan). *See* SAC Basic War
    Plan (BWP)

C-46 COMINT aircraft, 358
C-47 transport, 344
C-54D photoreconnaissance aircraft, 137
C-54E VIP transport, 137, 144, 238
C-54G photoreconnaissance aircraft, 76
C-54 transport, 55
C-97 transport, 33, 137
C-124 transport, 94, 131, 165, 203, 343
Cabell, Pearre, 127, 136
Caccola 6 (CIA agent), 61
Cambridge 5 spy ring, 127
Campbell Air Force Station, 53
Camp David, 2
Canada: cooperation of, with SAC, 33, 43, 107;
    forward tanker bases of, 134–35, 205–6, 254,
    257, 259–60, 267, 319; and overflight arrange-
    ments, 261; supplying of F-86s to United
    Kingdom by, 96
Canadian-UK-U.S. SIGINT sharing arrange-
    ments, 285
Canberra bomber, 271, 272, 273, 291, 295, 301
Carney, Robert, 169
Carroll, Joseph, 127
Carswell AFB, 128
Carter Doctrine, 7
Castle AFB, 66
Centerboard (Japan target selection), 12–14
CENTO (Central Treaty Organization),
    204, 246
CF-100 Canuck interceptor, 195
chemical warfare, 178
Chichi Jima, 364
China, Communist, 15, 71, 122, 171–77, 347, 352–
    53, 355; air defense system of, 178–79; NSA
    targets in, 285; SAC targets in, 98, 100, 165, 323,
    375, 377; support of, to Viet Minh, 164, 167;
    urban analysis of, 377–79
China, Nationalist, 164, 352; and overflights of
    Communist China, 170, 179, 358, 378; possible
    nuclear capability of, 352; and Taiwan Straits
    Crisis, 168
Christmas Island, 271
Churchill, Winston, 65, 69, 125

Killeen Base, 27

Killian Report, 276

Kim Il-sung, 389

Kinchloe AFB, 319

Kindley Air Base, 134, 206, 342, 469n52

King Shot (Operation Ivy), 75, 77

Kirtland AFB, 27, 53, 74, 77, 128, 233

K. I. Sawyer AFB, 319

Kissener, August, 36

Knife Rest (P-8) early warning radar, 141–42

Kola Peninsula targets, 307–9

Komaki Air Base, 102, 138, 359

Korean War, 3, 39–40, 54, 71, 74, 97, 164, 177; and biological warfare, 178; and nuclear weapons, 98–99, 100; Op Big Stick and, 108

Korolev, Sergei, 253

Kremlin, 68, 237, 241

KSR-2 air-to-surface missile, 194

Kunia bunker (CINCPAC), 188

Kusan Air Base, 360

Kuter, Laurence, 251–52; concerns of, over Alternative Undertaking, 334, 353, 354, 356, 377; and GEOP, 356–57, 380; as PACAF commander, 348; and Pacific command and control, 350–51; views of, on the Soviet Union, 348–49

Kwajalein Atoll, 76

Kyoto, 12–13

LABS (Low-Altitude Bombing System), 72, 145, 147, 165, 182, 207, 236, 243, 272, 281, 295, 296, 308, 324, 352

Lake Charles AFB, 133, 211

Lancaster AR reconnaissance aircraft, 195

Landon, Truman, 82–83

Lapp, Ralph E., 26

Large Charge delivery profile, 324

Lavochkin-7 interceptor, 70, 348

Lavochkin-11 fighter, 107, 348

"layercake" thermonuclear weapon design, 79, 116

Leavitt, Lloyd, 201–2

Lebanon Crisis (1958), 1, 215, 365

LeMay, Curtis, 15, 33, 37, 41, 43, 56, 63, 67, 74, 88, 106, 135, 145, 152, 154, 166, 200, 205, 213, 218, 279, 280, 355, 380; and Airborne Alert as signaling tool, 314; and Air Power Battle Target System, 192–99; and ASM program overload, 268; and B-52 weapons test, 116–17; and ballistic missile programs, 257; "Beagle problem" and, 96; and Berlin Crisis (1948), 36; and bomber penetra-

tion problem, 147–48; and Canada bases, 134–35; and concept of winning, 189; concerns of, about BW/CW, 178; concerns of, about espionage, 126–27; concerns of, about ICBMs, 148, 276; concerns of, about operations short of war, 135; concerns of, about Soviets, 25; concerns of, about tactics in Korea, 71–72; and core allocations, 125; Defense Emergency and, 216; on deterrence, 79, 111, 119–20; and Far East strategy game, 352–53; and George Kenney, 32; issues of, with U.S. Navy, 25–26, 169, 185; and Korean War nuclear targets, 98–99; and Mao Zedong, 170–71, 177; and MLC, 45; and Nathan Twining, 126; promotion of, 250; public profile of, 327; and RAF nuclear cooperation, 272; request of, for 60-megaton nuclear weapon, 114, 119, 262; and revolutionary reconnaissance system, 136, 201; and SAC as deterrent force, 43–44, 197; and SAC-SACEUR targeting, 85, 88–92; and special nuclear material, 48; and Sputnik effects, 254; State Department and, 58; and Taiwan Straits Crisis, 169–71; take over of SAC by, 28; and Target Panel, 45; and thermonuclear tests, 113; and Thomas White, 334; and Tommy Power, 333; and vulnerability of SAC, 133, 196–97, 212; and vulnerability of Washington DC, 74; World War II experiences of, 50; and WSEG, 46

Leningrad, 51, 56, 228

Library of Congress Air Studies Division, 30

Libya, 58

Limestone AFB, 130

Limited Test Ban Treaty, 113

Lincoln Laboratories, 286

Lindbergh, Charles, 28

Lockbourne AFB, 246

Long Look delivery profile, 324

look-down–shoot-down capability, 242

Loring AFB, 133

Los Alamos National Laboratory, 13, 75

Lovett, Robert A., 178

Luftwaffe aerial reconnaissance material, 30

MA-7 bomb-nav system, 243

MacArthur, Douglas C., 98–99, 256

MacDill AFB, 134, 207, 268

Maclean, Donald, 127

Malmstrom AFB, 206

Man-Chou-Li (Manzouli), 174–75

Talent intelligence material, 137, 201, 226, 228, 232–33, 289, 303, 305, 306, 307, 323, 324, 357, 369
Tall King (P-14) radar, 241
target (definition debate), 50–51
Target Coordination Conferences, 152–53
target coverage, 212, 218–19, 277, 332
Target Destruction Annexes, 45, 46
target folders, 45
Targeting Committee (1945), 13
target islands, 51
Target Panel (USAF), 45–44, 47
Taylor, Maxwell, 254
TB-47 training aircraft, 343
Technical Research Group, 178–79
Tehran summit, 16
Teller, Edward, 73, 331
Theater Joint Operations Center (FEC), 166
Thor (PGM-17) IRBM, 214, 276, 277, 280, 289, 336–37
Thule Air Base, 54, 59, 60, 129, 135, 205, 224, 244, 256, 322; nuclear component storage authorized at, 130, 316, 342; and Project Home Run, 139
Tibbitts, Paul, 28
Tinian, 13
Titan (SM-68) ICBM, 275, 276
Titan II (LGM-25C) ICBM, 261, 270
Token (P-20) radar system, 71, 142, 143, 145, 179
Tokyo fire-bombing raid (1945), 11, 16, 25, 213
Torrejon Air Base, 132
Travis AFB, 66
Trinidad, 286
Trinity nuclear test, 13–14, 51
tritium, 118
Truman, Harry S., 23–24, 35, 97, 108, 123, 124; authorization by, of nuclear weapon deployments (1950), 48; authorization by, of recon operations against Soviet Union, 65; and Dwight Eisenhower, 83–84; and H-bomb decision, 73–74; and Moscow targeting, 67–68
TU-2 Bat night fighter, 179
TU-4 Bull bomber, 31, 34, 43, 64, 65, 66, 67, 103, 133, 157, 162, 223, 367; in Chinese Communist service, 359; and nuclear weapon storage, 232; photographed by Haymaker aircraft, 139; shot down by SA-1, 149; TU-4A version of, 63, 79, 194; and Ukraine bases, 95
TU-14T Bosun torpedo aircraft, 224
TU-16A Badger bomber, 31, 66, 79, 157, 220, 222, 223–24, 225, 226, 228, 244, 287, 304, 305, 308,

323, 345, 359, 367, 368; and Arctic ops, 194–95; Bomber Gap and, 194; and nuclear weapon storage, 232; and test of RDS-37 bomb, 116
TU-16K-16 bomber, 194, 223–24
TU-22 Blinder bomber, 31
TU-22M Backfire bomber, 31
TU-95 Bear bomber, 3, 317
Turkey, 19, 131, 342, 437n68
12th GUMO (Soviet custodial organization), 234
Twining, Nathan, 12, 79, 91, 116, 166, 193, 212, 213, 257, 333; and Air Power Battle Target System, 192, 197; and ballistic missile programs, 275, 276, 277–78; and Canadian tanker bases, 205; and core allocation, 125; and Curtis LeMay, 126, 135; and deterrence, 126; and EWP 1-51, 42; and Pacific command issues, 350; and Plan 8-53, 108–9; promotion of, to JCS chairman, 250–51; and RAF nuclear capability, 272; and Taiwan Straits Crisis, 169–72, 186; and Target Panel, 45; visit of, to Moscow, 125–26, 251; and Yugoslavia, 58
Type XXI U-Boat technology, 86
Tyura Tam (Baikonur), 306, 317

U-2 reconnaissance aircraft, 28, 30, 31, 65, 66, 135, 139, 143, 189, 199–202, 226, 231–33, 243, 246, 290, 316, 357; and blow-by-blow SIGINT/COMINT coverage, 286; Bomber Gap and, 194; China overflights by, 357; and ELINT equipment, 242; limitations of, 285; May Day 1960 shoot down of, 324; operating locations of, 203–4; and poststrike reconnaissance operations, 343; and sampling ops, 195
Ukraine, 20
University of California Radiation Laboratory, 262
urban-industrial target category, 6, 52, 106, 377
U.S. Agency for International Development (USAID), 204
U.S. Air Force bases (UK), 35, 43, 52, 54, 56, 57, 87, 95, 107, 127, 134, 223, 292; "Beagle problem" and, 95–96; 49th Air Division and, 93; and possible cruise missile sites, 155
U.S. Air Force Commander's Conference (1957), 331
U.S. Air Force Command Post, 2
U.S. Air Force Director of Intelligence, Strategic Vulnerability Branch, 45
U.S. Air Force Pacific Air Forces (PACAF), 348, 354, 359–60, 370, 375

U.S. Air Force Scientific Advisory Committee, 276

U.S. Air Force Security Service, 286, 287

U.S. Air Forces Europe (USAFE), 84–85, 88–89, 154, 198, 221, 291–92, 321; and command relationships, 89–93; 49th Air Division and, 93; and intelligence collection, 137, 141; IRBMS and, 278–79; Spain and, 132; targets of, 219

U.S. Air Force Target Panel, 45

U.S. Air Force units: Second Air Force, 113, 196, 207, 223, 225, 319, 322; 2nd Bombardment Group, 87; 2nd Bombardment Wing, 95; 2nd Reconnaissance Technical Squadron, 201, 219; 3rd Air Division, 129; Third Air Force, 84; 3rd Aviation Depot Squadron, 361; 3rd Aviation Field Depot Squadron, 102, 165; 3rd Bomber Wing, 359; 3rd Strategic Support Squadron, 94; 5th Air Division, 84, 129; 6th Air Division, 268; 7th Air Deport Squadron and Detachment 1, 360; 7th Air Division, 65, 84, 95, 129, 201, 219–20, 221–22, 225, 226, 236, 244, 272, 280; 7th Bombardment Wing, 27, 60, 128; 7th Fighter-Bomber Squadron, 165; 7th Tactical Depot Squadron, 359–60; Eighth Air Force, 207, 221, 222, 223, 237, 319; 8th Fighter-Bomber Squadron, 165; 8th Fighter Wing, 359; 8th Reconnaissance Technical Squadron, 201, 219; Ninth Air Force, 21; 9th Bombardment Wing, 66, 98, 100, 101, 367; 9th Fighter-Bomber Squadron, 102, 103, 105, 165; 11th Bombardment Wing, 60, 128; 12th Aviation Depot Squadron, 361; 12th Aviation Field Depot Squadron, 165; 14th Aviation Depot Squadron, 361; Fifteenth Air Force, 113, 205, 207, 219, 227, 319–20, 322; 18th Tactical Fighter Wing, 359; 19th Air Division, 128; 19th Bombardment Group, 98, 99; 19th Bombardment Wing, 99, 167, 168; 19th Tactical Reconnaissance Squadron, 144; Twentieth Air Force, 20; 22nd Bombardment Wing, 207, 208, 343; 27th Fighter Escort Wing, 87; 28th Bombardment Group, 35, 98; 30th Depot Squadron, 130; 32nd Aviation Depot Squadron, 211; 42nd Bombardment Wing, 60; 43rd Bombardment Group, 33, 37; 43rd Bombardment Wing, 27, 57; 49th Air Division, 93, 155, 160; 49th Fighter-Bomber Wing, 102, 103, 165, 182; 55th Strategic Reconnaissance Wing, 343; 58th Bombardment Wing, 27; 72nd Strategic Reconnaissance Wing, 63; 92nd Bombardment Wing, 102, 104, 108, 168, 367; 93rd Bombardment Group, 33; 93rd Bombardment Wing, 66; 95th Bombardment Wing, 60, 361, 377; 96th Bombardment Wing, 319, 361; 97th Bombardment Wing, 58, 168; 98th Bombardment Wing, 167, 168; 99th Air/Aviation Depot Squadron, 273, 280; 99th Strategic Reconnaissance Wing, 104; 301st Bombardment Group, 35; 303rd Air Refueling Squadron, 206; 303rd Bombardment Wing, 200; 306th Bombardment Wing, 96, 207; 307th Bombardment Group, 35, 98; 307th Bombardment Wing, 167; 309th Bombardment Wing, 95; 310th Bombardment Wing, 207; 310th Tactical Missile Squadron, 360; 315th Air Division, 165; 320th Bombardment Wing, 208; 376th Bombardment Wing, 143, 242; 417th Fighter-Bomber Squadron, 155; 509th Bombardment Wing, 57, 58, 93; 509th Composite Group, 13, 27, 33; 544th Reconnaissance Technical Squadron, 219; 588th Tactical Missile Group, 353; 701st Tactical Missile Wing, 155; 868th Tactical Missile Squadron, 361; 1009th Special Weapons Squadron, 344; 2857th Test Squadron, 2; 3921st Reconnaissance Technical Squadron, 201, 219; 4060th Air Refueling Wing, 206, 267; 4061st Air Refueling Wing, 206; 4080th Reconnaissance Wing (Light), 200, 343; 4126th Strategic Wing, 367, 368; 4128th Strategic Wing, 373; 4130th Strategic Wing, 324; 4134th Strategic Wing, 361, 377; 4347th Combat Crew Training Wing (Medium), 343; 4373rd Refueling Wing, 342; 4925th Test Group (Atomic), 118; 6021st Tactical Reconnaissance Squadron, 358; 6091st Tactical Reconnaissance Squadron, 358; 6901st Special Communications Group, 286; 6902nd Special Communications Group, 286; 7499th Composite Squadron/Group, 137; Air Information Division, 30; Provisional Transport Squadrons, 345; Turkey-United States Logistic (TUSLOG) Detachment 8, 287

U.S. Air Force Weapons Board, 269–70

U.S. Army, 105, 123–24, 127, 166, 203–4, 333

U.S.-Japan Security Treaty, 359–60

U.S. Marine Corps, 171, 183, 360, 363

U.S. Naval Air Facilities: Naha, 363

over of TAC by, 252; and targeting of Soviet Union, 99–100, 327

Whalen, William H., 127

Wheelus AFB, 130, 134, 343

Whiskey-class submarine, 255, 304, 309

White, Thomas D., 46, 85, 88, 255–56, 266, 279, 311, 325, 331, 332, 340, 352, 355; Airborne Alert and, 314; Alternative Undertaking and, 327, 334–35; and ASM program overload, 268; ballistic missile programs and, 275, 276, 277; China expertise of, 171; and Curtis LeMay, 334; and pre-delegation, 254–55; promotion of, to USAF chief of staff, 251; Quantico speech of, 332–33; recommendation by, of single target list, 335; Sputnik and, 253–54; and Thomas Power, 333, 337

Whitehead, Ennis, 266, 328

White House, 124

Worldwide Coordination Conferences, 306

WS 122A decoy system, 146

WS 132A decoy system, 146

Wurtsmith AFB, 319

Yaeger, Charles (Chuck), 155, 296

Yak-15 interceptor, 70, 72

Yak-25 (Yak-25M, Yak-25P) interceptor, 31, 141, 221, 224, 242

Yak-35M interceptor, 370

Yalta Conference, 16, 252, 348

Yankee-class ballistic missile submarine, 391

Yellowknife seismic detection station, 195

Yokota Air Base, 33, 141, 167

York, Herbert, 117

Yo-Yo (B-200) radar system, 144–45, 148, 236

Yugoslavia, 21, 55, 58, 225

Zaragoza Air Base, 132, 310

Zhukov, Georgy, 126

Zimmerman, Carroll, 66–67, 113

Zulu-class missile submarine, 255, 256, 284

Zweibrücken Communications Annex, 286